This book is a gift of the
Friends of the Orinda Library

Join us at
friendsoftheorindalibrary.org

The Crusades of Cesar Chavez

The Crusades of Cesar Chavez

A Biography

MIRIAM PAWEL

BLOOMSBURY PRESS

NEW YORK · LONDON · NEW DELHI · SYDNEY

Published by Bloomsbury Press, New York

All papers used by Bloomsbury Press are natural, recyclable products made from
wood grown in well-managed forests. The manufacturing processes conform
to the environmental regulations of the country of origin.

LIBRARY OF CONGRESS CATALOGING-IN-PUBLICATION DATA HAS BEEN APPLIED FOR.

ISBN: 978-1-60819-710-1

First U.S. edition 2014

1 3 5 7 9 10 8 6 4 2

Typeset by Hewer Text UK Ltd, Edinburgh
Printed and bound in the U.S.A. by Thomson-Shore, Inc., Dexter, Michigan

Bloomsbury books may be purchased for business or promotional use.
For information on bulk purchases please contact Macmillan Corporate
and Premium Sales Department at specialmarkets@macmillan.com.

To the memory of my father,
who taught me how to write,
and to raise hell.

Contents

Part V: November 1978–April 1993

Prologue

The dark brown man's deep, sad eyes scanned the roomful of San Francisco's wealthy and worldly. Few assembled in the gilded splendor of the Sheraton-Palace Hotel on this fall day in 1984 had seen a lettuce field, or a farmworker bent over in pain. They had all seen the face of Cesar Chavez.

The city's political and business elite had come seeking wisdom from a man with an eighth-grade education and a passion that drove him to tilt at windmills until they turned. "He remains," said Michael G. Lee, the attorney who introduced Chavez, "a revered, almost mystical figure."

His thick black hair streaked with gray, his face and stomach gently rounded, Chavez stood just a few inches taller than his hostess, child-actress-turned-diplomat Shirley Temple Black. Unlike the presidents and Nobel laureates who typically addressed the Commonwealth Club, Chavez didn't own a suit or tie. He wore a white shirt and argyle vest. Nothing about his appearance was remarkable, except his eyes. People noticed Cesar Chavez's eyes.

In a speech that lasted a scant half hour, he traced the path he had traveled in fifty-seven years, from the cotton fields of Arizona to the pulpit of the nation's oldest public affairs forum, where Franklin Delano Roosevelt had once outlined the New Deal.

Chavez didn't dwell on his David-vs.-Goliath triumphs in founding the United Farm Workers union. His audience had grown up with the grape boycott, which forced the most powerful industry in California to negotiate contracts with its poorest workers.

Chavez was an improbable idol in an era of telegenic leaders and charismatic speakers. The cadences of his speech were flat, his phrases often trite. In his luncheon speech, Chavez described growers as punch-drunk boxers and spoke of chickens coming home to roost. His power lay not in words, but in actions. He had willed the future to be different for farmworkers and swept up thousands in his quest.

Chavez described his life's work as a crusade against injustice. He spoke of his anger as a child watching his parents humiliated in the fields, and his rage at the racist treatment of Mexican Americans. He traced his rise as a community organizer and his decision to walk away from a steady job to try to bring dignity to farmworkers.

Three days before Chavez spoke, his longtime adversary Ronald Reagan had won reelection to the White House by a landslide, carrying all but one state. The Reagan era was not kind to labor leaders and liberal movements. Many of Chavez's supporters had grown disheartened. Others had abandoned *la causa* in anger and disillusionment.

In the 1970s, the United Farm Workers had represented almost all who harvested grapes from California's vines and half of those who picked lettuce from its fields. As Chavez spoke in the Palace Hotel ballroom on November 9, 1984, the UFW had just one contract in the table grape vineyards and a handful in the vegetable fields.

While the audience dined on pork tenderloin with cranberry-mustard sauce, Chavez described farmworkers who drank from irrigation pipes and lived under trees. Children born to farmworkers were 25 percent more likely to die at birth. Their parents' average life span was two-thirds that of the general population. Laws protecting union activity in the fields went unenforced.

Chavez recited a litany of woes that testified to his union's failures. Then he waved away those facts, not as unimportant but as subordinate to a greater truth. He looked ahead to a twenty-first century when power would belong to people who looked like him.

"The union's survival, its very existence, sent out a signal to all Hispanics that we were fighting for our dignity," he said. "That we were challenging and overcoming injustice, that we were empowering the least educated among us, the poorest among us. The message was clear. If it could happen in the fields, it could happen anywhere: in the cities, in the courts, in the city councils, in the state legislatures. I didn't really appreciate it at the time, but the coming of our union signaled the start of great changes among Hispanics that are only now beginning to be seen."

As waiters cleared away the apple strudel, Chavez concluded his speech with the prescience that marked so much of his career. Within thirty years, he told the audience, the great cities of California would be run by farmworkers, their children, and their grandchildren. This radical vision—like his embrace of organic farming, yoga, and vegetarian diets—would become conventional wisdom long after he was gone.

"We have looked into the future," he said, "and the future is ours."

Twenty-five years later, Barack Obama entered the White House with a campaign slogan borrowed from Chavez: *Si se puede.* Yes, we can. And when the nation's first black president ran for reelection, he traveled to central California to place a red rose on Cesar Chavez's grave and declare his union headquarters a national monument. The gesture was both recognition of Chavez's heroic stature and an acknowledgment of the Latino political power that Chavez had prophesied.

Chavez's place in history is secure; the route he traveled from migrant worker to national icon has yet to be explored. The path has become well worn, so strewn with flowers and encomiums that reality lies half buried beneath the legends. Chavez nurtured those legends—yet he also took pains to ensure that each footprint might one day be unearthed. In thousands of papers and hundreds of tape recordings that he carefully preserved rest the intimate details of his remarkable journey.

Like the icon of the Virgen de Guadalupe, so omnipresent in his movement, the mosaic of Cesar Chavez viewed up close assumes a complexity absent from afar. Myriad pieces come together in an image illuminated not by myth, but by humanity.

"Unions, like other institutions, can come and go," Chavez told the Commonwealth Club audience in 1984, in what could have passed as a eulogy for his crusade. "Regardless of what the future holds for the union, regardless of what the future holds for farmworkers, our accomplishments cannot be undone. *La causa,* our cause, doesn't have to be experienced twice. The consciousness and pride that were raised by our union are alive and thriving inside millions of young Hispanics who will never work on a farm." Cesar Chavez's legacy would not be in the fields, but in the rise of his people.

The last question at the Commonwealth Club luncheon was whether, given the chance, he would do it all over again. The man with the deep, sad eyes that saw so much did not hesitate.

"I would thirty times over, yes."

PART I

March 1927–April 1962

CHAPTER 1

Home

Viewed from the air, the North Gila Valley is shaped like a boot, toe pointing west. Along the sole of the boot runs the Gila River, a name seized by the Spanish from an Indian word meaning "river that runs salty." The Gila empties into the Colorado River at the toe of the boot, on the border of California, just outside of Yuma, Arizona.

The valley on the Arizona side is a patchwork of fields and canals that irrigate this fertile stretch of the Sonora Desert. Cotton, alfalfa, and Bermuda grass tolerate the saline soil and flourish in the year-round sun.

In the foothills of the Laguna Mountains that line the eastern edge, about halfway up the back of the boot, are remnants of a once-sturdy adobe house and storage room built near the start of the twentieth century, when homesteaders first laid claim to the valley.

Three decades later, the household was headed by Librado Chavez, a forty-two-year-old cotton farmer. The family included his elderly mother, Dorotea, his wife, Juana, and their three small children, Rita, Richard, and Cesar.

The home stood on a dirt road alongside a small canal. The compound had no number; everyone just knew it as the house built by Papa Chayo. His eighty-five-year-old widow had inherited the farm, and Librado paid her $4 a month in rent. Like most families nearby, they spoke Spanish. The adults had all been born in Mexico, the children in Arizona.

Those basic facts recorded by a census taker on April 3, 1930, captured the skeletal outlines of the world in which Cesar Estrada Chavez grew up. Behind the dry statistics were the people and places that shaped Cesar's life, the physical and emotional geography of his childhood.

The boy born on March 31, 1927, never knew the grandfather he was named after, Cesario Chavez, better known as Papa Chayo. Cesario had grown up in Hacienda de Carmen, a small village in the Mexican state of Chihuahua. He was born around 1845, the same year as Dorotea Hernandez, who became his wife. Stories passed down through generations offered various accounts of why the family left Mexico and headed north. Papa Chayo ran afoul of landowners who ruled the Hacienda and fled rather than face conscription into the army. Or perhaps he served in the army and deserted. Or most likely he simply saw better prospects across the border. Whatever the circumstances, Cesario and Dorotea crossed into Texas in 1898 with eight small children, including Librado, their youngest son. They first lived in El Paso, moved a few times in search of work, and eventually settled outside Yuma, where Papa Chayo built a thriving business hauling wood. He employed much of his extended family, who transported wood in mule-drawn carriages to power the paddle-wheel steamers that plied the Colorado River.

On New Year's Eve, 1906, Cesario Chavez filed a claim under the federal homestead program and took title to the 120-acre farm in the North Gila Valley. He built his house with extra-thick walls, placing eighteen-inch adobe bricks sideways, to withstand the extreme summer heat. The adobe sparkled with small shells embedded to give the building greater strength. Inside, plaster covered the walls and open wood beams lined the ceiling.

By the time of the 1930 census, Dorotea lived in the main house with her one unmarried daughter, who had come to take care of her elderly mother. The house was connected by a wide breezeway to a large room that Papa Chayo had built to store food and grain. Librado and his family lived in the *galera*, or storeroom. It had two doors and four small windows, built for ventilation, not view.

The compound stood on a small hill, facing west toward the California border about a mile away. The house fronted on the North Gila Main canal, just a half dozen feet wide. To the south of the main house stood the outhouse. To the north was a small vegetable garden, and past that a large cypress that the children climbed and nicknamed the "umbrella tree." Further north along the canal were the homes of Cesar's aunts and uncles, Tia Carmen and Tia Julia on the same side and Tio Julio across the canal, alongside the Chavez family fields.

Librado and his brother Julio grew cotton, watermelon, alfalfa, and Bermuda grass, for the seeds. The crops were planted on eighty acres that sloped gently down from the west bank of the canal, so that gravity did the work of irrigation, pulling river water into the fields when a series of gates were opened. Small log bridges crisscrossed the canal and a wooden bridge in front of the Chavez homestead led to the corral for the horses that drew the plows.

Directly across the fields from Papa Chayo's homestead were three small buildings that Librado saw each day, a constant reminder of his failure. On November 25, 1925, a short time after their marriage, Librado and Juana had bought the cluster of buildings that housed a store, pool hall, and living quarters. To finance the purchase and stock the store, the couple took out mortgages totaling $2,750. Librado was the postmaster as well as storekeeper. He was a poor businessman and despite the multiple incomes soon fell into debt. Librado's children later blamed the financial problems on his generosity and willingness to extend credit at the store. Other relatives faulted Librado for lazy business practices, absenteeism, and a fondness for gambling. Within a few years Librado was forced to give up the store and pool hall to pay back the mortgages. On April 22, 1929, a few weeks after Cesar's second birthday, they lost the land. Juana was pregnant with her third child, and the family moved across the fields into the galera on the Chavez homestead. They brought with them two remnants from the failed business: a pool table and a three-hundred-pound ice chest.

Cesar grew up in a typical extended Mexican family—patriarchal in name, matriarchal in practice. Dorotea, nearly blind but mentally sharp, was the only literate elder. She had been orphaned at a young age and raised in a convent, where she learned to read and write. In the absence of a nearby church, she supervised her grandchildren's religious education and prepared them for confirmation.

Juana Estrada Chavez was the guiding force in Cesar's nuclear family. A dark-skinned, petite woman with Indian features, Juana was smart, strong-willed, and unusually independent for her time. She was born June 24, 1892, in Ascención in the Mexican state of Chihuahua and crossed the border as a six-month-old with her widowed mother, Placida, an older sister, and her uncle. He supported the family, working in the mines in Lordsburg, New Mexico, and then in a smelting plant in El Paso,

Texas. Juana's mother remarried and the family moved to Picacho, California, before settling in Yuma. Juana never attended school. She picked cotton, squash, and tomatoes and made mattresses from corn husks. As a young woman she worked as an assistant to the chancellor in the girls' dormitory at the University of Arizona in Tucson, where she sewed, cleaned, and did laundry for the coeds. The chancellor's wife gave her a recipe for turkey stuffing, which became a family Thanksgiving tradition, passed down through several generations.

Long before she married into the clan, Juana knew the extended Chavez family, connected through work and marriage. Juana's family operated boardinghouses in Yuma that housed workers employed by Papa Chayo's wood-hauling business. In 1906, Juana's older sister, Maria, married Julio, Librado's older brother. A half sister, Francisca, later married Papa Chayo's nephew. Papa Chayo often joked that Juana, too, would marry into the family one day, after he was no longer around. He died in 1921, and several years later his prophecy came true. Librado was thirty-seven and Juana was thirty-two, an unusually late marriage. Their first child, Rita, was born on August 21, 1925, and their first son, Cesar, almost two years later. Both times Juana returned to her mother's house in the city of Yuma to give birth.

While Cesar was still an infant, his grandmother began to suffer from dementia. After Mama Placida died in 1930, Juana said she never cried again, and she never wore black. Years later she would admonish her children not to wear black to her funeral.

Juana and Librado Chavez made a striking couple: Librado a husky man, about five feet eleven inches and 225 pounds, with poor eyesight and large Coke-bottle glasses; Juana a tiny woman, just four feet ten inches, slender with long black hair. The diminutive wife and mother made decisions for the family, and Librado went along. She ran a strict household in accordance with clear beliefs. She favored herbal remedies: Cesar did not see a doctor until he was almost twenty. As a child, his nickname was "Manzi," because of his fondness for the manzanilla tea his mother made to cure colic and other ailments.

Her children considered Juana to be more superstitious than religious, a person of great faith. Like many Mexicans, she believed in saints as advocates and lobbyists. She worshipped Santa Eduviges, an obscure Bavarian from the early thirteenth century known as the patron saint of brides, difficult marriages, and victims of jealousy. A duchess by birth and again by marriage, Eduviges (also known as Hedwig) renounced her worldly possessions when she was widowed and joined a convent. She practiced abstinence, fasted, and meditated on the supernatural. She ministered to the poor and earned sainthood for her generosity to the sick and feeble. Every year on October 16, St. Eduviges's feast day, Juana dispatched her older children to find homeless men and invite them to the house for dinner.

Juana instilled in her children the importance of helping others and the need for personal sacrifice. She raised her children with firm rules and *consejos* (advice) that underscored those beliefs: Never lend money to your relatives; if they need money, give it to them. When an uncle asks for an errand, perform the task without question. Favors, she told them, are just that; when the children did favors for neighbors, they were not allowed to take a nickel in return. She quoted *dichos*, or sayings, about not fighting and told them to just walk away from conflict. She insisted they share everything. She cut food in equal portions for the children; if someone complained they got the small piece, she took the food away from all. She told the children parables about good kids and bad kids: the disobedient son who was taken away by the devil; the drunk son who was about to hit his mother when the rock froze in his hand.

Mostly, life for Librado and Juana's children in the Gila Valley was carefree. They were not well-off, but they were comfortable, well clothed, and never hungry. Juana grew tomatoes, cucumbers, and hot chiles in the garden, turned sweet berries from the mesquite trees into drinks, and made fresh cheese from the milk of their cow. Even in 1932, in the depth of the Depression, when Librado could not sell his cotton and corn and had to trash his crops, the family had plenty of chicken. When Librado earned a few dollars, Juana used the money to buy salt to give the chicken flavor.

The children enjoyed the security of an extended family scattered across the tranquil Arizona valley. Two of Cesar's aunts lived in small houses on Papa Chayo's land. One of Papa Chayo's brothers had emigrated to America with him from Hacienda de Carmen, and over time the Chavezes intermarried with four families in the Gila Valley. Their surnames mingled—Arias, Rico, Quintero, and Arviso—and many ended up related to each other through multiple ties, whether cousins, in-laws, or double cousins. In the three-room schoolhouse that the children attended, Rita and Cesar were related in some way to almost every student.

The Chavez home had no electricity, and they stored food in the ice chest. They used water from the canal for drinking, cooking, and bathing. They heated water inside and washed in a big tub outside. As the eldest girl, Rita did much of the cooking, cleaning, and washing. She heated irons on the wood stove, attaching a cool handle each time the one she worked with became too hot. Juana was clear on gender roles: girls should not do men's work, and boys should not do women's work.

Cesar's chores included chopping wood, exercising the horses, harvesting watermelons, and feeding the animals. They had a cow, horses, and so many chickens that they couldn't give eggs away fast enough. During the Depression, Juana sent Cesar and Richard to trade eggs for goat's milk, flour, or freshly butchered meat. They hunted quail and rabbit and caught catfish in the irrigation ditches. When gophers became a problem for the canal and interfered with pipes, the irrigation district paid Cesar and Richard to catch the animals, a penny per tail.

Two years after Richard was born, Juana gave birth to a daughter. Helena was only about eleven months old when she fell ill, suffered severe diarrhea, and died. Juana was pregnant, and a few months later she gave birth to another daughter, whom she named after her patron saint, Eduviges. The youngest child was Librado, known as Lenny, born in the summer of 1934. By then the roof on the storeroom had begun to leak, and the family moved into a two-room cottage built next to the main house. The two adults and five children slept on three double beds.

The children viewed the outdoors as their playground. They rode horses, and in the summer the canal became their backyard swimming pool. Cesar and Richard shot pool on the table salvaged from the failed business. At night they gathered around fires and listened to the grown-ups tell stories. They measured time by when a horse gave birth, or how soon the first watermelon would ripen.

To get to school, the children crossed their fields, then turned right and walked about a half mile north to the Laguna Dam School, whose high steeple marked the skyline. The T-shaped building housed three classrooms—first through third grade in the left-hand room, fourth through sixth grade on the right, and seventh and eighth in front. Children were not allowed to speak Spanish, and when he entered school, Cesario became Cesar. Rita was an excellent student, but her brother chafed at the rules and discipline. His first few days in school, he insisted on sitting next to his older sister, rather than with his own grade at his assigned desk.

By the time Cesar began school in 1933, his family faced more financial difficulties. Librado had fallen several years in arrears on property taxes for the homestead. In December 1930, the state had put the family on notice:

the Chavezes had seven years to pay several thousand dollars in back taxes or lose title to the land. Librado made another short-lived attempt to make a go of the store and pool hall in rented space, hoping to capitalize on traffic generated by the building of the nearby Imperial Dam. The store again ended in failure. On March 14, 1936, perhaps as a sign that she lacked faith in Librado's financial responsibility, Dorotea deeded the farm to her youngest son, Felipe, although he lived in California.

Dorotea died in her home on July 11, 1937. Three months later, Yuma County auctioned off the Chavez farm for back taxes and penalties of $4,080.60. On December 6, 1937, Felipe Chavez filed suit against the county board of supervisors, charging they had improperly seized his mother's land because, as a widow, she should have been exempt from paying taxes. The legal action bought the family some time.

Librado had health problems in addition to his financial difficulties. He had suffered bouts of sunstroke since he was a young man. Doctors had warned him to move to a cooler climate or risk severe consequences. Librado had resisted leaving the Gila Valley while his mother was alive. After she died, he made a solo trip to California to scout out work. Then, in the summer of 1938, the family left the triple-degree heat of the Arizona desert and traveled to the temperate clime of Oxnard, California, where one of Cesar's aunts lived. Librado, Juana, and the five children all crowded into Tia Carmen's home, an hour north of Los Angeles. The older children attended Our Lady of Guadalupe school for five weeks, then the family returned to Yuma for the winter growing season. They moved back into the family homestead, now embroiled in legal foreclosure proceedings. Rita and Cesar finished another year at the Laguna Dam School, completing seventh and fifth grades, respectively.

The county reported its first bid for the Chavez land in early 1939: $1,000. Felipe Chavez reached an agreement with the county on February 6, 1939; the board agreed to sell the land to him for $2,300, providing he came up with the money in cash by March 15. He failed, and the county sold the land to the highest bidder, the local bank president, A. J. Griffin, for $1,750.

Cesar was twelve years old. He may have been oblivious to the complexities of the family finances or his father's business practices, but Cesar understood the injustice of losing his home. In later years, he never mentioned his father's health problems or questionable financial acumen. In Cesar's telling, and in the family lore passed down over generations, Librado fought heroically to save the family home. Whether Cesar was not privy to the details, forgot them, or found it convenient to gloss over certain facts, he focused on the clear and obvious villains: the bank, greedy lawyers, and the Anglo power structure.

A. J. Griffin owned land that adjoined the Chavez property. He knew the family and allowed the Chavezes to stay for a few more months, until the end of the school year. Before they left, tractors came to level the carefully terraced land and tear down the horse corral, a scene Cesar would later recall many times in anger.

The thick adobe walls withstood years of subsequent neglect from absentee owners who farmed the fields and ignored the home. Decades passed, water overflowed the canal bank and wind whipped through the valley, and slowly the abandoned house in the Gila Valley all but disappeared. The wooden roof disintegrated, the foundation crumbled, and all that remained were a few adobe walls buried under foliage at a bend of the canal. From time to time, Cesar talked about buying back the land, but he never did.

CHAPTER 2

Sal Si Puedes

The Chavez family packed what they could carry into their nine-year-old Studebaker President and headed west, entering a world that had just burst into the consciousness of the American public through the words of John Steinbeck. In May 1939, *The Grapes of Wrath* leaped to number one on the national bestseller list, selling ten thousand copies a week at $2.75 each. In the heart of the San Joaquin Valley, where much of the book takes place, Steinbeck's work was banned.

A decade of the Great Depression had taken an enormous toll in the rural towns of California, as Steinbeck's Joad family discovered. Thousands of people driven off their land in the Midwest had migrated to California, seduced by visions of bountiful pastures and a warm welcome. They found instead hundreds of workers for every job, pitiful wages, and horrible living conditions. Denigrated as "Okies," desperate families followed the crops, shunted into shantytowns where they competed for jobs that paid pennies.

This was the California that greeted Cesar Chavez when the twelve-year-old lost his Arizona home and joined the migrant stream. The shock of that transition, fighting for jobs that paid scant wages, was as bracing as the cold outside the tent he often called home. Memories of being poor, brown, and homeless in California would drive Cesar for much of his life.

The family left Arizona in early June 1939 and headed toward San Jose, working along the way. They picked avocados in Oxnard and peas in Pescadero. Along with Librado's family was his widowed niece Petra and her son, Ruben Hernandez. They traveled in two cars, reaching San Jose before Juana's birthday on June 24. In the Mexican section of the city, Juana knocked on doors until she found someone willing to let them stay in a garage. This was their first home in a neighborhood so poor and prone to floods that it was called Sal Si Puedes—get out if you can.

The crowded garage was among dozens of temporary homes, and far from the worst. During the next few years, the Chavezes lived in barns, tents, shacks, labor camps, and spare rooms, whatever shelter Juana could find. She always insisted the children go to school, though they worked in the fields on weekends and summers. Whenever anyone worked, they handed their wages to Juana, who functioned as the family banker.

The family spent the first winter in Oxnard, a small coastal city north of Los Angeles, where the Mediterranean climate fosters an elongated growing season. Even there, the winter offered little work. In the chill and fog, they camped out in the muddy backyard of another acquaintance Juana made. Home was two tents set up at right angles, with a wood stove between. The children retained vivid memories of those cold, wet winter weeks, where they struggled to keep clothes and shoes dry overnight.

The physical hardships left fewer scars than the emotional burden of adjusting to an alien, often hostile world. Where once they had roamed the Gila Valley, knowing everyone they met, Cesar and Richard now found themselves in a land of fences, locked doors, and strangers. Their classmates went to the movies and talked about the latest comic book, rather than swimming and speculating on when the mare would foal. Their poverty made the children the object of ridicule. Classmates made fun of Cesar for wearing the same gray V-neck T-shirt and blue sweat-shirt to school every day. (Rita washed them out each night.)

For the first time, they experienced pervasive discrimination and prej-udice. Decades later, they remembered the insults: the teacher who scolded children for not lining up straight by saying, "You remind me of the Mexican army"; the stores that refused to serve ethnic Mexicans; the segregated seating in restaurants and movie theaters that nurtured a life-long instinct to check where they sat; the rural towns controlled by white growers, bankers, and lawyers, each town divided by the railroad tracks—Mexicans on one side, Anglos on the other.

In the winter of 1941, the Chavez family moved to Brawley, an agricul-tural town in the southeast corner of California in the Imperial Valley, a center of the winter vegetable industry. Of the dozen or so schools Cesar attended, he spent the longest time at Miguel Hidalgo Junior High in Brawley, half of seventh grade and almost all of eighth grade. He was an average student, earning grades that were mostly S's ("satisfactory"). But he consistently received A's ("to be congratulated") in arithmetic, and often in social studies and reading.

At the end of his formal schooling, Cesar weighed 118 pounds and stood five feet two inches tall. He didn't particularly like school. Despite his mother's desire that he continue, he insisted on dropping out, in part so that she would no longer have to work. Cesar graduated from junior high in June 1942, a few days before his mother's fiftieth birthday, and went to work full-time in the fields.

By then, the family had learned some tricks for surviving as migrant workers, and the United States' entry into World War II had opened up more jobs. Gradually, the family figured out which jobs paid the best wages, and which caused the most pain. They also learned the one constant in the history of agricultural labor in California—a surplus of labor enabled growers to treat workers as little more than interchangeable parts, cheaper and easier to replace than machines. The Chavez family's ability to work the system more successfully did not lessen the hardship or humiliation.

Older workers often were rejected in favor of younger, stronger men. Librado was almost sixty years old when they arrived in California, and Cesar watched his father struggle to find work. After Librado was injured in a car accident and disabled for many months, Juana and Rita became the financial support for the family. They often had to take the worst-paying jobs, like tying bunches of carrots, which meant leaving the house at 3:00 A.M. to get a good spot and finish early enough to escape the worst heat. Supervisors frequently insulted workers, shaming them in front of their families. Women were sexually harassed, taunted, touched, and asked for favors. Farmworkers were exempt from most health and safety provisions that applied to other laborers. There were no bathrooms in the fields, and often no trees or buildings to hide behind. Women had to shield one another to try for a shred of privacy.

Jobs that required workers to stoop close to the ground caused the most physical pain. Often workers were required to use the eighteen-inch short-handled hoe, *el cortito*, an instrument of both physical and psychological oppression. To use the hoe meant bending over all day and left the body aching so badly that it was difficult to stand upright. Supervisors liked *el cortito* because they could look down the rows, spot anyone who stood up to stretch, and issue a sharp reprimand.

Wages were set by growers, and most jobs were filled through labor contractors, middlemen who found opportunities to skim off money and cheat workers. They undercounted the number of potatoes, or discounted the weight of cotton in the sack. In winter, when work was scarce and labor plentiful, wages dropped even lower. Often workers had to camp out in front of a labor contractor's house on Sunday just to get paid.

Wages varied with the season, the weather, the boss, and luck. In Sacramento one summer, the Chavez family earned $1,000 a week picking tomatoes. But the norm was far less, as little as a few dollars a day for planting onions or picking peas. They worked as much as they could in spring and summer, saving money for the winter months when jobs were scarce. Farmworkers did not qualify for unemployment insurance, nor were they covered by minimum wage laws.

At fifteen, Cesar supervised his family's work in the fields. While Librado was more likely to slack off or let others quit when they grew tired, Cesar set goals. Most of the work was piece rate—they were paid by the number of rows of onions planted or boxes of strawberries harvested. Cesar set a target that the family would make before quitting at the end of the day. Librado would grow tired and urge that they quit as the day grew long, but Cesar would tell his father to go wait in the car while the rest of the family finished. Working as a team, they always made the number. Even little things helped; when Lenny was too young to work, he served as the "water boy." With no water in the fields, each family had to bring their own. Lenny ran back and forth to the car to refill jugs so the others didn't lose time.

The Chavezes developed circuits, depending on crop conditions and weather. Each person had his or her favorites and crops they particularly disliked. In January, they thinned sugar beets and planted onions, which Richard argued was worst—bent over all day, pushing little matchstick-size plants into holes four inches apart, rows six inches apart. In a day they could plant about a quarter of a mile, which might earn $3.

In early spring came cauliflower, carrots, broccoli, and cabbage, and then melons in May. When school ended, they headed to Oxnard for beans, Beaumont for cherries, or Hemet for apricots. They packed apricots in Moorpark in June and then at Mayfair Packing in San Jose in July, picked plums around Gilroy, shook walnuts from the trees in Oxnard, and harvested grapes in the San Joaquin Valley, where the season began in mid-August. Late summer offered the most choice—lima beans, corn, chiles, peaches, plums, and tomatoes, which stretched into fall.

The moment the cotton came in, they rushed from grapes to cotton because the work was piece rate (paid by the weight of the bag) and more lucrative. Cesar preferred cotton because he could work as long and fast as he wanted. He felt the increased freedom was a good trade-off for the physical duress. There was more oversight in the grapes, where supervisors inspected boxes and criticized the pack, scolding if they spotted unripe grapes.

For entertainment, the teenagers relied on pastimes that cost little if any money. Richard and Cesar listened to Joe Louis's bouts on the radio. Boxing appealed to them as the only arena in which a poor Mexican could become a star. Cesar learned to play handball, a poor man's sport that required only a hard ball and a solid wall. When the family moved to the San Joaquin Valley city of Delano, they lived in a cluster of small cabins in a dusty courtyard next door to a handball court. Cesar and his brothers would duck underneath the fence in the evenings and play on a regulation court. He became skilled and would play with a fierce competitive spirit for many years. Just a block away from their cabin was the Comisión Honorifica Mexicana hall on Fremont and Seventh Street, where the teenagers went to dances most weekends. Rita taught her brothers to jitterbug, and Cesar chaperoned his sister.

Family was the one constant in Cesar's life, at play and at work. He and Richard were outsiders, shut out of ball games and marbles each time they moved to a new school. They grew even closer to one another. Gradually they assimilated to the pastimes in their new world. In Oxnard, where the movie theater showed the new episode of *The Lone Ranger* every Sunday, the boys scrounged tinfoil and bottles to raise pennies to buy tickets to the serial.

Another relative entered Cesar's life during this period, a cousin who became an important lifelong friend. They called each other brother, a Mexican tradition reserved for the closest of cousins. Manuel Chavez, two years older than Cesar, also had grown up in the Gila Valley. He had dropped out of school in fifth grade, lost his mother when he was fourteen, and lived with a succession of relatives, most of whom could not control the boy. Juana and Librado took Manuel into their home in Brawley. Where Cesar was quiet and shy, Manuel was bold and brash. He had not been raised by Juana and her strict moral code. At sixteen, he was grown-up and prone to trouble, but just as apt to charm his way out of scrapes. Along with Richard, the practical down-to-earth member of the trio, Manuel became Cesar's closest friend.

When he turned eighteen, Manuel joined the navy, following the path of many Mexican Americans who sought a way out of dead-end jobs and discrimination. He lasted less than six months before deserting. Manuel turned himself in eighty-five days later, served his punishment, and was restored to duty, only to go AWOL again after punching an officer. He was court-martialed and dishonorably discharged on April 18, 1945. By then, the war was winding down.

Cesar had just turned eighteen. Unlike Manuel, Cesar had stayed out of trouble, with only one arrest for fighting, charges that were dismissed. After the war ended, the United States still needed military to guard enemy territories and U.S. installations and solicited volunteers. On March 20, 1946, Cesar went to the recruiting substation in Bakersfield and enlisted in the navy.

On his application, he listed his most recent job as a field hand and tractor driver for $40 a week on the Delano farm of William Hailey, a job that had ended the previous spring. Asked his trade, he answered "none." He was five feet four inches, weighed 125 pounds, and had no health problems. He had 20/20 vision, perfect hearing, a resting pulse of 72, and a chest that measured thirty-three inches at expiration and thirty-six inches at inspiration. He listed his race as Mexican, but the navy called him white. He signed up for $10,000 in life insurance, at a cost of $6.50 a month, listing his parents as beneficiaries. The apprentice seaman was sent to the Naval Training Center in San Diego.

He completed training and shipped out to Saipan, where he reported for duty at the naval base on July 17, 1946. Six months later, he was transferred to the barracks at Guam, where he completed training to become a seaman first class and was promoted on May 1. Cesar's principal correspondent was his sister Rita, who wrote every day. She sent her brother letters and care packages on holidays. (She learned not to mail chocolate, after her first Christmas present arrived in less than edible condition.) Cesar loved Duke Ellington and big-band music, and Rita wrote out lyrics to new songs and enclosed them in her letters. Cesar wrote to her that he was painting ships and repairing damage caused by the war. He sent her a navy peacoat, which was a very big deal, and a hula skirt and shell bracelets, which were just for fun. He wrote her about his new acquisition, a 35 mm camera, and told her he had adopted photography as a hobby.

The Chavez family had settled in Delano, a small city at the southern end of the vast San Joaquin Valley, about 150 miles north of Los Angeles. The grape vineyards and cotton fields provided work many months of the year and drew a fairly stable population. Juana was close to a niece who lived there. As in most agricultural towns, the railroad tracks divided Delano: Mexicans, Filipinos, and Chinese on the west side, Anglos on the east side.

Cesar returned home to Delano on leave to celebrate Christmas with his family at the end of 1947. He went back to the naval base in San Francisco after New Year's and stayed just long enough to meet his two-year commitment. On January 19, 1948, he was honorably discharged, with a $100 mustering-out payment and $547.39 in separation pay—but no closer to figuring out his next step.

He talked to his sister about becoming a photographer or drawing cartoons and made some attempt to take advantage of the educational opportunities for veterans, but without a high school diploma, he could take only vocational courses. At twenty-one, he went back to working in the fields with his brother Richard.

In Delano, Cesar renewed his relationship with a young woman he had met a few years earlier. Helen Fabela, one year younger than Cesar, had been born in Brawley but grew up mostly in Delano, living in an old horse stable converted into rooms. Her family worked in the fields, and Helen often helped out on weekends and summer vacations. She was the middle child in a family of three girls and four boys.

Helen's mother, Eloisa Rodriguez, was born in Sombrerete, Zacatecas, in 1901. With one child from her first marriage, she had made her way to Los Angeles and met Vidal Fabela, a farmworker from San Jacinto more than thirty years her elder. They were married in 1923. Helen was born on January 21, 1928. Like Cesar's family, the Fabelas spoke Spanish at home, and Helen did not know English until she began school. Like Cesar, she was a mix of shy and spunky—quiet and reserved in public, but fiercely spirited in private.

Helen and Cesar had met in 1943 at La Baratita, a malt shop on Eleventh and Glenwood where Helen stopped to eat snow cones after school. She was fifteen, a freshman at Delano High School. Shortly thereafter, Helen left school and joined her older sister working in the packing shed of the DiGiorgio Company, where she earned 70¢ an hour. Sometimes she also worked as a clerk in local shops, including People's Market. Many commodities were rationed because of the war, and after she and Cesar started dating she saved him extra cigarettes and gas coupons.

Within a few months of Cesar's return from the navy, Helen was pregnant. Cesar's sister Rita was engaged to Joe Rodriguez Medina, a construction worker in San Jose. The two siblings had always joked around—you'll be my best man, Rita told her brother, and I'll be your bridesmaid. And so they were. The two couples drove to Reno, Nevada, accompanied by Librado Chavez. Helen and Cesar both wore checkered gray and black suits. The couples served as each other's witnesses, and they were married by District Court judge William McKnight on October 22, 1948. They returned home to San Jose the next day, stopping en route to take pictures by a snowy Lake Tahoe. Cesar and Helen took a short honeymoon, touring the old missions around California. Then they returned to Delano for the cotton harvest.

The extended Chavez family had by then left Delano and settled back in San Jose, near the Sal Si Puedes neighborhood where they had first landed in a kind man's garage almost a decade earlier. By the beginning of 1949, Cesar and Helen joined the Chavezes in San Jose. Their first child, Fernando, was born February 20, 1949. Sylvia joined the family a year later, on February 15, 1950. Cesar continued to work in a variety of agricultural jobs and saw no way to get ahead. No way out of Sal Si Puedes.

Cesar's cousin Ruben Hernandez, who had first traveled to California with the Chavez family, heard about timber jobs up north that paid good money. When he came home to San Jose to visit and told his cousins about the money he made stacking lumber in Northern California, Cesar and Richard went back with him. Richard built cabins, and their families moved up to join them, along with Rita and her husband.

Helen gave birth to her third child, Linda, soon after they arrived in Crescent City in January 1951. The men were earning good money—$1.50 an hour to saw, stack, grade, and sort wood. But there was little to do in the isolated northern town. Ruben and Richard played guitar and Joe Medina played maracas. Sometimes they played on the Spanish hour on the local radio station. The winter was cold and wet, they were homesick for their family, and they missed living in a Mexican community. They moved back south.

Librado and Juana had settled in a small house in San Jose, where they would live the rest of their lives. There was a second tiny house in back of 53 Scharff Street, and in 1952 Cesar and Helen and the children moved into the front house and his parents shifted to the smaller house in the rear. Cesar and Richard worked together picking apricots. Then they found work as lumber handlers at the General Box Company, sorting and stacking wood. The two brothers had children just about the same age, and they schemed about how to send their kids to college.

With Juana's strict guidance and years of hard work, they had made it out of the fields. But education seemed the only way out of poverty and into the middle class. Then suddenly, they discovered a different path out of Sal Si Puedes.

CHAPTER 3

The Priest, the Organizer,
and the Lumber Handler

I would do anything to get the Father to tell me more about labor history.

Father Donald McDonnell was only a few years out of the seminary when the priest settled in Sal Si Puedes, drawn to the barrio to help Mexican Americans get out. The tall, stooped, eccentric genius set out to build a church—literally and figuratively.

McDonnell's path to Sal Si Puedes could scarcely have differed more than that of the farmworker who would become his disciple. The priest was born two years before Cesar Chavez and grew up in an Irish Catholic working-class family in Oakland. His stepfather was a policeman who imbued his children with deep convictions about the sanctity of labor unions. Don met his best friend, Thomas McCullough, in sixth grade at Berkeley Parochial School, and in their teens the two boys gravitated to the church as a vocation. Together the "two Macs" entered St. Patrick's Seminary in Menlo Park, just as the United States entered World War II. The heavy stone walls offered quiet sanctuary during a turbulent time. As they worked in the seminary's victory garden, the Macs discussed the papal encyclicals and extracted lessons about labor and social justice.

McDonnell, with a gift for languages, picked up Spanish from the only Mexican student in their class and then bought a 10¢ catechism card with Spanish on one side and English on the other. He used the card to teach a few friends during lessons he dubbed "walkie talkies": as they walked through the gardens, McDonnell threw out basic Spanish phrases from the catechism for the others to answer. The Macs were joined on the walkie talkies by John Ralph Duggan, another son of an Irish family from the nearby San Francisco Bay Area. All three had grown up in homes with ironclad beliefs about supporting strikers and denouncing scabs, and they believed unions were not only a right but a necessity for working people.

Ordained in 1947, McDonnell entered the priesthood at a moment when the American Catholic Church was openly struggling with what clerics called the "Mexican problem." The sprawling diocese of San Francisco, fourteen thousand square miles that included some of the richest farmland in California, was home to roughly 147,000 ethnic Mexicans, the majority poor farmworkers. The Mexicans were largely ignored by the church, and largely ignored it in turn. McDonnell estimated that 80 percent of the Mexicans in the diocese never attended services. San Francisco archbishop John J. Mitty increasingly worried about losing parishioners to the Protestants, who offered popular Spanish-language services at conveniently located evangelical churches and capitalized on the Catholics' neglect of the poor Mexican parishioners.

In 1950, the two Macs, fluent in Spanish and committed to social justice, offered Mitty a proposal. Along with Duggan and a fourth friend from the seminary, they persuaded the archbishop to try a bold experiment: a new apostolate that would cross geographic boundaries with a mandate to minister to all Mexicans in the diocese. The priests had wide latitude, unique jurisdiction, and unusual independence. "Mitty saw the wisdom and the possibilities of this," Duggan wrote. "He gave us carte blanche to proceed as we saw fit. He had never done anything like this previously, and the Fathers were amazed." Mitty called the four priests the Spanish Mission Band.

McDonnell's territory was Santa Clara County, one of the major agricultural counties in the country. The rich soil and plentiful fruit in what would later become Silicon Valley earned the area the name "Valley of Heart's Delight." In Sal Si Puedes, McDonnell encountered conditions typical in barrios and *colonias* around the state—dirt streets, no sidewalks, second-class schools, few municipal services. There wasn't even a Catholic church. McDonnell found a shack on Tremont Avenue that was used as a community meeting hall and began to celebrate mass at the end of 1950 in a building known as Puerto Rican Hall. Just before Christmas, the leaking roof flooded the manger during a heavy rain.

McDonnell methodically divided his parishioners into different categories, in much the same way Chavez would later think about them:

Mexican Americans who lived permanently in barrios; migrants who worked the circuit and lived mainly in the labor camps; transients from New Mexico, Arizona, or Texas who came north just for the summer harvest; and Mexican guest workers, single men imported to work on specific farms. McDonnell used unorthodox tactics. He carried "Our Lady of the Fields," a portable altar, into labor camps to hear confession. He conducted mass on Sunday nights and weekday evenings to accommodate those who worked in the fields on Sunday mornings. The two Macs composed their own hymns in Spanish and substituted a Spanish liturgy.

McDonnell had developed a following by the spring of 1952, when a visitor from out of town showed up at the church on Tremont. Immaculately dressed and partial to plaid shirts, Fred Ross spoke in the clear, pedantic manner of an English teacher. He called himself a community organizer. Ross did things by the book—his own book. He formulated strict rules and followed them assiduously. Rule number one: when in a new place, go see the local priest. So on Wednesday, May 7, 1952, his first day in San Jose, Ross drove around the dusty streets of Sal Si Puedes and then paid a call on Father McDonnell.

Ross introduced himself to the priest and told his story. He had directed the government migrant labor camp in the San Joaquin Valley, made famous by Woody Guthrie and John Steinbeck. Ross helped resettle Japanese interned during the war. Then he established a grassroots group for Mexican Americans in Los Angeles called the Community Service Organization (CSO). The CSO registered voters, offered English classes, and filed discrimination claims, all in an effort to teach Mexican Americans to exert power. The group had made headlines with its massive voter registration drives and successful advocacy for victims of police brutality. Ross was ready to expand to Northern California, and he had chosen San Jose because of its large Mexican American community.

Like the priest, Ross was a striking figure, tall, angular, and unconventional. Both were native Californians immersed in the world of poor Mexican Americans and fiercely committed champions of the oppressed. At forty-two, Ross was almost a generation older. His Spanish was very limited and his accent as poor as McDonnell's was flawless. Where McDonnell was philosophical, Ross was pragmatic. Both men exuded charisma that attracted devoted followers, though both were reticent to talk about themselves. They preferred to stay in the background and push others forward.

After their first long talk, McDonnell referred Ross to a young nurse, Alicia Hernandez, who ran the well-baby clinic that shared space with the Catholic congregation. Once a week McDonnell pulled a curtain across the altar and the church became a clinic. Helen Chavez brought her children for checkups, and so did Richard Chavez's wife, Sally. Hernandez knew every family in the barrio with young children, and she agreed to help Ross set up what he called house meetings, small gatherings to meet the new guy in town.

Ross went back to see McDonnell, and the two schemed over lunch. "Map session with Father McDonnell. Fired him up to take me to families," Ross wrote in his diary. The next day McDonnell picked Ross up for back-to-back meetings, first a few parishioners at a family home and then a larger group at the Tremont Avenue church hall. The crowd was thin, so the priest rounded up more. McDonnell led the rosary. Then Ross delivered his pitch: "Who I was, why assigned to study San Jose, why asked Father McDonnell to call people together," he recounted in his diary. The residents told Ross how their children came home with sores on their feet from playing in the nearby creek that was polluted with refuse from the cannery, and about the streets strewn with garbage the city neglected to collect. Ross told them how a voter registration drive had propelled the first Mexican American onto the Los Angeles City Council. "That's [the] CSO story in LA. Do you think such an organization is needed here?" he asked them. "Do you have problems? Am I needed?"

Word of the house meetings spread. Cesar and Richard Chavez were skeptical about any gringo who claimed he had come to help. Surely he must want something in return. But McDonnell and Hernandez continued to vouch for Ross and spent time introducing him to potential leaders and recruits. One or the other took Ross to house meetings, usually two a night. At every session, Ross asked who would volunteer to host another meeting. At the end of his first month in San Jose, on Friday, June 6, Ross finished his 6:00 P.M. house meeting and tried to cram in a second at 53 Scharff Street, the Chavez home. But the hour had grown too late, he was politely turned away, and agreed to return the following Monday.

On Monday evening, June 9, 1952, more than a dozen family members and a few friends crammed into the green wood-frame house where Cesar and Helen Chavez lived with their four small children. Ross delivered a speech he had by now given dozens of times in dilapidated houses and shacks around Sal Si Puedes. His message was radical: the most powerless people could transform their lives if enough of them worked together.

As Alicia Hernandez translated his talk into Spanish, Ross explained the work he had done in Los Angeles with the CSO. He recounted the story of "Bloody Christmas," an infamous riot where Los Angeles police beat Mexican youths and then charged them with crimes. He detailed how the CSO successfully pressed for police brutality charges and mounted a defense that exonerated the Mexican youths. Ross told the people in the crowded living room they could change a system that had cheated them out of wages, shortchanged their kids, humiliated their wives, and stripped away their dignity.

That night, Ross recorded his first impressions of the man who would become his most celebrated student: "Chavez has real push, understanding, loyalty, enthusiasm, grassroots leadership qualities. From Kern City, now at Box factory."

Chavez was working at the General Box lumber yard. One day a week he unloaded wood from the railroad cars, and the rest of the week he sorted and stacked the lumber that was shipped off to a mill and made into boxes. For a bright, curious twenty-five-year-old, trapped in dead-end jobs, Ross's message was intoxicating. Cesar leaped at the opportunity. He volunteered to help Ross register new voters and work on a campaign to establish a CSO chapter in San Jose. From the beginning, Ross observed two important qualities in Chavez: an understanding of the nature of power, and a sense of urgency.

Soon after he began helping Ross, Chavez met McDonnell, and the trinity was complete. Chavez lived around the corner from the church on Tremont, but he had not been active religiously. Now the priest became a friend and teacher, Chavez's first model of servanthood. The close collaboration between the Spanish Mission Band and the CSO foreshadowed the way Chavez would later use religious leaders to great advantage in his own campaigns. McDonnell was a religious conservative who invariably began discussions with the admonition "Let's pray," followed by a lengthy prayer. He was passionately committed to social justice and his own version of liberation theology a decade before Vatican II. In his actions, he showed Chavez how the church could be an advocate for the working poor. With his words, McDonnell offered the theological underpinning for the Catholic Church's support of labor unions.

McDonnell gave Chavez copies of the two papal encyclicals that proclaimed the rights of workers to organize—Pope Pius XI's *Divini Redemptoris*, and *Rerum Novarum*, the 1891 encyclical from Pope Leo XIII, the "workingman's pope," who urged that workers form unions for the purpose of collective bargaining. The priest lent Chavez books, which sparked a lifelong passion for reading. In biographies of St. Francis of Assisi and Gandhi, Chavez gained his first exposure to nonviolent protest. "I would do anything to get the Father to tell me more about labor history," Chavez later recalled.

McDonnell experimented with novel ideas that left a lasting influence on Chavez. The priest set up a credit union and established cooperative housing for workers. Because funeral homes charged more than most workers could afford, McDonnell formed a burial association. He researched the law and discovered anyone could conduct a burial in California with a permit from city hall. Men in the parish built simple wooden coffins, lined with white linens sewed by their wives. McDonnell accompanied family members to the mortuary, where they demanded the release of the deceased relative. Chavez drove a station wagon, which they used to carry the body back to the church. Funeral services, McDonnell explained, served as a way to draw Mexicans closer to the church—particularly men, who often said the rosary for the first time when they attended the *velorio*, the wake that often lasted all night.

At the county jail, in one large room where prisoners made hot chocolate over open fires, Chavez helped McDonnell say mass. Chavez and another young CSO recruit, Herman Gallegos, often piled into the back of the priest's army-surplus jeep. McDonnell threw them rosary beads and told them to pray. "God will provide" was his favorite saying. Often the priest fell asleep from exhaustion before the rosary was finished.

The priest gave Chavez and Gallegos tutorials, drawing lines in the dirt to explain subjects such as Public Law 78. The federal law, signed by President Truman in 1951, extended the Mexican guest worker program long after the wartime shortages had passed, ensuring growers continued access to cheap Mexican labor. On weekends, McDonnell borrowed buses from parochial schools, called on Chavez and Gallegos to drive them to the labor camps, filled the buses with guest workers, and brought the Mexicans to the church.

Chavez helped McDonnell build the first real church in Sal Si Puedes. The priest had claimed an old church building—pews, stained glass windows, furniture, and all—and arranged to move it to a site he had acquired, just a few blocks from the Chavez home. Volunteers helped a contractor remove the roof, cut the old church into three pieces, and move them across town. They reassembled the building, and Chavez helped nail on the roof.

Our Lady of Guadalupe church opened on December 12, 1953, the feast day of the patron saint, the most important cultural icon for Mexicans. The new hall doubled as meeting space, recreation hall, and youth center, and housed a public health clinic one night a week. The sacristy often served as Father Don's bedroom. The church had no bell, so McDonnell used a megaphone and whistled a popular Mexican hymn, "O Maria, Madre Mía," to call people to mass.

McDonnell's childhood friend Tom McCullough had been building his own parish in Stockton, at the north end of the diocese. The more they ministered to farmworkers, the more the two Macs became convinced that a labor union in the fields was necessary. They became actively engaged in promoting the idea. McDonnell used any opportunity to speak out against the radical imbalance of power between the church's two key constituencies—wealthy agricultural landowners, and poor workers. In an address to a national organization of clerics who worked in Spanish-speaking communities, McDonnell spoke starkly of the two groups that would soon become locked in prolonged battle in the California fields. The priest invoked the image of the Mexicans' patron saint in an appeal for the Catholic Church to help rectify the injustice faced by farmworkers:

> In their meeting halls the picture of Our Lady of Guadalupe is enshrined. She is their Queen. They carry her picture in their wallets. On the other hand, there are already formed and have been operating for many years the gigantic multibillion dollar Growers' Associations in many of which Catholic growers play a considerable role. Will Our Lady of Guadalupe, the Mother of the Lord of Heaven, bring together and unite as brothers these two groups, the people of the land who seek to work in accordance with the dignity of their human nature, and the powerful economic interests that control the agriculture of the state? We pray that she will so that the good order and the peace of the kingdom of Christ may reign and the land and its people may give glory to God. But it is not enough to pray. This is the time for action.

The action would have to wait a few years, but when the time came, Chavez would build on all that he had learned from McDonnell and act with Our Lady of Guadalupe by his side.

CHAPTER 4

Cesar Finds His Calling

It's just single-mindedness, just nothing but that . . . I think I was born with it. I mean, I just, when I want to do something, I make up my mind I want to do it. I decide.

In the late summer of 1953, police arrested a Mexican teenager after a brawl in a Salinas Valley town, questioned him for more than twenty hours, and then charged the boy with the murder of a white high school football player. Fred Ross was asked to help calm racial tensions. Ross agreed to spend a few days in King City, two hours south of San Jose, and invited along his new protégé, Cesar Chavez. Helen was starting to go into labor with their fifth child. Cesar dropped her off at the hospital and went with Ross.

Ross approved wholeheartedly of Chavez's priorities. His commitment convinced Ross that he had found a young man with the makings of a first-rate organizer. Ross was impressed by the twenty-six-year-old's perseverance, his work ethic, and his "burning interest." He was a quick study, too. "As soon as you drew the picture, he got the point," Ross would recall a few years later. "The whole question of power, the development of power within the group."

Developing power within the Mexican American community was at the heart of the CSO mission. Ross had begun the organization in Los Angeles in 1947, after a promising young candidate, Edward Roybal, failed to win election to the city council in a heavily Mexican American district—because so few Mexican Americans were registered to vote. Roybal and Ross teamed up on a grassroots voter registration campaign, and Roybal made history in 1949. His victory helped the CSO grow, attracting people who had thought they were powerless to fight City Hall. The organization branched out and tackled police brutality, discrimination in the schools, and second-rate services in Mexican neighborhoods. Its success marked the beginning of the civil rights movement for Mexican Americans in California.

Even as he became deeply involved in building a CSO chapter in San Jose in 1952, Chavez did not imagine such work might turn into a paying job. But he saw himself as a natural fit. Describing the requisite characteristics for an organizer a few years later, Chavez said: "It's just single-mindedness, just nothing but that . . . I think I was born with it. I mean, I just, when I want to do something, I make up my mind I want to do it. I decide." The second important quality was another one he had grown up with: "Having the instinct to help, to work with people, to really want to help people."

Chavez plunged into this new world so intensely that the pastime evolved into a calling and then a vocation. His day job was stacking lumber. His night and weekend job was registering voters. He apprenticed himself to Ross, the master organizer.

Cesar and Helen had moved into a small dwelling at the rear of 2397 Summer Street, around the corner from McDonnell's first church on Tremont Avenue. The one-bedroom house was crammed with cribs: Fernando was three, Sylvia two, Linda one, and Eloise just a few months old when Ross came into their lives. The children slept in a spare, linoleum-floored front room, the beds leaving space for little more than a sofa. Each evening Chavez came home from work at the box factory, changed clothes, grabbed dinner, and went out with Ross. Even when Helen was sick with kidney problems, Cesar was waiting for Ross every night.

Ross taught through conversation, critiques, and debriefing, and by example. He adopted a routine in San Jose that he would follow the rest of his life, basic steps that soon became second nature to the young lumber handler who tagged along.

The house meeting was the cornerstone of the Ross technique, a sort of Tupperware-party method of organizing where each meeting spawned a few more. Chavez listened closely as Ross made the case for the CSO. Of the twenty thousand Mexican Americans eligible to vote in San Jose, Ross estimated, only two thousand were registered. He explained the influence they could have if they altered that equation. He gave examples of the changes that had occurred when Mexican Americans registered to vote in large numbers. Then he asked what problems people in San Jose would like to address. At the end, Ross asked for help in setting up more meetings: Maybe someone had a few friends they could invite over? The dozens of small meetings and one-on-one conversations built to a large general meeting to formally establish a CSO chapter in San Jose.

When the time came to elect the first slate of officers, Chavez nominated his friend Herman Gallegos for president. Herman nominated Cesar for first vice president. Herman had put himself through college working at gas stations in Sal Si Puedes and had just graduated from San Jose State with a degree in social work. The two men nervously practiced their speeches at Herman's house into the early hours of the morning the day of the vote. Herman walked with a limp, and in his speech he explained why. As a boy, the only place to play was by the railroad tracks. He had slipped under a train and lost part of his leg. Then it was Cesar's turn to speak. "I'm not good at speeches," he said. "But all I know is that the main reason we're here tonight is to keep that and a lot of other things from happening to our kids . . . to keep them from having to grow up like we did."

When the votes were counted, Gallegos and Chavez triumphed over several well-known names in the community. They ran to Ross, elated. He evinced no surprise. People can spot "phonies," he always said, and they know who is out there actually doing the work.

Chavez, soft-spoken and shy, took charge of the voter registration committee. A successful campaign could not only influence the outcome of the fall election but also cement the reputation of the nascent organization.

Ross directed Chavez with tactics the CSO had pioneered in Los Angeles. First they solicited CSO members fluent in Spanish to serve as deputy registrars, which would enable them to sign up new voters. Ross trained them and then they applied to be certified by the county clerk. The clerk balked. Ross and a local priest, with support from the local labor council, pressured her to cooperate. She swore in six volunteers, who would be paid 10¢ for every new voter. Ross combed through city directories, extracted Spanish surnames, and organized lists based on geography.

Chavez recruited family and friends into six teams and paired each with a deputy registrar. Every evening, Ross gave each team a map marked with assigned streets. Because the registrars could not go door-to-door, "bird dogs" knocked on doors of unregistered voters and dragged them over to the registrar's table set up nearby. Around 9:00 P.M., Ross picked everyone up and took them for coffee. He offered pointers and made adjustments for the next day. The CSO signed up about four thousand new voters. On election day, November 4, 1952, CSO volunteers made rounds of telephone calls and drove voters to the polls to ensure a strong turnout.

The CSO was nonpartisan, but Republicans had watched the registration efforts with alarm, assuming the new voters would support Democrats. Just before the election, Republican leaders warned that dozens of illiterate voters were preparing to cast illegal ballots. They posted poll watchers in heavily Mexican precincts, and election inspectors pulled Mexicans aside and subjected them to a "literacy test." Many were so flustered by the request to read a hundred words of the Constitution that they left, even though they could read English. The story made front-page headlines the next day: "Injection of a racial issue into the election is something we never expected in a democratic community like San Jose," Chavez said. "Our group has been struggling to prepare itself for a full share of civic responsibility. The blow dealt our effort is most discouraging and unfair. The assertion unqualified persons were registered as voters is false and malicious."

Work at the box factory slowed down in the winter months, and Chavez was laid off. He collected unemployment and spent his days in a small CSO office that Ross had opened. People came in with problems, and Chavez tried to help. He ran interference with county agencies, translated documents, and wrote letters for non-English-speakers. As Chavez explained how the organization could help improve their lives, he recruited new members for the CSO.

The high level of interest showed the time was right for organizing Mexican Americans in California, Ross argued as he lobbied for funds to expand the CSO throughout California. He estimated that one-fourth of the three million ethnic Mexicans in the United States lived in California, with "so much to feed upon in the way of accumulated wrongs, that once started [a movement] can't help but gain momentum." Mexican Americans had enlisted in the armed services, fought in Korea, tasted equality in the military, and returned home to find they were still second-class citizens. "The yeast of the ferment is supplied by the veterans," Ross wrote, "home now after fighting for a decent way of life, unwilling to fall back into acceptance of an indecent way, home now after being accepted on an equal basis by their Anglo buddies . . . ashamed to bring their war brides back to the 'barrio' and determined to *change* that 'barrio' for those wives and the children to come. These are the potential leaders."

Another factor made the time ripe for the CSO, an ironic by-product of the Cold War. As Chavez followed Ross around Sal Si Puedes in the early 1950s, the word McCarthyism became a part of the American lexicon, Julius and Ethel Rosenberg waited on death row, and Richard Nixon rose from junior representative to national prominence through his role on the House Un-American Affairs Committee. In response to red-baiting fears stoked by Sen. Joseph McCarthy, Congress passed the McCarran-Walter Act, which restricted immigration and allowed authorities to bar or deport suspected "subversives." President Harry S. Truman denounced the measure as "un-American," but Congress overrode his veto. The law, formally called the Immigration and Naturalization Act of 1952, reflected the isolationist and xenophobic politics of the time.

But the McCarran-Walter Act had a little-noticed provision that would prove a catalyst for the empowerment of Mexican Americans in California: immigrants older than fifty who could prove they had been in the United States for more than twenty years could take citizenship tests in their native language. The opportunities appealed to Saul Alinsky, the social entrepreneur and agitator who had pioneered the concept of community organizing in Chicago and founded the Industrial Areas Foundation (IAF) to spread his ideas across the country. Ross had worked for the IAF in the late 1940s when he established the CSO in Los Angeles. Pitching Alinsky to fund the CSO expansion in the summer of 1953, Ross reported the CSO could barely keep up with demand and had enrolled 1,200 Mexicans in citizenship classes in LA and 190 in San Jose.

Alinsky was excited by the opportunity to help the disenfranchised become citizens, vote, and make political demands. "I share your feeling that you are about to get your teeth into what might well be one of the most significant organizational programs in the nation," Alinsky wrote Ross on August 5, 1953, appointing him West Coast director of the IAF at a salary of $8,500 a year, plus $4,000 for expenses. "I believe that I am not overstating the fact." For the next decade, Alinsky and the IAF would provide most of the financing for the CSO.

Ross was eager to leave San Jose and jump-start his efforts around California. A coalition that supported his work put up $400 to hire an assistant for a few months. Ross offered the job to Chavez. In a folksy retelling, Ross described a hesitant Chavez who needed to be coaxed into accepting the offer. "I know I could *never* do what you're doing," Chavez told Ross in the parable. "Geez! There's nothing I'd like better. Get out there, you know, and start stirring the *raza* up like he's been doing. But right then, that same old failure-fear starts freezing my guts."

Ross was a master storyteller, not hesitant to embellish to make a point, a tactic he passed on to his protégé. It is difficult to believe that Chavez did not leap at the offer of a steady job with decent wages, working as an organizer for the man who had become his mentor. Soon after Ross began working for IAF, Alinsky hired Chavez as well. He began work as an IAF organizer on March 1, 1954, at a salary of $216 a month. He earned a regular paycheck, with no worries about seasonal layoffs. He was working with his mind instead of his hands, paid to go out and help Mexicans become citizens, vote, and learn to speak up for their rights. He had an expense account to cover gas and out-of-town meals. He bought a suit, and grew a mustache to look older. He was about to turn twenty-seven.

Chavez's first solo job took him from San Jose to nearby Decoto, an agricultural community that had been overwhelmingly rural and Mexican until a recent building boom brought an influx of Anglos. Ross, who had started the Decoto chapter, told Chavez to take over. The confident, outgoing Ross was a tough act to follow. In response, Chavez developed a tactic that became a key part of his repertoire. If people were unwelcoming, he worked harder. If they shirked responsibility, he did their jobs. "One of his little techniques has always been to shame people into doing something," Ross said a few years later. "To let them know how hard he was working or he and somebody else were working, and while they wanted and needed more help, well, if people didn't want to help, that was their decision and if they wanted to make that decision knowing how badly their help was needed and how it was going to hurt other people if they didn't help, well they could just go ahead and not help. I think that was one of the things he learned there."

The CSO expanded quickly in Mexican American communities around California. Word spread and spurred demand for more citizenship and English classes. Friends heard from friends: the CSO tracked down lost birth certificates, filled out immigration forms, fought deportation orders, and battled discrimination, all free of charge. By 1955, Chavez was spending many weeks on the road as he helped organize CSO chapters in Salinas, Fresno, Brawley, and San Bernardino. Ross kept moving his top organizer around. Wherever he went, Chavez carried a letter of introduction to the local priest from Father McDonnell: "I have always found him a man of sound principles, clear thinking, complete integrity and loyalty. I would greatly appreciate all the help and guidance you can give him in his work."

When Chavez moved to Madera, one of many small rural towns along the spine of the San Joaquin Valley in central California, his arrival made front-page news. "Cesar Chavez—seeking to make new Americans," read the caption under his photo in the *Madera Tribune*. Chavez estimated that three thousand Mexicans in the area qualified under the McCarran-Walter Act to take citizenship tests in Spanish. From the day he arrived, Chavez held house meetings every evening, usually two per night, building to a general meeting two weeks later. He was pleased with the turnout and the enthusiasm, but frustrated when the county clerk refused to deputize him to enroll new voters, on the grounds he had not lived there long enough. Ross told Chavez to try harder: "By going from door-to-door yourself you will be able to do an awful lot of organizing and selling people on the C.S.O—people that you will probably never meet otherwise."

By September, the Madera CSO had registered five hundred new voters and adopted a constitution. Chavez was enthusiastic. "It looks like the 'Giant' is wakening up more so every day, after that long long sleep," he wrote Ross. "The Politicians are getting interested in the Mexican vote."

Just before Thanksgiving, he moved on to Bakersfield, where three weeks of house meetings drew enthusiastic crowds despite competition from holiday gatherings ("It's getting harder for me to make sense when I speak of citizenship and voting and they speak of tamales and buñuelos and tequila," Chavez wrote Ross). The weekly CSO meetings attracted 100 people. More than 250 enrolled in citizenship classes. Chavez ran headlong into a new problem in Bakersfield—red-baiting. His initial meeting with county clerk Vera Gibson had appeared to go smoothly, and she agreed to certify ten deputy registrars. Chavez organized his team and was ready to go, but Gibson kept stalling. After a month, Ross urged Chavez to take dramatic action. Another month went by. "Break the thing wide open in the newspaper like you did in San Jose," Ross admonished Chavez, urging him to take supporters to a board of supervisors meeting to protest. Instead, Chavez enlisted the help of religious leaders. When Gibson told the local priest she had no intention of certifying registrars for the subversive group, Chavez demanded to know the source of her allegations and insisted she call the attorney general's office in Washington immediately to clear the CSO's name and reputation. After three months of fighting, he got his deputy registrars.

Strangers could easily underestimate Chavez. He was short, unremarkable in appearance, and unassuming in his manner. He was not an articulate speaker and often said "golly" to fill in space. But he had a way of getting people hooked. Everywhere he went, he impressed people with the single-minded intensity and focus that had struck Ross in their initial meeting. His empathy and compassion for those in need were equally evident. He was good at reading people. His deep, dark, expressive eyes focused intently on his listener. Then came a flash of gold when his lips parted into a warm smile and revealed the cap on his front tooth.

Wherever Chavez lived, work came first. At first he was on the road, away from home for days or weeks. Then came frequent moves. He uprooted his family from San Jose to Madera in July 1954, then to Bakersfield in November, to Hanford in April 1955, and in September back to San Jose. Linda, the third-oldest and still a toddler, thought of Ross as the tall man who came to take her dad away.

Chavez's dedication, and results, attracted attention from Alinsky. He bumped up his young organizer's salary from $3,600 to $4,000 a year—only to find that Chavez objected. Alinsky was amused, and somewhat appalled, by Chavez's protestations. "May I say that in the future there will be adjustments and that you most emphatically are not being overpaid," Alinsky wrote Chavez. "If you want to have an argument with me on the basis of your convictions in this matter I suggest that you have a talk with your wife first . . . Also a point of personal curiosity. I note that there is absolutely nothing charged for meals . . . were you on a diet, or did you carry a sandwich from home?"

Chavez's tendency to sacrifice did not perturb Ross. He wrote about a conversation with Chavez after he had helped a family get assistance from a government agency. The successful intervention, Chavez told his mentor, "made me feel like God, almost." The grateful family offered to pay for the help, but Chavez would not accept. "Might take a little bit of that God-feeling I've got away from me," he explained to Ross. Ross smiled. "What else is there?" he told Chavez. "You're an organizer."

Ross understood that Chavez thrived on the power to help people and the way that made him feel. He did not want to be poor, but he did not want to feel he was profiting from doing good. He had grown up with the idea that helping people was its own reward. He was Juana Chavez's son.

CHAPTER 5

Staying Organized

*We know we can't carry both programs and fundraising. We also know that if
the organization fails in programs, we will not have people around for the
fundraising . . . It's a big problem, and although we need both, we have to
decide on one.*

Saul Alinsky, the brilliant, acerbic founder of the discipline of community organizing, divided the task of building a successful entity into two phases: getting organized, and staying organized. From his Chicago base and during occasional visits to a second home in the Carmel Valley, Alinsky assessed the progress of the CSO, which depended almost entirely on financial support from his Industrial Areas Foundation. By the end of 1955, he decided the time had come to shift to phase two.

Alinsky saw a clear pattern: whenever Ross or Chavez left an area, the local chapter soon deflated. The two men spent their time riding the circuit and rebuilding chapters, only to have them fall apart again once they moved on. Alinsky, the witty and erudite son of Russian Jewish immigrants, requested time to address the annual convention of the group that had established itself in just a few years as the preeminent grassroots organization for Mexican Americans.

At first, Alinsky told the July 1955 CSO convention, the novelty of a new endeavor attracts people who enthusiastically volunteer time and effort. If the organization succeeds, after a while its mandate broadens. Administrative work multiplies with every success. Volunteers alone can't keep the organization running smoothly. If programs are run inefficiently, people lose interest. Eventually, the organization disintegrates. Alinsky described a scenario he had seen many times, and one that Chavez, in not too many years, would grapple with firsthand.

The CSO chapters had undertaken so many activities that they could no longer succeed without full-time staff, Alinsky said. The Industrial Areas Foundation would therefore shift its support, in the hope of forcing a long-range plan that would make the CSO financially stable. His organizers—Ross and Chavez—would no longer start new chapters. Their task was to unite the more than twenty existing chapters into one self-supporting national organization.

Chavez had shown he could land almost anywhere and make things happen. Now he needed to master the job of keeping chapters organized. For once, Ross was little help. As Alinsky observed, stabilizing an organization had never been Ross's forte.

In late 1955, Chavez moved back to San Jose, the city he considered the closest thing to home. The chapter he had helped build three years earlier had all but collapsed. Dues-paying membership had plummeted from about four hundred to eighty-seven. Meetings that once filled the school auditorium now drew so few members that they all sat up on the stage. Chavez spent the next year using his skills as an organizer not to help people solve problems but to try to rebuild the group on a secure financial foundation. His mandate was to raise enough money so that San Jose could hire a full-time organizer and Chavez could move on, confident the chapter would not fall apart again.

He worked twelve to fifteen hours a day, seven days a week, almost never taking a day off. He filled close to five hundred pages, largely handwritten, reporting his activities to Ross and Alinsky. Often he dictated reports to Helen, whose neat handwriting was far easier to read than Cesar's scrawl. He detailed failures as well as successes in an open and even-handed tone. To his basic tenet—work as hard as possible—Chavez added a second guiding principle: never give up. He would not admit failure, pushing long past the point where almost anyone else would have thrown up their hands in defeat.

With his single-minded focus, Chavez insisted that he must concentrate only on fund-raising, even at the risk of letting popular CSO services like English and citizenship classes slide. "We know we can't carry both programs and fundraising," Chavez told the local CSO president. "We also know that if the organization fails in programs, we will not have people around for the fundraising . . . It's a big problem, and although we need both, we have to decide on one." Throughout his career, this would be Chavez's mantra in critical times: to succeed, he must focus on one thing only.

Over the course of the year, Chavez opened a rummage store, staged a

three-day carnival, and sold Christmas trees. Each showcased his prob-
lem-solving skills and indefatigable energy, but also their limitations.

When the CSO board endorsed the idea of a rummage store, Chavez
scouted a storefront and bargained about the lease. He painted signs to hang
in the windows. He solicited donations and then borrowed a truck to pick
up furniture. He browsed secondhand stores to figure out prices and then
tagged the merchandise. He recruited volunteers to work in the store, which
they called "Macy's," and set up a schedule to cover the shifts. Each morning
Chavez picked up the volunteers and delivered them to the store. He drove
them home at the end of their shift. When his own car broke down, a
frequent occurrence, he borrowed wheels from his younger brother Lenny,
who was following brother Richard into the carpentry trade.

Chavez tended to every detail. Though one of his great gifts was enlisting support, he delegated little, not trusting others to get the work done.
Week after week, he recorded instances when committee chairs and
board members let him down. Chavez turned instead to his family, who
proved reliable and loyal. They never refused his appeals for help.

Chavez's idea for a three-day fair plunged him into new territory as
he searched for snow cone machines and scouted out-of-season baby
ducks. Throughout, he relied on the same small band of allies. His
brother Lenny and Herman Gallegos accompanied Chavez on a day
trip to San Francisco to visit carnival supply stores and investigate how
much Fun Land charged for games. When they needed wood to build
booths for the fair, Father McDonnell located a house that the owner
wanted to tear down. Chavez bought the structure for $80, his brothers
and father helped dismantle it, and they hauled the wood to the fairgrounds in a rented trailer.

Worried about how to attract an audience, Chavez came up with a
novel scheme: he sold tickets for the kiddie rides to merchants, who
handed them out to loyal customers. In a month, he had sold nine thousand tickets at 3¢ apiece. At a packing shed, he noticed discarded potato
sacks and inquired whether he could buy the burlap bags, which the fair
committee needed to make curtains for the booths. The foreman's parents
had legalized their status with the help of the CSO. He told Chavez to
take whatever he wanted. He left with two hundred bags, saving $30.

While volunteers dyed the burlap sacks four colors and sewed them into
curtains, Cesar scavenged for parakeets, goldfish, and cotton candy
machines. The final weekend of preparation, Helen made sandwiches and
brought them to the site of the fairgrounds to feed the volunteers; Cesar

feared that if the men went home for lunch, they would not return. Chavez ordered popcorn, candy apples, and beer. He played one distributor against another, threatening not to sell Lucky Lager until the brewer agreed to donate ten cases. Fred Ross came to help and located the elusive baby ducks. Ross went to pick up goldfish and then helped decorate the booths. On the day the fair opened, Friday, August 10, 1956, Ross "picked up ducks at post office, fed them and bedded them down," he recorded in his journal. Then he picked up Helen and the kids and took them to Juana Chavez's house, where they prepared food to sell that afternoon at the fair.

The free tickets proved such an attraction that dozens of kids showed up at 9:00 A.M., four hours before opening time. The food was not ready in time, inexperienced volunteers running the game booths gave away more money than they took in, and in the evening the fuses blew every time the lights went on. The highlight was the Panda Bear Pitch, which netted $60. Chavez called a huddle to debrief as soon as the gates closed. Ross was dispatched to buy more lightbulbs, and a volunteer went home to research the wiring. After a couple hours of sleep, Chavez was back early Saturday to help fix the lights with heavier-gauge wire.

By Sunday, they had worked out the kinks. The crowds swelled, the food was ready, and the fair grossed twice as much as the day before. Sunday night Chavez stood guard alone over the equipment. Father McDonnell showed up at 1:00 A.M. and kept him company for several hours.

When Chavez sat down with the treasurer a few days later to go through the bills and receipts, he checked and rechecked the math in disbelief. The costs totaled $2,400, the gross about $3,000. All that work for $600.

A Christmas tree sale offered the last chance to end 1956 with a sizable surplus. As soon as the idea surfaced, Chavez scoured the neighborhood for a suitable lot. The best spots had been reserved months earlier. On Thanksgiving afternoon, he rented a lot several blocks from Sal Si Puedes, for $25. The next day he went to Sears, rented a power posthole digger, and bought timber and lights. He worked all weekend to set up and wire the lot.

The best trees were also spoken for early, Chavez discovered. He had written away for lists of tree dealers from the Chambers of Commerce in Oregon and Washington and made more than a dozen calls before he found a dealer who still had trees at a reasonable price. The CSO board decided not to risk a $1,000 investment on a phone conversation; they dispatched Chavez to Oregon to check out the trees in person.

He left the next afternoon, driving straight through the night by himself to Eugene, almost six hundred miles. Chavez called eleven dealers. None had any trees left. He drove another hundred miles to Portland to visit the dealer who had made the original offer; as soon as Chavez voiced approval, the dealer raised the price. He spent the next day working the phones again. Finally he found Douglas firs for 65¢ apiece.

Now he had another problem—how to transport nine hundred trees to San Jose. On Saturday morning, December 1, Chavez hung out at a local truck stop until he found a driver heading to the Ford plant outside San Jose with an empty truck. The driver agreed to transport the trees for $150, no loading included. At 1:00 A.M. Sunday, Chavez began loading trees on the truck. He finished four hours later. He drove back through icy weather, arriving home at 2:30 on Monday morning.

At daylight, he rushed to the lot. No one had finished the work in his absence. He rigged a temporary extension cord from a neighbor's house to set up electrical poles and string lights. When the trees arrived, he unloaded them and stayed on the lot to protect the merchandise, sleeping in his car for three nights until the CSO president's mother-in-law lent him a trailer.

McDonnell blessed the trees, and Chavez gave him two for the church. Ross came and offered pointers about display. By Friday evening, the trees were arranged in size order, the power hooked up, and the city inspection passed. Chavez sold his first tree for $3.

"There isn't much more I can say about the Christmas tree sale except that most of the work is routine, by this I mean that it was a 24 hour operation from Dec 3 to 24," Chavez reported at the end of the month. "In the evenings after work one or two members would come over and help for a couple of hours, which would give me time to go get something to eat."

Chavez tried to price the trees attractively and the CSO took out ads to spread the word in the Mexican American community. But they had started late and faced competition all over town. They sold 480 of the 900 trees. The CSO ended up $280 in the red. The day after Christmas, Chavez cleaned the lot and discontinued the power. In a borrowed pickup truck, Lenny and his dad helped haul hundreds of trees to the dump.

Not even Chavez's relentless drive could change the bottom line from red to black. But the failure was not for lack of trying.

CHAPTER 6

The First Disciples

I told her I thought that I couldn't spend my life doing anything more worthwhile than working with poor people . . . People would come first. There wouldn't be any days off.

Chavez returned in early 1957 to the Imperial Valley city of Brawley, where he had graduated from junior high, to rebuild another CSO chapter. The office was filthy, and the membership roster slim. Fred Ross bought detergent, and Chavez and a visiting minister scrubbed the office floor. Chavez held house meetings until he was confident a general meeting would attract a decent turnout.

When the crowd was settled, Chavez played a game to jump-start a membership drive. He asked the audience to select four captains and stationed each one in a corner of the room. Chavez directed them to take turns picking team members, like a playground game, until everyone was standing in one corner or another. Each captain handed out membership books to their team, and each member pledged to fill a book.

The meeting lasted till almost 11:00 P.M. Over coffee afterward, the Rev. Gabino Rendon asked whether the process could not have been done more efficiently. "Sure, if we did it all," Chavez replied. "But then the people wouldn't learn anything. This way it takes longer, but the people do it themselves and learn. Next time, they'll be better at it."

In the five years since he had met Ross, Chavez had grown in confidence and in technique. Where Ross did the same things over and over, Chavez experimented. His success attracted attention. In schooling others, Chavez began to articulate tactics he had divined by instinct or developed through trial and error. He became the mentor for others that

Ross had been for him, and attracted followers of his own.

Rendon was among a group that became Chavez's first disciples. The California Migrant Ministry, a Protestant organization funded by the National Council of Churches, placed ministers and lay people in rural communities. The staff had served in traditional roles—delivering books and clothes to migrant camps, conducting Bible classes, and offering spiritual counseling. The Migrant Ministry director wanted to deepen their connection to the community, and Saul Alinsky arranged to send each staff member to train with Chavez and Ross for six to eight weeks. For Chavez, the mentorship marked the start of his relationship with an institution that would prove crucial to his future organizing. For the trainees, the encounter proved revolutionary.

"All my previous experience had been in starting from the top," Louise Bashford wrote after her apprenticeship. In the CSO approach, "always there was consideration of what the people themselves saw as needs." She observed how the CSO built leadership. She grew outraged as she gained insight into the lives of people she tried to serve: "The issue of civil rights takes on a new meaning when it is Mrs. Figueroa's home which the police break into without a warrant, when Mr. Botello gets no mail delivery because Kingman Street is unpaved . . . when twenty teenagers are picked up in a narcotics round-up and during the week in which they are held not one of the parents visits or knows that he can visit."

The trainees became attached to Chavez. He was as patient in answering their questions as he was with the CSO members who sought his help. The Migrant Ministry staff helped with typing and chores and tagged along as Chavez made his daily rounds. He offered Spanish lessons over breakfast, patiently explained what he did throughout the day, and finished late at night with a rehash of the day's events over coffee and *pan dulce*, Mexican pastries.

The ministry staff came away overwhelmed by Chavez's dedication and gentle manner. "He always had plenty of time for each individual," wrote Paul Cassen after his six-week stint. "He pursued every lead that was open to him." Chavez helped the epileptic vet who needed treatment, the man who wanted to bring his wife from Mexico, and the undocumented immigrant trying to legalize his status. A woman applying for citizenship brought in two sugar sacks full of papers and dumped them on the table. Chavez patiently sorted through the documents to find those that would establish her legal residency. The only time Cassen saw Chavez irritated was when a government agency stonewalled him.

"No one was told his situation was hopeless," noted Harold Lundgren, another Migrant Ministry worker. "No one turned away with that depressing statement, 'We can't help you.' Everyone was made to feel that *his* problem was very important, and without exception there was the note of optimistic confidence that something could be done."

One of the most important qualities that Chavez and Ross looked for in recruits, the trainees noted, was single-minded commitment. Divided loyalties of any sort were denounced as a distraction that drew people away from full participation in the CSO. Chavez set the standard that everyone else tried to emulate.

"How well I recall one night, after a very long and strenuous chapter meeting, Cesar Chavez accompanied Mr. Ross and myself to the motel where we were staying," wrote the Rev. Gradus Alberts. "In spite of the fact that Cesar had had only three hours of sleep the night before, he stayed until 2 o'clock A.M. searching his own mind for answers to knotty problems existing within the chapters. I was deeply impressed by his insight into each problem . . . At 2 o'clock we said goodbye and Fred Ross and I watched him vanish into the night, for another hour's drive so that he might be on hand for an early morning appointment."

In his 1957 datebook, Chavez noted his mileage at the top of every day, keeping a cumulative total. On July 28, he hit the fifty-thousand-mile mark.

He saw little of his wife and five young children, though he made it home to San Jose most weekends. When Helen went into labor with their sixth child, Cesar was at the national CSO convention in Fresno; his brother Lenny drove her to the hospital. In later years, to justify his lack of attention to his family, Chavez often told a story about a decision he made during this period. The details changed with each retelling, and the fuzziness of time and place suggested the tale was more apocryphal than factual. But the message was consistent, clear, and heartfelt: Chavez had been working hard for the CSO, without a day off, and planned to finally spend a Sunday relaxing on a family picnic. Just as they were about to leave, someone showed up asking for help. Sometimes when he told the story, a man had been beaten up by the police and thrown in jail. In some versions, Chavez went on the picnic anyway, felt miserable, and ruined the day for everyone else; in other versions, he cancelled the outing because he could not turn away people in need. The ending was always the same: he told Helen he felt torn and needed to make a clear choice between his work and his family. He had to either be of service to people, or be a servant. He chose to be a servant, and from then on, he was happy.

"I told her I thought that I couldn't spend my life doing anything more worthwhile than working with poor people," he recalled. "Once I made the decision, I didn't have any more problems. Because I wasn't torn . . . People would come first. There wouldn't be any days off."

The Migrant Ministry trainees were not the only ones won over by Chavez's commitment and his quiet, unassuming style; he also was building a loyal following among CSO members across the state. People trusted Chavez. Whether he hung out in a San Jose barbershop or a Bakersfield church, his informal, conversational style put listeners at ease. His understanding of people's problems resonated, his familiarity with political power impressed, and his confidence in poor people's potential to affect change left them inspired. Gilbert Padilla, working in a Hanford dry cleaner, switched his allegiance from the Junior Chamber of Commerce to the CSO, captivated by Chavez's sense of outrage at the prejudice against Mexican Americans and his certainty that together they could fight back. Juan Govea, who had come to California as a bracero and worked for the Santa Fe Railroad packing ice, turned his Bakersfield house into an unofficial CSO office and stayed up late night after night, translating the driver's license manual into Spanish.

To the Ross house meeting strategy, Chavez added a twist, which he called the problem clinic. Whenever he was in one place long enough, he established an office where people could come to him for help. Each time a grateful person offered thanks or payment, Chavez asked instead: Help organize the CSO chapter. Hold a house meeting. Tell your friends. Become a member. Volunteer at the new office.

Chavez put all volunteers to work. Some typed letters, some manned the phones, some cut stencils, others drove sick people to the doctor. They found meaning in the work, and they, too, became CSO champions. The volunteer model evolved into a key element of Chavez's repertoire, a tactic for drawing supporters close. He was so intent on keeping them involved that if he ran out of things to do, he made them up. He told another (perhaps apocryphal) story to make the point: On a very slow day, he told volunteers he needed them to cut up boxes of old papers into small squares to make raffle tickets. They obliged. Once they left, he tossed the boxes of cut-up paper.

As he quietly assumed more of a leadership role, Chavez began to chafe at the limits of his position as a staff organizer. He was on the payroll of Alinsky's IAF but worked for the CSO officers elected by each chapter's members. He had to adjust to their weaknesses, compensate for their failings, and follow their priorities. The latter proved most difficult.

The battle in San Jose underscored a philosophical issue that troubled Chavez: as the CSO achieved success and grew in popularity, its members became more middle-class, and their focus shifted away from the poor. In San Jose, as in many chapters, older members who had grown up with the CSO and shared a commitment to its original ideals found themselves pitted against newer, more self-interested recruits. In 1957, Chavez had to watch, powerless, as the split threatened to undermine all the hard work he had done during his yearlong stay in San Jose. As a result of his dogged fund-raising, the chapter had begun the year with enough money to hire an organizer for at least six months. But at two successive meetings, each time the motion to hire an organizer came up for a vote, opponents forced it to be tabled. They pushed through other expenditures that Chavez deemed low priorities, such as $250 to purchase two typewriters. "At this rate," Chavez wrote Ross in mid-March, "the San Jose group will be flat broke in the next six months."

Ross asked the San Jose chapter to transfer $1,000 to the national CSO to hire an organizer. That, too, was rejected. "This damn issue has created more dissension than I don't know what," Chavez wrote. After all his efforts, the money dissipated.

Chavez faced a dilemma. He was empowering people, and they chose to exercise that power toward goals he did not share. He disapproved, but he could not control. A decade later he would vividly describe his frustration, emotion that profoundly influenced his future endeavors: "You don't become an officer, you do all the work, you become their servant, you don't even have a vote . . . You build it, and you stand aside here, and then they have the votes, they destroy it, they send everything to hell. And you're standing over here just, you know, really mad at them, mad at the world, because you put all this goddamn work into building something, and then they get into fights among themselves and destroy things."

Just five years after the CSO had been his lifeline out of Sal Si Puedes, he began to outgrow the organization. A critical tone entered Chavez's reports. He expressed increasing unhappiness about the dominance of what Father McDonnell called "fur coat Mexicans." After the 1957 national CSO convention at the upscale Hacienda Motel in Fresno, Chavez voiced sharp disapproval: "At this rate in another two or three years the plain common ordinary member will not be able to attend this gathering. Imagine a couple having to pay $14 for the registration and banquet. At this rate it will soon become a convention for the privilege[d] few.'"

Ross shared Chavez's disdain for the influx of more highly educated CSO members. The Migrant Ministry trainees were struck by the sentiment, and most noted in their reports that Chavez and Ross were convinced that higher education was a hindrance to developing leaders. The leadership of the Fresno chapter had become too "respectable," Ross said. CSO leaders in Oakland were better educated, and as a consequence less interested in "bread and butter issues." In general, Ross explained, what had at first appeared to be a negative—a lack of education—turned out to be a positive attribute: "In a significant sense these people were not corrupted by a formal educational institution . . . They were not afraid of adventurous thinking, including the prospects of failures."

Education became a code word for middle-class values and lack of concern for the poor. Middle-class, once a lifestyle Chavez aspired to have his children reach, now became a dirty word. He became more militant in his commitment to sacrifice.

When Alinsky raised his young organizer's salary again, from $4,800 to $5,200 a year, Chavez objected that the money was "corrupting." Alinsky ignored the protestations. "I would appreciate your attributing your 'corruption' to Fred Ross rather than to myself," Alinsky wrote in his typically wry manner. "I was willing to respect your wishes, but you know as well as I do how persistent Ross can get. All this is by way of saying that I would appreciate your not resenting 'too much' your salary increase."

While he lauded Chavez's work, Alinsky saw little progress toward making the CSO self-sustaining. He spoke out forcefully at the 1956 national board meeting, then again in 1957. In 1958, Alinsky came up with an idea that would buy the CSO some time. His plan bought Chavez a reprieve as well.

Ralph Helstein, head of the United Packinghouse Workers of America (UPWA), was an Alinsky ally in Chicago, a close friend, poker-playing buddy, and occasional collaborator. The two men saw some advantages to teaming up in California. Helstein's union represented agricultural workers who packed fruits and vegetables in sheds where the produce was taken after harvest. Shed jobs were a step up from the fields, but the lines had become increasingly blurred. Workers had long gone back and forth, depending on the seasons—as the Chavez family had done during the 1940s.

As refrigeration trucks became available, growers shifted work out of the packing houses and into the fields, where workers were not subject to the National Labor Relations Act (NLRA) or wage and hour laws. The move lowered salaries by about 65¢ per hour, decimated the ranks of the UPWA, and enabled growers to substitute Mexican guest workers for the local union members.

Helstein's union had won several elections in the Oxnard area, using procedures laid out in the NLRA, and won the right to represent workers who packed citrus. But the companies balked at negotiating contracts. An Alinsky-Helstein idea took shape. Perhaps the CSO could help the Oxnard workers, in exchange for a much-needed financial boost. A strong CSO chapter in Oxnard that demonstrated the political power of Mexican Americans might give the labor union added leverage in negotiating contracts.

At first Helstein proposed a $10,000 grant. Ross rejected the offer and said he needed twice that amount to build a CSO chapter in one year. By August they had a deal. The UPWA would give the CSO $20,000. CSO would hire Chavez as director of organizing, Chavez would hire an assistant, and the two men would spend a year in Oxnard.

Ross was sad about losing his organizing partner. Though their relationship had subtly shifted as the student began to outstrip the teacher, the pair enjoyed each other's company and worked well together as a team. They happily shared the most mundane tasks: Ross bought soap, and Chavez scrubbed the walls; Ross bought stencils, and Chavez fixed the typewriter; Ross called information to get phone numbers for prospective members, and Chavez made the calls.

In early August 1958, Ross and Chavez went to Stockton for their final collaboration. As soon as the grant from the UPWA started, Chavez would move to the payroll of the national CSO and report to the president, Anthony Rios. Ross wrote Rios to let him know where Chavez would be when the time came for him to make the move. "Just in case that twenty grand should come hurtling through the air, your new director of organization wants to let you know where he'll be and when you can have him," Ross wrote. "Well," the older man concluded, wistful about the imminent loss of his star pupil and accomplice, "all I can say at this point is me and my big mouth. I guess I told one too many people I'd give Tony Rios my right arm. But, God, I never thought I'd end up doing it!"

CHAPTER 7

David vs. Goliath, Round One

This has been a wonderful experience in Oxnard for me and [I] never dreamt that so much hell could be raised.

The election night party on November 4, 1958, in the Quonset hut in the Oxnard colonia lasted until three the next morning. Sixty precinct walkers, tired after hours of shuttling voters to the polls, filled up on homemade tacos, sang songs, and cheered as they watched the results on television. They didn't care who won. They had declared victory as soon as the polls closed.

Chavez had arrived in Oxnard six weeks before a local election, determined to make a splash by producing a record turnout among Mexican Americans—not to influence a specific race, but to signal the political power of the community. Chavez had prepared one index card for each of the 1,425 registered voters in five heavily Mexican American precincts, recruited one captain and nine volunteers for each district, and plastered CSO SAYS VOTE signs all over a temporary office. On election day, he egged on the captains in a competition to see who could produce the most voters. The result was a 72 percent turnout, a city record.

After only a few hours of sleep, Chavez was back at work, cleaning up party debris. To capitalize on the election momentum, he had scheduled the first CSO organizational meeting for the next evening. More than fifty people showed up an hour early at the Juanita School, and Chavez greeted each at the door. A Boy Scout color guard led the audience of 230 in the pledge of allegiance. After two and a half hours of speeches, the appointment of a temporary president and secretary, and the formation of committees, a large group adjourned to the nearby Blue Onion bar.

On Sunday, November 9, Chavez took his first day off in almost two months.

Oxnard had not changed much in the two decades since Chavez had lived in the seaside city as a young teen. Mexican Americans lived in the colonia, on the east side of the tracks, connected somewhat perilously to the rest of the city by only one road that shut down every time a train came through. Agriculture was the dominant industry, and the fields, sheds, and related businesses were the most common source of jobs for Mexican Americans. The rich alluvial soil and temperate climate of the Oxnard plain boasted some of the best year-round growing conditions in California. Sugar beets and citrus had long been the primary industries, and growers had recently expanded into vegetables and flowers.

One significant change had altered the Oxnard landscape. The small city in Ventura County was home to the largest labor camp in the United States for Mexican guest workers, known as braceros. The number of Mexicans employed in the Ventura County fields had increased steadily, jumping 25 percent in the year before Chavez arrived, to 3,148 men. Chavez soon began to hear a lot about the braceros.

He had arrived in Oxnard on September 19 and launched a house meeting campaign the same evening. Two meetings a night was ideal, one acceptable, none a dismal failure. Some nights the living room of a small house overflowed with a dozen or more curious listeners. Chavez tried to position himself in a corner, to watch the most faces. He usually delivered his rap to the hosts and a few of their relatives and friends. Sometimes it was just Chavez and his host, slightly embarrassed that the invited guests had not materialized. "No matter how successful the day might have been, if the house meeting doesn't turn up a good attendance we feel as if the whole day was spoiled," Chavez fretted after a night of back-to-back meetings that turned into one-on-one sessions. "To me the most important thing are the house meetings and I will not leave them for anything in the world," he explained, turning down requests to attend other evening events.

As usual, work took precedence over his personal life. He despaired of finding a house for his family because no one wanted tenants with seven small children. He asked Helen to come down from San Jose to help. Cesar picked her up at the bus station and took her straight to a house meeting. While Cesar talked, Helen wrote down the names and addresses of the twenty-two people, a record crowd. The animated discussion ran so late that some excused themselves to dash to work at the 11:00 P.M. shift at the sugar plant.

Amid the typical complaints and queries at house meetings, the issue that piqued Chavez's interest was the braceros. Residents told him they were routinely passed over for jobs in the fields, and sometimes fired, so that growers could hire cheaper and more docile Mexican guest workers. Both practices violated federal law, but authorities did nothing. Chavez saw how the injustice angered people, and he knew that anger would fuel a campaign. Anger fueled him, too; he was back in the city where he had shivered in a tent and endured the ridicule of classmates for wearing the same shirt every day.

Until now, Chavez's work had revolved around social and political issues. In his problem clinics, he had focused on individual problems. In Oxnard, he saw an opportunity for the CSO to directly affect the livelihoods of an entire class of members—if the organization was willing to take on the economic goliath of agribusiness. During house meetings, Chavez took special note of complaints about how braceros displaced local workers. As the CSO set up its usual committees—Citizenship, Membership, Voter Registration—he added a new one: the Employment Committee. He told the workers that if enough people showed interest, the CSO would get involved.

When he had practically given up, Chavez found someone willing to rent to a family with seven children, who ranged in age from seven months to eight years old. A landlady in nearby El Rio agreed to take the family after raising the rent $10, to $70 a month. He moved the family from San Jose and settled in, ready to tackle something more ambitious than voter registration drives and citizenship classes. He chose a fight that seemed almost impossible to win.

The bracero program had begun as an emergency measure during World War II to import temporary laborers to fill jobs in the fields and railroads left vacant by the exodus of military recruits. Its name derived from the Spanish word for arm and reflected the lack of humanity: Braceros were viewed as extra hands, disposable and easily replaced. The agricultural industry found this new workforce so cheap and malleable that growers successfully lobbied to extend the program long after the veterans returned home. Braceros' livelihood depended on their sponsors, who could send them home at any time. So the men had little recourse when they were underpaid, cheated out of wages, or housed in deplorable conditions. By the end of the 1950s, an increasing chorus had been urging Congress not to renew the program, to no avail. An entire economy had grown dependent on the braceros—not only the agricultural employers but a host of ancillary businesses. Braceros could be overcharged for anemic meals and substandard housing, forced to patronize shady businesses and services, and cheated out of health insurance. They still earned more money than they would back home in Mexico, and competition for the jobs remained fierce.

Religious activists, including the Spanish Mission Band, were among the first to demand an end to the bracero program. Father McDonnell used every opportunity to argue Catholics had a moral responsibility to lobby against the use of braceros in California's $2.5 billion a year agricultural industry. A state that was the leading producer of fruits and vegetables, he said, should shun a program that depressed wages for the poorest workers, broke up Mexican families, encouraged gambling, drinking, and prostitution, and deprived locals of jobs. Sociologists chronicled the braceros' mistreatment and indignities, which led to media exposés that showed Mexicans packed into filthy barracks and fumigated at the border with DDT.

Organized labor viewed the Mexican workers as an impediment to unionizing farmworkers. Unions were enjoying a period of relative success nationally as the postwar economy grew, and although the seasonal nature of migrant farmwork posed particular challenges, some leaders had begun to press for a farmworker campaign. Alinsky's friend Ralph Helstein was one. Walter Reuther, the dynamic leader of the United Auto Workers, was another. "The unspeakable cruelty with which migrant workers are treated in the United States has for many years, I know, been an especial concern of yours," Reuther wrote to George Meany, president of the AFL-CIO, in November 1958, just as Chavez arrived in Oxnard. "I believe that a climate of opinion and a national awareness could be created at this time which would make an organizing campaign practical and effective. It can succeed, however, only if the entire labor movement is prepared to cooperate and to provide practical day-to-day support in addition to the moral backing of an aroused public conscience against this kind of human exploitation."

For several years, representatives of the United Packinghouse Workers union had been complaining to federal officials that growers employed braceros ahead of local workers, in flagrant disregard of the law. The practice had dramatic impact on the union's members: the average packing shed worker in California worked at most three months a year, less than half of what had been the norm. The bracero program had also driven an alarming wage discrepancy: while nonfarm wages had increased 56 percent in the previous decade, farm wages had increased less than half as fast, barely keeping even with inflation.

Dependence on braceros varied by region and crop, but abuses had been well documented around California by the time Chavez arrived in Oxnard. He had paid scant attention. The CSO targeted citizens and potential citizens. Its members were overwhelmingly Mexican Americans, many born in the United States, and they drew a sharp distinction between themselves and Mexican nationals. When the Immigration and Naturalization Service deported one million Mexicans during Operation Wetback in 1954, the CSO did not register any complaints. The CSO had minimal contact with braceros, whose contracts required them to return to Mexico at the end of each season. When Chavez was asked at house meetings in 1957 whether braceros were displacing local workers, he said he was not familiar with the issue.

A year later in Oxnard, the first meetings of the CSO Employment Committee turned into gripe sessions. Workers aired their grievances, and Chavez listened. After a few meetings, attendance dropped off sharply. "Don't know whether it's because of lack of interest or because they feel it's impossible to put the program over," Chavez noted. "There was a lot of discussion on the different approaches to the problem, but we came back to the fact that it looks almost impossible to start some effective program to get these people their jobs back from the braceros."

That Chavez persevered was a testament to both his indefatigable work ethic and a strategic intuition that enabled him to see beyond the despair. He could play out the contest far enough into the future to envision change, at a time when no one else could.

His first hurdle was to convince workers they had a chance. He suggested they start with a "registration campaign" to sign up all the unemployed farmworkers in Oxnard. He told the committee this would document the extent of the prejudice against locals and show that workers were not overstating their problem. He cut a stencil and ran off copies of a one-page "Application For Work" form that included more than a dozen questions: work experience, education, union affiliation, citizenship, marital status, military service.

Volunteers began helping people fill out the forms in the CSO office while Chavez answered questions. He explained they were not a labor union and allayed fears about strikes. All they were doing, he said, was asking to be hired before the braceros, to reclaim jobs that belonged to local workers. Soon the momentum built. Romulo Campos, an out-of-work field hand, arrived at the CSO office with thirty completed applications. As Chavez had hoped, the registration campaign built an esprit de corps. He stayed late most nights, eating dinner in the office with the volunteers.

The farmworkers taught him how the system worked. Growers belonged to large associations. Each association set wages and handled hiring. A grower would order a certain number of carrot toppers or tomato pickers. The director of the major growers association had his office right in Oxnard's Buena Vista bracero camp. In collusion with state officials, the director devised ways to circumvent the requirement that growers prove no local workers were available before they hired braceros. Local workers had to first obtain a referral card from the state Farm Placement Services office, more than ten miles away. By the time they had filled out the application and been sent to the Buena Vista camp, all the jobs for the day were taken. When they returned the next morning, they were told they needed a new referral card. Or they were offered the least desirable jobs, at the lowest pay. Most soon gave up.

Surrender, Chavez told the dispirited workers, was exactly what growers wanted. Besides, he reminded them, they had nothing to lose. They had no jobs. What they did have was the law on their side, and an argument that appealed to anyone with a sense of justice. As the registrations piled up, Chavez looked for opportunities to make the injustice public. He learned that Edward Hayes, the state director of the Farm Placement Service and a close ally of the growers, would be the guest speaker at a Ventura County Farm Labor Association lunch. Chavez wrote and circulated a leaflet urging unemployed farmworkers to show up and castigate Hayes for his failure to enforce the law. Hayes waved the leaflet angrily during his celebratory meal with the growers and declared, "This bulletin is a dastardly thing!"

Chavez's next move was to give the enemy a face. He chose Hector Zamora, director of the Ventura County Farm Labor Association and the man who controlled the most jobs in the area. Zamora had worked both sides of the bracero program, which made him ideally positioned to help growers collude with government officials. When the bracero program began, Zamora worked for the U.S. Labor Department as a recruiter in Mexico. Later he worked in the Washington, D.C., office and then as a field representative in California. When public criticism of the bracero program mounted, Zamora penned lengthy rebuttals, portraying the guest workers as grateful for the opportunity. His last federal post had been the chief enforcement agent in Southern California; now he helped growers flout the law.

"Zamora seemed to have a very satisfied attitude and frankly asserted his right to decide who is a qualified worker and who should be employed," reported a federal labor department official who visited Oxnard at Chavez's urging. Zamora admitted that he made life difficult for the workers brought to him by the CSO, and he asserted he had the right to assign them wherever he wished.

Once the CSO had amassed hundreds of registration forms, Chavez was ready to challenge Zamora. The CSO moved into the phase Chavez dubbed the "rat race." At 9:50 on Monday morning, January 19, Chavez arrived at the Farm Placement Service office with four workers. They asked for dispatches to the Fred C. King ranch, where they knew of good-paying jobs on the flower farm. Chavez helped the men fill out lengthy paperwork, and they were directed to Zamora's office. They arrived at 11:25 A.M., too late for that day's work, and the dispatcher told them to return the next day with lunch, ready to work. Back at 6 A.M. on Tuesday, Zamora told them there was no work at the King ranch. The workers drove out to the fields—only to find sixteen braceros cutting flowers.

Chavez drove the men back to the Farm Placement Service office to complain. The state official called Zamora, who said Chavez's crew had shown up too late. Chavez drove back to the labor camp to argue with Zamora. "You come back tomorrow morning and I'll send you where I want to, not where you want to go," Zamora retorted. Each step of the way, Chavez took notes.

A subsequent inquiry confirmed what he suspected: the complaints he filed were sent to the growers association to answer. Even when government officials drafted responses, they were often typed by secretaries for the growers.

All through March, Chavez led the rat race. He bombarded the newly elected Democratic governor, Pat Brown, with telegrams demanding action. "I have no work. Do something for us," wrote Romulo Campos, the worker who had helped collect dozens of registration forms. Chavez kept filing more and more complaints.

He was not alone in pressuring government officials. In early February, U.S. labor secretary James Mitchell found more than two hundred farmworkers picketing outside the Biltmore Hotel in downtown Los Angeles when he arrived to address a farm labor conference. Fathers Donald McDonnell and Tom McCullough led the workers into the hearing room, where they stood silently at the back, holding up protest signs. Mitchell, a Democrat appointed by a Republican president, had earned a reputation as the social conscience of the Eisenhower administration. He repeatedly expressed support for extending minimum wage laws to farmworkers and ending the bracero program. Mitchell noted the workers' presence as he began his remarks.

"First, the conditions under which far too many of our farmworkers live and work today are an affront to the conscience of the American people. This is both my personal and my official opinion," the labor secretary said. He pointed out the country had a large surplus of underemployed farmworkers. In 1957, more than two million people reported working in the fields an average of only 144 days—down from 180 a decade earlier. Total wages averaged $892, also lower than any year since 1951. Mitchell delivered a strong attack on the bracero system: "The foreign labor programs in themselves often permit employers to evade the necessity to pay the wages and to do the many other things needed to attract and retain domestic farm workers . . . This is no secret . . . Too many migrant farm laborers are living as no American should live in this abundant land."

State and federal officials had launched several investigations into abuses in the bracero program. In the midst of the rat race, the *Oxnard Press-Courier* carried front-page reports that detailed scams where growers had collected insurance premiums from workers but never sent them to the insurance company. When workers filed claims, the authorities stalled until the braceros were back in Mexico.

If Chavez could keep up the pressure and feed investigators more ammunition, he thought he could outwit the growers. He worked hard to keep up the spirits of workers, who knew by now the campaign was destined to make a case for the long term. They joked about the futile efforts as they shuttled back and forth. But Chavez and a small group kept going back day after day, compiling the damning evidence. In February the tomato season started, and Chavez put state officials on notice that he had men ready to take those jobs. On February 23, they saw braceros weeding and hoeing in tomato fields at Summerland Farms. When telegrams to the state yielded no action, Chavez called a federal labor official, who arrived and pulled the braceros out. Summerland Farms agreed to hire the locals.

"Called Cesar," Fred Ross wrote in his journal on March 1, 1959. "He had his first victory today. Forced the farm labor office to remove braceros from a large tomato ranch and replace them with the local boys he's organized. Almost had a riot on his hands. He's getting up at 5 am every day to go into the fields and gets to bed at 12 or 1 am." When Ross went to visit, he was shocked at how tired Chavez looked.

The confrontations in Oxnard came to a head in April during the tomato harvest at the Robert Jones ranch. First Chavez convinced Jones to hire the local workers. Zamora came the next day with braceros and fired the local men. Chavez summoned federal officials, who warned Jones he could lose his certification to employ guest workers if he continued to allow Zamora to displace locals.

Jones took a different approach. He told the local workers they were picking too slowly. He said he would pay them by the box instead of the hour, to force them to go faster. The workers protested that would cut their pay in half. When Jones did not relent, the crew of twenty-five local workers staged a sit-down strike in the fields. The forty braceros working alongside joined the strike at first. But the braceros had little leverage; they knew there were plenty more in the camp.

The next day, Chavez teamed up with the UPWA local in a protest march from the Farm Placement Services office to the Jones ranch, where the men burned the state referral cards that had proved so worthless. The protest made television news and forced a summit meeting with state and federal labor officials.

Slowly, Chavez made progress. A few labor contractors and smaller growers started to come to the CSO office in the early morning to hire workers directly. Chavez arrived each morning at five to help. By May, the CSO office was functioning like a union hiring hall. The national CSO leadership thought the UPWA should take over and Chavez should focus on the CSO's more traditional functions. "On May 14 the General assembly [of the Ventura CSO] voted to turn over the activities of the Employment Committee, Lock, Stock and Barrel, over to the United Packinghouse Workers of America," Chavez wrote in his monthly report.

"In the last two months many things happened in the employment field and the whole battle to secure employment for the domestic workers in the Oxnard area," Chavez summed up. "It started with a sit down strike, a thousand complaints to both the State Farm Placement and the United States Employment Service and then a protest march from the Farm Placement office (trailer) to the Robert Jones Ranch. This, plus almost six months of Headaches and Heartaches on numerous attempts to obtain employment for the local workers produced several minor gains for the people of this area."

The director of the state Farm Placement Service promised to enforce local preference, not to require workers to go to the bracero camps for referrals, and to allow direct hiring at individual ranches. Federal officials began investigating complaints promptly. The state employment service moved its trailer closer to Oxnard. The CSO won recognition to represent workers with complaints to state or federal officials. The governor pledged to help raise wages.

"Going back to November 1958 when we first started the program," Chavez wrote, "one couldn't [imagine] that all of these gains were going to be obtained for the workers."

The once-hesitant rookie had methodically set out to take on the agribusiness powers and fight an injustice that resonated personally. The battle showcased his ability to outwork, outlast, and outthink his opposition. Emboldened by his success, he also began to express another theme: he needed more control. He was frustrated with the UPWA organizers, frustrated with his bosses at the CSO, and frustrated with his deputy. None of them worked as hard as he did. "This has been a wonderful experience in Oxnard for me and [I] never dreamt that so much hell could be raised," Chavez wrote to Ross. But he needed to vent about his coworker. "I'll never want to work with anybody else on another project unless it's Fred Ross, otherwise I'll go at it alone. 'No me vuelve a llevar otra Gallina el coyote.'" ("The coyote is not going to take another chicken from me!")

Chavez returned to his first love, the problem clinic. From 5:30 A.M. till midnight, dozens of people came to the office each day "with every imaginable problem from traffic tickets to marriage problems." Most mornings, people waited outside for the office to open—a woman denied welfare benefits, a man seeking disability insurance, a family fighting a deportation order, an absentminded citizen who put a can of tuna in his pocket and was arrested for shoplifting. Chavez negotiated with merchants, interceded with the police, and arranged transportation to government offices.

On a typical spring day, Chavez arrived at 5:10 A.M. and typed daily reports until farmworkers arrived to register for work. He took eight men to a tomato ranch, where they were hired at 60¢ a crate. Then he took six women to a strawberry grower, who gave them cards for jobs the next day at 85¢ an hour. Waiting for him back in the office was a man who needed a visa for his brother and help for a crippled child; a local farmer looking for a few men to tend smog pots in the lemon groves for $1.25 an hour; and a man who needed a correction on his marriage certificate. McMann Furniture called to work out a deal for a member behind on payments. The Somis Labor Association asked for one worker to repair ladders at $1.25 an hour. A labor contractor called to say he would pick up workers the next morning.

In the afternoon, Chavez loaded six people into his old station wagon for the ten-mile trip to the government office complex in Ventura. One person needed to protest the loss of voting privileges. A widow applied for aid to needy children and general relief. One man needed a marriage affidavit. Another inquired about a missing social security check. One man filed an appeal on an unemployment claim. And the last visited the IRS to straighten out a tax problem.

"These are some of the small things that are always happening which are almost impossible to keep track of," Chavez wrote, "yet they are the important things that offer the people hope in their day to day living."

The Oxnard CSO had 650 paid members. Biweekly meetings drew several hundred people and lasted several hours. The citizenship class had graduated fifty people. A new committee, proficient typists, trained others in office skills so they could become more useful volunteers. A rummage store was providing some steady income, and the chapter had a charter to open a credit union.

Ross watched from afar and exulted in Chavez's success. Writing the annual report for Alinsky at the end of 1959, Ross used one superlative after another. For the first time, Ross stressed, local workers had been organized to successfully challenge powerful growers. "This project could make a publication in itself. Cesar Chavez, who left the Industrial Areas Foundation to go to work for the National Community Service Organization in order to carry out this project, has literally averaged five to six hours of sleep a night for the past 11 months! With it has gone all of his sympathies and a life long desire to organize the 'ones below the bottom,' the ever-shifting, fearful masses of 'unorganizables,' the field workers from whose ranks he came and whose misery he has never been able to forget."

CHAPTER 8

No Hay Mal Que Por Bien No Venga

I'll never get caught in this trap again. I'll never be used again by people that way. I never will. As long as I live. If I see it coming, I'll leave. I'll never be an instrument to being used by people, however poor, however good intentioned they are.

Cesar Chavez sat in a Los Angeles office, studying numbers. As the director of the national CSO in 1960, he faced a budget so bleak that his own salary was in jeopardy. Chavez had an idea for a plan that could buy some independence for the organization. He was trying to negotiate a life insurance plan sufficiently attractive that the CSO could collect dues and generate steady income. Like most aspects of his two-year tenure as CSO director, the insurance idea proved an exercise in frustration.

Chavez was fond of a Mexican saying: "No hay mal que por bien no venga" (There is no bad from which some good does not come). The proverb applied to his final years with the CSO. Largely unrewarding, they provided an important education. From his own mistakes and the actions of others, he took away lessons about what he would do differently when he ran his own show.

At the end of 1959, Chavez had hoped to stay in Oxnard and build on his success. Saul Alinsky had come close to arranging a deal with Ralph Helstein to extend the collaboration with the United Packinghouse Workers. But internal politics became too complicated, and at the end of 1959 Chavez moved to Los Angeles to assume his new duties as director of the national CSO.

The family moved into 2457 Folsom Street in Boyle Heights, the heavily Mexican neighborhood of Los Angeles. The house was less than a mile from the CSO office at 4th and Mott. The youngest of the eight children,

Anthony, had been born in Oxnard and was only a few months old. Fernando, the oldest, was eleven, and the move was his sixth in as many years. He didn't bother making friends at school; he figured he wouldn't be there long enough. The children all had nicknames. Fernando was so dark as a baby that he looked like a pollywog, and his nickname was Polly. Anthony was called Birdie because he had resembled a bird as an infant. Elizabeth pronounced her own name as Titibet. Paul was round like a bubble, which was shortened to Babo.

Chavez no longer worked on Alinsky's staff and now reported to Tony Rios, who had become secretary-treasurer of the national CSO. The change imposed new administrative responsibilities on Chavez, as well as restrictions. He had less freedom to dictate his own agenda, less contact with Fred Ross, and more friction with Rios, who also worked out of Los Angeles. Rios worked for a traditional labor union, and his personal trajectory mirrored that of the organization. Rios came to represent for Chavez and Ross the wing of the CSO that embraced the middle-class aspirations of its members.

Financially, the CSO had wobbled along for several years, never able to respond to Alinsky's challenge to become self-sustaining. By the spring of 1960, Chavez was "scared stiff over the budget." He wrote to Herman Gallegos, who was serving as president of the CSO: "As far as our budget is concerned, limited is not the word, depleted would be more like it . . . You and I, Tony [Rios] and a very few others really realize the financial condition of [the] organization."

The members, scattered around the state in two dozen local chapters, were largely oblivious to the problems and had repeatedly demonstrated their reluctance to pay dues or to chip in to support national staff. Chavez was forced to lay off organizers and scale back plans as his budget shrank.

Lesson number one: insist that members pay dues sufficient to support their organization.

Given its desperate situation, the CSO jumped at a temporary infusion of money from the state labor movement, which turned to the predominantly Mexican American group for help during the spring of 1960, a presidential election year. The California AFL-CIO gave the CSO $12,000 to conduct a voter registration campaign in six counties with large Mexican American populations. A second round of funds enabled the CSO to hire eleven full-time and nine part-time workers. In all, they registered more than a hundred thousand new voters. But once the AFL-CIO money was gone, so were the organizers.

Lesson number two: don't depend on outside money and short-term grants.

The voter registration campaign signaled the Democratic Party's recognition of the growing political power of the CSO and its members. In April 1960, a group of leaders, most with ties to the CSO, had formed the Mexican American Political Association (MAPA). Edward Roybal, whose election to the Los Angeles City Council had been the CSO's first major success in 1949, became the first president. In the November contest between John F. Kennedy and Richard Nixon, MAPA sponsored "Viva Kennedy" clubs around California that worked for the Democratic ticket.

The most significant event for Chavez during the campaign was his introduction to another Ross protégé, Dolores Huerta, who worked for Chavez enlisting new voters in San Diego. Huerta and Chavez had met a few times at CSO events, but knew little of each other besides that Ross held both in high esteem. Huerta had served as the first secretary of the Stockton CSO when Ross set the chapter up in 1955. Ross admired her passion, her devotion, and her intrepid personality.

"She's a real fire-brand, as I think you know, and does more work for the CSO than all the rest of the Stockton leaders put together," Ross wrote Alinsky in March 1960, urging him to put Huerta on the IAF payroll. "She's smart, articulate, self-starting. Her main fault is a tendency to take on too many CSO responsibilities and programs, fly off in all directions at once, and as a consequence bog down on some of them from time to time." Ross assured Alinsky that after long discussions on this issue, Huerta was improving.

She joined the staff at a time when the CSO was shifting toward the political arena, following both the money and the interests of its members. Huerta's quick wit and doggedness proved a good match. She was comfortable in any setting, happy to cultivate political allies in Sacramento, and ready to charm or badger anyone and everyone for support. She became the CSO's Sacramento lobbyist, the first full-time advocate for Mexican American interests in the capital.

The successful voter registration drive had enhanced the CSO's political stature and dovetailed with the organization's increased emphasis on state legislation. Huerta's top priorities in Sacramento were extending the minimum wage to farmworkers and granting state pensions to elderly noncitizens. Chavez worked to generate letters and support from chapters around the state, to help Huerta pressure lawmakers. The agricultural interests held too much power for the minimum wage bill to stand a chance. But after several years of falling short, the CSO successfully pushed the pension bill through both houses. Gov. Pat Brown signed the law on July 14, 1961, delivering pensions for the first time to thousands of Mexican citizens who were permanent residents of California. More than a hundred CSO members proudly attended the bill-signing ceremony.

The law became both a major CSO achievement and a key element in the organization's demise. Many members who had helped fight for the reform, satisfied with the financial relief they would receive, drifted away from the CSO. Chavez felt deceived.

"I go and see them and say, 'We need your help so we can help other people.' 'Well, no,'" Chavez later recounted. "And they had more money now than before. So I said, I'll never get caught in this trap again. I'll never be used again by people that way. I never will. As long as I live. If I see it coming, I'll leave. I'll never be an instrument to being used by people, however poor, however good intentioned they are."

Lesson number three: people must be taught the value of sacrifice.

As the pension bill headed for success after an eight-year struggle, Chavez redoubled his efforts to make the CSO financially stable through a life insurance deal. He penciled out numbers, contacted insurance agents, and publicized the idea. He needed to collect enough advance commitments to guarantee the insurance company a minimum number of customers. He worked so hard that at its July 1961 meeting, the executive board of the CSO noted that Chavez had not taken his vacation—and passed a resolution ordering him to take time off. (There's no indication he complied.)

He thought he had struck a workable deal: A CSO member could receive a $1,000 life insurance policy and $500 for his or her spouse, for a contribution of $1 a month. Chavez proposed that CSO charge dues of $2 per month, with half going to pay the premium and the other dollar divided between the national and local CSO chapters. He calculated they could hire two full-time organizers for every three thousand families that bought insurance.

After weeks more negotiation with insurance agents, the agreement fell apart. "I'm feeling so low I could crawl," Chavez wrote to the president of the national CSO board. The All American Insurance Company had imposed age limits that killed the deal. "I personally can't see how we can go into an insurance program and have our members kicked out at age 70 and their spouses at age 65."

The CSO executive board convened at the Alexandria Hotel in downtown Los Angeles the weekend of November 17, 1961, and the mood was glum. In addition to imposing age limits, the insurance company required a minimum of 2,500 participants. So far, the CSO had commitments from 650.

Lesson number four: don't count on things you can't be sure of delivering.

Once he saw the insurance plan would fail, Chavez began to lay the groundwork for his own escape. He turned his attention back to farmworkers as he pondered how to extricate himself from the CSO.

Chavez had studied the history of attempts to unionize farmworkers and the decades of defeats. Growers associations were convinced that a union in the fields would be ruinous, and they had fought off all attempts with money, guns, and political power. In 1961, agriculture was the largest industry in California, worth $3 billion a year. Eight counties in the San Joaquin Valley alone produced more income from farms than all but four states. Another round of organizing attempts had recently begun in Stockton, a farming community at the northern end of the San Joaquin Valley.

Dolores Huerta lived in Stockton with her second husband, Ventura, a former farmworker. Both had worked for the CSO, and although she had no firsthand experience in the fields, Dolores had become increasingly involved in farmworker issues. She joined one of the more unusual attempts in farmworker organizing when the Spanish Mission Band priests set up their own union.

Fathers McDonnell and McCullough had hectored labor leaders about the need for a farmworker union, even riding cross-country on McCullough's motorcycle to personally appeal to the AFL-CIO. The priests grew so frustrated that they took matters into their own hands. McDonnell wrote the by-laws for the Agricultural Workers Association (AWA), whose acronym they pronounced like the Spanish word for water, *agua*, to convey the idea that a union was as essential as water. The fifteen pages of by-laws spelled out election and grievance procedures, membership oaths, dues, and fines. Local 1 was to be in San Jose, but the cerebral McDonnell never actually got started. In Stockton, the more practical McCullough had Local 2 up and running. He conducted his version of house meetings, which he called "cell division." He worked closely with Huerta.

AWA passed resolutions calling for a minimum wage of $1.25 an hour and an end to the bracero program. As Chavez had done in Oxnard, AWA sent workers out to be rejected for jobs and reported the complaints. A young sociologist, Henry P. Anderson, jettisoned his academic studies of braceros and joined AWA as research director. His reports publicized the adverse impact of the guest worker program on farm wages. The priests were increasingly in demand as speakers and advisers to groups fighting for farmworker rights. McCullough learned to fly and bought a small plane they called *The Spirit of St. Patrick*. No sooner had AWA begun to build momentum than organized labor finally stepped in.

Calls to help farmworkers had been growing since the merger in 1955 of the more staid craft unions in the American Federation of Labor (AFL) with the socially activist leadership of the Congress of Industrial Organizations (CIO). In the absence of legal protection for farmworkers to form unions, the challenge was great and the financial rewards dubious. Yet Walter Reuther described conditions in the fields as "the one remaining blot on American democracy in an economy of abundance." California, with almost half a million farmworkers, a relatively strong labor movement, and a Democratic governor, seemed the logical place to start. In May 1959, the AFL-CIO officially chartered the Agricultural Workers Organizing Committee (AWOC), bringing a new player to California. Norman Smith, the first head of AWOC, set up shop in Stockton. Folding the priests' organization into the new union seemed only logical. Huerta went to work for AWOC, but her tenure there was short-lived.

Almost two decades earlier, Smith had worked for the UAW and organized a Ford auto plant, and he carried as a credential a photo of his bloodied face during a confrontation at the gate. He attempted, with difficulty, to apply the same methods he had used at auto plants to the fields. He knew no Spanish, nothing about agriculture or the culture of Mexican and Filipino workers. In the winter of 1961, AWOC and the UPWA joined in a strike in the lettuce fields of the Imperial Valley. The strike was a costly fiasco. The AFL-CIO temporarily withdrew support for AWOC after spending a half million dollars.

The 1961 lettuce strike claimed another casualty—the Spanish Mission Band. The two Macs appeared at a rally in the Imperial Valley, McCullough leading the strikers in prayer and McDonnell leading them in song, including "Solidarity Forever." Outraged growers pressured the bishops to abolish the apostolate. Huerta told Chavez the news, and he wrote Ross asking that he weigh in to support their friends. Bishop John J. Mitty, who had created and supported the Spanish Mission Band, was in failing health, and the group was disbanded. By summer, McDonnell was on his way to a new assignment, far away in Mexico.

Chavez watched from the sidelines and took away more lessons. A union should not strike before it had won the support of workers. To call a strike as a way to organize was to hold out a false promise. Watching the spate of negative publicity, Chavez also concluded that the violence common to strikes in the fields cast unions in a poor light.

He revisited his own experience in Oxnard to extract more lessons. After he had left, the United Packinghouse Workers union had converted the old Employment Committee into a new local and charged dues of $1 a month. Lacking Chavez's persistence and personal appeal, the effort fizzled. State investigations revealed widespread bribery at the Farm Placement Service, and several top officials, including Edward Hayes, were fired or forced to retire. But their replacements appeared equally willing to help growers circumvent the regulations. New state rules included mandatory thumbprints for workers and procedures that made the process even tougher for local workers. If a worker turned down two referrals for any reason, he could not reapply. "Some of the things that are going on made me sick," Chavez wrote to Ross. People still came to the CSO with complaints, but the chapter was hard pressed to help. "The same old thing," Chavez concluded, "who is going to help the people?"

Chavez went to talk with his old nemesis, Hector Zamora, who had dispatched braceros from the giant Buena Vista labor camp. Zamora had been fired by the growers association and was happy to turn on his old employer. He told Chavez that the CSO complaints had been effective, and had they kept up the pressure, they probably could have forced the braceros out at the Jones ranch. But one tomato ranch would not affect hiring practices of the larger growers. Braceros were obtained in the name of one grower, who supplied workers to others for a fee—an illegal practice that could be documented with careful work. The system would have to be taken apart over time, piece by piece, with extraordinary patience and commitment.

"To organize the workers into unions, Oxnard is the place," Chavez wrote Ross. "Will have to take one grower at a time and make an example of him. Will have to put [up] with all kinds of strike breaking tactics but in the long run the grower would find it more economical to make peace."

Chavez was realistic about the power and reach of agribusiness, yet he foresaw the possibility of creating sufficient economic uncertainty that growers would be forced to accept a union.

He focused on his future beyond CSO. The possibilities excited him, but he also was scared. "I wish I had time to tell you of some of my latest dreams," he wrote to Ross on January 25, 1962. Chavez decided on a last effort to move CSO where he wanted to go. He proposed that CSO launch an all-out lobbying push in Sacramento to extend the minimum wage to farmworkers, which would "get the organization to be indisputably recognized as THE organization for the farm workers." A lobbying campaign centered on farmworkers, he told Ross, "will add a lot of excitement to the drive and furthermore it will give us some semblance of a crusade . . . I hope you dig this—man!!!"

Then he made his plans even more explicit, and included an indirect appeal to Ross to join him in a new venture:

> I'm going to propose this matter to the officers at the Hanford meeting. If they don't move or come up with another plan, I am sure that they don't have another plan nor will they move, then I am going to try this on my own and get it off my *pecho* [chest] once and for all. To be sure I won't be cooped up in this little office any longer. Then again by the time I get to Hanford I may be forced to take a hard look at the situation and decide to latch on to the dear old paycheck for all it's worth and continue here in the little office and really enjoy it. What I need is an accomplice to go along with me.

At the Hanford meeting, the officers did have another plan. Chavez's success in Oxnard had impressed Katy Peake, a wealthy benefactor who lived nearby in Santa Barbara and was interested in the farmworker cause. Her husband, Clive Knowles, was a regional director with the UPWA. She had loaned thousands of dollars to finance the unsuccessful lettuce strike in the Imperial Valley. Now she wanted to invest instead in Chavez. Peake offered the cash-strapped CSO $50,000 over three years to organize farmworkers, under Chavez's direction. The idea appealed to Rios and the CSO board, hungry for cash, and they began to draw up plans and build their upcoming convention around farmworkers.

Chavez was wary. He had come to believe that money from donors had strings and time limits. Organizing went on only so long as the grant. When outsiders came in and threw around money, Chavez had concluded, the commitment was shallow on the part of the funders, the organizers, and, ultimately the workers. Rios knew Chavez was key to Peake's commitment. He also knew that AWOC, the AFL-CIO chartered union, would not appreciate competition. And he knew that a significant chunk of the CSO's membership had little interest in farmworkers' problems. He crafted a compromise three-stage plan.

The ninth annual CSO convention opened the weekend of March 16, 1962, in the landmark De Anza Hotel, an oasis of elegance in dusty Calexico, just a few miles north of the U.S.-Mexico border. Calexico had more in common with its sister city across the border, Mexicali, than with the rest of California. The Wild West feel was appropriate for the cast that assembled at the De Anza, ready for a brawl. Norman Smith and a group from AWOC arrived, determined to reaffirm their rightful place as the designated organizers of farmworkers. Saul Alinsky and Fred Ross came to try once more to impose a plan to turn the CSO back to its roots, away from middle-class objectives, and toward a self-sustaining financial base. Rios, the powerful secretary-treasurer, showed up eager for Peake's promised $50,000 and ready to push through a farmworker proposal, but suspicious of the Alinsky-Ross-Chavez alliance. And Cesar Chavez arrived prepared to make his dramatic exit after a decade in the CSO.

Herman Gallegos, who had known Cesar since the two ran for office in the first CSO in San Jose in 1952, had served as national CSO president and gone on to a job in the administration of Gov. Pat Brown. Gallegos was one of a handful who bridged two worlds: an old-timer, trained by Ross and personally committed to Chavez, Ross, and Alinsky, but also an educated, upwardly mobile member of the middle class. Shortly before the convention, Cesar had approached his old friend and urged Herman to challenge Rios at the convention. He was the only candidate who could defeat Rios, Cesar told Herman. The CSO needed him. Herman was reluctant. He had politely but consistently rejected the life that Cesar and Fred chose, where work came first at any cost. But Herman was indebted to the old CSO and believed in Cesar, so he weighed the idea and talked to a few CSO stalwarts in San Jose. Word got around.

As the board members gathered before the convention opened in Calexico, the physically imposing Rios came charging toward Gallegos, pointing at Chavez. Had that man, Rios demanded, put Gallegos up to the idea of challenging the secretary-treasurer? Gallegos looked at Chavez. Chavez looked down. Gallegos shook his head, covering for his friend. The revolt was now public.

The convention opened Friday afternoon with reports from officers and staff. Chavez told the delegates that the insurance program had failed, and he blamed state regulations. He mentioned he had spent a month investigating the possibility of organizing farmworkers. Louis Zarate, the CSO president, reported on the discussions with Katy Peake and the shape of the final plan: she would fund two full-time staff positions for three years and provide a $25,000 strike fund.

That evening, Alinsky made yet another attempt to resuscitate the CSO. At a meeting with the leaders, he offered $5,000 from the Industrial Areas Foundation if the CSO would raise dues enough to bring in another $10,000. Without that, he said, the CSO was a "charity organization." Rios stormed out of the room in protest, committed to the idea that CSO services should be free.

Zarate opened the Saturday session by reminding delegates of the convention's goal. "The theme of the convention should be the battle cry to bring about justice to the agricultural workers," he said. Zarate outlined proposals, including the idea that the CSO might eventually function as a labor union. After much discussion, the matter was tabled till the following day.

On Sunday, Rios moved that the CSO adopt a multistep plan to organize farmworkers, starting with a service center that would include a credit union, insurance, and a cooperative. The convention approved the plan, and then a second motion that the CSO establish a Farm Labor Committee that could function as a bargaining agent. The language about a union was sufficiently vague to pass muster.

Chavez rose to speak, but he did not address the farmworker organizing proposal. He said he wanted to clear the air and deny the rumor that he planned to quit if Tony Rios were reelected. That was not true, Chavez said. But he was resigning. He said only that he could not work for a board that was so divided.

Like most in the audience, Sue Carhart was stunned. She ran the Migrant Ministry office in Corcoran, and like the rest of the staff she had trained for six weeks with Chavez and Ross. The experience had affected Carhart profoundly, and she had become personally and professionally attached to Chavez.

Carhart had grown up in a Republican family in upstate New York, come west after graduating from Union Theological Seminary, and spent her first year in traditional ministry work. She ran vacation Bible school and teen clubs, and delivered clothes and food to farmworkers. Then she trained with Chavez. She went to house meetings, registered voters, and stood in supermarket parking lots gathering signatures on petitions. She was transformed. She shifted from a paternalistic view to an understanding that poor people could set their own agenda. She campaigned for low-cost public housing. She changed the role of the Migrant Ministry so radically that by the time she arrived at Calexico for the CSO convention, the grower-dominated church that sponsored her ministry had threatened to withdraw financial support.

Carhart had stayed in frequent touch with Chavez after her training. She respected his quiet authority and admired his unrelenting dedication. When he announced his resignation, she was crestfallen. As soon as she returned home from the convention, Carhart wrote to her boss, Chris Hartmire, the recently arrived director of the Migrant Ministry. Carhart described the scene in Calexico: "It seemed that a group was gaining control that didn't have the same goals as those we admire so much in CSO . . . Fred Ross was rather philosophical about the whole thing. Said that maybe they needed to go through this stage and lose Cesar in order to appreciate him."

Carhart knew Hartmire had developed a close relationship with Chavez, and she hoped the minister would talk with Chavez and learn more. "I didn't have a chance to tell Cesar so," she concluded, "but tell him I felt as if we had lost arms and feet and heart."

PART II

April 1962–July 1970

CHAPTER 9

Viva La Causa

This is what I tell the workers when we get together. I start out by thanking whomever is responsible for setting up the meeting and also those present. Also tell them that this is not a union and that we are not involved in strikes. Make sure they don't think I'm against the unions or strikes, but tell them that the way things have been handled by the unions makes me feel that unless they change their approach they'll never get anywhere. I start out by telling them this is a movement (un movimiento) and that we are trying to find the solution to the problem.

The man who had not taken a vacation in years packed up his family and headed to the beach. The Chavezes spent the third week of April 1962 camping at the state park in Carpinteria, just northwest of Oxnard. On Easter, Cesar took pictures of his young children playing in the sand.

The next day, Cesar and Helen Chavez returned to Delano, the city where they had met as teenagers. They arrived on April 23, 1962, with eight children, no jobs, about $1,200 in savings, and an impossible dream.

Chavez set out to form a labor union for the poorest, most powerless workers in the country, excluded from protection under virtually every relevant health and labor law. He confided his improbable mission only to a handful of close friends. To everyone else, he was conducting a census of farmworkers, to gauge their needs. No one had ever just asked them what they wanted. Outsiders always imposed their visions. Based on the response, he would develop strategies to help the workers. If he didn't, no one else would. That was his explanation to anyone who asked.

Chavez had no illusions about his task. His goal was to radically reshape the largest, most powerful industry in California, a $3 billion a year business whose leaders sat on the boards of banks and in the chambers of county and state legislatures.

Nor were field hands eager to rise up and jeopardize their fragile livelihood. Adversity had rendered many farmworkers exceedingly wary of taking risks. Years of exploitation, physical hardship, and searing indignities had beaten them into hopelessness and despair. Daily travails were all-consuming—the challenge of feeding a family, the struggle to survive. Farmworkers could not see a future for their children outside the fields. They could scarcely imagine a world where they had a right to refuse the filthy drinking cup with warm water on a 100-degree day, or demand a bathroom to avoid the indignity of squatting in an open field. They accepted as inevitable the need to wake before dawn and line up in parking lots to beg for the right to spend eight to ten hours in pain.

The pain varied from crop to crop and season to season: bending over all day with an eighteen-inch hoe to thin tiny beet seedlings to one every four inches, dragging a sixteen-foot cotton sack that weighed up to a hundred pounds, clipping thorny vines in below-freezing temperatures, or wading into cold, muddy fields to harvest broccoli, rushing so as not to fall behind. In the lettuce fields, pain was bearable for many only with drugs or alcohol, readily supplied by foremen.

The financial exploitation varied little. Labor contractors demanded two weeks' work before the first paycheck, skimmed off hours or entire days, and fired anyone who complained. Workers would be in debt to the company store for food and gas before they saw their first check. Labor camps were squalid and indoor plumbing scarce. More than two decades after *The Grapes of Wrath*, conditions had changed little.

For all the physical hardship, worst was the loss of dignity. Mexicans had a saying to describe the way Anglos viewed them as industrious but dumb, good for field work because they were close to the ground: *Como dios a los conejos, chiquitos y orejones*—the way God looks at rabbits, short with big ears. Children were told there was no point continuing to high school; they would have no use for education. Daily insults in the fields burned. Fathers were dressed down and humiliated in front of their children; women were taunted and sexually harassed in front of their husbands.

All this Chavez knew well when he launched his quixotic quest. He counted on anger to eventually overcome fear. He thought he could prevail if he were able to instill hope. He set out to win over workers, one by one.

Helen Chavez, who always suffered for her husband's crusades, understood fully the consequences of giving up a steady paycheck. She also appreciated the high stakes of the mission and offered unconditional support. "You know, when you have been a farmworker all of your life . . . I knew somebody had to do something about it," she recalled years later. "I had seen what my mother had gone through, what I had gone through."

They chose Delano because Helen still had family there, including two sisters. Cesar's brother Richard had also settled in Delano and established himself as a successful carpenter. Cesar knew his family would not starve. After a few weeks, they found a small two-bedroom house at 1223 Kensington, on the better side of town, for $50 a month.

Delano lies near the southern end of the San Joaquin Valley, a farming town with streets laid out in alphabetical order, bisected by the tracks of the Southern Pacific. Founded as a railroad outpost in 1873, the city was named in honor of Columbus Delano, secretary of the interior under President Grant. Almost a century later, fewer than twelve thousand people lived in wood-and-stucco homes on streets that trailed off into vineyards and cotton fields. In 1962, the city was largely segregated, just as it had been when the Chavez family lived there two decades earlier. On the west side, where the Mexicans lived, was the Fremont School, Our Lady of Guadalupe church, and People's Market. For most everything else, residents had to cross the tracks.

When Chavez had plotted his next move during his final months with the CSO, he had focused on Oxnard, where he had established a base. Oxnard's temperate climate and nearly year-round growing conditions had advantages over the sweltering summers and cold, foggy winters of central California. But after Chavez resigned from the CSO and spurned the financial offer from Katy Peake, she put her money into a new enterprise called the Oxnard Farm Service Center and hired Chavez's former assistant. Oxnard was out.

The choice of Delano, dictated by personal considerations, profoundly shaped the farm worker movement. The city in the heart of the table grape industry anchored Chavez to the vineyards and nurtured a sentimental connection to the people who worked in the grapes. Vines were not like lettuce or tomatoes, seasonal crops planted in one field this year and in a different place the next. In Delano, growers and workers shared an attachment to their land, often the only common bond. The permanency of the grapevines appealed to Chavez. Even in winter, the desolate vines made a good backdrop for strikes and protests.

From his base in Delano, Chavez had access to thousands of farmworkers who tilled millions of acres of farmland in the San Joaquin Valley. He had crisscrossed the valley many times during his CSO years.

He could call on a network of contacts scattered across towns where he had once set up chapters—Bakersfield, Hanford, Madera, Arvin, Lamont, Corcoran, Parlier, Mendota, Firebaugh.

Three days after arriving in Delano, Chavez held his first house meeting. He had already discovered some sobering facts: Delano growers paid the highest wages in the valley, $1.10 an hour during the grape harvest, a dime more than in other areas. Young men working piece rate on jobs like girdling vines could earn as much as $25 working from five in the morning until noon. A dozen labor contractors worked the area, middlemen whose ability to control their workers would make Chavez's quest even more difficult. "I'm beginning to think that if there ever was one place not to start in, this was it," he wrote to Ross.

Chavez became a prolific correspondent during his early months in Delano. He was not a fluid or comfortable writer, but he turned to Ross for both financial and emotional sustenance. Isolated and on his own, driven by his vision, by turns hopeful, overwhelmed, and scared, Chavez wrote Ross almost every week. Ross's encouragement offered a lifeline. "Sure happy to receive your letter this morning," Chavez wrote on May 2, 1962. "Cheque or no cheque, your letters will give me that hope which I need so badly right now."

Chavez's focus and work ethic kicked in. To start his census, he prepared a short explanation on a borrowed mimeograph machine. He distributed the flyer through the "leaflet committee"—his kids, plus his nieces and nephews. "The Farm Workers Association is conducting an extensive drive to register all of the Farm Workers in the San Joaquin Valley," his leaflet read. "The purpose to the census is to determine the exact number of workers in each community throughout the valley. In this Census information is being asked to find out from you, the Farm Worker, what ought to be the minimum hourly wage . . . to register with the association you must fill out the white card."

He chose four-by-six-inch index cards, inexpensive and easy to fill out. He scrapped the lengthy forms he had used in Oxnard and asked for only five pieces of information—name, address, permanent address, birth date, and number of dependents. He asked two questions: "In your opinion, what should be the minimum wage paid Farm Workers?" and "Would you be interested in a newspaper to inform the Farm Workers about their rights under the labor laws?"

Dolores Huerta was still on the CSO payroll, but her allegiance was to Chavez. She drove to Delano from her Stockton home at the north end of the valley and spent a day and a half with Cesar and Helen, mapping out the registration campaign. They spread out an atlas of the San Joaquin Valley, eight sprawling counties that ran 220 miles from the Sacramento–San Joaquin River delta south to the Tehachapi Mountains, which separated the valley from Los Angeles. Cesar, Helen, and Dolores marked all the small towns they would visit and divided up the territory. From Stockton, Huerta would register farmworkers in the northern part of the valley. "She, Helen and I decided on the name of the group: 'Farm Workers Assn.,'" Chavez wrote to Ross. "Decided to go ahead and use a name and try to take advantage of whatever publicity we may get during the registration drive."

Each week, Chavez drove all over the valley, forming small committees of workers who promised to circulate the registration cards and mail them back. He went into labor camps, including the one where Ross had worked in the 1930s. In Reedley, he followed three teenagers to the local swimming hole to talk to their friends, then waited an hour on the riverbank until the men emerged from the water. Usually, he surveyed a barrio and waited until around five-thirty, after dinnertime. He approached small groups at random, explained his mission, and handed out registration cards. Most times he found volunteers to set up a committee in one evening, left them with cards, and moved on to the next town.

By June, Chavez was printing cards by the thousands. "The local office supply store is running in circles trying to keep me supplied with white cards," he wrote Ross. "I know the guy wants very badly to find out what in the hell I'm doing." The cards began to pile up in his rented post office box. The average age of workers registering was thirty-six and a half. The demand for a newsletter was high. The expectations of a fair wage were disappointingly low.

Chavez started to define his target audience more narrowly. He divided farmworkers into categories, much as Father McDonnell had done a decade earlier in San Jose—migrants, temporary workers, guest workers, and "true workers." Chavez was not interested in braceros, unemployed construction workers or students earning extra money in the fields. "I tell them I'm looking for the true workers who depend 100% on farm work to make a living . . . I say that this worker is not recognized because he is white, brown or black but is recognized because his back aches with the tortures of farmwork and his shoulders are stooped with the weight of injustice."

Fear and hopelessness were his biggest hurdles. Chavez pondered what combination of psychological and practical incentives would persuade workers to pay money to join an organization that challenged the status quo, risking the ire of their employers on the chance that the new group might succeed. He vacillated between idealistic and pragmatic approaches. He wanted only the most committed workers who would willingly labor for the benefit of all. He was determined to demand sacrifice, to charge dues, and to avoid the mistakes of the CSO. "Otherwise we will be kidding ourselves and will again become slaves of those we are trying to help and will not be able to be effective."

By August, after three months in Delano, Chavez had settled on his approach. For the first time, he used the word "movement" to describe his work:

> My pitch has finally developed so that I don't have to be changing around everytime I give it . . . This is what I tell the workers when we get together. I start out by thanking whomever is responsible for setting up the meeting and also those present. Also tell them that this is not a union and that we are not involved in strikes. Make sure they don't think I'm against the unions or strikes, but tell them that the way things have been handled by the unions makes me feel that unless they change their approach they'll never get anywhere. I start out by telling them this is a movement *(un movimiento)* and that we are trying to find the solution to the problem.

In a May 28, 1962, letter to Ross, Chavez first closed with the salutation that would come to be known worldwide as the slogan of his movement: "VIVA LA CAUSA." He had defined his undertaking not as a job or a mission but as a cause.

As Chavez pursued his cause throughout the San Joaquin Valley, his family survived on savings, unemployment checks, work in the fields, and help from friends and relatives. When Chavez filed for unemployment in Bakersfield, his initial interview took three hours because he argued over how to classify his previous job at the CSO. The unemployment official tried "clerk," then "playground supervisor," then "intermediate 3rd class social worker with a second language." Chavez refused all three. He made them search all the code books and finally, with nothing close to "community organizer," he acquiesced to "public relations administrator, Class A." He was reasonably sure they would not succeed in finding him a job in that category. His checks began arriving on May 8, 1962.

As Chavez's project became better known, he received more offers. Katy Peake again offered financial support. On July 31, 1962, he was offered a job with the Peace Corps. He rejected both. He was still collecting unemployment, though he narrowly escaped a job selling used TVs after a store manager turned him down for lack of experience. The Chavezes moved next door, into a larger house owned by the same landlord. They paid the same $50-a-month rent for 1221 Kensington—856 square feet plus a screened-in porch where some of the children could sleep.

Helen worked in the fields to support the family. She thinned onions, ten hours a day, for a dollar an hour. She hated every minute. Her sister pulled strings to get Helen hired picking grapes at the DiGiorgio ranch, where she had worked as a teenager. Her sister was a crew boss and had more latitude at work, so she often was able to take care of three-year-old Anthony during the day. Helen woke up before dawn, made breakfasts and lunches for the older children, then left for work. In the afternoon she cleaned, cooked, did laundry, and took care of the eight children, ages three to thirteen. With Cesar seldom home, she tried to summon the energy to focus on the older children and respond to their stories about school.

Cesar occasionally worked in the fields when they ran short of money, labor that helped burnish his credibility with workers. In summer, Fernando went to work picking grapes at $1 an hour, earning $36 his first week. "This is his first big money," Cesar wrote to Ross. "The girls call him King and kid him about their willingness to take off his shoes and do anything for him, little favors. He came home and gave Mama all of the money and told her how it should be spent. Then he waited up for me until I came in and wanted to know how old I was when I earned my first $36 in one week."

The first winter was the hardest. Unemployment ran out, and bills piled up. They ate powdered eggs and beans. The kids began to show signs of malnutrition. Fred Ross's wife got angry when he told her how the children were hurting.

Chavez was determined that dues would eventually pay his small salary, or the organization would not succeed. In the interim, when he ran out of money, he relied on friends. He took Ross up on an offer to coordinate fund-raising. "Never thought the time would come when I would treasure a lousy piece of mimeo paper or a 4×6 card as much as I do now," Chavez wrote Ross. "As much as I didn't want to accept outside help, it is looking very much like I'll have to. Both Helen and I can't quite accept the idea of begging but it looks as if we will have to. So back to your gracious plan. We do need help if for nothing else but to buy material and pay for the gas expenses. I'm sure you know this. I will feel a lot better if you did the begging on my behalf."

The first person Ross appealed to was Alinsky. Ross outlined Chavez's plan, estimated the costs at $600 a month, asked for IAF support, and a personal contribution from Alinsky. Alinsky did not respond. Ross cobbled together a coalition of financial backers, mostly old-time CSO supporters. He extricated promises of monthly support—$5 here, $15 there—and sent Chavez encouraging notes along with contributions which he called "units of supply."

Among Chavez's most faithful supporters were Abe and Anna Chavez (no relation), who had founded the CSO chapter in Salinas during the 1950s, when he worked as a counselor at Soledad prison and she taught kindergarten. Abe had a master's degree from Berkeley and a state job as a parole commissioner. They had hosted Chavez, Ross, and Alinsky many times, and had grown to admire Chavez's special talents. At first he had impressed Abe and Anna only as quiet and unassuming. Then they watched him take command, soft-spoken, not particularly articulate, but so sincere and sure of himself. His presence made people listen to what he said, and want to help.

"Heard about your project and am pleased you have the guts to attempt that type of approach to help the farm workers," Abe wrote to Cesar. "I can only say that you deserve all the luck in the world and may you be able to put your idea across. I am sending a small check to help your luck, that's the least I can do. Will send something each week. Keep up the good work." In appreciation, Cesar gave Abe and Anna rosebushes, courtesy of farmworkers at a nearby nursery. Their roses were the envy of the block, Anna Chavez reported.

In communities where Chavez had admirers from his CSO years, word spread that he was working without pay. CSO members offered money for gas and food. "I remember how hard I used to find it to tell the people that I was being paid to organize CSO chapters," Chavez wrote Ross. "Now, I'm finding it much harder to tell them I'm not being paid. Most of the evenings someone somewhere will offer me food, and I take it right away. Sometimes I don't get any invitation so have to wait until I get home. Talk about being hungry."

He poured out frustrations and fears to Ross with unusual candor and awkward analogies ("Trying to determine who the Farm Worker is is about as hard as it once was to isolate the atom."). He wrote with elation when a young CSO member passed up a vacation in Mexico to help with the census and pride when his brother Richard organized a card-signing blitz in Delano. Two weeks later, Chavez was despondent. Committees had disintegrated, house meetings had fallen apart: "Dear Fred, All is not well. I'm going too fast and am having difficulty covering my tracks."

Ross was not the only one Chavez counted on for support. One of his early and most steadfast disciples was Chris Hartmire, the recently arrived director of the Migrant Ministry. Hartmire sent money regularly and stopped by Kensington Street whenever he passed through Delano. He became an important source of counsel, and the relationship offered Chavez an alliance with a religious group, which he knew would be important.

For Hartmire, the connection to Chavez had already been life-changing. The minister had arrived in California in late 1961, reluctantly leaving his urban East Coast roots and doubtful whether he could last two years. He had grown up in Philadelphia, graduated Phi Beta Kappa from Princeton in engineering, then entered the seminary to do good. He was arrested during the Mississippi Freedom Rides and arrived in California seeing no connection between the civil rights movement of the South and problems of migrant farmworkers. Then he met Chavez and Ross. Hartmire was entranced by their vision of organizing. A month-long stay in the Stockton boardinghouse owned by Huerta's mother gave him exposure to the CSO methods. He began to transform the Migrant Ministry, working closely with Chavez. Once Chavez left the CSO, Hartmire shifted his allegiance to the Farm Workers Association.

Hartmire invited Cesar and Helen to Migrant Ministry staff retreats to explain their plans and enlist support. He donated a mimeograph machine, which Chavez installed on his back porch, where the ink leaked in the triple-degree summer heat. Then Hartmire assigned his newest staff member, the Reverend Jim Drake, to work with Chavez. Drake came with a little red Renault, a credit card for gas and food, and an infectious spirit. He and Chavez hit it off immediately.

Chavez drew on political capital he had built up across the valley during his decade with the CSO. Several chapters donated money, and CSO leaders became the core of Chavez's committees throughout the valley—Roger Terronez in Corcoran, and Gilbert Padilla in Hanford. In

Bakersfield, David Burciaga held house meetings and registered about fifteen workers a day. In Hanford, Antonio Orendain helped with the census and scrounged reams of mimeograph paper. At the annual CSO convention in July 1962, partisans offered a resolution to support the "Chavez plan," and opponents argued the farmworker census might interfere with AWOC, the AFL-CIO union, which was active in several areas of California. Ross sent Chavez a blow-by-blow account of the convention: Tony Rios accused Ross and Alinsky of listening to the "lies of a bunch of snakes." Alinsky berated the delegates for their shabby treatment of Ross. Huerta lobbied for the Chavez plan. Orendain became so incensed by an AFL-CIO official's objections to the census that he waved a registration card in the man's face and "told him he didn't care what [he] or anyone else said, the Farm Workers were going to be organized 'with CSO or without CSO.'"

Chavez's efforts to downplay suggestions that his association might function as a union didn't stop the questions, which gave him opportunities to emphasize his differences with AWOC. He felt that strikes were often called by unions prematurely, at the expense of workers. AWOC exemplified that model—a union that called strikes it could not win "because they don't really care about the people and will sacrifice the workers on strikes before they are actually ready," he wrote.

Leaders of AWOC remained suspicious of Chavez's claim that he was merely conducting a farmworker census. AWOC opened a large office in Delano, and Norman Smith, the former UAW organizer sent to run AWOC, arrived to preside over an open meeting. Chavez packed the room with supporters. "I told the people there that the drive was to get information directly from the workers and find out how they feel on some of those questions that outsiders have been deciding for the workers for too damn long now," he recounted. Chavez was questioned by one of AWOC's strongest organizers, Larry Itliong, a cigar-chomping Filipino who headed the Delano office. Itliong asked if Chavez was conducting the drive around the state. Was he aware that a labor union was already organizing the workers? Did he oppose that? Chavez dodged the questions. "I'm almost sure though that Smith doesn't realize what we are really up to," Chavez concluded. "I'm sure he thinks we are still just conducting a little survey."

After eighty-six days and 14,867 miles, Chavez was ready to formalize his organization. He called a convention for September 30, 1962, in Fresno, the center of the valley. "Check the letterhead, paid for by my relatives, and which will be used for the credentials for the Fresno mtg," Chavez wrote to Ross on September 18, showing off his new Farm Workers Association stationery.

To help set up the convention and run the new organization, Chavez called on one of his most trusted accomplices—Manuel Chavez, the cousin he considered a brother. Manuel was not an easy recruit. He was working as a salesman at Guarantee Chevrolet in San Diego, where he bragged he earned as much as $2,000 a month, working four-hour days. Cesar first appealed to his cousin's sense of outrage, reciting the ways they had been cheated and humiliated as farmworkers by conniving labor contractors. Then Cesar reminded Manuel, who had had his share of encounters with law enforcement, how the police mistreated Mexican Americans. Still Manuel resisted. "Hell, let the farmworkers get out like I did," Manuel recalled telling Cesar. "He said, 'That's why the farmworkers don't get organized; all the farmworkers that get out of farmwork, they say the same thing once they get a good job.'" Manuel agreed to give it a try, and moved to Delano. Built like a wrestler, Manuel was smooth, charming, funny, and a natural salesman. He had a talent for making things happen and a hustler approach to life that complemented Cesar's strategic mind.

Even as he issued invitations to the Fresno convention, Chavez harbored doubts about the viability of his new venture. But he was clear in his expectations and unwavering in his demands. "As for me if the people in Fresno should vote not to pay dues and not to incorporate then I shall move out of state and begin the same thing in Arizona," Chavez wrote Huerta, who was helping plan the convention.

> If the workers vote to incorporate then I'll demand dues to live on and to hire more people and do a job. I will not be contented to have a large membership or to simply serve the people. I want something meaningful as soon as possible and I need the time in which to work at it. The dues and the membership and the service programs and the rest are only accessories to the main purpose of establishing some definite and concrete gains via collective bargaining contracts with employers. This sounds crazy but it is the ultimate goal and toward that goal I must work unflinchingly.

He realized he needed to offer something to make dues worthwhile. He decided to follow a suggestion from Ross and suspend the collection of dues until the association could deliver life insurance as a benefit "to *inspire* the workers to pay," he wrote to Ross.

Ross told Chavez that he couldn't attend the convention while on the IAF payroll, "but I'll be keeping all 10 fingers crossed and calling upon the saints of all good agnostics to bring you luck and success." Four days later, Ross decided he just couldn't stay away. He booked a flight arriving in Fresno on September 29 at four-thirty and "will stay over for the meeting if they let striking gabachos in."

Chavez had invited each of the small committees he had formed in towns around the valley to elect two convention delegates. About 150 workers and their families gathered at 10:00 A.M. on Sunday at the Edison Social Hall at 1405 California Street in Fresno. Huerta led the pledge of allegiance. Hartmire offered welcoming remarks, one of the few speeches in English. Chavez reported they had registered more than twenty-five thousand farmworkers. He thanked contributors, singling out several CSO chapters, Abe Chavez, and Fred Ross. Then he gave a short tutorial in parliamentary procedure—speeches should not exceed five minutes, no one should leave the hall during the meeting, only delegates could vote. He asked for a motion to formally organize the Farm Workers Association, which passed unanimously, followed by a lengthy debate on whether the name should be in English, Spanish, or both. Orendain, an immigrant more comfortable in Spanish than English, argued that they must use English in order to be inclusive of other ethnic groups. His motion carried the day.

The debate over dues was most heated. Proposals ranged from $1 to $3.50, and in the end the motion to assess $3.50 a month passed with the understanding that dues would not be collected until an insurance policy was offered. Jesus Martinez, an older farmworker from Sanger, delivered an impassioned speech about the need to levy sufficient dues to pay staff to carry out the work. On the strength of his oration, the little-known Martinez became the association's first president. His election would be the last time anyone in the farmworkers union spontaneously won office in an unscripted nomination. Chavez was elected general director. He had a commitment of $75 a week in salary and expenses, once the treasury had cash.

The dramatic highlight of the meeting was the unveiling of the association's new flag. The genesis of the black eagle exemplified Chavez's ability to meld Ross's attention to detail with a soaring vision. Chavez wanted an emblem that would be immediately recognizable, easily reproduced, and visually stunning. He thought about this for months. He studied marketing in grocery stores, cigarette packages, and advertisements on billboards. He researched which color combinations were most visually arresting and why Hitler chose the swastika and the Nazi flag. Chavez concluded that his flag, too, must be black, red, and white because the color combination attracted the most attention. He came up with the idea of an eagle from the "Blue Eagle," the New Deal–era symbol that was used to signify compliance with the standards of the National Recovery Administration, created by Franklin D. Roosevelt in 1933.

To execute the flag, Chavez turned to his brothers. He asked Richard, the craftsman, to sketch an eagle. Richard drew the thunderbird, with squared-off wings and feet so simple anyone could draw the symbol. Then Chavez asked Manuel, who could always find money to get things done, to produce a giant flag, large enough to dominate a meeting hall. Cesar wanted a black eagle on a red and white background.

They hung the flag at the front of the Fresno hall, hidden behind a curtain. Just before lunch, Manuel dramatically pulled off the paper to reveal the banner. Cheers drowned out a few gasps. Manuel was unprepared when asked to explain the significance, but he made up an answer on the spot: black was for the workers' desperation, white was for their hope, and red was for their sacrifice. The founding members of the Farm Workers Association shouted out the motto they had unanimously adopted: "Viva la causa!"

Ross could not have been prouder. "Well *mijo*, you've really done a fantastically wonderful job!" he wrote to Chavez three days later. "I know there's a long way to go, but with that marvelous *maña* (skill, cunning) of yours, and judging by the glory I saw pouring from the eyes of the farmworkers sitting around that table all afternoon, and with luck, you'll make it. I'm absolutely sure of it." Then Ross headed for a three-week rest at a favorite hotel in Puerto Vallarta, Mexico, his "spiritual home."

"The last day of September 1962 may well go down in California history as the beginning of a new era for the lowest-paid, worst-abused and the most unjustly treated group of people in our economy—the farm workers," read a press release announcing the official formation of the association. No member of the press yet evinced any interest in a meeting of farmworkers in Fresno. But Chavez had begun to shape the story of the movement, and of himself.

Who is organizing the FWA? the handout asked. "The Farm Workers, themselves. It all began in the mind of a man named Cesar Chavez, who at 17 left California's fields to go to war, came out and worked in a lumber yard in San Jose, helped build the civic action Community Service Organization (CSO) among the Mexican-Americans of that city . . . and finally in April 1962 resigned that job and went back to the fields in order to carry out his lifelong dream, organization of the state's Farm Workers for economic and legislative action." From then on, Chavez would back-date his navy service by two years, claiming he signed up in 1944 rather than in 1946, a small change reflecting his calculation that war veteran would prove a useful embellishment.

Who finances the organization? was the next question on the handout. "The answer to that one is brief and incredible: NOBODY. Nobody, that is, except two or three of Cesar's buddies who send him a buck occasionally, and Cesar and his wife, Helena, who are now working in the fields from 6 am to 2 pm picking cotton to support themselves and their 8 kids. The rest of the day and half the night Cesar devotes to organizing." In fact, his occasional field work did not support the family, the convention had approved a modest salary, and he would soon seek various additional sources of income.

Whatever details he bent and blurred, Chavez did not overstate the event's historic importance. The first successful union for farmworkers was launched in a Fresno social hall on September 30, 1962, along with the legend of Cesar Chavez.

CHAPTER 10

Chavez in Command

We must take risks if we are going to move forward.

In the beginning, Cesar Chavez said, only three people truly believed he could succeed: his wife, Helen; his mentor, Fred Ross; and Dolores Huerta, who became his indispensable, lifelong ally.

Huerta was fearless, loyal, and fanatical—qualities Chavez prized. She was a single mother of seven, living on $80 a month in child support from two former husbands and sporadic income from the CSO. Her car broke down, her babysitter vanished, the utility threatened to shut off water and power, but the Farm Workers Association always came first. When Huerta faced a choice between her work and her children, the children suffered. When her stepfather took back his typewriter, she wrote Chavez in pencil. When she landed in the hospital and needed a blood transfusion, she apologized because the illness interfered with her job collecting dues.

In many ways, she complemented Chavez. He was quiet, disarming, occasionally self-conscious about his lack of formal education, and not comfortable moving among the affluent. Huerta was assertive, voluble, college-educated, and always sought center stage. Her quick wit and charm attracted admirers and helped her weave social and political networks useful to Chavez.

Huerta was three years younger than Chavez. Born in Dawson, New Mexico, Dolores Fernandez was raised in California after her parents divorced when she was a young child. Her father served briefly in the

New Mexico state legislature. Her mother was the third generation of a family that emigrated from Spain; Dolores's great-great-grandfather Marshal St. John served in the Union cavalry during the Civil War. After the divorce, Dolores's mother worked in Stockton as a waitress, ran a luncheonette, and then took over a boardinghouse after the hotel's Japanese managers were interned during the war. Dolores grew up conflicted about her identity. She took music lessons and earned Girl Scout merit badges, but lived in the run-down El Dorado Hotel, on the edge of skid row. Her mother's family hated the "Indians" and made no distinction between Indians and her father's Mexican ancestry. Her mother's second husband, an Irishman, voiced equal hostility toward Mexicans. Dolores credited a trip to Mexico with her mother after high school for helping her avoid a nervous breakdown. "I saw a whole nation of Mexicans who weren't ashamed to be Mexicans," she recalled.

She started college but dropped out after she married Ralph Head, a high school classmate. They had two children, and she went to work for the county sheriff's office, using her bilingual skills. The couple divorced in 1952. Three years later, Dolores married Ventura Huerta. They shared an interest in community organizing. But her first allegiance was to her work, and he preferred that she stay home with the family. By the time she became involved with the Farm Workers Association, the marriage had ended. She kept her married name at the urging of Chavez; *huerta* means "orchard," and he told her she had a pretty and appropriate name: sorrows of the orchard.

Huerta's relationship with Chavez was tempestuous from the start, but their commitment to the cause trumped all else and grew into a mutual dependence that survived decades of discord. Huerta managed to be both subservient and assertive. She addressed Chavez as her leader, *jefe*, and general, deferred to his judgment, and routinely apologized for her poor performance and occasional outbursts. "I deserve the recriminations," she wrote Chavez after he apologized for critical remarks. "Furthermore I think I am still ahead when it comes to losing tempers."

She did not hesitate to voice complaints, particularly when she felt left out of discussions. "I am not the quiet long suffering type," she wrote Chavez, rather an understatement. "I also resent it when you are not honest with me . . . I do not mind playing the part of the heavy if I know why and when I am supposed to take on this role—please remember this for any future conspiracies. This is what I mean by your 'honesty' or sincerity if it sounds nicer that way."

Chavez delivered most of his criticism in private, but during an early meeting of FWA leaders he berated Huerta in public for the first time, ostensibly for her failures as a bookkeeper. He had planned the confrontation, Chavez explained to Ross a few years later: "I said, 'I run the show and I don't give a damn what you think or anyone thinks. I'm gonna run it the way I want to run it, and you don't like it, too bad. Get out! I don't want to argue with you. If you don't want to take orders from me, then get out. I've had it!'" People around Chavez soon grew accustomed to such public confrontations.

In the end, Huerta would always put aside her anger and her own travails and do whatever Chavez asked, whether dunning members for dues or selling motor oil. When Chavez broached the idea of selling engine oil in one of his early attempts at a cooperative venture, she replied in characteristic fashion: "On the oil, so help me I do not know what you are talking about. I gather that you have some oil that can be sold for 22 cents a quart. Yes I am game but will it be too expensive to send via Greyhound? You figure that out."

Chavez relished the freedom to figure things out and make decisions. He was in charge of his own organization and carefully set out to build the union he wanted. He assembled his tight-knit team of family and friends and added to the small circle for specific missions. He was determined to avoid the mistakes of the CSO.

This time the board would follow his direction, rather than the other way around. Chavez's closest associates had not run for office at the founding convention on the theory that this organization, unlike CSO, would be run by the staff and the officers were largely ceremonial. They proved so ceremonial that several—including the president—never showed up again. Early in 1963, Chavez called a second convention. A smaller group of delegates, representing roughly the same communities as the first convention, met in the hall of Our Lady of Guadalupe church in Delano, which Chavez rented for $15. He would recall the date many years later because the January 20 convention fell on the day before Helen's thirty-fifth birthday. The delegates scrapped the office of president. Chavez remained general director and Manuel Chavez was elected secretary-treasurer.

Chavez handpicked the rest of the board. He wanted two close allies as vice presidents, Huerta and Gilbert Padilla. But the constitution—which Chavez had written—required all the board members to be farmworkers. So he asked for, and obtained, a waiver.

"Padilla was my discovery," Chavez said a few years later, recalling how he found the dapper organizer working as a dry cleaner in the San Joaquin Valley city of Hanford. Like Chavez, Padilla came from a farmworker family. He was an army veteran and felt a visceral anger at conditions in the fields. Padilla was quick-witted, a natural mimic and storyteller, easy-going, heavy-drinking, and committed to both Chavez and the cause of helping farmworkers. Padilla's gifts for organizing impressed Ross, who arranged several stints for him working for the CSO. In Padilla, Chavez had a loyal friend on the board to back him up, and a strong voice for seconding any initiative.

Chavez's first focus after assembling the board was to find an insur-ance policy that would allow him to collect dues. Determined to avoid the CSO debacle, he made more pragmatic decisions. In the CSO, he had been unwilling to endorse life insurance that kicked people out at age seventy. He now faced the reality that the association would have to exclude any members older than fifty if he wanted to obtain insurance for farmworkers at an affordable cost.

"I hope I don't make the same mistake twice," Chavez wrote Ross. "In CSO, remember all the plans that were made (mostly by me) which were dependent on the success of our new membership dues and the insur-ance and so forth. Well, here too I'm planning (dreaming) of having enough money to get help on the organizing of the workers. And as before, everything depends on the insurance program and the credit union, at least to begin with."

Liberated from the constraints of working for the CSO board, Chavez plunged ahead. Right or wrong, he acted decisively. He did not waste time on lengthy consultations and deliberations. By the end of January 1963, he had hit bottom financially. He decided to start collecting dues even though the insurance would not start until March—if he finalized a deal. He borrowed ten dollars from his brother Richard to buy stamps to mail bills. When he ran out of stamps, Chavez instructed Huerta to call on members in the northern end of the valley and tell them to send in dues. He realized he was asking members to pay dues on faith, but he had no choice. "I know this is the risky part of the whole damn thing," he wrote Huerta, "but we must take risks if we are going to move forward."

Chavez declared that the first one thousand people to pay dues would be founding members "and will be placed in the archives of the Farm Workers Association for posterity." Their names would be displayed on scrolls in the organization's headquarters, though no office yet existed.

He also appealed for members on pragmatic grounds. "Let's face it, most of the workers will only join the association if they see that they can get immediate benefits," Chavez wrote in one of his periodic newsletters. "Only a small percentage of the people involved will really understand, at this point, what we are trying to do . . . you and I, maybe, can understand about causes, but most of us don't. So the INSURANCE BENEFIT is simply that something which we hope will encourage people to join and pay their monthly dues."

When the dues notices went out, membership plunged from 498 to 160. Chavez had promised the insurance company he could deliver 300, and he had promised the members life insurance as of March 1. By mid-February, the membership had inched up to 227. Chavez investigated more costly insurance options as a fallback. "I'm almost certain that we will get the coverage one way or the other," he wrote to Huerta. "Still the gut tearing fear of being refused by the Insurance commissioner looms large over me, especially when I lay down at night."

With three days till the deadline, he went to church on Ash Wednesday and pledged to give up smoking for Lent. He suggested his family do without television, an idea they rejected as excessive sacrifice. Soon he suffered the physical pains of withdrawal. When Hartmire stopped by Delano, Chavez told the minister the association had seven hundred members, with a potential of thirteen hundred more; he "overdramatized," Chavez confessed to Ross, because he didn't want outsiders to know the truth.

On March 1, Chavez signed an agreement with California Life Insurance, switching to a more expensive plan because he had only 253 paying members. When the first member collected on his policy a few months later, after his spouse died, Chavez presented the $500 check at a free barbecue for FWA members.

A little more than a year after he had moved to Delano, Chavez had stabilized the dues-paying membership of the FWA at around three hundred, sufficient to draw a $50-a-week salary. He was ready to move on to the next item on his list: a credit union. Members would be able to obtain small, low-interest loans to tide them through the lean winter months, credit they could not qualify for at banks. For Chavez, the credit union would help break the workers' dependence on labor contractors, often the only source of cash. And the credit union, like the death benefit, would bind members to the association year-round, even if they only worked in the Delano area for a few months. To keep up their insurance and to qualify for the credit union, they would have to pay dues all year.

When the federal government rejected his application for a credit union charter, Chavez called on political connections in Sacramento and obtained a state charter. But he lacked the requisite capital to start making loans. He turned once more to his family for help. His brother Richard was comfortably established as a carpenter and builder. Richard had bought a small house in Delano in 1955, taken out a construction loan, and added on to build his family a cozy two-bedroom home. Richard's house already functioned as an auxiliary office for the FWA since he had the only telephone. Now the house became collateral as well. On October 25, 1963, Richard took out a $5,600 mortgage against his house and lent $3,500 to jump-start the credit union. Next, Cesar needed someone trustworthy to run the bank. He persuaded Helen that she could learn enough accounting and drafted her as the credit union's manager. The credit union opened for business at the end of 1963, offering savings accounts to FWA members and loans at 1 percent interest per month. They had no rules and required no collateral. They made what they called "face loans"—they trusted people who had honest faces.

Chavez had much to celebrate as he presided over his association's annual meeting on January 26, 1964. The organization had survived sixteen months, delivered life insurance to workers who had lacked the means to properly bury their loved ones, established a credit union, and held on to its core membership. Farmworkers from hundreds of miles away began arriving in Delano at 5:00 A.M. for the one-day convention. They warmed up with menudo for breakfast and admired the colorfully decorated church hall. Crepe paper decorations hung from the ceiling, fresh flowers were arranged around the room, and musicians provided live entertainment. A ten-by-twelve-foot black eagle flag faced the officers, and a smaller version hung on a side wall.

For the first time, Chavez reached for help outside his immediate circle. Two idealistic young people from the East Coast, products of an entirely different world, became frequent visitors in the Chavez home. One plugged Chavez in to important networks beyond Delano, and the other helped spread his message. Soon a stream of young people would flock to Delano, enchanted with the cause and wanting to be of service. In 1964, Wendy Goepel and Bill Esher were the vanguard.

Goepel had grown up in a religious family in Hackensack, New Jersey. She was the first in her family to go to college and came west as a seventeen-year-old Mount Holyoke College sophomore on a Migrant Ministry summer internship. She fell in love with the foreign world of farmworkers. She met Chavez and Ross during the summer training and later stayed in Huerta's mother's boardinghouse. Goepel kept in touch with all three when she transferred to the University of California at Berkeley. She started graduate studies in sociology at Stanford, then quit to work on a California health department farmworker initiative. She found lots of reasons to stop by Delano, where she slept on the Chavez couch, displacing the two youngest boys, who moved to the floor.

In the summer of 1964, Goepel supervised a state-funded migrant health study. She hired Helen Chavez as an interviewer to survey farmworkers about health, housing, and economic conditions. The same summer, President Lyndon B. Johnson signed into law the Office of Economic Opportunity (OEO) and appointed Sargent Shriver as its first director. Millions of dollars in federal grant money to help poor people suddenly became available, and California wanted its share. Gov. Pat Brown hired Goepel to write grant proposals. She worked on a half dozen grants, but her personal priority was getting money for Chavez's association, which he now called the National Farm Workers Association, or NFWA. She spent days riding around the valley with Chavez, filling in details that would help craft a strong pitch. She attended house meetings and listened to workers' stories, then ended the day back at 1221 Kensington, eating Helen's corn tortillas at the red Formica kitchen table.

Chavez, the pragmatist, was willing to jettison one of his cardinal rules: don't take outside money. The application submitted to OEO asked for more than $200,000 to create seventy staff jobs, sixty-three for farmworkers who would work in the credit union, start a cooperative, and run a gas station. Chavez, as director, would receive a salary of $15,000.

With the credit union established, Chavez talked to Goepel about his next dream—a newspaper for farmworkers. "I'm still trying to get someone interested in being crazy enough to give up eating and join me to develop the newspaper," he wrote to a friend from the CSO. Goepel knew just the person.

"I'm writing because I hear you need some help with your newspaper, and I want to work for you, and the whole thing that you are doing captures my imagination very much," wrote Bill Esher, a tall, dreamy-eyed activist with strong opinions, a big heart, and a willingness to try anything. Esher had grown up in New York, moved to San Francisco after college, and met Goepel through the Catholic Worker movement. Drawn to the farmworker cause, he had tried operating his own labor contracting service. He picked up workers in Oakland, loaded them on an old bus, handed out sandwiches his girlfriend made, and drove them to jobs in San Jose. The workers became militant in their demands and were blackballed, and the project collapsed.

While Esher's friends headed south to Mississippi in the summer of 1964, he decided to pursue a civil rights fight closer to home. He became the only non-bracero on a cantaloupe crew in the San Joaquin Valley, filling ninety-pound bags with ripe melons as he carefully documented how the foremen cheated workers out of 25¢ an hour. Esher needed a place to stay while he worked in the fields, so Goepel let him sleep in the Bakersfield office that Helen Chavez used for her survey work. Esher liked Helen and heeded Goepel's urging to get in touch with Cesar about the newspaper job. Esher had worked nights on a newspaper in Syracuse, New York, in college and was confident he could produce a paper for farmworkers. Chavez asked Esher how much he needed, and he said only enough to eat. Goepel arranged to pay Esher $50 a week and procured an ancient trailer that Esher parked in Delano and called home. He became the first editor of *El Malcriado*, the farmworkers' newspaper.

Chavez picked the name and explained its significance: "The meaning is ill-bred. Also applied to children who speak back to their parents. During the [Mexican] revolution, one of the peoples' papers was called El Malcriado, and successively others since then have taken this name when they fight for the people." His intuition that a newspaper for poorly educated farmworkers could serve as an effective organizing tool quickly proved true; demand was so high they increased the print run from one thousand to three thousand copies. Workers who couldn't read heard the latest news from friends. Each story that exposed wrongdoing or reported a small victory won Chavez more converts.

They sold each issue for 10¢ to farmworkers and mailed subscriptions for $2 a year to supporters. Abe Chavez responded enthusiastically, buying a subscription for himself and offering to sell several more. "I liked the general tone and believe that a constant reminder to the worker as you have done in this issue will show how other people benefit by their poverty and hardship. Short, brief concise examples of how they are getting screwed out of their rightful share of their labor will arouse their concern and will enable you to work to help them improve their lot."

Esher found no shortage of such stories, which he reported and wrote and found someone to translate into Spanish. His first sustained crusade used information the NFWA had been collecting about systematic cheating of sugar beet workers. One labor contractor, Jimmy Hronis, had a particularly bad reputation, and *El Malcriado* began a campaign to expose him as an unscrupulous employer. The stories triggered state hearings and fines against Hronis. Farmworkers were astonished.

Chavez affectionately referred to Esher as "Guillermo Ceniseros," a quasi-literal translation of William and ashes. Esher took many meals with the Chavez family and became fond of the children. Occasionally he and Cesar picked grapes together, usually jobs arranged by Helen's sister. Esher did the layout on each issue, drove to Fresno, and slept in his car while he waited for the printer to run off the paper: a thousand copies for $43. Each time a new issue came out, the two men drove around distributing the paper to small stores that Chavez selected. They picked up the extras from the prior issue along with the nickel profit for each copy that had been sold. Esher designed a special hook that would hold ten copies and could be hung near the cash register. Chavez didn't like to drive, so Esher took the wheel and Chavez told him stories about his life. He talked about the CSO, about lessons he had learned, and about his ideas for a co-op for members. In spare moments, Esher helped Chavez experiment by selling tires and oil; members could buy tires for $7.99 plus a used tire; an extra $1.50 bought whitewalls.

Between the insurance program, the credit union, and the newspaper, the NFWA had outgrown its temporary home on Kensington Street, where Chavez would move the red Formica table from the kitchen to the living room to double as his desk. He had no phone, so people had to come find him in person. Even without the constant stream of visitors, there was scarcely any privacy with nine people plus frequent guests crammed into the two-bedroom house. When Huerta finally moved to Delano in the summer of 1964 with five of her children, they all stayed with the Chavezes until she found a house to rent.

For his first office, Chavez located an abandoned Pentecostal church on the far west side of Delano, where the streets ended and the fields began. Richard Chavez helped with plumbing and wiring, built cabinets and shelves, and partitioned off rooms. Supporters pledged to raise money for the $50-a-month rent. The grand opening of 102 Albany Street on September 26, 1964, featured refreshments, door prizes, and a raffle to raise money for the $850 in construction materials bought on credit. Helen and her sister donated plants, Goepel provided curtains, Huerta contributed vases, and Katy Peake delivered a conference table, chairs, and a filing cabinet. At the front entrance was a counter, like in a bank, and behind that two small offices, one for the credit union and one for *El Malcriado*. Chavez's office was just inside the front door, to the left, with a wooden desk that his brother had built. Chavez announced the office would be open from 9:00 A.M. to 8:30 P.M., Monday through Saturday, with an hour closed for lunch. He finally had the problem clinic he had always wanted.

One person missing from the celebration was Manuel Chavez. Cesar had delighted in the companionship of his irreverent cousin, who had traveled the valley talking up the association and gathering pledges. "Manny the Mostest is tearing around while I'm here banging away on the teclas [keys]," Chavez had written to Ross. Manuel bragged that he had never held a job longer than seven or eight months, but he stayed with the farm workers association because no one—not even Cesar—could tell him what to do. Manuel liked money, and even while working for his cousin at $50 a week, he always seemed to have plenty to spend. "Money's to roll, that's why they make it round," was one of his favorite sayings. By mid-1963 he had taken a job as a salesman at a grocery store and was helping Cesar in his spare time.

A year later, Manuel was arrested and charged with grand theft for cashing forged checks. His prior arrest record included time in federal prison for selling drugs and arrests for assault, disturbing the peace, and grand theft auto. The court was not inclined to leniency. At his sentencing, he said he had run up gambling debts, cashed checks to cover his losses, and intended to repay the money he stole from his employer, the Bakersfield Produce Company. He pled guilty to grand theft and was sentenced to prison in June 1964. Cesar missed him. Esher's office was kitty-corner to Chavez's, and the editor would see his boss there late at night, writing to his cousin.

Manuel Chavez was replaced as secretary-treasurer by Antonio Orendain, the only immigrant in the leadership of the association. Orendain was building up a following of his own through a television show he hosted. He had persuaded a local Hanford station to donate a fifteen-minute slot during which he delivered news in Spanish. He collected newspapers from all over Mexico by mail and read small items about different places. Little stories from workers' hometowns generated great interest, no matter how dated the news. As the NFWA grew, Orendain began mixing in news of the association. He worked as an irrigator during the day, then rushed each afternoon to the studio, where he donned a clean jacket and hid his muddy boots underneath the desk. His broadcasts reached farmworkers across a wide swath of the San Joaquin Valley, and the mustachioed Mexican became a familiar face.

During its second full year, the NFWA had more than doubled its income. The association reported collecting $12,947 in dues in 1964, another $771 in donations, and $2,414 in miscellaneous income, for a total of $16,133. Expenses had also doubled, to $15,487, including salaries for Chavez and Huerta, who each earned $65 a week. The other major expenses were $5,701 in insurance premiums, $1,229 in travel, and $447 for postage. Chavez decided he had built a sufficiently strong base to reveal his true agenda. He began to lay the groundwork for his first strike.

"The most exciting thing is our drive to get a contract this summer," he wrote to Ross in early 1965. "We have chosen McFarland rose industry for our efforts. Things look very good but still I can see all of the many problems we will have to overcome. If we are successful we will have something to crow about. If not we will probably lose a lot of ground, but I'm all for the risk . . . We need the fight right now."

On April 11, 1965, forty rose grafters met with Chavez, detailed their grievances, and asked for help in organizing a strike. Highly skilled and difficult to replace, rose grafters were what Jim Drake called "the watch makers of agriculture." Their work also was time sensitive, so they had significant leverage if they walked out. At a second meeting on April 20, they agreed to strike two companies—Mount Arbor and Conklin. On Sunday afternoon, May 2, they met and took the strike vote. Workers were handed slips to mark an X in the box that said "I agree to strike my employer, Mount Arbor nurseries." Then Chavez had them all swear on a crucifix not to break the strike.

Chris Hartmire was sent to speak with the owner of the Mount Arbor nursery and urged him to recognize the union, to no avail. Drake was detached to work full-time on the strike along with Chavez, Huerta, and Padilla; Hartmire agreed Drake was "on vacation," knowing how outraged the churches that funded the Migrant Ministry would be to learn that one of their organizers was leading a strike.

"With the strike in the roses in McFarland, the Association has declared open war against the growers of California whose cruel exploitations must end after more than a hundred years," declared *El Malcriado*. The workers struck on May 3. When Huerta saw lights on in a worker's house the first morning, she blocked his car with hers so that he could not go to work. On the fourth day, the grower offered a raise; the workers decided to go back without a contract.

El Malcriado reported the strike as a great victory nonetheless, and the strike spurred more outside interest in the union. Helped by *El Malcriado* and friends like Goepel, news was slowly making its way out of the valley to the cities. Anecdotes about the short, quiet, determined leader with big plans drifted north into political circles in Sacramento and west into the activist communities in the San Francisco Bay Area. Progressive labor advocates who longed to do something for farmworkers murmured about Cesar Chavez, the new hope.

The abysmal conditions and poverty of farmworkers had periodically flared into the national consciousness, from *The Grapes of Wrath* in 1939 to Edward R. Murrow's *Harvest of Shame* in 1960. Now the farmworkers' plight elicited comparisons to the civil rights struggles in the South. Berkeley and Oakland emerged as the hub of farmworker activism. Henry Anderson, who had first worked with Fathers McDonnell and McCullough and then served as AWOC's research director, launched a new support group, Citizens for Farm Labor. The advisory board included a familiar cast: Chavez, Ross, Peake, Hartmire, several CSO leaders, and two of the former Spanish Mission Band priests.

Mike Miller, a field secretary for the Student Nonviolent Coordinating Committee (SNCC) in San Francisco, approached Chavez about potential joint projects. Miller arranged to visit Delano with three national SNCC leaders—Robert Moses, Stokely Carmichael, and Ivanhoe Donaldson. Chavez declined to attend but delegated Huerta to meet with the group. As the internal politics of SNCC made the organization increasingly inhospitable to whites, more young activists returned to California from the South and cast about for a new cause. Miller proposed that SNCC formally endorse Chavez's association. "Urban support within the state can be very important to success or failure," he wrote to supporters.

Shortly after the rose strike, Drake and Padilla led a rent strike to protest abysmal conditions in a Tulare farm labor camp, where families lived in one-room, eleven-by-sixteen-foot tin shacks, with holes in the walls and no indoor plumbing. The protest drew support from SNCC and others in the Bay Area. Handbills distributed in Berkeley advertised a protest march to support the rent strike under the headline "Tulare County—California's Selma." Sponsors urged people to join the march and show support for "a new mass movement of farm workers in California who are fed up with the feudal conditions of California agribusiness."

Despite Chavez's best efforts to control his own destiny, external events began to shape his future. In May 1965, another labor action started in the vineyards of the Coachella Valley, the southeast desert area of California where the first table grapes of the season ripen.

The bracero program had finally died at the end of 1964. Growers had greeted the change with alarm, insisted they would never be able to harvest all their crops, and demanded some other form of guest worker program. The government obliged. Under the terms of the new program, growers had to pay the prevailing wage in order to qualify to import guest workers. In Coachella, the wage was set at $1.40 an hour. Filipino members of AWOC demanded the same wage for working in the short, labor-intensive grape harvest. When the growers denied them, they struck. After a week, the growers caved. "There was a strike that had much success," El Malcriado reported. "Between 500 and 1,000 workers were affected. The companies had to raise wages to $1.40 an hour."

Fred Ross was among those who now relied on El Malcriado for news about the farm worker organization. Ross had reluctantly taken a job in Syracuse, New York, when funding from the IAF ran out. He had a family to support, and Chavez determined that the NFWA did not have the funds to pay Ross a sufficient salary. He eagerly read El Malcriado and continued to correspond with Chavez. Learning that Chavez had been seriously ill with pneumonia, Ross scolded his star student for working himself to exhaustion:

> Hey, bub, sounds like you had a pretty narrow squeak. And whomever wrote the piece in El Malcriado about the 12 and 14 hours a day bit, hit the nail on the head. Check the calendar, man—it's later than you think! If they'd asked old Doc Ross I could have diagnosed it without a second thought as "don't-know-when-to-quititis." Some of the rest of us have had a touch of this but, brother, you've always had the worst case I've ever heard tell of. Well maybe this will scare some of that can't-quit virus out of you—hope, I hope. Well, the main thing—thank God—you made it through. I don't know what in hell we'd do if you cashed in your chips!

Ross asked Chavez to think about what he was doing differently in his current campaign and how to avoid the problems that had doomed the CSO. "I have been giving a lot of thought, in my spare moments, to your questions Re: avoiding pitfalls when starting all over again," Chavez replied. "I can truthfully say that there isn't anything one can do unless all human nature is redone over again. I guess the best thing is to keep organizing new groups until they become rotten with personalities, then just move over and begin another group. I really don't know. The only one suggestion I have is to make sure there is always one person who is in charge . . . I think this way the work of the group moves forward always."

Ross arranged for Chavez to come speak at Syracuse University. Ross suggested Chavez structure the talk around how and why he got involved in the CSO and then the NFWA and what lessons his experiences held for organizers. "When you're on the plane, between naps, jot down some of the ideas and concepts you've developed over the years," Ross wrote. "For instance, your idea about how peoples' organizations can be spoiled by too much democracy."

Chavez was booked on a flight to Syracuse on September 16, 1965, but he was forced to cancel. Instead of pondering lessons about democracy as he winged cross-country on Mexican Independence Day, Chavez found himself in a Delano church, surrounded by hundreds of farmworkers who chanted the Spanish word for strike: "Huelga, huelga, huelga."

CHAPTER 11

The Strike

We have to find some cross between being a movement and being a union.

Cesar Chavez stood in the front of Our Lady of Guadalupe church hall, dressed in his usual plaid shirt, a few strands of jet-black hair falling into his face. Behind him was the giant flag with the black eagle. In front of him stood hundreds of expectant farmworkers. Fresh from celebrating Mexican Independence Day, they crowded excitedly into the church annex, overflowing the large room and the upper balcony along the back wall.

You, the members, have asked for this meeting, Chavez began. Then he reviewed the tumultuous events of the past week, events that had turned his world upside down.

Filipino members of the Agricultural Workers Organizing Committee had migrated north after their brief May strike in Coachella ended with a wage of $1.40 per hour plus 25¢ per box of picked grapes. The workers expected the same wages in Delano but lacked leverage: the lengthy season in the San Joaquin Valley gave growers ample time to find replacements. Because Delano growers did not employ guest workers, they faced no imperative to pay the higher wage. They paid what they wanted, usually $1.25 an hour and 10¢ for each box.

On the morning of September 8, 1965, Filipino workers refused to leave their camps to harvest grapes at ten Delano vineyards. Word spread quickly, and workers streamed into Chavez's office at 102 Albany Street, asking what to do. "All I could think was, 'Oh God, we're not ready for a strike,'" Chavez would recall a few months later.

For a few days, growers waited for the strike to end, like so many earlier job actions. Then they began recruiting scabs. Larry Itliong, head of the AWOC office in Delano, went to Chavez for help. If Mexicans broke the strike, the Filipinos' action was finished. Chavez called a meeting for September 16, Mexican Independence Day, unhappy he was forced into action, but aware he had no choice. All he could do was buy a few days to prepare.

Word of mouth, radio announcements, and last-minute flyers inserted in *El Malcriado* helped draw a large crowd to the church hall. As he addressed the workers, Chavez embraced the symbolism of the historic day. He compared their struggle to that of the Mexicans who fought more than 150 years earlier to free themselves from Spanish oppressors. We will defeat the growers, Chavez told the crowd, just as the Mexicans vanquished the Spaniards. The fifth item on Chavez's agenda for the meeting was the question he told the workers they must decide: would they strike? The seventh item was his explanation of the HUELGA signs they soon would carry. He had never doubted the outcome of the vote. The workers shouted their approval: *Vivan los trabajadores del campo. Viva la huelga. Viva Cesar Chavez.*

With those words, everything changed—for Chavez, for his fledgling union, and for Delano.

He had little money in the treasury and a small membership. His first foray into economic action, the rose strike, had ended with higher wages, but no contract. He had been warning for years against unions that called strikes before workers were ready. Now he faced a strike called by a rival union, not on his timetable, and not under his control. He had to hope that three years of organizing had developed a strong enough base to sustain the union, not tear it apart. He saw an opportunity, and he took a risk.

On Sunday evening, September 19, Chavez assembled his small staff and volunteers and made assignments for the following day. He listed growers the union would target and mapped out destinations for the first picket lines. Then Chavez went home, gathered his family in a circle, and said a Hail Mary for each grower.

The next morning, some two hundred strikers gathered at four-thirty in front of the NFWA office. Each was handed a cup of coffee, a round sign saying HUELGA, and a slip of paper with a crossroads—the address of their assignment. The first mission was to flag down workers as they headed to the fields and persuade them to join the strike. Once the work-day began, action shifted to the roads alongside the fields. Mexicans walked picket lines alongside Filipinos, shouting at workers to join the strike. They stood on top of cars and yelled through megaphones to coax, shame, or occasionally threaten workers out of the fields.

This was no ordinary strike. "It's like striking an industrial plant that has a thousand entrance gates and is 40 square miles large. And if that isn't bad enough, you don't know each morning where the plant will be, or where the gates are, or whether it will be open or closed, or what wages will be offered that day," Terence Cannon wrote in the *Movement*, the West Coast newspaper of the Student Nonviolent Coordinating Committee, reporting from the picket lines the first week. Strikers spent much of their day jumping into cars to chase around the miles and miles of fields, trying to locate scab crews who were whisked to work stations with police escorts to evade the picketers.

The logistics were daunting. Chavez divided the strike zone into four quadrants and assigned picket captains and crews to each one. To make best use of the limited number of pickets, Chavez and Itliong developed a system of roving lines that they moved among the twenty or so ranches affected by the strike. In the predawn, cars cruised hundreds of acres of vineyards to locate crews, then called back to strike headquarters so a makeshift picket line could be dispatched. During the day, Chavez drove from place to place, relaying messages, updates, and new assignments.

As each picket line sprang up, the growers responded. They blasted music to drown out pickets' chants, ran trucks to stir up dust clouds, and sprayed strikers with the sulfur used to fertilize the fields. Sometimes the growers drove close enough to nip the pickets' heels. Cars were forced off the road. Fights broke out. Growers unleashed dogs, hired armed guards, and used physical and verbal threats, trying to provoke a violent response from the strikers. Chavez insisted that pickets resist the temptation to fight back. He believed a nonviolent posture was essential for the union's reputation. "We are stopping them and we are hurting them," Chavez told a large rally a few days after the strike began. "If we can keep our great strike peaceful, non-violent and strong, we cannot lose."

Whether nonviolence was a core belief, a tactic, or both, Chavez used the doctrine to great advantage. He had watched the power of the Selma marches and the clashes in Birmingham and seen the value of an antagonist like Birmingham sheriff Bull O'Connor. The more the growers taunted protesters, sprayed them with sulfur, and shoved cameras in their faces to intimidate, the more the union could claim the high moral ground.

With strikers scattered among the vast vineyards, Chavez looked for ways to make them more visible—to each other and to the outside world. Sunday was the workers' one day off, and Chavez invited Itliong to participate in a unity march the first Sunday, in an effort to bring together two groups that did not ordinarily mix. Hundreds rallied in Ellington Park and then marched around the west side of Delano. Children whacked piñatas and adults ate tacos as the strikers carried colorful signs and flags emblazoned with the black eagle and urged onlookers to join their cause. The day ended with a joint meeting in Filipino Hall, strike headquarters for the better-financed AWOC. The crowd heard pledges of support from labor leaders who came to help Itliong's union, their colleague in the AFL-CIO.

Chavez's union had no institutional support, so he had to improvise. In many ways, he preferred that position. With no outside oversight, he had freedom to pursue original strategies, respond to events and throw the opposition off guard. Chavez was convinced they could never win a traditional fight on the grower's terms. "No one in any battle has ever won anything by being on the defensive," he told a group of workers. "The idea is to stay on the offensive, always."

Within a few weeks, the initial excitement of the strike began to wear off. Chavez sought novel ways to stay on the offensive, spread his message, and gain attention. He called on one of the rare priests willing to embrace *la causa*—Father Keith Kenny, a Sacramento priest with a commercial pilot's license. Kenny flew to Delano in his Cessna 180 and picked up Chavez. The men flew low over the vineyards to take stock of who was working where and spot crews the growers had moved far inside the fields. The priest had mounted a portable loudspeaker system on the plane he called *El Macho*, and on the second pass above the vineyards Chavez began to broadcast to the workers. Kenny skimmed the fields, careful to stay above the legal floor of six hundred feet, while Chavez exhorted the workers to join the strike. Everyone was leaving the fields, he told them, and the strike had the support of his pilot, a Catholic priest.

Two growers and a deputy sheriff were waiting at the Delano airport when they landed. Chavez was charged with violating a county ordinance against broadcasting from the air, and complaints were filed with the FAA. Fresno bishop Aloysius Willinger demanded that the Sacramento diocese keep the rebel priest home where he belonged. "The strike at Delano involves more than civil rights," Willinger warned. "Considerations involved, if not most carefully handled, could well ruin farmers and growers."

Growers formed the financial pillars of Catholic congregations, and only a handful of priests dared to support Chavez in those early, critical days. Responding to Willinger from Rome, where the fourth and final session of Vatican II was winding down, Sacramento bishop Alden J. Bell apologized for the renegade: "These are troublesome days for Ordinaris when priests manifest such presumption and unpredictable conduct."

Chavez had another unconventional weapon to use in his unconventional strike: *El Malcriado*, which had developed a devoted following. Bill Esher moved his trailer from behind the noisy union headquarters to a secluded spot a few miles away where he could focus on writing, editing, pasting up, and distributing a fourteen-to-sixteen-page paper every two weeks. The paper became essential for spreading news and keeping spirits high. Each issue found a victory to trumpet. "The Strike Gets Stronger Every Day," proclaimed the front-page headline above a photo of Dolores Huerta standing atop a car with her HUELGA sign aloft. "They have the money and the power," Chavez declared, "but there are thousands of us and very few of them."

When pickets marched outside the homes of scabs carrying signs that said STRIKEBREAKER LIVES HERE, *El Malcriado* published the full text of Jack London's withering essay, "Definition of a Strikebreaker." The short piece begins: "After God had finished the rattlesnake, the toad, and the vampire, he had some awful substance left with which he made a strike-breaker. A strike-breaker is a two-legged animal with a corkscrew soul, a water-logged brain, and a combination back-bone made of jelly and glue. Where others have hearts, he carries a tumor of rotten principles."

On the morning of October 17, the Rev. David Havens, one of the Migrant Ministry staff working full-time on the strike, led a group of pickets who set out to read London's words through a megaphone to shame workers out of the fields. Kern County sheriff Sgt. Gerald Dodd warned that he viewed this as subversive and criminal behavior. Dressed in suit and tie, Havens stood on a pickup truck and read from *El Malcriado* until he was hauled away. Dodd wanted to arrest this man London too, Havens later noted, and was disappointed to hear the author was dead.

A month into the strike, Chavez's talent for improvisation found an important kindred spirit in another son of farmworkers, who brought his creative passion to the picket lines as they began to flag. Luis Valdez was born in a Delano labor camp in his grandmother's bed and returned to his hometown twenty-five years later as a promising young playwright and actor. Valdez shared Chavez's anger about farmworkers' lives and the treatment of Mexican Americans. In elementary school, when Luis questioned why a boy named Jimmy always got to be the hall monitor, the teacher explained: Jimmy's father is a grower. He needs to learn how to give orders. Your father is a farmworker. You need to learn how to take orders.

Luis's parents moved to San Jose, determined that their children receive a decent education. He found a literary mentor in his high school English teacher. But Luis enrolled in San Jose State on a math and physics scholarship, the more practical way to make a living. When his first play was produced, Luis switched majors. In a column he wrote for *El Excéntrico*, an alternative weekly, he described Delano and gave voice to the anger that would soon fuel *la causa*:

> As a Mexican, I have felt the sting of life among the gringos since the day I was born, some twenty-four years ago in a classic example of the American "small town." It had a main street, called Main Street, a cotton gin, a Greyhound bus depot, a Purity Store, a high school, a few churches, and a proverbial length of railroad tracks separating the White Protestant elite from "minority groups" . . .
>
> Life sometimes poses difficult questions. Once they are asked, there is no effective way a man can ignore them. He can prod at them like live scorpions. He can suppress them till they turn to acid in his gut. He can drink beer or cheap wine and sing dirty songs or sad corridos til he's drunk and he forgets, but they always come back. The shame, the pride, the hate, the love—a fierce mosaic of paradoxical emotions; and always, under them, the same basic questions: "Why do they treat me this way?"

After graduation, Valdez joined the San Francisco Mime Troupe, which nurtured his interests in writing, acting, and radical politics. He traveled to Cuba and met Fidel Castro. When the grape strike began, Valdez was on the verge of moving east to enroll in graduate school and see his first play, *The Shrunken Head of Pancho Villa*, produced off-Broadway. His grandmother still lived near Delano, and she had been sending him copies of *El Malcriado*. Valdez felt the pull. He went back for a weekend soon after the strike began, and then sought out Chavez at an appearance in the Bay Area. Valdez offered to come start a street theater. Chavez was clear: they had no money, no equipment, no actors. Valdez signed on.

He became a picket captain and saw that the strike was losing steam. Valdez started doing skits with workers on the picket line. He explained theater to farmworkers who had never seen a play. They wrote out signs—PATRÓN (boss), ESQUIROL (scab), CONTRATISTA (contractor), HUELGISTA (striker)—and hung them around their necks to create the basic characters. They started with a familiar situation, added satire, and improvised dialogue as they went along. Each *acto* lasted ten to fifteen minutes and was performed mostly in Spanish. At first the skits were a way to educate workers about basic concepts like seniority and dignity. Then the humor became a tool to break tension, ease fears, and lift spirits. The crowd cheered the heroes and booed the villains. The Teatro Campesino was born.

They performed on the back of a flatbed truck and soon they moved from the picket line to the union's Friday night meetings, where the Teatro became the highlight of the evening. The skits were brilliant and caustic, whether lampooning a grower or skewering the governor. Just as Chavez improvised tactics, the Teatro improvised skits, using comedy to score points about the latest outrage or victory. Chavez delighted in the humor. "The teatro appeals to its actors for the same reason it appeals to its audience," Valdez wrote as his theater's popularity grew. "It explores the meaning of a social movement without asking its participants to read or write. It is a learning experience with no formal prerequisites . . . In a Mexican way, we have discovered what Brecht is all about. If you want unbourgeois theater, find unbourgeois people to do it."

Valdez cut a dramatic figure—dark, olive-skinned, cultivating a Che Guevara image with beret and cigar. With more swagger than most of the recent recruits, he did not treat Chavez with unquestioning reverence. But the playwright, too, looked on the movement leader with respect bordering on awe: "Here was Cesar, burning with a patient fire, poor like us, dark like us, talking quietly, moving people to talk about their problems, attacking the little problems first, and suggesting, always suggesting—never more than that—solutions that seemed attainable. We didn't know it until we met him, but he was the leader we had been waiting for."

The growers and leading citizens of Delano were blind to the anger that Valdez expressed and thus equally oblivious to the power of Chavez's leadership. Decades of bias and comfortable dominance rendered even the sharpest of the growers incapable of assessing their adversary, or of comprehending the simmering outrage of workers who had been mistreated for generations. The growers were not even confident that Mexicans could fill in competently for the Filipinos who traditionally did the more delicate work of packing grapes that Mexicans picked.

The idea that a poorly educated Mexican American farmworker was masterminding this labor action was inconceivable. The strike, which had limited impact in the fields but was gaining public attention, must be the work of subversive, outside forces, the growers concluded. Some branded Chavez a Communist, but most saw him as a stalking horse. "The civil rights forces have taken over, although they continue to use Chavez and his FWA as a front," the Council of California Growers newsletter reported in the fall of 1965. "The lesson to be learned from Delano is that this is *not* an isolated case; that it *will* be continued, and that other areas of the state can expect similar efforts as crops are ready."

Earlier strikes in the fields had been easily broken. Between 1960 and 1962, AWOC had staged 158 job actions around the state, many ending with higher wages but no contracts. Several growers grasped that this strike was different, and they began to worry. They turned their wrath on Chris Hartmire, attacking the Migrant Ministry as a "third force" that conspired with the two unions.

The Migrant Ministry had indeed become an important adjunct of the NFWA. In the absence of support from the Catholic Church, Chavez relied heavily on the Protestant ministers to show frightened workers they had powerful allies. Hartmire and Jim Drake, both eloquent writers, played key roles in crafting Chavez's message. He no longer wrote his own newsletters. Hartmire and Drake drafted important statements and speeches, both in the name of Chavez and the union and under their own signatures.

The earnest, boyish-looking Hartmire became the face of the union's religious support. Chavez used the thirty-three-year-old cheerleader to full advantage. "There is no way for me to over emphasize the importance of the Delano strike," Hartmire wrote in his first official communication to a group he called his action mailing list. "A movement is underway in Delano!"

Drake, a large man with stamina that rivaled that of Chavez, coordinated events, walked picket lines, ran off leaflets, and wrote mailings. In the Coachella Valley, where he had grown up, Drake now found himself denounced as a Communist by childhood friends. The church that had given him an Interpreter's Bible demanded the thirty volumes back. In 1960, Drake had voted for Richard Nixon over John F. Kennedy because he could not imagine voting for a Catholic; now he marched with Catholic farmworkers who had signs on their front doors that read: "This is a Catholic home; we don't accept propaganda from Protestants or other sects."

The Protestant ministers' support became even more critical as the growers turned for help to their allies in law enforcement. Kern County sheriff deputies kept index cards on thousands of picketers. Judges sympathetic to the growers issued injunctions that limited picketers, often to absurd degrees. Rather than acquiesce and retreat, Chavez challenged the legal restrictions. He welcomed the ensuing confrontations as an opportunity to showcase his unorthodox mix of supporters—workers, students, and ministers.

When the Kern County sheriff warned pickets that shouting "huelga" was illegal because the noise interfered with commerce, Chavez selected a group of women, including his wife, called them to a secret meeting, and asked if they were willing to go to jail for a few days. Hartmire did the same with a group of ministers. On the morning of October 19, Helen Chavez, seven other women, a dozen ministers, and another two dozen farmworkers and supporters gathered outside the W. B. Camp ranch and prepared to challenge the latest restriction. Sgt. Dodd turned on his tape recorder at 10:53 A.M. as the pickets shouted "huelga" with all their might. Dodd arrested all forty-four and charged them with unlawful assembly and disturbing the peace.

Like most things in the union, media strategy was improvised as events unfolded. Drake had made sure reporters were on hand to witness the confrontation, and Hartmire was dragged off to the police wagon in the middle of an interview with the *Los Angeles Times*. The forty-four prisoners were taken to the Bakersfield jail, where union officials declined to post bail. Drake led a prayer vigil outside the jail that evening, accompanied by more than three dozen children whose Mexican American mothers had become heroines behind bars. In one of Helen Chavez's rare moments in the spotlight, her action emboldened other women and enhanced her stature as a role model.

Chavez had timed the "huelga protest" to coincide with a speech he was to deliver on the Berkeley campus. He addressed a crowd of around five hundred who gathered in Sproul Plaza, which had become known worldwide since arrests a year earlier had touched off the Free Speech

Movement. Someone handed Chavez a slip of paper, and he announced that his wife and forty-three others had been arrested hours earlier. The union did not have money to post bail, he said—neglecting to mention that they would not have done so in any case. He appealed to the audience to share whatever they could. Volunteers passed cans and students dropped in change while faculty members wrote checks. They collected more than $1,000.

Around the same time as the arrest of the Huelga 44 came news that could bring the union a far greater supply of cash: the federal Office of Economic Opportunity had approved the $268,000 OEO grant for which Wendy Goepel had applied the previous spring. Although the grant was for training programs, outraged growers and elected officials demanded that public money not fund the strike. The local congressman, Harlan Hagan, requested an FBI investigation of this dangerous and potentially subversive group. FBI director J. Edgar Hoover opened the inquiry at once and began surveillance of Chavez and the union that would last for years. Chavez turned down the grant and requested a delay, saying he could not run the strike and administer the programs at the same time.

In mid-December, labor leaders from around the country convened in San Francisco for the annual meeting of the AFL-CIO. The grape strike started three months earlier was more than 250 miles away but very much on the minds of delegates. Many saw in the struggle of the farmworkers echoes of their own early battles to bring the benefits of union contracts to industrial workers, and they wanted to help. The convention passed a resolution in support of the striking farmworkers, sponsored by UAW president Walter Reuther. Long the strongest labor advocate for farmworkers, Reuther was the prime reason that the federation had given AWOC a charter four years earlier. Reuther wanted to see the strike for himself and lend his personal support. He chartered a bus and invited the national press corps covering the AFL-CIO convention to take a road trip to Delano.

Reuther faced a delicate situation. Chavez's union was not part of the AFL-CIO nor affiliated with national labor in any way, yet in less than three months Chavez had clearly emerged as the leader of the strike— and possibly the leader Reuther had been seeking for years.

Reuther landed at the Delano airstrip, and he suggested a march through town to celebrate the one hundredth day of the strike. Told that the Delano City Council had barred marches without permits, Reuther pressed ahead. He carried a brand-new HUELGA sign and led strikers and supporters on a march through Delano, Larry Itliong on one side and Cesar Chavez on the other. Reuther's stature was such that no one stood in his way, and the mayor instead invited him into city hall. The march ended in Filipino Hall, where Reuther addressed an overflow crowd. "You're going to win this strike," he told the workers. "And we're going to stay with you till you do." Reporters from around the United States captured the scene, providing the first significant national publicity for la huelga.

Chavez had heard earlier that Reuther was likely to announce financial assistance. Chavez had sent word back that unless the money was evenly split between the Filipino and Mexican unions, he would not accept a cent. "We're poor, but we're proud," he said. As he wound up his speech, Reuther pledged support of $5,000 a month for as long as the strike lasted and an extra $5,000 as a Christmas bonus—all to be equally divided between AWOC and the National Farm Workers Association. The announcement was not only recognition of Chavez's growing importance but also a tribute to his instinct for brinkmanship.

Manuel Chavez had made sure the room was filled with supporters, and the crowd cheered loudly. "Here for the first time we were being made a part of it," Chavez said afterward. "We were always on the outside . . . People sense these things. So they felt like they were equal now."

He went home that night relieved that there would be a reliable stream of money to pay bills. But at an impromptu celebration at Richard Chavez's house, Cesar also noted, "Tonight we lost our independence." The mixed emotions characterized Chavez's ambivalence about the national labor movement, an ambivalence he never shed.

Even as he grew dependent on organized labor, Chavez insisted he would never lead a typical labor union. He described himself as a community organizer, not a labor leader, and he emphasized that distinction over and over. "When you read of labor organizing in this country, you can say there is a point where labor is 'organized,'" he said in a speech to the California Student Nonviolent Coordinating Committee state meeting in Fresno a few months into the strike. "But in community organizing, there never is a point where you can say, 'It is organized.'"

For Chavez, the tremendous difficulty, the high rate of failure, and the need to never walk away or rest were the lessons of the CSO: "A community organization can disintegrate right from under you . . . the only way I know is to spend an awful lot of time with each individual—hours and hours—until he understands and you've got him going." The only way to organize successfully, he said, was one person at a time.

Even in the first hectic days of the strike, Chavez focused on the difference between a union and a movement, between labor organizing and community organizing, between what had been done before and Chavez's conviction that he could and must create something new to bridge that divide.

"We don't want to model ourselves on industrial unions; that would be bad. We want to get involved in politics, in voter registration, not just contract negotiation," Chavez said. "We're experimenting." He mused about potential structures and finding ways to ensure that the members maintained control. "We have to find some cross between being a movement and being a union."

CHAPTER 12

Beyond Delano

I want each of you to know that something very special is beginning to happen here and I would like you to join your brothers.

Chavez had read widely about dozens of earlier, failed strikes in the fields of California. He knew he could not win a strike in the vineyards of Delano. From the start, he looked far beyond the valley.

In the early weeks, he sought help from urban supporters just to survive—to feed the strikers; pay for gas, picket signs, and mimeograph paper; and make sure babies had milk to drink and children had shoes for school. His first appeals went to allies Chavez had cultivated for several years.

Wendy Goepel had been working for the state and living in the foot-hills of the Sierra Nevada mountains when the strike began. She had been shocked to hear Chavez's voice when he called; he had no phone at home and only rarely made calls from his brother's house. When he told her the news, she headed to Delano. "Without hesitation," the twenty-six-year-old wrote to Saul Alinsky, "I quit my state job." She told her boss she was too busy to return the state car. With single-minded devotion, she answered phones, solicited help from contacts in Berkeley and Washington, and walked picket lines, conspicuous in her brown plaid skirt and monogrammed white blouse.

Chris Hartmire had also gotten an early call, and he made the 140-mile drive north to Delano from his Los Angeles home again and again and again, energized by each visit. Hartmire put the Migrant Ministry staff of more than a dozen at Chavez's disposal and protected them when they were attacked by conservative Protestant clergy. He expanded his mailing list, issued urgent appeals for specific foods needed in the strike kitchen, and solicited monthly pledges of support.

Terence Cannon had exchanged letters with Chavez just days before the strike began, to plan joint projects between the Student Nonviolent Coordinating Committee and the farm workers union. Cannon switched gears and threw himself into the strike. His dispatches in the SNCC newspaper the *Movement* became the primary way that news about Delano reached an activist community eager for a new cause to embrace.

Chavez had hesitated to even meet with SNCC leaders earlier in the year; now he welcomed them as crucial allies. They were steeped in the language and practices of the civil rights movement. The SNCC veterans taught classes in nonviolence and passed on their mailing lists. They brought lessons from Mississippi—along with two-way radios, which proved just as essential in Delano for communication and protection.

After the organization he now openly called a union had survived the first chaotic weeks, Chavez had begun to think long-term. The strike might last a year, he predicted. He needed a different kind of help. He turned his focus to recruiting bodies to do everything from cook food to repair cars, but most urgently to bolster the sagging picket lines.

Hundreds of workers had walked out on strike at the start (the union estimated thousands while growers said five hundred, and no one really had an accurate number). Within weeks, the vast majority of strikers had either found jobs in other crops, left Delano, or returned to their original employer. Some went back out of necessity, some out of loyalty, and others out of fear. Growers increased wages to undermine the union and paid as much or more than the union's original $1.40-an-hour demand. Bills came due, and strikers had no money. Cars broke down from all the driving. The number of picketers plunged, and tensions grew. As the Civil War had split families, so did the strike; children faced parents across picket lines, friendships ended when strikers turned scab. Brothers ended up on opposite sides of the struggle. Luis Valdez found himself on a picket line facing his uncle, a foreman who had helped finance his nephew's education.

"*Estimado amigo*," Chavez wrote in a "dear friend" letter seeking volunteers to shore up the picket lines. "We can provide a floor to sleep on and three meals a day." He described a movement "which has the spirit of Zapata and the tactics of Martin Luther King" and asked for food, donations, and, above all, volunteers to join the fight. "Please consider this letter and my proposal carefully. I want each of you to know that something very special is beginning to happen here and I would like you to join your brothers."

The response came quickly. Most of the early arrivals came to Delano from the San Francisco Bay Area, which had become a magnet for politically engaged young people. Protests on the Berkeley campus, San Francisco demonstrations against racial discrimination, and recent anti–Vietnam War marches had imbued a generation of youth with a sense that they could change history. Delano became their latest cause. Many recruits began as weekend warriors, joining one of the caravans that arrived in Delano each Friday evening with food, money, and fresh faces. Chavez welcomed the guests to the Friday night meeting, holding them up to strikers as evidence their cause was generating support hundreds of miles away. The visitors listened to Chavez's updates, joined in the singing, and laughed at the Teatro Campesino. Afterward they treated strikers and staff to pitchers of beer at the NFWA hangout, People's Bar, where the Rolling Stones' new hit song "Satisfaction" played on the jukebox all night long.

Kathy Lynch, a Berkeley student who helped edit the Citizens for Farm Labor newsletter, had drifted through her young life searching for ways to be of service. She hung out with worker-priests in France, packed apricots in a San Jose shed, returned to finish her studies at Berkeley, and gravitated toward the Catholic Worker movement before embracing the farmworker cause. She joined an early caravan to Delano, walked a picket line on Saturday morning, and met Chavez later in the day at the union office, where he poured wine for the visitors. For several months she spent most of her waking hours collecting food, money, and clothes in Berkeley during the week and trekking to Delano on Fridays. After a few months, she moved in.

People flocked to Delano with no expectation beyond a place to sleep and a cause to believe in. Eddie Frankel, a nineteen-year-old from Pittsburgh, Pennsylvania, who wanted to be a poet, slept underneath a big table at 102 Albany Street, while someone else slept on top. He was so caught up in making history he never thought to take any photographs, and only realized the oversight years later. Ida Cousino arrived from San Jose, where the twenty-five-year-old had been helping draft dodgers and had worked with Luis Valdez. She stored her possessions in a church basement, never saw them again, and never thought twice.

More and more people heeded Chavez's siren call as news of the strike spread through the *Movement* and *People's World*, a Communist newspaper published in Los Angeles. They slept on the floor of the office and then, as the union expanded, next door in the building christened the "Pink House." For decades, those early volunteers' first association with Delano was a floor covered with sleeping bags. Berkeley radicals, Protestant ministers, college dropouts, earnest do-gooders, and monolingual farmworkers began to coalesce into the quasi-union, quasi-movement Chavez envisioned. By the time the harvest season wound down in late fall, a community had formed in Delano. They had a nursery for kids, a store with donated goods, and a makeshift clinic with one nurse.

The mix of people was exhilarating, if occasionally problematic. Radicals had to be reminded that their political beliefs and antiwar campaigns had no place in Delano. Irate farmworkers' wives blamed coeds for corrupting their husbands. Disheveled hippies played into the stereotype that growers used to stir up antiunion feeling. Illegal drugs, officially banned in the union, were readily available.

But for the most part, the melding of cultures and values in the tiny farming town was a heady mix that raised spirits and propelled *la causa* forward. Cousino, who knew no Spanish, took the small children of the family she lived with to San Jose for their first meal in a restaurant. Catholic farmworkers who had never met a Protestant walked picket lines with Jews and Communists. Suddenly Mexican farmworkers of all ages glimpsed a future that might include something other than being a worker or a foreman, the exploited or the exploiter.

"We begin to believe that this is the time for a real movement among farm workers to begin," Chavez wrote in a letter to supporters. "And people are beginning to talk about the Movement instead of a strike."

By the end of 1965, the temperature had dropped below freezing in the valley and just a handful of crews pruned vines in the cold and fog. To maintain a token presence, pickets marched halfheartedly outside railroad cars that sat on the tracks, loaded with grapes. They kept a twenty-four-hour vigil and set fires in big tin cans to keep warm in the rain and cold. Police refused to renew the one-week fire permit and confiscated the cans.

Chavez needed to maintain enthusiasm and find an outlet to exploit the energy of the eager young people before they drifted off to the next cause. Grapes were not on the vines, but they were in the stores. The boycotts of Greensboro, North Carolina, lunch counters and Birmingham, Alabama, merchants had made headlines only a few years earlier and were still fresh in the mind of Jim Drake. He suggested a boycott, and Chavez agreed.

Chavez put Drake in charge of a venture that both viewed as an experiment. At least the project would keep their supporters busy, a lesson Chavez had learned in the CSO when he asked volunteers to cut up squares of paper when he ran out of other tasks. He chose as the first target Schenley, a major liquor distributor that owned a relatively small wine grape vineyard near Delano. The *Movement* published a special boycott supplement listing Schenley brands, which included popular labels such as Dewar's, and an eight-step guide to setting up a boycott committee, in time to hurt Christmas sales. Hartmire came up with a $1,000 contribution, which Drake spent on phone calls to solicit support around the United States.

Chavez framed the strike and boycott as a civil rights struggle, an approach crucial to translating the movement to a broader audience unfamiliar with the farmworker cause. In New York, James Farmer, director of CORE, staged a protest outside Schenley's Manhattan headquarters. He drew parallels between the farmworkers' fight in California and that of blacks in the South: "Police controlled by the growers, phones tapped, sulfur sprayed on pickets, prejudiced juries."

Hartmire invoked similar comparisons in his appeals for religious support. "There is no relevant middle ground on a moral issue that is as clear as the farm workers' fight for opportunity and self respect," Hartmire wrote. "Silence and neutrality inevitably become the allies of the established, unjust way of doing things . . . The issue of human worth is as central in Delano as it was in Selma."

In addition to boycotting Schenley liquor, Chavez wanted to figure out a way to depress the sale of table grapes, harvested on the majority of vineyards where the union had called a strike. He thought if grapes could be tracked on their journey to market, the union could position picket lines at the destination to block trucks from unloading.

Eddie Frankel, the poet, and a few strikers began to tail trucks carrying grapes to the produce market in Los Angeles. The drivers caught on, so the pickets switched tactics. Frankel waited in a car with a two-way radio at the top of the Grapevine, the mountain pass that separates Los Angeles County from the San Joaquin Valley. Strikers in Delano staked out the trucks and wrote down license plates as they left the vineyards. They radioed the information to Frankel and used codes that Chavez set up to indicate different stations: Delano was "Mother," Bakersfield was

"Father," and Mojave was "Titibet," the nickname of one of Chavez's daughters. Frankel picked up the chase, followed the trucks to the market, and set up picket lines. Depending on the sympathies of other unions, whose drivers unloaded the grapes, the pickets caused costly delays and sometimes blocked the delivery entirely.

Grapes headed to markets across the United States were loaded in Delano onto "reefers," refrigerated train cars kept cool with ice that was replenished every day. If the union could trace the grapes, they would know where to throw up picket lines as soon as grapes arrived. Chavez decided they needed to follow the grapes nationwide. He asked at a meeting if anyone had experience riding trains.

Bob Coffman was just out of high school, enough of a ringer for a young Bob Dylan that people asked for autographs. He had spent the summer of 1965 working for SNCC in Mississippi, hitchhiked home to San Francisco, heard about the grape strike, and headed to Delano. He slept on the floor of the Pink House, drove Chavez when he needed a ride, stood guard over the Cessna 180 that the Sacramento priest flew down to Delano, and did whatever he was told. Like others, Coffman was a little in awe of Chavez, but he also saw him as a regular guy, often scruffy with a day's growth of stubble, and with a sense of humor. The first time Coffman was alone with him they were driving in Wendy Goepel's Volkswagen convertible, equipped with the latest features. Chavez asked if Coffman wanted to see Wendy pee, then delightedly played with the automatic windshield-wiper fluid squirter. Coffman knew he was part of something big. They were making history.

Coffman had jumped a train in Memphis on his way home from Mississippi, so he raised his hand when Chavez asked for volunteers. Chavez sent Coffman off with $50, a bottle of whiskey, a small sign, and instructions to jump off in Chicago and form a picket line. Under cover of darkness one December night, he clambered aboard a train in Delano and found the only place he could ride—leaning against the back wheels of the reefer where the trailer sat on the flatbed. By dawn they were in Fresno. He escaped detection as the train was re-iced, but the cold and wind were punishing. At the next stop in the giant switching yards in Roseville, railroad police spotted Coffman. They had to carry him off the train; his legs were too frozen to move. Coffman headed back to Delano and told Chavez they'd have to find another way.

Chavez had more success drawing attention to the strike in a different arena. Democrats in Congress had drafted legislation to amend the

National Labor Relations Act to include farmworkers so that the national rights, procedures and protections for union elections would extend to the fields. Sen. Harrison Williams, a New Jersey Democrat who chaired the subcommittee on migratory labor, scheduled three hearings in California in March 1966. While the legislation had little chance, the hearings would focus attention on the plight of farmworkers. The third hearing, in Delano, succeeded beyond all expectations, largely because Walter Reuther had urged that the junior senator from New York, Robert F. Kennedy, attend.

Mexicans felt a strong affinity for the Kennedy family, and the CSO and other groups had worked hard for the election of the first Catholic president in 1960. The day before the Williams hearing, Sen. Kennedy came to Delano and toured a labor camp with Chavez. "We need to be recognized; not just in the union sense, but as human beings with human rights," Chavez told Kennedy, again framing the ongoing struggle as one about dignity. The senator visited the union office and the strike kitchen and addressed a mass meeting in Filipino Hall. "We are here to help farmworkers help themselves—not just to improve wages, but housing, living conditions, and educational opportunities as well," Kennedy told a cheering crowd.

A mix of farmworkers, growers, and students packed the Delano High School auditorium for the Senate hearing the next morning. Martin Zaninovich was the only grower on the witness list. He insisted that virtually all of the grape workers had remained at their jobs and refused to walk out and the strike was a public relations myth. "The simple truth is, gentlemen, that there is no strike in Delano," Zaninovich told the senators. Kennedy asked if Zaninovich would allow his workers to join a union if they chose, and the grower responded he would honor an election if an acceptable set of rules could be established. "We have the ability to get to the moon," Kennedy replied, "so I think we can establish machinery so people can vote."

The most memorable exchange came just before lunch, when Kennedy, the former U.S. attorney general, quizzed Kern County sheriff Leroy Galyen about why his deputies photographed people on picket lines. "I can understand you want to take pictures if there's a riot going on," Kennedy said, "but I don't understand why if someone is walking along with a sign you want to take pictures of them. I don't see how that helps." Peaceful picketing, Kennedy insisted, was not the same as riots.

GALYEN: Well if I have reason to believe that there's going to be a riot started and somebody tells me that there's going to be trouble if you don't stop them, it's my duty to stop them.

RFK: Then do you go out and arrest them?

GALYEN: Yes.

RFK: And charge them.

GALYEN: Charge them.

RFK: What do you charge them with?

GALYEN: Violation of—unlawful assembly.

RFK: I think that's most interesting. Who told you that they're going to riot?

GALYEN: The men right out in the field that they were talking to said, "If you don't get them out of here, we're going to cut their hearts out." So rather than let them get cut, we removed the cause.

RFK: This is the most interesting concept, I think, that you suddenly hear or you talk about the fact that somebody makes a report about somebody going to get out of order, perhaps violate the law, and you go and arrest them, and they haven't done anything wrong. How can you go arrest somebody if they haven't violated the law?

GALYEN: They're ready to violate the law.

To roars from the crowd, Kennedy suggested that during the lunch break the sheriff read the Constitution of the United States. Like the arrest of the Rev. David Havens for reading Jack London on the picket line (a charge that was dismissed), Kennedy's exchange dramatized the extreme measures the ruling class of Delano used to protect its way of life. For farmworkers, the sight of a revered United States senator ridiculing a local sheriff became a seminal moment in the strike, and in their education.

Chavez's next move was, again, born out of necessity and a desire to bring the strike to the world outside Delano. It was still winter. There would not be workers in the vineyards in large numbers for months, nor grapes headed to market for months after that. At a brainstorming retreat at a supporter's Santa Barbara home, Chavez kicked around ideas. Again the civil rights movement provided inspiration. At a moment when the strike was nearly on life support, Chavez embraced a suggestion for a march, an idea that would catapult *la causa* into national consciousness.

Chavez had read vivid accounts of Mao's long march in *Red Star Over China*, by Edgar Snow, and paid particular attention to the way the Red Army organized along the route. Martin Luther King Jr. had recently organized the March on Washington. Chavez preferred Mao's model of a march that traveled, rather than a group that converged on one place. He believed that walking lent itself naturally to organizing, with daily goals and visible results. He rejected the suggestion of a march to Schenley's headquarters; what if no one were there? Instead he opted for a march to Sacramento. The three-hundred-mile route from Delano to the state Capitol would pass through dozens of farmworker communities. Workers outside Delano knew little of the strike and had not identified with the strikers; Chavez decided to take the strike to them. Lent was approaching, he pointed out. So the march became a pilgrimage, or in Spanish, a *peregrinación*. Their slogan reflected the mix of religious and revolutionary fervor: "Peregrinación, Penitencia, Revolución."

Buoyed by Kennedy's support and performance, about fifty marchers, mostly farmworkers, set out the morning after the hearing on the long trek to the state Capitol, sleeping bags slung over their shoulders and clothes carried in paper bags. Chavez began by staging a confrontation, to show the workers their own power. The route out of Delano ran straight north on Albany Street from the union office, and that had been the route agreed to with police monitoring the march. Two blocks north of 102 Albany Street, police stopped traffic on Garces Highway, a major east-west route, to allow the marchers to cross. Instead, Chavez moved to turn east onto Garces, which would take them across the railroad tracks and toward the center of town. Police blocked the way. Marchers knelt in prayer. With images of Selma still fresh, the Delano cops backed down from a fight they realized they could not win. "They wanted us to arrest them," Delano police chief James Ailes said. "It would have made them look good if we arrested them with all that press and TV there." Chavez triumphantly led the marchers through the east side, the heart of the growers' domain.

The route had been planned to pass through as many small towns as possible: twenty-five days, thirty-three cities, about fifteen to twenty miles per day. Strike captains enforced rules and regulations. Alcohol was forbidden. Song sheets were distributed to the marchers. Manuel Chavez, out on parole, was supposed to avoid working for the union as a condition of his release. But he came back to help, going ahead each day to handle advance work, turn out crowds, and organize food and shelter. He promised Cesar a crowd of at least five thousand in Sacramento.

As the marchers bravely walked single file up the spine of the San Joaquin Valley, along Highway 99 and on small roads that cut through acres of fruit, cotton, and citrus, people came to cheer the workers on and offer food and drink. With tears in their eyes, farmworkers joined the march for a block, a mile, or a day.

"Walking along the freeway? If you'd suggested that to a farmworker a year ago, a year and a half ago, they would have thought you were a little unbalanced," Luis Valdez said to a filmmaker. "I think anybody would have thought you were a little unbalanced. Walk along the 99? With a flag?" Just four years after its dramatic unveiling in the Fresno social hall, the black eagle flag had become more than a union emblem: it was a symbol of grassroots struggle and cultural pride. Each day of the march, the sense of solidarity grew, along with the crowds. "Like, we're not alone," Valdez said.

Chavez battled to overcome fear and instill hope, and the march furthered both goals. "There is now a movement throughout the state," Chavez told high school students who interviewed him along the way. "See, in the past the only time workers were organized was only in those cases where paid organizers came in and got them organized. Now that is not the case. Now the people are striving for organization and they are making this organization themselves."

Each evening as marchers straggled into another town, they were greeted with cheers as they paraded by candlelight to a local hall for dinner and a performance by the Teatro Campesino. Valdez had written the "Plan de Delano," modeled on Emiliano Zapata's "Plan de Ayala," the 1911 manifesto of the Mexican revolutionary. In his deep, resonant voice, Valdez read the fiery declaration in Spanish and English each night:

> This is the beginning of a social movement in fact and not in pronouncements . . . We are tired of words, of betrayals, of indifference. *We shall be heard* . . . We are not afraid to suffer in order to win our cause . . . We draw our strength from the very despair in which we have been forced to live . . . Our revolution will not be armed, but we want the existing social order to dissolve . . . Our pilgrimage is the match that will light our cause for all farmworkers to see what is happening here, so that they may do as we have done.

Just as Zapata's forces had carried images of the Virgen de Guadalupe into battle, the pilgrims marched each day behind a banner with a portrait of the saint, the most important cultural symbol for Mexicans because, as the Plan de Delano proclaimed, "she is ours, all ours, patroness of the Mexican people."

Whether they were practicing Catholics or cultural Catholics, Mexicans knew the story of the Virgen, who appeared in a vision to the peasant Juan Diego on a hill in Mexico City in 1531. The virgin mother was brown like the Indians, and she spoke gently to Juan Diego in his language, Nahuatl, at a time when the Spanish conquistadors treated the Aztecs like dirty savages. She commanded that a church be built in her name, and when the archbishop dismissed the peasant's vision, the Virgen reappeared and supplied Juan Diego with an armful of red roses. He dropped the roses in front of the bishop, revealing an image of the saint imprinted on Diego's cloak. That icon hangs in the basilica built on the spot where the Virgen appeared. Millions of pilgrims journey to the Mexico City shrine on her feast day, December 12, some traveling for weeks. Penitents often walk the final miles on their knees. Thousands line the road and offer refreshment, just as Mexicans throughout the San Joaquin Valley did for the farmworkers who marched to Sacramento in the spring of 1966. "The Virgin of Guadalupe is more Mexican than Catholic," Chavez said. "She is our mother, and she's Mexican."

By harnessing the power of the Virgen, Chavez reached out and embraced the church, leaving its reluctant sentinels no choice but to return the gesture. Priests opened their doors, welcomed the penitents, and said mass in each new town. The church's imprimatur conveyed safety, emboldening more people to join la causa, especially women. As the march wore on, the physical suffering enhanced the religious aspects. Limping along, Chavez stressed the value of the physical hardship and talked about the importance of admitting sin: "The penance part of it is, to me, the most important thing of the pilgrimage."

Valdez watched the suffering, observed with a writer's eye how Chavez endured pain and used that image for maximum advantage. After the first day, when both men's feet were blistered from walking miles in work boots, Valdez switched to sneakers and urged Chavez to follow suit. Chavez declined. He saw the power of the suffering image, and he embraced it. He was sidelined with a swollen ankle, blisters, and fever for a day or two, then resumed the march, hobbling with a cane. "Every step was a needle," he recalled.

Bill Kircher, the director of organizing for the AFL-CIO, did not know much about farm labor and had never talked to Chavez. But Kircher was a good Catholic who understood the appeal of penance, and a good organizer who grasped the potential of Cesar Chavez. Kircher put on old clothes and joined the march. He learned the words to the movement songs and went to mass every morning. After a few days, they arrived in a town where the local paper ran a story saying that AWOC and the AFL-CIO were boycotting the march. Kircher went ballistic and ordered his own reluctant union to participate. Kircher's determination to demonstrate his organization's commitment stemmed both from personal conviction and from a deep, decades-long animosity toward Walter Reuther and other top officials of the autoworkers union. Chavez became the beneficiary of that feud, as the leaders of the AFL-CIO and the UAW vied to prove themselves the farmworkers' most loyal labor ally.

The UAW had donated a radio-telephone, and Terence Cannon rode in a truck with the primitive mobile phone to handle public relations for the march. The phone worked by calling operators, a different one as they moved from zone to zone, and Cannon got to know them all. Each day he typed up a statement and called reporters at all the national papers. The first week he had no bites beyond the local press. Then the *New York Times* picked up the story on March 25, 1966 (only the third time the paper had mentioned Chavez's name—first when Reuther visited, then once in a boycott story). Cannon's phone started to ring. In the towns where Chavez had struggled just a few years earlier to turn out a handful of people, they now showed up in droves.

The growers looked on with a mixture of bafflement, apprehension, and anger.

"The simple truth is that there is no strike in Delano," Martin Zaninovich said once more to the annual meeting of the California Grape and Tree Fruit League in San Francisco on March 24, one week into the march. "More than 5,000 of the people who regularly, year after year, picked our crops, stayed on the job. In fact, they picked the largest crop in history." For a brief period, he acknowledged, the two unions "succeeded in frightening perhaps as many as 500 workers away from their jobs." But within days, most had returned.

Zaninovich was the son of one of three brothers who had emigrated from Croatia and each started a Delano vineyard in the 1940s. His Jasmine Vineyard was far from the largest, but Zaninovich had quickly emerged as a leader among the grape growers. He had helped form a Delano group

called the South Central Farmers Committee a few years earlier, anticipating a union drive. In January 1966, the committee leased an office at 1224
Jefferson Street on Delano's east side—almost exactly one block over from
the Chavez home on Kensington. Growers met daily to exchange information and plan strategy. Along with a handful of other growers, including his
brother-in-law, Jack Pandol, Zaninovich became the public face of the
employers. Pandol was frank and profane, Zaninovich more statesmanlike.
Both were angry and confused by the attack not only on their often-
precarious financial situation but also on their way of life.

On April 3, as the marchers arrived in Stockton, Chavez received a
message that a lawyer for Schenley wanted to meet. First he thought the
call a hoax. But Sidney Korshak, a well-known lawyer to mobsters, said
he was empowered by the chairman of Schenley to negotiate as soon as
possible. For Schenley, a multinational company with only a small fraction of its business in Delano, one small vineyard was jeopardizing the
sale of dozens of major liquor labels. Schenley officials had proposed selling the vineyard, but Korshak suggested they could reap good publicity
by signing a contract instead.

Chavez slept in the car as Hartmire drove him to Los Angeles. They
met Korshak at his Beverly Hills home the next day, and after a minor
skirmish about the role of the AFL-CIO in the pact, they had a deal. They
signed a recognition agreement with contract negotiations to follow
within sixty days. "Labor history was written here today," said Kircher,
who cosigned the agreement.

Chavez reached Cannon on the mobile phone, and he stood on top of
a car and announced the news to the cheers of the marchers. Four years
after he had moved to Delano with little more than a dream, Cesar Chavez
was on the front page of the *New York Times*. Chavez sent a letter to
boycott supporters to share the news—and told them to switch focus
immediately to the giant DiGiorgio Corporation, the union's next target.

The union had made sleeping arrangements for nine hundred people
in Sacramento, in a gym, churches, and union halls. On Easter, the
marchers crossed the Tower Bridge into Sacramento, the crowd so large
it took almost an hour for the last person to cross. More than eight thousand cheering farmworkers and supporters massed in the park in front of
the state Capitol. The *originales*, those who had marched the whole way,
had a special place of honor. Hartmire led the crowd in prayer. Chavez
spotted Fred Ross, who had just joined the march, and called him up to
the makeshift stage.

The union leader addressed the crowd only briefly. "It is well to remember that in defeat there must be courage, but also that in victory, there must be humility," Chavez began. He thanked the many organizations that had lent support, and the farmworkers who had the courage to walk out on strike. Prolonged applause followed his introduction of the only person he thanked by name: "And I want to introduce to you someone, when we started organizing four years ago, in fact one of the very few people that thought that this could be done—my wife, Helen."

Governor Pat Brown had declined Chavez's request to meet and spent Easter with his family at the Palm Springs home of Frank Sinatra. That only made the rally stronger. Chavez rejected the governor's offer to meet the next morning. Sunday or not at all, he told Brown. My way or the highway, a hallmark of Chavez's negotiating style that growers would soon see again and again.

The farmworkers had shown their strength, to the outside world and to themselves. They could walk through the heart of enemy territory in Delano, and they could rebuff the governor's overtures. The *Delano Record* might report on its front page that the rally on the Capitol steps fanned "the flames of class struggle and suspicion and bitterness and hatred," but the marchers had carried their message far beyond the parochial barriers of the valley: Farmworkers were no longer willing to be treated as second-class citizens.

"We are still in an age of symbols and heroes and so forth," Chavez said in an interview, downplaying his own role. "For many years I was a farm worker, a migratory worker, and, well personally, and I'm being very frank, maybe it's just a matter of trying to even the score, you know."

Now that he was gaining national attention, Chavez took care to shape his own life story. He began to embellish his evolution as an organizer in small but pointed ways. The history melted into mythology, the better to draw people into *la causa*. In particular, Chavez recast two key junctures in his life—his decision to join the CSO, and his decision to leave.

When Chavez recounted how he became an organizer, he was still a farmworker, picking apricots, not a lumber handler. Where Fred Ross had been too late for the Chavez house meeting the first night and returned the following week night, Chavez massaged the facts to say he dodged Ross several times and made Helen cover for him, assuming Ross was a nosy sociologist studying the habits of Mexicans. Chavez erased his parents and family from the house meeting that night and replaced them with a bunch of rowdy friends he recruited to give Ross a hard time. He had told them he would give them a signal, Chavez said: when he switched his cigarette from one hand to the other, they were to drive Ross out. While in real life Ross brought an interpreter along, in Chavez's version Ross spoke fluent and impressive Spanish. One detail remained true to the history: Ross was such a great organizer that Chavez was immediately impressed and ready to join the CSO.

Ross did his part to fuel the myth building. He invented a diary entry and told interviewers that when he went home that night he wrote: "I think I've found the guy I've been looking for."

The end of Chavez's account of the fateful meeting was equally fictional. The first thing Chavez asked Ross, according to the revised history, was, What will CSO do for farmworkers? If we get strong enough, Ross replied, we will form a union.

In his revisionist account of leaving the CSO, Chavez likewise altered the facts. Frustrated that the CSO helped middle-class Mexican Americans and ignored farmworkers, Chavez said, he decided to go off on his own and do the job. In fact, at the March 16, 1962, convention where he announced his resignation, the CSO adopted a program to help farmworkers. Chavez rejected the plan and believed he needed to organize on his own terms, reporting to no one and free to work in the way he thought best. He submitted his resignation letter on April 16.

As more national reporters began to express interest in where Cesar Chavez came from, he added one more significant detail to the evolving legend. He began to repeat that he quit CSO on his birthday, March 31, 1962. Not too many years later, that date would become an official union holiday.

CHAPTER 13
The First Big Test

It's tough enough just fighting a company. Or it's tough enough just fighting another union. But when the company and the union are working hand in glove, it's a hard combination to beat.

As soon as Chavez announced the Schenley agreement, some marchers on the *peregrinación* tore up their BOYCOTT SCHENLEY signs and tossed them in the air. Others crossed out SCHENLEY and wrote in DIGIORGIO.

DiGiorgio was not only the largest grower in California but also a symbol of corporate agricultural power. With ties to the Bank of America, offices in the hub of San Francisco's business district, and a history of violently putting down labor strife in the fields, DiGiorgio offered Chavez an attractive villain.

The DiGiorgio empire had been built by Joseph DiGiorgio, who arrived in America as a fifteen-year-old Sicilian fruit peddler at the end of the nineteenth century and rose to run a multimillion-dollar food company. By 1966, his four nephews had taken over and expanded from vineyards, a winery, and a shipping and distribution network into canned goods and juices. DiGiorgio was the largest grape, pear, and plum grower in the United States. As with Schenley, only a small percentage of DiGiorgio's business was directly affected by the strike. The company had been shifting more and more investments out of agriculture; only about 20 percent of DiGiorgio's $100 million annual revenue came from farming. Most came from sales of well-known brands such as S&W Fine Foods and Treesweet. So the threatened boycott caused concern.

Robert DiGiorgio, one of Joseph's nephews, had been trying to convince his partners to get out of the fields altogether. Farming was too perilous, dependent on factors outside the grower's control, and yielded only a modest income at best. If a union contract proved unworkable, he could use the labor problems as an added incentive to sell the DiGiorgio land. Robert DiGiorgio threw down the gauntlet: he called for an election among workers in his grape vineyards.

Chavez had no choice but to accept. He knew the challenge was fraught with problems. Who would be eligible to vote? What were the rules? Who would enforce them? But he had been demanding elections for months, and his supporters would not have understood had he turned down the opportunity.

As Chavez faced the first significant test of his union's power in the fields, he drew on everything he had learned. Unlike his campaigns in the CSO, he did not have to rely on his relatives, nor did he have to do everything himself. He had a team of savvy, dedicated advisers and dozens of zealous volunteers, including farmworkers, students, nuns, and ministers, eager to carry out any request. And once again, he had the help of "Papa Ross."

Fred Ross had returned from Syracuse and moved to the Bay Area, where he worked as a consultant for several community organizations. One group had asked him to research Chavez's death benefit plan, so Ross took the opportunity to visit his old student in Delano a few weeks after the march to Sacramento. Chavez was heading into a meeting with DiGiorgio officials to discuss election protocols, and Ross tagged along. The April 20, 1966, meeting was interrupted by a phone call about a violent confrontation on a picket line outside DiGiorgio's Delano ranch. Chavez and Ross rushed out to investigate.

At the center of the disturbance, crestfallen, stood Ida Cousino. Ross realized they had met a week earlier in Sacramento. Cousino had sought out Ross when he arrived on the final day of the *peregrinación* and introduced herself. "She wants to be an organizer," Ross had written in his journal. Now he and Chavez found the young woman looking desolate as two farmworkers nursed injuries, one with bad wounds to his head. Cousino had been picketing when Hershel Nuñez, a DiGiorgio security guard, drew his gun and pointed at the picket line. Cousino announced she was making a citizen's arrest. That brought DiGiorgio managers to the scene. One shoved her roughly out of the way, she fell to the ground, and pickets scrambled to her defense. They tussled with the DiGiorgio supervisors, who struck two workers in the head. Chavez publicly denounced the company and broke off negotiations, then called a meeting for that evening. At the standing-room-only session in the Negro Pentecostal Church, he chastised his members and lectured for almost two hours on the importance of nonviolence: "If we return the growers' violence with our violence, we will lose." They were only defending the honor of a woman, protested the men, one with a bandage covering ten stitches in his head.

"Through it all, Ida had sat slumped down, head bowed and desolate. She looked so pitiful sitting there as the battle roared around her," Ross wrote. "Sad, I'm sure, that the men who sprang to her aid were being punished, hurt that the brave thing she had done out there in the field had gone unrecognized. I thought I would see her after the meeting and give her a word of cheer. But the moment the meeting was over, she was gone." Ross found his introduction to the strike dramatic and exhilarating. He decided to stick around for a while, much to Chavez's delight. He gave instructions to put Ross on the payroll at whatever terms he wanted, a rare order. Ross and Cousino began to spend time together. Soon they were romantically involved, one of many couples who formed in the charged ambiance of the shared fight.

As talks over the terms of the election continued, union organizers worked to get DiGiorgio employees to sign cards pledging support to the National Farm Workers Association. Suddenly they heard a disturbing report: Teamsters were circulating cards in the fields as well. The DiGiorgios had recruited the Teamsters, a scandal-scarred union that had been expelled from the AFL-CIO and had a record of signing contracts that allowed management to retain most of its prerogatives. DiGiorgio supervisors began urging workers to sign Teamster cards.

With no agreed-upon rules for the election, Chavez faced long odds and a well-financed campaign by twin antagonists, DiGiorgio and the Teamsters. DiGiorgio fired workers at will, targeting Chavez supporters. Even if fired workers were ultimately ruled eligible to vote in an election, most would be long gone and far away by the time of the vote. The NFWA had no official lists of employees and no access to workers in the fields of the Delano ranch, which was crisscrossed by eleven miles of roads that divided the vineyard into one-mile squares. Neither Chavez nor Ross had ever run a union election campaign. Their budget was so precarious that when the phone bill was too high one month, Chavez put a lock on the phone.

"It's tough enough just fighting a company. Or it's tough enough just fighting another union," Chavez said after DiGiorgio had abruptly laid off

190 workers in crews where the NFWA had strong support. "But when the company and the union are working hand in glove, it's a hard combination to beat."

Ross and Chavez teamed up again to do what they did so well—win over one person at a time. The campaign combined Ross's meticulous attention to detail and discipline with Chavez's creative genius and instinct. Through the ups and downs of the next four months, they used all the tactics they had employed in the CSO, and many new ones. The union dispatched "submarines" who worked on DiGiorgio crews and quietly talked up the union's cause. DiGiorgio workers who voiced support but were afraid to walk out were schooled in ways to help from inside. Women who packed grapes pricked them with pins so they would rot.

Joe Serda had grown up in a migrant family and picked grapes since he was a small child. He had worked his way up to foreman at DiGiorgio, a good job. Now his daughter was on the picket line. When she came home with bruises on her legs where the company trucks had deliberately bumped the picket line, Serda began to attend the union's Friday night meetings. Chavez, Ross, and Orendain came to Serda's home one night and appealed for help. Don't walk out, Chavez said; smuggle out information. Chavez gave clear instructions: find out who was being hired and fired, where grapes were being shipped, and how many were in storage. Serda decided to risk his job for the cause. At Chavez's instigation, the foreman collected trash from the DiGiorgio office and brought the crumpled paper to the Pink House each night, where union leaders taped together torn documents to gain valuable intelligence. When he was eventually discovered and fired, Serda proudly joined the union full-time.

Barred from the fields and blocked by anti-picketing injunctions, the union came up with a novel way to circumvent the restrictions and reach laborers as they left the fields. Richard Chavez built an altar to Our Lady of Guadalupe on the back of a station wagon. The car parked across from an entrance to the DiGiorgio fields; a religious shrine did not violate the injunctions. The shrine drew people for prayer, especially women. Volunteers wrapped themselves in blankets to stay warm during all-night vigils and served hot chocolate and tamales to the penitents—and handed out union cards to sign.

When he needed to up the ante, Chavez called on Chris Hartmire and a Catholic priest to accompany him into one of the DiGiorgio camps in

San Diego from which striking workers had been evicted. Chavez called Valdez, too, who arrived at night and found Chavez rolled up in a blanket, sleeping in a park. The next morning, the union leader, the priest, and the minister accompanied strikers into the DiGiorgio camp. They were arrested for trespassing, strip-searched, and held for hours. Chavez "was, of course, not overlooking the strategic importance of such a confrontation," Hartmire noted in a letter detailing their arrests. The publicity helped raise money, and the stories inspired loyalty and emboldened workers. Here was a leader, Valdez said, who was one of us, sleeping in a park, risking arrest to help farmworkers.

The greater the challenge, the more people looked to Chavez for direction. When they panicked, he remained collected. Their education and experience had not equipped his volunteer staff with a fraction of the understanding of power and human nature that Chavez demonstrated. Their awe grew each time he calmly counseled a distraught forewoman who had lost her job or turned a setback in the fields into a public relations success.

Ross was astonished by how Chavez had grown, his ability to make decisions and to think several steps ahead of the opposition. "Jesus, I had thought of him as a brilliant guy, but I felt he went beyond that," Ross recalled a few years later. "He could do in thirty minutes what it would take me or somebody else thirty days."

Chavez had to think fast when DiGiorgio suddenly announced the company would conduct an election on its own terms—clearly designed to end in a Teamster victory. "They're animals," Chavez said angrily about the DiGiorgios. "You can't trust them. The other growers tell you something and you can be fairly sure they'll do it. Not DiGiorgio." Chavez obtained a court order to remove his union's name from the ballot. Then he switched messages and began urging workers to abstain in protest.

On June 24, 1966, the day DiGiorgio had selected for the vote, hundreds of protesters stood outside the polling place. Each time a bus pulled in carrying workers to the polls, a priest prayed and the protesters dropped to their knees. Many DiGiorgio workers defiantly refused to disembark. Joe Serda's crew returned to the fields and embraced one another for their courage in standing up for their rights. Almost half of the workers refused to vote; of 385 who cast ballots, 281 voted for the Teamsters.

Chavez and Huerta called in every political favor to persuade Governor Brown to intervene and negotiate terms for a fairer election. Brown was facing Ronald Reagan in a difficult campaign for reelection. The governor had been criticized for his handling of the Berkeley student protests and the 1965 Watts riots, and he was anxious to make amends for his decision to snub the farmworkers on Easter. Chavez's request also coincided with Brown's appearance before the Mexican American Political Association (MAPA) to seek the group's endorsement. MAPA made clear that its support was contingent on Brown's intervention. The governor agreed to appoint an independent mediator. The mediator concluded that the first election was invalid and promulgated rules for a second vote. All parties agreed. The campaign was on.

Chavez explained the terms to a packed meeting at Filipino Hall. In less than two months, on August 30, 1966, farmworkers would vote in an election supervised by the American Arbitration Association. The union had to stop boycotting DiGiorgio. If they lost the election, they could not attempt to win recognition at the vineyard for at least a year. "We had to give up a lot to get this," Chavez told the crowd. "I think it's a good thing."

They also gained a lot. Each union now had access to the DiGiorgio property at certain times and was given company lists of employees. Most significantly, any worker who had been on the payroll when the strike began, or had been employed for at least fifteen days since, was eligible to vote. With those ground rules, Ross was in his element—one three-by-five index card for each voter, three meetings a day, nothing taken for granted. Ross taught a new generation of organizers the lessons he had taught Chavez a decade earlier.

One of those novices was Eliseo Medina, a twenty-year-old farmworker from Delano who had joined the union the day after the strike vote in Our Lady of Guadalupe church, so caught up in the fervor that he broke open his piggy bank to pay three months' dues. The son of a former bracero, Eliseo had emigrated from Mexico as a child and lived on Fremont Street, near where the Chavez family had lived a generation earlier. He loved to read and excelled at school even though he had arrived in fourth grade speaking no English. But when teachers explained that Mexicans should enroll in vocational classes in high school, he saw no point. Like Cesar, Eliseo had left school after eighth grade to help his mother support the family. He had first been drawn to the union through the early editions of *El Malcriado*, impressed by the saga of Jimmy Hronis—an Anglo labor contractor brought to justice for cheating sugarbeet workers. For a farmworker such as Eliseo, being cheated without recourse had seemed until then an inevitable part of life. Medina had volunteered for picket duty early in the strike and tasted for the first time the power that came from collective action. Cesar Chavez became more than an inspiration; he was a hero.

Medina's intelligence had impressed Jim Drake, and his good spirits and loyalty caught the eye of Dolores Huerta. When Medina inquired about working under the new Schenley contract, she recruited him instead to work on the DiGiorgio campaign. Now he reported to Ross.

Each day began with a meeting in the Pink House to discuss the day's message. Organizers from each union were allowed into the DiGiorgio vineyard for an hour at noon. Workers ate lunch in the shade of walnut trees outside the commissary, a grassy area that quickly became known as the "bull ring." Ross drummed into his organizers that their job was to explain the benefits of the union, not engage in name-calling with the Teamsters. But the lunch hour invariably ended with the two sides hurling insults back and forth. The Teamsters called their adversaries the "Viet Cong" and threw in frequent references to Cuba and Fidel Castro.

DiGiorgio bosses had access to workers all day. They could threaten, cajole, and promise, and each time they fired a union supporter, the action reminded others of the risk. DiGiorgio handed out leaflets urging a pro-Teamsters vote: "The Teamsters do not want support from beatniks, out-of-town agitators, or do-gooders." Like most growers, DiGiorgio had one camp for women and separate camps for Mexican, Filipino, black, Anglo, and Puerto Rican men. They justified the segregation based on ethnic food preferences, but the divisions helped growers play one group against the other, bestowing such favors as better food on certain camps. Union organizers were allowed access to the camps between 5:30 P.M. and 7:30 P.M. During the same evening hours, Ross sent a different team to fan out across Delano and track down workers who lived outside the camps or had quit when the strike began.

Dozens of the early strikers had left the area long ago, many returning home to Texas. Chavez had fought to get them included in the election; now he had to find them. The Rev. Gene Boutillier from the Migrant Ministry took one list. Gilbert Padilla took another. Hartmire sent a letter to religious leaders in Texas asking for help. They located eligible voters, persuaded them to return, rented a bus, paid their transportation, and promised food and shelter until the August 30 election.

Each day, the union mass-produced bulletins featuring a character called El Mosquito Zumbador, who "buzzed" around with a simple, clear message of the day. In the final weeks, the union bought dozens of one-minute radio spots on Fresno and Bakersfield stations, most featuring El

Mosquito Zumbador buzzing with the latest news. As the Teamsters increased their red-baiting, El Mosquito Zumbador responded with cartoons that showed former Teamster president Jimmy Hoffa behind bars. The AFL-CIO purchased and distributed dozens of copies of *The Enemy Within*, Robert F. Kennedy's account of corrupt practices within the Teamsters. On the Sunday before the election, Medina and his partner drove into the camp and were surrounded by Teamsters who began punching him through the car window. He got out with a busted lip. The NFWA quickly churned out another leaflet about Teamster violence on the Lord's day.

Chavez had taken charge of the DiGiorgio campaign, but Larry Itliong and AWOC also helped, focusing on the Filipino camps. Bill Kircher, the AFL-CIO director of organizing, had been spending his time not with his own organizing committee but with Chavez's union. Since they had talked on the march to Sacramento, Kircher had worked to soften Chavez's resistance to joining the labor movement. They had been discussing terms of a possible merger ever since.

As the election neared, the two separate unions became increasingly unwieldy. Kircher negotiated the terms of a merger, and then he explained the arrangement to workers at several large meetings. Kircher had a big blackboard and recorded the tallies as members voted their approval. The new union would also be an organizing committee of the AFL-CIO, a status that carried a monthly subsidy. They agreed on a new name: the United Farm Workers Organizing Committee (UFWOC).

For AWOC, the merger was an official recognition that the Filipinos had long since ceased running the strike they had bravely launched. Itliong became the assistant director of the new union. For Chavez, who had eschewed and denigrated traditional labor unions, the move also represented a bow to reality. For the foreseeable future, he was dependent on the labor movement, though he never embraced it, nor did most labor leaders ever shed their wariness about him. As with his decision to join the strike, Chavez didn't really have a choice, so he worked to turn events to maximum advantage. One immediate benefit was badly needed financial help; by summer, the DiGiorgio campaign was costing $25,000 per month, $4,000 in gas alone. The AFL-CIO provided an immediate $10,000-a-month subsidy.

The merger was not universally popular among Chavez's staff, and ideological splits on the picket lines widened. Many of the volunteers who had come out of leftist political groups looked on the labor movement with abhorrence. The AFL-CIO had recently purged unions for alleged Communist ties, and AFL-CIO president George Meany staunchly supported the war in Vietnam. At People's Bar, where the staff gathered to drink beer and shoot pool, many of the committed leftists reacted with disgust. Chavez had sold out to a corrupt institution, they said. Chavez's response was clear: "I told them that the grassroots had to run the strike. I said they were here as servants of the union, not to run the show, and that they had to work disinterested in the politics of the union."

Chavez was leery of labor leaders for his own reasons, and continued to talk derisively about many. But he was also the ultimate pragmatist. He needed the help, and he recognized there was a price. When you get down in the gutter, he told Cousino and Frankel, you're going to get dirty.

The merger, designed in part to unite two ethnic groups that had little contact and some friction, had another lasting repercussion. Filipinos ended up feeling like second-class citizens in a Mexican-controlled union. Despite Chavez's efforts to stress the multiracial nature of the organization and his occasional overtures to the Filipinos, the divisions widened. Chavez made some public efforts to include Itliong and a few other Filipino leaders, but their backgrounds and interests clashed. They were too materialistic, Chavez complained, and he had nothing in common with them, nothing to talk about.

For the moment, however, those differences paled in comparison with the stark contrast between UFWOC and the Teamsters. The Teamsters ostentatiously arrived in the DiGiorgio fields at lunchtime in brand-new Cadillacs and boasted about their wealth. Their organizers camped out at the Stardust Motel, gathering each night to drink beer, compare golf scores, and swim in the pool. They were confident of victory, relaxed up until the night before the election. The famous bookmaker Jimmy the Greek put the odds of a Teamster victory at 3–1.

Unlike the Teamster office, which was deserted on election eve, Filipino Hall was full of energy and excitement, trepidation and laughter. The Teatro Campesino skewered DiGiorgio and the Teamsters. The crowd sang songs. Finally, Chavez spoke briefly. "I think we have done all the work that is necessary. I hope that with the help of God, we will be victorious."

On August 30, 1966, cars lined up outside union headquarters at five o'clock in the morning, waiting to take voters to the polls when they opened an hour later. All day cars shuttled voters back and forth, just like election day in Oxnard in 1958. Teams of poll watchers with lists of eligible voters crossed off names and sent others to find the missing voters before the polls closed. At 8:00 P.M., the ballots were locked up and escorted by members of the California Highway Patrol to San Francisco to be counted. Joe Serda went along as the delegate to stand guard. Huerta gave him a Dexedrine to make sure he stayed alert.

On the morning of September 1, union members gathered in Filipino Hall to await the results. Of the eighteen hundred eligible voters, only seven hundred currently worked at DiGiorgio. The outcome could well hinge on how many of the fired workers had come back to cast votes. Jon Lewis, a talented photographer who had lived around the corner from Luis Valdez in Haight-Ashbury, had followed his friend to Delano and been shooting pictures ever since. He captured the tension in the hall as they waited, the unusual sight of Chavez calming his nerves with a cigarette. Then Chavez stepped up to the microphone, resting on a stand almost as tall as he was, cigarette still in one hand, in the other a paper with scrawled numbers.

There were two separate tallies: an election among a small unit of workers in the DiGiorgio shed, and the big vote for the field workers. First Chavez read the results for the shed unit: Teamsters 94, UFWOC 43. With his usual dramatic flair, Chavez saved the best for last. The results in the election for the field workers: Teamsters 331, UFWOC 530. The room exploded. They lifted Chavez up high in the air and paraded him around the room. Priests, students, and workers were cheering and crying and screaming, throwing themselves at Chavez. A woman handed him a statue of Christ and he held it above his head.

They could not know that the victory would hasten the DiGiorgios' exit from the fields and put hundreds of workers out of jobs only months after they signed a contract. The downside of targeting a large publicly traded company, as would become apparent again and again, is that shareholders care only about the bottom line. Unlike the Delano growers, who lived on the land and had a personal connection, the corporate entity had no such sentimental attachment.

But for the moment, all that mattered was the remarkable underdog victory. There were 513 votes cast from strikers and laid-off workers, who did not have to fear repercussions for their support; though some of those votes were challenged, they clearly swung the election in the UFWOC's favor. Many workers had already sacrificed their jobs to speak out for the union. They sacrificed again to journey back to Delano. Workers who had received only a mimeographed letter from Chavez had returned from as far away as Mexico, walking into the union headquarters in rubber-soled sandals and saying, "Quiero votar por Chavez" (I want to vote for Chavez). They had traveled back to Delano because they believed Cesar Chavez's struggle would improve the lives of farmworkers everywhere, and the victory was sweet revenge.

For Chavez, the victory vindicated his strategy and affirmed the depth of his support. The Teamsters might have had reason to be confident about winning among workers in the fields; they never imagined Chavez and Ross could conduct such a methodical search and persuade so many former workers to return to Delano and vote.

If he had lost the election, Chavez said a few years later, that would have been the end. "We didn't have the credibility with the people yet, we weren't established, we were just beginning. I think the public wouldn't have supported us after that."

CHAPTER 14

Chavez the Leader

There are about five people in the union that are like that: they just look at me and blink their eyes and do it. I may be wrong, they still do it. But it's also a reciprocal thing, they have more influence with me than most anybody else.

His leadership burnished by two big victories, Chavez began to assert his vision more forcefully and assemble a team that shared his values and met his needs.

As the strike entered its second year, his public persona remained the patient, soft-spoken, collaborative leader. He talked with many people, elicited information, consulted a handful of close advisers, and made decisions. During deliberations, he was so engaged and solicitous that many participants mistook the process for democracy.

One of his early decisions became a linchpin for all that followed. In Fred Ross's model, the organizer was the spark, always in the back of the room pushing others forward to be leaders. Ross's star pupil adopted a different model, one that grew out of his frustrations in the CSO and his difficulty trusting others to do anything as well as he could. Chavez saw himself as both the leader and the organizer-in-chief. He must play both roles, he argued, because he alone had the requisite commitment.

"The organizer has to work more than anyone else," he said. "Almost no one in a group is totally committed. And in the initial part of the movement, there's the fear that when the organizer leaves, the movement will collapse. So you have to be able to say, 'I'm not going to be here a year, or six months, but an awful long time—until when they get rid of me, they'll have leaders to do it themselves.'"

The twin roles showcased different facets of Chavez's personality. As the organizer who wanted to persuade people to act, he was charming, attentive, and humble. As the leader who wanted an order carried out, he was single-minded, demanding, and ruthless. "Nice guys throughout the ages have done very little for humanity," he told a group of volunteers. "It isn't the nice guy who gets things done. It's the hardheaded guy."

He made his values clear: loyalty and hard work topped the list. You earn your place in this union, Chavez said repeatedly, with hard work. He divided people into three categories. He reserved the highest accolades for those in the first group, "the guy who can go out there and turn the whole thing upside down, and get production, and get results. To me, this guy is very valuable. I have something in common with him. I like him."

In the second group was "the guy who works his head off and can't get things done. Fine, he can be taught."

The third group was the lazy, and laziness was a cardinal sin. Chavez marked those people, and sooner or later, they would be purged. "That guy has no business in the union," he said. "If we don't do that, then we destroy ourselves."

His closest advisers remained Chavez's family and the friends he had trusted and relied on for years—Helen, Dolores Huerta, Gilbert Padilla, Manuel Chavez, and Richard Chavez, who had joined the union full-time. Chris Hartmire and Jim Drake had earned spots in the tier just beneath the inner circle. Fred Ross had a special place, the mentor turned student, always treated with great respect. As needs arose, Chavez drew in new disciples. Almost all were Anglo men.

Two key players came from nearby Bakersfield. Brother Gilbert, a Christian brother who had met Chavez a year before the strike, resigned as assistant principal at Garces High School and dropped out of graduate school in November 1965. His assignment was to build a service center— the tool that Chavez had developed during his years organizing in the CSO and which he valued so highly as a mechanism for attracting and binding followers to the movement. Brother Gilbert soon reverted to his given name, LeRoy Chatfield. Tall and rail thin, with white-blond hair and piercing blue eyes, Chatfield was an exceedingly capable and equally loyal presence. Chatfield raised funds and oversaw a service center that soon included the newspaper, the credit union, a health clinic, and various properties. Chatfield, then thirty-one, was respected for his access and efficiency, though his authoritarian demeanor often clashed with the more freewheeling spirit of the movement. Chatfield considered Chavez his closest friend.

Marshall Ganz was a recent graduate of Bakersfield High, where he had starred on the school debate team and knew Brother Gilbert as coach of a rival squad. Ganz was the son of a Bakersfield rabbi who had tried to help Chavez procure deputy registrars a decade earlier. Ganz had dropped out of Harvard after going to Mississippi in the summer of 1964, worked for SNCC, and returned home to discover a civil rights battle in his backyard. A generation younger than the others, the twenty-three-year-old was the only Anglo in the inner circle who made a concerted effort to learn Spanish. He soon spoke flawlessly, enabling him to organize in the fields. He loved to brainstorm and had played a key role in organizing the *peregrinación*, plotting out the route, handling logistics, and drafting Chavez's explanations of the march.

As growers became more skilled at using the courts to restrain picketing and cripple the strike, Chavez wanted a lawyer who would fight back. He could not have found a better match than twenty-six-year-old Jerry Cohen, who made up for his lack of experience with a fighting spirit that rivaled that of his new boss. Brash, fast-talking, and brilliant, Cohen saw the law as a tool and loved to find creative ways to turn it against the ruling class. Chavez always said you don't win by playing defense, and Cohen, an avid sports fan, shared that conviction. Only one year out of law school, he immediately saw ways to wage an offensive battle even in a legal system rigged against the union. Bill Kircher arranged for the AFL-CIO to pay Cohen $750 a month.

As Chavez brought more players into his emerging kitchen cabinet, others were gradually pushed aside. Larry Itliong, technically the number two person in the union, felt cut out and grew angry. Many of the earlier generation of CSO leaders had faded in importance; some were turned off by the religious pageantry or frustrated by the lack of militancy, while others found themselves marginalized. Antonio Orendain, the union's secretary-treasurer, remained the only Mexican immigrant in the leadership ranks. He treated Chavez with a certain formality, an outsider's reserved respect. Unlike most people, who called him "Cesar" (Chavez used the English pronunciation, CEE-zer), Orendain always addressed the union leader as "Chavez," or "Sr. Chavez" in writing. Orendain referred to Chatfield and the others as "the twelve apostles." (Chavez also used the term on occasion; when Cesar prevailed upon his brother to join the union full-time, Richard Chavez recalled, "He said, 'I want you to be one of my apostles.'")

But Orendain appreciated the value of Chavez's leadership. Sent to Texas to straighten out disorganized factions after a rogue melon strike broke out, Orendain explained, "In California, just one man makes all the decisions—Cesar Chavez. You never hear anything about an executive board calling the shots. You hear only one name. People like to have one flag; people like to have one leader, one name."

With the exception of Huerta, women remained in the background and played traditional roles. They typed, answered the phone, took notes at the Friday night meetings, ran mimeograph machines, took care of the children, and worked as secretaries and nurses. Chavez had absorbed his mother's lessons about gender roles, and the nascent women's liberation movement had not affected his ingrained views. "Of course, I never change our kids. I never even learned how to put a diaper on," Chavez boasted. He believed that women needed to be involved in the strike to make sure they supported their husbands. He wanted women transcribing notes and doing other secretarial work because they were "made for this kind . . . [of] tedious work."

Chavez also found women useful for public protests. On one occasion, he asked Helen to lead a group of women staging a sit-in at the office of the new Fresno bishop, Timothy Manning. Manning had made overtures to the union and assigned a young radical priest to minister full-time to the Delano farmworkers. Father Mark Day began his ministry by celebrating mass in a bright red robe emblazoned with the black eagle and led worshippers in "Solidaridad Pa' Siempre" (Solidarity Forever) and "Nosotros Venceremos" (We Shall Overcome). Growers expressed outrage. Manning acquiesced to pressure and reassigned Day.

When Chavez found out, he dispatched his wife and a group of women to the chancery. Informed that Manning was out, the women politely brushed past the receptionists and made themselves comfortable in his office. One mother changed her baby's diaper. Helen Chavez installed herself in the bishop's chair, and when they got hungry, she carefully cut a candy bar into small pieces on the bishop's desk. Meanwhile, supporters sent dozens of telegrams to Manning, beseeching him to reconsider and allow Day to remain in Delano. At the same time, sympathetic reporters were asked to make calls—but not write stories—inquiring about the rumored transfer. By the end of the day, Manning had relented.

Helen Chavez preferred to stay out of sight as much as possible and avoid the limelight even during events like the march to Sacramento. "Her sense of privacy is what I like about her," Cesar said to an interviewer. "I mean, I like *everything* about her, but I really like that a lot." Helen spent much of her time taking care of their large family in a house that was always spotless and smelled of Hexol. She cleaned, cooked, and battled cockroaches. She also continued to manage the credit union, having learned basic accounting techniques. Reserved and closed in public, in private she was outspoken and funny. Ida Cousino especially loved spending time with Helen and her small circle of women friends— her sister Petra and a few others. In private, they let down their hair, drank beer, and cracked jokes. They were boisterous and salty, gossiping about staff members and friends. They shared stories about their husbands, who were gone more than they were home, and often that was just as well. "He wants to make the babies," Helen would say about Cesar, "but he doesn't want to take care of them."

The adjective used most often to describe Helen was "fierce." The facial feature people remarked on were her fierce eyebrows. She was fiercely loyal to Cesar and would not tolerate any griping about her husband. And she could be fierce in her condemnation of others: women she viewed as poor mothers, or young volunteers she considered floozies out to seduce married men. She was equally strong as a champion for the women she liked, for whom she served as an important role model. Despite her crowded house, she welcomed volunteers who lived in the Chavez house at various times. When Kathy Lynch moved in, she wanted to teach Helen to drive so she would feel less isolated, but Cesar did not approve. Others thought Helen enjoyed the dependence, knowing there were always people happy to give her rides.

Chavez exhibited a fondness for smart, aggressive women who demonstrated impeccable loyalty. The first to win admittance into the inner circle was Marion Moses, a nurse who had been taking pre-med courses in Berkeley when she first visited Delano. "Can you type?" Drake asked the first time Moses walked into the office. She could, and she did. But as a nurse, she brought professional expertise of greater value and soon was working in a makeshift clinic. Like Chatfield, she had strong opinions but knew when to keep them to herself. She proved herself by her willingness to unquestioningly take on any assignment and deliver. When Chavez suspected someone was stealing money from the union, he handed the problem to Moses. When he grew frustrated that the strike kitchen refused to save scraps of meat to feed his worm farm, Chavez turned to Moses, knowing she would both understand his passion for organic fertilizer and solve the problem.

Decades before organic vegetables commanded premiums in supermarkets, Chavez was a committed home gardener. He cultivated his own compost and grew worms to produce nitrogen that would fertilize the barren soil. The writhing box ("this little hole where you have some worms") bothered people, Richard told his brother. But Cesar persisted in his efforts to get scraps thrown out by the strike kitchen each night. When he put Moses on the case, he reported triumphantly, the worms ate well. "Marion has never said no to an assignment," Chavez said. "No matter how shitty it is, she gets it done."

Moses exemplified many of the qualities Chavez valued most highly: intelligence, initiative, efficiency, and loyalty. "There are about five people in the union that are like that: they just look at me and blink their eyes and do it," Chavez explained. "I may be wrong, they still do it. But it's also a reciprocal thing, they have more influence with me than most anybody else."

Almost all of the inner circle were paid basic wages from the Migrant Ministry, the nonprofit Service Center, or foundations. Supporters seeking to make tax-exempt donations were directed to foundations that funneled the money to help the strike. Hartmire chaired a nonprofit called the Center for Change and Community Development (CCCD), one of several ways government and foundation grants were quietly directed to the union cause. A grant from the federal Office of Economic Opportunity supported a program run by the CCCD called the Self-Help Service Corps Project, chaired by Richard Chavez. The project trained volunteers to organize and essentially provided staff for the strike, until Governor Ronald Reagan vetoed the funding. At one point, Fred Ross was on the payroll at $1,250 a month and Manuel Chavez at $500 a month.

For some time after the strike began, Chavez continued to say the union needed a paid staff, supported by members, to ensure the organization didn't collapse. He pointed frequently to his experience in the CSO as a lesson in the perils of relying on volunteers and outside funds. "If you don't have a paid staff, and that staff isn't in any one place long enough to make the thing strong, you're not going to get anywhere," he told an audience in November 1965.

But soon thereafter, Chavez jettisoned that conviction. The sleeping bags perpetually covering every available inch of floor space were testament to his power to attract people willing to work for free. So he turned his tenuous financial situation into a strength and began to spin the romantic tale of an all-volunteer movement: "None of our staff is salaried, but we can provide a floor to sleep on and three meals a day," he wrote in a form letter. He instituted a tradition that became a hallmark of the movement: the $5-a-week volunteer. Chavez proudly explained that his staff worked for room and board and five bucks a week because it was a movement. Each Friday, Kathy Lynch went to the bank and withdrew a stack of $5 bills, which were handed out ceremoniously at the end of the Friday night meeting in Filipino Hall.

The young people who flocked to *la causa* and burnished the legend of the $5-a-week volunteer continued to come primarily through political circles, though more began to be recruited through religious groups and social services internships. The newer arrivals expressed a desire to serve and voiced fewer ideological convictions. They were overwhelmingly Anglo and drawn by Chavez's unconventional magnetism. "The pay is five dollars a week and no one seems to mind—all are too busy doing what they feel they must do," wrote four students from the University of Oregon, who spent a month-long spring break in Delano. They found Chavez "such an exciting person" and described his address to a packed crowd in Filipino Hall: "Cesar spoke as only a man who is truly the leader of his people can speak. His demands were simple, so reasonable, yet they spelled human dignity and success to his brothers—higher wages, double time for Sunday work, no more labor contractors (loud cheers), better working conditions for women, a fifteen minute paid break in the morning and one in the afternoon, job security in the event of illness."

A handful of people knew that not everyone lived on $5 a week, but that knowledge was closely guarded. There was no formal discussion about policy. Practices evolved. Chavez was pragmatic. People's needs were met. The union made arrangements to pick up car payments and student loans for valued volunteers. The few farmworkers who went to work for the union full-time as volunteers worked out supplements for their families.

In the summer of 1967, the frantic pace that had characterized the first two years slowed just a bit. Finances stabilized; a handful of wine grape growers had followed Schenley's lead, and the union secured half a dozen contracts and several thousand members. Over the course of the year, dues would total more than $82,000—still a small fraction of the overall budget, but steady income. Contributions, mainly from labor organizations, totaled more than $439,000. The Service Center was bringing in additional revenue through grants and tax-deductible contributions.

Chavez also achieved a truce that gained him breathing room. After the DiGiorgio election, UFWOC had continued to spar with the Teamsters, who were recruited by several growers anxious to avoid Chavez. The growers could claim a union contract; the Teamsters, who already represented shed workers and truck drivers, could pick up members without expending any effort. But organized labor frowned on such raids, and the Teamsters came under pressure to negotiate a peace treaty that left farmworkers to Chavez's union. After UFWOC barely finessed an election victory over the Teamsters at the Perelli-Minetti vineyard, Jerry Cohen negotiated a pact that got the Teamsters out of the fields. Chavez was ready to turn his attention back to table grapes and take on the Giumarra company, the largest grape grower in the valley. First, though, he cleaned house.

He had welcomed all the help that came to Delano in the early months and employed volunteers without asking about politics or ideology. It was understood the union came first, just as the demand for undivided loyalty had been clear to the Migrant Ministry interns who followed Chavez and Ross around a decade earlier in the CSO. Most people who learned about the strike and offered help in the early years were involved in leftist politics, and their convictions were no secret. The first wave of volunteers tended to be smart, strong-willed, passionate, and independent-minded. That, more than their politics, proved a problem. After almost two years, Chavez could afford to be more selective. As he had observed to Ross years earlier, too much democracy in an organization was not a good thing.

In June 1967, Chavez initiated the first purges. A half dozen individuals were targeted for different reasons, but the common denominator was the accusation that they had become disloyal, created dissension, and undermined the leadership. The cover story became ties to the Communist Party and leftist groups, a plausible justification given the relatively recent, high-profile purges within the labor movement. Chavez had been red-baited from the start, and the McCarthy era was still recent history. Any taint of Communist influence could hurt the union.

In each case, however, Chavez had long known the political leanings of his staff and never found them troublesome. Even the FBI found no evidence of Communist infiltration in the union. The bureau's reports duly noted that those with leftist leanings were quite public. For Chavez, red-baiting became a convenient excuse to get rid of people who asked too many questions, grumbled about the drudgery of picket work, objected to the AFL-CIO alliance, broke up marriages, exhibited too much independence, or drew too much attention to themselves. In some way, their absolute loyalty was in doubt.

Wendy Goepel had already disengaged. She worked for the OEO and spent time in her home in the Sierra foothills an hour from Delano, sometimes taking with her the youngest Chavez children to give them a break. She felt Chavez was being "managed" into someone less appealing by people who wanted to satisfy their own needs. She had become involved with a doctor at the Delano clinic, David Brooks, a medical resident in Fresno who worked for the union nights and weekends. Brooks began to challenge Chavez's ideas about the clinic, to advocate moving the clinic to a different location, and to insist he must treat all patients, not only strikers. Chavez asked him to leave, and then told Goepel she had to make a choice. She left with Brooks, and they soon began their own farmworker clinic.

Ida Cousino and a leftist volunteer named Eliezer Risco were kicked out shortly after they returned to Delano from a party at the San Francisco office of Sam Kushner, a reporter for the Communist Party newspaper, *People's World.* Dolores Huerta also had attended the party. Cousino and Risco had questioned her about negotiations, Huerta reported. Kushner's coverage had been enormously helpful to the union, and he was considered a good friend to the cause. A soft-spoken man with a pipe always dangling out of his mouth, Kushner was so disturbed by the suggestion that Cousino and others had anything less than union's best interests at heart that he wrote to Huerta when he heard people had been accused of "dual loyalties" and told to leave. "Everyone I know who is associated with the strike places the welfare of the strike above all else," Kushner wrote, asking Huerta to share the letter with Chavez. Whether Chavez purged Cousino because of her politics, her earlier relationship with Fred Ross, or her perceived disloyalty, the net result was the same. She went numb when she heard. She left, and did not discuss the reasons for years.

Donna Haber had worked as one of Chavez's secretaries and then moved over to the *El Malcriado* staff. Chavez called Bill Esher to an executive board meeting on June 26, 1967, and told him that Haber had been conspiring against some of the union leaders. Esher disagreed but said he would abide by the board's decision. Haber was fired, and walked down Albany Street in tears, dazed, back to the house she shared with her boyfriend, Luis Valdez. For decades afterward she thought she was the only person who had ever been asked to leave the union.

Valdez, however, did not shy away from a showdown. Unlike almost everyone else, he had the standing to fight back. Valdez formed a unique bridge between two worlds—the farmworkers he had grown up among and the radical activists who now flocked to Delano. He understood both and occasionally tried to interpret or even mediate. Leftists shuddered at the farmworkers' cars with HUELGA bumper stickers on one side and SUPPORT OUR BOYS IN VIETNAM on the other. Valdez did not need an explanation about why the Teatro should stay away from antiwar skits.

The Teatro was enormously popular and important to the union for both organizing and fund-raising. Its reputation had spread beyond Delano, and the group had been invited by Pete Seeger to perform in the Newport Folk Festival. East Coast appearances had been scheduled around the prestigious Rhode Island event and the Teatro was about to leave on its first national tour when Valdez was called to an executive board meeting on June 29, 1967.

Tension between Chavez and the Teatro had been growing for months, on both ideological and practical grounds, and the troupe's headquarters had become a magnet for airing gripes. Farmworkers found out some staffers were paid, and some strikers resented the discrepancy. Valdez had set up a meeting so that Chavez could hear the complaints; the meeting went badly. Drugs, officially banned though commonly used, were particularly prevalent among the theater crowd. Teatro members found the AFL-CIO abhorrent and had objected to the decision to become part of the federation. Some had been students at Berkeley during the Free Speech Movement and were equally opposed to Chavez's support for Governor Brown, who had condoned harsh actions in the campus confrontations a few years earlier.

Perhaps most annoying for Chavez, the Teatro was getting more and more national acclaim. At the board meeting, Chavez told Valdez the Teatro needed to be disciplined. Everyone would be put to work on the upcoming Giumarra campaign, and the Teatro would be disbanded. When Valdez protested they were about to leave on tour, Chavez at first denied he had approved the trip, then acknowledged he had but said circumstances had changed. Valdez told the board that a hundred people had been involved in planning the fifteen-city tour. Wasn't helping the farmworkers more important? Huerta asked. The tour would truly help farmworkers, Valdez responded.

Chavez told Valdez the Teatro would be resented if its members received special privileges. Then he moved closer to the real rationale: members of the Teatro had unfairly criticized LeRoy Chatfield. The strikers had their own minds, Valdez replied; they had the right to criticize.

Antonio Orendain moved that the Teatro be allowed to go on the tour, but his motion failed by a 3–2 vote. Handed an ultimatum, Valdez responded in kind: the Teatro would leave the union. In his anger, he made one final point: He supported the union 100 percent, but he was a playwright and would help in his own way.

Philip Vera Cruz, a Filipino board member, voted to cancel the tour, though he voiced private skepticism about Chavez's rationale. "Cesar suspects that there is a conspiracy against him and would like to suppress it now. This is the main reason, not the Giumarra campaign," Vera Cruz wrote in his notes after the board meeting. "Whether the suspicion is real or imagined couldn't be adequately substantiated." At a meeting for the strike community on July 6, Chavez repeated his assertion: Some people had been conspiring against the union and had been asked to leave. By denouncing them as conspirators, he effectively silenced any debate about the issues they had raised; conspirators had no legitimacy or standing to raise questions. Chavez could not afford a confrontation about the volunteer system, which had become central to the union's public image and to Chavez's vision of the union.

The Teatro traveled east and earned rave reviews in the *New Yorker*, the *New York Times*, and a host of other media. They performed on Thursday, July 13, at the Newport festival, along with Judy Collins, Bob Davenport, Jimmy Driftwood, and the New Lost City Ramblers. They professed total allegiance to *la causa* and performed at fund-raising events. Valdez made one last overture when a television station asked to film their Delano homecoming, but Chavez rebuffed the attempt at rapprochement. He had to take the idea "to the board," Chavez told Valdez. Anyone who knew Chavez knew what that meant.

Chavez sacrificed an important part of his organization because he could not control the Teatro. For him, no Teatro was safer than an independent-minded group that might question his actions and whose acclaim might rival his own. Though Valdez was a playwright and actor with no interest in leading the union, he posed a threat as a rival voice for farmworkers. He did not unquestioningly accept any order. He had a constituency and a future apart from the union, but that made the parting no less emotionally difficult for the young playwright. The two men ultimately remained on good terms, and in later years the Teatro performed often on behalf of the union. Many months had to elapse, however, before they could bring themselves to sing and act about *la causa*.

The purges passed largely unnoticed outside the union. An alternative paper in Berkeley reported that the Teatro left because of interference and censuring from AFL-CIO leaders, rather than a breach with Chavez. Even within the union, the silence of those kicked out ensured that the changes made few waves. But they sent a clear message about the importance of loyalty. The internal explanation was that the Teatro members had shirked their responsibility to the strike. Told they must choose between loyalty to the union or to a performing troupe, they chose the latter. This, too, would become a persistent message: anyone who left was putting his or her own interest ahead of the cause. Asked by an interviewer to name the best volunteers who had left, Chavez said: "The best ones are still here."

David Brooks had been the family doctor for Tomasa Zapata, one of the strongest strike leaders. When Brooks was asked to leave, Zapata was told she must choose: drop the doctor or quit the union. Sooner or later, in one form or another, everyone working for the union would face a variation of that ultimatum.

Some first-generation volunteers left on their own volition. Bill Esher had not approved of the purges, and he quit the following week. *El Malcriado* had morphed from a Spanish-language newspaper written for farmworkers into an English-language paper aimed at supporters who could donate money, appear on picket lines, and help the grape boycott. Like most early arrivals, Esher had not planned to spend his life with the farm worker movement; *la causa* had come along at the right time, it was the fight of the moment, and he signed on. The Cesar that Esher first knew was fun to be around, a person he expected might become a lifelong friend. He danced the jitterbug at parties late into the night and delighted in the occasional meal at his favorite Chinese restaurant. By the time Esher left, Chavez had begun to distance himself from people, even as his magnetic attraction grew.

Chavez also was developing something very tangible, apart from the strike, that was integral to his vision of himself as the leader of more than a labor union. He had acquired a parcel on the western edge of Delano that would be the new headquarters for the union, which had outgrown 102 Albany Street and the Pink House. Its ravines overgrown with weeds and littered with debris from the city dump next door, the land was known as Forty Acres.

Chavez planned to turn the barren land into a lush "farmworkers' cathedral" that would be the spiritual center of his community. "It should be a place where the spirit and the body come together, where being there, if we're successful, it'll accomplish two things," he said at a planning session. "One is a place to come to, to generate, pick up energies, and at the same time it's a place where we go forth from."

He spent hours thinking through the smallest details for Forty Acres, from selecting drought-resistant plants that would grow in alkaline reclamation soil to debating the design of the parking lots. He wanted to transform the hot, dusty plot into a physical and spiritual oasis with trees, ponds and flowing water, arbors, sculptures, monuments, and shrines. Plans called for a chapel, a market, a gas station, and an Olympic-size swimming pool. The land would be ringed by high walls "so that we're going to be looking constantly from the inside out, instead of being looked at from the outside in," he explained. He debated the merits of keeping cars outside the walls versus building parking lots inside to preserve the sense of entering a walled city. "What would give one a greater sense of being in a womb?" Chavez asked Chatfield. "Driving at 10 or 15 miles an hour thru a huge gate? Very plain, but very beautiful, mission-style gates. Or, you get out and you walk thru a small gate?"

Volunteers disced the land and planted thirteen hundred pounds of vetch and oat seed. Richard Chavez was in charge of construction. After he leveled the ground, he began to build the gas station, which would offer service at reasonable rates to union members. Richard designed a Mission-style building constructed of the adobe bricks that Cesar requested, the same kind used in the old Chavez homestead where they had grown up in the Gila Valley.

Chavez had specific ideas for the interior as well. He wanted scrolls to hang on the walls during meetings. Each scroll should have a picture of Gandhi, surrounded by poor people, and quotations in Spanish on one side and English on the other. They must be a certain curved shape, made of cloth and paper and mounted on burlap, propped on a steel-rod stand. After each meeting, the scrolls would be taken down, rolled up, and stored in a locked aluminum box.

One day, Chavez said, Forty Acres would be the headquarters of a national union. But he stressed that this goal was secondary to developing a spiritual center to preserve the essence of his movement:

> We want to keep what we have now. That's the most crucial thing. We have what I would call a Christian radical philosophy . . . We know that movements, sooner or later they're successful, they turn into institutions. But I think that it's possible to really affect lifetimes of people, especially the poor as they begin to organize

and begin to get a better way of life, that they don't grow compla-
cent and think, "Well, this is it," you know. But that they will
always be concerned about the other men, and about the other
problems, and about all the burning issues we're faced with on
discrimination and peace and exploitation. So Forty Acres, we
hope it will be the spiritual center of the union . . . Obviously, we
have to win the fight first.

To his followers, who grew in number by the day, the big plans were
yet another testament to Chavez's grand vision, and to their own ability
to achieve under his leadership the seemingly impossible. "The project
seems at times fantastic and unrealistic, and we often wonder why and
how we continue under the pressures of the strike," read a Delano newsletter to supporters. "But building our organization to the point we have
now reached once seemed a dream. The organization started with one
man, and he organized another, then they organized some more, and so
on, one man at a time. It is the same with The Forty Acres. One nail, one
block, one shovelful at a time, and it is begun. Much material is donated,
and the labor is by our own hands, often a welcome relief from the picket
line. Slowly, but definitely, each day, we are closer to the dream."

CHAPTER 15

The Fast

It is my deepest belief that only by giving our lives do we find life. I am convinced that the truest act of courage, the strongest act of manliness is to sacrifice ourselves for others in a totally non-violent struggle for justice. To be a man is to suffer for others. God help us to be men.

As cold and fog settled over the San Joaquin Valley in the third winter of the strike, the bleak Delano landscape mirrored the spirits of even the union's most stalwart supporters.

At the start of 1968, the union had signed no new contracts in more than six months. The DiGiorgio corporation was in the process of pulling out its table grape vines, rendering the contract a hollow victory. Lukewarm support for the strike in the fields and injunctions that severely curtailed picketing had enabled table grape growers to complete the harvest with little problem. Attendance at the union's Friday night meetings had declined so badly that the assembly passed a resolution in January to fine no-shows $2 per meeting.

Chavez had read widely about power. He studied Machiavelli, Mao, and Hitler, and borrowed tactics from each leader. But the man Chavez adopted as his role model was Gandhi. Chavez's admiration for Gandhi went beyond his steadfast adherence to nonviolence. Chavez was fascinated by Gandhi's personality and ability to wield power. His embrace of voluntary poverty, his ideas about community, and his penchant for fasting intrigued Chavez and spurred him to emulate the Indian leader.

"He made up his mind, this is what he's going to do. But he made experiments with truth," Chavez said about Gandhi. "I like the whole idea of sacrifice to do things. If they are done that way they are more lasting. If they cost more, then you will value them more." In early 1968,

Chavez was preparing to undertake a sacrifice so significant it would become an inflection point in the history of his movement and irrevocably transform his image.

Nonviolence had become a selling point of the farm worker movement for critically important outside supporters, and the doctrine held particular appeal for religious audiences. In many ways, compared to labor strife in the first half of the twentieth century, Chavez's union was indeed peaceful. He was able to defuse anger that threatened to degenerate into violence, which he knew would hurt the cause. But there was plenty of destruction—and not just on the part of rogue picketers.

Within the movement, participants drew an unspoken line between violence against people and destruction of property. The latter was tacitly condoned and in some cases actively promoted. Grape storage sheds were burned to the ground, vines that took years to mature were hacked down with machetes, irrigation pumps were decapitated, and tacks that tore up tires were strewn across entrances to vineyards. Few incidents were conclusively or officially linked to the union. When confronted publicly, Chavez denied any allegations. In private, the man who controlled the smallest details of his operation made clear that there were some things he preferred not to know.

In one of the more clearly coordinated campaigns, the "Research Committee" attempted to disable refrigerator units on railroad cars, so that grapes either froze on the journey through the Sierra Nevada or roasted in the desert. Manuel Chavez was in charge of the southern routes, while Fred Hirsch, an activist plumber from San Jose known as "Fred the Red," teamed up with Antonio Orendain on the northern routes. Supplied with guns and dynamite, they passed as hoboes in rail yards to cut wires and shoot at refrigerator units when trains slowed on steep inclines. Rudy Reyes, a Filipino striker who worked closely with Manuel Chavez, climbed on trains and cut the electrical wires to refrigerator units.

At the center of most accusations of stealthy, untoward conduct was Manuel Chavez. Cesar took full advantage of his cousin's illicit talents and tolerated behavior he would not have condoned in anyone else. As Cesar said about Manuel a few years later: "He's done all the dirty work for the union. There's a lot of fucking dirty work, and he did it all. He did all the dirty work for the union in the beginning."

Any hint of sanctioned violence would tarnish the union's image and affect its ability to attract volunteers and raise funds. By early 1968, growers believed they had evidence that could tie the union to criminal conduct. On February 13, the Giumarra company, the largest table grape grower in the San Joaquin Valley, obtained a contempt citation against Chavez. Giumarra charged that the union threatened and intimidated the company's employees, picketed in illegal numbers, trespassed, threw clods of dirt and chunks of concrete, and spread inch-long roofing nails on the driveways of scabs and at entrances to the ranch.

Chavez knew the general demoralization had spurred talk that nonviolence was a losing strategy. Rumors circulated that Manuel Chavez and others wanted to escalate attacks to scare growers into negotiating. Chavez was due in court to respond to the contempt citation on February 26. He needed a way to shift the debate, and he needed to restore momentum and reenergize his troops.

"What you've got to keep in mind all the time about him is that his whole life is in the strike, and I mean in the whole movement, and that's the thing that he had uppermost in his mind at all times," Fred Ross said a few months later. "He thought that things were slowing down and had to be zoomed up. Something had to be created that would zoom things up, just like the march did."

On February 13, 1968, the day Giumarra filed its legal papers, Chavez stopped by for dinner at the home of Fred and Ginny Hirsch and ate a hearty portion of pasta. LeRoy Chatfield spent the next day with Chavez, driving him to meetings in San Francisco. From 4:00 A.M., when they left Delano, till 11:00 P.M., when they returned, Chavez didn't eat. On Thursday, Chatfield checked around and talked to Jerry Cohen. They concluded Chavez had probably started a fast. On Sunday, visitors took Cesar and his brother Richard out to lunch at Abbati's, one of their favorite local spots. Cesar didn't eat. Richard talked to Helen, then confronted his brother. Cesar told him he had been fasting for five days, as penance, because he was afraid things were getting violent on the picket lines.

The next day Chavez called all the union staff, volunteers, and strikers to a noon meeting. Manuel Chavez drove his cousin to Filipino Hall. Cesar sat at a table on the stage at the front of the simple hall where strikers and union volunteers took their meals, a room that smelled of peanut butter, mystery meat, and fish heads. When everyone had assembled, Chavez spoke for about ninety minutes about the importance of nonviolence and explained that he had begun an indefinite fast to reaffirm the movement's commitment to the principle of peaceful protest.

"He told us that he was fasting as a prayer—it was not a hunger strike and its purpose was not strategic but as an act of prayer and of love for us," Marion Moses wrote in a letter the next day, struggling to find words to convey the emotion of the moment. "He felt that he was responsible as the leader of the union for all the acts of any of us."

He told them he was afraid they might be losing the will to win, and he spoke of his fear that people might turn to violence. He warned about the danger of taking shortcuts. He compared their fight to the civil rights movement in the South and pointed to ways the recent shift away from nonviolence had hurt that struggle. Many in the audience opposed the war in Vietnam, and Chavez said they must be just as adamant in their opposition to senseless killing back home. No victory was worth endangering a human life.

"The most important thing that he said, in my opinion," Moses wrote, "was that we as a union and as a movement have aroused the hopes and aspirations of poor people . . . and we have a duty and responsibility to those people . . . we cannot by resorting to violence crush their hopes and destroy what we have done. He said that even if all of us in the room were to disappear the movement that had been started would still go on."

He told them he planned to stay at Forty Acres, the barren patch of land on the outskirts of town that would someday be the union's headquarters. The fast was a spiritual experience, he said, and although they had so far built only a gas station on the site, Forty Acres was the spiritual home of the union. The last thing he said was that he was doing this because he loved them all. Then he left and started walking west. Helen followed, and they walked together the three miles to Forty Acres.

Larry Itliong took over the meeting, angry that he had not known about the fast and impatient with the theatrics. Itliong protested that Chavez had made his decision without consulting the board. He said the union must continue its work and endorsed a resolution calling on Chavez to stop. People began talking at once, angry, offended, close to tears. Some expressed concern about his health; others thought Chavez was playing Gandhi, or God. They took a vote on the resolution to urge him to stop, and the motion failed. Even if they had trouble understanding Chavez's rationale, his supporters argued, they owed him that effort. After all, his decisions had proved sound in the past.

Those who knew him best realized that when Chavez made up his mind, he would not change. Cesar was an old Indian and it was no use arguing with him, Manuel Chavez said. Chatfield berated Itliong and the other skeptics, furious that they did not appreciate the reverence of the act and incredulous they could talk about union business at a moment like this. For Chatfield, Chavez was the union, and whatever he decided to do, that was the business of the union. Pointing his finger at Richard Chavez, Chatfield declared in a loud voice that for the duration of the fast, Forty Acres was "sacred ground." He ordered Richard not to allow any cars onto the property.

Richard, Manuel, Marion, and LeRoy headed to Forty Acres. They spent the rest of the day cleaning out rooms in the adobe gas station building. They moved heavy machinery, oil, tires, and surplus clothes. Chatfield found a bed, mattress, and heater for the room where Chavez reclined on a canvas mat, and they hooked up an electric line from the outside utility pole. Chavez told them he had no deadline, nor idea how long he would fast.

Father Mark Day announced that mass would be said every night, a decision that transformed the private penance into a communal religious celebration. Within days, Forty Acres became a shrine. Offerings were tacked up on a huge union banner hung against the wall; the Chatfields brought a picture of John F. Kennedy, and Richard Chavez's wife brought a photo of their oldest son, who had died in a car crash in 1966. Votive lights, crucifixes, and a picture of the Virgen de Guadalupe sat propped on a card table that became an altar.

Women painted the windows of the gas station, mimicking the stained glass of chapels, with designs and peace symbols and Our Lady of Guadalupe. The number of people at mass doubled overnight from 100 to 200, then jumped to 450, then 600. Traffic backed up on Garces Highway, the two-lane road that led to the union headquarters, and cars parked as far as a half mile away. When they entered the edge of Forty Acres, women carrying candles walked on their knees.

"A lot of people thought Cesar was trying to play God," said Dolores Huerta, who was in New York working on the boycott when the fast began. "They just couldn't accept it for what it was." She understood the Mexican tradition of penitence and accepted Chavez's action without question. Ross was in New York, too, and he was shaken. "Fred was hit very hard," Huerta said. "Fred reacted very strongly because I think Fred probably loves Cesar, I think more than anybody in the world, maybe even more than his wife and children." Huerta and Ross flew back to California.

Each night, Chavez came out from his room around seven-thirty for mass, which was held indoors at first, and then outside, despite the winter cold, to accommodate the swelling crowds. Father Day searched biblical indices for references to penance and sacrifice and read a different passage each night. Special guests were called up to speak during the mass, including Fred Ross, Walter Reuther, and Jerome Lackner, Chavez's physician. Protestant clergy and Jewish rabbis participated, and Chavez wore a mezuzah around his neck. Each night, people brought "relics" to present to Chavez during the offertory. He held up each one and named the donor family. Then they were tacked up on the walls, till the walls were full and the extras placed on tables.

They sang songs, sometimes "We Shall Overcome," and usually "O Maria, Madre Mía," the song Father McDonnell used to sing to summon parishioners in Chavez's old San Jose neighborhood of Sal Si Puedes. The singing usually ended with "De Colores," a Spanish folk song that was becoming the anthem of the farmworkers. Everyone crossed arms in front, held hands with their neighbors, and swayed to the music

After about a week, another ritual was added to the evening mass. Someone suggested tacking up a cross for each day that Chavez fasted, a visible record of the length of his penance. It was pruning season in the grapes, and Richard Chavez collected fresh cuttings from a nearby Giumarra vineyard and twisted the canes into small crosses, each a few inches high. Each night a family member or friend presented another cross to Cesar, and then the symbol was pinned up above the door.

The longer the fast, the more impressive Chavez's sacrifice, the more emotional the response. His willingness to risk his life moved people of all faiths, and the ecumenical touches gave the services universal appeal. But the outdoor masses and colorful rituals resonated most deeply with ethnic Mexicans. Catholicism was a part of their cultural identity, and in the ceremonies at Forty Acres they saw their church, el pueblo, the people. Sacred ground was where they chose to worship, not within the confines of the brick-and-mortar church. The fast played into the deepest traditions of Mexican Catholicism, infused with spirituality, penance, and a sense of community.

After mass each night, people milled around. Some prayed. Others gathered around the campfire that burned around the clock, close enough to the building that Chavez could see the shadows cast by the flames at night. People told stories about their lives and about la llorona, the Mexican version of a female bogeyman. Women served hot chocolate as temperatures dipped near freezing.

Father Day had swiped a few boxes of vigil candles from the local church, but they soon ran out. They bought out all the candles they could find in the nearby cities, and Chatfield sent for more from Los Angeles. "I'm playing for all the marbles on this one," Chatfield said to Cohen. "We're going to make Huntley-Brinkley," referring to the national NBC-TV nightly news report.

An impromptu campground sprang up on the dusty land that surrounded the gas station. First to pitch a tent at Forty Acres were Nick Jones and Virginia Rodriguez, one of many couples who had met through the union. Nick worked for the Migrant Ministry. He had grown up in Fargo, North Dakota, and had been working for leftist causes in Chicago when he heard the farmworkers needed help. Virginia was one of the few union staff members who had worked in the fields. As a child, she had to ask the school bus driver to stop at the fields where her parents worked so that she could help in the afternoons. She knew the indignities firsthand, and she believed fervently in *la causa*. As soon as Nick and Virginia pitched their tent, others followed. Chatfield rented tents, first all he could find in Bakersfield, then Fresno, and then Los Angeles. Each slept eight people. More than two hundred tents filled the lawn, some occupied for just a night, others for a week.

Rotating guards restricted entrance to the room where Chavez stayed. During the first days he did some routine work, met with union officers, and wrote letters. "Please pray for me," Chavez wrote to Fresno bishop Timothy Manning, explaining why he had chosen to fast. Manning came to visit and said he appreciated Chavez's commitment to nonviolence and urged him to obey doctor's orders.

Chavez remained in seclusion during the day, but after mass his door stayed open late into the night. He talked one-on-one, his specialty. "He sacrifices for us!" read a flyer urging workers to come to Forty Acres. "The fast of Cesar Chavez has moved farm workers throughout the state to come to talk with him this week. He turns away no one. He desires to see the people." The people waited as long as two hours to see him, farmworkers mingling with politicians, religious leaders and supporters. Chatfield kept a guest register but stopped after a few days because of complaints that the lists served a more sinister purpose: attendance became another loyalty test.

One of those who condemned the fast was a former member of the Spanish Mission Band, John Ralph Duggan, who had left the priesthood and now worked full-time for Chavez. Duggan saw the fast as a spectacle that offered Chavez a welcome escape from the mounting drudgery of running the union. If Chavez wished to fast in a truly religious manner, Duggan argued, he should have gone off by himself, rather than turn the fast into a public drama that provided an excuse for everyone else to stop work. "I expressed my amazement to Jerry Cohen, the lawyer of the union, the day the fast began," Duggan wrote, "and he explained that the fast could become a great propaganda instrument; in a very short time I saw what he meant."

Orendain, the union's secretary-treasurer, shared Duggan's view. Manuel Chavez had asked Orendain for money to buy items for the fast. Orendain refused. Chavez had said the fast was a personal, religious matter, Orendain said. He would authorize no expenditure of union money. Chatfield controlled ample funds through the Service Center and approved any expense necessary. By the end, they had spent more than $20,000 on food, drink, tents, candles, and transportation. "Had Cesar the right to decide as he did alone and without the consent of the executive board or the membership while the fate of the union was at stake?" Philip Vera Cruz wrote in his journal in the midst of the fast. "This question has been and still is being debated among strikers and volunteers alike."

Most of the people who were among the presumed targets of Chavez's plea for nonviolence, including Orendain and Hirsch, reacted negatively to the fast. Hirsch was initially shocked: "His new emphasis on nonviolence was a wholly irrational reversal from the Cesar Chavez I had spoken to only a few days previously," he wrote three months after the fast. Beyond any personal offense, Hirsch and others tended to be more militant and agnostic, and uncomfortable with the religious overtones. The masses brought "enforced respect and reverence," Hirsch wrote. The message was clear: go along or get out.

Manuel Chavez, of course, was different. "One of the things he [Cesar] was trying to accomplish was the redemption of Manuel," Jerry Cohen wrote in his diary. Whether or not Manuel was repentant about his own misdeeds, he spent a lot of time with his cousin and supported him in every way. He no doubt saw the benefit of the fast from an organizing point of view, and he also played his usual role of cheerful prankster. Once when someone was waiting to come in to see Cesar, Manuel called out, "He's not finished eating yet." On another occasion, as Cesar lectured him about great nonviolent leaders and mentioned Gandhi and King, Manuel called out, "And Hitler." Only Manuel, with his disarming smile, could get away with that degree of irreverence in a way that made everyone laugh.

Cesario and Dorotea Chavez, Cesar's grandparents, who homesteaded the family farm outside Yuma, with their youngest son, Felipe, and a grandchild. (Walter P. Reuther Library, Wayne State University)

Placida Estrada, Cesar's maternal grandmother, with her son, Jesus. (Walter P. Reuther Library, Wayne State University)

Cesar Chavez at his eighth-grade graduation in 1942, the end of his formal schooling. (Walter P. Reuther Library, Wayne State University)

Chavez poses in navy uniform at home in Delano, circa 1946. (Walter P. Reuther Library, Wayne State University)

Fathers Tom McCullough (left) and Donald McDonnell (right) wrote Spanish liturgies and hymns and organized a union for Mexican American farmworkers in 1959. (Courtesy of Steve McDonnell)

Chavez (first row, second from right) at the founding convention of the national Community Service Organization in 1954. Others in the picture include CSO's key financial backer, Saul Alinsky (far left); CSO founder Fred Ross (center in plaid shirt), flanked on the left by Edward Roybal, the first Mexican American elected to the Los Angeles City Council, and on the right by Herman Gallegos, who joined the CSO with Chavez in 1952; and Helen Chavez (third from right, back row). (Walter P. Reuther Library, Wayne State University)

Chavez, with clipboard, organizes the Community Service Organization's get-out-the-vote campaign in Oxnard, November 1958. (Walter P. Reuther Library, Wayne State University)

The short-handled hoe, *el cortito*, caused backbreaking pain and came to symbolize the exploitation of farmworkers. (Walter P. Reuther Library, Wayne State University)

Chavez, in his first Delano office, consults a dictionary as he writes on his Royal typewriter. (Farmworkermovement.us)

Helen Chavez goes door to door in the summer of 1964, surveying migrant workers for a state-funded health study. (Courtesy of Wendy Brooks)

Chavez, with Gilbert Padilla on his right, conducts a house meeting with Fresno farmworkers. (© George Ballis/Take Stock/The Image Works)

Chavez talks with a farmworker at the front counter of the union's 102 Albany Street office. (Jon Lewis/farmworkermovement.us)

At the start of the grape strike, union pickets spread out at the edge of a field, trying to convince workers deep inside the vineyard to join the strike. (Jon Lewis/farmworkermovement.us)

An enthusiastic crowd greets Chavez as he rises to speak at a Friday night union meeting in Delano. (Jon Lewis/farmworkermovement.us)

Music played an important role in the movement. Donna Haber, Luis Valdez, Chavez, and Wendy Goepel (far right) lock arms and sway as they sing "De Colores" at a Friday night meeting. (John Kouns/farmworkermovement.us)

UAW president Walter Reuther (center), who provided crucial support for the grape strike, parades through Delano with Chavez and Larry Itliong on December 16, 1965. (George Ballis/Walter P. Reuther Library, Wayne State University)

Chavez and Robert F. Kennedy talk in the parking lot during a recess in the March 16, 1966, Senate hearing in Delano, where the two men first formed a bond. (Courtesy of Wendy Brooks)

Chavez shows the route of the three-hundred-mile pilgrimage to Sacramento that the farmworkers began the day after Kennedy's visit to Delano. (Jon Lewis/farmworkermovement.us)

Chavez walked in pain for much of the march to Sacramento; he said penance was the most important part of the *peregrinacíon* for him. (Jon Lewis/farmworkermovement.us)

Farmworkers celebrate their victory over the Teamsters when the results of the DiGiorgio election are announced in Filipino Hall on September 1, 1966. (Jon Lewis/ farmworkermovement.us)

Luis Valdez (center) performs with the Teatro Campesino, the farmworker theater troupe he founded on the picket lines. (John Kouns/Walter P. Reuther Library, Wayne State University)

Chavez and Jim Drake enjoy the Teatro Campesino skit at a Friday night meeting. (John Kouns/farmworkermovement.us)

Jerry Cohen confronts a deputy sheriff in the Imperial Valley. (Cris Sanchez)

Gilbert Padilla, one of Chavez's early and key lieutenants, talks to a worker in the union office. (Walter P. Reuther Library, Wayne State University)

LeRoy Chatfield speaks at a Friday night meeting as Larry Itliong looks on. (Walter P. Reuther Library, Wayne State University)

Chavez breaks his twenty-five-day fast with Senator Robert F. Kennedy on March 10, 1968, as Helen Chavez looks on. (Richard Darby/Walter P. Reuther Library, Wayne State University)

Jessica Govea, at left, leads a boycott march through Toronto in December 1968. (Courtesy of the Govea family)

During the second week, Chatfield suggested they put up a large symbol to remind them of the fast in years to come. They settled on a cross. Richard Chavez scavenged old power poles from the utility and constructed a thirty-foot-high crucifix. They figured the solemn, white-washed cross would make a dramatic backdrop when Chavez finally broke his fast.

As the days passed, Chavez grew weaker. He needed more support to walk to the bathroom. Richard could tell his brother was in great pain. He begged him to stop, to think of others, including his family. Librado Chavez also asked his son to end the fast, saying he had sacrificed enough. Helen Chavez, in typical fashion, had two reactions, one public and one private. In private, she was furious. She had argued with Cesar on the walk to Forty Acres and vented to friends throughout the fast about how angry she was at Cesar for jeopardizing his health. In public, she supported her husband unflinchingly, as he had known she would. She also knew that when he made up his mind, there was no point arguing.

Cesar's mother, Juana, had a similar response. Richard, apprehensive about his mother's reaction, talked to her out of Cesar's earshot and asked if she thought they should ask him to stop. Her response caught him by surprise: "She said, 'No, he knows what he's doing. Just pray to God.'" She told Richard she had confidence because of Cesar's faith. "When he believes in something, you know your brother," Richard recalled his mother saying. "He believes very strongly in things, and he knows that God is with him . . . I will not ask him to stop. This will be his own decision.'"

As the fast neared the end of the third week, his doctor urged Chavez to stop and warned he risked serious damage to his kidneys and liver. After the twenty-first day, Chavez agreed to take light liquids in addition to water. On Wednesday night, March 6, 1968, Chatfield urged Chavez to end the fast. You can't get the people here till Sunday, Chavez responded. As soon as he heard that, Chatfield announced the fast would end in four days. They began to plan for a mass event.

One of the first calls went to Sen. Robert F. Kennedy. Drake had noti-fied Kennedy's staff when the fast began, before it became national news. Kennedy expressed concern about Chavez's health and asked for updates each day. He knew he might be asked to fly out to Delano on short notice; as Chavez's health worsened, his staff considered asking Kennedy to appeal to Chavez to stop. As soon as Chatfield set a date, Kennedy was invited to be the guest of honor at the celebration to break the fast on the twenty-fifth day.

Chavez's top aides had viewed King's telegram as an overture indicating that the civil rights leader wanted to visit. They deliberately did not extend an invitation. As Cohen wrote in his diary, King was "someone on the way down trying to attach himself to someone on the way up." Kennedy, widely rumored to be a presidential contender, would enhance the movement's national stature.

On Sunday morning, March 10, Kennedy flew into Los Angeles and dodged a dozen questions about his political plans from reporters who followed him onto the tarmac, where he boarded a private plane. Huerta and Jim Drake picked up Kennedy at the Delano airstrip and brought him to Forty Acres. Everyone was nervous. What do you say to a guy on a fast? Kennedy asked as he came in. He stayed with Chavez only a few minutes. Kennedy asked for a glass of water and a bathroom. They had no water, and no one could find the key to the bathroom. They were all embarrassed. Kennedy went to Drake's house to wait for the ceremony. On the plane ride from Los Angeles, the senator had told his top three aides that he was going to run for president.

A rainstorm a few days earlier had turned the ground so soggy that the ceremony had been moved from Forty Acres to a city park. Chavez sat on a makeshift stage on the back of a flatbed truck, between his mother and Kennedy. Thousands of people poured into the park, and dozens of photographers and cameramen from around the United States jostled for space. Kennedy asked to move so that he did not have to speak on the truck decorated with crosses and the Virgen, but the crowds made it impossible to shift. Kennedy broke the tension when he began his speech in Spanish, acknowledged he was mangling the language, and drew tremendous applause.

"When your children and grandchildren take their place in America, going to high school and college, and taking good jobs at good pay," Kennedy said, "when you look at them, you will say, 'I did this, I was there at the point of difficulty and danger.' And though you may be old and bent from many years of hard labor, no man will stand taller than you when you say, 'I was there. I marched with Cesar!'"

Chris Hartmire handed Chavez the bread to break his fast. Then Chavez reached out to share the bread with Kennedy. The photographs of Kennedy and Chavez became among the most enduring images of the movement.

Chavez was too weak to talk and asked Drake to read a statement, which Drake had largely drafted. The text spoke of what the fast meant to

Chavez, and concluded: "When we are really honest with ourselves we must admit that our lives are all that really belong to us. So it is how we use our lives that determines what kind of men we are. It is my deepest belief that only by giving our lives do we find life. I am convinced that the truest act of courage, the strongest act of manliness is to sacrifice ourselves for others in a totally non-violent struggle for justice. To be a man is to suffer for others. God help us to be men."

The crowds mobbed Kennedy, reaching out to touch him, shake hands, and ask for his autograph. He took almost half an hour to make his way eighty yards to the car where Drake waited to take the senator back to the airstrip. Drake started to leave, but Kennedy jumped out and climbed on top of the car, leaving a dent in the blue Chevy Nova's roof that the Drake family treasured. In his Boston accent, Kennedy shouted the union's battle cry: "Viva la huelga! Viva la causa!"

Chavez was whisked away to recuperate at a twenty-five-hundred-acre ranch north of Santa Barbara, owned by Katy Peake's sister, Helen Pedotti. Pedotti cleared out rooms for Cesar and Helen, six of their children, and a nurse. Chavez read Gandhi and recovered quickly in the crisp ocean air. In appreciation for the hospitality shown to her son, Juana Chavez sent Pedotti a set of hand-embroidered towels.

Two days after Chavez ended his fast, Minnesota senator Eugene McCarthy, running on an anti–Vietnam War platform, nearly defeated President Lyndon Johnson in the New Hampshire Democratic primary, an upset that effectively forced the incumbent into retirement. Four days later, on March 16, 1968, Robert F. Kennedy announced his candidacy for president. When Kennedy called to ask Chavez to run as a delegate in the California primary, he convened a membership meeting to solicit the farmworkers' approval. Putting the question of an endorsement up for a vote gave Chavez cover with the AFL-CIO, which supported Johnson and was displeased by Chavez's decision. Presenting the endorsement as the members' choice, like taking decisions "to the board," was Chavez's preferred form of democracy—a process where the outcome was never in question.

Kennedy had a late start in California, a state whose large delegate bloc was crucial. Many liberals had already committed to McCarthy. The farmworkers union had never endorsed a candidate or worked on a political campaign. Chavez and Ross had never explicitly urged support for a particular candidate, but they had plenty of experience turning out the vote. Democratic registration had fallen dramatically in California, by a million votes in the previous year. Ross led a registration drive in Los Angeles that signed up eleven thousand Democrats in three weeks and about forty thousand across the state. They paid 25¢ per signature and gave cash prizes to those who signed up the most new voters.

Chavez blocked out May to campaign and make speeches around the state. He traveled through cities in the San Joaquin Valley where just a few years earlier he had struggled to attract a handful of workers to meetings. He marveled to Drake as people turned out in droves. On college campuses, where McCarthy had strong support, Chavez told students that Kennedy was the candidate the farmworkers wanted. "And some people would say, 'All right, if that's what the workers want, we'll work for Kennedy,'" Chavez recalled.

In the final weeks, Chavez took a hundred farmworkers and volunteers to Los Angeles and ran the campaign in the heavily Chicano areas of the city. He divided East Los Angeles into precincts and assigned several workers to each precinct. They, in turn, were assigned to blocks, where they walked door to door, hitting every registered Democrat four times. The first visit was to test the waters, and they found strong support for Kennedy and for their own cause. "We were extremely popular," Chavez said. "They knew all about the farmworkers and they liked them very much because they're only about a generation removed from farm work." The second visit was to ask for volunteers, the third to drop off literature, and the final visit, a few days before the election, was a reminder to vote.

For Chavez, the only thing unusual about this campaign was that he did not have to worry about finding money for gas, food, or supplies. The career politicians running the Kennedy campaign, on the other hand, found his organization astonishing. When Walter Sheridan, a Kennedy campaign coordinator, first met Chavez, he had a typical reaction: Chavez did not look like a leader of anything. He was short and slouched over, with small hands and a weak handshake. Then Sheridan watched Chavez run a meeting. The discipline was complete. Whatever he told them to do, they did. At the end of every meeting, when he had carefully explained what they should do, Chavez put the plan up for a vote. Then they broke into the rhythmic applause that had become the farm worker movement clap—starting slow and gradually speeding up, growing louder and louder as the clapping grew faster and faster.

On election eve, Chavez organized a fiesta with a mariachi band, which cost the Kennedy campaign $500. Sheridan invited Chavez to bring all the workers to the party the next night. Chavez said they would be delighted, and could they bring the mariachis as well? There was no room, the word came back. Well, then they would go someplace else, Chavez told Sheridan sweetly. It was no problem. It was just that the workers had voted, and they wanted the band. Sheridan told him to bring the mariachis.

On election day, twenty cars with loudspeakers drove through the streets of East Los Angeles making announcements in Spanish while teams knocked on doors and offered rides. In some precincts, the turnout was 100 percent—more than twice the normal rate. Kennedy carried the city, and the results in Los Angeles propelled him to victory in the state.

Chavez, a couple of hundred farmworkers, and the mariachi band all arrived at the Ambassador Hotel on Wilshire Boulevard for the victory party. The candidate was still upstairs in his suite, but the results were already clear. Chavez was tired, and he slipped out early. Kennedy requested that Chavez be on the platform for the victory speech, but he was nowhere to be found. So Dolores Huerta took his place. She was just a few feet from Kennedy when he was shot.

Within two months, two iconic American figures had been assassinated: King, already a legend, and Kennedy, heir of the Camelot dynasty. In Delano, they mourned the death of Robert Kennedy for political and personal reasons. And they began to worry about Chavez's safety. As Jerry Cohen wrote to a friend: "The attitude now is that sooner or later Cesar or Ted Kennedy or anyone who speaks out for the poor will get it."

At Forty Acres, they wrapped the thirty-foot cross in black crepe paper.

CHAPTER 16

The Celebrity

It got to where, you know, I was, well in many places I was introduced as a saint and it went on and really just went on and on . . .

By the time he flew to New York to serve as a pallbearer at Robert F. Kennedy's funeral, Chavez had been catapulted into the stratosphere. Nothing had prepared him for the leap from little-known, eccentrically charismatic labor leader to national celebrity.

Journalists from around the United States began to make pilgrimages to a tiny city so remote they had trouble pronouncing its name (de-LAY-no, the *New Yorker* explained). Chavez had been conscious for some time of his place in history. Now he was in a position to be selective about how his story was told to a wider audience. He chose to grant extraordinary access to two chroniclers, both of whom became advocates and penned sympathetic, influential profiles.

Peter Matthiessen, writer, naturalist, and cofounder of the *Paris Review*, knew of Chavez's work and was happy to help when a friend asked Matthiessen to draft an anti-pesticide manifesto for a fund-raising appeal in the *New York Times*. Chavez liked the advertisement and asked to meet the author. Matthiessen traveled from his home on the East End of Long Island to Delano in the summer of 1968. The two men were born just months apart, and Matthiessen felt an instant kinship, though their worlds could not have been more different. Matthiessen spent weeks working on what became a lengthy two-part profile in the *New Yorker*, and later a book, *Sal Si Puedes*. He deftly captured Chavez's humanity and the essence of his remarkable appeal as well as the euphoria of the young movement: "[Chavez] has an Indian's bow nose and lank black hair, with sad eyes and an open smile that is shy and friendly; at moments he is beautiful, like a dark seraph . . . There is an effect of being centered in himself so that no energy is wasted."

The second journalist to whom Chavez entrusted his story was Jacques E. Levy, a reporter who had taken a leave from the *Santa Rosa Press* in Northern California. Levy had begun his writing career at the *Harvard Crimson* and worked for several papers before ending up in Santa Rosa. He had covered farm labor issues, become interested in Chavez, and persuaded him to cooperate with a biography. Levy taped and transcribed hundreds of hours of conversations with Chavez's family and closest advisers. Chavez steered Levy to the right people to interview and included him in strategy sessions. Often Levy interviewed Chavez on long car rides; Levy drove, while Chavez held the tape recorder.

Levy was more intellectual than activist, but he admired Chavez and blended in well as he accompanied top union leaders to rallies and private meetings. Chavez trusted Levy, correctly, to omit material that might make the movement look bad or cast Chavez in an unflattering light. Chavez also knew he could review and censor the book before publication, so he allowed Levy unfettered access. At first Chavez kept the journalist somewhat at arm's length. Their relationship deepened when Levy, an experienced dog trainer, presented Chavez with a German shepherd and showed the union president how to train the animal. Chavez loved Max, and several German shepherds that followed. The dogs created an emotional bond between Chavez and Levy.

With Levy and Matthiessen, Chavez was warm, funny, low-key, and self-effacing. But beneath his patient demeanor, Chavez struggled to cope with enormous new pressures. The increased adulation brought heightened expectations to achieve victories in a war that had reached a stand-off. Describing the response when he made his first public appearances after the fast, he said: "It got to where, you know, I was, well in many places I was introduced as a saint and it went on and really just went on and on . . ." A priest wrote to Chavez that "Cesar" had become a popular confirmation name.

His fame generated reverence and resentment that deepened fissures in the union. He had less privacy and more demands. The fast had been not only a way to "zoom things up," as Ross put it, but also in some sense the ultimate time-out. By the fall of 1968, Chavez needed another escape.

His health worsened, and recurring back problems became acute. In early September 1968, Helen Chavez called Bill Kircher in tears, saying she could not get Cesar to stand up. Kircher flew to California, called Chavez's doctor, and checked him into O'Connor Hospital in San Jose. Dozens sent get-well cards and a parade of visitors stopped by, including Father McDonnell, who made everyone in the room recite the Hail Mary, Glory Be, and Apostles' Creed.

In the wake of the King and Kennedy assassinations, fears about Chavez's safety increased. When his physician, Jerome Lackner, was not present to act as gatekeeper, two elderly nuns guarded access to the hospital room. In the early morning hours of September 13, a mysterious caller asked for Chavez's room number. The operator alerted Lackner, who had Chavez transferred to another room and called the San Jose police. From then on, an officer was stationed outside his room from midnight till 6:00 A.M.

There had been vague threats earlier. Just after Martin Luther King Jr. was assassinated, a newspaper reported rumors that growers had offered a $10,000 bounty for Chavez. After Robert Kennedy was shot, union officials received various reports of threats, all unsubstantiated but worrisome in the climate of 1968. Union officials relayed the reports to county law enforcement, the FBI, and the White House. Chatfield wrote twice to Bishop Manning, suggesting he keep other bishops informed and implying he should speak to growers.

Front-page newspaper stories about the potential threats while Chavez was in the San Jose hospital precipitated a debate in Delano about his security. Chavez professed not to want any protection, but he also wanted to see how people responded. The security issue became another test of loyalty. "Cesar is creating a crisis for the leadership of the union," Chatfield wrote in his diary on September 15, 1968. "He is using the threat on his life, which has been blown up by the press, to force the officers to make a decision about whether they are going to see that Cesar is protected or not."

Chatfield talked to judo experts and guard-dog trainers. Chavez played down the need for security and resisted entreaties that he travel with guards. With friends, he adopted a fatalistic attitude. After another threat was reported by a Filipino labor contractor in Northern California, Chavez was worried but told Huerta he had decided that "it's going to happen sooner or later, there's nothing I can do."

Others worried more. As she watched the emotional reaction of a crowd when Chavez spoke to a rally in Coachella, Huerta said to Ross:

"This kind of feeling for him the people have, this is exactly what's going to get him killed . . . The guy sounded like a messiah or something."

Whatever his feelings and fears, Chavez again turned a difficult situation to his advantage. The threats became a convenient way to escape from public view when he felt the need. The threats fueled more comparisons to the two martyred heroes of nonviolence, King and Gandhi, which enhanced Chavez's prestige and leverage. The comparisons, however, also increased the pressure to succeed. After the fast, Drake said years later, "he was too saintly to make mistakes."

When he was discharged from O'Connor Hospital, Chavez moved to a small room at St. Anthony's seminary in Santa Barbara to recuperate. He hung a photo of Gandhi and a Mexican straw crucifix on the wall and wore a mezuzah around his neck. Helen and Peggy McGivern, the first nurse who had gone to work for the union, shared a room next door. Matthiessen came to visit, and Chavez greeted the writer propped up in a hospital bed in white pajamas. For therapy, he soaked in a tub with 97-degree water. Matthiessen, his back aching from a touch football injury, joined Chavez in the water. Using his ill health as an excuse, Chavez persuaded Matthiessen to read his draft of the *New Yorker* stories out loud. That way, Chavez could truthfully say he had never read the glowing profiles before they appeared in print.

Chavez's health improved dramatically, which he attributed to the hot soaks. Matthiessen offered to pay to install a similar facility in Delano. Arrangements were discreetly made to heat the pool at the home of a nearby union lawyer to exactly the same temperature. Matthiessen quietly wrote a $900 check.

Chavez moved back home, where he had a relapse. He was cross and impatient with those closest to him, even as he was tolerant and kind to others. He had so much trouble resting in the small house filled with children that he moved a bed into his office at Forty Acres and asked McGivern to take care of him.

Just as Luis Valdez had observed on the march to Sacramento, Chavez leaned into the suffering. The pain was real, and he exhibited courageous willingness to endure physical hardship. But the suffering image also proved an effective tactic. Now Chavez experimented with a variation—the crippled leader, conducting business from his hospital bed at Forty Acres. Chavez's bad back gave him another way to control situations. He could beg off from meetings and engagements or terminate conversations quickly, pleading pain. He gave interviews from bed, in his pajamas.

Some in his inner circle harbored doubts, not about the genuineness of his pain but about the strategic timing. He seemed to take to his bed at convenient times, and they wondered whether some of the suffering was psychosomatic. Chatfield thought Chavez was experimenting with the image of a great man working through pain to establish his authority. A decade earlier, Chavez had grown a mustache and worn suits to look older as a CSO organizer; now he talked to Chatfield about the idea of wearing pajama-like clothing as a symbol of sacrifice until workers had a union. Chatfield thought the idea a "bold stab of genius."

Chavez also talked to Chatfield about the importance of symbolism at union meetings. He wanted to restore liveliness to the Friday night meetings. Chavez proposed they schedule in the midst of each meeting the *abrazo de solidaridad*—essentially the traditional kiss of peace used in the Catholic mass—to help "get everybody involved in the act of strengthening the community." Chatfield enthusiastically agreed. "Easier to get it now than it will be a couple years from now," Chatfield observed. "Oh yes, it'll be too late," Chavez agreed. "Even now there will be some that are going to be reluctant to get into it. It's pretty hard for some people to love people. They can't let go. Why should it be that hard? . . . There's going to be a lot of complaints because we won't have enough time for business."

"And therefore we're not running the union democratically and all that stuff," Chatfield added.

Chavez's celebrity coupled with his medically enforced semiseclusion had already inflamed unhappiness among those shut out of the inner circle. Larry Itliong, Antonio Orendain, and others renewed complaints that the president was more interested in playing God than running a labor union. They clashed more openly with the apostles.

Itliong had to go through aides just to talk with Chavez, and when Bill Kircher chastised the Filipino leader for not taking more responsibility in Chavez's absences, Itliong responded angrily: "How in hell can you expect me to give an order to those volunteers? . . . Every time I ask them to do a little something, they look at me like I'm crazy. They look at me like, 'Who the hell are you? . . . we work for Cesar Chavez.'"

The clashes grew more open. Chavez condemned Itliong and others as lazy, materialistic, and jealous. The problem, Chavez told Itliong, is that "you won't obey my orders."

Meeting at his house with Richard, Manuel, Hartmire, Drake, and a few other close advisers, Chavez warned he was headed for a confrontation. Chavez had begun to tape meetings and conversations. He liked technology and felt the need to preserve his own history. He told his advisers he wanted to "put this on the tape." Then he recounted a recent, heated conversation with Itliong and other unhappy union officials: "They said that it was a one man union. I said, 'Yes, that's true. If I leave, I bet you that most of the volunteers who work with me would leave.' I said, 'They're here mostly because of me.'"

This was not the first time he had found himself in this situation, Chavez continued, speaking softly and sadly. "This is my problem. I've lived with this everywhere I go . . . In CSO, I was just an organizer. If I said something, they did it. There was just this kind of loyalty. When I came to the valley, man, I had to build loyalty because we needed loyalty. That's the way I do it."

Loyalty had always been a clearly stated prerequisite for union staff. But in earlier years, the issue had been undivided loyalty to the cause. Nothing should interfere with dedication to work—not family, outside interests, or competing causes. Now there had been a profound shift: the union was synonymous with Cesar, and loyalty was to Cesar. Subtle changes ensued. Supporters were called "Chavistas." Some mythologies Chavez encouraged, like the story that he started the union on his birthday. Some he professed to view with dismay: "Every time they say 'Cesar Chavez's union,' it cuts you inside."

Despite that, he told the group at his house, he feared there was no way to live with the split that had developed among the union's top officials. Chavez's preferred tactic for getting rid of people was to be passive-aggressive. As Orendain said, Chavez didn't tell anyone to leave; he just opened all the windows and doors and waited. Chavez feared a confrontation not because he doubted the outcome but because he preferred to avoid the fallout.

"In a confrontation, I can beat them," he said. "I can beat them because they haven't been around organizations, they don't know how to stab each other, and I know how to do every fucking stab. But once you do that, so you do it to save the union, then every time there's opposition developing, boom, you get them because, well, you want to save the union. And I've done it twice now, and I don't want to do it again. Even if it means the union goes to hell."

Chavez, the ultimate pragmatist, was not about to let the union go to hell, nor could he afford to have the showdown yet. Itliong had strong allegiance among Filipino workers, and Chavez needed their support. So he arranged a rapprochement after his outburst. He made overtures to Itliong and publicly condemned the lack of attention to the Filipino leader.

From time to time Chavez raised his biggest threat, sometimes in anger, sometimes in weary resignation, sometimes in good humor. He would leave soon, he said, because he disliked the politics of running an organization. Chavez told Kircher that once the political infighting started, he would resign. He would like to head a team that went from place to place, organizing workers and then moving on, he told Chatfield a dozen times, and might leave as soon as the strike was settled. Chatfield wondered about his own fate; would he stay with the union or go on with Chavez to his next venture? He was inclined to go. They discussed organizing in East Los Angeles, Texas, and Florida.

Chavez voiced similar sentiments to Matthiessen as they drove around the San Joaquin Valley. "He sees himself not as a union leader but as an organizer," Matthiessen wrote, "and he told me once with cheerful fatalism that when his union is established and his own people, aspiring to consumer status, find him too thorny for their liking and kick him out, he may go and organize somewhere else, perhaps in the Chicano slums of East Los Angeles." A decade before similar issues would surface in a defining moment for the union, Chavez foresaw an eventual split.

Chavez was anything but cheerful when he raised the threat of leaving with the small group of advisers in his living room in January 1969. Chavez saw no good alternative: "In order to put it together, I've got to become a real bastard, more than I am now. Just go around and crack the whip and get people out of the union. In other words, I got to pull a Joseph Stalin, to really get it. And I don't think I want to do that. By the time I do that, then I'll be a different man. Then I'll do it again for some other reason. More and more and more, you know. What I'd like to do is, just leave the organization. I've had so many damn disappointments . . . It's been one after the other. Organize great things in my life, and they all come down to the same thing. Obviously I do a horrible job going in, you know. If I did a better job, we wouldn't have these things. But boy, the moment that leadership develops and that struggle starts, it's time to leave."

The more the union became synonymous with Chavez, the hollower the threat. The only way to leave would be to destroy the very thing he had built, and even those who disliked or resented him did not want to see that happen.

"I've never taken the kind of shit that I've been taking in this organization in my lifetime," Itliong told Jacques Levy, quotes that stayed buried in Levy's notebook. "But I do it because I think it's bigger than me for the farm workers to have an organization." Itliong called Chavez a brilliant, magnetic leader who distrusted his own friends and advisers. "Cesar is afraid that if he shares the authority with the people, he's afraid that they might run away from him . . . If you have a one man organization, once the man is gone, the organization is gone."

Increasingly, Chavez surrounded himself with people who simply could not imagine the union without him. His lament to the advisers about pulling a Stalin was met by great concern, and Hartmire responded that the only solution was to recruit "more people of heart into the struggle" so that they would overwhelm any volunteers who lacked the proper attitude.

Hartmire was prophetic. Where the first generation of volunteers had been political activists who saw Chavez as the best vehicle to help farmworkers, newer recruits were drawn by the man. They came because they had heard about the mystical leader, and they stayed because they found him charming, humble, sweet, and caring. He seemed in some ways just like them—physically unprepossessing, almost shy, not above doing the most menial jobs—and yet in other ways almost saintly. When he talked one-on-one, he focused intently on his listener, and he pulled them into *la causa* just as he had organized recruits for the CSO at house meetings. The new generation was more in awe and less likely to question decisions. When new volunteers asked Jim Drake what they could do, he sometimes told them to sweep the floor and clean up. That weeded them out quickly.

"One thing which characterizes Cesar's leadership is that he takes full responsibility for as much of the operation as he is physically capable of. All decisions are made by him," Fred Hirsch, the leftist plumber, wrote in a twenty-five-page, single-spaced resignation letter in June 1968. Decisions were rubber-stamped by the board, workers had little input, dissent was discouraged, and volunteers were treated with contempt, as interchangeable parts, he wrote. People whispered that Chavez surrounded himself with Anglos because he feared encouraging young farmworker leaders who might prove less malleable. "More than anyone else, I love and admire Cesar for what he has done in the past and for what he can do in the future in organizing. He is a man who will not easily be matched anywhere," Hirsch wrote. "But he is a man."

Philip Mason was both a student and a collector of history. As a young archivist, he had pioneered a labor history library at Wayne State

University in Detroit, with the support of Walter Reuther. In 1966, the UAW gave Wayne State money to build a home for the library, which was later named after Walter P. Reuther. One day Reuther told Mason he had arranged for him to go to Delano. History was being made there, Reuther said, and Mason needed to meet with Cesar Chavez and arrange for the Reuther Library to collect the archives of the farm worker union.

His first night in Delano, Mason went to a Mexican restaurant that Chavez recommended. They were expecting him, and Mason dug into a green sauce he thought was guacamole. His mouth caught fire. The next morning, Chavez was eager to know how Mason liked the meal. The archivist learned the union leader had a sense of humor. That began what Mason considered a real friendship. They met at least once a year, usually around Chavez's birthday, when Mason was sure to find him at home. The two were one month apart in age and talked about everything from their astrological signs to poetry. Mason sent Chavez law books and a tape recorder. Chavez agreed to preserve all the materials from the movement and send them to the Reuther Library. From then on, he saved notes, letters, minutes, and tapes.

Mason knew he was not only collecting history but watching it unfold. He thought the movement was particularly important for young people. Disillusioned by the tragedies of Vietnam, assassinations, and riots, they found hope in Delano. Not only did Chavez have a great sense of history, Mason said, but "he comes awfully close to feeling he has a mission. Almost a fatalistic view." Mason saw how people idolized Chavez after the fast, and he accepted the hero worship as necessary, though he worried about the consequences. "I have some serious doubts," Mason confided in Levy, "whether if anything happened to Cesar, whether that union would survive."

Chavez had never had close friends outside his family. Some in the inner circle, like Chatfield, Moses, and Cohen, considered him a close friend. Others, including Hartmire, did not mistake the bond they shared for friendship, despite the many trials they endured and the tributes Chavez lavished on the minister. If you had friends, Chavez said, your decisions were influenced by your feelings and your desire to protect your friends. Personal relationships became a distraction. "I don't have any friends," he said. "I'm single-minded, one-track minded. I came here with the idea of building a union for workers. That's what I intend to do."

By the time Peter Matthiessen's profile appeared in the *New Yorker* in late June 1969, Chavez had acquired a guard dog named Boycott. Security guards were stationed outside his house on Kensington Street. On July 4, Chavez's portrait appeared on the cover of *Time* magazine, which hailed him as "a one-time grape picker who combines a mystical mien with peasant earthiness." The magazine included an "Anglo-Chicano Lexicon" that defined more than a dozen terms associated with the movement, including la causa, anglo, bracero, and barrio.

Matthiessen donated his $1,500 fee from the *New Yorker* to the Service Center. His stories provided an enormous boost to Chavez's credibility and status on the East Coast. As he returned to Delano that summer to do further reporting for his book, Matthiessen presciently captured Chavez's predicament:

> As his leadership inevitably extends to the more than four million Mexican-Americans in the Southwest, Cesar will necessarily become more lonely, more cut off in a symbolic destiny. Already, sensing this, he puts great emphasis on loyalty, as if to allay a nagging feeling of being abandoned, and people who are not at the Union's disposal at almost any hour of the day or night do not stay close to him for very long. It has been said that he is suspicious of Anglos, but it would be more accurate to say that he is suspicious of everybody, in the way of people with a tendency to trust too much . . . The very completeness of this trust, which makes him vulnerable, may also have made him wary of betrayal.

CHAPTER 17

The Boycott

So how do we generate the power? . . . We can't move till we understand power.

As the strike wore on, the Delano growers grew more fiercely determined not to recognize the union. On their turf, where they controlled not only the fields but the courts, schools, city hall, and even the church, they believed they could outlast Cesar Chavez. Most had never met the man they considered the devil incarnate and hoped they never would. For this among other reasons, they underestimated both his perseverance and his tactical skills.

In theory, the union was on strike at more than a dozen vineyards. In reality, Chavez carefully picked one fat target after another: Schenley, then DiGiorgio, and then Giumarra. He calculated that if he defeated the largest domino, others would follow. After the early modest successes in wine grapes, Chavez had turned to the thornier problem of the table grape growers. The Giumarra company, the largest grape grower in the San Joaquin Valley, became enemy number one.

Giumarra was a family conglomerate founded by Joseph Giumarra, a Sicilian immigrant who began selling fruit in the early 1900s, first from a pushcart in Toronto and then at a stall in the Los Angeles produce market. By 1939, Papa Joe had purchased his first vineyard in the San Joaquin Valley and formed Giumarra Brothers with his siblings, John and George. By the time of the strike, Joseph's son Sal supervised work in the fields, John was running the family business, and his Stanford-educated son John Jr. worked as the company lawyer. The Giumarras kept to themselves and did not socialize with the close-knit Slav growers, many of whom found the "Grape King" arrogant and aloof. Yet size alone made Giumarra the dominant agricultural player in California. Giumarra owned more than twelve thousand acres of land, half planted with grapes. The company sold more than $12 million worth of fruit a year.

Chavez had first announced the strike against Giumarra on August 3, 1967. Four days later, the company won a temporary restraining order banning the use of bullhorns on the picket line. Jerry Cohen challenged the ruling. Unlike other labor unions, the farmworkers' representatives had no legal right to communicate with workers and thus were forced to rely on shouting from the side of the road. "To take away petitioner's right to speak to the workers is to take away their only weapon," Cohen wrote. The appeals court agreed and threw out the injunction. The victory had more impact on morale than on the picket lines, which dwindled after the first few weeks.

Chavez recognized he would not defeat Giumarra in the fields, and he turned again to the boycott. Earlier boycotts of Schenley and DiGiorgio had proved effective, but they were quick and easy, focused on specific brands of liquor or canned goods. Boycotting table grapes was far more complicated. Boycotting grapes from one particular grower posed even more challenges.

Chavez made a strategic gamble that changed the nature of the boycott, and the movement. He sent farmworkers out to cities across the country with nothing but a mandate to stop the sale of Giumarra grapes. Most of the boycotters, as they called themselves, were young and had never been east of California. Many did not speak English well. They ventured out with money to cover the first week and the names of a few supporters in labor and the churches. Marcos Muñoz, who could not read or write or speak English, went to Boston. Eliseo Medina, who had never been on a plane, was sent to Chicago with the name of one contact, $100, and a bag of UFWOC buttons to sell. Joe Serda, who had been the submarine at DiGiorgio, went to Detroit. The Herrera family moved to Denver, Julio Hernandez took his wife and seven children to Cleveland, and Al Rojas took his family to Pittsburgh, not knowing where or how they would live.

Suddenly the boycott was not long-haired college radicals but hungry farmworkers far from home. They had given up jobs and uprooted their families to ask consumers not to buy grapes. They gave the struggle in the California fields a human face in cities and suburbs around the country. At the same time, the boycott became a training ground that offered promising leaders a chance to grow, learn, and experiment, the way Chavez had done in his early CSO years. No one came back from the boycott quite the same.

Initially Chavez instructed boycotters to focus on the major distributor in each city: pressure that agent to stop buying Giumarra grapes, and failing that, block the grapes from being unloaded at the produce terminal markets. That strategy met with little success. The Teamsters, whose drivers delivered produce to the terminal markets, had no reason to cooperate. Giumarra's agents had no financial incentive to acknowledge the boycott.

At Christmastime in 1967, Chavez called the boycotters back to Delano for brainstorming sessions. Happy to be home, they talked good-naturedly about disorganization and mistakes and sang off-key renditions of "Solidarity Forever." Chavez joked that although he could not leave home, he was the only one who had truly suffered. "Where's the nail?" Marion Moses shot back. Chavez entertained the group with stories about his special dispensation to violate the dress code during the recent AFL-CIO convention at a fancy Miami hotel, because the labor bigwigs knew Chavez never wore a tie. He told a story about lining up his small children and coaching them to perform a skit for Marshall Ganz. Chavez asked questions and taught his children the responses: Who am I? You are Chairman Cesar. What is the huelga? The huelga is the people. Can the huelga be against the people? No, because the people are the huelga. Who are you? We are the future leaders of the socialist revolution!

With the boycotters, Chavez engaged in a more subtle Socratic dialogue. He elicited information as he guided them toward the right answers. "Where do we stop the grapes?" he asked, prodding the boycotters to identify one big, fat target. "One specific place, if we're going to make Giumarra call up tonight on the phone and say he'll settle? . . . Which one person in the entire United States is the most key?"

Because farmworkers were not covered by the National Labor Relations Act, Chavez explained, the union could boycott not only Giumarra grapes but anyone who sold them. A few boycotters got excited about throwing up picket lines outside stores. But Chavez rejected that idea and focused again on the distributors or agents, to stop grapes before they reached the stores. "This is not a consumer boycott," he told them. "Supermarkets—that's just a tiny tiny drop in the bucket. Because there are thousands and thousands and thousands of those stores."

They inched closer to the idea Chavez clearly endorsed—sending everyone to New York, the biggest market for Giumarra grapes. He asked what would happen if they concentrated all their efforts on Victor Joseph, the Giumarra broker in New York. Marcos Muñoz replied that either the agent would tell them to go to hell or they would succeed. Chavez's tone changed suddenly.

"If you were to concentrate all your time, every bit of your time, blindly, like Dolores does, she just puts on shutters like this and she goes directly in a straight line, you could get anyone . . . you generate power," he said sharply. "No one's going to tell you to go to hell if you have that power . . . So how do we generate the power? . . . We can't move till we understand power."

His answer was simple: work single-mindedly, day and night, searching for the most vulnerable place to attack. Do not even entertain the idea of failure. "You find out which is the most sensitive part and you go after it. You'll get it. I'm sure you'll get it. If you put it on the basis of, 'If I don't get it then I'm a failure, if I can't get this done, I'm a failure,' then you'll do it. Your mind's made up that nothing's more important."

He imbued them with a sense of their own power, and they left with renewed commitment—to the cause, and to Cesar. He told them they were fanatics, just like him, and the notion filled them with pride. They did not want to let him down. "Cesar is the main reason we are alive today," Eliseo Medina told an interviewer. "We have not been wiped out like other unions that have tried to organize the farm workers." Farmworkers who only a few years earlier had not seen a future outside the fields now met with congressmen and mayors, flew cross-country, and debated growers on radio shows.

As soon as the New Year's holiday passed, the boycotters set off for New York. Father Mark Day blessed a school bus that had no heat, and fifty boycotters traveled cross-country to work under Fred Ross's direction, with the mission to get Victor Joseph, the Giumarra broker. They generated publicity and persuaded New York City mayor John V. Lindsay to support the boycott. But Giumarra continued to sell grapes with little difficulty.

After several months, the union figured out that Giumarra was borrowing labels from other growers and easily shipping grapes under dozens of other names. Since there was no way to distinguish where grapes in the supermarket originated, Ross and Huerta urged Chavez to extend the boycott to all California grapes, whether or not they were harvested from a vineyard where the union had ever set foot, much less certified a strike.

The union redeployed boycotters to more than a dozen cities, the largest markets for grapes. In early May, just as the first grapes from the Coachella vineyards reached the market, Chavez went on the *Today* television show and announced a boycott of all California grapes. This far more ambitious goal enabled the union to spread a simple message: don't buy grapes, so that farmworkers in California can win better wages and working conditions.

Given that mandate, boycotters quickly went to work. While Chavez nursed his bad back, labor and religious leaders helped boycotters build coalitions among students, politicians, housewives, and business tycoons. They created serious havoc and soon demonstrated that the consumer boycott Chavez had rejected a few months earlier offered the best prospect for success.

The creative peskiness of the best boycotters knew no limit. Priests sat in produce aisles and prayed over grapes. Picketers held candlelight protests outside the homes of supermarket executives. Supporters bought shares in Safeway and Jewel supermarkets and disrupted annual meetings. Boycotters stalled cars to block supermarket parking lot entrances. Shoppers loaded carts with frozen goods on the bottom, piles of cans on top, and then asked at the checkout counter whether the store carried grapes. Receiving the affirmative answer they expected, they abandoned their carts in protest.

Again, Chavez had taken a law his adversaries had seen as protection for the industry and turned it against them. Farmworkers were excluded from the protection of the National Labor Relations Act—but that meant they also were immune from its prohibitions against secondary boycotts. That allowed the union to picket entire stores. Instead of asking consumers not to buy grapes, they could ask them not to shop at stores that sold the fruit. The mantra of the boycott became one that was difficult for many people to ignore: please don't shop at this store so that farmworkers can earn a decent living and have toilets and water in the fields.

Chavez, a skilled pool player who had learned the game as a child on the table left over from his father's failed store, used the boycott as a carom shot. By pressuring a few major supermarket chains, the boycott aimed to make life so uncomfortable for the stores that they in turn would pressure growers to solve their labor problems.

The new boycott alarmed growers. They appealed for help to a sympathetic Republican administration in Sacramento, where Ronald Reagan had become governor in 1967 after defeating Pat Brown.

"They are immoral to boycott grapes!" Reagan exclaimed at a June 5, 1968, cabinet meeting when his agriculture secretary, Earl Coke, explained the boycott.

"We have little to fight with," Coke explained.

"This is simple blackmail," Reagan replied. "What will it do to the grape market?"

Coke told him prices were already $1 less per crate than a year ago because of the threat. Reagan said he would reach out to the Teamsters, with whom he had a close relationship, and see if they could help the growers. Coke's sympathies were clear; he had been vice president of Spreckels Sugar and had run a company that imported braceros. "We don't know how to get at it," he told Reagan a few weeks later. "If the boycott spreads, we will have growers who are innocent go broke."

In 1969, after suffering through the boycott for one season, a handful of growers in the Coachella Valley asked for mediation help from the administration of President Richard Nixon, who had proudly eaten grapes a year earlier during his campaign. The Federal Mediation and Conciliation Service set up the first direct talks, a milestone, although they mainly convinced each side of the other's intransigence. The Delano growers, unhappy about any negotiations, turned the talks to their advantage: the Whittaker Baxter public relations firm assured supermarkets that a resolution was imminent and they should restock grapes. The boycott's effectiveness dipped precipitously, from affecting 18 percent of sales to only 3 percent.

Chavez did not attend talks with the Coachella growers. He did not think they were serious, and he was holding out for the more important Delano growers. "We are the ones who should be negotiating from power and they are the ones acting as if they have all the power," Chavez said as he broke off negotiations.

The 1969 harvest was unusually large. Grapes ripened late in Coachella, so the early season overlapped with the harvest further north, forcing Delano growers to keep more grapes in cold storage. Prices for the fruit dropped sharply. After the Coachella talks fell apart, the boycott regained strength. Some growers began to soften their opposition to legislation, feeling unionization was inevitable and a law might at least give them ground rules to better fight off Chavez, a man they feared more than the union itself.

"Chavez has created an image for himself," John Kovacevich, one of the key Delano growers, reported to the Commonwealth Club. "In a recent trip east, New York and Boston people said that if the attitudes of the churches and the Kennedys could be neutralized, the growers' position would have a chance." Other unions were also interested, Kovacevich said, a reference to the Teamsters. "So unionization may come about whether we like it or not. Legislation fair to both sides is needed."

Once he decided the boycott was key to winning contracts, Chavez directed all his strategic moves toward that end. If the boycott needed more strike action, he threw up picket lines in the fields. If the boycotters needed a new hot issue, he found one. If supporters needed an explanation of why grapes were still being harvested despite the strike, he created a justification. If an organizer needed a prominent endorsement or help from major labor leaders, Chavez made a phone call.

The boycott also built leadership on college campuses, where the first generation of Chicano activists was beginning to emulate black student groups and demand attention to their issues. At the University of Washington in Seattle, a record thirty-five Chicanos enrolled in the fall of 1968, doubling the number on campus. The black eagle flag became their trademark and the grape boycott their focus; after months of protest, helped by boycott leaders sent from Delano, the university residence halls voted overwhelmingly to ban grapes from dining halls.

In cities around the United States and Canada, supermarkets and in some cases whole chains succumbed to the boycott pressure and declined to stock grapes, though some put them back on the shelves once the pickets moved on. Supermarkets were worn down by the bad publicity and the relentless pressure the boycotters generated, the outcry from mayors and city councils, the telegrams from local and national labor federations, and the denunciations by congressmen and religious leaders. Supermarket managers lost time and money because they needed emergency squads to handle picket lines and protests. Executives tired of candlelight marches outside their homes that demonized them as people who kept farmworkers impoverished. Grapes were a luxury item that accounted for a very small percentage of total produce sales for supermarkets. Executives began to tell growers they needed to resolve their labor problems.

Grape growers hired a public relations firm to fight the negative publicity. Teams of growers crisscrossed the country, urging supermarkets not to honor the boycott. In May 1969, ten growers made sixty-nine appearances in the United States and Canada. If stores gave in to pressure and stopped carrying grapes, growers warned, supermarkets would face no end to the demands to boycott different products. John Giumarra Jr. told members of the New York State Food Merchants Association that Chavez was a "New Left guerrilla" who hoped to topple "the established structure of American democracy." Supermarket executives cautioned growers to tone down their language. "You can't do business with Cesar Chavez," Giumarra said, "any more than you could do business with Hitler."

Chavez read the growers' response as evidence they were hurting. He was optimistic that an all-out push when the 1969 harvest hit stores, from May until the end of the year, would finally break the deadlock. Writing to Marshall Ganz in Toronto, where he ran the boycott, Chavez was upbeat and blunt. "I guess by now you know that the growers are bleeding re: the sharpness of the boycott. The bastards are really screaming and my hope is that if we do a boycott as good as we did last year and some action in Delano the bastards will be coming to UFWOC for a blood transfusion (signing a contract). At this point it's either them or us. We miss you very much and the ranch committees are a mess but don't worry the boycott is more important."

A week later, Chavez received even better news. Marion Moses had arranged for Dr. Janet Travell, who had been the White House physician and treated President Kennedy for back problems, to visit Chavez in Delano. She arrived in time to be introduced briefly at the Friday night meeting on March 14, 1969. Travell stood in the back of the hall and drew a series of sketches as Chavez leaned against the platform in front. She watched him walk, in great pain, and Travell lit up with excitement. By the time she arrived at his house the next morning, the doctor had a strong suspicion she knew what was wrong. Chavez lay flat on his back, unable to sit up without help. Despite his pain, he made sure to tape-record the session, preserving for history his consultation with the Kennedy family doctor.

"You can see that the left foot is considerably larger than the right," Travell explained to Moses. "You can also see that lying straight, the points of his ankle bones don't meet. The left leg comes way down. The difference in size of the foot is very striking." The disparity went beyond his legs: His left arm, pelvis, and side of his face were all significantly larger than the right. He had been born with an extreme case of asymmetry, Travell explained. His vertebrae were slightly fused, so his skeleton resembled that of a gorilla. Lastly, Chavez had a condition she called "Venus de Milo foot," because the gods that Michelangelo sculpted always had a second toe longer than the first. In mere mortals, that configuration caused acute pain on long walks.

Chavez was elated with the diagnosis as well as with the simplicity of the solutions—a rocking chair to keep muscles moving and prevent spasm, electric blankets to keep his legs at an even temperature, and pads under his shorter foot. Just like putting a shim under one side of a door to even it out, he said repeatedly to his brother Richard, the carpenter. "Isn't that fantastic!" Cesar said happily. Richard was crooked too, Travell observed, but to a far lesser degree. "You're a freak too!" Cesar said laughing. "We can be in a carnival."

Travell showed Moses how to apply ethyl chloride spray to ease the pain and allow muscles to be stretched out. By afternoon, Chavez could raise his knee to his chin and sit up by himself. He called in top aides to hear Travell's diagnosis and recommendations. With two-minute breaks to stand, stretch, and apply heating pads, Chavez should be able to resume a full schedule. "He's got to work," Travell said, "otherwise he's not going to be happy."

To even out his legs temporarily, Travell put a book under his right foot and flipped a handful of pages at a time until she found the proper height—about three-quarters of an inch. Moses set out to buy an electric blanket before stores closed for the weekend but was stymied by a recent Chavez edict that no check could be signed without a vote by the entire board.

"For the first time I bring an honest-to-God feeling of hope to the prospect of complete recovery," Chavez wrote to a friend two weeks after Travell's visit. "Not only do I feel better, but I know why the pain has been so intense."

Chavez began to work in a rocking chair in his new office at Forty Acres. Construction had progressed, though in a far more prosaic fashion than Chavez's original grand plans. Thanks to a $40,000 contribution from the United Auto Workers, an office building and meeting hall stood on the site, along with a trailer donated by the International Ladies' Garment Workers' Union that housed the medical clinic. The elaborate plans for a walled oasis, fountains, and recreational facilities gathered dust. The gas station had only briefly been open for business. Chavez's new office was sparsely decorated, with a painting of the Virgen de Guadalupe behind his desk, a straw crucifix on a facing wall, busts of John F. Kennedy and Abraham Lincoln on shelves, and large photographs of Gandhi and Martin Luther King Jr.

Although Forty Acres was home to "boycott central," neither Chavez nor others who helped to coordinate actually exercised much central control. Communication was limited. Chavez discouraged calls. He viewed the phone as expensive and had an aversion to phone conversations. When he did talk, he assumed the lines were bugged. In discussing a campaign against pesticides, he used the code name "fishing expedition."

Resourceful boycott leaders didn't need Chavez to tell them what to do. Those with good instincts emulated Chavez's fanatical work ethic and plowed ahead, trying different approaches until they found the most vulnerable spot in their market. Chavez felt in control, but the distance and decentralized operation afforded boycott leaders an unusual degree of independence. They made dozens of strategic decisions each week that determined their success or failure. In many cities the effort was weak, but the boycott did not have to succeed everywhere. The union needed sufficient pressure on three major chains—Jewel in Chicago, Stop & Shop in Boston, and Safeway in Los Angeles.

Boycotters relied on Chavez and the Delano crew for a steady stream of fresh outrages to generate consumer support. The "fishing expedition" Chavez referred to, for example, was just that: Jerry Cohen requested data from Kern County on pesticide use. Before county officials responded, a judge issued an injunction blocking the release of the information. What were they afraid of? Chavez demanded. The growers handed him a perfect issue for the boycott: if consumers didn't want to stop eating grapes to help farmworkers, they should stop for their own health. Chavez dispatched Moses on a tour to boycott cities to talk about the dangers of pesticides.

Enterprising researchers turned up another statistic that gave Chavez a new line of attack. The Nixon administration had almost doubled the amount of grapes purchased by the Defense Department, exporting many to troops in Vietnam. The Defense Department's purchase of grapes increased from 6.9 million pounds in 1968 to 11 million pounds in 1969. The amount shipped to Vietnam jumped from 555,000 pounds in 1968 to 2,047,695 pounds in the first six months of 1969 alone. "The Grapes of War," the union proclaimed, turning the statistics into a double whammy: Nixon used tax dollars to subsidize growers so desperate to find new markets that they unloaded grapes in an increasingly unpopular war.

Chavez had finally taken a position on the war, after avoiding the subject in earlier years. For one thing, he believed that the growing opposition to the war extended to the fields of California. An antiwar stance, which aligned him with outside supporters, had become more palatable with the union's members. For another, the war had become personal. His eldest son, Fernando, had applied to be a conscientious objector. The decision surprised Chavez, who had a somewhat rocky relationship with Fernando. Chavez talked about his son with rare bitterness, Peter Matthiessen noted, calling him a "real Mexican American," a withering epithet he reserved for those with middle-class values. Fernando liked to play golf, his father noted with scorn.

Cesar refused to give Fernando a letter of support in his application for conscientious objector status and told his son that if he truly believed in the principle of resisting the draft, he should be willing to go to jail. Fernando followed that counsel. On April 22, 1969, Richard Chavez, who had taught his nephew to play golf, accompanied Fernando to the Selective Service office, where he announced he would refuse induction because he did not believe in war. A crowd turned out despite the rain, and Father Mark Day led them in prayer. Helen was there with some of the younger children; Cesar stayed in his sickbed.

Many responded with plaudits, but others urged Cesar to persuade his son to change his mind. Two weeks later, Chavez attended the Friday night meeting, despite a bad day of pain. In both Spanish and English, he explained why he would support Fernando's decision to risk prison rather than serve. He framed the issue in terms of a commitment to nonviolence:

> This has nothing to do with the union, only that he is my son and I am the director of the union so it has become part of the union . . . I know I'll be willing to give all my time and all my work and my health and my life, if you think that's needed, but I never really knew there was something I wouldn't give the movement. And I found today that I'm not willing to give the union my principles . . . I'm willing to leave the movement, I'm willing to be asked to leave, but not to sacrifice my principles to anyone, because if you do that, then of course there's nothing left to give your life meaning.

A few months later, Chavez participated in a mass at the National Cathedral in Washington, D.C., to commemorate the death of Robert

Kennedy. Ascending the ornate, ten-foot-high pulpit, from which Martin Luther King Jr. had delivered his final sermon four days before he was assassinated, Chavez spoke publicly for the first time against the Vietnam War.

Chavez's Washington appearance marked the start of a three-month tour, his first major national appearances since the fast and his illness. To push what he hoped would be the final boycott season, Chavez decided to visit all the major cities. He traveled in a Winnebago accompanied by a small entourage that included a nurse, a guard, and Chris Hartmire, who functioned as spokesman, speechwriter, and general campaign manager.

Boycott leaders eagerly lined up events and jostled to secure more time. They counted on Chavez to fire up supporters and to raise money. (In addition to shutting down grape sales, boycott leaders were expected to raise enough money to support their own campaigns and send some back to Delano.) Between September 25 and December 21, Chavez spoke at dozens of rallies and fund-raisers, visited supermarket picket lines, addressed students and labor leaders, and gave interviews in thirty-three cities.

He disliked public speaking and recognized he was a poor speaker, though he had a knack for sensing what audiences wanted to hear. "It makes you feel like you're a little monkey in a cage," he said to Jacques Levy before departing on the tour. "They take you out and put you out front. You do your trick and then they put you back. It's really mean. I leave half of my soul every time I speak."

Dressed most days in gray work pants and a plaid wool shirt, Chavez gave the same speech over and over, and always told the same joke: a woman was shopping in a store with her little boy, and as they passed the grapes he tugged on her arm and said, "Mommy, when are we going to be able to eat some of those boycotts?" At one stop Chavez was so tired he left out half the joke and then wondered why no one laughed.

What he said made no difference. He was greeted like a rock star and applauded for what he had done, not what he said. At a Chicago rally, speakers compared him to Gandhi and King. "There were cries of 'Cesar' in the Coliseum Wednesday night for a small, brown-skinned man with a bad back," the newspaper account began. Chavez spoke briefly to the crowd of more than a thousand people, to deafening cheers. "We are going to win the strike soon," he said. Helen, who had joined the tour for a few days, stood behind her husband.

Chavez found time while on the cross-country tour to see the National Zoo and take pictures of fall foliage in New England. The highlight, he told Levy, was attending a performance of *Hello, Dolly!* on Broadway. "For the opening scene all of these girls come out, mostly black girls and your eyes leave their sockets they grow about that big. Wow, beautiful color and then Pearl Bailey is just fantastic, just fantastic."

He still paid attention to the smallest details of the operation. On a drive between cities, Chavez wrote to his brother Richard and told him to enforce rules at Forty Acres, keep the bathrooms clean, and make sure the phone was answered. He wrote to Helen the same day: "Todos bien g.a.d." (Everyone is OK, *gracias a dios*.) "Mi encanto, it's important to think about modernizing the c.u.[credit union]. You need to have more help. Also you need to direct people better. You have to become a manager to operate in the future."

Chavez called the boycotters the vanguard, and the best ones embodied two qualities Chavez talked about more and more—relentless determination, and a willingness to sacrifice. In Montreal, Jessica Govea sometimes cried herself to sleep from loneliness and lived on candy bars when her money ran out. She kept on organizing picket lines to persuade supermarkets to stop selling grapes. Jessica's father was a leader in the Bakersfield chapter of the CSO, and she had known Chavez and Ross since she was a small girl. She had formed a Junior CSO and helped on voter registration drives. In her first year of college, she had gone to hear Chavez speak and was so drawn to the cause that she dropped out of school, promising her parents she would only stay with the union for a year. She had been on the boycott in Canada for several years, first with Ganz in Toronto and then on her own in French-speaking Montreal.

"One of the most important things that I have learned is that you never give enough of yourself," she wrote. "I feel that I have grown and become a better person because our movement has grown and become a stronger and more determined movement. I no longer belong to myself but to the thousands of people who are struggling to be free."

As the possibility of ending the strike began to seem within reach, Chavez talked less about contracts and more about the sort of lofty and less tangible goals that Govea embodied. He had shifted his thinking from earlier years. He no longer believed political power would bring economic justice for farmworkers. Even a successful labor union would achieve that goal for only a small percentage of the poor. Political power for minorities, he said repeatedly, was a myth. He had seen little change in the balance of power since he began organizing almost two decades earlier. The solution he began to try to articulate was a broader poor people's movement.

"It is incumbent upon us to lead the movement into bigger and better things, to the end that all of us develop more as human beings and that we become more and more aware and concerned with broader issues," he wrote to Ganz in Toronto.

> I think that without real economic power on our side . . . we will develop a small, elite group of workers with a lot of benefits, surrounded by mass unemployment, welfare, war on poverty, old people, etc., which will not be able to participate simply because they are not members. The only way to correct this is by organizing in the rural areas on a broader scale.
>
> Please understand that the Union is still the first concern. I see it as the tip of a drilling bit, making its way through a solid wall of granite. But behind that bit, there are other things that must be done . . . You know I have always been interested in the cooperative movement . . . I'm convinced that cooperativism, when free association is the order of the day, and the democratic process is established, could have many beneficial results for all of us.

Chavez struggled to reconcile conflicting beliefs. He abhorred the kind of involuntary poverty he knew so well. He was committed to a movement that brought dignity and a decent standard of living. At the same time, he viewed the middle class with contempt. He feared a repetition of his experience in the CSO, where people moved out of poverty, became focused on material wealth, and adopted middle-class values. He sought a way that poor people could gain economic independence without becoming materialistic.

He glorified boycotters like Govea, who found happiness through sacrifice. Giving up a paycheck, he argued, was a liberating experience. He looked to some form of cooperatives for a longer-term answer and talked about his ideas with Hartmire, Chatfield, Matthiessen, and Mason. He avoided the subject with those who would raise their eyebrows in dismay or lack of understanding—Bill Kircher or Jerry Cohen. Chavez asked Chatfield to look for a large, remote tract that might be suitable for an educational center. Although Chavez had envisioned Forty Acres in that role, he now believed its location in the heart of the farmworkers territory compromised its value as a retreat.

Chavez studied why the civil rights movement faltered and thought about how he would motivate people in Delano to come to meetings in future years. Like his commitment to find some cross between a movement and a union, he believed collectives offered the possibility of middle ground between the failed systems of capitalism and communism. He thought they held the promise of preserving a spirit of community.

"We go up and down, you know," he mused to Jacques Levy. "My illness brought the community closer together. The fast really pulled it together, the strike, the first one, the march, all those things pulled it together. But it's like the kind of glue that wears off. You've got to come back with more glue."

He was just starting to research cooperatives. "I'm at the point where I was in 1965 about organizing farm workers unions," he said. "I was just talking about ideas and what could be done and a lot of people thought I was nuts."

First, though, he needed to end the strike.

CHAPTER 18

Contracts

I think that we set an example for those who wanted to help us, that we said that we're not going to abandon the fight, that we were going to stay with the struggle if it took a life time. And we meant it.

The denouement of the grape strike began where the battle had started, in the vineyards of the hot, dry Coachella Valley.

The Coachella growers had been an afterthought for Chavez. They were not involved in the labor dispute for the first two and a half years. But when Chavez called on consumers to stop eating California grapes in May 1968, the season was still months away in the San Joaquin Valley. The only grapes in supermarkets came from Coachella, the desert area around Palm Springs, where the union had almost no presence. There had been no strike there since the short-lived Filipino action three years earlier.

Eager to start the boycott, Chavez called a strike against the startled Coachella grape growers at the height of their 1968 season. He hastily threw up picket lines and called them off just as fast, blaming anti-picketing injunctions. The union must focus on the boycott, he declared. "We're talking about going 80 miles an hour and throwing the machine in reverse gear and not even a squeak, it just starts paddling back," he boasted about his ability to switch tactics without missing a beat.

The boycott hurt badly in Coachella. The season was short, profit margins slim, and options limited. Unlike in Delano, growers in Coachella could not turn their surplus grapes into wine or raisins if the market turned bad. They counted on a relatively high rate of return because the early, sweet Thompson grapes were highly prized.

Kelvin Keene Larson was a small but influential Coachella grower, known for high-quality fruit and innovative techniques. When Chavez announced the boycott, the price of Larson's grapes dropped by $1 a lug overnight. Larson was angry and baffled that his fruit had become a casualty of a war in which he had been a bystander. Larson epitomized the small grower caught in the middle. He became the most articulate and persuasive speaker against the boycott, traveling around the United States to make his case.

Larson also did what they had taught him to do in the navy when he had a problem: he went to his minister. The Rev. Lloyd Saatjian knew next to nothing about the strike when the first pickets hit Coachella, so he traveled to Delano. He found Chavez lying in bed, courteous but firm about the need to boycott all grapes. Saatjian spoke with some of the Delano growers, too, and was taken aback by the animosity. Saatjian compared the enmity between Chavez and the Delano growers to the irreconcilable hostility between his own people, Armenians, and the Turks. He rued both conflicts, and hoped he could help find common ground.

His hometown soon was riven by the same conflicts. Saatjian's Methodist congregation included Palm Springs families whose children had spent summer vacations together but now faced each other across picket lines. Growers who expressed a willingness to negotiate with Chavez became ostracized by those who held out. Sheds burned down. Friendships ended.

As Larson tried to figure out an accommodation that would keep him in business, he teamed up with the largest and most liberal grape grower in Coachella, Lionel Steinberg. A staunch Democrat, Steinberg wanted to make peace with the union for economic and political reasons. U.S. Rep. Phil Burton arranged a secret meeting between Steinberg and Chavez soon after the Coachella strike began. They met at a Sambo's chain restaurant. Steinberg invited Chavez home to continue the conversation and offered a tour of his extensive art collection. Chavez made snide comments about the visit for years. Steinberg was the type of wealthy elitist who made Chavez uncomfortable and angry, but the grower became the union's first and most lasting supporter among the table grape growers.

By the end of 1969, after two seasons of the boycott, the number of grape growers in Coachella had dropped from eighty-five to fifty-two. Some small growers were bought out by larger ones, but 1,000 out of 8,800 acres went out of cultivation. "It just gradually closed in, closed in like a noose around the necks of the vineyardists," Steinberg said a year later.

The Larsons were unable to pay off the principal on the mortgage for their 160-acre ranch. Corky Larson, Keene's wife, began private negotiations with the union, working with Reverend Saatjian. The two met with Jerry Cohen and then drove to Santa Barbara and talked with Chavez, the three of them walking around on a track outside the mission where Chavez liked to stay.

At the same time, the Catholic Church began to play a more aggressive role. Though the Church held itself out as a neutral broker, the sympathies of key clergy had shifted toward the union. The march to Sacramento, with the Virgen de Guadalupe leading the way, had forced churches to open their doors. The fast had marked a turning point, elevating Chavez in the eyes of religious leaders. The boycott appealed to Catholics as a peaceful, inclusive form of protest. Many clerics outside of California, less subject to pressure from agribusiness, openly praised Chavez. Robert Lucey, archbishop of San Antonio and an early supporter of the Spanish Mission Band, endorsed the boycott and removed grapes from diocesan institutions. "You and your associates are writing history in California," Lucey wrote to Chavez.

Closer to home, clerics showed more caution. The national bishops conference adopted a position paper that endorsed the struggle of farmworkers for justice, but in deference to the California bishops from agricultural areas, an endorsement of the boycott was deleted from early drafts.

Roger Mahony, a young monsignor in the Diocese of Fresno, emerged as the key liaison with Chavez. Fluent in Spanish, Mahony had worked on farm labor issues since his ordination and knew the players well. He reported back to the bishops as the boycott gathered strength, and urged them to maintain neutrality. In November 1969, Mahony became secretary to the bishops' newly formed Ad Hoc Committee on Farm Labor, a position that gave him great influence and shaped both the negotiations and his career.

Although Delano growers were increasingly unhappy with church leaders, they also were running out of options as the labor strife passed the four-year mark. In early 1970, members of the bishops' committee met with about forty growers in small groups. The most hostile response came during a lengthy conversation with eleven members of the Giumarra family. "There was no disposition to do anything that would in any way recognize the existence of the union," the bishops reported.

Bishop Joseph Donnelly from Hartford, Connecticut, chair of the farm labor committee, expressed amazement at the lack of communication. Many growers had still not met Chavez. "As in the early days of the industrial organization," Donnelly wrote, "they are convinced that their workers are very happy and do not want a union."

Mahony was more blunt. "I don't like to use the word racism, but a feeling really exists between the growers and their Mexican American workers," he said in an interview. "The growers . . . [are] not used to sitting down and talking with their workers; for decades they've just been telling them this is the way it's going to be. They're not used to dealing with workers on an equal plane."

The bishops arranged separate meetings with growers and with the executive board of the union on March 23, 1970, and then a joint session with both. They invited any grower serious about negotiating to remain in the afternoon. Only Steinberg returned after lunch.

Chavez was reluctant to sign contracts with a few growers, for fear that might complicate and weaken the boycott. Steinberg and the Larsons made a persuasive case that it would only help. Having union grapes available would give stores an alternative, and they could more easily refuse to carry nonunion fruit.

Two days later, Mahony sat in on all-day negotiations between Chavez and Steinberg at Saatjian's Palm Springs church. They scrawled numbers on the blackboard and negotiated till late at night, then agreed to resume on March 30 in Los Angeles. After around-the-clock sessions at the International Hotel at Los Angeles International Airport, they reached a deal: a three-year contract that began with wages of $1.75 an hour plus 10¢ for a health and welfare fund, along with seniority protection, grievance procedures, and protections against pesticides.

The announcement was made at the Los Angeles Archdiocese, presided over by Bishop Timothy Manning, in whose Fresno chancery Helen Chavez had once led the sit-in to keep Father Mark Day in Delano. The union's black eagle would now mark boxes of table grapes. Chavez and Steinberg jointly autographed the first wooden crates imprinted with the union label. Union grapes immediately commanded a premium, and Chavez promised to use the boycott machinery to promote the fruit.

The Steinberg contract marked the turning point the Delano growers had feared. They had long viewed Steinberg as a weak link, and now he had become a traitor. Several Coachella growers called Mahony to say they wanted contracts quickly, in time to get the black bird on their grapes, too. Second to sign was Keene Larson, after lengthy meetings mediated by Mahony and Saatjian. Larson wanted a face-saving election; Chavez was reluctant to set a precedent. Finally Chavez agreed to an election, provided they signed a contract in advance, rendering the election a formality. The Larson contract followed the terms of Steinberg's pact.

Bruno Dispoto and Tony Bianco were next to call, large growers who had acreage in the San Joaquin Valley as well as Coachella. "In the beginning, I didn't think the conflict would last three weeks," Dispoto said after he signed a contract. "But it lasted three weeks, then three months, then three years and it was still going on. It was a lot like Vietnam. It kept escalating and it was jungle warfare." From the earliest days, when he filed charges against Chavez for broadcasting from Father Kenny's plane, Dispoto had been one of Chavez's most rabid opponents. Now he blamed himself. The refusal to even acknowledge Chavez, Dispoto said, allowed the union leader to successfully appeal to the American public as a reasonable man trying to sit down with intransigent, irrational employers.

Hollis Roberts, a Texan with a three-hundred-pound frame and an outsized personality to match, was one of the largest growers in the San Joaquin Valley. He, too, signed a contract after negotiations mediated by the bishops. "I learned to like Chavez and I found that a lot of things we had been told about these people were not true," said Roberts, who gave Chavez a tour of his home, complete with personal chapel. "I had been told they were Communists, and I had been advised never to talk to them in person . . . Now I don't think we could have been any more wrong."

The first contracts covering vineyards in central California brought the union about three thousand workers. John Giumarra Jr. was so angry he suggested that the bishops' involvement might violate the separation of church and state. In fact, the growers' conviction that the bishops were quietly on the union's side was not far off. By May, Chavez was sending Mahony lists of supermarket executives who might, with a little push from church leaders, be willing to "put the squeeze on the growers." The more growers who signed, the easier for stores to shun nonunion-harvested fruit.

In negotiations, Dispoto, Bianco, and Roberts had not been particularly concerned with economic issues—most growers already paid close to or above the $1.75-an-hour wages in the union contracts. The trickier issues revolved around how much control growers would retain over their workforce. They worried about losing the ability to hire their own workers and having to rely on the union hiring hall.

Those concerns were not ill-founded. The new contracts created massive logistical problems for the union. All workers would be dispatched from UFWOC hiring halls, in seniority order. At a time when the union needed to figure out how to administer contracts and plan for a future with tens of thousands of members, Chavez instead picked a new fight. As Jerry Cohen had said presciently some months earlier: "Cesar couldn't bear to sit in an office and administer contracts. If he got the grape industry signed up, he'd take on the Jolly Green Giant."

Chavez's new target was an old ally—Cruz Reynoso, head of California Rural Legal Assistance (CRLA), a federally funded organization that advocated for farmworkers. The skirmish between the two men was barely noticed and quickly resolved, but the dispute presaged Chavez's ruthless demand to be the sole voice for farmworkers. The man who believed in single-minded concentration was willing to take time out from his fight with the growers to battle a respected colleague who, like the Teatro Campesino a few years earlier, had shown signs of being too independent and winning too much credit.

Reynoso was a few years younger than Chavez, one of eleven children from an Orange County, California, farmworker family. When he was eight, Cruz had started working as a *rata*, a rat, picking oranges into the basket of his older brother. When Cruz was old enough to have his own social security number, a younger sibling became his rata. Cruz stayed in school, won scholarships, and decided to become a lawyer to fight the kind of injustice he had witnessed growing up. He had been active in the CSO, supported Chavez when he left to organize farmworkers, opened a private law practice, and then taken over running CRLA.

Chavez had been on the original board of CRLA. Now he sent a picket line to march outside the organization's office. He summoned Reynoso to Delano, where the attorney found himself facing not Chavez but Dolores Huerta, who informed him the union intended to treat him like a grower. They had a committee that would present a list of demands.

The ostensible trigger for the dispute was the action of one CRLA worker who had intervened in a union dispute. The charge was an excuse to provoke a confrontation with Reynoso and make demands in typical Chavez fashion: ask for the moon. The union demanded that CRLA place sixteen staff members in the union's service centers, make the staff of the nonprofit available to perform union work, and allow union attorneys to determine what cases CRLA would pursue—all clearly illegal under the terms of CRLA's funding, and in some cases violations of the legal canon of ethics.

"California is not big enough for CRLA and the union," read notes from a meeting Chavez held to prepare the committee that met with Reynoso. "We have no alternatives but either that they phase out or we wipe them out."

CRLA had begun to make headlines and win praise with several class-action lawsuits. Chavez did not appreciate the competition. Reynoso realized that Chavez was willing to sacrifice an organization whose actions helped the people he represented if he thought that necessary to further the cause of the union.

"The power goes to the head," Chavez complained about CRLA, boasting to Jacques Levy that he had forced the organization to back down, though in fact Reynoso had done no such thing. Chavez's brinkmanship with CRLA did not succeed, but neither did he lose anything. Reynoso quietly prevailed but allowed the union to save face. Chavez turned his attention back to the growers.

Howard Marguleas, head of the Tenneco ranch in Coachella and a major player, wanted to talk. Marguleas and Chavez had gotten together once before for a meal at Denny's. Chavez had explained why he would win: You're on the top rung of the stepladder, Chavez told Marguleas, and I'm on the bottom; you have a long way to fall, and I have nowhere to go but up. On June 19, 1970, the two men began negotiations, with the bishops' committee facilitating, in a twelfth-floor hotel conference room overlooking the runway at Los Angeles International Airport. Talks broke down and were rescheduled. Key players were in Bakersfield instead of Los Angeles. Marguleas sent a private plane to pick up Monsignor Mahony, Chavez, two of his sons, and his dog Boycott.

During the final negotiating session, Jerry Cohen drew two ships on the blackboard, one carrying Marguleas and the other with the Giumarras sinking and calling out to Marguleas, "Don't give up the ship."

The Marguleas contract meant the union represented about 65 percent of the workers in the Coachella vineyards, 60 percent of Arvin, a small area near Bakersfield, and 20 percent in Delano. Union leaders were giddy and started a $1 pool on when Giumarra would call Chavez to negotiate. Mahony and Donnelly joined the betting.

Chavez made a behind-the-scenes strategic move. He suggested that Hollis Roberts contact the head of the Farm Bureau and explain why it was in the economic interest of all growers to settle at the same time. After a flurry of calls and meetings, Governor Reagan proposed on June

29, 1970, that the state conciliation board supervise secret ballot elections in the fields. Giumarra and Zaninovich held a press conference the next day to endorse the plan. Chavez rejected the idea as too little, too late—growers had had their chance for elections years ago and he would not give them "two bites at the same apple." But the announcement signaled a major shift on the part of the governor and the growers. "All they need now is a little push, if my reading is correct," Chavez said. "They don't want any more war . . . If things go the way they're going, we should have them all!"

Waiting for movement from the Delano growers, Chavez fasted for several days during the first week in July, to strengthen his resolve. Chavez was resisting pressure from national labor leaders to soften his demands, end the boycott, and sign more contracts. He told the bishops' committee he would agree to nothing weaker than the contracts already signed and would refuse to participate in elections to determine representation. He would consent to contract ratification votes as a face-saving measure. He waited for the Delano growers to come to him. "I seldom like to go see my opponent unless I have some power over him," he explained to Levy. "Some blue chips."

Chavez broke his fast with matzoh, which had become one of his staple foods since the first fast. He went through phases where he ate only matzoh and Diet Rite cola. He had become a vegetarian a month earlier. Helen, accustomed to cooking Mexican food that relied heavily on meat, was having difficulty figuring out meals. Chavez ended up eating cheese sandwiches when he was on the road.

His strategy for the end game was twofold: promote union grapes and help growers sell them at a premium, and boycott hard in Los Angeles, where Giumarra sold much of its produce. The union had about one-quarter of the industry under contract. "With all the guys we've got signed up in Arvin, if Giumarra doesn't come in, man those guys will make a mint!" Chavez said. "And he's going to be completely out."

LeRoy Chatfield took charge of a team in Los Angeles that made a push on Ralphs, picketing almost all the chain's supermarkets in the city. Chatfield not only urged shoppers to avoid Ralphs but directed them to other stores nearby that carried fruit harvested under union contracts. Within a few days, Ralphs caved.

On July 15, Philip J. Feick, an attorney representing the Delano growers, spent three hours talking with the bishops' committee. Feick agreed to ask his clients if they would participate in negotiations moderated by the clerics. At 7:45 the next morning, Feick returned to the bishops' suite at the Hill House motel in Bakersfield and said the growers had assented. Bishop Joseph Donnelly called Chavez to convey the good news. Chavez made Feick get on the phone, state his name, list every grower he represented, and repeat their willingness to negotiate.

At noon, the bishops met with Chavez and delivered the written agreement from Feick with the list of his twenty-five clients. Chavez excitedly summoned everyone he could round up for an afternoon meeting, keeping the purpose secret. They gathered in the big hall at Forty Acres. Chavez called for a mass. Midway through, he said he had an announcement. He read out loud the short letter: "The table grape growers listed below have authorized Philip J. Feick Jr., Western Employers Council, Bakersfield, California, to negotiate on their behalf with the United Farm Workers Organizing Committee for the purpose of affecting a labor agreement between the parties." The room erupted in cheers. He read the list of growers, and each name elicited more cheers. The crowed lifted Chavez and carried him around the room.

At 7:00 P.M. he moved to Marshall Ganz's office in the Pink House and settled in to share the news with boycotters who had been away from home for years, working for this moment. The first call went to Jessica Govea in Montreal. Chavez read the letter from Feick and then began to name the growers. Jasmine Vineyards . . . M. Caratan . . . Pandol and Sons . . . "Are you kidding?" Govea screamed. "Oh wow. Oh, this is like heaven . . . Oh my God . . . That's amazing, how did that happen?"

"I don't know, I think the boycott," Chavez replied.

"I'm not going to be able to sleep tonight!" Govea exclaimed.

"We recorded your impressions!" Chavez told her happily, as Jacques Levy handled the tape recorder to capture the historic calls. For three hours Chavez made calls, reading the same announcement over and over, each time with pure, undisguised delight, and then shared joy as the boycotters reacted. Chavez reminded them not to let up. The union was going to be tough on the growers in negotiations, he warned. In between, as he waited to catch the boycotters at home, Chavez celebrated with Monterey jack cheese, matzoh, and water. He and Larry Itliong took turns reading the Feick announcement, saving the best for last and eliciting squeals when they hit the key names—Zaninovich, Pandol, Caratan, Giumarra. "Beautiful, beautiful," Eliseo Medina exclaimed over and over, on the phone in Chicago.

Chavez made one more call. He invited Fred Ross to come to Delano and sit in on negotiations. "I don't think I've ever seen him as happy," Ross's son, Fred Jr., wrote to Chavez about his father's reaction.

Bill Kircher arrived the next morning and reviewed with Chavez, Cohen, and Itliong their demands and strategy. Chavez told Kircher there were two nonnegotiable demands: the contract signing must be at Forty Acres, and the agreement must resolve a problem at Delano High School.

Tensions at the school were not new; the "huelga kids" had encountered hostility since the start of the strike. Administrators refused to register students who wore UFWOC buttons, and backed down only when the union threatened to picket the school. In 1969, students had staged a sit-down strike after Richard Chavez's son Freddy, the senior class president, had been suspended for making "disrespectful" comments to faculty. In the spring of 1970, the conflict boiled over. On May 6, 1970, dozens of Mexican American students walked out of Delano High School to protest teachers' use of racial slurs, the lack of Hispanic faculty, and the scant attention to the educational needs of farmworker children. Teachers called Mexicans "beaners," students testified in affidavits, and told them that if they didn't like school, they should go back to Mexico. For weeks students and parents picketed the school as well as businesses owned by school board members. Many students were disciplined, and a dozen seniors were denied the right to graduate. Among them were Cesar Chavez's daughter Eloise and his niece Dorothy.

At the graduation ceremony on Friday, June 12, police guarded entrances to the school. They barred the sister of a student strike leader from entering, and a melee ensued. A dozen students were arrested and held in jail over the weekend. For weeks, angry charges and countercharges were leveled in exchanges on the streets, in the local newspapers, and in court.

When Chavez sat down to open formal negotiations between UFWOC and the growers at noon on July 18 at the Bakersfield Holiday Inn, he insisted that the school issue be part of any settlement. Kircher and Feick gave opening remarks, each voicing the same goal: total peace and an end to the hostilities. Each also acknowledged the difficulties in moving from an emotional, adversarial position to a working relationship. Kircher pleaded with the baffled growers to understand why expulsions at the high school, where one grower sat on the school board, were so important.

Several days of proposals and counterproposals, caucuses, and recesses followed. Dissatisfied with Kircher's pressure on the union to end the boycott as a good-faith gesture, Chavez replaced him as chief negotiator with Dolores Huerta. She presented a list of sixteen demands, including a wage of $1.85 a hour the first year, 10¢ more than the other contracts signed so far. Feick responded that the growers viewed this as "uncalled for and vindictive" and told the bishops they were leaving. Feick expected the bishops would encourage the union to soften its deal and appeared surprised when they refused. Feick "over-played and over-bluffed," Mahony noted.

The next morning, Feick reached out to Kircher to ask if there were flexibility in the union's economic proposal. Kircher checked with Chavez and said yes. Feick had coffee with Mahony, who made clear they could not help get a better deal but would mediate if talks resumed. The bishops left town.

The union intensified the boycott against Giumarra in Los Angeles. Chatfield tried a new tack—he tested grapes for sugar content. Two days after the talks had broken down, Jacques Levy prepared a press release for the *Los Angeles Times* claiming Giumarra was shipping "green grapes," with sugar content less than the 17 percent federal requirement.

That evening, Jerry Cohen returned home from a late meeting to find two urgent messages from John Giumarra Jr. He wanted to meet to negotiate, immediately. Chavez was en route home from San Rafael, north of San Francisco, where he had lent support to a strike by the typographical workers union. When he arrived in Delano, he responded to Cohen's message to call at any hour. They called Giumarra back. He was leaving town soon and urged that they meet at once.

At 2:30 A.M. they gathered in room 44 of the Stardust Motel—the elder and younger John Giumarras, Chavez, Cohen, Levy, and Marion Moses, who massaged Chavez's back. Chavez made another bold gamble: He told Giumarra he would only negotiate with all the growers at once. The Grape King said he would make arrangements. Within hours, they assembled in the auditorium at St. Mary's School.

Now Chavez felt pressure as well. Farmworkers around the state, inspired by his success in the vineyards, were starting job actions on their own. Chavez had from time to time assured workers in the vegetable and melon fields that their turn would come once he concluded the grape strike. Now workers in Santa Paula, Salinas, and Stockton were walking out on strike and calling on Chavez for help. He told Huerta they needed to reach an agreement by the end of the day.

Cohen went through the remaining issues, working them out without great difficulty. Then he said they wanted a meeting with the grower on the school board. Giumarra told them to call directly. Chavez became angry. "That was one of the conditions we raised this morning," he said. "We listened to your peculiar problems and we had only one . . . We cannot accept no for an answer . . . We want a resolution of this problem. I have kids who didn't get their diplomas, who didn't get credit for the work they did at school, and the roots come from the conflict of the strike . . . The day is gone when you can isolate a problem."

He walked outside during the recess, visibly upset. He would not sign without resolving the school problem, he reiterated to his team. Cohen met privately with Giumarra and the situation was resolved: Louis Lucas, the youngest member of the growers' team, said the school board member was a relative by marriage. He would meet with a small group to work things out. Cohen and John Giumarra Jr. met the next day to finalize contract language.

Two days later, on July 29, 1970, hundreds of workers and supporters crowded into the hall at Forty Acres and overflowed on the lawn outside. At the front of the room were the bishops, Chavez and a few of his team, and John Giumarra and his son. The elder Giumarra signed with a flourish, and threw up his hands for the camera in mock surrender. All the growers were there; Chavez had made that another condition. They were painfully aware of their status, the vanquished army capitulating in the citadel of the victors.

"You are a new union and you have tremendous responsibility," said John Giumarra Jr., who spoke eloquently on behalf of the growers. The world's eyes were on Delano, he said. "If it works well here, if this experiment in social justice, as they call it, or this revolution in agriculture, however you want to characterize it, if it works here it can work elsewhere. But if doesn't work here, it won't work anywhere."

Chavez made a joke, saying they were surprised to see the growers didn't have horns, and the growers were surprised to see the union leaders didn't have tails. He, too, hailed the beginning of a new day and hope for millions of farmworkers. "We will not disappoint them," he said.

Chavez said the contracts were a tribute to the success of nonviolent protest and thanked supporters around the world. He spoke of strikers who had lost homes and cars. "I think that in losing those worldly possessions they found themselves," he said, "and they found that only through dedication, through serving mankind, in this case serving the poor and those who were struggling for justice, only in that way could they really find themselves."

He was asked afterward why he had succeeded where others had failed, and Chavez gave credit to those far from Delano: "I think that we set an example for those who wanted to help us, that we said that we're not going to abandon the fight, that we were going to stay with the struggle if it took a lifetime. And we meant it. And I think that this gave our friends around the country and around the world the encouragement that they needed to come to our aid."

July 1970–June 1975

CHAPTER 19

A Very Different Strike

Jails are made for men who fight for their rights . . . They can jail us, but never the cause.

In Salinas, the Salad Bowl of the World, the differences began with the land. Unlike the torrid, bleak landscape of central California, the Salinas fields were cool and lush, nestled against the foothills and drawing moisture from the nearby ocean. Most everything grew in the Salinas Valley, a hundred-mile strip sandwiched between the Gabilan and Santa Lucia Mountains, beyond which lay the tourist meccas of the Monterey coast. Vegetables, tree fruit, and strawberries flourished in the temperate clime. But lettuce was the "green gold."

Lettuce cutters were the elite of the fields, trios who harvested and packed in carefully choreographed movements. Their skill and speed commanded respect. The most successful growers depended on their *lechugueros* and recognized the workers' power: if they withheld labor at crucial times, or picked and packed sloppily, the price of the produce plummeted. Many workers returned to the same company each season, but others jumped around. They worked piece rate and renegotiated wages frequently in response to changing conditions in the field. The militancy of the vegetable workers was clear to Chavez from the start. Unlike in Delano, where the union had to coax or threaten reluctant grape workers out of the fields, the lechugueros led the charge.

The Salinas growers were different, too. In the industry they were sometimes called "blue-blood farmers." Many came from families of greater means than the immigrant ancestors of the Slav farmers in the San Joaquin Valley, who had scrabbled hard to buy their vineyards. With a few exceptions, the major vegetable growers rented fields or harvested crops grown by others. They planted row crops, tore them out, and moved on to new fields whenever necessary. They had little attachment to a particular piece of land.

Ninety percent of the lettuce produced in the United States, 2.28 billion heads of iceberg annually, came from California and Arizona. Growers planted, irrigated, thinned, and hoed the lettuce. Packers harvested and packed the produce in boxes. Shippers stored it in coolers until the lettuce was loaded onto boxcars or trucks. And sellers made deals to market the green gold. Most major companies packed, shipped, and sold. A few grew their own lettuce as well. The growers and shippers made deals with one another in fields, bars, and back offices. They were accustomed to adjusting quickly as circumstances changed. Their business depended on being mobile and nimble.

Chavez needed to modulate his tactics to suit the Salinas dynamic: militant workers and a more unified industry better positioned to outmaneuver the union. The Salinas growers worked closely with one another and acted through a central organization, the Grower-Shipper Association, that dated back to the 1930s. They had followed events in Delano and moved quickly to preempt Chavez, catching him by surprise.

A week before he sat down to sign the grape contracts, Chavez had sent telegrams to twenty-seven vegetable growers, announcing that the United Farm Workers Organizing Committee represented their workers and wished to negotiate contracts. The July 23, 1970, telegrams reached Salinas as the Grower-Shipper Association was in the midst of renegotiating contracts with the Teamsters Union, which represented their truck drivers. The day Chavez's wires arrived, all the vegetable growers signed agreements authorizing the association to "feel out the Teamsters and explore the prospects of negotiating an agreement for agricultural workers." The next day, a committee reported back that the Teamsters were interested, and twenty-nine companies signed recognition agreements. They worked through the weekend and finalized contracts on July 27.

Chavez had spent the day meeting with citrus workers near Oxnard, unaware of the machinations in Salinas. Emboldened by UFWOC's success in the vineyards, lemon pickers had spontaneously walked out on strike and called the union for help. Chavez and Bill Kircher spoke at a rally at Our Lady of Guadalupe church in Santa Paula, promising support. "The workers will no longer make a few men rich by their sweat and suffering," Chavez said. "Above all, the workers want to be treated with the respect and dignity that befits every man."

Driving back to their hotel, Chavez and Kircher heard a radio report that the Teamsters had signed contracts with dozens of major lettuce growers in the Salinas Valley. Kircher was sure it was a mistake. Worried about wiretaps, they drove to a gas station and called Eric Brazil, a reporter for the Salinas newspaper, from a pay phone. Brazil confirmed the story. Chavez and Kircher drove straight to Salinas.

At a press conference the next morning, Chavez compared the Teamsters' act to the Japanese bombing of Pearl Harbor and declared "all out economic war against the conspiracy by the Teamsters and the growers, who have signed a totally illegal contract." From the beginning, Chavez made this fight about race, not missing an opportunity to point out the white leadership of the Teamster union: "Two Anglos got together maybe at the Taj Majal in Burlingame [Teamsters headquarters] or maybe at one of the grower association offices here and they are determining the life of the farm workers for the next five years and this besides being unethical, it is politically pretty stupid."

Despite his tough talk, Chavez was despondent on the ride back to Delano. His mood finally brightened, not at the prospect of signing the historic grape contracts the following day, but as he brainstormed a plan of action for Salinas. Chavez relished the prospect of a good fight against a clear enemy.

Jacques Levy, Chavez's biographer, drove him home from Salinas. Levy had become part of the core group, blending in unobtrusively as he collected notes and tape-recorded interviews. He helped draft press releases and handle media calls and often attended negotiations, taking notes. Levy noted the difference in the Salinas workers right away, particularly their response to Chavez. After the union leader met with workers in a labor camp, Levy noted: "The workers listened intensely. But there was not the furor or the adulation, at least it wasn't as apparent as at some of the rallies." He talked over the reaction with Kircher. "Kircher found that very significant . . . He said 'Yes, well, it's obvious that they support him . . . maybe this quiet attitude is stronger.'"

They quickly discovered Kircher was right. The workers wanted to know how they would support their families, but they were prepared to strike without hesitation. They felt sold out by the growers and

Teamsters, whose weak contracts contained only a half-penny increase over five years. Fred Ross and Marshall Ganz set up headquarters in an old post office and helped farmworkers organize committees at each ranch, elect strike captains, and prepare to walk out.

In an impressive display of strength, thousands of workers from the four corners of the valley marched toward the center of Salinas on August 2, each group carrying a homemade banner that identified their ranch. To counter the Teamsters' flag-waving patriotism, the UFW bought all the red-white-and-blue banners within miles, and American flags mixed with huelga flags as proud workers paraded through the streets shouting "Viva Chavez!" Addressing the cheering crowd that converged at Hartnell College, Chavez talked again about race. "The time has passed when a couple of white men can sit down together and write the destinies of all the Chicano and Filipino workers," he said. The farmworkers took a strike vote by loud acclamation. Union organizers circulated membership cards during the rally, collecting more than 650.

In the next few days, workers streamed into the UFW office with hundreds more cards. They also offered accounts that bolstered the union's legal claim as the legitimate representative of the people. Workers at Mann Packing, the largest broccoli grower, swore they knew nothing of the Teamsters until a supervisor informed them one morning that the company had signed a five-year contract and all workers must join within ten days or lose their jobs. "Three days later, UFW organizers came and we all signed cards," the Mann workers wrote in an affidavit. When the supervisor told them they must sign with the Teamsters, "we told him we had already signed with the union of Cesar Chavez. We all shouted 'Viva Chavez, viva la union' and went to work."

Chavez announced he would call the first strike against a few large growers. He estimated a general strike would cost $125,000 a week and asked Chris Hartmire to tap religious supporters and raise enough money for six weeks. If they could not win by then, the union would switch to a boycott. Chavez had already chosen the first target, United Fruit, which had recently bought out seven small growers in Salinas and formed Interharvest, the largest lettuce grower in the valley. United Fruit also owned Chiquita, whose bananas would be an attractive product to boycott.

The strike deadline coincided with the wedding of Cesar's third-eldest daughter, Eloise. Helen, running the household in Delano while Cesar spent most of his time in Salinas, had been leaving notes for her husband to remind him of the date. Before the church ceremony began on August

8, Jerry Cohen caught Chavez's attention and motioned with his eyes that he needed to talk. Chavez went and kneeled by Cohen. Cohen told him the leaders of the Teamsters wanted to talk immediately. Talk or deal? asked Chavez. Cohen made a phone call and returned with word that they wanted to negotiate a truce. National leaders of the union were interested in rejoining the AFL-CIO and not eager to antagonize labor leaders. They pressured the Teamsters organization in California to negotiate with Chavez. Cesar went to the wedding reception at Filipino Hall, called Helen aside to explain, and took the second dance with his daughter. Then he left with Cohen, Dolores Huerta, and Manuel Chavez and sped a hundred miles to the Black Oak Inn in Paso Robles, halfway between Delano and Salinas.

At 2:15 A.M. Chavez called Monsignor Roger Mahony to say the two parties had reached a verbal agreement. To give both unions cover, Chavez asked the bishops' committee to issue a statement calling for negotiations. Mahony headed to Salinas to set up a meeting.

By the time Monsignor George Higgins arrived from Washington—his thirteenth trip in six months to mediate farmworker disputes—talks had broken down. Higgins and Mahony found Chavez in bed with back pain. He revived sufficiently to hold a press conference at the union office to denounce a temporary restraining order against the strike, issued by a local judge at the request of growers. Chavez announced he had begun to fast and would go to jail rather than obey the order. Mahony and Higgins shuttled between Chavez and the Teamsters, and talks went on till dawn. By 5:00 A.M. they had hammered out an agreement that averted the strike. The Teamsters agreed to relinquish the contracts, and both unions granted the growers six days to acknowledge the UFW and begin negotiations. At Higgins's discretion, the deadline could be extended four days.

Unlike the early days of the grape strike, Chavez now headed an established union, and his church and labor allies urged him to make peace. Chavez had to balance his instinct to stay at war and hold out for all he wanted with his need to appease his financial and political supporters. Chavez fasted at an undisclosed location (the apartment of a friend), conveniently unavailable to speak with Higgins, Kircher, or anyone else who wanted to exhort him to be more reasonable. When Higgins agreed to extend the peace treaty for the extra four days, Chavez was upset. He sent Cohen and Huerta banging on the priest's hotel room door late at night to convey his displeasure at a decision he knew the workers would not like.

Chavez's secret weapon turned out to be the intransigence of the growers. They held some general discussions with the union but had no intention of letting the Teamsters renege on their deal. The growers were confident about prevailing in a court system heavily weighted in their favor. Their argument was simple: they were victims of a jurisdictional dispute between two unions, and California law forbade strikes in such a situation.

Only the two companies threatened with boycotts—Interharvest and Freshpict, a subsidiary of Purex—expressed interest in negotiations with the UFW. As the ten-day moratorium expired, Interharvest agreed to allow Monsignor Higgins to conduct a card check election so workers could choose between the Teamsters and the UFW. As Higgins counted almost a thousand cards, an Interharvest official hovered nearby. Finally he beseeched the priest to make sure the UFW won. The company wanted to avoid a boycott, but Interharvest would be ostracized if the company betrayed the industry and signed with the UFW. They needed a UFW victory for cover. Higgins obliged. He never announced the vote totals, and only years later acknowledged that the union had fallen short of a majority.

The ten-day truce expired, with no agreement other than that with Interharvest. Thousands of workers rallied again at Hartnell College and enthusiastically approved a general strike. Chavez was recovering from his fast and declined to attend. He had lost seventeen pounds and gained some time to himself, but failed to achieve the peace of mind he sought. "That fast was not like a spiritual fast," he said later, "it was mostly because I was distressed and because I needed strength. And I had been going very fast, you know, from negotiating the [grape] contracts and all right on thru the other . . . It was really like a rest more than anything else."

On Monday morning, August 24, some five thousand workers picketed the fields, shutting down the Salinas lettuce industry in the largest strike of its kind. Production the following week plummeted to a quarter of normal. The price of lettuce doubled.

The growers were stunned. "It took everybody several days to catch on that it was a totally new ball game, that the workers were into it 100 percent," Tom Driscoll, a large strawberry grower, told Jacques Levy a few weeks later. "The second shock was that the workers stayed out, they didn't go back in two days like everybody thought they would."

The vice president of the Grower-Shipper Association wrote an article called "How to Handle Your UFWOC Problem" in which he recommended that each grower form a "citizens committee," set up a public relations department and a legal team, obtain a temporary restraining order, prepare to evict workers from company housing, procure a heavy convoy to transport workers in and out of fields, play loud music to drown out pickets, take down license plates of pickets, and decide on "combat pay."

During the first week of the strike, judges issued fifteen restraining orders against the pickets, covering thirty-six growers. The union quickly exhausted its appeals, and arrests began. By September, legal sanctions started to mount. "I would have to be in a monastery in Tibet not to know that neither Cesar Chavez nor his union intend to obey any court order," commented San Mateo County judge Melvin Cohn.

Chavez was running out of money, growers were bringing in scabs, and the injunctions that limited or restrained pickets multiplied daily. "I have to call a boycott," Chavez told his staff. "See, that's the only card that we have that we haven't played."

Chavez knew that people who had been out in the cities for years on the grape boycott had looked forward to coming home once the contracts were signed. He had called all the boycotters to Salinas, ostensibly to help in the strike. He knew the action would likely be short-lived, and he needed to persuade them to reenlist. Eliseo Medina had driven from Chicago, eager to help with the strike and then return home to Delano and the grape contracts. Jessica Govea had driven from Montreal, equally glad to be back in California, reunited with her boyfriend, Marshall Ganz. Both Govea and Medina noticed the difference in the Salinas workers immediately. "These were young men—rough-and-tumble guys who worked piece rate, who had a work life expectancy of 10 years, who lived in labor camps in the growers' land, who worked hard, lived hard and partied hard," Govea wrote in her journal. "They were unafraid."

Chavez broke the news to the boycotters gradually. On September 8, he met with them in a church hall and spoke about the power of the boycott. He told them the union could afford two more weeks of the strike at most. They had spent more than $300,000, paying $15 a week to single strikers and $25 to families. Gas cost another $1,500–$1,800 a week. Hartmire had arranged a $125,000 loan from the Franciscans and was working to come up with more.

On September 16, State Superior Court judge Anthony Brazil declared that a jurisdictional dispute existed and issued a permanent injunction against the strike. Chavez called the boycotters to a beach picnic that afternoon to celebrate Mexican Independence Day, the fifth anniversary of the historic meeting in the Delano church that launched the grape strike. He used all his charm to persuade the tired boycotters to go out into the cities again. Medina wanted badly to stay in California and help his own people, the grape workers. But he decided that as long as he worked for the union, he had to go where he was most needed. He told Chavez he would return to Chicago.

Few vegetable workers volunteered to join the boycott. They did not want to leave their jobs and lose their livelihoods. Many had families living in the Imperial Valley or in Mexicali, just across the border. Disappointed in their lack of interest, Chavez attributed the reluctance to their concerns about money.

The boycotters dispersed. Violence flared between Teamsters and Chavistas. After a UFW picket was arrested in connection with a shooting in Santa Maria, Jerry Cohen wrote in his diary: "Manuel Chavez is not controlling (I suspect he is encouraging) the violence of the people. My fear is that there will be retaliation against members of our union and Cesar." Dolores Huerta was trying to negotiate contracts with two companies that had agreed to recognize the union, Freshpict and D'Arrigo, but talks broke down. Kircher and Higgins expressed frustration with the UFW's intransigence. Higgins sent Chavez a telegram to try to goad him into taking charge. "Kircher shares my view that Dolores has mismanaged the negotiations—to put it mildly," Higgins wrote to Monsignor Mahony.

Kircher was perturbed about Huerta's involvement for another reason. He had found out she was six months pregnant. An unwed pregnant woman as the lead negotiator and key figure in the union was a major crisis, Kircher told Cohen. Kircher hoped Chavez would remove Huerta from her public role, before news of her pregnancy spread. For Cohen and others in the union, the situation was more complicated: Huerta had become involved with Richard Chavez. Their relationship, kept quiet for some time, became public during her pregnancy. Many women, Helen Chavez chief among them, were livid. Richard's wife, Sally, had been Helen's close friend since childhood. The betrayal seemed particularly cruel because Sally had never recovered from the trauma of losing their eldest son in a car accident a few years earlier. Richard, in his grief, had turned to Huerta. "One of the interesting events to contemplate is the confrontation between Dolores and Cesar if that ever took place," Cohen speculated in his journal about Huerta's pregnancy. "Perhaps Cesar is waiting for Dolores to tell him. A confession?" The new liaison became a subject of widespread gossip, and Helen voiced her anger to many people. Two of Richard and Sally's daughters showed up in the union office and roughed-up Dolores. But Huerta and Chavez's relationship survived, and she relinquished none of her power within the union.

With the boycotters settled in cities around the United States, Chavez announced his next target—the Bud Antle company, which shipped $25 million worth of lettuce a year. Union researchers had dug up some tenuous connections to Dow Chemical, which produced the napalm used by the United States in the Vietnam War. Pictures of Vietnamese women and children disfigured by napalm bombs had triggered anti-Dow protests on college campuses. Antle was one of the three big lettuce growers in the valley, and the Dow Chemical connection, however distant, made the company an attractive boycott target.

Bud Antle, who gave his name to the company, was known as an innovator who often broke with the pack. Rather than hire braceros for certain field work, he had signed a contract in 1961 with the Teamsters. For that treachery he was thrown out of the Grower-Shipper Association. Antle's contract with the Teamsters had not covered workers who hoed, thinned, irrigated, and drove tractors. But when other growers signed Teamster contracts, Antle hurriedly extended his pact to cover all agricultural workers. He took the lead among the growers fighting Chavez in court, charging that a strike would cost his company $100,000 a day.

When Chavez suspended the strike, Antle went back to court and obtained an injunction on October 8 ordering the union to stop boycotting his produce. When the UFW showed no sign of complying, Antle asked for a bond to protect against the company's losses. On November 17, Judge Gordon Campbell ordered UFWOC to post a $2 million bond. The union ignored that, too.

Six days later, Antle's attorneys met with Chavez to take his deposition. Just before the lunch break, Chavez was asked whether the union was boycotting Antle lettuce. He readily confirmed the boycott and volunteered that the union had every intention of continuing. Antle's lawyer immediately took that statement to a judge. When the deposition resumed shortly after 1:00 P.M. at the Royal Palms Motel in Bakersfield, Chavez was handed an order to appear in court to answer contempt charges for defying the anti-boycott injunction. He could not have been more pleased.

At the end of the nine-hour deposition, Cohen gleefully warned Antle's attorneys that they would be treated to a repeat of the scene at the Bakersfield courthouse in 1968, when Chavez had appeared on the thirteenth day of his fast, accompanied by thousands of farmworkers. Chavez chimed in: "You see, the only way we can get the fact that we are being persecuted by Bud Antle and Dow Chemical is to have our people get it on the cameras and let the people throughout the country react to that. That is the only defense we have. We wouldn't do it, but I don't see what else we can do. I also want to have them there because if I go to jail I want them to witness. They get pretty upset and they want to go on the boycott, and we want to use the public awareness of the persecution."

Chavez flew to New York, where he appealed for support to two thousand Sunday morning worshippers at Riverside Church. Addressing the nondenominational service in the Gothic cathedral in his customary attire—plaid shirt, olive pants, and work boots—he asked them not to buy lettuce without the black eagle on the label and called nonviolence "truly the essence of Christ's teaching." The next day, he delivered the St. Thomas Aquinas lecture to a packed auditorium at Manhattan College, then debated the vice president of the growers association on the *Today* show. On Thursday, December 3, Chavez arrived back in Salinas, so tired he could barely keep his eyes open. Due in court the next morning on the contempt charge, he huddled with his lawyers at the sparsely furnished apartment of Bill Carder, a recent addition to the legal team. Carder had read Peter Matthiessen's profile in the *New Yorker*, gone to see Chavez speak, and run into his old law school classmate Jerry Cohen. Within weeks, Carder was in Salinas, his living room dominated by the big red IBM typewriter he used to prepare dozens of court filings.

Just as Cohen had promised, hundreds of farmworkers stretched out the next morning in a mile-long march from the union office at 14 South Wood Street to the massive concrete courthouse. For three and a half hours, men, women, and children stood and knelt silently in the courtyard and hallways on all three courthouse floors.

Inside Judge Campbell's chambers, attorneys for both sides asked that the hearing be postponed. AFL-CIO president George Meany had set up a meeting the next day with the Teamsters and they thought the dispute might be resolved. Belatedly, Antle's attorney had recognized Chavez's ploy. He did not want to see Chavez in jail, "possibly causing national repercussions," Richard Maltzman told the judge.

Judge Campbell listened impatiently. No agreement reached between the parties outside of court would affect the question of whether Chavez had flagrantly violated the judge's order: "The question still remains as to whether or not there has been a contempt of court," he told the lawyers. He ordered the case to proceed.

Chavez sat in the courtroom and listened as his lawyers argued that the judge's order was confusing and impossible to obey. Ultimately they rested their case on the same legal argument they had presented in fighting the injunction. The order "was in excess of the court's jurisdiction and unconstitutional," Carder told the packed courtroom. Chavez had the right to discuss the labor dispute and to tell people Antle's workers were not represented by the union of their choice. "That is pure speech," Carder said, "and if that is not protected by the First Amendment, I don't know what is!"

When Maltzman gave a convoluted response, Cohen and Carder laughed, and Campbell admonished them for unbecoming conduct. The union put on no witnesses; no evidence would change the fundamental question of constitutionality, Carder argued.

Maltzman swore himself in as a witness and testified that Chavez had told him the union would continue to boycott Antle lettuce and had tied the company to Dow Chemical for the sole purpose of harming Antle. "We know that Mr. Chavez has the power and the ability to call these people off," Maltzman said in his closing statement. Rather than see Chavez in jail, getting the publicity once accorded Martin Luther King Jr., Maltzman asked the judge to set Chavez free and order him to return to court the following week with a notice calling off the boycott.

Campbell recessed only briefly before he delivered a ruling he had drafted in advance. "No man or organization is above or below the law," the judge began. He briefly reviewed the facts and concluded Chavez was clearly in contempt. Campbell ordered the labor leader jailed for ten days on three counts of violating the order and held indefinitely until Chavez ordered an end to the Antle boycott. "Mr. Chavez shall remain in the county jail until that notification has been proven to have been done," Campbell told the audience.

"If an objective is a noble objective," the judge concluded, "and many people can say there is a noble objective here, improper and evil methods cannot be justified to achieve those noble ends and objectives." With that he remanded Chavez to the custody of the Monterey County sheriff.

Deputies took Chavez one block north on Alisal Street and booked him into the Monterey County jail. His black pants, blue shirt, and work boots were deposited in Locker #216. He declined an offer for special treatment and donned the regulation prison denim. His cell was in the rear of the second floor, so he could not see the round-the-clock vigils that began immediately in the parking lot across from the entrance to the Gothic Revival–style jail. A truck decked out with flowers and a brown-and-gold Our Lady of Guadalupe became a shrine. When darkness fell, votive candles lit the night.

Helen Chavez arrived for a brief visit the next morning, bringing her husband a book on Gandhi. They spoke on a telephone, sitting on opposite sides of a glass wall. Afterward she read a short statement from Cesar to the crowd across the street: "I am fine and in good spirits. They are being very kind to me. I was spiritually prepared for this confinement." The workers must have their choice of union, he said. "Jail is a small price to pay to help right that injustice."

Chavez's incarceration quickly exposed a national audience to the ugly fissures that split Salinas. As in so many communities that revolved around agriculture, the farm worker movement posed both an economic threat and a challenge to the social order. Mexican farmworkers were suddenly visible, empowered, and making demands on a system whose Anglo leaders had relegated them to the lowest possible status. Farmworkers wanted not only better working conditions and pay; they wanted health care, education for their children, dignity, and respect. As Chavez had declared on the *Today* show: "These workers are all brown and black workers and they want our union. They don't want to be led by white men who don't understand their needs."

On Chavez's third night in jail, Robert F. Kennedy's widow, Ethel, arrived for a visit and rally. Hundreds of angry Salinas residents turned out to protest, waving American flags and signs that read CARPET BAGGER and KENNEDY GO HOME. Ethel Kennedy marched in a candlelight procession down Alisal Street to the shrine across the street from the jail, where thousands of farmworkers gathered to celebrate mass. They sang "De Colores," the movement's unofficial anthem, to drown out the rhythmic chants from the crowd: "Reds go home, reds go home."

Kennedy placed a candle on the altar and climbed on the flatbed truck, adorned with a Mexican flag, a huelga flag, and four American flags, one at each corner. The Rev. James McEntee celebrated mass, lit only by the spotlights from a dozen television cameras. "We are here today to seek justice for the campesino," the priest prayed, and the crowd across the street booed loudly. "We are here to seek justice for all mankind. We are here to ask prayers, the help of God, for our leader Cesar Chavez." The farmworkers' applause drowned out the protests, and workers lined up to take communion at the base of the truck.

Kennedy held a candle and smiled grimly as she walked toward the jail, accompanied by Huerta and Olympic decathlon champion Rafer Johnson. The farmworkers sang "Bendito Sea Dios," a Mexican hymn, and the chants along her path changed to "Ethel go home, Ethel go home." Boos echoed off the concrete walls of the courthouse as she entered the jail around 7:15 P.M. After a ten-minute visit, she left through a back door to avoid the gauntlet of protesters. Cohen visited Chavez later and reported that he was pleased by the account of the scene outside. "He's going to be in there as long as it takes," Cohen said. "He's feeling fine. He's perfectly happy in there and he thinks he can continue." When reporters pressed Cohen on how soon the courts might spring his client, the lawyer could barely stifle a grin. Chavez wanted to stay right where he was.

With Chavez in the national news, the boycotters went to work. A quote of dubious origin, attributed to Chavez as he was taken to jail, became the new mantra: "Boycott Antle, boycott Dow, boycott the hell out of them!" Jessica Govea worked as a boycott coordinator and sent daily updates to cities around the United States. A Dow executive sat on the Antle board, and years earlier Dow had produced cellophane wrappers for the Antle lettuce; that was enough for the boycotters to invoke the much-maligned company as they urged consumers to avoid Bud Antle lettuce.

Chavez's willingness to endure imprisonment on their behalf moved even workers who had been cautious about the movement. Chava Bustamante worked in the lettuce fields, hating every minute. Their father had taken Chava and his older brother Mario to a union meeting when Chavez first came to Salinas. The other two had been enthusiastic converts, but Chava had been skeptical. Seeing Chavez in jail won him over. "Our hearts at this moment are heavy and full of sadness to see the injustice that has been done to you by a judge who does not understand the cause of the workers," read a December 8 petition signed by dozens of farmworkers. "We know that no matter how many obstacles they try to put in your path, they will not be able to find a way of stopping your fight for justice and respect for all of us, we who have suffered so much in the camps of exploitation. Cesar, we want you to know in these moments of suffering, our hearts are with you, and that our faith is so great, we are firm in our conviction that you will triumph once again for the good of the workers. We are with you till the end."

Letters to Chavez poured into jail and the union office from celebrities, friends, and strangers. Good wishes arrived from U.S. Reps. Phil Burton and Edward Roybal, old CSO friends, the Rev. Ralph Abernathy, the Sisters of St. Joseph, and housewives in Kalamazoo, Michigan. "Dear Cesar, you don't know us but we feel like you are one of our oldest and dearest friends," began one missive.

Carder emerged from his daily visits with messages and requests for books. Chavez also passed along small favors for inmates he had befriended. A few days after he was jailed, Chavez handed Carder a note from another prisoner: "Mr. Chavez, would it be possible for one of your friends to get me just one hearing aid battery? I am without any funds. It would cost .52c and give me hearing for 10 days." Carder bought the battery and kept the note.

On the second Saturday, eighty-nine people visited the jailed leader. On the third Saturday, supporters found out Coretta Scott King was in San Francisco and invited her to Salinas. "I expressed to him the fact that my husband had great admiration for him, and he said that my husband had been an example for him and to all of his people," King said after her jailhouse visit.

King joined union leaders for dinner at nearby Rosita's Armory Cafe, their favorite hangout. They returned for an evening rally at the parking lot shrine, where workers maintained a constant vigil even as temperatures dropped to near freezing. In a black fur coat and leather gloves, King stood on the flatbed truck as she addressed the large crowd. "For more than 30 years farmworkers were thought to be unorganizable and so powerless they could not demand and achieve security and dignity," King said, as Huerta translated into Spanish. "But Cesar Chavez challenged the tyrants, organized the working poor, and became a threat. So they jailed him." She paused for the long and loud applause. "But as my husband often said, you cannot keep truth in jail. Truth and justice leap barriers and in their own way reach the conscience of people."

"Cesar Chavez is not an accident. He is a genius of his people, and their union, the farmworkers union, is a hero union . . . You are demanding your place in the halls of men. You are saying, there are no lowly people, there are only people who are forced down."

Helen wrote Cesar regularly. She fretted about his back pains and whether his clothes kept him warm. She passed on news: so many people took out loans before Christmas that the credit union was broke; the cold, wet weather had stranded two of their children overnight in Los Angeles when snow closed the Grapevine pass, which connected the city with the San Joaquin Valley; and his "poochies," Boycott and Huelga, missed him. She wrote wistfully about their brief visits, cut short to make time for dozens of others waiting to see Chavez. "You know Honey when Sat. approaches I am all excited and glad to go see you but when I have to leave you behind it's really hard," she wrote. "I sure wish I could visit with you in the morning and afternoon after all it's only once a week. Well I guess this is part of the sacrifices."

Helen's last letter was dated December 22:

> The kids are out of school for two weeks, Christmas vacation. I don't know what else to tell you about here, you probably know more of what's happening than we do. People in other places know more about what is happening then us. But that has always happened here. Well my love, hope you are fine and your back isn't giving you much trouble. Marion [Moses] told me that you were having some pain. Take care and we are praying so that you will be home soon. The kids all send their love, your poochies too. And me as always.

The next day, the California Supreme Court voted 6–1 to dissolve key parts of the injunction and ordered Chavez released from jail. The crowd outside the Salinas jail swelled in anticipation. At 7:30 P.M. Marshall Ganz announced that the sheriff would not free Chavez without a copy of the order. At 10:10 two union volunteers arrived from San Francisco and hand-delivered the high court's ruling. Chavez emerged from the jail fifteen minutes later, in the same clothes he had worn ten days earlier but with considerably longer hair. "Jails are made for men who fight for their rights. My spirit was never in jail," Chavez told the crowd. "They can jail us, but never the cause. I'm well and fit, and I was treated very kindly by the deputy sheriffs . . . I made a lot of friends inside." He said the jail was badly lit, cold, damp, and leaky—much like a labor camp. He expressed gratitude for the visits of Kennedy and King and the outpouring of well-wishers. "But no matter how much support you have outside, a jail is still a jail."

Christmas Eve was only a few hours away. "It will soon be 2,000 years ago that the prince of peace was born and brought to this world the message that blessed are those who struggle for justice," Chavez said. "It seems to me that those words say, if you are fighting for justice, he'll be with you. I'm happy to be with you."

"And us with you," the crowd responded. Chavez drove home to spend Christmas in Delano.

CHAPTER 20

Nuestra Señora Reina de La Paz

*We'll organize workers in this movement as long as we're willing to sacrifice.
The moment we stop sacrificing, we stop organizing. I guarantee it . . . We're
not going to do it by paying wages.*

Far from the Salinas picket lines and the Delano vineyards, Chavez was
fashioning an isolated compound in the foothills of the Tehachapi Mountains into the improbable heart of the farm worker movement and a
special sanctuary for its leader.

The detailed blueprints for a walled-in oasis at Forty Acres in Delano
had long ago been scrapped, replaced by utilitarian plans. The grape
contracts increased traffic to the headquarters exponentially. Hundreds
of workers sought jobs, argued over seniority, and filed grievances. The
medical clinic averaged seventy visits a day. From around the world,
farmworkers and dignitaries showed up seeking an audience with Chavez.
He wanted a more remote setting, free from daily demands, where he
might experiment with ideas about education and communal living.

In a conversation during his 1968 fast, Chavez had discussed his ideas
about an educational center with Ed Lewis, a wealthy Hollywood movie
producer. Chavez was interested in cooperatives, and he questioned
Lewis about Israeli kibbutzim. Lewis offered to help finance a purchase if
Chavez found a suitable retreat. Two years later, LeRoy Chatfield saw a
flyer advertising a county auction for an abandoned tuberculosis sanatorium thirty miles east of Bakersfield. He called Lewis. The producer
toured the 180-acre parcel with Richard Chavez disguised as a chauffeur,
so that the carpenter could secretly get a firsthand look at the property.
Lewis bought the parcel from Kern County on April 3, 1970, for $208,350.

No one knew he was fronting for the farmworkers union, and an uproar ensued when the news broke.

Chavez named the complex with care. He wanted a moniker with religious meaning that also conveyed his aspirations for a peaceful movement. He christened the site Nuestra Señora Reina de la Paz, or Our Lady Queen of Peace. The property quickly became known simply as La Paz.

Chavez envisioned a retreat center for workers, staff, and above all himself. To begin the process of transforming La Paz, he turned to Kathy Lynch, the former Berkeley student, and her husband, Lupe Murguia, a farmworker on the payroll of the Migrant Ministry. The Murguias happily became the first residents of La Paz. Lupe learned to operate the boiler, plumbing, and sewage treatment plant, while Kathy figured out how to furnish the accommodations. The property contained a half dozen small houses, two large hospital buildings, and assorted smaller structures. Richard Chavez, an experienced carpenter, worked on the dilapidated buildings. Kathy compiled lists of items they needed and circulated requests among supporters: 240 sheets, 60 mattresses and covers, 100 blankets, 400 towels, 200 pillows, commercial washer and dryer, commercial heater, commercial floor buffer, D-6 tractor, jeep, chain saw, large coffeemaker, white latex and enamel paint.

Chavez wanted to bring farmworkers to La Paz for intensive three-day retreats modeled on the religious *cursillo*. Literally a "short course," the cursillo was a strict, immersion program for lay Catholics based on a movement that had originated in Spain and become popular in the United States. Chavez met with Hartmire to sketch out ideas for farm-worker retreats. As always, Chavez had big plans, and his enthusiasm was infectious. The sessions should be inspirational and fun, Chavez explained, with time set aside to learn movement songs and to act out skits. Activities should involve the whole family, especially children. He wanted to videotape the role-playing and show the videos at night. "Information must be presented in such a way that it comes to life," he told Hartmire. Lessons should be short on theory and long on examples. He wanted equipment for simultaneous translation, like at the United Nations. He estimated the educational program would cost $5,000 a month.

"Educated" had been a pejorative word for Chavez since his days in the CSO. Now he wanted to redefine and transform education into a force that suited his purpose. He wanted to rip up the CSO equation—educated equals middle class—and turn education into an appreciation of sacrifice. "In other words, instead of being all that competitive, instead of being all that worried about the new house, the new car, the new clothes and all those things, to sort of talk to them about the other things that are important," he explained to a group of students. "Things like concern for people who suffer. Concern for people who are discriminated against. Concern for social justice. These kind of things that are really important in life. And not the other stuff. So we call that education: learn how to be people."

He was unsure where to start. He rejected education programs run by other unions. He knew what he did not want to teach: reading, writing, Robert's Rules of Order. Then, from the militant lechugueros in Salinas, Chavez found inspiration.

A group of active union members at Interharvest had missed work to attend a UFW rally in Sacramento, and the company had fired one of the leaders for the unexcused three-day absence. The workers responded with *la tortuga* (the turtle), a slowdown. They worked so slowly they cut production to 20 percent of normal. They were willing to sacrifice earnings to establish a principle: the union contract meant something more than a set of rules and regulations. The union meant power, and the contract meant they would no longer be treated like second-class citizens. Frustrated company officials complained and filed grievances, but finally gave in to the workers' demands. Chavez was thrilled. He vowed to replicate the model he called "Ranch Nation," which would teach the value and power of sacrifice.

"If the workers are not liberated, they don't have the power, they're not equipped to learn," Chavez said. "They don't understand what the hell you're talking about because everything you deal with in the movement is about power: either retaining or making it or employing it or using it wisely or rationing it or duplicating it." If they did not succeed in teaching workers to subvert the contracts, he concluded, "first of all they don't deserve a union, and we don't deserve to be leading it."

Chavez planned to use La Paz for mainstream education—English and Spanish classes, and lessons in contract enforcement, negotiation, and grievances. But he made clear that sort of practical knowledge was secondary: "The idea that we're turned on to mostly is the idea of having workers come here and talk to them about the important things, the important qualities that people must have really to have a long life and to be happy."

Though public attention was focused on Chavez's goal of signing labor contracts, he talked openly about his sweeping ambition to extend the movement far beyond farmworkers. The vision especially resonated with religious audiences. "There are hundreds of thousands of rural poor people in our country who need the dignity and security of an organization of their own. We intend to reach them," he told two hundred religious leaders in Delano. "Our goal is a national union of the poor dedicated to world peace and to serving the needs of all men who suffer."

Chavez had thought long and hard about how to avoid a repetition of his CSO experience, where he empowered poor people who moved into the middle class and abandoned their efforts to help those less fortunate. He was convinced the solution lay in the power of sacrifice. When he thought and read about qualities of great leaders, he saw sacrifice. He observed the way people responded to his own actions. "When people sacrifice, you force others to sacrifice. It's a very powerful weapon," Chavez said. "Somebody stops eating for ten days or for a week and people just come. They just want to be part of that. Somebody goes to jail, people just want to help him. You don't buy that with money."

He grappled with how to instill sacrifice as a value in the union's staff, as well as its members. Each posed different hurdles. How could he counsel workers not to ask for more money when they saw their employers reaping profits and looked to the union to even the imbalance? "It's a very difficult question," Chavez said. The staff must set an example, he explained. "Then the workers who are in leadership positions may begin to get the idea of self-sacrifice. Then we will really have something. Like everything else, it has to begin in your own life and in those people who have given their lives to build the union."

Chavez believed the commitment to the voluntary life of poverty had propelled the movement to its success. Now he saw danger signs. Staff members who had accepted the subsistence lifestyle during the grape strike asked whether the union should start paying salaries now that the contracts generated significant income from dues. Staff still received $5 a week plus room and board. Some had asked for an increase. "I'm very worried," Chavez said in October 1971 to a group of religious leaders visiting La Paz. He singled out for criticism the farmworkers on the union staff. Under the grape contracts, they could earn as much as $3.50 an hour during the harvest season. The lettuce workers earned more. "So if you want to make that kind of money," Chavez said, "we tell the workers, 'You go back. That's where the money's going to be. Not here.'"

He was adamant in his opposition to paying wages. "We'll organize workers in this movement as long as we're willing to sacrifice. The moment we stop sacrificing, we stop organizing. I guarantee that . . . We're not going to do it by paying wages."

Chavez thought communal living might offer a solution to the looming problem about compensation. He talked about Saint Francis as a model for building community and read books on Scandinavian co-ops. Chavez focused most sharply on Gandhi's experiments with ashrams because the Indian leader had harnessed power from spiritual communities and used it for political ends. "I'm at heart an experimenter," Chavez said. "I hate to do things routinely. I want to experiment in forming a community."

The potential to build a community in La Paz, with its wide-open spaces and abundant housing, was much of its attraction. The first time he visited the site, Chavez had talked to Chatfield about kibbutzim and other forms of cooperative living. Chavez envisioned a commune that offered volunteers an alternative lifestyle, providing security and community in exchange for their financial sacrifice.

For farmworkers, Chavez argued, the stakes were even higher. Contracts alone would not lift millions of people out of poverty; owning land was the key to economic stability. La Paz could serve as his laboratory. Chavez talked to Jacques Levy about how the black Muslim movement acquired land. He researched Wall Street corporations to explore how he might pool the credit of many people to purchase more property. Referring to Mao's saying that power comes out of the barrel of a gun, Chavez said, "Power also comes out of credit. In a capitalist society the biggest gun is credit, and credit in a society like ours means people."

Gradually Chavez invited more families to join the Murguias in the ramshackle buildings on the rolling hills of La Paz. The UFW headquarters remained at Forty Acres, but Chavez shifted more of the union's business out of Delano. He took his computer expert, Dave Smith, to see La Paz, and Smith picked out a perfect home for the union's new computer system—a T-shaped building where the minicomputer could sit in the middle, the keypunch operators on one side, and the programmers on the other.

Chavez convened a group at La Paz to restart *El Malcriado*, which he had shut down years earlier because of unhappiness with its independent and often provocative stance. Chavez allocated funds for an $18,000 press and a $7,000 structure to house a printing operation. He appointed a new editor and asked Levy to hold weekly sessions to critique prototype papers. They planned three versions: English for farmworkers, English for liberal supporters, and Spanish for farmworkers. Chavez invoked Gandhi as a model and said *El Malcriado* should break news that the mainstream media would follow. Like Gandhi, they would print only a small number of papers but gain outsize influence. To distribute the paper, Chavez looked to the model of the Jehovah's Witnesses and sent aides to collect information on how the group operated. He wanted to find "fanatics" to distribute *El Malcriado* with equal religious fervor; perhaps they should have a uniform, too, with white shirts.

The linchpin of Chavez's growing network of nonprofit entities remained his first entrepreneurial venture, the National Farm Workers Service Center. Groups like the Catholic Church could funnel money to Chavez through the Service Center and avow that not one penny was going to the union. "The whole game since 1966 has been to use the Service Center to defray much of the cost of running the union, because it was easier to raise the money there," Frank Denison, the lawyer who handled the nonprofits, explained to the union's leaders.

The Service Center paid for cars driven by union staff, ran the clinics, owned Forty Acres, and acted as the movement's landlord, charging rent to the union and other entities for office space. Chavez served as president, and Ross, Hartmire, and Chatfield sat on the board. Chavez assured donors they maintained the requisite legal separation. In reality, the lines blurred whenever necessary. When the union ran short on funds, the Service Center paid for conferences and expenses, effectively extending a $90,000 loan. A Field Foundation grant to the Service Center paid the salaries of lawyers, who then "volunteered" to help the union.

When an inflammatory quote from a union lawyer appeared in the *New York Times*, Field Foundation president Leslie Dunbar grew alarmed. "To you, it may seem artificial to distinguish the Union from the Center," Dunbar wrote Chavez. "If it is, in fact, an artificial distinction, then I believe we may be in trouble." The Field Foundation contributed hundreds of thousands of dollars, and Dunbar viewed the movement as "a vital and good spirit and force for America and for humanity." Chavez assured Dunbar that union leaders had "final say" over the policies of all related entities, but "this does not mean that we are inflexible when it comes to accommodating ourselves to the needs of those who are helping us." Dunbar eased his conscience by asking that the Field Foundation contribution be shifted from the lawyers' salaries to other purposes.

The fuzzy lines between the union and the Service Center set the pattern for Chavez's future financial dealings, which increased in complexity as he created more corporations and gained access to larger sums of money. His fundamental disregard for the legal strictures increased along with his reputation. So did donors' willingness to over-look red flags in their eagerness to help the movement.

A year after the union acquired La Paz, Chavez made his most signifi-cant move: he proposed relocating the national headquarters out of Delano. Like all his suggestions, the idea was readily approved by the board, despite some trepidation. La Paz was about an hour southeast of Delano, surrounded by desert and mountains, not fields. Chavez told the board that he needed to be outside Delano to carry out his larger mission. In effect, he argued that proximity to the union's members made his job more difficult. In Delano, he had become bogged down in the adminis-trative work of the union, which now had tens of thousands of members in the area.

"I was getting a lot of problems," he explained. "I was being forced to do a lot of work. Though the leadership was there, workers wouldn't talk to the guy in charge of Delano, wouldn't even talk to the ranch committees."

Not everyone shared his enthusiasm for the remote rolling hills of Keene, a crossroads with a post office and coffee shop, where the nearest city, Tehachapi, was even smaller than Delano. Some objected to the life-style imposed by the mountain retreat, and others questioned the wisdom of removing Chavez and other leaders from the fields. "There is a mystic bit in all of this, something that pulls him off into a dream of a small, perfect community," Bill Kircher observed. He saw that as a weakness that distracted Chavez from the hundreds of grape contracts the union held and the dozens more they hoped to win in the vegetable fields. Chavez should focus on Delano, Kircher thought, instead of La Paz.

Jerry Cohen was reluctant to leave Delano and felt he would be cut off from the action. Helen Chavez, who knew the place well, was adamant in her refusal to move. As a child, she had shown signs of anemia and malnutrition and been sent to live for months in a program for children housed in the tuberculosis sanatorium that was now being converted into the union headquarters. She had vivid, negative memories.

Some of Chavez's champions and funders expressed concern about the retreat from the fields. "Even those of us who have been 'outside support-ers' of the movement cannot help but feel a slight bit of trauma at Cesar's decision," John Moyer, a United Church of Christ official and leading supporter of the Migrant Ministry, wrote to Jim Drake.

Chavez's trump card was security. A convoluted tip about an assassination plot from a petty criminal turned informant evolved into months of intrigue. Chavez used the threat as a rationale to move permanently to La Paz, where his security could allegedly be ensured with a guarded entry and regular patrols of the compound.

In the summer of 1971, an informant went to the local office of the U.S. Bureau of Alcohol, Tobacco, and Firearms (ATF) and said he had been solicited in an arson and murder plot against Chavez. Larry Shears had provided accurate information to the ATF on a separate arson plot, and he asked for a $10,000 contract. The ATF signed him up, but he would receive the money only for information leading to an arrest. He told them that his source, a drug dealer named Richard Pedigo, had said that a grower had put up $25,000 for the killing. On July 28, federal officials notified the UFW and provided a picture of the alleged hit man, a mobster named Buddy Gene Prochnau. The ATF agents wired Shears and assigned an undercover agent who went along to meetings with Pedigo and offered to work as a substitute for Prochnau, who had been arrested in an unrelated case. But Pedigo, who appeared to be high and suffering withdrawal symptoms, said the deal was off because the growers had backed out.

On August 21, ATF agents busted Pedigo for drugs. The lead agent tracked down the grower Pedigo had named, who denied any involvement in a Chavez plot. The ATF told Shears they no longer had jurisdiction in the case and passed their files to the local authorities.

In December, Shears went to a Bakersfield television station with his story. They called UFW officials for comment. Cohen talked to Chavez, and Chavez called Jacques Levy with an urgent request. For the first time in the three years he had spent time with Chavez, the union paid Levy to fly to Bakersfield. Cohen, Richard Chavez, and Larry Shears met Levy at the airport. Shears told his story about the plot to kill Chavez, produced a Treasury Department check to corroborate his informant status, and told them he had tapes of all his conversations with targets of the investigation and ATF officials. He offered to sell the union the tapes. Levy went with the others back to La Paz to report to Chavez and the board.

The union bought the tapes with the intention of using them to publicly denounce authorities for their failure to pursue the investigation. With the help of Sen. Edward Kennedy, the UFW raised a $10,000 reward for information leading to an arrest. At a press conference, Cohen outlined the plot according to Shears, naming both Pedigo and Prochnau.

Meanwhile, Levy contacted Jann Wenner, editor of *Rolling Stone* magazine. Elaborate negotiations between Levy, Cohen, Wenner, and Shears ended in an agreement that Levy would write a magazine story and *Rolling Stone* would get exclusive use of the tapes, finance a private investigator, and pay Shears $2,000 for his cooperation. When Cohen and Levy went to explain the deal to Chavez, Cohen reported, "Cesar objected to paying 'the little bastard' any money, but at the same time asserted the Union should get 95% of the movie rights . . . Cesar then lied, saying that he had never authorized the payment of money to Shears in the first place, and that every morning when he woke up he felt that he had lost a little bit of his principles. He then walked out of the meeting."

In the end, the tapes were largely unintelligible, *Rolling Stone* killed the story, and the investigations went nowhere. The union's charges of cover-ups were never corroborated, despite extensive federal reviews by multiple agencies over the next several years. The only financial beneficiary was Larry Shears.

But the threat of assassination had seemed plausible, only a few years after Kennedy and King were shot. A group of people living at La Paz were given guns and taken to the police shooting range in Tehachapi for practice. They patrolled the perimeter of La Paz at night with shotguns. One night Lupe Murguia pointed his gun at a rancher who had permission to cross the land, and that ended the official experiment in armed defense.

The threats persuaded Helen. She gave up her resistance, and the family left Delano at the end of 1971 and joined Cesar in La Paz. Soon after, a heavy snow blanketed the complex, which sat at thirty-five hundred feet above sea level. Cesar caught the flu but recovered in time to throw a New Year's party for the growing La Paz community. "Helen and the kids moved up just before Christmas," Chavez wrote to a friend. "I think she may even like it here now. On her birthday the whole staff came to sing Mañanitas to her."

As more people moved to La Paz, they added trailers. Chavez was content, happy to live on a rural ranch for the first time since he had left Arizona as a child. He added beehives. "I eat honey like a bear," he said. He spent five minutes a day training his dogs, using lessons from Jacques Levy.

"We've built sort of a community of sorts here," he told a group of students who came to visit. "The reason we came here is, we're, like, alone, you know." People came from all over the world to visit, he explained. "There's a lot of love here. And that love generates power. Generates spirit. A generator throwing out this beam of light . . . When I go away, I can't wait to come back. When I come thru that gate, at night, when I'm back, I feel great . . . You really feel like you're coming home. To your house, but to a bigger home."

He wanted someday to replicate the La Paz experience so that poor people could find solidarity and happiness through communal life. He invoked as models Gandhi, St. Paul, and Christ. Living together forced people to share, rather than retreat into their homes and watch TV, Chavez argued. "Here, there's not too many places you can go," he said. "It's easy to get together and share with one another . . . So this is serving as a model. You strengthen one another. You bring support. Unlike working separate and apart. There something about the spirit. Something happens to people when they work together and have a community like we have here."

CHAPTER 21

Staking a National Claim

The great myth is broken. The myth is shattered. The farmworkers can win.

Scott Washburn, a twenty-two-year-old UFW volunteer, showed up for work at his boss's home as usual on the morning of May 12, 1972. He saw guards in front of Gustavo Gutierrez's small concrete house in suburban Phoenix, which doubled as the union's Arizona office. Washburn went around the back. His entrance startled a short man sleeping on the floor in his underwear. He jumped up and introduced himself, and Washburn met Cesar Chavez.

Chavez had arrived in the early morning after driving almost five hundred miles from La Paz to demand a meeting with Arizona governor Jack Williams. The legislature had just become the first in the United States to pass a bill designed to keep the UFW out of the state. Williams was expected to sign the measure, which would criminalize boycotts and make union elections in the field virtually impossible. Chavez wanted to respond in dramatic fashion. The Yuma native's return to his home state marked the union's first major farmworker campaign outside California and the start of Chavez's effort to stake a national claim.

A local priest said mass for the small group in Gutierrez's living room, which included Dolores Huerta and Richard Chavez. Chavez had already decided to begin another public fast. He outlined options and consulted his top advisers. Then he turned to Washburn and softly asked the junior volunteer, What do you think? With that simple gesture, Chavez cemented Washburn's loyalty.

The Republican governor declined to meet with Chavez and signed the bill less than an hour after the legislature had voted. Jim Drake told supporters that Williams had looked down at the farmworkers rallying outside his office and said, "Those people don't exist as far as I'm concerned." The quote drew outrage and spread quickly in press releases and speeches—despite no evidence that Williams ever said those words.

Workers massed on the lawn of the state Capitol in protest, and the UFW leaders arrived for a rally in the afternoon. Chavez stood by quietly as others made fiery speeches. In his typical low-key manner, he explained his decision to fast, calling it a rare opportunity to "show our love by sacrificing ourselves." He would fast, he explained, "to erase from the minds of the men and women who are here in the state Capitol that fear, that distrust that they have against us."

He condemned the legislators who had rebuffed farmworkers' attempts to meet and the governor's decision to sign the bill without the courtesy of a conversation. "It's not only a question of injustice; it's even more importantly a question of not respecting our people when they came to the state Capitol in a very humble and human way . . . They were not permitted the decency of presenting a petition to the people who are supposed to be representing them. And that's more shameful than passing the law."

Chavez announced the union would sue to overturn the unconstitutional law. Jim Rutkowski, a former seminarian who had gone to law school to help farmworkers, had drafted the suit and driven round-trip to La Paz the day before so that Jerry Cohen could review the filing. Chavez wanted to sue immediately, and there was no other way to get Cohen the documents fast enough.

One of the decisions made in Gutierrez's living room was that Chavez would fast in the Santa Rita Center, a small hall used by a local Chicano group. Chavez stayed during the day in a room just off the chapel, lying in a hospital bed, with a fan to ease the hundred-degree heat. As in the Delano fast, Chavez came out each night for mass, sitting quietly as hundreds of people crammed into the small chapel and overflowed into the dirt yard. Union organizers asked boycotters and workers to send telegrams to Chavez, and a few were read aloud each evening. During the day, Chavez meditated and read. He set no time to end the fast. "He's a pretty stubborn guy," Gutierrez told reporters.

On the third day, Chavez talked to Hartmire about the message he wanted the minister to disseminate. Arizona farmworkers were being denied fundamental rights and rejected by society. Chavez wanted the fast to underscore the need to show courage in the face of such oppression. Farmworkers must shed their fear of the bosses and the ruling class, understand their own dignity and demand their rights. For politicians, Chavez's message was about a different sort of fear. "The issue isn't the law, the issue is the fear of recognizing human beings as human beings," Chavez told Hartmire. Chavez played off the politicians' actions to make the union appear more powerful. Williams had used the highway patrol to bring him the bill, because he knew Chavez was on his way to Phoenix. Why was the governor so afraid?

The union announced a recall campaign to oust Williams from office. Just as the Giumarra court hearing had mobilized supporters during the Delano fast, the recall campaign took advantage of the enthusiastic response to the fast and put people to work. They needed to collect more than a hundred thousand signatures to qualify the recall initiative for the ballot. Eager volunteers like Washburn were sent out each day with petitions. At the evening mass, Drake delivered a progress report and pep talk on the campaign. The recall campaign helped rejuvenate a dispirited Democratic coalition in Arizona. "All have been crushed so many times by the [Sen. Barry] Goldwater machine that they had all but given up hope," Hartmire wrote from Phoenix to boycotters around the country. "The most common phrase was, 'No se puede,' 'It can't be done.' But they have caught the fire of the farm worker movement."

"Si, se puede!" Huerta threw back at the naysayers. The union gathered more than enough signatures. The Republican attorney general disqualified the recall petition, a move later overturned in court. The farmworkers adopted Huerta's phrase, and by the end of the fast a giant SI SE PUEDE banner hung across the Santa Rita Center. *La causa* had a new slogan.

Chavez had more trouble with this fast than in 1968. He had eaten his last meal a few hours before arriving in Phoenix and felt unprepared. He attributed some of his pain to the unfamiliar water in Phoenix and the extreme heat. He became quite sick, his blood pressure dropped, and on the nineteenth day he was hospitalized. His physician, Jerome Lackner, reported that Chavez's vitamin levels had dropped sharply and his heart muscle showed weakening. "As someone who has taken care of him . . . to look at his cardiogram today and yesterday brings tears to my eyes," Lackner said. "We want him to terminate the fast."

Chavez held out a few more days; he had planned to break the fast at a memorial mass to mark the anniversary of the death of Robert Kennedy. LeRoy Chatfield took charge of the event, each detail carefully planned, from the placement of microphones to the seating arrangement for the dignitaries. Crowds poured in when the doors of the Phoenix Convention Center opened at 1:00 P.M. on Sunday, June 4. Mariachis played. Yaqui Indians performed a special dance for Chavez, and Joan Baez sang. She sat next to Chavez, the two dressed in matching white Nehru-collar shirts made of manta, a coarse cotton fabric. Helen sat on Cesar's other side.

Joseph Kennedy began his speech in broken Spanish, as his father had done in Delano in 1968, and spoke of that historic trip. "He went to Delano because he believed that what the farmworkers were doing was right," Kennedy said. "He went to Delano because he believed that nonviolence was right. He went to Delano because he believed that Cesar Chavez was right."

Hartmire read Chavez's statement in English, and Gutierrez read it in Spanish: "I am weak in my body but I feel very strong in my spirits . . . The fast was meant as a call to sacrifice for justice and as a reminder of how much suffering there is among farmworkers."

Hartmire, who had long ago turned his ministry into an adjunct of the union, now played an increasingly important role for Chavez on the national stage. At Chavez's instigation, Hartmire had transformed the California Migrant Ministry into a nationwide, ecumenical group of religious supporters. Chavez did not want religious support for farmworkers to be diffused among multiple causes, and he wanted to head off potential competition. Hartmire convened a planning session to launch the new group, and Chavez attended to reinforce the goal: support for his union, and his union only.

In Hartmire, Chavez had a most willing disciple, one who employed skillful rhetoric to maneuver religious leaders into line as they founded the National Farm Worker Ministry (NFWM). "I hope that there will be one national farm workers union under the leadership of Cesar Chavez that will continue to give leadership to the whole country on what it means to serve the poor effectively," Hartmire wrote. In making his pitch for the new group to support only Chavez, Hartmire compared the challenge that the UFW offered supporters with the challenge that Jesus posed to his disciples—to join in their complete dedication to helping farmworkers. At Chavez's request, Hartmire also proposed that the UFW have veto power over any future endeavors of the religious group. Even with Hartmire's clout and Chavez's personal appeal, the mission statement drew some skepticism and heated debate. They prevailed on a 14–5 vote, with 8 abstentions.

One prominent supporter reacted with dismay to Chavez's position. "He made it abundantly clear that what he wants is a national organization of religious leaders who will support UFWOC 1000 per cent with staff and funds and will do so without asking any questions or offering any advice," Monsignor George Higgins wrote in a confidential memo. "In my judgment, he appealed very crassly to the guilt feeling which so many Protestant social actionists seem to harbor in their souls and even went so far as to threaten them with the enmity of the poor (meaning, in this case, farm workers) if the religious community fails to measure up to his expectations. All in all, I thought it was a miserable performance on his part." Higgins, however, remained a stalwart supporter. There was no alternative.

Chavez expressed optimism that the union was on the verge of a breakthrough not only in California but across the country. The victory in the grapes had demonstrated the power of si se puede. "The great myth is broken," Chavez said. "The myth is shattered. The farmworkers can win."

He noted that the farmworkers' success inspired others in the budding Chicano movement, although by and large he kept his distance from that movement and its leaders. He condemned the violence endorsed by some Chicano movement leaders, and he showed little interest in some of their goals. "What's happening now is no big thing to me, this identity," he said when asked about the Chicano movement. "I've lived with it; it's been my life." As a dark-skinned Mexican, he said, he had no choice: "The darker you are, the more Mexican you have to be. So if you're dark and poor, you have to be more Mexican."

The Arizona fight was only the first in a series of legislative battles for the union. The Farm Bureau, aided by the Nixon administration, introduced bills modeled after the Arizona statute in several key states. Thirteen labor bills related to farmworkers had been introduced in Congress. Chavez's strategy was twofold—to fight off the bad laws, and to use the publicity to gain footholds in other states.

Drake elaborated in speeches to religious leaders and boycott supporters: "What we're trying to do is at least stake a claim in certain states where if we don't get there right away, we know that somebody else is going to do the organizing, and we're never going to have a national union." Already, a college student named Baldemar Velasquez had set up the Farm Labor Organizing Committee (FLOC) and negotiated a handful of contracts in northwest Ohio. Efforts were under way in New York as well.

So despite the ongoing battles in Salinas, the hundreds of grape contracts, and the melon, citrus, and tomato workers in California clamoring for attention, Chavez spread the union thinner by setting up a token presence in Washington, Oregon, Idaho, Texas, and Florida. "There are about eight or ten major states . . . where we have to show we're doing something," Drake said. He outlined ambitious plans for recruiting forty organizers in the Midwest, taking aim at the cherry harvest in Michigan, and targeting orange growers in Florida. "There's no limit to where we should organize."

When the Oregon state legislature passed an anti-farmworker bill, Chavez dispatched Cohen to persuade the governor to veto the measure. Cohen disregarded advice from liberals who urged him to gently approach Gov. Tom McCall, a moderate Republican. Hardball was more Cohen's style, and he drew on tactics he had learned from Chavez. Cohen orchestrated a prayer vigil on the Capitol steps and bombarded the governor with letters and calls. "If you work with Cesar for a while you get a pretty realistic view of politicians," Cohen said. "No matter if they're liberal Republicans or liberal Democrats, if there's an issue they don't feel any pressure on, and it's a little hard for them to make a political decision, they're going to make the easiest political decision." McCall vetoed the bill.

Cohen hoped the union could break through outside California "We are at a crossroads—could become a national union," he wrote. But he worried the expansion had come at the expense of organizing in California. In 1972, a year of near-record dues, the union spent $230,000—about half its income—on political campaigns. When Cohen looked for plaintiffs in a suit against Bud Antle, he had trouble finding a farmworker because the union had pulled everyone out of Salinas. Fred Ross shared Cohen's concern, and the lawyer urged Ross to talk to Chavez.

"Oh hell, he won't listen to me," Ross said.

"He'll pretend not to listen to you, but he'll listen to you," Cohen responded. "I mean it'll be in his head, and then in about a week he'll come up with the idea."

The Salinas situation remained a stalemate; the UFW had only a handful of contracts and the Teamsters held the rest. At the request of the AFL-CIO, Chavez had suspended the lettuce boycott to see if a settlement could be negotiated with the growers. After eight months of meetings, Cohen reported, "they agreed to the bulletin board clause," the most minor provision in the contract. Chavez declared an impasse and prepared to relaunch the lettuce boycott, a decision that would bring the farmworkers into conflict with the AFL-CIO.

AFL-CIO president George Meany felt liable for the actions of the farmworkers as long as their union remained an organizing committee under the federation's umbrella, rather than an independently chartered union. The rest of the labor federation was covered by the National Labor Relations Act, which barred secondary boycotts. Meany was concerned the AFL-CIO would be accused of violating the law if the farmworkers boycotted supermarket chains.

Chavez was displeased about the prospect of losing the $10,000-a-month subsidy from the AFL-CIO that came with the organizing committee status. But he needed the boycott, so he made a pragmatic decision and formally requested a charter. "When a guy named Nixon came into office, he began to change the labor board," Chavez explained. "He is going to do anything and everything he can to screw unions. We're one of their big targets . . . In order to keep boycotting, we have to get a charter to save the AFL-CIO the headache they think they're going to have."

Then a new crisis derailed not only the boycott, but all other plans, and drew Chavez away from his national expansion plans and back to California. The most serious legislative fight came on home turf, where growers qualified an initiative on the November 1972 ballot that would effectively ban the boycott in California and cripple the union. Chavez summoned all the California volunteers to La Paz in late summer to launch the campaign against Proposition 22.

"The only time we come together is when we're in trouble," Chavez said as he opened the conference. He told them the union faced a life-or-death fight, and the boycotters responded. Ellen Eggers had just graduated from college and was on her way home to Indiana after a summer internship arranged through the National Farm Worker Ministry. She had heard about Chavez all summer and had recited the details of his life dozens of times as she asked people not to buy lettuce. When she finally visited La Paz and saw him in person, she was starstruck. His speech was rambling, his manner alternately funny and stern, but his presence was utterly compelling. Eggers gave up her plans for graduate school and her boyfriend back home and joined the fight against Prop 22. She cried as she tried to explain to her mother that she would always regret it if she abandoned the union in its time of need.

"The minute you meet him, you know he's special," said Margie Coons, a twenty-three-year-old boycotter in Los Angeles, struggling to find words to explain her feelings about Chavez to a reporter. "He's so patient and forceful at the same time."

Chavez tapped Chatfield to run the campaign against Prop 22 and Chatfield recruited Hartmire to help in Los Angeles, where they set up headquarters in the office of the National Farm Worker Ministry. Chatfield's wife, Bonnie, discovered the opposition had collected signatures for the initiative under false pretenses and in some cases had forged names. Dozens of volunteers scoured the petitions, interviewed signers, and collected affidavits. Chavez and Chatfield appealed to Secretary of State Jerry Brown, son of former governor Pat Brown, to throw the initiative off the ballot. Brown declined, but launched investigations that provided ammunition for the farmworkers' campaign. More significant, the meetings forged a tie between Chavez and Brown and drew the Democratic politician into a cause with which he would soon become closely identified.

Chatfield masterminded a brilliant "No on 22" campaign that featured human billboards at key intersections across Los Angeles, along with radio and television ads, newspaper endorsements, and a massive get-out-the-vote campaign. On election eve, exhausted, he sat with Chavez in the Los Angeles campaign headquarters late at night. Both men were nervous.

"Cesar spoke very softly and with a friendly but nervous edge to his voice," Chatfield wrote.

> He simply explained to me that if we lost the election tomorrow, I would have to take the blame. I couldn't answer. I was totally silenced by the harsh reality of what he had said. I was completely helpless. My closest friend, almost 9 years now, had just explained the political facts of life to me. I had worked on this "life and death" campaign full time since July, barely had any time to even see Bonnie and the girls unless she was in the office working, working late into the nights on the telephone plotting strategy with my staff directors in other California cities and then worrying half to death about everything because of the stakes involved for Cesar and the union. And now, to top it all off, I had been reduced to a fall guy. I didn't answer Cesar. I just nodded and gave sort of a shrug of the shoulders.

Prop 22 lost overwhelmingly, 58 percent to 42 percent. Chavez threw a victory party and heaped praise on Chatfield. Chatfield left the union some months later for a combination of personal and professional reasons. But his departure was clearly influenced by the election eve conversation.

Only a few years earlier, Chavez had told Jacques Levy there were five people he demanded more from than anyone else because he knew they could take it: Helen and Richard Chavez first, then LeRoy Chatfield, Marion Moses, and Jerry Cohen. By the time Chatfield had his November 6, 1972, conversation, Moses was gone, too. Chavez had quarreled with her over her interest in attending medical school and kicked her out. She left immediately, without saying any goodbyes. Chavez soon made amends, and they stayed in close touch. But her abrupt departure shocked people throughout the union and served as a warning. No one was immune from Chavez's displeasure.

His increased profile, the higher stakes, and the competing pressures combined to make Chavez more openly ruthless in his drive to be the one and only farm labor leader. As a national figure, Chavez felt he could not afford to make mistakes.

Chavez sometimes used a juggling analogy to explain his work:

> When you start organizing, it's like a guy who starts juggling one ball. You start, you have one ball. You go at your own speed. You're doing your own thing, you know, nobody is after you. After a little while, you got to get two balls, and you start juggling two balls. Your own speed. Because even up to that point, you've got everything under control. Then after a little while, more people come in, you've got to take three balls. And then four and then five and then six. And pretty soon you can't deal with it. And the organization breaks because the guy who's supposed to be leading wants to juggle a lot of balls and he can't do it. So he's got to make up his mind he's going to let some of the balls drop. But even more important, he's going to multiply himself to have more jugglers to handle all the balls that are coming at him.

The union had expanded so quickly in so many directions, and Chavez had great difficulty delegating. He struggled with the prospect of passing off to more jugglers. But as his talk with Chatfield showed, if a ball dropped, someone else would take the blame.

CHAPTER 22

Brother Against Brother

This will create more criticism but we must not be afraid of it. Workers have to handle their own problems—we have to organize, they have to put in their share of sacrifice.

When the Teamster fight erupted in the vegetable fields and the leadership decamped to Salinas, Richard Chavez was left in Delano to administer the dozens of grape contracts his brother had triumphantly signed.

Richard's first job was to get workers to ratify the contract that had already been approved, a formality required under the terms of the agreement. None of the workers had voted for the union. Many were suspicious. Richard needed signed cards from a majority at each ranch. His helpers were a college professor and twenty young interns from Los Angeles sent by Chris Hartmire.

At first they summoned crews to the hiring hall to sign union cards, but with only two windows the workers had to wait on line for hours. Richard ended up with thousands of cards stacked all over the room and little idea which cards matched what ranch. Richard tried taking his staff into the fields instead. Some of the interns gave cards to the foremen to have the workers sign. Richard had to go back and get them signed all over. At the Giumarra ranch, drunken workers threw beer cans at him. Both sides knew the contracts would be ratified one way or another. But the process did nothing to help the union's image. A few years later, Richard shuddered at the memory: "It was the most terrible two weeks in my whole life."

Richard was kindhearted, practical, and a natural entertainer. Where Cesar strained to tell jokes, Richard was genuinely funny and loved to tell stories. He shared his brother's commitment to the movement, but Richard did not share the commitment to material sacrifice. He enjoyed playing golf, and his family was the first in the neighborhood to have a color television. Yet time after time, Richard gamely took on whatever task his older brother called on him to perform.

With everyone else absorbed in the Salinas fight, Richard struggled to bring order to a tense and chaotic situation in Delano. Skeptical workers now had to pay monthly dues. Hostile foremen tried to sabotage the agreements, which deprived them of their power to hire and fire, practice favoritism, and demand bribes and sexual favors in exchange for employment. The union had not been terribly efficient at managing only a handful of wine grape contracts; now tens of thousands of members expected service and dozens of growers expected competent laborers. With a skeleton staff, Richard struggled to administer about two hundred contracts covering fifty-five thousand jobs. He kept appealing to his brother for help, to no avail.

The centerpiece of the contracts was the hiring hall, designed to be the only source of job referrals and eliminate the labor contractors, who had so often cheated and exploited workers. Growers now requested workers and the union dispatched them in seniority order. This required the union to keep accurate seniority lists and to quickly muster workers to meet each grower's demand. Both tasks proved difficult.

On top of the normal growing pains, the union had adopted several policies that generated confusion and animosity. Rules crafted in La Paz by Cesar, in consultation with LeRoy Chatfield and Marshall Ganz, were intended to transfer the workers' loyalty to the union. The plan backfired badly.

No worker could be employed on a union ranch without an up-to-date membership card, and members were required to pay the monthly dues year-round, regardless of whether or where they worked. A migrant family returning to Coachella for the harvest season after eight months in Mexico or Texas or other parts of California might owe hundreds of dollars in back dues. To secure their experienced workers, employers often lent families money to pay the dues.

The union's seniority rule caused further outrage. In an attempt to reward longtime supporters, seniority was measured by number of years as a union member, rather than the length of time worked for a particular employer. That meant workers returning for the grape harvest might be denied jobs at a vineyard where they had worked for years. The seniority rule also affected families whose members had different tenures and found themselves split up. They often had only one car and no way to get to jobs on different ranches. "What a mess it was," Richard said. "What a mess. I think about those times and I just . . . bad times."

By the second season of the contracts, in the summer of 1971, the hiring hall problems were well known. Jerry Cohen, who was resisting Chavez's entreaties to move to La Paz, attributed some of the difficulty to the isolation of the new headquarters. Cohen explained to Jacques Levy during a break in the Salinas negotiations that everyone knew the hiring hall rules worked badly but were afraid to confront Chavez. Among the board members, only Huerta tried to argue with Chavez, and their fights became so personal that they produced only recriminations and hurt feelings. "Cesar is a gentle intimidator," Cohen wrote in his diary. "He can change a man's report for example with a slight change of expression. The man noting displeasure will anticipate what is wanted and deliver it. This is bad. Some do not like to be the bearers of bad news."

Chavez was stubborn about charging dues year-round. "We have a policy; we collect back dues," he said flatly. He reminded those who complained that $3.50 a month was an arbitrary number adopted by the first convention in 1962, long before the union had contracts. Starting out the new contracts by raising dues would have been unpalatable, so the compromise was to charge dues year-round. "You have to understand, you cannot run a union on $3.50 a month," Chavez said. "But politically, we were in a bind."

Tension grew between the small band of longtime supporters in Delano and the bulk of workers who were new to the union. Each ranch elected a five-member ranch committee, which was to be the governing body and the intermediary with the union office. In a few places, strong ranch committee leaders helped coworkers understand how the contract should work and sold them on the benefits. But in most cases, the union's policies generated so much hostility that the workers most loyal to the union failed to win election to the ranch committees. When they complained to Chavez, he voiced no sympathy. Their service on the strike and boycott did not entitle them to special privileges. "They consider themselves a step above the other workers because they struggled," Chavez explained. "It's the same problem that any revolution has anywhere. If you've read anything about revolutions you know that the guys that won are the guys who want a little extra. And we're saying, 'No, you're no different.'"

On other hand, he viewed workers who had not supported the union early on as ungrateful, taking for granted benefits of contracts that others had sacrificed to win. "If they want a union, goddamn it, they've got to do something for it," Chavez told a meeting of boycotters. "We never educated them . . . they think the boycott is a gift from heaven." Borrowing a concept from the Spanish cursillo, he asked farmworkers to offer a *palanca*—which he translated as "a small sacrifice"—for the success of the boycott. ("If I were making a palanca for New York so that New York can win its boycott," Chavez explained, "I'd stop drinking Diet Rite. That's a palanca.")

Chavez imposed more demands. To support the Salinas strike, the union created a voluntary $1-a-week strike fund assessment on members. "This will create more criticism but we must not be afraid of it," Chavez said at a meeting of hiring hall administrators. "Workers have to handle their own problems—we have to organize, they have to put in their share of sacrifice."

Some, who looked to exculpate Chavez, attributed problems to his relative isolation at La Paz, where he made decisions insulated from workers who might have alerted him to the consequences. But Chavez had worked in the fields himself and knew the issues well. In large part, he insisted on the rules because he believed they would, over time, establish the union as the source of power and eradicate the labor contractors. He underestimated the workers' response, and then angrily dismissed complaints when others tried to tell him—even his brother.

"I started telling Cesar, 'Look Cesar, this and this is happening in the office, you know. We do not have the qualified people to enforce those contracts,'" Richard recalled. "'The membership is getting a little, ah, disturbed at us, you know. They're starting to raise complaints, and we have to do something about it.'" Many farmworkers occasionally worked in packing houses under Teamster contracts; they saw the differences between the two unions. The Teamsters might be less interested in workers' rights, but they did not demand that employees spend weekends on political campaigns or boycotts. The Teamsters were a business union, and for some workers that held appeal.

While Cesar escaped to his retreat in the Tehachapi Mountains, the issue boiled over in Delano. In early 1972, Richard and Cesar had it out. Richard told his brother the union was antagonizing workers so badly and managing so poorly that they were sure to lose the contracts when they came up for renewal in a year unless they acted quickly. They shouted at each other. Cesar called Richard names and said he was a fatalist. From then on, they had shouting matches every few months. As the time to make amends to workers grew shorter, Richard became more upset. "I said, 'Look we're not doing the organizing that we have to do. We're in right now, we can organize our people, but we need staff and we need this.' Well, everything was denied. I was always being told that we had more staff than necessary, we couldn't get cars, you know, all that, everything. So it was a constant fight, constant fight."

Richard told his brother he was losing touch with the union's members. They expected to see Cesar, and he was never around anymore. He was resting in La Paz, or fasting in Phoenix, or fund-raising in New York, but not talking to workers in Delano. Later, when the union was a full-fledged national organization, Richard said, other leaders would emerge and the workers would not expect to see Cesar. But now his presence mattered. "He was getting away from the people," Richard said. "And I used to tell him, 'Cesar, you know, we have contracts and everything but . . . you're staying away from the people. They're complaining. They want to see you.' . . . Well, he'd make all kinds of excuses."

Cesar was focused on his latest project and the next fight. He wasn't accustomed to having workers complain to him about the union. He had patience for their complaints about others—but not about his own operation. He rationalized their anger and set out to deflect it: "I was thinking this morning, I got up at 6 o'clock, it was colder then hell. Workers going to work at 7--no amount of money is going to make that worker feel good when the weather is very cold. Or very hot. So when they react, who do they react against? They don't react against the employer. Many times they react against the union. When the union wasn't there, they didn't react. So our job is to make damn sure they know who to react against."

Frustrated with the Delano workers, Chavez found enlightenment in Salinas, at the "liberated ranches" where workers had taken matters into their own hands with the tortuga. More militant from the start, the vegetable workers had embraced the power of the ranch committees and needed no encouragement to turn their anger against the employer. They willfully violated the contract to show the foremen they no longer could exert the kind of unilateral power they had enjoyed in the past. "Finally, the vegetable people began to make us understand what the hell was going on!" Chavez exclaimed, recounting with delight to a group of boycotters the experience of the union in Salinas.

Richard, the practical builder, saw the need to adapt to peacetime, to stop demonizing the growers, and to live by the contracts. "I said, 'Cesar, that tortuga is going to come back and kick us right in the teeth, you know.' And they thought it was very funny. Because they had the growers by the balls. A little slowdown and the grower goes berserk, he doesn't know what to do." The union should let growers fire the workers who willfully violated the contract, Richard said.

He warned his brother the grape workers did not believe in *la causa* the way Cesar thought they did. The union was turning them off. In the Delano hiring hall, Richard bent the rules. While he was in charge of the other field offices, he encouraged others to follow suit. Cesar responded by moving Richard out of Delano.

The Filipino workers were even unhappier than the Mexicans; they resented the hiring halls and felt they were treated like second-class citizens. Larry Itliong, who had launched the grape strike and hung in despite his ongoing differences with Chavez, finally resigned in frustration in October 1971. He was no longer willing to put up with the treatment he had suffered for several years, and he denounced the "brain trust" that surrounded Chavez.

Others warned Chavez as well, and he greeted their critiques with equal disdain. Monsignor Roger Mahony, who had played a key role in the negotiations with both the grape and vegetable growers, traveled throughout the San Joaquin Valley and became concerned. "I thought you should be aware of the increasing animosity towards the UFWOC efforts, in particular by many Mexican-American groups in our parishes," he wrote Chavez. The ratification votes had been rammed through, workers did not understand how the union operated, and the hiring halls were staffed largely by young, inexperienced volunteers. "I am bringing this to your attention because of the very wide-spread resentment. In all honesty, I can say that we never came across one single parish in the Diocese in which any group of Mexican-Americans voiced support for the unionization efforts."

Chavez's response was curt: "I have your letter. I was very surprised at the contents. You must know things that I don't."

He dismissed the complaints as grower propaganda, feeding on the bad attitude of a small group of ungrateful workers. There was no shortage of people eager to deliver an upbeat message and assure Chavez that workers loved the union. In fact, many workers angry with the union policies still worshipped Cesar and believed the problems stemmed from inept staff. If only Cesar knew, they said, he would fix the problems.

The young Anglo volunteers running the hiring halls often had little if any experience in the fields or knowledge of agriculture. Chavez moved his staff around often, and each new person felt the need to "rewrite the contract," Mahony reported to the bishops' committee. Growers had long lists of complaints about the staff's attitude, lack of experience, and lack of authority. When problems arose, "no one at the local level has the authority to make decisions; in all cases, Cesar or Richard must be contacted."

Compounding the problem, the union operated like a fire department: whenever a new alarm went off, Chavez shifted everyone to help with the latest crisis. In the spring of 1972, between the Phoenix fast, the lettuce strike and boycott, and the presidential primary in California, "it was almost impossible to locate any top union leader," Mahony wrote. "Local union operations were virtually abandoned." He wrote to Chavez again with growing alarm about arrogant and inept young personnel in the hiring halls.

Chavez responded this time at greater length. Growers were not complaining to the union, Chavez said, but only to the bishops. He dismissed the grievances as a strategy to strengthen the growers' negotiating position when the contracts came up for renewal. Mahony was so concerned by this response that he appealed immediately to Bill Kircher: "Something has to be done at the local hiring hall level to get this union functioning, or I am afraid they are all finished. There are so many problems at the local level you cannot believe it."

Despite Chavez's claim, growers did complain to the union. In Salinas, Andy D'Arrigo, one of only four vegetable growers who had signed a UFWOC contract, wrote in frustration when he could not reach Richard in June 1972 after repeated calls. The union had been unable to provide D'Arrigo with enough workers, so he was allowed to bring in labor contractors. The union workers harassed the labor contractors. The contractors now refused to work for him, and he was losing crops. He had scrapped plans to expand and would instead plant fewer fields next season. "Why is there such hostility on the part of this local office to the extent that without even taking the time to seek out the existing facts that hell is being raised first?" D'Arrigo wrote to Richard. "What are you trying to prove?"

In Coachella, grape grower Keene Larson wrote to Chavez in bewilderment. The first two years, he had enjoyed a good relationship with the union office. The union raised valid complaints, like the lack of clean toilets, and he took corrective action. Larson could live with the frustrations of the hiring hall, but not with the constant harassment. He had even been ordered out of his own vineyard by a UFWOC volunteer. His time in the fields was what made his grapes so sweet, said Larson. "It is as if the union were at war with me. This kind of action has been unreasonable, capricious, and hostile," he wrote to Chavez, appealing for help. "The worker, the union and management are like a troika . . . in the final sense, we all 3 must live off the vine."

Lionel Steinberg was among the union's biggest supporters, and his large ranch attracted some of the union's strongest worker-leaders. Because he had signed first, his wages went up to $1.90 an hour while his competitors were paying only $1.75. He, too, encountered endless frustration dealing with the local union office. "There is not one grower that I know who would have a good word to say for the Coachella Valley UFWOC organization," Steinberg wrote to Chavez. He copied the letter to Mahony, adding: "While Cesar is busy elsewhere in the nation, he has several on-the-ground organizers who are destroying all the good work that we all did together."

Howard Marguleas, head of the large Tenneco ranch, had been an early supporter of the union. "I've never been so disgusted," Marguleas said about the union's operation. Families returned to Coachella for the grape season and had to pay eight months' back dues, more than $100 per family, before they could start work. His company policy was that no one worked in the fields over age sixty-five; the union grieved the rule and he had to hire Filipinos in their eighties, despite medical exams that suggested the work could be dangerous for their health. He put in an order for eighty people, and only fourteen showed up.

The final straw came in the fall of 1972. Contracts gave the union the unilateral right to decide who was a member in good standing. Only members could work on union ranches. If the union required members to skip work to attend a Sacramento rally or a Salinas picket line, anyone who refused lost union seniority and faced fines and even expulsion. Negotiations with the new owners of the Schenley ranch, site of the union's first contract, had broken down. The union called a strike at what was now called the White River Ranch and ordered workers under contract at other vineyards to take time off from work and to join the strike lines at White River. Hollis Roberts discovered one morning that he had no crews because 657 of his workers had been ordered to picket at White River. The work stoppage cost Roberts $200,000 a day. Marguleas faced a similar situation, a walkout that shut down his Ducor Ranch with no warning.

Chavez stubbornly tuned out the increasing chorus of complaints. Once he took a position, he rarely if ever backed down.

Word of problems trickled down to the boycott staff in California. In anticipation of a conference at La Paz, the San Francisco boycott office staff sent Chavez a letter that enumerated complaints they had heard and asked him to address each one. Chavez responded by opening the conference with a withering, personal attack on the principal author of the letter, a passionate twenty-six-year-old volunteer named Kit Bricca.

Bricca had been teaching third grade to Mexican American kids in East Los Angeles in the late 1960s and watching their older brothers come home from Vietnam in body bags. In 1969, Bricca went to a Joan Baez concert where Baez's husband, David Harris, talked about draft resistance. Bricca went home and tore up his draft card. He moved to the Institute for the Study of Non-Violence in the Bay Area, founded by Baez and Harris, and worked with a group of draft resistors to prepare their appeals. One by one, his friends ended up in jail. Bricca volunteered to help on the grape boycott while he waited. His case was never called. He rose within the boycott ranks to run the Bay Area boycott, supervising twenty full-time staff. He had made frequent trips to Delano and was at Forty Acres when the contracts were signed in July 1970. At that moment all things seemed possible; a national union no longer seemed a dream. Farmworkers from around the world came to visit for inspiration. Then the union moved to La Paz, and Bricca began to see problems. He felt the union leaders were losing touch, far from the fields.

"According to the report, there's a lot of concern in San Francisco because the contracts are not being enforced," Chavez said to the boycotters assembled at La Paz in December 1971. He read from Bricca's letter a list of familiar complaints: Grievances were not being promptly handled, back dues were a problem ("I don't know what that issue is," Chavez commented), the medical plan did not pay claims promptly, Chavez was isolated in La Paz and had lost touch with the workers, the "brain trust (Chatfield and Ganz)" had too much power, and there was no room for complaint in the union. "These are all strictly grower lines," Chavez said. He called up various union officers who rebutted the charges and attacked Bricca.

Bricca walked around the hills of La Paz, crying. He asked Ganz to offer Chavez an apology. After the conference ended, Chavez met with the San Francisco boycotters. He told them he felt like there was some sort of cancer he had to stop before it destroyed the union. He referred to the purge in the summer of 1967, when the Teatro left, and said there had been a group in the Bay Area that tried to take over the union. He was afraid that might be happening again, Chavez said. He said he didn't care if everyone left and he started all over—he was determined to do it the right way. Complaints from the boycotters ceased.

By the end of 1972, Richard Chavez was sure the union would lose the contracts when they expired in April. There were already signs of Teamster organizers in the fields. As he grew more worried, he badgered his brother. "Finally one day, we had a blow out," he recounted to Levy. Richard shouted at Cesar, stomped around, and grew so angry he began to throw things around Cesar's office. "I said 'Okay, goddamn it, it's coming, we're going to lose the goddamn contracts, there's no way we can save them now.' . . . I said, 'Screw you, I'm going to quit, I'm not going to stay with this outfit anymore.'"

Richard left Delano, and Huerta went along. They had two young daughters, and their relationship had turned into another source of tension, a pressure point Cesar could use. He excelled at playing people against one another and knew he could count on getting a rise out of Richard by accusing him of bending to Dolores's will. Cesar's fights with Dolores had become legendary; they were frequent, loud, and personal. Her relationship with his brother became more grist for their verbal sparring. In December 1972, Huerta worked in Chavez's office, an assignment that lasted barely a month. He gave her directions on how to prepare for contract negotiations along with specifics on how to fix cracks in the outside pipes— "take gunny sack and baling wire that should do it"—and criticized her child care arrangements. They fought about Richard. "If the pressure in my office is unbearable let me know," Chavez wrote to her. "The very least clean your desk and let me know if you're quitting. Maybe you should be assigned to something not so demanding as my office—the problem of accountability and sticking with something is too much for you."

Richard and Dolores were gone from the union only a short time. Both brothers felt bad. Cesar sent word and asked what would make Richard come back. Richard said he wanted a meeting with all the top people. "I want to tell everybody what's happening, because you don't listen to me. You always say that I'm crazy, that it's not happening. That . . . all the people love us and that all the people are content and everything, and it's not, you know."

They met in Santa Maria and had one more emotional argument in front of the other union leaders. Cesar told Richard things were not going to change and suggested he go out on the boycott. Richard jumped at the option and headed for New York.

The Teamsters prepared to make their move. At the invitation of Teamster president Frank Fitzsimmons, the bishops' committee met with leaders of the Western Conference of Teamsters at the union's California headquarters. Teamster leaders questioned the bishops about Chavez, his commitment to a "social movement," and the difficulties administering the grape contracts. "It was evident that the decision had been made [by the Teamsters] to enter the farm labor field seriously once again," Mahony reported.

At La Paz, Chavez was philosophical. He told Mahony he was confident about renegotiating the grape contracts, just a few days after he explained to a group of students that he expected the growers to try not to sign again. "There's a lot of forces against us," Chavez said. "If we make it, it's going to be a great miracle. The moment we get over the hump, the moment the growers begin to accept the union as just another headache they have to deal with, and the workers begin to feel secure in that change of mentality, from then on, it's just a mechanical thing from there on. The excitement's going to pass. I'd like to be alive to see that day. It's going to take a long time."

On March 16, 1973, Keene Larson wired Bishop Donnelly, chair of the bishops' committee, to tell him the Teamsters were invading the Coachella fields. Donnelly called Kircher, who called Chavez, who said to send the message back to Larson that if he wanted to sign with the Teamsters, "we'll come beat their brains out."

John Giumarra called Chavez the same afternoon. He had returned home after two days to find Teamsters all over his fields. Chavez delivered the same message: if this was a negotiating ploy, Giumarra would get his brains beaten out. Giumarra assured Chavez he was genuinely concerned and wanted to avoid problems, and he urged that they start negotiations as soon as possible: "This Teamster thing in the Coachella Valley . . . it's a spreading cancer." Chavez said he wanted to negotiate a master contract with the whole industry, and Giumarra said he would convene a meeting.

He wasted no time. They met at on April 5 at the Riviera Hotel in Palm Springs. Giumarra led off by talking about the hiring hall: "I can't emphasize enough the alienation it causes on all sides." It was disruptive and disorderly, wasted time, and angered people by making them apply for jobs they already had.

"We can prove beyond a doubt that the hiring hall works," Chavez retorted. "You've had three years of the hiring hall and you made money. We're not going to give it up."

Giumarra and Martin Zaninovich said that their foremen still did the hiring—they put together crews and sent them to the hiring hall so they could be dispatched back to the ranch. "It's a paper mill," Zaninovich said.

"We're telling you, the workers want the hiring hall," Chavez asserted.

"Are you sure?" Zaninovich challenged.

Giumarra tried to reason. He articulated the union's goal—to make sure labor contractors did not return and to police seniority—and suggested they could find ways to modify the hiring hall to make the system work more efficiently. Cohen thought they were making progress toward compromise, but Chavez kept deflecting the conversation into other areas. The meeting ended with no agreements other than meet again. The Coachella contracts expired in ten days.

Richard had no doubt when he left for the boycott in New York that the Teamsters would take the contracts away, and he believed the union was to blame. "We didn't do proper administration," he told Levy. "We did many mistakes, you know . . . We did a terrible job. Sure the growers are bad, you know, but we also made a lot of mistakes and we could have corrected them, and we didn't."

Richard's comments were the only passages that Cesar censored from Levy's book.

CHAPTER 23

The Perfect Villain

Every little thing that happens we blame the Teamsters for, because, we can! . . .
it's just like magic.

Chavez liked to call himself the leader of the "non-violent Viet Cong."
His guerilla movement depended on neither money nor contracts, he
said. He needed only three ingredients to succeed: "First of all, a very
disciplined group about work . . . number two, we have the people with
us . . . number three, we have the villain."

In the spring of 1973, he lost the grape contracts and gained the
perfect villain.

On April 10, five days before the first contracts expired, Chavez's religious and political allies gathered in the Coachella Valley to mount a
last-ditch show of force in hopes of scaring off the Teamsters. Led by
Monsignor Higgins, they conducted a carefully orchestrated election.
Chris Hartmire marked off teams on his clipboard as he paired priests
with farmworkers and sent them into the fields to hand out ballots. They
were directed to crews where the union's support was strongest. Higgins,
ostensibly neutral, presided over a spectacle with an outcome more
predetermined than the vote he had helped sway at Interharvest. "We
have come to the Coachella Valley because we believe in justice for farmworkers," Higgins declared in his booming voice. "Because we believe
that farmworkers should be represented by a union they believe in."

Higgins announced the results: United Farm Workers 795, Teamsters
80, no union 78. "It is clear to us in the light of these figures that the vast
majority of farmworkers in the Coachella Valley want to be represented

by Cesar Chavez's United Farm Workers union," he said. U.S. Rep. Edward Roybal, one of several Democratic politicians on hand, described the reception in the fields: "The first thing they said to us was 'Viva Chavez!'" Bill Kircher denounced the Teamsters and pledged the full support of the AFL-CIO in the labor strife that now seemed imminent.

Two days later, Chavez arrived at a union rally in the Coachella high school auditorium, accompanied by nine security guards with telltale bulges under their jackets that the Riverside sheriff deputies spotted at once. After a short speech, Chavez asked everyone in favor of authorizing a strike to stand, and the workers rose to their feet.

Over the next few days, he finalized contract renewals with Lionel Steinberg and Keene Larson. The first growers to sign with the union three years earlier were the only ones to re-up; everyone else signed with the Teamsters. Unlike the Teamsters' hastily written and poorly received 1970 Salinas contracts, these pacts included a 15 percent wage increase, health and welfare benefits, and four paid holidays. The issue for the growers, as they had made clear, was not financial. Under the Teamster contracts, growers hired their workers directly.

The Coachella contracts expired on Palm Sunday. The strike began Monday. "They've got the contracts, we've got the people," Chavez repeated confidently many times. The accuracy of his contention was never tested; instead, the Teamsters, a union notorious for violence and corruption, became the perfect foil to Chavez's nonviolent brigade.

To help growers harvest the grapes and shield workers from the taunts and threats of UFW pickets, the Teamsters hired the largest, loudest thugs they could find and paid each one $67.50 a day to set up a counterpicket. The Teamsters arrived every morning on a flatbed truck the local deputies dubbed the "Animal Wagon." They were armed with chains, clubs, knives, and baseball bats. They forced UFW cars off the road, shouted threats and insults, and beat up UFW supporters. When UFW pickets assembled outside a field, the Teamsters formed a counterpicket, and then sheriff's deputies formed a third line to keep the two sides apart. During the first week of the strike, the sheriff department's overtime bill was $91,235.

Chavez visited the picket line and walked silently between the two sides, each trying to drown out the other: "Chavez si! Teamsters no!" answered by "Teamsters si! Chavez no!" As Chavez walked the gauntlet, the 250-pound goons towered over the diminutive leader and screamed crude insults: "You're nothing but a rotten Commie! You rotten bum! I can smell you from here!"

Chavez had found a villain even better than the growers. "Every little thing that happens we blame the Teamsters for, because, we can!" he exclaimed. "We're safe you know, we're outside. And it's really, I mean, it's just like magic . . . We've got this great villain, the Teamsters, and everything that's wrong is because of the Teamsters . . . The Teamsters and the growers become one and the same, you put them together, tie them together, and there's no way they can get out of that fix, there's no way!"

A core group of grape workers supported the strike and left the vineyards, but the picket lines were primarily staffed by workers and volunteers from outside Coachella, including a large contingent from Salinas. The union staged dramatic confrontations that took full advantage of the Teamster thugs. Scene after scene was captured on tape by a film crew that Chavez had dispatched to Coachella before the strike began. Anticipating a summer of unrest, Chavez had instructed a young filmmaker working for the union to spend the next six months shooting a documentary in the California vineyards. Until they were unmasked, the crew masqueraded as news reporters and gained damning footage of Teamsters and growers.

The opinions of rank-and-file workers rarely surfaced amid the vivid demonstrations of the Teamsters' brute force. To the public, the workers' support for Chavez became a given. In private, Chavez said complaints about the hiring hall were an excuse for growers to ditch the union. "They had to pick on something," he explained to Levy. "The hiring hall becomes an issue when the employer doesn't want to cooperate. If the employer wants to cooperate, it works beautifully . . . the issue is, just among us chickens, you know, who's going to control the workforce." He also saw racism in the collusion between the growers and the Teamsters. "A lot has to do with this great fear that we're a movement, not a union. But really, deep roots lie in the racism of both groups. We are a non-white union . . . They have been the superior race, not only race-wise but economic-wise. They have had total say over the work force."

The UFW's religious supporters offered the ideal contrast to the Teamster goons. Hartmire brought religious leaders from around the country to Coachella to bear witness, and the Teamsters obligingly staged displays of violence that rendered the question of the workers' choice moot. A UFW supporter's trailer was burnt to the ground. A Teamster leader broke the nose of a priest while he was being interviewed in a diner by a *Wall Street Journal* reporter.

A group of United Church of Christ delegates discussed the strike during their annual assembly in St. Louis, Missouri. They offered to take up a collection and send money. Send people instead, Hartmire told John Moyer, who was spearheading the UCC effort. The ministers chartered a plane, left St. Louis late at night, and arrived in Coachella before dawn, in time to observe Teamster goons gathering up their weapons. When the visitors arrived at the park where the strikers assembled every morning, the bleary-eyed clergy were welcomed with cheers, tears, and hugs. They split up to visit picket lines, and one group witnessed Teamsters run a UFW car off the road, pull the picketers out, and beat them. "I can say truthfully that you couldn't have been here at a better time," Chavez somberly told the ninety-five delegates after they reassembled that after-noon. "Things have really escalated. The tensions as you can see are very high and the violence is rampant at this point."

Chavez ran down the incidents of the past three days—six men hospi-talized, thirteen injured, one house burned down, fifteen cars stopped and people dragged out and beaten. "A month and a half ago, a month ago, a week ago, people on the picket line hadn't been in a strike before. And they're now striking and they're being asked to change their life radically and to make this very difficult commitment to non-violence . . . Our main concern right now is not in winning the strike, although we'd like to. The most important thing today, and it's going to be for the next few days, is to be able to remain on those picket lines, to remain non-violent, but not to become frightened."

Sterling Cary, president of the National Council of Churches, responded on behalf of the clergy who had journeyed to Coachella to reassure the farmworkers they were not alone: "Your struggle is our struggle. It is the struggle of America itself as America tries to finds ways to be on the side of those who are locked out of the system."

Cheers greeted the United Church of Christ delegates when they marched into the St. Louis assembly forty-eight hours after they had departed, sleepless but exhilarated. They delivered emotional accounts of the valiant struggle of the Chavistas. Then the "Coachella 95" returned home to twenty-five different states, and each formed a UFWOC support group.

The more important Delano contracts could still be salvaged, but Chavez was determined to negotiate on his terms. He foresaw victory no matter the outcome: if they lost the contracts, another boycott would force the growers to come crawling back.

"Organizing is a gamble," Chavez told Moyer, who interviewed the union president during a car ride, sitting in the backseat with Boycott and Huelga as they slurped up ice cream cones. "I bet there are more failures in organizing than in any other endeavor you can think of. It's a very risky business."

Chavez made several gambles during the 1973 strike that would shape the future of his union. The first was a deal with AFL-CIO president George Meany. Meany had denounced the Teamsters' raid on the grape contracts as "tantamount to strike breaking," and Chavez asked for financial help. Meany agreed, on one condition: Chavez would push for state legislation to govern the rights of farmworkers to organize. Meany wanted to put an end to the unrest and free-for-all in the fields.

Chavez did not want a law; he much preferred to operate as a nonviolent guerilla force. But he needed money for a strike fund, and advocating a law when Ronald Reagan was governor of California seemed a safe bet. Reagan would never sign a law unfavorable to his agribusiness allies. Chavez turned to Cohen and told him to start drafting a law that incorporated several key principles on which they would not compromise.

Cohen became Chavez's gambling partner all summer—in courtrooms, on picket lines, and at the negotiating table. For Cohen, Chavez's willingness to take risks made the lawyer's job immensely appealing. Both men loved the action, and the bond between them had grown as each came to appreciate the other's talents. Cohen proved masterful at devising strategies to make the law work for the union, turning even defensive situations into offensive advantages. "Cesar has told me I fit the union like a glove," Cohen wrote in his journal. The young attorney's mind was always racing ahead, and he often spoke as fast as he thought. He had been drawn to the law by heroic attorneys in *To Kill a Mockingbird* and *Anatomy of a Murder*. His favorite movie was *McCabe and Mrs. Miller*, about a gambler who teams up with a prostitute to run a brothel. Cohen looked the part of the angry young crusader, shirttail hanging out, hair unkempt, toothpicks in his mouth since he had given up smoking. He reveled in defying conventional wisdom and did not feel bound by legal tradition or strictures. He was precisely the type of lawyer Chavez wanted, and one of the very few outside professionals whose expertise Chavez valued.

"Must gamble daily," Cohen wrote down as he tried to analyze Chavez's style and success. Chavez could gamble, Cohen noted, because there was always a way to turn a loss into a victory. The strike in Coachella offered a prime example—the Teamster war generated an outpouring of public support. "Cesar has been able to breed amazing confidence in some of us who naturally believe and act on the proposition that there is no ill from which some good will not flow."

Cohen's legal gambits played an increasingly important role in Chavez's strategy. Shortly before the strike began, the union had won a major victory in the highest court of California. After more than two years of appeals, the Supreme Court threw out the injunctions that had ended the 1970 Salinas lettuce strike. The court concluded the vegetable growers had signed sweetheart contracts with the Teamsters with no input from workers, who clearly preferred the UFW. Therefore, no jurisdictional dispute existed. "The crippling injunction is dissolved," Chavez declared. "Salinas is a prime example of how the politics of a local community interfere with the courts being able to administer this justice. We are very, very disturbed because had the courts been able to administer justice equally . . . we would have won the fight two years ago."

As soon as the decision was announced, the union went on the legal offensive. Based on a novel theory promulgated by Bill Carder, the UFW sued under federal antitrust laws, accusing the Teamsters and growers of colluding to artificially depress wages for farmworkers. The suit had the potential to cost growers and the Teamsters millions of dollars and force them to divulge sensitive information during depositions and interrogatories.

But Chavez had to focus on the crisis in the vineyards before he could return to Salinas. With a $1.6 million strike fund from the AFL-CIO, the union paid pickets $75 a week. By June they had increased pay to $90, and still the picket lines were relatively thin. When the filmmakers shot footage of farmworkers shouting "Viva la huelga!" as they were carted off to jail, the arrestees came from Salinas. At ranches where the union still had contracts, such as the Almaden winery, workers were ordered to rotate two-week stints on the picket lines as a condition of employment.

By July the grape season was over in Coachella. The conflict followed the harvest north into the San Joaquin Valley, where the union faced a more hostile legal system and draconian anti-picketing injunctions. Cohen suggested another legal gamble that Chavez quickly embraced: civil disobedience and mass arrests. In law school, Cohen had studied a recent California Supreme Court decision that established the principle that one could challenge the constitutionality of an injunction by violating the ruling. The tactic carried risk: a loss brought contempt-of-court charges that could carry severe penalties. But a victory would swiftly overturn a bad injunction, much faster than through standard appeals.

In July, hundreds of workers and supporters openly defied anti-picketing injunctions in the vineyards of the San Joaquin Valley. They filled the jails, first in Kern County, then Tulare, then Fresno. The protest-ers refused to post bail, and the jails overflowed. When they were released, many returned to the picket lines to be arrested again. Sheriff's depart-ments quickly exhausted their overtime budgets and looked frantically for places to house the prisoners. While Teamster leaders signed more contracts and bragged they had 221 growers, Chavez hailed the UFW pickets in jail as true heroes, willing to sacrifice for others. "This is our entire life," Chavez told a rally in a Delano park. "We have nothing else to live for."

Eighty-five priests and religious women attending an International Symposium on Ignatian Spirituality in San Francisco decided to go to Fresno and join the picket lines; half of them volunteered to go to jail. They were soon joined by Dorothy Day, the seventy-six-year-old founder of the Catholic Worker movement, one of 443 arrested as they violated an injunction that limited pickets to one every hundred feet. In her olive-green jailhouse dress and wide-brimmed hat, Day explained why she had flown across the country to go to jail: "I think Cesar Chavez and his United Farm Workers union is the most important thing that has happened to the U.S. labor movement. The working poor in the fields have banded together through free choice to work out their own destiny." She talked about Chavez's sacrifice, his humble lifestyle, and her visits to his house, which lacked the trappings customarily associ-ated with labor leaders.

A recalcitrant judge refused to release Day and the other prisoners from out of town. The Fresno jail took on a festive air, with an all-night prayer vigil, a twenty-four-hour fast, and celebrity guests. Chavez climbed on a chair in the barracks-style jail and thanked the prisoners for their sacrifice. The union was at a crossroads, Chavez said, that would deter-mine whether it survived. Joan Baez sang in the prison courtyard, and Daniel Ellsberg offered updates on the bombing in Cambodia. All the women signed Day's dress in marker, and she asked to keep the prison garb as a souvenir. When the prisoners finally were set free after two weeks, they celebrated mass with singing and huelga chants. With a flourish, Chavez added his signature to Day's prison dress.

At the negotiating table, Chavez had undertaken another gamble when the expiration of the Delano contracts neared. The Delano grow-ers had suffered for five years through the first strike and boycott, and they badly wanted to avoid a repeat. But they needed changes in the hiring hall. John Giumarra Jr. had again taken the lead. Cohen met alone with Giumarra and felt they made good progress on structuring a compromise.

Ten days before the contracts expired, Chavez was suddenly optimistic. A boycott leader had called to report that several major chains in Los Angeles had agreed to tell Giumarra they would not carry his grapes without a UFW contract. "It's all over!" Chavez announced, beaming, to the group working on contract language in a Bakersfield hotel room. He thought they now had the leverage they needed.

He left a few days later on a four-day whirlwind tour of Midwest cities, making speeches to raise money and support for the boycott. Chavez spoke to packed crowds in Michigan and Ohio. He marveled at how the strike helped educate the workers, which he called the most difficult part of his job. "We've learned that there's a great difference between a member who has never been on the picket line and had a contract handed to him and a member that had to fight for his contract," Chavez said at a Cleveland rally. The picket line was the greatest educational tool he knew. "They have learned more about concern and solidarity than they would have learned if we had put them in a school for three years. I have never seen love develop among human beings as I do on the picket line."

Chavez was buoyed by his reception. Around the country, millions of people felt good about themselves because they refused to buy grapes, walked on a picket line, or donated to the union. "I was talking to a group of supporters, one of them said, 'Hell, you know it's our strike, too. We've got a lot of years invested in it,'" Chavez recounted on his return to Delano. "So it seems to me that the concern comes from the recognition that if we were to lose here this would be the end to a very important and a very unique movement among farmworkers."

He had lost thirty-one contracts in Coachella, twenty in Lamont, and fifty small ones in Fresno. His optimism about the twenty-nine Delano contracts dimmed. But the losses did not faze Chavez. "It's not that serious, that they are going to destroy our union," he said. "All we have to do is go back to the pre-contract days." The strain on the union, he said, was balanced by the lift from "the tremendous support that we get throughout the country."

Chavez wanted the growers to come as supplicants, the way they had in 1970. If it took another boycott to beat them into submission, he saw advantages to that strategy. In the final negotiation session with the Delano growers, Chavez made a gamble that caught even Cohen by surprise.

Cohen had made good progress. He was so confident they were about to sign a deal that he had called for a typewriter at the hotel to finalize contract language. A half dozen growers, twenty-one farmworkers, and union leaders began to negotiate the evening before the deadline, prepared to work through the night. They went clause by clause, and Cohen checked off each one on his list as they reached agreement. After a break, they resumed negotiations just after midnight, and came to the section on housing. Chavez took over.

He attacked the growers for the conditions in their labor camps, in particular for allowing gambling on cockfights and prostitutes to visit. "We have a responsibility to the membership to change the quality of life," Chavez said in a speech that became known to his baffled aides as the "whores in the camps" attack. "There's a hell of a lot of gambling that results in fights and deaths. The foremen make money from controlling gambling, chicken fights, prostitutes . . . We feel we have to change the quality of the life in the camps."

After his tirade, talks fell apart. Chavez declared they would not budge on the hiring hall. "In 1969, we waited one more year just for our hiring hall," he told the growers. "You have no choice, the die is cast. We have certain things we need in this contract. You did OK for three years, and you're throwing it away. This industry has no way to go but with us." When the growers came back, Chavez vowed, "we'll screw them to the ground and they can go to hell." This time, though, the growers did have an alternative. Giumarra and Zaninovich were not enamored of the Teamsters or the prospect of another boycott. They would have preferred to avoid further strife and stay with the UFW, but not at any cost.

The talks that had been expected to go through the night recessed. The next morning, Chavez predicted the boycott would force growers to sign in early 1974. He did a Zorro imitation, jumping on a table and brandishing an imaginary sword. Marshall Ganz began to list the boycott cities where they would need to send more people. "They're going after our balls," Chavez said as they waited for the last formal session. "I don't know about you guys but for the few years I have left, I don't want to go around without them."

Shouts of "huelga" and "boycott" filled the room as the talks officially ended. "Brothers and sisters, if you're ready for the strike, let's go," Chavez said to the farmworkers. "They won't be able to sell their grapes," he said confidently.

Chavez's performance was typical of the way he treated the grape growers, who had come to expect he would dress them down at every opportunity. "He knows how to make them feel small," observed the union's business manager, Jack Quigley, one of many who believed the contracts could have been saved. The "whores in the camp" speech left Cohen baffled and angry. Not only had Chavez's actions cost the UFW most of its members, but he had also signaled that he did not necessarily share the same priorities and agenda as key members of his team.

Those differences, however, were quickly submerged in the strike and escalating violence in the fields of the San Joaquin Valley, where Chavez found his new villain. The Teamsters had not reprised their thug tactics as the harvest moved north, but they did not need to. Growers had their own security, and guns were common. Unlike the sheriffs in Coachella, law enforcement officials in Kern and Tulare counties were openly hostile to the farmworkers union. They taunted, harassed, tear-gassed, and occasionally beat the UFW pickets.

"We charge that the arming of the strikebreakers and the growers is with the consent and with the knowledge and with the encouragement of [Tulare County] Sheriff Wiley," Chavez said angrily at a Delano press conference after a picketer was shot in the shoulder. "They have known that the men are armed inside the fields and they've done absolutely nothing to try to correct the situation and take the guns and the rifles away from them."

Union supporters sent dozens of telegrams demanding that the U.S. Justice Department investigate alleged civil rights violations. Cohen brought witnesses to the FBI and the Justice Department's civil rights division, charging local authorities stood by and did nothing to keep order or stop attacks.

"In Kern County, we've had now a series of beatings by the police," Chavez said. "They have very consistently used profanity against men and women on the picket line . . . that they're going to kill them and that they're no good son of a bitches and that they're Mexican greasers. It is, I think, to the everlasting glory of the farmworkers that they've been able to hold back and to continue to espouse the whole idea of nonviolence."

In the early hours of August 15, a group of drunken men entered the Smoke House in Lamont, and a barroom brawl ensued. The bartender called police, and three sheriff's deputies responded. A beer bottle thrown by Nagi Moshin Daifullah hit Deputy Gilbert Cooper in the face, and he chased Daifullah into the street and struck him with his flashlight.

Daifullah, twenty-four, fell from the curb headfirst, and never regained consciousness. He died at 1:00 A.M. from a massive concussion.

Daifullah turned out to be a UFW striker; overnight he became a martyr. The police reported that the deputy hit Daifullah on the shoulder and he fell on his head, but Cohen announced he had witnesses who saw the officer hit Daifullah on the head. He would only identify the witnesses to federal Justice Department officials, Cohen said, because he did not trust the local police. Cohen worked the phones, talking to witnesses, arranging to have the body released to the custody of the union, and calling Sen. Edward Kennedy's office to initiate a federal probe. In the end, there was scant evidence to challenge the official report, but that mattered little.

Daifullah had come to the United States hoping to study medicine but ended up working in the fields. He had written his father in Yemen, describing the brutal conditions for immigrant farmworkers: ten men sleeping in a room, small portions of poor food, pesticides in the fields, labor contractors treating workers like virtual slaves. Then Daifullah wrote home about helping organize workers to join a revolution led by a man who did nothing but work for his cause, had no outside life, wore simple clothes, ate no meat, and earned but $5 a week. "In comparison to other leaders, he most resembles the great Indian leader Gandhi," Daifullah wrote. "Finally, father, we are participants in a revolution. The revolution is strong and moving along the path to victory."

Chavez announced he would fast for three days to honor the martyred Daifullah and asked all UFW members, strikers, staff and friends of the movement to join him. More than five thousand people marched through Delano behind the casket of the young farmworker, carrying black-and-white union flags. The traditional three-color banner wrapped the casket.

On August 16, sixty-year-old Juan de la Cruz was walking a UFW picket line with his wife when shots were fired from a passing pickup truck. De la Cruz died in surgery the same day. The sheriff arrested two men and charged them with homicide. Charges were later dismissed.

Once again, thousands of mourners took to the streets. "He was a humble farmworker," Chavez said in his eulogy. "And yet in his dying, thousands of people have come to pay honor to his life."

During a candlelight procession the night before, Chavez said he thought back to the very early days, when people like de la Cruz believed in the union long before contracts had seemed a realistic possibility. "We live in the midst of people who hate and fear us. They have worked hard to keep us in our place. They will spend millions more to destroy our union. But we do not have to make ourselves small by hating and fearing them in return . . . We are going to win. It is just a matter of time."

The week of the funerals, the U.S. Attorney General's office received about three thousand letters, many from religious organizations, demanding the Justice Department intervene to protect the striking farmworkers. Chavez announced he would have to call off the strike until the federal government guaranteed the safety of the picketers. Justice Department memos recorded no request for protection from Chavez. Officials noted that Chavez was out of money, and they concluded he was using the safety issue as an excuse to end a losing strike

Chavez blamed police for colluding with growers, making allegations he felt no compunction to substantiate. "There have been over 200 cases of shootings. And we know the cops are behind it," Chavez said. His own son Fernando had ducked behind a parked car to escape bullets during a rock fight on a picket line. "So when the two people got killed, we knew the cops were behind it. They weren't pulling the triggers, but it was a plan. They were losing the strike. The only way they could do it was to shoot at us. And they had to have the agreement of the police. If the police had acted halfway reasonably, that strike would have been won."

Chavez ended the strike. The civil disobedience gambit had produced more than thirty-five hundred arrests and generated widespread sympathy for the union. "You have no idea how far we have brought the workers," he explained. "That is why when people ask if I am discouraged, how can I be discouraged? In 1962 people were afraid to even look at you, you know. Now they are not only not afraid of the flag, they accept the strike as an important part of their lives, then they are willing to go to jail . . . that kind of commitment you cannot destroy."

The union had just a handful of contracts. Interharvest was the only vegetable contract left; Steinberg and Larson in table grapes; one strawberry grower; eight wine grape growers. But as he lost members to the Teamsters, Chavez gained public esteem—and contributions. In February 1973 the union had collected slightly more than $30,000 in donations and ended the month $84,000 in the red. In July, donations exceeded $300,000, a record for a single month. In December, a direct mail appeal that included stories about Juan de la Cruz's funeral netted thousands more. The UAW, which had suspended contributions in 1971 because the UFW had large assets relative to its membership, resumed its help, sending $10,000 a week. By the end of 1973, the union had raised more than

$4.3 million since January and spent more than $5 million—an enormous sum for a tiny union with almost no members.

Chavez had bought recognition, empathy and support. From top labor leaders to nuns to housewives, thousands felt personally invested, emotionally and financially, in his success. He had also raised expectations. As he had long ago discovered, when people give money, they expect things in return.

Despite his commitment to Meany to press for legislation, Chavez was determined to operate on his own timetable. Asked when he thought the union might regain the contracts, Chavez answered: "We don't know. We don't have a time limit. We don't set time limits. This is our work. We're committed to do it the rest of our lives. It takes whatever it takes, we'll do it. It will be done."

CHAPTER 24

The Seeds Are Sown

We have demonstrated to the whole world our capacity for sacrifice. We have demonstrated for many years our willingness, our commitment, and our discipline for nonviolence, and even more important than that we have demonstrated to the whole world that nothing is going to stop us from getting our own union.

At the end of a marathon day presiding over the first constitutional convention of the United Farm Workers of America, Cesar Chavez paused to reflect on the historic occasion. After a celebratory evening of music and dancing, Chavez chatted in the early morning hours of September 22, 1973, with Jacques Levy. The union leader was pensive, expressing pleasure tinged with regret. On one hand, Chavez told Levy, the convention was a dream come true. Hundreds of farmworker delegates, debating resolutions, learning Robert's Rules of Order, building their own union. The next day, delegates would elect the first executive board, and that milestone would usher in what Chavez called a "so-called democracy." From now on, he said with resignation, his strongest colleagues would inevitably become his enemies.

Your best people always turn out to be the opposition, Chavez explained, because the strongest leaders have the most ambition. In this "so-called democracy," he would be forced to get rid of potential challengers, otherwise they would get rid of him. He would have to eliminate those who showed the greatest promise, and inevitably be left with the second-rate. "I don't like it," Chavez said. "It makes me puke." But he had no doubts: "It has to be done." The convention, he said, had sown the seeds.

Levy tried to reassure Chavez. Next week, the writer pointed out, the top union leaders would disperse to cities around the country to organize the boycott, a diaspora that would stymie potential opposition. Chavez shook his head. "No," he said, "the seed is there. It will not be stopped."

In public, Chavez displayed none of this concern. In a blue guayabera, an embroidered Mexican shirt, he reveled in the music and art commissioned for this special occasion. Religious and labor leaders came to speak and pay respect. Congratulatory telegrams poured in from around the world. Each speaker was escorted to the podium by a farmworker honor guard marching in a double line, while the rhythmic stomping of feet reinforced the applause. In substance and style, the event symbolized the triumph of the UFW's spirit. They had but ten contracts, had just buried two martyrs, faced war with the Teamsters, yet remained ebullient.

The delegates met in the Fresno convention center, which dwarfed the small social hall a few miles away where Chavez had held his first convention eleven years earlier. A giant 16-by-24-foot mural by a rising young talent, Carlos Almaraz, hung behind a podium draped with flags. The painting was in the style of the great Mexican muralists: Teamsters attacked farmworkers, who used picket signs as their shields, while the Virgen de Guadalupe protected workers, a small boy sold *El Malcriado*, Anglo supporters stood ready to help, and the word *huelga* was carried on the wind to the four corners of the earth.

More than a year had passed since the AFL-CIO approved a charter for the farmworkers, and the 1973 convention was the final step in the transition to become a full-fledged union. The UFW needed to elect an executive board and adopt a constitution. Delegates worked for seventeen hours on Friday, September 21, 1973, ten hours the next day, and then twenty-three hours on Sunday straight into Monday morning.

"We are the only ones that can determine whether we are going to win or lose," Chavez declared. "We have demonstrated to the whole world our capacity for sacrifice. We have demonstrated for many years our willingness, our commitment, and our discipline for nonviolence, and even more important than that we have demonstrated to the whole world that *nothing* is going to stop us from getting our own union." The applause went on for more than a minute, until Chavez motioned for the cheers to stop.

The strike and the violence of the summer of 1973 had forced the UFW to turn once more to "our court of last resort—to go to the American public and put the case before them," Chavez told the audience, reading a speech Jacques Levy had helped craft.

The constitution that delegates approved, section by section, had been printed at La Paz the night before the convention and rushed to Fresno—a timetable that ensured few would have time to analyze or question the document. Several who did, including Antonio Orendain, now effectively exiled in Texas and cut out of the leadership, saw that the constitution vested enormous power in the president and almost none in the rank-and-file workers or their elected representatives.

Chavez had drawn once again on his experience in the CSO, taking that group's constitution as a model of how not to do business. "It was so democratic that nothing could be done," Chavez explained a few years later. "One of the hang-ups of the formers or founders or drafters of that constitution was that they believed that power corrupts; they were misquoting Lord Acton who said not power corrupts but power *tends* to corrupt. They were a group of liberals mostly and in their wisdom they did not give the president or any officer any power to really do things. All the power was vested in the membership so that it became almost impossible to act."

When Chavez had drafted his first constitution in 1962 for the Farm Workers Association, he had been determined not to accept any outside funds and to make the union self-supporting. He used a preamble drawn from a papal encyclical and wrote the constitution for the farmworker members. When Chavez composed the new constitution in 1973, the union depended almost entirely on outside financial support. So he aimed much of the new document not at the farmworkers but at his wider public audience. He took particular care with the preamble, judging that the most likely section outsiders would read. "It doesn't speak to the members, it speaks to the public," he explained at a meeting with union staff, where he analyzed line by line how he had crafted the brief preamble:

> We, the Farm Workers of America, have tilled the soil, sown the seeds and harvested the crops. We have provided food in abundance for the people in the cities the nation and the world but have not had sufficient food for our own children.

"We're making a statement on justice in that paragraph," Chavez said.

> But despite our isolation, our sufferings, jailings, beatings and killings, we remain undaunted in our determination to build our Union as a bulwark against future exploitation.

"That comes from one of my favorite speeches in the beginning of the movement when I talked to the public. That was hope. Nothing but an expression of hope."

> We devoutly believe in the dignity of tilling the soil and tending the crops and reject the notion that farm labor is but a way station to a job in the factory and life in the city.

"Every time people say, 'Let's train farmworkers to get them out of that awful work in farm labor,' it always gripes me. I just can't stand it."

> And just as work on the land is arduous, so is the task of building a Union. We pledge to struggle as long as it takes to reach our goals.

"That came from a little speech that I prepared for the members, this is in 1966 . . . we were losing strikers, losing hope . . . I ended the speech by saying, 'If all of you leave, you can go, I don't give a shit. We'll win the strike if I have to be the only guy out there, if it takes me 30 years, I'll be out there with a fucking picket sign by myself. You guys can take off. Who needs frightened people. Take off, I don't need you. I'll do it by myself.' It rallied them."

The delegates adopted several substantive changes. They scrapped the $3.50 monthly dues in favor of a more traditional structure, 2 percent of income, which would provide more money to the union and eliminate fights about back dues. A second provision was far less traditional: volunteers who worked for the union more than six months would become members with certain voting privileges. Anyone who sacrificed for the movement should have the right to set policy, Chavez said. "Some of the best people we have working in the movement are not farmworkers. They're volunteers. And a lot of them are not brown or black, they're white . . . We have seen too many movements where they're used, and after a while they're taken for granted."

Chavez extended the same reasoning to his choices for the executive board: the majority did not come from the fields. In addition to Dolores Huerta and Gilbert Padilla, who had obtained waivers when first elected in 1963, Cesar invited his brother Richard to join the board. Chavez rounded out the slate with two of the Filipino leaders, Philip Vera Cruz and Peter Velasco, and a young black farmworker, Mack Lyons, who had been working for the union full-time since the DiGiorgio strike. For the "Anglo spot" on the board, Chavez tapped Marshall Ganz, who excelled as an organizer on the boycott and in the fields. Chavez had approached LeRoy Chatfield and Jim Drake, who both declined, believing that only farmworkers should serve on the board.

The slate had been carefully composed ("All colors, all shapes, all sizes," Chavez told the convention, "Mexicanos, Filipinos, a black brother, a Jew, a woman") with no input from workers. At the convention, a rump group of young Mexican workers formed an opposition slate to challenge Ganz and the two Filipinos, arguing there should be more Mexican farm-workers on the board.

Only one person was briefly on both slates, a reflection of his popu-larity, as well as his naiveté. Eliseo Medina, now twenty-seven, had grown from the scared kid who arrived in Chicago with a bag of buttons to an accomplished organizer who stood out wherever he landed. His indefatigable work ethic, warm smile, and ingenious strategies had produced impressive results and won him followers. When Medina ran the Chicago boycott with seven full-time staff, sales of grapes had dropped 42 percent and one of the major chains in the country pulled the fruit off its shelves. During his tenure as director of the Calexico field office, he had streamlined a chaotic operation and found ways to deal with problems at the hiring hall and back dues. Sent by Chavez to establish the union in Florida, Medina had publicized a slave trade operation in the vegetable industry and organized opposition that killed an anti-farmworker bill. After the 1973 strike, Chavez sent Medina to run the boycott in Cleveland.

Medina was flattered at the invitation to join the Chavez slate. When he arrived at the Fresno convention, some of his old friends asked him to join the opposition slate and run against Ganz. Medina agreed, oblivious to the political implications. As soon as Chavez heard, Medina was bumped off the official slate, and new lists were typed up with his replace-ment. Medina was stunned. Finally Manuel Chavez intervened and held a hallway meeting on Saturday afternoon to explain the political realities. Medina quickly withdrew from the opposition slate and went back on the Chavez team.

Elected by acclaim, Medina took the oath of office and joined the victory lap as the new board members walked around the convention hall to cheers. His reverence for Chavez bordered on hero worship. The immigrant farmworker from Zacatecas would never have imagined that Chavez could find anyone in that assemblage a threat, least of all him.

After the convention, Chavez returned to La Paz and tackled the job of running the operation he had conceived. Even with only a handful of contracts and members, the bureaucracy had grown. He reviewed more than eighty budgets each month for thirty-three boycott offices, twenty-six field offices, a dozen departments at La Paz, the Service Center, and the health group. Each day, the president's office received an average of eighty letters, four to five speaking requests, and one call every three minutes. Each time Chavez left La Paz for trips, he fell further behind. Letters went unanswered, phone requests were mislaid, budgets did not add up. As he prepared for the first meeting of the new executive board, Chavez vowed to make drastic changes, confront people about their sloppy habits, and impose order. Rather than delegate more, Chavez concluded the problem stemmed from delegating too much. Much as he had done years ago in the CSO, Chavez decided the solution was to perform each task himself, at least until he understood exactly what had to be done.

He started his day around 3:30 A.M., opening each piece of mail and sorting letters. He took his pile and dictated answers on tape for his secretaries to type. Starting around 8:00 A.M., he met with people and returned phone calls for the rest of the day, often working until 10:00 P.M. He did not believe in appointments and enjoyed what he called "the exchange, the human part," of conversations, unconstrained by any clock. "People should come, you deal with the problem till it's done," he said. "There's no way to know how long it will take."

When Jacques Levy arrived at La Paz in mid-November 1973 to continue his interviews, he found Chavez sprawled barefoot across his bed, complaining bitterly to Jerry Cohen and Anna Puharich, a well-connected New York socialite who had raised money for the union and then moved to La Paz to run the Service Center. Chavez ranted about inefficiency and overspending. "Cesar says he must get control," Levy wrote. "This is now a Union. Before he was king, but now there are forces and factions keeping track of what he is doing, and he will be held accountable. So he must straighten out La Paz. Can't allow sloppiness and independence that exists. I'll fire everyone, if necessary, he says. I'll start from scratch. But it must be done."

In some instances, Chavez forced out the most competent staff members, much as he had foreseen. Quigley, a former seminarian with an accounting background, had been recruited to the union by Hartmire. When Quigley arrived at La Paz as the business manager in April 1972, no one had kept financial books for the union or the Service Center since the last accountant left six months earlier. Quigley set up systems and instituted quarterly budgets. Chavez was pleased, and the two men enjoyed a good rapport. Chavez helped Quigley, paralyzed in a surfing accident, raise money for a motorized wheelchair. When Chavez was absent running the strike during much of 1973, Quigley made decisions, kept tight control on the budget, and administered the $1.6 million strike fund. When Chavez returned to La Paz, he felt Quigley had usurped too much power. Chavez turned the budget functions over to a trusted aide who had no financial background. Puharich took over the Service Center, throwing her weight around with demands that reduced some of Quigley's coworkers to tears. Quigley understood that Chavez didn't fire people; he just made situations uncomfortable and waited. Quigley resigned in early December 1973.

Chavez's basic mistrust of almost anyone with outside expertise complicated his efforts to structure an efficient operation. "We haven't yet mastered the whole idea of administration," Chavez acknowledged to a group of boycotters. "Administrating things is very difficult for us. Either because we don't like to do it or because we don't see the necessity of doing it or because we're just too pressed doing other things."

With some sixty thousand index cards in the files from past members, no one knew for sure how many members the union had, who paid dues, or whether dues corresponded correctly with the hours worked. Similar problems plagued the medical plan, an innovative insurance program set up by LeRoy Chatfield and designed to meet the needs of seasonal workers. Chavez had the foresight to invest in a computer system, and he pinned his hopes on programmers who were laboriously writing language and punching cards to create programs to computerize the union's files. Dave Smith, the computer whiz, had been close to Quigley. When he was forced out, Smith left as well.

When the first meeting of the national executive board convened on December 17, 1973, Chavez faced a new dynamic—a roomful of strong personalities, experienced organizers, and smart minds unafraid to voice opinions. He set out to structure meetings to ensure that he maintained control.

The board met at least four times a year, each meeting lasting several days, often ten hours a day. Discussions on the most mundane matters could take hours, while significant policy decisions often were made quickly, or ratified after the fact. If Chavez sensed resistance to an idea, he changed the subject and deferred the discussion. He skillfully played one member against another to build coalitions that supported his ideas and break apart allies who might form an independent bloc. If he found himself backed into a corner and all else failed, he lashed out at Huerta. If a discussion veered off course, he suggested they take a walk or tell war stories into the tape recorder, which he kept running throughout the sessions. When emotions ran too high, he defused the situation with a joke or a song. From the beginning, Chavez, the master organizer, organized the board to do his bidding.

Most of the board members were stationed in the field or boycott cities, and an us-versus-them dynamic with La Paz emerged from the start. They wanted to explain their problems and frustrations dealing with the inefficient union headquarters. Chavez wanted them to appreciate his challenges as president of the union. The tension played out in dozens of small, mostly good-natured exchanges: Medina asked that La Paz send out background on candidates seeking endorsements before the board members were asked to vote. Chavez said nobody was available to pull material together. Medina persisted, saying that a simple recommendation would suffice. He didn't want to vote blind. "What I had forgotten was that there was a new board," Chavez replied, gracious and patronizing at once. "Because on the old board they all knew these things and I could just send them and they would act on them. But that much we can do."

When he became frustrated, Chavez frequently fell back on his two favorite bugaboos: "The biggest problem is car and telephone. That's the single biggest problems we have in the union. You can't control those." For two weeks, he told the board, he had negotiated with Jerry Cohen about the legal department's phone bill. He wanted the board to adopt rules so he would not face these situations. "I'm just making you guys responsible for what I've been responsible for all this time," Chavez said. "I've got to force all of you, including you, Dolores, to make some rules so we can run this goddamn union. If we had rules, there wouldn't be any problems."

Board members protested that rules invented in La Paz did not work in the real world. For example, Chavez told them not to accept any more eight-cylinder cars as donations because they used too much gas; they told him the boycotters would have no cars. He presented a formula for

car repair budgets that added up hypothetical averages, which were irrel-
evant when the clunkers broke down. "So I get one-tenth of one brake
shoe per month?" Medina asked. Chavez told them the budget assumed
twenty-four thousand miles per set of tires; they laughed and said they
were lucky if tires lasted fifteen thousand miles.

"When you call me on the phone, I don't tell you my problems; I
try to help you," Chavez finally said in annoyance. "This week is my
week. You have to know what problems we have in La Paz so you can
help me."

Occasionally, philosophical arguments broke out—and remained
unresolved. One of the most persistent revolved around the question of
how to compensate union staff. Several times Chavez had tamped down
suggestions to pay wages. At one board meeting, Medina and Richard
Chavez argued that eventually workers would have to be paid for the
time they spent on union business if farmworkers were to truly play
important roles in running the union. Other board members dismissed
the suggestion as the start of a slippery slope toward paying salaries,
which would destroy the movement spirit. "That discussion is the one
that's going to give us the biggest problems. See, that discussion goes to
the whole movement," Chavez said, noting the question was moot until
they won back contracts. "We have enough sense," he said calmly. "We'll
know what to do when the time comes. We always do."

Chavez complained that his long absences from La Paz had wreaked
havoc with the administration. Board members told him he needed
competent help. "I doubt anyone else but me can do it," Chavez said
defensively. "You can't take your eye from it. Not one minute."

"We're playing hardball now," Richard said. "We're not Little League
anymore. We're so good at kicking ass."

"Richard, just give me some time to be in La Paz," Cesar replied. "I can
do my job. I don't need any help. When the strike's over, when the boycott's
over, then I want you to come to La Paz."

"The day the boycott's over, we're going to have a nightmare," Huerta
warned. "Getting contracts negotiated, setting up enforcement . . .
We're going to not only have this little problem, we're going to have a
statewide problem."

"The problems are going to multiply," Richard added.

"They'll be different problems," Cesar said.

"It's the same problems over and over," Huerta responded.

Just as the inept management of the hiring halls had alienated workers, the chaotic administration at La Paz—dubbed by its detractors "Magic Mountain"—frustrated everyone who dealt with the union office. Financial practices remained murky. The state threatened to shut the credit union because half its loans were delinquent, the bank lacked sufficient reserves, and it commingled investments with UFW funds. Board members heard complaints from supporters, staff, and funders about poor management. The disorganization of the union was an open secret, they told Chavez. He rejected the idea of problems in his own office as firmly as he had dismissed complaints about the hiring hall.

Fred Ross, who often sat in on executive board meetings, always treated Chavez with great respect, proud of the student who had outstripped his teacher. The older man almost never challenged Chavez. But Ross had been watching the union drift and the boycott flounder, and in the fall of 1974 he finally spoke up in his typical no-nonsense manner. La Paz gave no direction, boycotters were confused, half the cities had ineffective operations, and no one on the board knew why. "I think it's absolutely insane the way we're organized," Ross said. The boycott needed a director who could ride herd on cities, spot problems, offer advice, and move people around when necessary. Someone needed to ride the circuit, the way he and Chavez had done back in the CSO.

Chavez blamed the board for not wanting centralized direction and insisted the boycott was working well. Ross chastised Chavez for overconfidence. Then Ross compounded the challenge, suggesting they put Medina in charge. He had written a lengthy pamphlet on how to run a boycott that Ross used as his training template. "I think Eliseo has a very nice way with people, I think that he's not going to rub people the wrong way, and I think that's half the battle right there, besides all the rest of his smarts," Ross said.

Medina, the only Mexican farmworker on the board, was the last person Chavez wanted to elevate to a position of greater power. Chavez reacted instinctively: Medina was irreplaceable in Ohio. "We're not going to have a director if the board doesn't want one," Chavez said. "Over my dead body we're going to have a director!" Ross told Chavez he was acting like the manager of a supermarket chain who had not felt enough pressure from the boycott to take grapes off the shelves. "You're not hurting enough," Ross told Chavez.

Ganz tried to ask Medina whether he would take the job, but Chavez cut him off. "We're not going to force a decision down no one's throat and then make that goddamn decision the source of some conflict on this

board. You understand? Not while I'm here. You take that into consideration. It's a new ball game in this movement. It used to be when I gave
orders, it was done and no one asked questions. It's not like that anymore.
Sure, people will do something if I say something. Next meeting I don't
want to come and be accosted. When you do things democratically, it
takes a lot more time."

Medina finally spoke, quietly. He would rather stay in the Midwest, he
said, but he was willing to do whatever the union needed. Chavez assured
him he need not move, then changed the subject. They sang some union
songs, and laughed as Padilla, a great mimic, performed imitations of
their negotiator. They watched the first cut of the documentary about the
summer of 1973 and adjourned for the night, the question of the boycott
left unresolved.

Chavez was unwilling to relinquish control over even the smallest
details of the operation, much less the boycott. No one understood that
better than Richard Chavez. He had not joined in the boycott discussion. But he led the charge on the administrative disarray. He saw the
problem as twofold—Cesar's unwillingness to delegate or trust anyone
else, and his attachment to an ideological movement at the expense of
running a union.

"Let's start looking at it as a labor union," Richard urged. "Let's
divide the authority, divide the responsibilities . . . if somebody wants
to buy a battery for a goddamn car, you don't have to know about it."
His brother, Richard said in frustration, insisted on knowing about
every spark plug that was purchased. "You can't do that, not unless
you don't trust people. If you don't trust me, I'm your brother and you
know that I would go to hell for you . . . I'm sure nobody is going to
work against you, if that's what you're afraid of or whatever. Nobody
is going to politic against you."

But his brother was not taking any chances. Chavez met privately with
Ross, and by the next board meeting, announced happily that the veteran
organizer had agreed to direct the boycott. In a reference to the earlier
dispute, Chavez spoke about the evolution of the union since the days he
and Jim Drake could decide one afternoon to launch a boycott.

"You have to understand," he said pleadingly. "I'm watching here, and
I know what the difference is between now and then. You want to know?
You want to be reminded? You've erased it, but it's there. It's a truth . . .
The difference is that now we have an executive board." Decisions might
be approved by majority vote, he said, but even unanimous tallies masked

underlying disagreements. "You've got to understand this," he said again. "I must discipline myself to think constantly that unity is more important than winning tomorrow. And we didn't have that before. From where I sit here, it's an entirely different ball game. I see it. And I play it that way. See, when you get all eight, nine minds working together, if you don't watch what you're doing, you get in trouble. So whatever we do, always constantly think about that unity."

CHAPTER 25

The Saint and the Sinner

It was recognition for us, and a tremendous joy. Something I never thought would happen.

The headline in the Sunday *New York Times Magazine* in the fall of 1974 posed in large capital letters the unspoken question hovering in the minds of even faithful supporters of *la causa*: "Is Chavez Beaten?"

Cesar Chavez was portrayed as a sympathetic, charismatic figure, but the story concluded that his prospects for building a successful union looked bleak and the high point might well have been behind him—the 1970 contracts. Farmworkers still worshipped Chavez, but they increasingly worked under Teamster contracts.

"La Causa is good and its time will come again," a worker named Hernandez told the *New York Times* reporter at the end of a fifteen-hour day thinning lettuce with his wife and six children. "When I hear the cry of 'Huelga' I want to, you know, walk out of the fields, to screw the grower right at harvest time, to help Cesar in this hard time he has. But look around you, at all these open mouths to feed." The Hernandez family had four yellowed magazine pictures tacked on the wall of their small house: Abraham Lincoln, Emiliano Zapata, John F. Kennedy, and Cesar Chavez. The Hernandezes had gone on strike for the UFW in 1973; this year, they signed Teamster cards. "I like the Chavez union most, but they made some mistakes," Hernandez said. "The Teamsters are not as bad as he says." The Teamsters now printed literature in Spanish and staffed service centers to help workers obtain food stamps and other benefits. "Maybe in our hearts," Hernandez's wife added, "we still are with Chavez."

One year after the emotional strikes and mass protests of 1973, after burning through millions of dollars in strike benefits and related expenses, Chavez's union was broke again, and no closer to regaining hundreds of lost contracts. The Teamsters had pulled out their goons and become increasingly savvy. The boycott was floundering. National labor leaders wondered about the UFW leader, who seemed more successful as a candidate for sainthood than as a union president. AFL-CIO president George Meany said the 1973 strike "was almost a disaster," and by inference a waste of money. "It was Chavez's own people who went to work behind picket lines in Coachella last year, and that didn't indicate much support," Meany said. His comments provoked questions among union supporters, and problems for boycott leaders. "We bought a goddamn strike, you know," Richard Chavez told his brother. "I had a hell of a time explaining that $90 a week [payment to strikers]. A really, really bad time explaining that."

If Chavez's confidence wavered, he never let on. "I don't ever get tired of fighting the Teamsters," Chavez said. "That is what you are here for, so it is not work, and you don't get tired." The closer people were to him, the more they believed; the more they believed, the greater their outrage against the doubters. Hartmire wrote a response to the *New York Times* called "The United Farm Workers Are Alive and Well" and circulated the mailing widely to movement supporters.

The day after the *New York Times Magazine* piece appeared, Chavez boarded a plane for London. He had completed three tours of boycott cities within the United States, looking for the next great villain that would help him break through one more time. He had negotiated a deal with Meany, who refused to support the secondary boycott because his federation could not sanction a boycott of stores where union members worked as clerks and butchers. Chavez agreed to boycott only specific produce in exchange for an endorsement from the AFL-CIO, a potentially important boost for the grape and lettuce boycott. Now he headed to meetings with European unions to talk about blocking the produce overseas.

Chavez received a cautious, disappointing response. "I don't think the trip was as successful as I thought it was going to be," he said on the plane ride home. "I kidded myself along the way that it was just like sweeping money with a broom, but far from that." In a dozen speeches and press conferences in London, Oslo, Stockholm, Geneva, Hamburg, Copenhagen, Brussels, and Paris, Chavez was asked how many members were in the union, why he had lost the contracts, and what he expected from Europeans. He explained the trouble was a lack of labor laws in the fields and the collusion between the growers and the Teamsters. He blamed the Nixon White House. He claimed that fifteen hundred people worked full-time on the boycott (there were no more than five hundred at the height during summer), which was so successful that growers now looked to Europe as a place to "dump grapes." He struggled to explain the unique nature of his union, so different from the well-established trade unions he addressed.

If the response from labor groups was underwhelming, the reception in Rome more than made up for any disappointment. Chavez was in Stockholm, due to fly in two days to Rome, when Monsignor George Higgins found out that Chavez had been granted an audience with the Pope the next morning. The last flight for Rome had already departed Stockholm. After hours of phone calls, Chavez finally found an evening flight to London that connected to a Nigerian Air flight to Rome. They landed at 2:00 A.M., Chavez recounted, "and there stood Monsignor Higgins in this big empty airport with his nose up against the window, and when he saw us he made a sign of the cross and uttered a sigh of relief."

A few hours later, Cesar and Helen, with Higgins and Bishop Donnelly, observed the pontiff's public audience from a balcony at the Vatican, and then had a fifteen-minute private meeting. Pope Paul VI commended both Chavez and the work of the Bishops' Ad Hoc Committee on Farm Labor, then spoke about the importance of the Mexican American community. The Pope gave Helen rosaries and medals for the kids. Cesar gave the Pope a large UFW flag with the black eagle and the word HUELGA sewn across the red banner. The pope asked what the word meant as the Vatican photographer took pictures of the group with the flag. (Strikes were rampant in Italy, and the Vatican never released that picture.)

At a meeting of the pontiff's Council for Justice and Peace the next day, Archbishop Giovanni Benelli, one of the top officials in the Vatican, surprised the gathering when he pulled a statement out of his pocket to add his own commendation: "We are all indeed grateful to Mr. Chavez for the lesson which he brings to our attention. It is a very important lesson: to know how to be conscious of the terrible responsibility that is incumbent on us who bear the name 'Christian.' His entire life is an illustration of this principle."

After a day of sightseeing ("I fell in love with Rome"), Chavez's party drove the winding roads to Assisi, where a bishops' synod had convened.

Addressing the group, Chavez said simply: "We've experienced some of our greatest joy the last two days here in Rome . . . We were overjoyed with the audience, just more than we'd ever hoped we'd get."

On the flight home, Chavez tried to articulate his feelings about meeting the Pope. "It's such a personal experience that I have difficulty expressing it . . . To us, to Catholics generally, he is probably the most important person in the world. Not only religiously but also historically. So we were elated." Chavez was particularly gratified that the Pope had made favorable comments about Mexican Americans. "It was recognition for us, and a tremendous joy. Something I never thought would happen."

While Chavez was enjoying encomiums from the Catholic hierarchy, back at home Manuel Chavez launched a project decidedly not in keeping with his cousin's saintly image and steadfast commitment to nonviolence. As soon as Cesar left the United States, Manuel set up the "wet line," a private UFW patrol along the Arizona border designed to stop workers who routinely crossed illegally in search of work. The philosophy behind the wet line (as in "wetbacks," the common term for those who crossed the border illegally) was consistent with the union's position that illegal immigrants should be blocked from working as strikebreakers. Ostensibly, the wet line existed to strengthen a citrus strike in the Yuma lemon groves by convincing Mexicans who might work as scabs to turn around and stay home. But the UFW night patrols did not stop to ask Mexicans walking across the open border where they planned to work, nor did the private patrol use verbal persuasion on those tempted to scab. By the time Cesar was en route home from his audience with the Pope, stories had begun to surface about widespread violence and beatings along the wet line.

With union money and some additional support from Chris Hartmire's credit card, Manuel Chavez purchased seventeen tents and set them up along twenty-five miles of the border, near the city of San Luis, Mexico. He enlisted fifteen crews to patrol the border in three shifts, paying $60 a week to about three hundred people. Anna Puharich, Cesar's trusted fund-raiser who had been running the Service Center, moved to the border to manage a special "payment team" that Cesar set up for his cousin. As the union rapidly depleted its reserve accounts, Manuel spent $80,000 a week on the wet line and the lemon strike.

A steady drumbeat of stories about violence appeared in the *Yuma Daily Sun*. On October 8, a seventeen-year-old crossing illegally reported being beaten by a UFW patrol; on October 11, five cars were torched and a lemon picker was attacked with a blackjack; on October 13, a twenty-three-year-old Mexican said he was stopped by three men just north of the border, who beat him with a hose and stole $10; on October 21, two workers told sheriff's deputies they were robbed of border crossing cards, $350 and their car; the same day, deputies found a man hiding under a bush, nude, who said he had been taken from a grove by three men. On November 10, two men were beaten, one whipped with a plastic hose, the other burned on the soles of his feet, then thrown in the Colorado River.

The Mexican papers carried stories about more pervasive violence on their side of the border. In San Luis, newspapers reported that cars were firebombed daily, houses set on fire, and families threatened. On November 30, 1974, *La Voz*, a Mexicali paper, reported thirty-seven confirmed beatings. Another Mexicali paper, *La Tribuna*, published pictures of victims who said they were beaten by the "*cesarchavistas*."

The willingness of illegal immigrants to voluntarily report crimes to U.S. authorities, generally unsympathetic to the migrants' status, reflected the severity of the violence. The Mexican labor federation, the Confederación de Trabajadores de México (CTM), which had worked closely with Manuel for years and initially supported his lemon strike, broke with the UFW and denounced the wet line as a campaign of terror. CTM director Francisco Modesto estimated there were hundreds of beatings, most unreported, and that two men had been castrated and one drowned in the river. "They had control of San Luis," he told a reporter. "They bought off the police . . . even the taxi drivers were under Manuel's control."

In Yuma, citrus growers went to court seeking injunctions against the strike. Witnesses testified that a radio station rejected ads from growers after eight employees received threats from the UFW. One picker suffered a broken neck when he was pulled out of a tree. Buses used to transport workers were gutted with gasoline bombs. Oscar Mondragon, one of the strike leaders, was charged with setting fire to labor contractors' buses in the Imperial Valley. Police described the simple mechanism: a cigarette taped to a matchbook formed a makeshift fuse, which was placed in a plastic water bottle one-quarter full of gasoline. Mondragon and two other UFW workers were convicted after testimony that they poured gasoline on the hood of the bus, placed the bottle on top, and lit the cigarette. When the cigarette burned, it ignited the matchbook, which melted the plastic and set the gasoline on fire. The same brands of water bottle and matches were found in other arson investigations.

Hundreds of miles away, in the quiet sanctuary of La Paz, Manuel's reports to the executive board at its October and December 1974 meetings were upbeat. The lemon strike was shutting down the fields, costing the growers thousands of dollars, he reported. In his gruffly charming manner, Manuel provided entertaining accounts and urged board members to visit Yuma and see for themselves the damaged trees and empty lemon groves. He was certain the growers would soon capitulate. They were losing money, and the weight of the overripe fruit was causing permanent damage to the trees. "We don't win this one," he told the board, "we'll never win a strike!"

The only reference Manuel made to violence along the border was a passing mention of a recent court case. In another example of the ridiculous nature of justice in Arizona, he said, two UFW members of the wet line were convicted of beating three illegals and robbing one of $227. How could an illegal have been carrying that much money? Manuel asked. He did not mention that at the trial, the victims testified they were beaten with sticks and a battery cable. "There is no justification for stopping these people, robbing them, beating them and throwing them back across the line," Judge William Nabours said, sentencing the men to probation. "If I thought for a minute sending you to prison would stop this activity, I wouldn't hesitate . . . This sort of activity has got to stop."

At the CTM's instigation, Mexican authorities from the state of Sonora conducted an investigation that concluded San Luis city officials had been bribed to cooperate with the UFW. At the executive board meeting in December 1974, both Manuel and Cesar tacitly acknowledged the truth of the bribery allegation. Cesar asked Manuel how he could cut expenses.

> MANUEL: If we can get some people to man the lines on the other [Mexican] side of the border, police it. Because we've got them very well under control now. But if we turn down the tents, they'll flock in. Maybe we ought to leave the tents . . . and just sort of bluff. But then we have to put surveillance on the other side . . .
>
> CESAR: How much if you got Mexican people to do it over there?
>
> MANUEL: If we pay the police over there on the other side— which they accused us of already anyway—like we had before, we had five of them guys doing it, just going back and forth, if

they catch any illegals, they take them in, and then they just get them away from the line, then we don't have as many people on this side. But we can't stop that line completely. Once they get into those groves, they sleep in them . . .

CESAR: Can you cut the line down to 100, on this side? And then put . . .

MANUEL: Yes, then we got to pay at least three shifts . . .

And then he asked that the tape recorder be shut off.

After an inquiry that included hearings where men testified about a range of brutal incidents, the Sonoran Judicial Department issued arrest warrants—including, according to Mexican news reports, one for Manuel Chavez. Manuel offered a different explanation to the executive board. The growers had bought off the Mexican authorities and the CTM, he said. Then *El Malcriado* had the poor judgment to write something critical about the Mexican president, so the irate government picked Manuel up and held him in jail for three days. With rampant corruption in Mexico, the story was plausible enough to pass.

But even with allowances for Mexican corruption and one-party rule, the evidence was overwhelming. News reports, official complaints, and investigations on both sides of the border confirmed the victims' stories and documented the pattern of brutality. So did the similar scars on the backs of victims beaten with chains, and the stories of workers beaten with hoses, robbed of petty cash, stripped of clothes, and left naked in the desert.

"The moment Manuel came here, he started buying everybody off," Enrique Silva Calles of the San Luis district attorney's office told a reporter. Calles said he had a stack of complaints about Manuel involving bad checks, burnt cars, and beaten bodies. "What I can't understand," he said, "is that Cesar Chavez continues to reward that son of a bitch. He knows about the checks and the complaints against Manuel. Why is he still supporting him?"

By the end of 1974, word had begun to trickle out to the group most likely to be appalled by the stories. "Church folks visiting Yuma and San Luis are being told some mind-boggling stuff about arson in Sonora, UFW pay offs to the police chief of Sonora, charges being brought against the police chief, etc etc," Hartmire wrote to Chavez. Cesar sent Manuel a Spanish translation of the letter—removing Hartmire's name—with a note saying, "let's talk." Hartmire assured the church folks that the stories were based on antiunion propaganda from the local sheriff.

As always, Cesar protected Manuel at all costs. When checks bounced and reports surfaced of forged union checks, Cesar told board members the banks' computers had screwed up the account. He blamed Puharich for cost overruns and said he had fired her. As Chavez combed through individual budgets to cut $10 here and $20 there and berated officers for their phone bills, he gave Manuel a virtual blank check, long past the time when it was clear how the money was being spent. "It's like playing poker," Cesar told the executive board as he asked for approval to commit more money. "We've got $800,000 in the pot. Do we go all the way, or do we pull back? . . . I don't see how we can stop the damn strike."

Manuel offered no accounting, though simple arithmetic showed that $80,000 a week was more than the cost of supporting even twice as many strikers as he claimed. By the end of the year, the union had spent more than $1 million. Manuel agreed to reduce his weekly budget to between $25,000 and $30,000. "We told Manuel to go do something goddamn difficult!" Cesar exclaimed angrily when board members argued about cuts to their budgets. "Now trying to cut a piddly dime, I get all sorts of grief."

Cesar acted out of protectiveness, love, and admiration for Manuel. As Peter Matthiessen had observed several years earlier, "Cesar forgives Manuel what he will not forgive in anybody else; he loves him, but he also depends on him." From their teen years on, Cesar had looked up to his charming, troublemaker cousin. Like Cesar, Manuel could beguile people into helping him even when they knew better; like Cesar, Manuel loved action. He took risks. He could make things happen. He could walk into a field and start a strike just for the hell of it. Manuel was willing to do "the dirty work," Cesar acknowledged. Cesar also depended on Manuel's judgment about people and relied on him for internal intelligence. Those qualities, plus loyalty, bound the two cousins. Cesar was ruthless in placing the success of his movement above all else, but he deemed Manuel's value far greater than any risk. Telling the story of how Manuel had been there when needed and given up his job as a used-car salesman in 1962, Cesar said: "As far as I'm concerned, they don't make people any better than Manuel."

Whatever doubts executive board members harbored—and those with experience working along the border knew something of Manuel's methods—they kept silent. They, too, knew Manuel was useful, and preferred not to know too much about how he accomplished his organizing feats. An October field trip to the Yuma strike offered proof of Manuel's lavish lifestyle and sparked internal griping: he ate and drank well, often operated out of bars, and had women around at all times. But board members' visit to the strike was cut short when Manuel relayed a death threat—never substantiated—against Cesar, who took to his bed instead of appearing at a mass rally. He feigned back trouble and held a press conference from his hotel bed. He dismissed questions about violence on the part of union members as the reports of paid provocateurs.

Beyond loyalty to his cousin, Chavez supported the wet line for ideological reasons. His current villain was illegal immigration. He had seized on immigrants as the latest explanation why the union could not win a strike. A few months before the wet line, Chavez had launched the "Illegals Campaign," an effort he deemed second in importance only to the boycott. He berated the Nixon administration and the Border Patrol for turning a blind eye so that the growers could keep their illegal workforce. Chavez declared the UFW would identify illegal immigrants to force the government to deport them. He reported they had identified twenty-two hundred in East Fresno alone.

To coordinate the Illegals Campaign, Chavez turned to a nineteen-year-old protégé, Liza Hirsch. Liza had worked for the union in one way or another since she moved to Delano as a twelve-year-old with her parents, Fred and Ginny, in 1967. When the rest of the family returned to San Jose a year later (the occasion of Fred Hirsch's long critique of the union), Liza moved into the Chavez family home for the following year. Unlike his own children, who resented the union and showed little interest, Liza was committed to *la causa* at an early age. Fluent in Spanish, she stood on picket lines as a teenager and took notes at Friday night meetings. An aspiring cellist, she gave up music because Chavez told her outside interests would interfere. She was raised as a secular Jew, but Chavez secretly arranged to have her baptized, an act that would have particularly enraged her father. When Liza watched the Democratic National Convention with Chavez in the summer of 1968, he told her she would grow up to be a lawyer for the union. From then on, she worked toward that goal. She finished college early and was about to enter Boalt Law School when Chavez put her in charge of the Illegals Campaign, a task he knew she would not like. He also knew she would accept without question. He gave the assignment while doing yoga, standing on his head.

Hirsch distributed forms printed in triplicate to all union offices and directed staff members to document the presence of illegal immigrants in the fields and report them to the INS. The "Report on Illegal Alien Farm

Labor Activity" forms included space for names, the Border Patrol office, the field where the illegals worked, home addresses, the grower, names of those who gave them food, transportation, and housing, how they had crossed, and what they were earning. The statistics served another function: they helped boycotters explain why, despite the strikes, nonunion lettuce and grapes were plentiful. "If we can get the illegals out of California," Chavez said repeatedly, "we will win the strike overnight."

Chavez reacted scornfully to criticism of the Illegals Campaign, particularly from his liberal allies. When Chicano activist Bert Corona staged a protest against the wet line, Chavez directed Jerry Cohen to retaliate with an investigation of the funding of Corona's group. The National Lawyers Guild refused to allow summer interns to participate in the Illegals Campaign, and Chavez angrily broke ties and rejected the interns. Some UFW field offices refused to cooperate in tracking and reporting illegal immigrants, and even some board members expressed concerns. Huerta supported the campaign but suggested they change the terminology because some people found the words wetback and illegal offensive. "The people themselves aren't illegal," she said. "Their action of being in this country maybe is illegal."

Chavez turned on Huerta angrily. "No, a spade's a spade," he said. "You guys get these hang-ups. Goddamn it, how do we build a union? They're wets, you know. They're wets, and let's go after them."

The issue of illegal immigration touched deep chords for Chavez, going back to his experience with braceros in Oxnard. As he had campaigned against the guest workers in 1959, he again charged that immigrants were taking jobs away from local workers. Like the braceros, the immigrants came north to make money. Chavez dwelt on that point frequently, lamenting the difficulty in organizing people who cared about money. They needed to be educated to appreciate sacrifice. Immigrants "come here to become rich, you know," he told Levy. "It is so ingrained in them. Although they're sympathetic and they want to help you, goddamn, they miss one day's work and they think they're going to die."

Reports of violence at the border abated somewhat after Manuel's arrest, though they persisted into the new year. On January 6, 1975, a seventy-three-year-old man from San Luis reported that one of his companions disappeared after crossing the border at night. They saw car headlights, and he hit the ground; he heard three shots and shouts of "stop" in Spanish, and then the cars took off. He searched for his friend without success.

Four days later, the United Auto Workers union presented Chavez with a $50,000 check at a Yuma press conference, to support the strike during the final weeks of the lemon harvest. Chavez estimated that four hundred members were now receiving strike benefits, and he dismissed questions about violence on the wet line. "I read one report of an illegal who said he was robbed of $200," Chavez said, echoing Manuel's comments to the board. "Where does an illegal alien from Guadalajara get $200?" He promised that any union member guilty of violence would be expelled or removed from the strike, but no one had been found to have committed violence in Yuma. "Violence is against our constitution."

Cesar appeared with Manuel three weeks later at a rally in front of the UFW hall in San Luis, Arizona. Cesar charged that the police had beaten pickets, and he said the union would sue. He announced that Manuel would run a melon strike. "I strike the cantaloupe crop every year just for sport," Manuel joked. The same day, one of the UFW strikers pleaded not guilty to robbery and aggravated battery for beating four Mexicans who had tried to cross the border illegally in September.

For those who believed in Chavez, the idea that he might condone such behavior was unthinkable. His noble and sincere public image gave credibility to the denials and enabled him to convincingly dismiss as grower propaganda the persistent rumors of untoward behavior.

Just as he had learned the magnetic power of suffering in the march to Sacramento and in the fasts, Chavez now capitalized on the power of his increasingly saintly image. Once a smoking, drinking, meat-eating campesino, he had adopted habits more in keeping with his new persona. He rejected fatty Mexican foods as sapping energy. In his diet, as in other arenas, he was constantly searching for the magic bullet. He drank carrot juice, which he said filtered out impurities found in water, and only used water to brush his teeth. He credited his strict vegetarian diet with helping his back, though he said he adopted the diet for moral reasons: "I wouldn't eat my dog, you know. Cows and dogs are about the same." He shunned fish, processed food, and dairy except cottage cheese, and studied Arnold Ehret's "mucusless diet healing system." His diet included avocados, low-fat cottage cheese, black bread, apple cider vinegar, pumpernickel bread, tomatoes, cucumber, red onion, watercress, romaine, mango, papaya, grapefruit juice, carrot juice, celery juice, strawberries, cantaloupe, lemon, black olives, and whole green Ortega chiles. Although his wife and children remained militant meat eaters, Helen learned to make vegetarian versions of traditional Mexican stews. Whenever Cesar traveled, his security guards brought along a box of fruit and vegetables and an Acme juicerator.

Many admirers emulated Chavez, especially in La Paz, where he converted followers to his carrot juice regime and vegetarian diet. Increasingly, the movement became synonymous with the man. Supporters were Chavistas. Direct mail appeals carried the return address of "Cesar E. Chavez," not the United Farm Workers. When he described his activities in conversations and reports, Chavez adopted the royal "we," even when chronicling personal events: "During this period we spent two days at San Jose for a physical examination and some tests, and were hospitalized for four days. We also attended our parents' 50th wedding anniversary."

His image helped in some circles and hurt in others. When Chavez met with labor leaders in Washington, D.C., to discuss a possible agreement with the Teamsters, Seafarers Union president Paul Hall lectured Chavez about the need to act like a labor leader, not a saint. "Get up off your fucking knees. Let's not make it a cause. Let's make it a fucking union," Hall told Chavez. "We'll buy you fucking knee pads if you want to fight a holy war." If Chavez could move beyond fighting and consolidate his leadership, Hall said, he could play an influential role in the labor movement, comparable to civil rights leader A. Philip Randolph. Be a labor leader, Hall urged Chavez, instead of "a fad—the poor man others can support to expiate their sins."

Some executive board members heard similar sentiments in their boycott cities and shared Hall's concern. "We're trying to build a union to better the lives of a lot of people, but we have to start thinking this is a business," Richard Chavez said. "People say, 'Cesar is a saint, he never was a union leader, he can't administer, he should be a monk.'" Progressive unions in New York managed to help people with housing, retirement, and health care, too, but operated in more businesslike fashion, Richard pointed out. "In New York City I can't get help with labor [leaders] because they're turned off at Cesar."

Cesar did not much care what labor leaders in New York thought. He, too, was thinking about the future of his organization. But he envisioned growing in an entirely different direction. The UFW was strongest in faraway cities and weakest in its own backyard. Poor white people in the San Joaquin Valley, who should be natural allies in the struggle for economic justice, hated the union. Chavez wanted to win them over by including them in the union.

"I'm proposing we should organize a PPU, for lack of a better name, a Poor Peoples Union," he told the executive board at the end of 1974. Senior citizens on fixed incomes, who needed help, services, and community, would be his first target. Seniors could become dues-paying members of the PPU and use the credit union, the clinics, and the service center. Membership would be limited to those receiving some form of government aid, in order to keep out the middle class and avoid the problems that plagued the CSO. Members of a PPU local in Los Angeles, for example, might be eligible to move into a union-sponsored retirement community, which Chavez envisioned building in a rural area. The communal home would have a garden, grow food, and participate in a biweekly union-sponsored farmers market. His level of detail made the dreamy proposal sound almost convincing.

"The potential to make real ardent followers and supporters, the potential to make a *causa* out of this, is fantastic," he said. "Besides, we don't have a choice . . . We've got to go out and organize those people, just for our own salvation." He looked ahead to a time in the near future when the farmworker cause would become passé, once they won back contracts or succeeded in passing the state legislation he had committed to support. The union's political power did not come from its members but derived from urban centers many thousands of miles away. A transition away from the boycott to a more straightforward labor union for farmworkers would jeopardize all that power.

"The more we win, the weaker we're going to get," he warned the board. "The moment we pull our troops from the cities, back to our own, we lose power. We're going to lose a hell of a lot of power . . . it's borrowed."

Chavez followed up a few weeks later in a meeting with Fred Ross and directors of the Service Center and field offices. He suggested they issue plastic photo identification cards to senior citizens in exchange for a fifty-cent donation. He wanted to aim for a Poor Peoples Union convention in early spring of 1975, with a few hundred seniors from around the state, all eligible for social security and "not too middle class." The majority should be Anglo and black, and not farmworkers. He hoped the convention would help restore the spirit of the early days of the union, the lure of being involved in the start of something big. He told the staff to read about Mao's Long March.

Chavez described himself as a pragmatic organizer; others viewed him as a grand dreamer. Part of his peculiar genius lay in his ability to see as realistic what others deemed improbable. Like many of his schemes, the

Poor Peoples Union was both an impossible dream and a practical solution to a problem that Chavez accurately anticipated.

For true believers, Chavez's ambitious dreams were an inspiration. "In the midst of a desert of apathy, cynicism and self-centeredness, Cesar Chavez and the farm workers with him are a visible, believable, concrete sign that life can have meaning, that love is possible and that justice can be done," Hartmire wrote to supporters.

For skeptics, Chavez's grand visions detracted from his effectiveness. "I admire him," said George Meany, reaffirming his support for the UFW in the summer of 1974. "I think he's an idealist. I think he's a bit of a dreamer. I still admire him, but the thing that I'm disappointed about is that Cesar never got to the point that he could develop a real viable union . . . We're not writing him off by any means."

More and more, people used the word saint in conversations and interviews. Chavez sometimes appeared slightly embarrassed, but he did not demur. He drew a distinction between saints and angels. Gandhi was difficult to work for, he said, and Martin Luther King Jr. was difficult to live with. He saw himself following in their footsteps, and he was indeed both hard to work for and hard to live with. "There is a big difference between being a saint and being an angel," he told Sally Quinn of the *Washington Post*. "Saints are known for being tough and stubborn."

Chavez claimed to hate the public parts of his job, the awards and accolades, the need to make appearances to return favors. He said Helen made sure he did not get carried away by the idolatry. Those who knew Helen well concurred. ("The only ones who might scare him are God and his wife, Helen. But besides that, he's not afraid of anyone," Huerta said.)

At home, Chavez said, "I am just like a plain human being. I get reminded of this constantly like at the house . . . I am just the same old guy, you know. She [Helen] lets me know that I am just Cesar, you know, not that public figure. She has an advantage. She is not part of it. She is removed from that public part and she lets me know very definitely who I am. I think that is sometimes, although I don't enjoy it, it is a good thing, that reminder at home . . . to us he is just a plain old guy."

CHAPTER 26

The End of the Nonviolent Viet Cong

*The whole fight's going to change. Because once you're recognized . . . then the
essential fight of recognition . . . is no longer there. Then from that point on,
you're talking about wages, you're talking about money, you're talking about
benefits.*

Near the end of the legislative session in the summer of 1974, Jerry Cohen
called Chavez from Sacramento with big news: the union's elections bill
had passed the Assembly. Chavez said he felt sick to his stomach. Cohen
quickly offered reassurance: the Teamsters would kill the measure in the
Senate. Chavez, however, was thinking more long-term.

From the start, Chavez's response to even the most favorable laws
governing union activity in the fields was one of great ambivalence. He had
protested the exclusion of farmworkers from national labor laws, so he had
no choice but to support the idea of a fair elections bill. But Chavez never
relished the prospect of playing by someone else's rules. Each legislative
victory that he hailed in public, he bemoaned in private, worried that a law
would cramp his style and divert energy from his broader goals.

His predicament had begun when he promised to push for legislation in
exchange for accepting the AFL-CIO's $1.6 million strike fund during the
Coachella strike in 1973. Cohen was eating dinner at a Denny's restaurant
in back of the Date Tree Motel in Indio when Chavez cut the deal at another
table. Afterward they went for a ride, and Chavez told Cohen to start drafting a measure that would set up a procedure for state-regulated elections in
the field. The bill would be similar to the National Labor Relations Act but
take into account the unique needs of seasonal farmworkers.

Chavez acted to fulfill his commitment to the AFL-CIO, but he
directed Cohen to delay as long as possible. Cohen met with labor

leaders, worked on drafts, and played for time. By the end of 1973, when he met with the new UFW executive board, Chavez said he could stall no longer. Jack Henning, the secretary-treasurer of the California Labor Federation, was pressing the UFW to introduce a measure early in the 1974 legislative session. The Teamsters and growers were drafting their own bills.

The pressure came from many sides. Labor leaders wanted an end to the interunion fights and costly strikes. Growers wanted an end to the boycott. County officials were tired of the protests and mass arrests. Church and liberal leaders worried the movement was losing steam. The *New York Times Magazine* story had taken a toll. The 1960s were over, the protesters had moved on. In New York, Richard Chavez used to attract thousands to a rally on a few days' notice; now if two hundred people showed up to support the boycott, he considered the event a success. "We've run out of time," he said. "Let's face it."

"How do we introduce a bill that we're committed to but postpone it from getting through, and not draw suspicions?" Chavez asked.

"One way to do it is to introduce a bill that can't be passed," Cohen responded. "See what reasonable sounding things we can put in there that are impossible."

Chavez liked that idea. "We should put a bill that if it passes, it's damn good. Then we tell Henning, 'No compromise. This is what we need.'"

The bill Cohen and his legal staff drafted, AB 3370, included four provisions Chavez considered essential: elections only in peak season, when the most workers could vote; expedited elections first with objections heard afterward; a bargaining unit that included all agricultural workers; and the right to boycott. When Cohen asked whether they were willing to modify a section after the bill had been introduced, Chavez told him to hold firm. "They're gonna kill everything," he said confidently.

When Cohen called with the news that the Assembly had actually passed AB 3370 on August 19, 1974, Chavez felt queasy. He realized the measure had little chance of surviving in the Senate and even less chance of being signed into law by Governor Reagan. But Chavez saw the inevitability of legislation. He needed time to prepare.

The UFW was not in position to wage campaigns in the fields. The most sustained strike activity had been in Yuma, where the lemon strike cost more than $1.2 million and ended with no contracts. Most of the union's energy had been directed toward the boycott, fund-raising, and events designed to build public and political support outside the fields, and in many cases outside California. *Fighting for Our Lives*, the documentary about the 1973 strike, had finally been completed, with a script written by Peter Matthiessen and narrated by Luis Valdez. The dramatic footage of Teamster confrontations, worker rallies, and arrests provided riveting propaganda. The union coordinated screenings to raise funds around the country. While thousands of people cheered as the Teamster goons were pilloried on the screen and *Fighting for Our Lives* received an Oscar nomination, tens of thousands of farmworkers worked under Teamster contracts. "If we don't get those bastards out pretty soon, they're going to start creating roots with those workers that they're representing now," Chavez warned.

Much of Chavez's brilliance as a tactician stemmed from his ability to respond quickly and decisively to external events. After their bill passed the Assembly, Chavez switched gears. The pressure to find a legislative solution to end the chaos in the fields had proved greater than he had anticipated. He foresaw that pressure would continue to build. He needed to stake out a negotiating position.

"I've come to the conclusion that the only way we're going to build a union . . . we don't have to be defending every two years or every three years, is going to be through legislation," he told the executive board in October 1974. "We have to introduce legislation again this coming year. We're expected to and I think we have to. We introduced a little chicken-shit bill [in 1974] that really didn't amount to anything." In 1975, he wanted to submit the most ambitious possible measure, a broad, sweeping farmworker bill of rights. He directed Cohen to draft a law that would include collective bargaining rights, unfair labor practices, even unemployment benefits for farmworkers. They would line up as much support as possible and fight hard for the measure, banking on the idea that they had crafted a bill too strong to pass.

"Then in 1976, we'll go directly to the voters in a referendum," Chavez explained. In a presidential year, the turnout would be particularly high. An initiative would enshrine the farmworkers' rights in the California constitution, so no successive legislature could undo the measure. "I think the voters will give it to us . . . what it means is, then we'll start organizing workers left and right."

Huerta, who had the most experience with Sacramento lawmakers, cautioned Chavez they had better line up strong commitments in advance: "Once they start wheeling and dealing, they are liable to do anything." Marshall Ganz was taken aback by Chavez's shift and worried a law would change the nature of the movement. Chavez's scenario would inevitably trap the union in political gamesmanship, he said: "When you make so much of your power dependent on legislation, that becomes the focus rather than the organizing and the other kind of work. You become so preoccupied with politics."

Chavez agreed, but he saw no alternative. "We're like, isolated over here. We can win, but we can't protect what we've won. If the law passes, you're right, immediately, it's a completely different ball game."

Jerry Brown was the Democratic candidate for governor on the November 1974 ballot and held a comfortable lead in the polls. Chavez sent Cohen to meet with Brown and seek a promise to veto any bill the union did not like. Brown was knowledgeable on the issues and vague on his commitment.

When Brown won an easy victory, farmworkers' rights suddenly took center stage in the state Capitol. Brown had helped the union as secretary of state during the "No on 22" campaign. He had joined UFW protests and endorsed AB 3370 (though not until Cohen dispatched his second in command to stage a sit-in at the candidate's office). LeRoy Chatfield had worked on the Brown campaign and would join the new administration as a top aide. Labor leaders expected Brown would be sympathetic to their cause. Religious leaders had high hopes for the new governor, a former Jesuit seminarian.

Brown did not disappoint. He devoted two paragraphs of his fifteen-paragraph inaugural address to the needs of farmworkers. He declared it was time to extend unemployment insurance to those who worked in the fields and "to extend the rule of law to the agriculture sector and establish the right of secret ballot elections for farmworkers."

Chavez dispatched a full-time staff person to Sacramento to track legislation, hunt down lawmakers on a moment's notice, and keep Chavez informed of developments. He felt confident Brown would not sign a bill over the union's objections. But he did not trust his own allies. Labor leaders, for one, would not fight to protect the UFW's right to secondary boycotts, a tactic allowed no other union. "The problem is going to be our friends," Chavez said repeatedly, anticipating they would pressure him to accept compromises. He asked Hartmire to start making the rounds of church groups to stress the importance of the union's tough stance.

Chavez also did not particularly want elections; he hoped that the growers would be equally averse to the prospect and cut a deal. He planned to stress that setting up elections would be a complex and time-consuming task that would delay the end of the boycott, which was what mattered most to growers. On this one he misjudged. Growers were willing to take their chances with elections, and the governor viewed secret-ballot elections as a centerpiece of the law.

The shift toward a legislative solution drove a change in the boycott, which now needed to pressure growers into accepting a good law rather than signing contracts. The grape and lettuce boycotts had built popular support and served as an ongoing nuisance but never had the same devastating economic impact as the first grape boycott in 1969. Lettuce was a staple, not a luxury item like grapes. Supporters were confused about which brands to boycott. The most promising target was Gallo wine, which had been added to the boycott list on the strength of its well-known name. The E. J. Gallo winery, which had signed with the UFW in 1967, had switched to the Teamsters in 1973.

The Gallo boycott was popular with college students. Though the union had invested few resources, the campaign had proved surprisingly effective, judging from Gallo's response. The company hired a public relations firm, took out newspaper ads, and paid representatives to stage informational counterpickets wherever the union appeared. Chavez liked the idea of focusing on Gallo for an easy win. "Just do one thing—go after Gallo. Nothing else," he suggested to the board.

In public, Chavez portrayed a different image. When the bishops' committee came to California for a series of special meetings early in 1975, Chavez discussed the boycott and legislation but also talked at length about Yuma, claiming that three thousand lemon workers were still on strike. He predicted more strikes would occur and that the union would ultimately prevail. "Chavez presented a very forceful and self-confident picture of himself and the forces of their union," concluded Roger Mahony, who had just been appointed auxiliary bishop of Fresno.

Mahony's career had in an odd way paralleled that of Chavez, and the cleric's rise was due in no small part to the role he played in the farm labor struggle. Nine years younger than Chavez, Mahony had grown up in North Hollywood and learned his first Spanish shoveling chicken manure with Mexican workers at his father's poultry-processing plant. As a seminarian in the late 1950s, he accompanied priests who went to say mass in the labor camps around Oxnard. His Spanish became fluent and he gravitated toward ministering to Mexican Americans. He was ordained on May 1, 1962, one week after Chavez moved to Delano, and assigned to the Fresno diocese. He earned a master's degree in social work, special-izing in community organization. By the time the grape strike started in 1965, Mahony was in charge of social welfare programs for the diocese of Fresno. As secretary to the bishops' committee, Mahony had made himself the most knowledgeable cleric on the issues and became a broker during key disputes.

He chose "To reconcile God's people" as his episcopal motto, and wrote to Martin Zaninovich that the motto reflected the new bishop's desire to heal wounds among Catholics in the valley. Mahony knew Zaninovich exemplified those wounds: the grower had angrily pulled his third-grader out of St. Mary's Catholic School in Delano when the diocese adopted a new catechism that included passages on Cesar Chavez. Mahony invited Zaninovich to his ordination and mentioned the new governor's pledge to support a farmworker bill that would require compromise on all sides.

The Delano growers were more open with the bishops than Chavez had been. They told the committee they thought legislation was inevita-ble. Grape growers had turned to the Teamsters as a last resort, in hope of fending off a boycott, and were not particularly happy with the result. They hoped for certain provisions in the law and were ready to take their chances to end the years of chaos and strife. Ernest Gallo also told Mahony that he wanted a law; the vintner had only 250 year-round work-ers and another 250 during the season, and was tired of being the poster child for greedy, exploitive growers. The boycott was hurting, too; Gallo's wine sales in California dropped 6 percent during the first quarter of 1975, while other brands were up 13 percent over the prior year.

On February 24, 1975, a UFW rally in San Francisco kicked off a four-day march to the Gallo headquarters in Modesto. Fred Ross Jr., son of Cesar's mentor, had been running the San Francisco boycott office and pulled together the march in response to Chavez's call to focus on Gallo. The event succeeded beyond expectations, in part because the crowd swelled to many thousands, and in part because of Gallo's response. Underneath the windows of a hotel overlooking Union Square where the marchers assembled, the company hung a banner that read: GALLO'S FARM WORKERS BEST PAID IN U.S . . . MARCHING WRONG WAY, CESAR? The UFW should aim its protest at legislators in Sacramento, Gallo argued. The company took out full-page ads urging that farmworkers be placed under the National Labor Relations Act.

After four days and 110 miles, the marchers reached Modesto. The crowd grew to about ten thousand and rallied in Graceada Park. "As the song says, we're going to roll this union on," Chavez said as he addressed the cheering crowd. "No doubt in our minds and our hearts that we're going to win . . . Together, we're going to stop drinking Gallo wines, and together we're going to win!"

He concluded his speech with a pointed jab: "Brothers and sisters, we have a final message to another person." He reminded the crowd that candidate Jerry Brown had pledged to support a farm labor law, but Governor Brown had yet to consult with the union. "We want to tell him, 'Dear Governor, you know, we once went to Sacramento to visit your Daddy.'" Cheers of "Si se puede" greeted Chavez's reference to the legendary 1966 *peregrinación*, when Pat Brown had snubbed the farmworkers and stayed in Palm Springs on Easter. "We want to make Modesto the furthest we go. But we're not going to let anyone introduce legislation because they think they know what's best for us!"

Within twenty-four hours, phones began to ring. Monday morning, the farm labor bill dominated the agenda at Brown's weekly meeting with legislative leaders. On Tuesday, Chatfield placed an urgent call to Cohen, saying Brown wanted a complete briefing on farm labor legislation in time for his Friday cabinet meeting. A week later, Chavez and Cohen spent most of Saturday at the governor's house in Los Angeles, the three of them alone for an hour, joined later by various aides.

"Jerry [Cohen] and I made a plan when we went there," Chavez told the board a week later. "Say very little. Find out where Brown stood. Let him know that legislation wasn't what we were after. We wanted damn contracts more than anything else. Legislation could screw us." Chavez said he would support legislation, but only a very strong bill. He ran through the issues that were important—one unit for all workers, quick elections, recognitional strikes. Brown seemed fine with most of them and not overly worried about Teamster support. He thought growers would pose more difficulty.

Brown recognized Chavez was posturing, but the governor also sensed Chavez's genuine and well-founded fear. "He knew that the legal structure favors the status quo, and farmworkers are not the status quo," Brown said later. "They are marginal participants in the economy." Around three o'clock in the afternoon, Brown suddenly invited Chavez to take a walk. Cohen was somewhat surprised when Chavez readily agreed; he ordinarily avoided situations where he might find himself trapped. But Chavez had a degree of faith in Brown. "We walked out, and that's where we made some deals," Chavez recounted to the board a week later.

Brown said he was serious about a law, and Chavez said he was, too, but they needed a law with teeth that protected the workers' right to decide on the union of their choice, with penalties on employers who interfered or failed to negotiate in good faith. Brown asked Chavez if he was sure the UFW could win elections. Chavez said of course. Brown asked a second time. Then they agreed on the outlines of a strategy. Brown would introduce his bill, and the UFW would support a more radical alternative and attack the governor's measure, trusting him to ultimately negotiate a law that included the union's bottom lines. Chavez wanted a three-member board; Brown argued for five. Chavez said the law would work only if the people enforcing the rules were sympathetic, aggressive, and hardworking. Brown said he thought that could be arranged. He understood that Chavez needed to create enough pressure so that a law appealed to all parties as preferable to continued chaos in the fields.

The next two months were a whirlwind of statements and counter-statements, late-night meetings, and strategy sessions, a wild ride that showcased Cohen's legal and negotiating talents. Playing the game he had learned from Chavez, the lawyer gambled for all the marbles. He had nothing to lose. The UFW had mastered a strategy of confidence that bordered on arrogance, which enabled Cohen to act without concern about whom he might insult or offend. He referred to the Assembly Speaker as the kind of leader who made him puke, then shared a drink with the lawmaker the next day. When a UAW lobbyist questioned the UFW's negotiating strategy, Chavez sent back word that "if he doesn't trust brown people to make their own decisions and make their own strategy he can go fuck himself."

Brown's bill, his first as governor, was introduced by Assemblyman Howard Berman and Senator John Dunlop at an April 9 press conference. Brown and Chavez talked twice that day. The governor held a press conference the following day and called friends of the UFW to report that Chavez was close to endorsing the new measure. Chavez unleashed Cohen, who held his own press conference to attack the bill as deceptive and unacceptable.

By then, Mahony was in on the game. He explained the strategy to Cardinal Timothy Manning, president of the California Catholic Conference, before testifying at a committee hearing in favor of the governor's bill. The cardinal should not be alarmed when the UFW packed the hearing with several thousand farmworkers and loudly denounced the bishops. "That is part of their plan and we should not be fazed by it. At some point, attention will turn to the governor's legislation, and after much public noise, it is expected that the governor's approach will prevail."

Brown negotiated among the parties, ending with round-robin talks in his chambers—the UFW in one room, the Teamsters in another, the growers in a third. On May 5, 1975, they had a deal. With all the parties assembled in his office, Brown called Chavez on the speakerphone and asked him if he would support the compromise. Chavez feigned hesitation before he agreed, though the growers were not fooled. The room broke into applause.

The law contained so many provisions favorable to the union that the growers lost track and mistakenly announced in their trade magazine that the boycott had been outlawed. Farmworkers would have the right to support a union without fear of retribution, and employers would face penalties if they violated those rights. Workers would vote in expedited secret-ballot elections and could trigger an election within forty-eight hours if they walked out on strike. The union could still boycott under certain circumstances. Growers who failed to negotiate in good faith faced severe penalties, including back pay to all their workers. No other union in the country had the right to unilaterally determine the good standing of its members.

Growers needed the governor's help on other issues, such as water, and Brown exerted his political clout to add another twist: the legislature must approve the exact measure he had negotiated, with not a single change, or the deal was off. In a last-minute trade, the UFW agreed to allow the Teamster contracts to remain in effect until elections took place, and in exchange the bill would be passed in special session and go into effect ninety days later, in time for the late summer season. Brown signed the Agricultural Labor Relations Act on June 5, 1975. The law became the shared legacy of the two men who had gone for a short walk in Los Angeles less than three months earlier.

Brown understood the law marked a profound turning point for the UFW, a milestone that risked draining the energy from the movement if the union could not make a successful transition from guerilla warfare. That was the argument he had used with growers: that a legal structure worked to their advantage. Some growers supported the law because they believed they could beat the union in elections; others calculated they could outlast Chavez.

Chavez had been well aware of the pitfalls, and now, at his moment of great triumph, he was apprehensive. Congratulations poured in as the outside world hailed the improbable victory: the farmworkers had negotiated the most favorable labor law in the country. For Chavez, the future appeared far more cloudy.

He sighed when Jacques Levy asked if the law would do to the farm worker movement what federal legislation had done to the civil rights movement—rob the struggle of its spirit. "The whole fight's going to change," Chavez said. "Because once you're recognized, that's essentially what the law does, then the essential fight of recognition, which is the one that appeals to the human mind and the heart, more than anything else, is no longer there. Then from that point on, you're talking about wages, you're talking about money, you're talking about benefits, you're talking about . . . something more diffuse and not as crucial and critical."

He predicted that growers would sign contracts as long as the union was negotiating with an entire industry, so that no individual was at a competitive disadvantage. He foresaw that growers would improve wages and benefits in order to convince the workers they did not need the union. The great challenge that worried him was whether he could sustain a movement. "The only thing that will keep us going will be if we get into, if we can develop the movement into a real commitment to giving. By that I mean giving to other people who need to struggle, giving them help, but giving them substantial and real help. If we can do that, we can continue to have a movement."

He talked vaguely about helping build unions in Europe, the Philippines, and Latin America, in countries where people thought they were too poor to organize. The farm worker movement could serve as a model that taught poor people how to organize and demand rights when they had no resources with which to fight, except their own lives. "If we can set ourselves up so we can give," Chavez said, "then we'll keep our movement. Short of that, nothing can keep us going."

PART IV

June 1975–November 1978

CHAPTER 27

Elections in the Fields

*We knew that the new legislation was going to have an impact on the union,
but we had no way of knowing how big it would be . . . We have to find a way
of enduring.*

With just ten weeks to prepare for elections in the fields, Cesar Chavez
deployed his best organizers to areas of California where competition
would be most fierce. Alone in La Paz after everyone had fanned out
across the state, the union leader struggled to define his role in this
new world.

He traveled to a meeting in Calexico and watched the UFW film *Fighting for Our Lives* with a group of workers. He had seen the movie about
the brutal summer of 1973 dozens of times, and his mind wandered.
"During the film, you know, I was thinking, well, what am I going to do?"
Chavez recalled a few weeks later. He couldn't envision himself behind a
desk at La Paz while everyone else was in the field, though he realized
that might be helpful for coordinating the campaigns. "I've got to be out
there," he said. If he drove from place to place, he would spend most of
his time in the car. "And right there I said, 'March!'"

Chavez began to plan his route that night. He decided to begin at the
San Diego border and walk up the coast. Starting at the southern end of
the state would give organizers in the battleground areas of Salinas,
Oxnard, and Delano more time to build support before he arrived. "It's
just being with the people," he said about the appeal of the long walk.
Workers were less afraid to join a march than attend a meeting. Walking,
like singing or praying, was participatory. Families and children could
join. "It's like a common language, especially with the Mexican worker. I

can't explain," he said. "I know that if you walk, something happens to people. If they walk, something more beautiful happens."

No one knew what would happen when the law went into effect on August 28, 1975, creating a state agency to oversee union activity in the fields. A lot would depend on the five-member Agricultural Labor Relations Board (ALRB) and the general counsel to the agency, who supervised elections. Governor Brown made good on his commitment to Chavez and appointed a sympathetic board, including former UFW official LeRoy Chatfield. To chair the historic board, Brown persuaded Bishop Roger Mahony to temporarily forsake his clerical duties. The board immediately faced dozens of crucial decisions about eligibility of voters, union organizers' access to workers in the fields, and election procedures. Some policies would be decided by regulations, and many would ultimately be decided by the courts. "The first month is going to be incredibly chaotic," Jerry Cohen predicted when he briefed the union staff. "It's unbelievable the problems the state is going to be faced with, they have no notion of what's going to happen to them. We may not have any notion of what's going to happen to us either," he added with a laugh.

Chavez summoned to La Paz the executive board members, boycott leaders, field office directors, and key volunteers so that Cohen could explain the intricacies of the law and walk them through the cycle. Elections had to take place during peak season, when more than half the company's total workers were employed. The union needed to collect cards—nonbinding pledges of support for the UFW—from more than half the workers to file for an election. Once the board certified the petition, an election would be held within seven days. At every step of the way, there could be violations, problems, challenges, and appeals. "That's the campaign . . . it's chaos!" Cohen said. "Remember, we thrive on chaos!"

For a decade, Chavez had argued that his union represented the workers and would win in any fair contest. Now he faced pressure to live up to those claims. He warned his staff the union had a short window to succeed, and he outlined the challenges realistically. If the union won elections and did not negotiate contracts fast enough, workers would get discouraged. If strikes became necessary to convince recalcitrant growers to sign, workers would equate a vote for the UFW with a strike. Growers would begin to match union wages and argue workers did not need the UFW. "Our best time to win elections is this year," he said.

Chavez suggested a campaign modeled on those the union had

conducted for Robert F. Kennedy and Proposition 22. "We'll make it a movement election and get the people involved," he said. The first set of rallies should focus on the law and the workers' right to the union of their choice. A second set would feature *Fighting for Our Lives*. In between, the Service Center would help workers with medical, immigration, and other non-work-related complaints—a version of Chavez's old "problem clinic."

His best organizers had other ideas. They faced tight deadlines, dozens of quirks in the law to master and litigate, and hundreds of workers to win over. Only a targeted approach would yield enough cards to file petitions on August 28. Then they would need to hold on to supporters, in the face of strong campaigns from the Teamsters and the growers, to win elections.

The UFW leaders debated major strategic choices, often with insufficient information. Should they focus on taking contracts away from the Teamsters or file for elections at ranches that had no existing contracts? How would they compile accurate lists of eligible voters at each ranch? Who would inform workers of their rights and protect them if employers retaliated against union supporters?

The issue that aroused the most passionate debate would prove more peripheral to their ultimate success: whether illegal immigrants should vote. The law did not address the question, and Cohen asked whether Chavez wanted to seek clarification from the new state board. Cohen was not optimistic about the chances of a regulation that would bar undocumented workers from voting and unsure the idea made sense from a legal or political perspective.

Chavez grew agitated. He warned that illegal immigrants posed a threat to the union's election chances, especially in areas where the Illegals Campaign had been most active. Huerta agreed: "All an employer has to do, all he has to say is, 'If the union wins, you guys are going to be out of a job.' And that is true. Everybody knows it's true. We know it, they know it, the other workers know it."

Chavez went further, making accusations that reflected the depth of his feelings on the immigrant issue. He charged the federal government had made a deal with Mexico to look the other way and leave undocumented immigrants in the fields in order to create an informal bracero program. "It's a union busting operation of the biggest goddamn order. And the CIA is part of it," Chavez declared. Mexican leaders had warned the United States that if the border was sealed, "the Communists will take over Mexico," thus triggering the involvement of the CIA.

He offered neither substantiation nor concrete suggestions. Manuel Chavez, who had engineered the wet line to keep immigrants from crossing the border when he believed they were breaking his strike, now cheerfully switched positions. The UFW must win their votes, he declared: "I'm not afraid to have an election with illegals."

Manuel dismissed his cousin's hand-wringing and accused the naysayers of looking for excuses to fail. "Let's go at it! Let's go fight and see if we win!" he said. "Let's not be afraid of the people. The people will respond. If we're a good union, they're going to vote for us. If we're a bad union, they're not gonna vote for us."

Manuel's bravado received support from Richard Chavez, who backed up his cousin with more down-to-earth arguments. Several field office directors had said the majority of the workers in various areas were undocumented. "If they're the workers, we should organize them," Richard said simply. They may have been strikebreakers in the past, he said, but now "they're not breaking strikes because nobody's breaking strikes. They're the workers, and were going to go out and organize whoever's working in those fields."

For Cesar, the issue was as much an emotional flash point as an organizing challenge. He dismissed the possibility the UFW might win over undocumented Mexicans, whom he viewed as a monolithic group, beholden to the grower or the labor contractor. Chavez rejected arguments that immigrants would be open to embrace the union for the same reasons as other workers. He clung to his vision of illegal immigrants as a threat, as well as a convenient scapegoat for election losses. The man who had adopted "si se puede" as his motto spoke like a defeatist.

"What do you have if they vote for you?" he pressed. "You still don't have a union . . . they're not going to support you in the contract . . . Anyone here who doesn't think that the growers are going to use the same work force to destroy the union on elections that they use on strikes has to take a real good look at themselves. It's there. That's what they've been using to break the union. You think they're going to stop now?"

Cohen pointed out ways the new law would help protect undocumented workers' right to vote and urged that they focus on strategies for pressuring growers to allow workers to freely support the union of their choice.

"Brothers and sisters, we have a real problem," Chavez warned again. "The illegals aren't going to vote for us just because we're there."

"That's right," shot back Manuel. "You've got to work for it."

The split mirrored a deeper division among the union leaders—one group anticipated elections with enthusiasm, the other with trepidation. Younger organizers like Marshall Ganz and Eliseo Medina were eager for the fight, confident they had strong arguments to persuade workers to vote for the UFW and excited about the first-ever secret ballot elections in the fields. Many of the older organizers took their cues from Chavez, who voiced obvious ambivalence about the new law.

When Cohen explained how they would challenge any elections the UFW lost, and then added, "Of course we're not going to lose elections," Chavez cut him off: "We're going to lose elections. It's going to be the hardest fight we're ever going to have. I hope you're just kidding when you say that. You guys get it through your head." He spoke of workers in Coachella refusing to sign cards supporting the UFW and predicted that growers would hire experienced antiunion propaganda experts. "It's going to be hard. It's going to be hard getting those cards signed. Imagine what the elections are going to be like."

While his staff worked frantically to collect signed cards, Chavez marched. All through July, he walked as much as thirty miles a day, attending evening rallies organized by his staff along the route. Unlike the 1966 march to Sacramento, with its striking visual imagery of farm-workers stretched out single file along the highways, the central attraction of the "1,000 mile march" was Chavez. This time he wore tennis shoes for comfort. His aides helped wash and bandage his sore feet. Security guards drove him to the rallies at night and to and from his accommodations. Instead of the Teatro Campesino and the "Plan de Delano," each evening featured *Fighting for Our Lives*. As he talked with workers along the way, he did not need to mention too much about the law, Chavez told Jacques Levy midway through the march. His presence was enough. "The sacri-fice, they understand," he said. "Mostly women will come, some men. And they will embrace me, and they cry, and they say, "Stop walking. It's too much sacrifice. It's too much. Five hundred miles is just too much. We'll do it from now on."

Medina saw that response when he met Chavez on the outskirts of Oxnard. Chavez had assigned Medina to handle elections in a Teamster stronghold—the only area where the rival union had won contracts on their own, rather than sweetheart deals signed to preempt the UFW. "You got a real fight on your hands," Chavez told Medina. The assignment was a vintage Chavez gamble: If Medina succeeded, the victory would help the union. If he failed, the loss would dim Medina's luster. Medina joined the march and walked with Chavez ten miles across the Oxnard plain. Tired after only half a day, Medina was impressed again with Chavez's willingness to sacrifice.

From Oxnard, Chavez continued to Santa Barbara, where the local paper sent a part-time photographer to cover the march. Cathy Murphy's first impression was how small Chavez looked, how incongruous his body seemed with his dauntingly large mission. Then she saw the piercing, determined eyes. She went back to shoot more pictures the next day, drawn in by his power. Chavez liked her photos and invited her to join the staff. The thirty-three-year-old dropped her photojournalism studies, quit her job, sent her six-year-old son to live with his grandparents for the rest of the summer, and joined the movement. After three days on the march, her feet were so blistered that she asked permission to ride with the security guards for a day. Instead, Chavez called for a tub of hot water with salts and sat while she soaked her feet. He broke the blisters with a needle. She thought of Jesus and Mary.

Another hundred miles north, Chavez entered the Salinas Valley in King City, where he had gone with Fred Ross in 1953 to investigate a race riot. The lettuce workers in the valley turned out in full force to cheer Chavez. He reminded them of the great struggles the union had endured in the past decade to reach this milestone, and of the fights no one had thought they could win. "It is because of these sacrifices that we have a law, and not because the politicians all of sudden wanted to give us a law," he said. "We are involved in this campaign for one reason—At stake is the dignity of the worker." Chants of "Viva Chavez!" punctuated the speech. "For the first time, the worker has come to realize that he has a lot of worth. And that realization has made him stand up and be proud and be counted."

Chavez timed the first part of the march to end in the second UFW convention, designed to build enthusiasm for elections. "We have survived jailings, beatings, professional goons, biased judges, racist law enforcers and the violent deaths of two of our brothers," Chavez said in his opening speech. "We have learned to match our opponents' riches with our blood, sweat, dedication and hard work. For all their money and sordid influence, the growers and Teamsters have not been able to destroy our movement. Now our time has come."

Several hundred boycotters had traveled back to California to join the celebration. Jessica Govea had left Toronto on a bus with about twenty boycottters at midnight on Sunday, August 10, joined up with boycotters in Detroit and then Chicago, and spent four days in a bus caravan to reach Fresno on the eve of the convention. She was known for her beautiful singing voice, and when Chavez called upon her to sing for the audience, Govea apologized for being hoarse from the long trip. Along with many of the boycotters, Govea stayed in California after the convention and joined the frenetic election preparations.

Chavez left the convention to complete the last lap of his walk through the San Joaquin Valley. As critical questions arose, staff members had to drive to find him on the march and walk with Chavez to discuss the issues. Cohen was already frustrated by Chavez's lack of interest in the strategic details. The two men had testified at a hearing on proposed regulations, and when the meeting was simultaneously translated into Spanish, Chavez became overwhelmed with emotion. He teared up at the sign of respect and told Cohen they had won a great victory. Cohen, intent on lobbying to get symbols on the ballot because many workers could not read, was dismayed by Chavez's lack of interest in the nitty-gritty decisions.

In the field offices, nitty-gritty decisions had become all-consuming. The evening before the ALRB was to spring to life, a crowd of workers gathered outside the board's Salinas office. A priest said mass and the workers settled in for an all-night vigil to make sure they would file the first, historic petition. When the doors opened and a state agent tried to escort a Teamster representative into the building, a near-riot ensued. The start was every bit as chaotic as Cohen had predicted.

Workers who had never cast a ballot in their life lined up to vote for "*la union de Cesar Chavez*," marking an X next to the picture of the eagle. In Oxnard, Medina's staff assembled cards from twenty-two companies he had targeted, half of which had Teamster contracts. In Salinas, Cohen's second in command, Sandy Nathan, was in the board office every day, screaming at the state agents about unfair access for Teamsters and demanding that they protect workers from retaliation. When police and immigration agents raided a labor camp a week before elections and tried to deport thirty-two undocumented workers who supported the UFW, Nathan went to find them in the detention center. He ended up under arrest, handcuffed to Ganz. The workers who had been in danger of deportation were allowed to cast ballots.

For weeks, the results of many elections remained secret because growers persuaded state officials to seal the ballots pending legal challenges. State agents were untrained, many unfamiliar with agriculture, and none accustomed to the feverish pace. In the first month, more than thirty-thousand workers voted in 194 elections.

The union hired five hundred organizers, many of them farmworkers, for $100 a week. Chavez decided where to throw resources based in part on the Teamsters and in part on what he called psychological reasons. He poured resources into losing campaigns at Gallo and Giumarra, the vineyards that had been poster children for the boycott. In private, Chavez regretted the decision, which he blamed for diverting resources that hurt in Delano, where the union lost all but a handful of contests. "This one breaks my heart, Delano," Chavez said sadly, as he reviewed the record. In public, Chavez blamed Teamster-grower collusion for the union's defeats. "There is now a reign of terror, especially in the Delano area," he said. "There are no free elections in Delano." He claimed UFW supporters refused to vote out of fear, despite the secret ballots.

Chavez called the executive board to a meeting at La Paz to plan a different kind of campaign, one where he felt on sure ground: an attack on the new state agency. Many of the three dozen state board agents had been making decisions that favored growers and Teamsters. Chavez wanted to expose the conspiracy between growers and the board, he said, calling the past two weeks "the most frustrating in the history of the union," with the sort of hyperbole that had become second nature.

His view was not universally shared. In Oxnard, Medina had won eight elections to the Teamsters' two, taking companies away from the opposition's strongest organizers. In Salinas, Ganz had successfully adjusted his tactics in response to the growers, who had initially advocated a "no union" vote and then switched to supporting the Teamsters. Ganz urged that union leaders evaluate their own performance. "It's not a depressed scene," he told Chavez. In San Diego, Scott Washburn won five out of six elections. The competition with the Teamsters forced UFW organizers to articulate reasons why workers should vote for the black eagle. The successful organizers applied the lessons they had learned from Chavez: listen to the workers and respond to their needs.

Chavez dismissed their victories. If a grower supported the Teamsters, the UFW could not win, Chavez told the group. "Harder, but not impossible," Ganz countered. "Impossible," Chavez repeated. "A miracle," Huerta added.

Chavez interrupted the meeting to take a call from Roger Mahony and warned the bishop that the UFW would attack the board and the governor if the situation did not improve. "I told him, we're working fulltime.

We don't want to win elections any more. We want to prove to you and everybody else that the whole thing stinks."

"We're better at that anyway," Jim Drake replied, and everyone laughed.

They all agreed that the ignorance of many board agents posed impediments, and organizers wanted to pressure the state to correct egregious favoritism toward growers and Teamsters. The process needed to be streamlined so that results and appeals were handled expeditiously. If workers had to wait months for justice after they were unfairly punished or fired, confidence in the new law would erode.

"What the hell are we going to do?" Chavez asked. "Boycott the elections? Cry? Continue to cry about what they're doing to us?"

"Go after the board," Ganz responded.

"Go after Brown," Cohen said. "Fuck Brown."

"Brown, Brown, Brown," chanted Chris Hartmire. "Get him! . . . It's a big feather in his cap. Let's put mud all over it!"

Chavez liked the idea of attacking the governor. He wanted a villain, and he found one—Walter Kintz, general counsel of the Agricultural Labor Relations Board (ALRB), who supervised board agents in the regional offices. They must force Kintz out, Chavez declared. His mood brightened. He was back in his element, planning a campaign. He told Hartmire to organize religious observers to visit and document abuses. Chavez would go on television, hold press conferences, and demand Kintz's resignation. The union would organize a letter-writing campaign to Brown, and if necessary stage sit-ins to increase the pressure. The governor was contemplating a run for president; Hartmire suggested they could tarnish his reputation around the country. "Get a few people who want to run for president to come here," Chavez added.

Chavez spent a day in San Francisco for media appearances in which he attacked Kintz. He persuaded Meany to send several top AFL-CIO officials to Delano to witness the problems. Hartmire brought two religious delegations. Brown appointed a task force to investigate the problems and report back, but Chavez was dubious that would achieve real results. Farmworkers picketed an appearance by Kintz, and Chavez warned that the governor would face pickets, too, unless he removed Kintz. Huerta suggested they enlist legislators from East Los Angeles and other heavily Chicano areas to pressure Brown. "If we can just get the Chicano community on his ass, that's all we need to do," Chavez agreed.

When the governor did not relent, Chavez sent Washburn with a delegation of farmworkers who had been fired from jobs in San Diego to stage a vigil outside Brown's Sacramento office. More than fifty workers camped out, first on the floor and then on couches in the governor's reception area. When Brown returned to the office around midnight on the third night of the sit-in, he spoke with the group for three hours, and they finally dispersed.

The task force corrected many of the problems. During its first three months of operation, the ALRB conducted 329 elections, handed down fifteen formal opinions, and scheduled three hundred hearings around the state. Of the 38,164 ballots cast, only 16 percent were for no union. In head-to-head contests, the Teamsters outpolled the UFW, but overall the UFW won more elections than it lost.

Winners and losers also became clear among the union staff. During the boycott, no one had known if an organizer failed to set up picket lines one weekend or fudged his numbers. "When it comes to elections, you win them, or you lose them," Ganz said during an argument over the competence of certain staff members. "You either do the work, or you don't. There's no bullshit about it." Mistakes were glaring, and costly. One error could have statewide ramifications. The winners were those who applied all they had learned from Chavez to navigate the new state rules. The losers were those who had always counted on Chavez to tell them what to do; they looked to him for guidance, but he struggled to find his footing.

Much as he loved a fight, Chavez never mastered the new game. He was immersed in the smallest details about the administration of La Paz, but not the minutiae essential to winning elections. He was uncomfortable playing by someone else's rules; his past successes had depended on the ability to spring surprises, pivot 180 degrees on a moment's notice, and make outrageous demands and bluffs. Elections called for methodical organizing. The best organizers could predict election outcomes within a handful of votes.

"We knew that the new legislation was going to have an impact on the union, but we had no way of knowing how big it would be," Chavez said in an interview. "It changed everything. It affected everything we do, even our way of thinking . . . We now are faced with trying to find out how to maintain the vitality we had, so that it goes beyond just shouting, 'Viva la huelga.' . . . We have to find a way of enduring."

The union's center of gravity shifted inexorably away from La Paz and Delano, toward the coastal regions of Salinas and Oxnard where the bulk of the new members worked, and the Imperial and Coachella Valleys.

Chavez resisted the message in the early election results, which would become increasingly clear: The union's greatest strength was among the vegetable and citrus workers. He clung to a sentimental attachment to the Delano area and a determination to win in the vineyards where he had begun his quest. "It's in the valley towns where we have our strength," he insisted. "People will sacrifice . . . They've been in the union longer . . . They have less love for money than the others. That's the difference."

Organizers in the field pressed to consolidate their victories with contracts. "What kind of time schedule are we looking at for negotiations and who's going to be doing it?" Medina asked at the fall 1975 board meeting. "I don't have it quite worked out in my mind," Chavez replied. In the meantime, he said, organizers should work with ranch committees to form negotiating committees, compile seniority lists, and preliminary lists of demands. Medina and Ganz said they had already done that.

"I think it's important for us to go out there and get a contract so that we can show some concrete results," Medina said. "Not just winning an election and then sitting there and sitting there and sitting there with nothing happening." Inaction would hand the Teamsters a campaign issue: the UFW didn't deliver. "It sounds to me, we're talking about a month or more. And I think waiting can be very harmful."

"No not a month," Chavez said. "We're talking about doing it right away."

Medina persisted: "What do you mean by right away?"

Chavez said they needed to discuss strategy before he could answer that question and promised the timetable would be clear by the end of the night.

But nothing was clear by the time they adjourned. Medina had developed a strategic plan for Oxnard and targeted dozens more companies for elections. A month later, Chavez decided the priority was fighting the Teamsters. He moved Medina to Coachella, one of the most difficult areas for the union because of the short season, the transitory nature of the workforce, and resentment among grape growers who had chafed under the 1970 contracts.

Even in Coachella, Medina and his troops found moments to savor. John Gardner, one of Medina's strongest organizers, wrote to Fred Ross in late December, describing election night at Valdora Produce Company. David Valdora got very drunk, bet thousands of dollars that his workers would reject the UFW, then watched in astonishment as ballots were counted and the union triumphed. "You deserve a Christmas present,"

Gardner wrote, "and maybe one of the best ones is the reassurance that everything is proceeding smoothly, at least for the moment, without your presence for impending emergencies and general directions."

Perhaps if Chavez had been in the middle of campaigns instead of isolated at La Paz, he might have shared in the excitement and found a way to direct his talent for organizational jujitsu toward winning elections and gaining converts. Instead, he grew frustrated at the welter of deadlines and pressures imposed by the state law and competing requests from organizers around the state. Separate power bases developed, harder for Chavez to control from La Paz. He had always been able to aim the union machinery at one goal—the boycott, No on Proposition 22, the Teamsters. Now different demands had to be juggled, under tight deadlines.

"You know what made the movement?" he asked rhetorically in a pensive moment. "The one thing that helped us all the time is that we've had all the time we needed, and more. We've never had any deadline. The moment we get into deadline things, like [publishing] the *Malcriado*, like having the reports on time—we screw up. But when we have all the time in the world . . . See, the difference here is that time is not going to be as good a friend as it's been in other cases."

At the beginning of 1976, Chavez caught a break. The initial appropriation for the ALRB had been $1.3 million. The board blew through that quickly and received a $1.25 million emergency appropriation. Over five months, the board had conducted 423 elections. Preliminary results gave the UFW 192 victories, while the Teamsters won 119. Twice as many workers voted for the UFW as chose the Teamsters. In only 25 contests did workers reject both unions.

When the board's funds ran low again at the end of 1975, growers prevailed on the legislature not to authorize more money. On February 6, 1976, the ALRB shut down. The closure looked like a defeat and handed the UFW another public campaign issue. In reality, Chavez welcomed the breathing room. Time was on his side again, for a while.

CHAPTER 28

The Crosby Era

We need help. It's like somebody growing up in the Depression. All of a sudden, the Depression ends. But he's attuned to being in the Depression, and pretty soon it's prosperity, and he doesn't know how to deal with it.

Chavez took advantage of the respite from elections to focus on the administration of the union that had grown so large, so fast. He needed to consolidate, much as Saul Alinsky had urged back in the CSO days. Just as in San Jose in 1956, Chavez struggled with the "staying organized" phase. He recognized he had no expertise in organizational structure. "We're people people," he said. "We know how to deal with people and organize people. When it comes to shuffling papers . . . we're lost."

Determined to conquer this new world, Chavez made an unusual move. In early 1976, he turned to a stranger for help. Crosby Milne, a retired navy man and self-taught management consultant, had been drawn into the UFW by his son, who dropped out of college to join the boycott.

Chavez and Milne shared certain bonds. Milne had grown up poor in rural Canada, in a house without indoor plumbing. He was deeply religious and largely self-educated. He had joined the navy as a mechanic, discovered a knack for devising systems to straighten out troubled situations, and became a systems expert. His outsider's perspective and homespun comments appealed to Chavez. Every person is a creator, Milne often preached. He had learned three principles from an admiral, which he said would guarantee control and success: never take yourself too seriously, don't get into a pissing match with a skunk, and never let an SOB know you know he's an SOB. Chavez loved that line and prompted Milne to repeat it often.

During the summer of 1975, Milne had gone to visit his son, hoping to persuade him to finish college. Milne attended a rally along the 1,000 mile march and watched as Chavez climbed on a park table, then realized that half the crowd was behind him no matter which direction he faced. As the crowd good-naturedly chanted the union slogan "Which side are you on?" Chavez jumped down and moved the table back so that no one else need move. Milne was sold. He offered his services to the union for a year, which he viewed as a gift to his adopted country during its bicentennial.

To introduce Milne to the executive board, Chavez called a special meeting at the Mission San Antonio de Padua, toward the southern end of the Salinas Valley. Chavez explained that he had invited Milne to the retreat to help figure out a structure to make the union work. Over the next four days, Chavez raised logistical and philosophical issues that would become flash points over the next two years: his wish that the leadership move to La Paz, his desire to train young Chicanos in disciplines like the law, the need for a process that allowed union staff members to air grievances before they became festering problems, the difficulty in finding the right person to restart El Malcriado, and above all the need for more contracts so the union might become financially stable. "Members aren't paying for it," Chavez told the board. "And as long as that's the case, we can't really say we have a union."

At the outset of the retreat, Medina asked Chavez how they knew they could trust Milne with the most intimate workings of their organization. Ganz questioned his military background. Chavez verbally shrugged. He said he trusted Milne but could not vouch for him unreservedly. He thought, however, that they had no choice. Milne might turn out to be a spy, Chavez said, but he definitely knew his stuff.

"We need help," he told the board. "It's like somebody growing up in the Depression. All of a sudden, the Depression ends. But he's attuned to being in the Depression, and pretty soon it's prosperity, and he doesn't know how to deal with it . . . We grew up under tremendous stress. Everything we did was like fire drills. We ran from one fire drill to another. All of a sudden, either actually or because the press began to say that we're successful . . . we're successful. Yet, we're not successful."

The executive board voted unanimously to accept Milne's help and spent four days immersed in flow charts and lists. The heart of Milne's program was what he called SAMS—specific, attainable, measurable goals. Milne used his favorite example to explain goals and objectives:

President Kennedy had a goal to explore outer space, and he set an objective to land a man on the moon. Under Milne's tutelage, Chavez told the board, he had become convinced that to meet objectives, the union must centralize power. Officers should have broad statewide functions rather than regional responsibilities. Chavez announced new assignments: Ganz to run the organizing department, Medina to head contract administration, Padilla for financial management, and Richard Chavez to direct the Service Center. Huerta was assigned temporarily to the Personnel Department. The executive board enthusiastically endorsed the new structure.

Chavez's insistence that union leaders should live at La Paz met with a decidedly less warm response. He persisted, pressing an issue that would take on increasing importance. Few were swayed when Chavez prompted a testimonial from Padilla, who said he had never been happier living anywhere else. "Everybody's moving to La Paz, it's going to be so crowded, I'm willing to give up my happiness to somebody else," Richard Chavez said, arguing that an assignment should not require officers to live in the compound. People who lived on the outside were ostracized, Cesar responded, because they were rejecting the community.

"Being honest about it, some of us just don't want to be at La Paz," said Jerry Cohen. Chavez had recently acquiesced to Cohen's personal considerations and allowed him to move the legal department to Salinas, hundreds of miles from union headquarters. Chavez was having second thoughts. "We're having one hell of a problem," he told the board. "We're going to work it back."

Milne showed no reluctance about La Paz and moved there with his wife. He spent many hours with Chavez, who discussed his dream for a broader Poor Peoples Union and his determination to avoid the failures of the CSO. They shared meals and attended mass. On Easter, Chavez washed Milne's feet. Over several months, the two men held a dozen conferences, each lasting several days, with every department—legal, boycott, contract administration, political action, data processing, security, financial management, even the National Farm Worker Ministry. They charted goals and objectives for each department and for the union as a whole, so that people could see how their work fit into the larger picture.

"God, we never knew we would have to go into all these things: law, initiative, politics, SAMs, goals, budgets . . . If I'd known that I would have said, 'Screw it,'" Chavez said at the Organizing Department conference. "But it was essentially the organizing which I loved and I still like, but I can't do it these days. It's like candy behind a glass counter." They sketched out short- and long-term goals. "We must be missionary," Chavez said. "If we are missionary and visionary, in ten years we will be in Asia, Latin America, Africa . . . organizing farmworkers of the world."

At the moment, however, the union had only fifteen contracts and a few thousand members. The UFW had won 207 elections and been certified by the state board at half those ranches but had yet to start negotiations in most places. In Delano, for example, the union had one contract that covered fifty-three jobs; five thousand other workers had voted for the UFW and now clamored for attention. Chavez latched on to Milne's system as a solution to propel the union out of a morass that threatened to become overwhelming.

Chavez confronted a paradox. The more elections the UFW won, the more resources had to be diverted toward serving new members, and the less expansion they could afford—delaying his dreams of a broader movement. He did not want to stagnate like other unions. He needed contracts to stabilize the union's finances, but contracts imposed new demands. "Once you get a contract, you get a string around your neck," Chavez warned a young farmworker organizer from Ohio who wanted to affiliate with the UFW. "Right now, we have a clear shot at California, and goddamn it, we're being held back by our own success. We got to go into all kinds of other things. Servicing, negotiating, getting involved in guarding our right flank and our left flank and the rear flank. When other unions used to tell us that, we didn't believe them."

Chavez embraced Milne's boxes and charts and began to implement change, in a somewhat stilted fashion that clashed with the union's free-wheeling style and prompted parodies. Chavez set up a numbered system for administrative divisions and sent out memos creating a Personnel Relations Department, code 40000. He issued directives, beginning with Instruction 1:0001, which he promised would codify the policies of the union. He instructed staff members to place the directives in a loose-leaf binder, filed by code and subject; they eventually totaled more than a hundred pages.

Milne asked Chavez to list all the people who reported to him. They stopped when he hit fifty. Chavez headed a labor union, a Service Center, a pension trust, a health insurance program, a credit union, two political action committees, a death benefit insurance program, and several other nonprofit entities. More than a hundred people lived and worked at La Paz. Hundreds more worked in the union's two dozen field offices and thirty boycott offices—and most reported directly to Chavez. Milne told Chavez that would have to change.

The new structure established clear lines of authority. Department heads would have decision-making power. "This is what's going to save you," Chavez told his staff. "You have to delegate more and more things to your people, and hold them accountable. The big thing is that you have to be able to let go."

Chavez had trouble following his own advice. He accepted the trade-off in theory: he could delegate more authority and maintain control by demanding accountability. In practice, Chavez gave subordinates full authority—provided, as he spelled out in Instruction 1:0003, that they "cut in" the president on any decisions involving the budget, priorities, programs, policies, schedules, personnel, and procedures. That language covered virtually all decisions that a department head might make, leaving Chavez free to overrule at any time. Sometimes he intervened on significant policy issues. Other times he chastised subordinates over petty matters. He monitored use of phone lines to determine who made the most calls. He still wanted to know, as his brother Richard had said a few years back, when anyone needed a new battery for a car.

A dispute with West Foods, a major mushroom grower in Oxnard, illustrated both the potential strength of the union and Chavez's difficulty adapting to the new management system. That tension would only increase as the union expanded.

From the start, West Foods had defied Chavez's predictions. By his calculation the union should never have won the election—about 80 percent of the 220 workers lacked legal papers. But Medina had successfully organized the workers he called *visitantes* (visitors) during his stint in Oxnard in 1975. When the border patrol raided the mushroom grower a few days before the election, Medina denounced the action and UFW lawyers made sure the workers were able to stay and vote. The UFW won a resounding victory, taking an important contract away from the Teamsters. The win was one of Medina's most satisfying because his campaign had focused on the contrast: the Teamster organizers are labor leaders, he told the workers; we are farmworkers, like you.

Now in the summer of 1976, Medina was head of contract administration and his staff had been trying to negotiate a contract with West Foods. When talks stalled, he called a press conference to announce that workers intended to escalate their protest. He had routinely taken similar steps as a boycott leader.

"A large banner on a wall in the administration building reads, 'Let there be no surprises,'" Chavez chastised Medina in a note complaining he had not been informed of the press conference. "You surprised the hell out of me . . . You must clear with me on these matters before you act."

West Foods workers voted to go on strike, and Medina kept Chavez informed. All but ten workers walked picket lines in two 12-hour shifts that began at 4:00 A.M. and 4:00 P.M. Community supporters delivered more food than the pickets could eat. When Chavez returned to his old stomping grounds for a rally, arriving late on a foggy night, "the first thing we saw was the outline of a flag," he recalled happily. Then he heard the singing. "All these guys with serapes, and hats. The moment we got there they were passing around a big basket with tacos, steaming hot burritos."

West Foods lost nineteen tons of overripe mushrooms during the strike. After a twenty-hour marathon negotiation, the company and union reached agreement. "The first contract we've gotten by a strike!" Richard Chavez exclaimed.

To workers like those at West Foods, immigrants without legal papers who harvested mushrooms in dark, stiflingly hot rooms that smelled of manure, with no clean drinking water or adequate ventilation, the victory of *la union de Cesar Chavez* was nothing short of miraculous. "*Nuestro Moises*," workers in the fields began to call Chavez—our Moses.

Chavez continued to enjoy widespread popularity outside the fields as well. In a Harris poll, seventeen million people—12 percent of all adults in the United States—said they had boycotted grapes. The public favored Chavez over the Teamsters by a margin of six to one, and supported Chavez over the growers as well, by a narrower 34 to 29 percent split.

"Out of the ruin of the 1960s, one remarkable institution and one remarkable leader survived," Jack Newfield wrote in the *Village Voice* on May 10, 1976.

> Martin King, Malcolm X, and Robert Kennedy were assassinated. SDS, SNCC and the Beatles fell apart. Rennie Davis discovered a teenage guru. Tim Leary became an informer. Huey Newton beat up an old man and jumped bail. Rap Brown is in prison for armed robbery. *Ramparts* expired. Jimi Hendrix, Janis Joplin, and now Phil Ochs are dead. But Cesar Chavez and the United Farm Workers endured, and grew, and faltered, and rallied, and became the one tangible thing we could point to and

say yes, this is good, this works, this is an example of the world we want to create.

By the time he was interviewed by Newfield, Chavez's stories about his early years had strayed farther from the facts. He said he had attended sixty-seven schools by seventh grade and that he had been trained by Fred Ross as a teenager.

"We're here to stay," he said in a newspaper interview. "We don't have to do now what we've been doing for 13 years. But we've got to sharpen up our management. I understand this now, and it's exciting. It's creative. It's an experiment we're doing." On Tuesdays, he had instituted a communal lunch at La Paz. At five o'clock each day, they had "situation time," where about thirty people joined him to act out management situations. Milne's lessons and the idea that there was a science of management theory had piqued Chavez's natural curiosity. He was self-educated, deeply knowledgeable in certain areas and with enormous gaps in others, and disinclined to analyze information. When he embraced a new idea he swallowed it whole; he was convinced, for example, that the key to computerizing the union's files was to find the right hardware system. No amount of argument from others that the problem was software and programming could shake him from his conviction.

In the summer of 1976, Chavez faced a public test of his new management structure. After the state labor board had shut down in February and elections stopped, Jerry Cohen had prepared an initiative for the November ballot that would make the rights and regulations established under the Agricultural Labor Relations Act part of the California constitution. An initiative had been Chavez's original plan, before the governor threw his support behind legislative efforts. A campaign would capitalize on the union's support in the cities. By the end of February Chavez had told board members he wanted to proceed even if behind-the-scenes efforts to restart the ALRB succeeded.

The union passed the first hurdle easily. A petition blitz collected far more signatures than needed to place Proposition 14 on the ballot. Chavez celebrated the success of the union's new structure and increased efficiency at a meeting to debrief staff who had run the petition-gathering campaign. Medina hailed the union's new maturity. "In the past there was a fire and all of us grabbed hoses and buckets and we ran and left everything hanging," he told the boycotters. "We didn't do that this time." With the new structure, Medina predicted, "we're going to become not only the strongest but perhaps the largest Union in this country during the next four or five years."

A month later, the state legislature approved $6.5 million to reopen the ALRB, and the UFW faced a crucial decision: whether to invest money and resources to actively campaign for Proposition 14. Elections in the fields would start again within months, and the union was ill-prepared. Ganz and a dozen of his staff had been on loan to Jerry Brown's short-lived presidential campaign, which scored several upsets in Democratic primaries. The union had been steadily signing contracts, but still represented only a small fraction of the workers who had voted for the UFW. Ranch committees were just beginning to function effectively. A statewide campaign would sap all resources away from those efforts, at the very time the union had to gear up for more elections.

Chavez estimated a Prop 14 campaign would cost more than $1 million and have only a 40 percent chance of success. In mid-June 1976 he laid out to the board the arguments against proceeding: Only a small percentage of comparable initiatives had ever passed. A no vote was much easier to win than a yes vote. The initiative had started as a tactic to prod the state to refund the ALRB; now there was no necessity to pursue a costly and risky fight. Most board members agreed the union's limited resources should go toward negotiating and administering contracts. "Workers are getting antsy," Medina said, pointing to places where elections had been won a year earlier and the union had yet to return. "They see time passing by and they see nothing happening."

Fred Ross voiced the strongest dissent. He urged an all-out campaign for Prop 14 and challenged Chavez's lack of conviction.

"But see, Fred, if we lose the damn initiative, that's goodbye to everything," Chavez said. "To the board, and to the law. And we're in trouble."

"Cesar, if we don't do that, and we think we won, we're kidding ourselves," Ross responded. "In my opinion, we're going to be right back to the same spot. Those growers are never going to give up."

"Then we do exactly the same thing," Chavez said.

"We can't do the same thing. We'll have lost credibility in the eyes of the public," Ross said. If they backed off now, people would not take the union seriously. "Right now that ace is in the hole. We can bluff this year. We are bluffing this year. Next time we try to bluff, I don't think it's going to work."

Chavez postponed the decision.

A few weeks later, he flew to New York to attend the Democratic

National Convention. Eight years earlier, Chavez had watched Hubert Humphrey accept the nomination for president that he had hoped would go to Robert F. Kennedy. Knowing Humphrey would not mention the farmworkers, Chavez got down on his knees in front of the television and begged for a bone, much to Jerry Cohen's amusement. Now Cohen was in New York to watch Chavez deliver a nominating speech for California governor Jerry Brown, and the UFW was the most popular ticket in town. On the spur of the moment, Marshall Ganz and Jessica Govea put together a $10-a-ticket fund-raiser to precede Chavez's speech. They began planning Monday; Wednesday afternoon, crowds waited up to thirty minutes for the ancient elevators in the McAlpin Hotel to ascend to the party on the twenty-fourth floor. Chavez and Brown waded through crowds to the front of the room to make brief remarks. New York papers ran photographs of Jane Fonda auctioning off six autographed copies of Jacques Levy's book. The books sold for $1,100, and the event netted the UFW more than $8,500.

At 7:00 P.M. the party ended, and an hour later an estimated fifty million viewers watched Chavez nominate Brown, a speech carried in its entirety by the networks. Jimmy Carter won the nomination, but the UFW received credit for Brown's upset victories in several state primaries. The hottest item on the convention floor was the black eagle flag.

One week later, the UFW executive board met at La Paz to decide how to proceed on Proposition 14. They were riding high after the convention, confident of their political prowess. Chris Hartmire took notes in the front of the room as Chavez asked the board and staff to list pros and cons. The cons far outweighed the pros. The union's strongest argument—farmworkers were being denied the right to vote—had been undercut as soon as funding for the state board was restored. Opponents had seized on provisions in the initiative that allowed union organizers access to workers and framed the vote-no campaign as a defense of private property. Everyone agreed that had powerful appeal. Ganz presciently outlined the opposition's advertisements: "There will be a woman sleeping in bed, and all of a sudden the window will open, and in jumps Roberto Garcia . . . I'd take a picture of a grower's wife—'You mean they can come into my home?!'"

Chavez sidestepped the question of whether a $1 million campaign was the best use of the union's resources as he steered the board to the conclusion he had already reached. Can we win? he asked. Yes or no? At first, no one spoke. "I guess you got your answer!" snorted Richard

Chavez, the lone skeptic. "It's gonna take a big miracle and a big chunk of money."

"Yes or no?" his brother insisted. "Could it be won?" No, Richard answered.

The only other naysayer was Nick Jones, the national boycott director. Hartmire voiced some concern, disabusing Chavez of the idea that religious groups and editorial boards would understand the rationale now that elections were resuming. But the minister joined the chorus, confident that the union could once again overcome all odds. Imbued with the si se puede spirit, how could the answer be anything but yes? The vote was 8–1.

The governor called Chavez to urge that the union reconsider. Brown warned the campaign could backfire and energize opponents. Growers would launch a multimillion-dollar campaign that would be difficult to overcome. "I think it is a real problem," Brown said. He predicted the campaign would polarize communities and cost many of the UFW's allies a lot of political capital. "I don't see how the initiative can be justified in view of the fact that the money was appropriated and there is a board."

Chavez defended the decision with a standard line: "It is a mandate of the membership. I am not going to go against their wishes." Brown asked for an opportunity to speak with the board. Chavez said he was welcome but that it would be a waste of time. Brown and Assembly Speaker Leo McCarthy met with the UFW board the following weekend. McCarthy warned that Democrats from rural areas could not afford to support the controversial measure. He offered the UFW a deal: drop the campaign, and the Speaker would promise to fund the ALRB in time for elections to begin in late summer, and to protect the law for the next two years. As Chavez had predicted, the politicians' arguments fell on deaf ears.

Ganz took charge of the campaign, with Hartmire as second in command. Jones was told to bring boycotters to California to help. By the middle of September, Hartmire was worried. "We're getting burned already in the press," he said. Cohen and Drake agreed. The union had allowed the opposition to define the measure. Prop 14 was being portrayed not as the farmworkers' right to vote but as the union's right to trespass on private property. The California Supreme Court had upheld an ALRB rule that allowed union organizers access to workers in the fields three times a day, but that mattered little. Hartmire warned that the union needed to move fast to launch its own media campaign.

The era of door-to-door campaigns had given way to television advertising, and the UFW was caught unprepared. As Brown had predicted, the growers unleashed a well-funded television, radio, and print campaign. Harry Kubo, a Japanese American farmer interned during World War II, had formed the Nisei Farmers League in 1971, frustrated by the UFW's pickets and penchant for destructive acts. Within a year, he had four hundred members, who formed night patrols to protect against damage to irrigation pumps and fields. By 1976, Kubo was widowed with two teenage daughters. He hired a guard to watch his house while he spearheaded the opposition to Prop 14. He traveled thirty thousand miles between June and November and raised $1.8 million for a sophisticated multimedia campaign. Kubo talked about how he had lost his land during the Japanese internment and had no intention of giving up property rights again. Other commercials featured white farmers making thinly veiled appeals to racist fears: "I don't scare easily, but Prop 14 is an invasion of my property rights. I've raised my family and daughters on this farm and we feel threatened."

The UFW followed a consultant's advice and withheld its limited media buy until the last few weeks. Although Brown stood by the union and filmed commercials, Speaker McCarthy sent his constituents a letter urging them to vote no on Prop 14. Chavez made dozens of appearances the last six weeks, but house meetings, rallies, bumper stickers, and Chavez's personal appeal were no match for the growers' aggressive media blitz. Chavez found himself in violation of one of his cardinal rules: never be on the defensive.

Proposition 14 lost by more than a two-to-one margin. Carter failed to carry California, and Democrat John Tunney narrowly lost his U.S. Senate seat to S. I. Hayakawa, an outcome some blamed on the UFW's losing crusade. "Our experience in this movement is that we never lose," Chavez told the disappointed crowd that gathered on election night at Mount Carmel High School in Los Angeles. "There may be temporary setbacks, but we never lose . . . Don't be bitter."

Since the ALRB was set to reopen anyway, the immediate setback for the union was not particularly significant. The damage to Chavez was more severe. He had not had to take responsibility for a strategy gone awry in many years, not since he had become a national celebrity. Earlier setbacks caused by judgment errors, like the loss of the contracts in 1973, had been apparent only to a small circle. To the world at large, the UFW leader had been a heroic victim who brilliantly turned every loss into a victory. He had not made a losing gamble—until now. Prop 14 was a very public rejection and an avoidable loss. He would have to face people who would tell him one of the things he most hated to hear: I told you so. On top of that, he would have to be nice to them and make amends, because he was now even more dependent on them for the future of the law.

Chavez had been fasting before the election, as had his driver and chief of security, longtime union volunteer Ben Maddock. On the drive back to La Paz on the night of the defeat, they had to stop the car on a cold mountain road because both men were sick to their stomachs.

CHAPTER 29

The Cultural Revolution

We're prepared to lose anyone that wants to leave. We're prepared for that.
We're also prepared to have people here who when I ask them to jump, they're
going to say, "How high?" That's how it's going to run.

The failure of Proposition 14 stripped away one of Chavez's surefire fall-backs: go to the people in the cities for support. Struggling to reconcile his faith in the union's popularity with the dramatic loss, he looked for explanations—and then for scapegoats. Chavez began to lay the ground-work before the votes were cast.

Nick Jones had grown up in North Dakota, dropped out of college, and joined the Students for a Democratic Society. He registered as a conscientious objector during the Vietnam War and discovered the boycott in Chicago soon after the grape strike began. At twenty-four, he moved to Delano in the summer of 1966 and went on the payroll of the Migrant Ministry. A few months later he met Virginia Rodriguez, a farm-worker kid who had been working as a secretary when she saw an advertisement for a training program to help *la causa*. She ended up at the nonprofit Center for Change and Community Development, where Manuel Chavez was working when he was out on parole. Manuel convinced Rodriguez to join the union full-time, and she went to work as Cesar's secretary in early 1967. She and Jones were married that summer. When the fast started in February 1968, they pitched the first tent at Forty Acres. A few months later, they headed to Portland with their six-week-old daughter to work on the boycott.

Chavez trusted Jones with a variety of assignments over the years, including undercover missions and one of the first security details to protect the union leader, a job that required familiarity with weapons, devotion, and discretion. Jones's success as boycott director in Boston and then Chicago propelled him to his position as national boycott director in early 1976. Jones had recruited a lot of the boycotters and developed a loyal following around the country.

"My whole life is the union," Jones said in a July 1976 interview at La Paz, the day the executive board voted to move ahead with the Prop 14 campaign. "I can't imagine what I would have done had I left the movement . . . Virginia and I have never had a day that we've looked back on that we've felt we shouldn't have been here. So I mean, we made our life out of it and will live and die in the movement, I think."

Chavez often marked people he wanted to purge and then waited for an opportunity to move against them. As Ross observed, Chavez preferred passive resistance to confrontation, subjecting people to "a certain type of ostracism, embarrassment, to the point where they just can't stand it anymore." As part of his technique, Chavez became skilled at weaving complicated Machiavellian webs, tying together unrelated events to form patterns. His distrust often prompted comments or actions that verified his suspicions, and the prophecies became self-fulfilling. What distinguished Chavez's attack on Jones was the prominence of the target and the ensuing outcry.

Jones had been the only union staff member to publicly voice doubts about the wisdom of pursuing the Proposition 14 campaign; that alone became grounds for suspicion. He did not get along well with Ganz, and the two had clashed during the signature-gathering phase. What Ganz wanted from Jones was his staff. Some boycotters were reluctant to move across the country for another grueling campaign, and Ganz was known as a tough taskmaster. Jones turned over his staff, but not as quickly as Ganz wanted. Their disagreements fueled speculation that Jones wanted to challenge Ganz for his seat on the board. In mid-September, Chavez told the executive board at a private meeting at his house that he believed Jones was out to sabotage Prop 14 and the union. To strengthen his case, Chavez dragged in two people Jones had recruited in Chicago.

Kathleen McCarthy was a nurse who had worked on the Chicago boycott, where she accused a farmworker of attempting to rape her during a driving lesson. In 1976 she joined the staff of the Delano clinic, where she had run-ins with her supervisor. At a September 9 meeting of the board that ran the health group, Chavez said people at the clinic were undermining the union and singled out McCarthy as a probable spy. The next day, Chavez met with McCarthy and accused her of being an agent. When she burst into tears, he viewed her response as confirmation. As she wandered around La Paz dazed by the encounter, she ran into Joe Smith, who had worked on the boycott with her in Chicago. He gave her a ride to Bakersfield and then spoke to Chavez on her behalf.

Like Jones, Smith wanted nothing more than to spend his life working for the movement. Unlike Jones, Smith had neither political ambitions nor a radical past. He grew up in Indiana, came out of the Catholic Worker movement, and found his home in the boycott, first in Chicago and then San Diego. When Chavez decided to restart *El Malcriado* for the third time, Crosby Milne had suggested Smith as the editor, and Jones endorsed the choice. "I think Joe Smith is a fantastic idea for the newspaper," Chavez said at the February 1976 retreat. "I don't know why I didn't think of it myself." Smith worked closely with Milne and Jacques Levy to assemble a staff, well aware the board had been unhappy with the paper and shut it down twice before. "The best thing about working in La Paz is getting a chance to work directly with Cesar," Smith told a journalist he recruited as managing editor in the summer of 1976. "Cesar and the union will delegate a lot of responsibility to someone and not be looking over his shoulder and second-guessing him. Because Cesar understands that if you delegate responsibility to someone that also means giving them the right to make some mistakes, too, and understanding that's going to happen, and giving people room to grow."

The first issue of the new *El Malcriado* was about to go to the printer the Friday that Smith intervened with Chavez on McCarthy's behalf. Over the weekend, Chavez reviewed the pages, expressed some concerns, and asked for changes in two stories he thought made the union look bad. When the executive board reviewed the printed paper on Tuesday, September 14, Chavez explained the problems he had spotted and stressed that board members needed to guide the newspaper staff, who could not be expected to understand the subtleties of union politics. He talked about plans for a Spanish edition and asked the editors to schedule a weekly meeting for board members to give input. "I think it's a beautiful paper," Chavez said. "It's the best, well-written paper we've ever had . . . Considering the circumstances, I think they've done an outstanding job, and I think they should get a hand." The board gave Smith and his staff a rousing farmworker applause.

When the board reconvened the next day and Smith asked for input for the next issue of the paper, Chavez abruptly reversed himself. Whether he had received information that caused him to distrust Smith or simply had decided that Smith needed to be discredited to further tarnish Jones, Chavez turned on the astonished editor of *El Malcriado*.

"I have some very serious questions about the first fucking edition. And I'm pissed off at you very much," Chavez said to Smith. "Cause you couldn't have fucked up. We laid it out, we told you exactly what to do . . . It's a fucking game you're playing. It's not a mistake . . . This board tells you what to do in the first edition, and you don't do it. Don't tell me you forgot. I'm not going to buy it. You must have had some special reasons for doing it."

"I'm not trying to run a game on the board!" Smith protested, baffled by the sudden attack.

"You'll have a hell of a time convincing me different," Chavez said. "I wasn't born yesterday."

Smith's voice rose and his tone grew agitated as he realized that both his competence and his integrity were under attack. "I didn't ask for this job! You called me and you asked me to do it and I came up! I made a lot of mistakes. I was confused. Four years on the boycott doesn't prepare somebody for this kind of job . . . I have never tried to fuck with the union. Never. In any way! You ask anybody I worked for if I have tried to fuck with the union. Never once. And I'm not trying to fuck with the union now." A train rumbled by, and Smith yelled to be heard above the racket. "I didn't understand the dynamics of how we were supposed to put the paper out. Because I would not have deliberately created any problems for the union." His voice rose even higher, in alarm and indignation. "Why would I want to do that?"

"I want to know why," Chavez said calmly. "You tell me why." Then he turned to Jones. "Nick, you'll recall it was on the strength of your recommendation that we hired Joe. You recommended him at the meeting at the mission."

By the end of the afternoon, the board had killed the paper. When the meeting continued that night at Chavez's house, he launched into an attack on Jones.

Two weeks later, with polls showing Prop 14 in trouble and only a few weeks left before the election, Chavez confronted Jones. "I had a very shattering phone conversation with Cesar yesterday," Jones wrote to Chris Hartmire. Chavez suggested Jones was part of a left-wing conspiracy to undermine the union. The UFW president pointed to Smith as an example and also accused Charlie March, the New York boycott director, of sending volunteers with Communist leanings to mess up the Prop 14 campaign. "I recruited them both," Jones wrote about Smith and March, "and have as much faith in their integrity as I do yours or Helen Chavez. I expect the next accusations to fall on my head . . . Cesar believes there is a conspiracy within the union and now I do. Someone in leadership is doing some vicious and unprincipled witch hunting."

After Proposition 14 lost, Chavez lashed out at those upon whom he could most easily vent his anger. He directed Ganz and Ross to interrogate everyone who worked on the campaign, ostensibly to decide on new assignments but with orders to root out the "assholes," the term of choice for spies, agitators, or malcontents. During a debriefing session for campaign volunteers at La Paz, Chavez eavesdropped outside the meeting room and suddenly climbed in a window to denounce those who criticized the leadership of the ill-fated campaign. Ganz, who might have been the logical scapegoat for the loss, was far too valuable to Chavez to sacrifice.

Jones had one final meeting with Chavez, who accused him of bringing spies into La Paz. On November 14, 1976, Nick and Virginia Jones resigned, saying they no longer had the trust of the union leaders. In a two-page letter, they outlined Chavez's charges against them. "We are deeply concerned about what we perceive to be serious internal destruction of the United Farm Workers of America," the Joneses wrote. They urged the board to take a stand against the "accusations and firings of full time staff based on the flimsy say-so, whims and innuendo which the accuser(s) are not held responsible to substantiate."

The day he received the letter, Chavez fired Joe Smith. Similar charges would be leveled against many others in the years to come: problems could not be innocent mistakes but must be a deliberate attempt to sabotage the union. Smith was outraged as only a naive, dedicated believer could be. "I do not question Cesar's right to fire me. His authority is quite clear," Smith wrote after he was fired, asking the board for a hearing. "However, I also believe that the way in which I was fired presents a clear danger to the safety of the union." Despite everything, all he wanted was a chance to stay. "The union has become the most important thing in my life."

Jerry Cohen said Smith had no rights under the constitution ("We're fighting the Teamsters, the growers . . . we don't have to be screwing around with chickenshit hearings of staff people when it's the prerogative of the president to fire people," Cohen said impatiently), but Chavez magnanimously insisted that Smith be heard. Chavez wanted a public forum to deny allegations that the firing was politically motivated and to discredit Smith.

"I've been fired, that's one thing," Smith said. "But the other thing is that I've been accused of being an agent, of deliberately sabotaging the paper, and of deliberately attacking the union."

"Who accused you of that?" Chavez said with feigned surprise.

"Well that's what you told me in your meeting," Smith replied, taken aback.

"I didn't tell you that at the meeting. I didn't tell you you were an agent."

"You said I was in conspiracy with other people."

"I didn't tell you that. You know what I told you. The only thing I told you was that all of the screw-ups in the paper were deliberate as far as I was concerned. I didn't tell you you were an agent or a spy."

Smith held his ground, reiterating that Chavez had said the editor was part of a group of leftists conspiring against the union. Chavez grew irate and accused Smith of using the red-baiting line to cover his incompetence. "You said that my friends had come to you with information about me that led you to distrust me," Smith insisted. Sooner or later, he warned the board, they would have to find a way to deal with staff. A union fighting for the rights of workers denied its own workers any recourse.

Most board members said nothing. They understood that Smith was a pawn in a larger chess game. None of them had objected to Chavez's decision to force out Jones. Jones had no strong allies on the board and Chavez's assertion that Jones was "politicking" against Ganz was reason enough for the dismissal.

If Chavez had thought these firings would pass unnoticed, like his earlier housecleaning in 1967, he misjudged. The union's profile was much higher, the investment of its supporters greater, the reach of the boycotters and former staff members wider. A Denver weekly did a lengthy story on a volunteer who had been thrown out during the Ganz/Ross inquisitions. The Los Angeles Times ran a story based on the Joneses' resignation letter. Letters poured in from religious supporters and staff in many boycott offices who had worked with Jones, Smith, and others who had been dismissed. The letter writers were baffled, hurt, and full of questions: either there had been some grave mistake or Chavez needed to reveal information that supported his decisions.

Chavez offered different explanations to different audiences. With those who appreciated the importance of keeping the political left out of labor unions, he accused Jones of a left-wing agenda. With people who would never believe that Smith and Jones were part of a Communist conspiracy, Chavez dismissed the idea as silly, denied having made such accusations, and said Jones had been fired for politicking. Chavez said Jones had schemed to challenge Ganz at the next convention, an explanation that allowed those eager to exculpate Chavez to blame Ganz for purging Jones out of self-interest.

As far as Chavez was concerned, people who complained were questioning his judgment, and that alone was enough to warrant their dismissal. As Fred Hirsch had pointed out as early as 1968, Chavez viewed almost everyone as expendable. He prided himself on his unmatched work ethic and the union's ability to chew people up and spit them out. "I'm a son of a bitch to work with," he told a group of volunteers. "And most of you could not work with me side by side. You could not keep up my pace. I work every day of the year. I just sleep and eat and work. I do nothing else."

Before Prop 14, Jones had supervised 329 boycotters in thirty-four cities. A month after he resigned, 57 of them had been reassigned, 92 had been fired, and 23 had taken an extended leave of absence. Almost all boycott leaders had left or been transferred, and eleven offices were closed. "We are still having problems vis-a-vis Nick's resignation with virtually all boycott [office]s," the new director, Larry Tramutt, reported to the board. He read them a letter from the New York boycotters who charged that staff were "dealt with in a manner reminiscent of McCarthyism."

In their confusion and anger, many boycotters turned to Chris Hartmire. Chavez turned to the minister, too, first to find out what was being said, and then to send back a message. Hartmire summarized the reactions among those perturbed by the departure of Nick and Virginia Jones: "(1) Somebody fingered Nick and falsely accused him of leftist activity—without foundation; (2) it smacks of McCarthyism (3) If Nick can be dealt with that way, it can happen to anyone (4) no one will tell us what really happened." The minister urged Chavez to meet with the staff to clear the air. "Some very solid, serious people have had their sense of security shaken by the events or by the lack of explanation of the events. They want to stay for a long time (or for life) but they have a hard-to-define worry that maybe there will be more firings in the future."

Chavez offered explanations that enabled the minister to rationalize the dismissals of people he trusted. First, no one knew as much as Chavez did. Workers called him all the time. No one else sat where he did. Second, he might be wrong about one person. But even if firing Smith had been a mistake, for example, the damage to one person paled in comparison to the risk to the union if Chavez's conspiracy theory was correct. Everyone knew the union had been under FBI surveillance at various times. Jerry Ducote, a former Santa Clara County sheriff's deputy, had pled guilty to breaking into union offices and stealing documents, allegedly at the behest of growers. Conspiracies did not seem far-fetched. Hartmire accepted the reasoning and dutifully spread the word.

Hartmire's explanations did not convince his close friend John Moyer, the United Church of Christ minister who cared deeply about the cause. Moyer knew Nick and Virginia Jones well, was aware of their unswerving loyalty to the union, and rejected Chavez's accusations as absurd. Though he cared about the Joneses, Moyer focused on Chavez and the union. "The real issues here deal with the future of the UFW and the NFWM and go far beyond Nick and Virginia," Moyer wrote Hartmire. "They have to do with trust, loyalty, delegation of authority, leadership, the movement from organizing in the fields to an established union, from powerlessness to power, from Fred Ross to Crosby Milne, from youth to maturity, from idealism to disillusionment, from smallness to bigness."

Moyer recalled a 1966 talk that Chavez had delivered in New York, where he asked church leaders to stick with the union when it gained power and the inevitable internal struggles emerged. "All of us were amazed at the depth of his perception of human nature and of what we in the church call sin," Moyer wrote. "There is a basic conflict between Cesar's academic perception and his emotional ability to deal with it. In that respect he is a very normal human being."

His distance and his wisdom gave Moyer greater clarity than most observers. Chavez was increasingly annoyed that even simple orders turned into debates. "Following orders is a gift," Chavez said. "It's very hard to find a group of people who will follow orders." His decisions were challenged, rather than obeyed. When Chavez ordered the Delano day care center closed, staff members helped the parents organize a petition to keep the program open. Union clinics continued to dispense birth control pills, despite a union policy prohibiting the practice. After finding contributions in envelopes unopened for months, Chavez ordered that all mail to anyone at La Paz be opened by a central office unless marked "personal." His brother returned the memo to the mail administrator with a note that read: "B.S. Any mail that says Richard E. Chavez on it must not be touched or opened by anyone."

Cesar did not confront his brother about the mail policy, nor was he ready to take on other members of the board, who had once accepted his edicts and now grew more confident as they gained experience and expertise. But he could continue to clean house in the area where he had control.

"We have never really been that clear about democracy in the union, and I think we mislead people," Chavez told the executive board in March 1977. "We don't make it clear to the staff that they don't have the same rights. They don't. Face it . . . we bullshit about democracy, but they don't have it."

Chavez divided the staff into two categories: those for whom the movement way of life represented a step up, and those from more privileged backgrounds who had taken a step down to join the union. Complaints about the lack of democracy, Chavez said, came from those who had taken a step down. If they didn't like it, they should leave. The objections did not come from the farmworkers, he maintained: "They could care less." In a few years, he would find out differently.

When the criticism did not abate, Chavez escalated his attacks. For the first time, he purged people in public, humiliating ways. Drawing inspiration from Mao's Cultural Revolution, Chavez used "the community" to do the dirty work. He carefully scripted roles for the community meeting he called at La Paz on April 4, 1977. The meeting, which became known as the Monday Night Massacre, was chaired by Gilbert Padilla and his wife, Esther, a major figure in La Paz.

"We know who you are," Esther Padilla began ominously. "And we're sick and tired of it. We want some action. We want you to get the hell out of La Paz. We want you to get the hell out of the union. Cesar has been busting his ass off for so many years to build this union. So many people have been sacrificing. The whole Chavez family. You have the *audacity*, the *audacity* to try to destroy our union. What we have built. What we have sacrificed for. It is sickening. We want some action. We want it now."

The roles had been rehearsed. Most of the half dozen targets were too shaken to say much in their defense and simply agreed to leave. Several were women who shared one of the dilapidated kitchens in the old hospital building. They had not been happy, they admitted, but they had never acted to sabotage the union. Denials only brought more screaming. Some of the loudest attacks came from Cesar Chavez's son and Dolores Huerta's daughter. "This movement is based on trust," Paul Chavez yelled at one of the malcontents. "Who are you not to trust this man? Who are you?"

The only one to fight back was David McClure, a plumber who had recently arrived to help with badly needed construction projects. Accused of being a spy, he denied the allegations with screams as loud as those of his attackers. And he refused to leave. Chavez intervened, triumphantly offering as evidence McClure's daily calls to the office of the conservative senator S. I. Hayakawa: "We got the goods on that, David. We got the goods. We got the witnesses. Documented. We got the hours."

"They're engineers, Cesar!" McClure said in disgust. "It's not that Hayakawa." The Tehachapi consultant working with him on the heating project was named Hayakawa.

Cornered, Chavez lashed out in his nastiest voice. "We know what you're up to. You're a fucking agent."

"I am not!" McClure shouted

"You're goddamn right you are. You're a fucking agent and we want you out of here right now."

Mary Ann Coffey saved them the trouble of throwing her out. She came to the defense of her friend Deirdre Godfrey. Godfrey had already submitted her resignation because she felt burned out. Coffey broke down in tears as she objected to the attacks on Godfrey's loyalty. "I just don't believe what's going on here. I've known Deirdre and her family since we joined within a day of each other, three years ago." Godfrey came from a large family, who all supported the union. "Her mother didn't eat lettuce, which is no big deal, millions of people don't eat lettuce. Except Deirdre's mother was dying at the time. It was on her diet. She constantly argued with the dieticians at the hospital and told them to take it back."

Gilbert Padilla jumped in angrily. "My mother died during the campaign, I took three days off . . . My sister died, I took two days off. My aunt died, I took one day. Don't pull that guilt trip." Then he explained Godfrey's real offense: she had not accepted his explanation about why Nick Jones was fired, and instead pursued the question with Chavez.

> I said, "Deirdre, you have no concerns. Nobody's after you. I like your work. Don't worry about it." . . . It never went away, Deirdre. It's still in your mind . . . You didn't trust me.

Since 1961, when Cesar has asked me to do something, I never questioned it. You tell me, "Go, do this," I go do it. Whether I do it well or don't do it well, but I do it. So it hurts me to see people who've been here six months, three months, up in arms, doesn't like policy. If this union's going to run under the leadership of this man, the board of directors follow his leadership. When we sit down here in this room, and Cesar says, Eliseo go to Coachella, Eliseo doesn't question it. He doesn't question it. He says, "When do I leave?" Marshall, you go to Calexico. Richard, you take your family to Delano. They don't question it. Why should people here have a hard time following policy? . . . You have some people here questioning the leadership of this man. It's just crazy.

Chavez had remained in the background most of the time. Now he spoke up. "Let me tell you what's happening. You know, we're not dumb. We've been at it for a long time. We built a movement because, I think, we're pretty fucking smart about what we do and we know people, and we know politics, and I've been around even before some of you were born." When he asked Padilla to do something, he acted without question. From now on, Chavez expected the same of everyone at La Paz. "We're prepared to lose anyone that wants to leave. We're prepared for that. We're also prepared to have people here who when I ask them to jump, they're going to say, 'How high?' That's how it's going to run. We've got a responsibility to do something for the workers over there and the only way we're going to do it is if we have some goddamn rules and when I give an order or Gilbert or Dolores or anybody in authority, you just do it . . . Beginning tomorrow, when you get an order, if you don't carry it out, out."

Godfrey and the others thrown out of the union were not allowed to use the pay phone at La Paz after the meeting. "I have never spent such a fearful night," she wrote the board members afterward. Security people loudly patrolled the halls all night and threatened to throw her out on the street after she went to Tehachapi to make a call. "I shall never forget the frenzied, hate-filled faces and voices of people who had been warm and friendly with me right through to the hour of the meeting."

When McClure refused to leave La Paz, the union called police and had the plumber arrested for trespassing. Liza Hirsch, the law student Chavez had mentored, was working for the union as a negotiator in Oxnard. She knew McClure through her father, who was active in the plumbers union, and when McClure was thrown out he went to stay with

Fred Hirsch in San Jose. When the UFW refused to give McClure back his truck, his portable plumbing shop, Liza called Chavez to intervene. In doing so, she cast a cloud of suspicion on herself. Though he had known her since she was a child and groomed her for a future in the union, Chavez began to monitor her actions for evidence of treachery. A year later, during the wedding of Gilbert Padilla's daughter at La Paz, Chavez denounced Liza as a Communist and ordered her thrown out.

The Monday Night Massacre did not make the newspapers. Internally, the purge was discussed in muted tones. Hartmire did more damage control. He compared Chavez's leadership style to that of Castro, John L. Lewis, Mao, and Gandhi. "What did the Cultural Revolution look like up close?" Hartmire wrote to reassure his staff members. "From one viewpoint it must have been clumsy, ugly, and painful: young militants attacking established leaders, people being demoted, removed from positions, sent to the villages, attacked in wall signs, beaten by the red guard, etc . . . Clearly, Cesar has embarked on a mini-cultural revolution within the UFW . . . he is determined to carry it through and he is certain that it will help the movement, while at the same time knowing that it may not always be right or accurate or wise in particular cases."

The Great Leap Forward, the structure that Chavez had struggled for a year to build with the help of Crosby Milne, gave way to the Cultural Revolution. For all intents and purposes, Chavez abandoned what he had built with Milne. Chavez took away union-wide responsibilities from the executive board members and reassigned them to geographic areas. He consolidated the organizing and contract administration departments (what he called "the heart and soul of the union") and put himself in charge.

Milne was gone, too. One of the people thrown out during the Monday Night Massacre was the girlfriend of Milne's son. Milne bore no ill will about the purges and understood the necessity, he wrote to Chavez. His year was up, and it was time to move on. A short time later, Chavez turned Milne into a co-conspirator, falsely accusing him of having absconded with tapes from the restructuring conferences. Medina had been right to question Milne's trustworthiness, Chavez lamented.

With Milne's departure went the last best chance for a workable management structure that would allow the union to function efficiently. As John Moyer perceptively wrote to Hartmire: "The delegation of authority, which Cesar so often talks about and which Crosby's reorganization demanded, involves the relinquishing of power and responsibility to others with whom the leader still has to relate. This is very, very difficult to achieve. It puts severe stress on the psyche of the leader. Things happen over which he no longer has direct control but for which he is still responsible. Trust relationships become strained, and a certain degree of paranoia becomes inevitable."

CHAPTER 30

Slough Off the Old

All the elements are there to fulfill the dream of a strong and democratic national union except one: We have not yet learned how to work as one towards a common goal. We are convinced that the game will help, and we are grateful to you for the opportunity to learn and use it.

The UFW board members looked distinctly out of place as they walked around the immaculate grounds of a well-appointed residential compound in the foothills of the Sierra Nevada mountains, greeted warmly by bald men and women in orange overalls. The leaders of the farm worker movement had been summoned by Chavez to a planning meeting, and the eerily similar appearance of their hosts was just the first surprise.

Chavez had intended to call a special board meeting at Sweet's Mill, an old logging camp in the Sierra Nevada where the union had retreats. He wanted somewhere without phones or distractions so he could keep the board focused on his agenda. Then in mid-February 1977 he visited Synanon founder Charles Dederich at the headquarters of his drug-treatment empire, a showplace community high in the mountains east of Fresno. Dederich invited Chavez to bring his board to the Synanon compound for his planning session, and the UFW president accepted.

Dederich was called Chuck, or "the Founder," or "the Old Man." He was a charismatic con man with a rags-to-riches story, a large man with an outsized personality, a big ego, and a booming voice. The reformed alcoholic had developed a drug-treatment program that earned national praise for its seemingly remarkable—but vastly overstated—results. On the strength of Dederich's salesmanship and testimonials from experts, journalists, and celebrities, Synanon had grown during its first decade from a small storefront in 1958 to an oceanfront complex in Santa Monica. In the 1960s era of drug experimentation, families gratefully sent their teenagers to Dederich's facility, lauded on the floor of Congress as the "miracle on the beach." By the 1970s, Dederich had parlayed Synanon's reputation into vast wealth and a devoted following, upon which he experimented at several highly regimented communities around California. He no longer believed addicts could "graduate" and successfully reenter society. The only way to ensure their continued health was for them to remain at Synanon. He moved the headquarters to a complex in Marin County. At its height in 1972, about seventeen hundred people lived in Synanon communities, which included separate children's dorms, communal dining, and private schools.

The Santa Monica facility had been familiar to UFW staff members for many years because Synanon offered free medical and dental care for union volunteers. Only Chavez, however, had been in close touch with Dederich recently and understood how Synanon had changed. In a deliberate manner, Dederich had transformed the drug treatment program into a cultish movement, open to anyone willing to pay for the privilege of living in one of his structured communities. In 1975, Dederich declared that Synanon was a religion, in part an effort to shield his finances from public view, in part to enhance his status as the Founder. He abandoned an earlier commitment to nonviolence and trained a weapons corps to discourage interference from public officials or private individuals.

The manicured complex where Chavez brought the UFW leadership was Dederich's latest community. The most privileged residents lived in an isolated group of buildings with its own airstrip. By 1977, most long-term Synanon residents were what Dederich called "squares"—people with no history of addiction. They paid rent and donated large sums of money to the religion, often turning over real estate and savings. Dederich continued to experiment with new rules, such as the requirement for shaved heads. One month before the UFW board met at the compound he called "Home Place," Dederich declared there were too many children in the world and ordered mandatory vasectomies for all men in Synanon.

Dederich, just a few weeks shy of sixty-four, had a salesman's talent for hooking people into his vision. He spoke with the cadences of a revivalist preacher, and his followers included comedian Steve Allen, jazz musician Art Pepper, and Connecticut senator Thomas Dodd. "I say this with as much humility as I am capable, which isn't very much, but when I sit down and start to talk, people start gathering," Dederich said in a deposition. "It is inevitable. No matter where I do that, it just happens. I can't stop it."

Chavez found much to admire in Dederich and his iron-clad grip on the planned community. Both men considered themselves experimenters and rebels and shared a disdain—and often disregard—for established authority. Dederich believed in communal living, where people worked without salaries for the common good (although he himself collected a six-figure income). Dederich ostensibly dedicated himself to rehabilitating the poor, the addicts, and the outcasts of society, a group that Chavez daydreamed about recruiting into the Poor Peoples Union. Although Synanon increasingly courted "squares" with ample wealth, Dederich kept enough ex-addicts around to maintain the fiction of operating a treatment program. He was an authoritarian who had built an efficient operation, with luxury cars, an electronic intercom system that replaced telephones, and access to so much money that he claimed Synanon had not needed to bother with a budget.

Dederich also had successfully navigated a transition similar to the one Chavez now struggled to achieve. The Old Man had taken his first creation, the drug-treatment facility, and radically reshaped the organization into a social community. He offered to share the secret of how to manage such change, build a communal society, and maintain firm control. Slough off the old and groom the new, Dederich told Chavez. Root out those who resist change.

The essential tool Dederich used was the Game, an encounter-group-type therapy at the center of Synanon's daily life. In the Game, players accused one another of real or exaggerated misdeeds, in order to correct faults and improve communication. One person was "indicted" for either professional or personal misbehavior and others joined in the attack, screaming and using as many obscenities as possible. The target escaped only by shifting the indictment to someone else. Other drug treatment programs adapted variations of the Game as a therapeutic practice, but Dederich had moved in a different direction, using the Game as his daily management tool. The Game, Dederich told Chavez, was the key he needed to reshape the UFW.

Aside from Chris Hartmire, in whom Chavez had confided some thoughts about Synanon, UFW leaders knew none of this when they drove up the winding roads to the tiny town of Badger on February 25, 1977. They shared Chavez's sense that the union had been drifting and looked forward to the meeting as an opportunity to develop new strategies. Marshall Ganz wanted to make a pitch for the union to focus its energy on consolidating victories among vegetable workers in the Salinas and the Imperial Valleys. Eliseo Medina, now in charge of the Coachella office, hoped for resources to wage a strong campaign in the vineyards and citrus orchards when the season reached its peak in another month. Jerry Cohen had just finished negotiating an agreement with the Teamsters to leave the fields, a huge step that eliminated the rival union and established the UFW as the sole dominant union for farmworkers.

The pact grew out of the antitrust suit that the UFW had filed in federal court in early 1973, accusing the Teamsters of colluding with Salinas vegetable growers to depress farmworkers' wages. The defendants had grown weary of responding to dozens of pages of interrogatories that required hundreds of hours of high-priced legal talent. As the trial neared, they faced the prospect of divulging sensitive information and the possibility of millions of dollars in damages. Farmworkers were a marginal group for the Teamsters, and their relatively low incomes did not generate enough dues to warrant a continued fight. Cohen negotiated a settlement that would give the UFW sole jurisdiction in the fields in exchange for an end to all litigation.

Chavez made clear as soon as the board assembled at Home Place that he had no interest in discussing the Teamster pact, problems with the ALRB, contract negotiations, or election strategy. He wanted to talk about *his* problems, he said, which revolved around the union's philosophy. Questions about everything else could wait until the next regular board meeting.

As they gathered Friday evening, Chavez explained the weekend would include a discussion with Chuck, communal meals with "the Synanon family," and a demonstration of the Game, Dederich's great innovation. "In all of this there's a tremendous amount of discipline," Chavez said. "But also an awful lot of really tough, good management. No nonsense. Which we need."

Chavez opened the meeting with a statement that drew no disagreement: "We're at a crossroads about our philosophy . . . The crossroads right now is whether it's a movement or it's a union. We're at that stage where we have to make a decision. Because it's neither right now. With the new law coming in California, it's changed us completely."

He reminisced about the early years and appealed to those who had been with him from the start, recalling the good times when they had struggled together, united against a common enemy. Now they battled an anonymous state agency, instead of evil growers. The adrenaline that fueled the early fights had evaporated, leaving the movement deflated. They had achieved a great labor law, won elections, and driven the Teamsters out of the fields. "The road is open, and we ran out of gas," Chavez said. Again, no one disagreed. "Here's this tremendously great opening to just charge through and get the job done. Look, there's nothing between us and getting the workers organized right now . . . All the obstacles are removed. And we finally climbed the hill and we're at flatland, and we can't go."

The crisis was deeply personal for Chavez, and he believed the only path involved radical change. Using a favorite tactic, he insisted the executive board choose between two options: the UFW must either pay wages like a regular union or build a community like Synanon. He refused to allow discussion of any middle ground. He was confident the majority would support his commitment to the volunteer system. He also knew the UFW's shaky finances would make salaries unrealistic. So he really offered no choice. "I'm just convinced that the way for me, at least, for me personally, the way to go is to have a community like Synanon, or close to that, and start truly cooperative ventures," Chavez explained.

Framing the choice so starkly drew out those who would pose the greatest obstacle. "I want to take a clear position," Cohen said. "And my clear position is that we're going to have to pay people." Cohen argued the volunteer system created a revolving door that crippled the union's ability to negotiate and administer contracts, conduct research, and operate efficiently. Only departments where people earned small wages, such as the legal department and the Migrant Ministry, did not suffer from debilitating turnover. Paying wages would not cost more in the long run, Cohen contended.

Richard Chavez, an early advocate of paying wages, raised his concern about long-term security. He had young children. He understood the union could not afford to pay salaries now, but he needed some guarantee about his future.

"I came to this outfit when there was nothing," Cesar responded scornfully. "I literally went goddam starving. I had eight kids. Don't you goddamn ever forget that. None of you . . . I'm not afraid of security. That's the difference between me and most of you. I think that God will provide."

"Then tell him," Richard snapped back. "Cause I'm kind of worried.

I'm a practical man. I am asking a question because other people feel the same way but they're afraid to say it. I'm saying it because other people are thinking it but they're afraid to say it."

Encountering resistance, Chavez upped the ante with another familiar move: "I'm going to tell you something. It's not threatening, it's just plain fucking fact. If this union doesn't turn around and become a movement, I want no part of it. I'll help and everything, but I don't want to be in charge. I want to do something else. I tell you because that's the way I feel."

He became more explicit about why he had brought them to Home Place. He wanted to bring the Game to La Paz. Dederich had arranged for the UFW leaders to watch a demonstration, and join if they desired. They gathered in the Game Room and sat on bleachers. The Synanon players sat below in a recessed pit. As soon as the screaming began, Richard Chavez walked out. Hartmire, Huerta, and Cohen joined in the Game. The Synanon players gamed Cohen for having moved from La Paz to Salinas and abandoning his friend Cesar. Chavez had brought up the issue of the legal department's location at the planning retreat with Crosby Milne a year earlier; now the complaint surfaced in a much more volatile forum. Cohen realized the Synanon players had been briefed in advance. He scored points by responding with a reference to Dederich as "Chuck the schmuck."

Dederich met with the board the next morning for a two-hour chat. He explained the triangle and the circle. The triangle represented one's day job, because people worked in a hierarchical system. The circle was the Game, where everyone was equal. "I consider myself an experimenter. I'm in the business of researching and developing human relationships," Dederich told them. "I manipulate the environment. That's my triangle job."

He spoke with pride about the Game and how his invention allowed him to manipulate people and build the Synanon empire. "I would not know how to run an organization without the Synanon Game," Dederich said. He had offered to train a dozen UFW staff members at Synanon, and Chavez had gratefully accepted. He had already broached the idea at a community meeting in La Paz and solicited volunteers. Now Chavez revealed this to the executive board, whose permission he sought. Eventually, he told them, he wanted everyone at La Paz to play. Current residents might seek exemptions, but the Game should be mandatory for anyone moving in after March 1. "I'm going to fight like a goddamn tiger inside that Game, because that's my nature," Chavez said. If people did not take him on, "they'll be told, they're chickenshit."

How would this help with the citrus campaign or the grapes? wondered Ganz numbly. Chavez ignored the question. He wanted to build a community at La Paz, he told the board members, who listened in a state of semishock. Padilla asked how long that would take. Two years, Chavez replied. "I have a hard time believing that's the best use of your time," Ganz said. "If that means you have to stay in La Paz and be the father of the community there in La Paz, what about all those farmworkers out there that also need you to go out there and talk to them?"

Board members did not embrace the Game, but they did not object to Chavez's plan. Some were appalled but saw no point in a public challenge. So Chavez left Synanon with what he sought: tacit agreement to bring the Game to La Paz. Everyone else left with monogrammed pens that Dederich gave them as they left Home Place.

"We are tremendously impressed with your community," Chavez wrote Dederich a few weeks later, thanking him for the hospitality. "The dedication, happiness, discipline and cleanliness are qualities we admire and which we have thus far been unable to achieve." Chavez explained the landmark agreement with the Teamsters. "The settlement is something of a miracle. We can reclaim the members we lost and have an open shot at organizing the rest of the industry. All the elements are there to fulfill the dream of a strong and democratic national union except one: We have not yet learned how to work as one towards a common goal. We are convinced that the game will help, and we are grateful to you for the opportunity to learn and use it."

Dederich had amassed an impressive business and real estate empire. Synanon's most lucrative venture was selling small advertising gifts, like monogrammed pens. In 1975 the distributing business grossed more than $8 million, and Synanon reported assets of more than $30 million. In addition, hundreds of corporations, including many Fortune 500 businesses, received tax write-offs in exchange for donating excess goods to Synanon— everything from Thomas' English muffins to Adidas sneakers. After Chavez's first visit to Home Place, Dederich sent a forty-foot semitruck to La Paz with twenty-two thousand pounds of food, children's clothing, building materials, and paper cups. Dederich disparaged Chavez's "orange crate mentality," and the Old Man liked to impress UFW staff members by ushering them onto private planes to hop around the state. On occasion, Dederich showed up with his entourage for lunch at La Paz in a fleet of Cadillacs.

For Dederich, a shrewd businessman, the affiliation with Chavez offered several potential advantages. Increasingly Dederich depended on wealthy liberals, often from the west side of Los Angeles, where Synanon had scored its initial success. An association with Chavez would burnish Dederich's reputation with a key constituency, who held the farmworker leader in the highest esteem. Dederich also knew of Chavez's interest in building communities, and the Old Man schemed about joint real estate deals. Two months after the UFW board meeting at Home Place, Dederich told the Synanon board of directors that he intended to discuss with Chavez their future relationship to "see what Chavez wants to do and what's in it for us—imagewise, investment wise." Dederich proposed a joint venture that might be called "Synanon House, UFW #14," a communal farm where workers lived according to Synanon principles and the union supervised their work.

Dederich made the offer the next time Chavez visited Home Place, wandering into the Game Room after the UFW group had finished playing. "I see some mutual advantages in a merger between Synanon and the United Farm Workers," Dederich said. He assured Chavez they would have no trouble raising funds to purchase land for communal farming. He described Home Place with false modesty and suggested Chavez could end up in a similarly comfortable setting. "This is a nice little place on the side of a mountain for me and my friends to get old in," Dederich said. "That's what it's for. All these young punks that you see around here have one mission in life: that's to wait on me and make me feel wonderful. Because if I feel wonderful, they'll feel wonderful. If I don't feel wonderful, they'll feel rotten. I am going to put you in a position like that in about 15 years."

"I like it," Chavez replied.

Chavez was dazzled by Dederich. "He is a genius in terms of people," Chavez told the board. He marveled about Synanon's success in turning the dregs of society into happy, productive citizens: "If these guys who are ex-prostitutes and dope fiends and thieves and every imaginable kind of criminal you can think of, if they can . . . not only rehabilitate themselves but become truly great human beings in the process, not only that but build an unbelievable community, not only that but develop a work habit that is hard to conceive . . . they're so skilled in what they do, so eager to learn, so happy with what they're doing. And so effective."

Chavez entrusted Hartmire with pursuing discussions about land deals with Matt Rand, the Synanon official who became the primary liaison to the UFW. Rand "made it clear they were not in a charity game," Hartmire reported to Chavez. "They expect a return, tit for tat." In the end, the real estate partnership went nowhere. For all his admiration, Chavez had no interest in ceding to Synanon the degree of control Dederich wanted.

The Game, however, became an increasingly important part of life at La Paz. "The Synanon Game represents a revolutionary concept that can turn the union around and facilitate the kind of effective, efficient and cohesive organization that will enable us to reach our long-term objectives," Chavez explained in a memo.

He did not share all his reasons. The real point of the Game was not communication, but control. Dederich had explained how to use the Game to dramatically reshape an organization. Each time he moved Synanon to a new phase, Dederich created a model community, then offered everyone the opportunity to sign on to the new vision. Those who did not enthusiastically embrace the change were forced out. He used the Game to shape behavior, root out disloyalty, and break up "contracts," personal relationships in which people backed each other up and, in effect, formed coalitions. The Game was an important tool to subvert any potential coalitions or alternative power bases. Dederich referred to his underlings as "trained seals," and he focused particular attention on training young people, often children of residents.

Following Dederich's advice, Chavez carefully chose the first eleven La Paz residents who traveled to Synanon with him to learn to play the Game. The young people he hoped to groom into a faithful cadre included his son Paul and son-in-law David Villarino; Richard's daughter Susie; Huerta's daughter Lori and son Emilio, and Kathy and Lupe Murguia's son Joaquin.

From the start, the Game proved an effective tool to shape behavior. Unlike the other young people, Joaquin Murguia had chosen to attend a local college. The decision frustrated Chavez, who arranged for Joaquin to be indicted for his lack of commitment to the union. "The Game started, and we got on him," Chavez recounted to the executive board. "Boy did he open up . . . he broke down and cried." Joaquin quit school and went to work full-time in the UFW accounting department. "It works real nice," Chavez said. Matt Rand cited Joaquin's decision approvingly as "testimony to the power of the thoughts and feelings of their peers when expressed in the Game."

More players were trained at La Paz, and they played multiple Games on weekends. Playing became a badge of status, although many people dreaded the humiliation and some found the ordeal so traumatic they stopped. Religious people particularly objected to the obscenity, which included every possible curse and derogatory term. Nothing was too personal. People were gamed for being fat, dirty, and smelly. They were ridiculed for their sexual preferences and queried about their sex lives. They were attacked for being bad mothers, disloyal workers, lazy, stupid, old, and useless. In theory, the indictments contained only a kernel of truth and much exaggeration, and in theory the insults stayed only in the Game. But in a community where everyone lived and worked together twenty-four hours a day, that separation became purely theoretical.

Four months after the board meeting at Home Place, Chavez reported that several dozen people played on Sunday mornings from nine to noon with "fantastic results." The Game, he enthused, had done its job "as a tool to make us better people and make us better workers." He claimed the Game was almost universally popular, with a waiting list of forty people. He acknowledged that Richard and Helen Chavez were among those who steadfastly refused to play. "The biggest opponent here is my wife," Chavez said, recounting how Helen watched a Game in which the others indicted her son Paul for having too many girl-friends. "She thought that was awful."

Paul, known to most by his nickname, Babo, seconded his father's endorsement. He looked forward to playing, Babo told the executive board, for two reasons: "I get a lot of feelings out," he said. In one Game, "me and the old man had a good cry." Also, the Game produced results. After gaming the head of the Service Center about why the Game Room was so hot, for example, the air-conditioning improved.

"People shape up," Cesar agreed. "It is a tool. It's a good tool to fine-tune the union, to get those things that are important, to get the work done . . . We look forward to playing . . . You begin to crave it."

The differences in behavior in and out of the Game narrowed. Chavez described an incident when he attended a fund-raising dance in Bakers-field with a group of people from La Paz. They were drinking beer and got into a fight. Asked at a board meeting how he intended to deal with them, Chavez used the language of Synanon: "Brother, we're going to have a fucking haircut. We're going to kick somebody out of La Paz. We'll bring some of our tough people and we'll have a meeting in my office and we just chew their fucking ass out. Scream at them and point out their mistakes. If they don't want to admit it we just ram it down their throat you know. Make them feel like fucking shit. It helps. You take one of those, you don't want to go through that fucking haircut again."

The once collegial tone of board meetings grew more tense. Chavez and Huerta's fights intensified. Not a meeting went by that she did not resign or get fired. Chavez had always modulated between gentle and harsh; now harsh became the dominant tone. The board resisted Chavez's invitations to play the Game, but meetings morphed into wrenching, personal discussions. People talked about quitting. They confessed they could not follow where Chavez was going with his insistence that community was the solution.

"It's unthinkable to me that after twelve years of work we're going to blow it out the window right now," Ganz said. "It's incredible to me . . . we're going to blow it right now if we don't get it together."

Chavez did not discuss his ideas with farmworkers, on the increasingly rare occasions when he met with the union's members. The workers were not to be told about the Game, he warned. He spoke often of the need to train workers, both in practical aspects of administering union contracts and in the movement philosophy that would help them embrace the need to sacrifice for others. But time after time, he thwarted plans for training conferences. Medina and Milne had each scheduled conferences several times to train ranch committees, only to have Chavez decide they should be postponed.

In private, he worried that workers cared primarily about money and did not appreciate values he believed essential to the future of the movement. When staff members at a conference talked about the need to bring farmworkers into the union leadership, Chavez warned that they had to first teach them the value of sacrifice. "You don't want farmworkers managing the union right now," he said. "With the attitude they have on money, it would be a total goddamn disaster, it would be chaotic. Unless they're taught the other life, it wouldn't work."

Those sentiments contrasted sharply with Chavez's public rhetoric. The less he trusted the workers, the stronger his statements about their importance in the union. "We are convinced that the vanguard of this movement must be the workers themselves," Chavez said in his address to the third UFW convention in the summer of 1977. "We must completely turn over the task of running the union to them."

Jessica Govea understood better than most the CSO experiences that had shaped Chavez, both the successes and failures. Her father, Juan, had been one of the early leaders in the Bakersfield chapter that Chavez organized in 1955. As an eight-year-old, Jessica attended CSO meetings that Chavez led in her backyard. She made chalk marks outside houses to help with voter registration drives. She watched the CSO transform her mother from a shy housewife into an effective community organizer. As a young adult, Govea witnessed the rifts that tore the CSO apart and the middle-class agenda that ensued. She understood the roots of Chavez's ambivalence about the leadership emerging from the fields.

Govea worked closely with farmworker leaders in the Imperial Valley, where she had been developing a health plan and clinic. She met daily with ranch committees and was impressed by the workers' strength, courage, and dedication. When she traveled to La Paz, Govea watched the Game with dismay. She had been brought up to treat people with dignity and respect, and nothing about the Game conformed to that moral code. The gulf between the reality in the fields and the Game in La Paz troubled her deeply. She spoke up in the midst of one of the executive board's soul-searching sessions and challenged Chavez on precisely the point where he was vulnerable.

"Maybe in a lot of ways and in the overall way, CSO failed. But I think in some ways it didn't. Because I know it's given a lot of meaning to my life. You all have taught us, a lot of us. You're the sparks, you know, in my family's life, in my life." Her voice began to crack as she spoke about the history the people in the room had made, the agonizing point they had reached, and the doubts they faced about whether the union's promises would mean more than rhetoric: "We've sparked stuff. I'm not saying we owe it to keep on holding the union together, if you will, or to keep on getting good contracts, if you will. But we owe it to people, to what we've sparked . . . And right on if they take it and run with it, because in all the time that I've been here, that's what I thought we wanted to do. Right on if the [ranch] committees come together . . . It's a really beautiful thing that's been built over the years . . . I really hope we're going to pull it together."

CHAPTER 31

Mecca

See, this becomes the mecca, and people come here to touch and to feel, you know. Otherwise, I'm telling you, it's not going to work.

Chavez's birthday had always been a festive occasion at La Paz, but the March 31, 1977, celebration took on new significance. Mariachis serenaded Chavez outside his window at 6:00 A.M. as the community sang "Las Mañanitas," a traditional Mexican birthday song. He joined them for hot chocolate and *pan dulce*, Mexican pastries, followed by a menudo breakfast. Chavez celebrated with a midmorning ceremony to sign a contract with an Oxnard nursery. At noon, everyone attended a special mass.

As Chavez turned fifty, the movement marked its own milestone—the first celebration of Founder's Day. "It is, in fact, the day that the Chavez family left the CSO and turned toward building a farmworkers union," a memo to the staff explained (although, in fact, it was not). Founder's Day "should be a time of memory and celebration for all union groups and offices." Staff members were directed to spend at least an hour learning the early history of the union, recounting stories, and conducting religious celebrations. A few months later, the UFW convention ratified a resolution approving Founder's Day as an official holiday.

As he had promised the befuddled leaders of the union when he brought them to Synanon's Home Place, Chavez focused on building a community at La Paz. Formal celebrations and rituals played an important role.

He turned increasingly inward. In public statements, he framed his commitment to La Paz as a vital step for farmworkers. "We are giving the worker all the material things but nothing of the spiritual," he said in an interview in the spring of 1977. "Together with the material has to come some kind of a bond, a community, a discipline, an understanding. In fact, one of our biggest challenges right now is to experiment with build-ing communal living among some of us here in La Paz. Some of us, a few, just a minority, feel that the salvation in this country will come through living together. There is no future in living the way we are right now. It creates fear and suspicion and fighting."

At sea in the new world of elections and laws—and outshone by some of his staff—Chavez devoted his energy to La Paz. In some ways, his interest mirrored his desire a decade earlier to transform Forty Acres in Delano into a beautiful oasis. But the plans for Forty Acres had sketched out a special place for farmworkers to relax, recharge, and learn. Chavez's vision for La Paz had little to do with workers. "We've got to have a mecca," he told the board members, a place so attractive that staff would vie for the privilege of working in the rolling hills of the Tehachapi Moun-tains and volunteers would retreat to La Paz after tough election campaigns. Chavez already hated to leave home, he said. He no longer wanted to visit workers in the heart of the union, in Salinas or Delano or Coachella; he wanted the heart of the union to come to him. "There's Washington, D.C., there's Mexico City, there's Rome, there's Mecca . . . We have a place here where it's comfortable, people from the outside can come, we can really take care of them."

Chris Hartmire again became Chavez's collaborator and confidant. The two men had talked for some time about collectives. At Chavez's request, Hartmire researched the Hutterites in the Midwest, the Commu-nity of the Ark in southern France, and kibbutzim in Israel. At one point Chavez sketched out an idea for a communal farm that could serve as a "mother house" for a new religious order. He proposed buying land in Oxnard where they could grow vegetables, cotton, wheat, and alfalfa, with room for dairy cows and a chicken coop. People would live in small houses but eat in a communal dining hall. The commune would include a church, a school, and craft shops. Chavez had picked out a name for the communal farm and the new order: Los Menos, "the least." He took the name from the Gospel of Matthew: "Inasmuch as you have done it to one of the least of these my brothers, you have done it to me."

Los Menos would be another movement entity, Chavez said, a varia-tion on the Poor Peoples Union. Chavez would select farmworkers and

people committed to the movement idea, not too "Anglo and educated."
Residents would be required to work on UFW campaigns and might
need to live there for a year before working for the union. Chavez wanted
Hartmire to serve as the religious leader and the National Farm Worker
Ministry to help run the new community. At Chavez's request, the Protestant minister contacted Catholic officials to inquire about the possibility
of forming a new religious order.

After his visits to Synanon, Chavez modified the plan. Instead of
dreaming about a farmworkers' commune in Oxnard, Chavez asked
Hartmire to help transform La Paz into a model community. The project
was no longer a haven for farmworkers, any more than Synanon cured
drug addicts. Money from the union's Martin Luther King Jr. trust fund,
negotiated in contracts to fund educational services for farmworkers,
was used to buy furniture and expand the Game rooms. Although
workers were not to be told about the Game, part of their wages subsidized the activity.

"Everything that we do is for the worker," Chavez complained. "The
worker is getting so much fucking benefits, and we're having other kinds
of problems. OK—that's what we're here for, to get them benefits. But
we're not getting hardly anything. And while I still resist very strongly the
idea of getting paid, I think we can live a little better . . . It's an atrocity to
have to come to this goddamn conference room, and it's so cold."

Hartmire felt pressure from Chavez to join the La Paz community, but
he could not move until his youngest son graduated from high school. So
Hartmire split his week between his Los Angeles home and Keene, where
he became head of the new community life department. In weekly meetings, he and Chavez discussed how to set up a communal laundry, when
to begin communal meals, and whether residents would be required to
say grace. Hartmire compiled lists of union holidays and appointed
committees to help run La Paz: Outstanding Citizen Committee, Birthday Committee, Welcoming Committee, Pet Committee, Beautification
Committee, Training Committee, Medical Committee, Liturgy Committee, and Work Day Committee. Weddings and baptisms became major
community celebrations. Hartmire composed the UFW prayer, which
was published in the second issue of the President's Newsletter, a publication that had replaced *El Malcriado*. "Show me the suffering of the most
miserable, so I may know my people's plight," began the nine-sentence
prayer. The prayer did not mention farmworkers.

Many of Chavez's conversations with Hartmire revolved around the

Game—who should game whom, how to spread the Game to Delano, what issues and policies needed to be raised in the Game. Some were straightforward rules, such as that all gifts to volunteers were to go to the movement. Others involved philosophy. When Chavez found out board members and many delegates to the union's 1977 convention stayed in hotels instead of supporters' homes, as he had requested, he ordered the issue be raised in a Game. He reacted with the same disgust he had voiced back in the CSO when conventions became more upscale: "This is a people's movement! . . . Assholes. You've got to watch them every step."

In a gentler moment, he acknowledged that hustling room and board was a "hassle" but an essential one. When staff members questioned how to get by on the $2-a-day travel allowance for meals, he talked about his experience in the CSO when he refused reimbursement for meals (to Saul Alinsky's dismay) and depended on hand-outs. "You force yourself to be with the people," he said. "If we don't do that, very fast we get separated from people . . . That's how you make the movement alive and keep it alive. You keep it in people's hearts and minds by doing that."

Following Dederich's advice, Chavez continued to groom young people who had grown up in the movement. He drew up a curriculum for a six-month negotiating class and ran his ideas past educators at four universities, with mixed reviews. Some were perturbed by a unit on "mind control," one of Chavez's recent interests. Others applauded his commitment to teach labor history, as well as practical negotiating techniques. As in his earlier fascination with the science of management, Chavez seized on the idea that there was a "scientific way" to train negotiators and organizers. He spent hours researching the curriculum. He combined lessons on parsing contracts and simulated negotiations with playing the Game.

Chavez, who had once called true organizers a rare breed of "fanatics," now argued that almost anyone could be effective if properly trained. He deliberately recruited "just plain folk to do it. Not the real bright ones, because we don't have too many of those around." His principal criteria were likelihood to remain with the union and loyalty. "The life of the union depends on teaching people," he told the board. "And unless they're really, really, very, very dumb, you know, I think they can be taught." Chavez selected a dozen students for the negotiations class, including his son Paul, son-in-law David Villarino, and Huerta's son Emilio. The class was to be the first piece of a school that the board voted to name after Fred Ross.

Breaking his long-standing rule against taking government money,

Chavez applied for more than $500,000 in grants from the U.S. Department of Labor and the Community Service Administration for the school and other projects. Six years earlier, he had proudly declared, "We don't take one plugged nickel from the government . . . We don't want to have any strings attached from Washington." Beyond the uncertainty of living grant to grant was a core belief he had articulated consistently since his days with the CSO: depending on members for financial sustenance forces organizers to pay attention to workers and deliver services they are willing to support. "With government money, you don't even have to talk to them," he said about workers. "That's the difference. If you haven't got the money, you've got to really go and put your ear to the ground and listen very, very intently."

In 1978, Chavez acknowledged his reversal, but did not explain. "I think things have changed," was all he told the board. All that had changed was the UFW's financial need and the party in power. Democrats controlled the White House for the first time in eight years, and the Carter administration encouraged Chavez to apply for funds.

Chavez focused on negotiators because he needed more contracts to bring in more dues. Fund-raising had slowed dramatically. "We're a thirteen-year-old cause," Eliseo Medina observed. Labor organizations thought the farmworkers, who had the best labor law in the country, should be self-supporting. The UAW had begun to phase out its subsidy, reducing weekly payments of $6,200 to reach zero by the fall of 1978. Chavez could not move forward on his expansive ideas—or move outside California—until the union was on a more stable financial basis. That required more contracts. He grew impatient with discussions about why contract talks took so long and scolded others for not making more compromises. He pushed negotiators to accept contracts under almost any conditions, even if that meant excluding workers from the discussions or acceding to demands he once would have rejected out of hand. In 1977, dues accounted for only 60 percent of the union's income.

Repeatedly, Chavez made clear that what excited him was not elections, contracts, or negotiations (which he called "non-missionary" work), but building a community so that everyone would love being in La Paz as much as he did. "If we don't do that," he said, "then we don't have a movement."

About 150 people lived at La Paz, depending on campaigns, boycotts, and departures. Singles and a few couples lived in the old hospital building, a ramshackle dormitory with small rooms, coed bathrooms, four shared kitchens, lots of cockroaches, and no central heating. Just in front of the hospital was the one-story administration building, where Chavez and his staff worked. He and Helen lived in a two-bedroom wood frame house a few hundred feet to the west, surrounded by a chain-link fence and guarded by the two German shepherds, Boycott and Huelga. An unpaved road led down a hill to a dozen more small houses and trailers. At the western end of the property, a five-minute walk from the administration building, was the old North Unit of the hospital, an elegant stone building that had been rehabilitated for conferences, parties, and special events, including the Games. Along the northern perimeter of La Paz ran the tracks of the Southern Pacific, and the noise of the trains lumbering up the Tehachapi Mountains often forced a pause during meetings and conversations. In the spring, the grounds were covered with wildflowers, and Chavez often climbed the rolling hills early in the morning.

Union leaders who worked elsewhere had hoped Chavez's concentration on community life would prove a short-lived phase. Instead, his preoccupation with La Paz became harder to ignore. La Paz played the Game on Sunday mornings and Wednesday evenings, and Chavez ordered staff from around California to attend the weekend sessions. Those who complied traveled long distances for the privilege of being cursed and trashed for everything from personal hygiene to work habits. At its height, about a hundred staff members played each week. Hartmire sent Chavez lists of several dozen people at La Paz who refused to play, which included most of Cesar's family. "It is not helping people," Richard Chavez told Hartmire. "In fact the people I relate to are being screwed up by the game." Authoritarian tactics originally designed to shock drug addicts into going straight did not translate well when superimposed on a civilian community that had not bargained for this therapy, or even for communal life.

"Those of us who were on the boycott, we did live in communities," Richard explained to his brother. "We already had a taste of that... When they say community, man, I just start shaking. I don't want any part, I had such miserable experiences."

"You put your finger exactly where it is!" Cesar responded. "We're all afraid of it." The communities he had researched, Cesar assured his brother, achieved incredible results, generating the sort of excitement the farm worker movement had enjoyed in its early years. When Chavez cited Synanon, the Hare Krishna, and the Moonies (followers of Rev. Sun-Myung Moon), the response was not what he had hoped.

"When you talk about that, you scare the shit out of all of us," Jim Drake said.

"We're trying to do things for *other* people," Richard said. "It's not us. We could build a beautiful community if all we had to do was live in La Paz . . . We are doing some things trying to help other people."

"Those are losers," Drake said about the groups Chavez cited. "Bad losers. Including Synanon."

"Jim, those are the only ones I can point to," Chavez replied. "Synanon has new cars and airplanes . . ."

"Yeah, and they have a whole lot of people who can't cope with the world and that's why they're there," Ganz interrupted. "Let's be realistic. Folks are there because they can't handle reality."

Long-standing jokes about La Paz and disparaging comments about the "Magic Mountain" intensified, infuriating Chavez. Some of the movement's outside supporters visited La Paz and left alarmed. Father Edward Donovan, a Paulist priest who worked with the union in Los Angeles, spent a Sunday at La Paz. "He saw it as a disaster area," one of Hartmire's staff members reported, "where people walk around in fear and act like zombies or robots."

John Moyer spent a few days at La Paz. The minister talked at length with Chavez, as well as twenty others, all loyal to the union. They confided to Moyer that they felt ill-used, second-guessed, and not treated like adults. They lacked sufficient freedom to do their jobs, sensed they had lost Chavez's trust, and felt pressure to play the Game, which they found destructive and emotionally scarring.

"I sense that Cesar is having a real struggle with his leadership role," Moyer wrote to Hartmire. "Like many other founders of movements, organizations, revolutions, he is having trouble letting his child grow up. He speaks eloquently of enabling people to grow and make their own mistakes, and then he fails to do what he speaks of. He gives people responsibility, then does not give them the freedom to do their job, even becomes paranoid when he does not know everything that is going on. And, of course, the paranoia grows as the union grows because there is more and more that he *cannot* know. Delegating responsibility is the hardest task for any leader: to let go, to hold people accountable, but to *let go.*"

Moyer cared deeply about the movement, and viewed its success as vital not only for farmworkers but for social activists and for the Protestant Church. He urged Hartmire to step in and guide Chavez on a midcourse correction.

Hartmire dismissed the criticism. Like many, his identity was tied too closely to Chavez for him to acknowledge the looming problems. Hartmire enjoyed the Game and valued his position of responsibility and trust. To question Chavez's leadership in any way would have put that relationship in jeopardy. Hartmire's steadfast defense of Chavez underscored the question that had clouded the formation of the National Farm Worker Ministry: was the NFWM too close to Chavez? When the UFW president visited the Philippines in the summer of 1977, the ministry's blind support faced a severe test.

The UFW had been largely rebuffed by Filipino workers in elections. Andy Imutan, who had served on an early NFWA board, told Chavez that a trip to the homeland would help. Imutan offered to arrange for Chavez to travel to the Philippines as the guest of President Ferdinand Marcos. Chavez asked the board members for input.

"Cesar, I really don't think much of the idea," Richard replied. "I don't think people here know too much about Marcos, and those that know would probably get turned off at the idea." Hartmire cautioned that Marcos's military regime had been accused of torture and human rights violations. Nonetheless, Chavez decided to go.

From the moment he landed to a royal greeting at the Manila airport, Chavez was escorted by top officials, wined and dined, accompanied by honor guards and motorcades, and whisked around the islands as a high-ranking dignitary. A range of government officials extolled the virtues of agrarian reform and collectives, which they said had been made possible through the imposition of martial law. Chavez stayed at deluxe hotels, played handball, met with labor leaders, rode a water buffalo, and planted rice. He received an honorary doctor of human letters from the Far Eastern University in Manila and a special award from Marcos. The most visible sign of martial law, Chavez said, occurred while he was having a late-night drink after a banquet at the hotel. As the clock approached midnight, everyone suddenly vanished—to comply with the government curfew.

In an interview with the *Washington Post* a day after he met Marcos, Chavez praised what he had seen of the Philippines under martial law. He said he had spoken with sixty labor leaders "and every single one of them said that it's a hell of a lot better now" than before Marcos imposed martial law.

Monsignor George Higgins read his morning paper and was appalled. He fired off a letter to Chavez the same day, assuming he lacked adequate information. "I have the uneasy feeling that you may have spoken out of turn during your recent visit to the Philippines . . . If I were you I would look for an early opportunity to clear the record. I honestly don't think you can afford to let the *Washington Post* story stand without some sort of official clarification. Again, I must ask you to forgive me for writing to you about this matter so bluntly, but that's what friends are for."

When Chavez returned home, he refused to back down. He would not criticize those who had shown him great hospitality. "We asked the sixty-four-dollar question about martial law," he told a group of boycotters. "I'm convinced by what I saw that the people support martial law. Ninety percent support it. I have no way to prove it."

The outcry intensified, especially among religious groups. Cases of civil rights violations and torture were well documented. "This is a *very* serious situation. It will *not* go away. It cannot and should not be minimized," Moyer wrote to Hartmire. "Mistakes were made. They are going to have to be admitted and some face-saving opportunities will have to be made."

Acknowledging mistakes was not part of Chavez's character. As the complaints mounted, he told Hartmire to invite all critics to a public forum. He arranged for five high-ranking Philippine government officials to attend and invited them to speak from the stage, while everyone else had to talk from the floor. "I called this meeting to set the record straight," Chavez told hundreds of people who crowded into the Delano High School auditorium. "I did not praise martial law. I did praise President Marcos' action in calling for elections."

The heated five-hour exchange only hardened positions. Chavez denounced the *Post* reporter. He insisted the trip was not managed and that he did not see any evidence of human rights abuses or torture. His critics said that was naive at best. At a Mexican restaurant after the meeting, Higgins refused an invitation from Hartmire to sit at Chavez's table. "I said, 'Your problem, Chris, is a very serious one,'" Higgins recalled. "I said, 'You've got yourself so enmeshed in this union, you can't—you don't own your own soul any more.'"

Chavez's handling of the controversy eroded support from a key constituency. His stubborn refusal to consider information that ran counter to his convictions upset religious leaders, who began to reevaluate other criticism they had dismissed, such as allegations of red-baiting and purges.

Chavez retreated to La Paz. "It's in a way a little kind of cultural revolution," he said. "We're experimenting. It may lead us to damnation. It may lead us to heaven. La Paz is a place to experiment, to experiment about people. Not with, but about."

One of his favorite experiments was the community garden. For two consecutive years, the union received a $50,000 annual grant from the federal Community Services Administration, which funneled the money through a local nonprofit group. Chavez decided everyone living at La Paz should spend Saturday morning working in the flower and vegetable garden. "I noticed when I did that, things changed," he said. People talked to one another informally, free of guilt that they should be at their desks. He talked happily about the garden as a small but significant part of his experiment.

His top organizers saw the experiment very differently. "On Saturdays I can't get any business done because everyone's in the garden," Medina complained. "Yeah, it's a problem," Ganz agreed. "It's bullshit . . . you call on Saturday and you can't get through—because everyone is in the garden."

Chavez tried to explain the importance of the garden and the need for events that generated excitement at La Paz, so isolated and removed from the action. "What are you going to do? The staff here doesn't go to a bar, they don't have outside friends, they don't talk to workers . . . We don't have elections . . . The sun sets, and the sun rises."

Perhaps, Drake suggested gently, Chavez was making an argument for moving the union's headquarters elsewhere. Chavez just rejected that as impractical, and returned to his idea of experimenting with community.

"Cesar, let me be real upfront about that," Ganz said. "I really question the value of working at building a community here in La Paz. If there's any kind of meaningful community going to be built in this movement, it's got to be built out where the struggle is."

Chavez's voice took on a hard edge. "Well you're against it, you don't understand it." He tried once more. "See, this becomes the mecca, and people come here to touch and to feel, you know. Otherwise, I'm telling you, it's not going to work. Let me tell you something, I can't operate like in a vacuum. I just need to see things and touch things and know exactly . . . In the beginning of this movement, I didn't go and ask your ideas, I did it myself. It's not that the idea is great, it's that everybody gets behind it, see what I mean. The idea may not be the best idea, but if we set a community here, isolated, it's going to be very fantastic if everybody gets behind it. What makes it great is that everybody's behind it, not that it's such a good idea."

Fred Ross understood. Ross, now sixty-seven, was also out of his element in the post-ALRA world. He privately questioned the Synanon connection, but he steadfastly supported his greatest student. Traveling the country to recruit volunteers, Ross echoed Chavez's grand vision of a time when the two men would return to their roots. "Like Martin Luther King, we have a dream," he told students at Harvard in May 1977. "And our dream is a Poor Peoples Union, a union of the unemployed in the cities." He and Cesar had done this before, he said. They would set up service centers, cooperatives, clinics, and schools in every major city. He conceded that the idea sounded far-fetched. "But don't forget," he admonished the audience, "We've had several dreams in the past. We had a dream back in 1962 of having a farm workers union."

CHAPTER 32

Trapped

When I came here, I had total, absolute power. That's how it got done. The whole cake was mine. Well, it was a little cake. But it was mine. And then the cake keeps expanding. I try to keep being a proprietor. After a while, everybody built it. After a little while, if you have absolute total power, can you go to more total power? No. The only way to go is to go down. To go down, to have less power, is tough.

By the middle of 1977, Chavez had whipped La Paz into shape. Families with small children appreciated the ready-made community, complete with day care center, church, and shared kitchens. Chavez loved celebrations, and he threw parties for the numerous couples who got married. The community passed a rule that everyone should wear a UFW button at all times, and those who forgot were dinged 25¢ to raise petty cash. People who did not enjoy working in the garden on Saturdays and playing the Game on Sundays either left or kept complaints to themselves. The message from the Monday Night Massacre had been clear: when Cesar said jump, people asked how high.

Top union leaders, however, remained less compliant. Chavez was frustrated by their questions and challenges. He had not persuaded the board to endorse his idea, largely because he could not articulate a plan that went beyond La Paz. Meetings degenerated into anguished debates and circular arguments. Board members left bewildered, retreating to Salinas, Delano and Coachella with no clearer sense of the future of the unwieldy union.

"We have come to the crossroads where we have to make up our minds, are we going to be a labor organization or a movement?" Richard Chavez said, voicing a familiar refrain. "We have to decide before too long. What are we going to be? We can't be both. It's clear."

Perhaps they could have done both, as some argued, and as Chavez once had vowed to do. "We have to find some cross between being a movement and being a union," he had said one week after the 1965 strike began. Twelve years later, paralyzed by a law he could not embrace and a bureaucracy he could not master, Chavez no longer tried to envision that path. He had found that any serious attempt to meld a union with a movement required him to relinquish control and delegate authority to an extent he was unwilling to do. He agreed with his brother's assessment, but he reached the opposite conclusion. For Cesar, the movement came first, at the expense of the union if necessary. He had been the first to see the split among the leadership looming; now they all grappled with the implications. For the moment, no one was prepared to force a showdown. The stalemate continued.

Chavez found himself in the position he had been so determined to avoid: "This reminds me of *exactly* the CSO meetings, before the union was born. You feel like incapable of moving, you feel like you can't move, like there's just nowhere to go."

But this time, he was in charge. To walk away as a young staff person, as he had in the CSO, was a far different proposition than to walk away from a world-famous organization often called simply "Cesar Chavez's union."

The business of the union kept intruding on his experiments at La Paz. Rarely did those intrusions bring welcome news. The state was demanding more than $100,000 in back unemployment taxes, rejecting the union's argument that staff were members, not employees. The paralegals working for Jerry Cohen sent Chavez a petition asking for salaries. Richard told his brother the health clinics had become known as "pill mills." Eliseo Medina pointed out that translations of contracts were so poor that the Spanish versions said something different than the English originals. Dolores Huerta complained the ranch committees were still not receiving any training. Cohen warned that workers under contract were angry that they received so little attention from the overextended union staff in field offices. Marshall Ganz begged Chavez to read Ganz's forty-page plan for organizing the vegetable workers. The governor wanted to know why the union did not have more contracts. Brown advised Chavez to start organizing more workers, lest the landmark labor law become an issue in the governor's 1978 reelection campaign.

The weightier the issue, the less interest Chavez evinced in public debate. He discussed with the executive board the new car inspection program, noting with interest the percentages of cars with dirty air filters and low oil. But the decision on whether to wage an organizing campaign in vegetables or grapes Chavez passed off to a committee. Gilbert Padilla reported that the committee recommended the union focus on grapes. Chavez engineered a vote when Ganz, Medina, and Richard Chavez were all absent, ensuring that the motion passed without discussion. Chavez was tired of the debates.

"I'll tell you why we're screwed up," he said. "Every time I give an order, it's challenged . . . It's not followed. It's negotiated. So pretty soon, the executive board is really administering the union . . . There's no one head. I'm totally frustrated."

The veterans waited for him to snap out of his Synanon-inspired dreams and lead with the inspired, creative passion that had gotten them this far. Instead, in the summer of 1977 they received a form letter. Chavez asked all staff members to answer two questions: What is our union business? And what should our union business be? "For our own salvation," he wrote, "we must raise the question of what is our business clearly and deliberately, and answer it thoughtfully and thoroughly."

That Chavez felt compelled to ask such questions generated anger, derision, and confusion. Jim Drake experienced all three, perhaps more than most. He had been there from the start, when the Chavez family moved to Delano in 1962 and Hartmire sent his young recruit to drive Cesar around for a few weeks. The weeks turned into months, then years. Drake directed the first boycott from a desk built over a toilet in the Pink House. He uprooted his family to New York, New Jersey, Los Angeles, and La Paz, losing two spouses along the way. He went to jail, celebrated babies born in boycott houses, and marched hundreds of miles with farmworkers. He hung out with Chavez at the adobe ruins of Papa Chayo's homestead in the Gila Valley. Drake signed Cesar's name so often that the bank once rejected a check that Cesar himself had signed.

Now Drake ran elections in Lamont with Scott Washburn, who had joined the union just before Chavez's fast in Phoenix, when the leader turned to the rookie and asked for his advice. The mass mailing about the "union business" was the first request for input that Drake or Washburn had received in many months. "I have wanted to leave the union for some time because I just feel sometimes that I'm rotting away," Drake wrote. He fought through his anger and disappointment to compose a serious response. The union must consolidate, negotiate more contracts, build a dues base, and establish an efficient structure that would allow further growth. Most of all, Drake pleaded, Chavez must lead again: "For all your studying and slaving over administrative methods, you could be out doing what you do *naturally*, which is leading and inspiring."

At a board meeting, Drake elaborated. He traced the emotional arc that had kept him and many others in the union. "Since 1962, I've gone from this situation of being absolutely incredulous that you were going to go out and do what you were going to do," Drake told Chavez. "I thought you were fucking crazy. Then I saw, some of the things he was predicting he was going to do, he actually did. The guy must be some kind of genius. There ain't too many of these guys around who say they're going to do something for the first time in history, and then they go out and do it. I got this tremendous awe." The awe had driven Drake to do crazy things, too. He woke at 3:00 A.M. to picket produce markets, drove cross-country in January in a bus with no heat, and marched through the Coachella Valley in triple-digit temperatures. Now the adrenaline rush of facing down the enemy was gone, relived through the taped reminiscences that Chavez often asked them to record. "The march to Sacramento, all those things we talk about—now they're all part of history."

Drake articulated feelings that Chavez struggled to express. The movement had achieved its early victories, against great odds, by inspiring a small group of militant farmworkers and a small percentage of consumers who agreed to boycott grapes. Success was defined differently now: winning 51 percent of the votes at ranch after ranch, among a more conservative group of farmworkers. "Now we are the shadow of the law," Drake said. "Everything is by the book."

Like Chavez, Drake wanted to organize the poor. He shared the concern that the UFW, at best, would help a small fraction of the rural poor. He sympathized with Chavez's impatience with the welter of state rules. But Drake did not see how Synanon and the Game could solve the problem. In the field offices, they wondered how people in La Paz had time to play games. Just as in the troubled administration of the 1970 contracts, the handful of staff in the field could not handle the demands of the workers under contract. The Game only widened the gulf between La Paz and the fields.

"The glory of this union used to be when we just risked everything we had," Drake said. "The reason I used to stick around years ago was because I didn't understand what the hell he was doing but I figured, well, it always seems to turn out right. I never understood why, but it did, you know. So, I just think, Cesar, if you've got a plan, you ought to lay it out and we should get back to the place where we follow your leadership again."

By the time Drake arrived at the June 1977 UFW board meeting, he had decided to resign.

Chavez came to the summer meeting with several goals. He wanted to show off the La Paz community. He needed to reassert his leadership; never had he faced the kind of rumblings and open challenges that had surfaced. He also confronted a more personal challenge: Helen Chavez had moved out of La Paz. Her absence had been noted, and Chavez needed to offer an explanation. Over the course of three days, he cajoled, threatened, berated, and pleaded with the union leadership, playing one card after another.

He opened the meeting with the farmworker prayer. He announced that two members of his staff, including his son Paul, would wait on the board, fetch drinks, and relay messages. Meals would be served in the room next door. They sat in new comfortable reclining chairs, specially ordered for the refurbished Game room.

Shortly after the meeting began, Chavez played a demonstration Game for the board with the others who had trained at Synanon. He began by announcing he was firing his secretary "for fucking up and making me feel so fucking embarrassed." (She was only fired in the Game.) For more than half an hour, the group shrieked at each other, yelling at one person for being fat, another for failing to make sure the room was properly cooled, and a third for neglecting to finish a financial report on time. They yelled over one another most of the time, stopping only when Chavez spoke. They acknowledged that even in the Game, they deferred to the player they called "the Chief."

That evening, Chavez invited the La Paz community to listen as board members reminisced into the tape recorder. He stressed the importance of preserving their history for posterity. Until midnight, they spoke about the good old days. Chavez asked each person to describe how they had come to the union. Richard, the best raconteur in the family, regaled them with stories about vacuuming up cockroaches in the middle of the night at the New York boycott house. Medina recalled how he had no idea where Chicago was when Chavez told him to go there for a few weeks. Four years later, Medina finally came home; no one in the office recognized him. Chavez reminisced about driving out to the first rose strike in May 1965 with Drake in his little red Renault.

With the heady victories of the past and long-standing bonds fresh in mind, Chavez tried to lay down the law the next morning. As he worked through the agenda, he dismissed objections to his decisions and ruled out of order people who complained. He was not going to brook the kind of challenges to policy decisions that had been slowing things down.

"I haven't really said, 'Fuck it, this has got to be done,'" Chavez explained. "Jim, in the past, I used to do that, you remember," he appealed to Drake. "We're gonna do this cause I think it's gotta be done. And I think I was right most of the time . . . I used to just get in my mind, it's gonna be done. And I just command it be done. And make myself a fucking nuisance. But, the value was, we were really going someplace. And that's happening less and less."

What some considered micromanaging, he defined as essential prerogatives of the president. He planned to interview every prospective applicant in California. He demanded letters of reference from employers, dismissing objections that no employer would give a farmworker a recommendation to work for the UFW.

His new buzzword was "concentrate," which elicited confusion. He had decided that the union could only do one thing at a time successfully. History showed that they succeeded when they focused on only one thing. They must do that again. The choice he offered was to negotiate contracts, organize more workers, or administer the contracts. He left no doubt that negotiations was the correct response. No amount of protest shook him from that position, though most board members objected that the choice itself made no sense. Padilla said they needed to sign contracts, but they also needed to organize new workers and to enforce the existing contracts. "Growers are laughing at us because we're not organizing," he said.

"If we're thinking we can do one and not do the other, we're kidding ourselves," Richard Chavez said. "We have to do both."

Ganz and Medina argued that organizing *was* negotiating contracts; the two could not be separated. Challenged on the definition of organizing, the thing he once knew best, Chavez refused to debate. Ganz suggested they concentrate on one region or crop instead of an activity.

"There's no other way to define it," Chavez said flatly. He had been agonizing over the decision for months, he told the board. "The biggest problem in my mind has been: what the fuck's gone wrong. Really just trying, day and night, thinking about, what the hell's happening. I'm convinced after looking at it, after sleeping on it, after looking at it, after reading, after reviewing, after analyzing, that it's very simple. We're not concentrating," he said.

Chavez acknowledged he faced a group that no longer accepted what he said without question. In part, they had grown up and had ideas of their own; in part, they could not understand or accept what Chavez was trying to do. Padilla thought he might resign, confused about where Chavez was leading. Richard Chavez felt burned out, torn between his practical beliefs, his older brother, and his partner, and frustrated that he had been unable to build a legacy or train another generation. Even Chris Hartmire, the faithful disciple, was confused. He had recently made a startling confession to Drake. Hartmire said he was afraid to speak his mind for fear he, too, would be branded one of the "asshole" conspirators.

The assholes, Chavez and Huerta insisted, had infiltrated the union and now were attempting to undermine friendships and marriages. They recounted again the alleged espionage of Kathleen McCarthy, the nurse, and David McClure, the plumber. Huerta charged that the assholes were now sabotaging her relationship with Richard. "Richard and I have been having fights about this for the last two months," she said. "They're going to fuck other people's relationships up. We're stupid if we think it's not happening . . . They're starting to live with the members. They're doing it just to fuck us up . . . They're going to marry people just to fuck this union up."

Richard ran the Delano office. He just did not see the conspiracy that his brother and partner wove. "For God's sake, open your eyes and see what's happening!" Cesar said. "They've got you and Dolores fighting like never before. Don't say no, Richard!"

Hartmire screwed up his courage and challenged Chavez and Huerta. The minister had been disturbed by the firing of Joe Smith, but he had accepted Chavez's explanations. Now Huerta had targeted a woman named Shelly Spiegel, a teacher for a small school in Delano that the farmworker ministry sponsored. Hartmire knew Spiegel was not an infiltrator. "When somebody gets focused on as being a problem, all sorts of unrelated facts, incidents, relationships, begin to automatically fall into place as an indictment on that person which would never fall into place if someone wasn't focusing attention on things," Hartmire said. "And those pieces may or may not add up to something. But they add up to something because someone with power has indicted them. All I'm pleading for is that we also listen to another interpretation of those events. So we don't screw good people who shouldn't be screwed. And Cesar, let me tell you, we're afraid."

"My God, what are we?" Drake exploded. "What are we? What have we become? If Chris Hartmire is afraid to express things openly because he's afraid he's going to be accused of being part of a conspiracy, what more is there to say?"

"I'm afraid of you, too," Richard Chavez told his brother. "Everybody's afraid. But we're too goddamn chickenshit to say. I'm afraid, because I might be one of the conspirators."

Chavez played masterfully on their fears—the fear that he would reject them, and the fear that he would abandon them. In a poignant, rambling soliloquy, he said calmly that perhaps the time had come for him to work out a transition and leave. He did not want to stay until he was forced out. He talked about Churchill's defeat after World War II and about the fate of movement founders who were overthrown. He wanted to leave gracefully and go on to his next project. He was committed to his vision, and he would rather leave than compromise.

"We've come to a stop, kind of. I see certain things in the union that I think have to be dealt with. But, most people don't agree with me. They don't. Let's face it, they don't. The Game, they don't agree with me. This idea that we're being had. They don't, you know. That's just the way things happen. So what I want to do, this union would be a lot better off if we could have an orderly transition."

He gambled that despite their discontent, no one in the room could envision the union without Chavez. As Hartmire observed, they defined themselves in terms of their relationship to their leader. In the end they were willing to compromise their principles to preserve that central relationship. Once he brought them to that realization, Chavez was halfway there.

"If I stay," Chavez continued, "I have to stay on my own terms and I have to fuck the organization to the extent that I become a real dictator, if I'm not one right now. That's just natural." He would only stay, he repeated, on one condition: "I got to be the fucking king, or I leave."

"When I came here, I had total, absolute power. That's how it got done. The whole cake was mine. Well, it was a little cake. But it was mine. And then the cake keeps expanding. I try to keep being a proprietor. After a while, everybody built it. After a little while, if you have absolute total power, can you go to more total power? No. The only way to go is to go down. To go down, to have less power, is tough."

No one said a word. He told them he had been fasting. He pleaded with them to understand. "What you're saying, you've grown up. You have grown up. And now it's very hard to face me on an equal basis. As it should be. And all of you are growing up . . . You're sure, you now own the union, you've done enough, you feel like, 'I have a right now to say.'"

Chavez knew the group functioned best when they faced a common enemy. "When we had a visible opponent, we had unity, a real purpose, it was like a religious war." He conjured up a new villain, just as he had done at other key junctures. He spun a web of innuendo to strengthen his case about infiltrators and cover his own misdeeds.

Philip Vera Cruz was the eldest member of the board, the quietest, and the least popular. Although he had been on the board since 1966, he remained an outsider, separated by language, culture, and ideology. He was more left-leaning than the others, and known as the "philosopher" because he often gave discourses to students who visited Forty Acres. He had refused to leave Delano for a boycott assignment and clashed with Chavez over the construction of a retirement home for elderly Filipinos. Vera Cruz had privately questioned Chavez's authoritarian leadership for some time. His distrust pushed him further outside: when the board had discussed Nick Jones, Chavez engineered an emergency call to send Vera Cruz out of town. Recently Vera Cruz had questioned the purges. Word had gotten back to La Paz that the seventy-three-year-old planned to introduce a resolution condemning the firings at the union's upcoming convention. He needed to be discredited.

Chavez charged that Vera Cruz, who took copious notes at meetings, planned to write a book in which he would criticize the union. Chavez accused Vera Cruz of having turned over his notes to the Communists, more commonly referred to as the "assholes," or simply "them." They knew he stayed in San Francisco with left-wing radicals, Chavez told Vera Cruz. He was accused of sabotaging Agbayani Village, the retirement community (in fact, Chavez had insisted on charging rents and imposing conditions that made the accommodations unattractive to the elderly Filipinos). Vera Cruz denied the accusations but said little in his own defense. "Those assholes got Philip. They organized and they fucked him up," Chavez told the board and two dozen staff members in the room. "You got to watch out 'cause they're very fucking smart."

People in the room were angry, eager for someone to blame for the union's travails. The proud Filipino leader made a good target. They heaped curses and epithets on Vera Cruz. They accused him of turning over internal documents to his girlfriend, an Anglo volunteer, and alleged she had seduced him to gain information. "Philip, we started a movement together," Chavez said. "You know how those Commies work. They come and they probe everywhere until they find a weakness. They came and they buttered you up. Everyone's seen it."

Chavez produced a one-sentence oath, written by Cohen and designed to trap Vera Cruz: "We, the undersigned agree that the matters discussed today were confidential and in consideration of the mutual promises made herein covenant with each other and with the UFW AFL-CIO and agree not to disclose the matters discussed at today's meeting in any manner whether by written publication or orally." The board members pleaded, shouted, and threatened Vera Cruz, but he refused to sign. Chavez trumpeted his refusal as evidence of the Filipino's treachery, whipping the crowd into a frenzy like a revivalist preacher. The other thirty-five in the room signed the oath. Almost everyone was won over.

Those who harbored doubts about the conspiracy theories eased their consciences with two arguments. There *had* been spies; often the plants were so clumsy they were quickly spotted, but perhaps others had infiltrated more successfully. And Cesar had usually been right. For years, as Drake had pointed out, his vision and instincts had guided the union to success.

"I think if we don't know where it's at, there's something wrong with us," said Richard Chavez, who had done a 180-degree turn and now enthusiastically supported his brother, marveling at his perspicacity. "I feel that I know exactly where it's at. No doubt in my mind why he's where he's at. What happens is he might be months ahead of us, or years . . . He's way out there in front, way in front."

The most important thing, Chavez said after Vera Cruz was escorted out of the room, was to have convinced the board that the threat from infiltrators was real.

The victory also gave Chavez more credibility in painting his own family troubles as part of the conspiracy to bring down the union. "I don't even know if I'm married right now," he said. "Helen just took off."

Helen Chavez had filled in for her husband's secretary one day and opened the mail. She found a love letter to Cesar, sent by an eighteen-year-old who lived in Mendota, a small agricultural community west of Fresno. The teenager came from a farmworker family. She had gotten involved in the union through her mother, helped on the picket line during a Mendota melon strike, and then spent a summer in La Paz along with three classmates. Helen's first instinct when she read the love letter was to seek out a friend and ask her to drive to Mendota to confront the teen. Talked out of that plan, Helen left La Paz and moved in with her daughter in Delano. When Helen asked the secretary who normally opened the mail if she had seen similar letters in the past, the secretary lied to protect Cesar and said no. The woman later confessed to Hartmire.

Chavez's infidelities had become common knowledge in certain circles, particularly among those who spent time around him at La Paz. The threats against him, his ability to disappear for unspecified reasons, and his need to travel with trusted guards all facilitated his liaisons. His affairs were not discussed, in part out of deference to Helen, in part because extramarital affairs were common, and in large part because such behavior would not have squared well with the image of the saintly founder and devoted Catholic family man. Just as people did not talk about internal conflicts or purges out of fear the revelations might hurt the movement, they kept quiet about his flirtations and sexual indiscretions.

On a few occasions, Chavez made a point of talking about how women approached him, painting himself as a hapless victim in stories that may have been intended to counter any rumors that surfaced. In the CSO days, he told a story about an angry husband who interrupted a house meeting with a knife and threatened Chavez. "The moment you're sort of different from other men, there's a natural attraction," he told a group of union volunteers in the early years. "It has nothing to do with your looks . . . Some women, they get attracted."

Helen's anger over the love letter and her absence from La Paz forced the issue into public view. The letters, Chavez claimed, were intended to frame him. He had warned his wife that something like this would happen. "My marriage is on the rocks right now, on the fucking ice. I told Helen, 'I bet you, whatever you want, you're going to be approached, you better watch out.' Sure enough, two fucking weeks later, there's a fucking love letter. In perfect Spanish. It just sort of appeared. When I came back, she's just going out of her mind."

Chavez hoped to resolve the situation at a meeting to be moderated by Manuel Chavez. Manuel, whose own affairs were legion, would support Cesar's testimony about the ways that infiltrators seduced or framed union leaders to gain information. "I have to meet tomorrow at nine to find out if I'm still married or not," Cesar told the executive board meeting. "It's really fucking ridiculous. I can't believe it. But it's there."

Chavez extended the cover story to protect his son-in-law Arturo Rodriguez. A volunteer in Coachella had recently been publicly purged after she held meetings among women staff members to discuss security and other issues. Among the accusations Chavez now leveled against her was that she suggested Rodriguez was cheating on his wife, Linda. "I'm feeling some pressure," Chavez said. "They're fucking over with my daughter, her marriage. They fucked with Helen, you know. I told Helen this was going to happen. She believed, but didn't believe it . . . That's what they do. They're experts. They're doing it now. They're doing it to my wife. They're doing it to my daughter."

He cast the net wider. "They almost fucked over Fred Ross in San Francisco," Chavez said, an apparent reference to Ross's early affair with Ida Cousino. "Your dad," Chavez said, turning to Fred Ross Jr. "Remember?"

The only board member who really understood was Huerta, Chavez said. She jumped in to back him up. She talked about men who had approached her over the years with the intention of spying on her and the union.

By the end, everyone went along, some out of conviction, others accepting the inevitable. They wanted to put it behind them and get back to the place where they had once been. Almost as an afterthought, they agreed on the need to "concentrate" on negotiating contracts, at the expense of almost everything else. Only Ganz voted against the resolution.

At the end of the meeting, Drake announced his resignation. Everyone ganged up on him, begging and challenging him to stay. He said it was like being at his own funeral. He agreed to stay.

Two days after the meeting, Cesar and Helen talked at their daughter Eloise's house. Cesar prepared notes for what he called "My Marriage Meeting." His opening statement indicated that he did not expect to be believed. He wanted to know at the end of the discussion whether he was still married. Number two on the agenda, "My Affair," included a discussion of the young woman and the letters. Number three was evidence in his defense, which included Manuel and the guards. He ended with some "observations," including thoughts about the assassination threats, the lack of security, and Helen's changing role.

Helen moved back to La Paz, ending their most public separation. Some months later, Hartmire presided as the community gathered to pay tribute to the first lady of La Paz on her fiftieth birthday. "Through all of it," Hartmire said, "she and Cesar, through all the ups and down, they seem to still like each other! It always amazes me. I think the thing that kind of draws us to her most quickly is, she is just so damn real. There isn't an ounce of phoniness in her being."

The roller-coaster summer meeting of the executive board was prominently featured in the president's newsletter, with a front-page picture of the board and Cohen. The caption read: "The meeting progressed almost without pause and proved to be the most productive in the movement's history."

CHAPTER 33

The End Game

*It is not difficult to get rid of total failures. They liquidate themselves. Yester-
day's successes, however, always linger on beyond their productive life. We must
seek out those sacred tasks of the past that drain needed resources and scarce
time, and prune them ruthlessly so we can focus on the future.*

When Chavez had lamented the "so-called democracy" that would
require him to sacrifice his best people before they turned on him, he
singled out Marshall Ganz as a special ally. When they come after me,
they will take Ganz out as well, Chavez told Jacques Levy in their late-
night conversation at the union's 1973 founding convention.

For more than a decade, Ganz had enjoyed a special closeness to
Chavez, a father-son dynamic resented by some and envied by others.
Ganz's father had been a rabbi, and his religious upbringing helped form
an early bond with Chavez. Ganz's relationship with Jessica Govea linked
him to a CSO family that had been among Chavez's earliest supporters. A
high school debate champion, Ganz spoke his mind more freely than
most. He and Chavez quarreled from time to time but always made up.
After Huerta, Ganz had been Chavez's strongest ideological supporter,
committed to the importance of the movement philosophy and strongly
opposed to paying wages.

Since the ALRA had passed, however, Ganz had felt increasingly
estranged. He was unable to get Chavez's attention and confused by his
preoccupation with the La Paz community. Thrust into the unknown
world of elections with little guidance, Ganz learned fast. His fluency in
Spanish and comfort in the Mexican culture helped him form relationships with workers in Salinas and figure out the complicated vegetable
industry. He immersed himself in strategies to win elections, negotiate,
and administer contracts. He was excited by the strength of the ranch

committees and his success in building leadership. Ganz was eager to share his new knowledge, but Chavez rebuffed discussions, resenting the intrusion of "real world" issues on his work at La Paz.

In February 1978, without notifying Ganz, Chavez announced that Ganz would be shifted to organizing—a department all but abolished after the decision to concentrate on negotiating more contracts. The switch was motivated, Chavez said, by concern from state officials that if the UFW did not pick up the pace on elections, the Agricultural Labor Relations Board's budget would be cut.

Ganz responded to the abrupt about-face with a thirteen-page, single-spaced letter that detailed everything he found troubling in recent months: Chavez's lack of interest in substantive issues facing the union. His response to the loss of Prop 14, "the first time the public really rejected us." The focus on purging "assholes" as "a substitute for dealing with our own problems of administrative incompetence." Chavez's annoyance when problems arose. His desperation to sign contracts at any cost, and the message of weakness that sent to employers. His veiled comments at recent meetings about board members having "political interests" that conflicted with Chavez's plans.

"It was like you locked yourself up in La Paz with your people over there and that the trust which should be shared with the rest of us who worked all these years to help you build this movement is transferred to your 'co-game players' and your La Paz folks," Ganz wrote. "What the fuck political interests are you talking about? Does someone on the board have ambitions to replace you? If so, I don't know about it. Are those of us on the board some kind of threat to you? If so, I don't know what it is."

Ganz felt he had lost Chavez's trust by questioning his decisions. "If my thinking for myself and arguing for my position is a threat to you and to the union, then I'm ready to leave rather than create an internal division. But I think it's a bigger threat to the union if you can't tolerate independence and self-direction among top staff and officers. You cannot build a national union out of 'yes men.'"

In his anger and hurt, Ganz wrote with more accuracy than he realized; though Ganz found the idea almost inconceivable, yes-men were what Chavez wanted. Rather than respond privately, Chavez brought up the letter at the March 1978 executive board meeting—a further breach of the intimate relationship Ganz had enjoyed. Ganz asked for a private conversation. "He's the president of the fucking union, Marshall," Cohen said in annoyance. "He's not your father." Ganz was coaxed into repeating the points of his letter in a long monologue. Chavez took notes. He scrawled four words on the bottom of his pad: "Let me run union."

To run the union, he repeated, he needed the Game. Ganz's unhappiness became another opening to convince the board to play. The Game, Chavez promised, offered the perfect forum to voice grievances and clear the air. The first Game would be painful, he warned. But "a two, three hour rip-roaring game" would free them to make better decisions. "It's like hunting two tigers with one bullet," he said. "You want to take a chance." Almost everyone who played at La Paz enjoyed the Game, Chavez insisted. Gilbert Padilla immediately disagreed. Plenty of people had confided in Padilla that they found the Game upsetting and destructive. "They come because it's part of the community; if you don't come, you're an asshole," he told Chavez, who vehemently disagreed. "Let's go play," Chavez urged the board. "We'll record it for posterity."

And so they did. The players knew each other well, knew their vulnerabilities, and knew which attacks would appeal to Chavez. The ten players (Cohen played with the nine board members) included two brothers and two couples—Huerta and Richard Chavez, and Ganz and Govea, who had replaced Philip Vera Cruz on the board.

Chavez had mentioned off and on for two years that he wanted the legal department at La Paz, not Salinas. Ganz gamed Cohen: "The real problem is he's got his own union going in Salinas. How many unions have you ever heard of that the general counsel, the legal department of the union is 300 miles away from the union? How many of you ever hear of that? But see, he's got his own thing going."

Huerta gamed Ganz on developing an independent power base: "I think you're trying to start your own union." Then she turned on Govea and accused her of being Ganz's sidekick: "At the convention we should have just passed a resolution to give Marshall two votes."

Padilla and Ganz gamed Medina about his ambition and accused him of campaigning to be the union president. "He doesn't believe in God . . . and he wants to be president of the union!" Huerta said. If he assumed power, she warned, he would bring all the assholes in with him.

Cohen and Huerta gamed Padilla, who had gone around to all the others in recent months in a futile attempt to get them to agree that Chavez had gone crazy. "'Nutsy,' is the word, Dolores," Cohen said.

But they saved their strongest indictments for Chavez. The anger and unhappiness and confusion of the past months spilled out in attack after attack on the union leader. They gamed Chavez hardest on being out of touch with the workers. "He doesn't know the goddamn members," Ganz said. "He doesn't know shit about contract administrations," Huerta added, recalling the early days of the union when Chavez drove from town to town and spoke with farmworkers all the time.

"He hates the fucking workers," Richard Chavez said. "He doesn't know a fucking thing about the field office. He's trying to make policy for the workers and doesn't know a goddamn thing about them." He chastised his brother for shunning the workers whose dues supported the union. ("Think of them as dues-units," Cohen chimed in sarcastically.) "The workers don't know who he is anymore. They just know his name."

They made fun of Founder's Day, the La Paz committees, and the royal "we" in the president's newsletters, "a substitute for going out there and really dealing with the problem," Ganz said. Huerta gamed Chavez for not learning from the 1973 debacle and again failing to make sure the field office staff could handle the contracts. "We're going to get screwed," she warned. "Whores in Giumarra's camps!" Cohen shouted, a reference to Chavez's tirade that blew up the 1973 negotiations with Delano grape growers.

The new owners of Interharvest, the largest lettuce grower, had come to meet Chavez the prior week and found him fasting. "Here's these agribusiness guys who want to talk about problems," Ganz said, and instead "they got all this weird stuff . . . In the car going back to the airport, [Interharvest owner] Howard Marguleas says to me, 'What was that all about?'"

The Steven Spielberg science fiction movie *Close Encounters of the Third Kind* had been recently released, and the board members made fun of Chavez by humming the five-tone melodic theme that scientists used to communicate with extraterrestrials who landed in a UFO: "Doo do doo do doo. Doo do doo do doo."

Chavez had recently taken a six-day mind-control class in Los Angeles and then announced he could cure ailments by laying on hands. The board members ridiculed him as "the Great Healer." Padilla described a recent scene where Chavez "cured" someone, and they all began humming the *Close Encounters* theme again.

"Why don't you start eating like a regular person, and why don't you start sleeping like a regular person!" Mack Lyons yelled.

"He wants to be like Gandhi," Ganz replied. "Watch this, Gandhi led the independence in India. But then when it got down to the real problems, of starting to build a country, the real problems, he went off in this cloud."

"He talks about how when you touch someone in the dark, the sparks fly . . . Cesar, do you think you really can heal people?" Lyons asked.

"Yes," replied Chavez, who made almost no effort to defend himself.

Chavez did not need to fight back; the Game was a way for him to elicit information that would give him greater control. People said things in the Game that they were "too chickenshit" to say in another context. Their comments gave him clearer understanding of who stood in his way. "It is not difficult to get rid of total failures. They liquidate themselves," Chavez had said in his address to the 1977 union convention. "Yesterday's successes, however, always linger on beyond their productive life. We must seek out those sacred tasks of the past that drain needed resources and scarce time, and prune them ruthlessly so we can focus on the future."

The legal department was next to play the Game. At Chavez's urging, Cohen ordered his staff to travel to La Paz for training. On Saturdays, the eighteen lawyers and several paralegals boarded a van in Salinas at 3:00 A.M. for the five-hour ride to La Paz, unhappier each week.

The legal department was in Salinas because in 1974, Cohen had decided he could no longer live at La Paz and wanted to raise his family in Monterey County. Cohen had offered to resign as general counsel, but Chavez rejected the offer. He liked and trusted Cohen, relied on him for advice, and appreciated the law as a weapon. Chavez delighted in Cohen's legal gambles, his irreverence toward authority, and his winning record. Like Chavez, Cohen turned defensive situations into opportunities that cost growers money and forced them to divulge information.

Once the ALRA passed, however, the role of the legal department changed dramatically. They became more traditional labor lawyers. They filed election objections and unfair labor charges, fought for back wages for fired employees, and litigated to define the parameters of the new law. For the lawyers, the chance to set precedents and shape the best labor law in the country was exhilarating. For Chavez, the work held little appeal. The legal department became less crucial to him, and the location in Salinas more problematic. "They're not plugged into the union," Chavez told the board. "They don't have the same hopes that we have. The department should not be in Salinas. It's a mistake."

Chavez knew the lawyers would make strong Game players. "The guys that have words, have an edge," he said. "If you have a lot of words you don't have to scream too much; if you don't have words, you scream." For four weeks, the legal department played the Game under the watchful eyes of Chavez and his trusted staff. In their naiveté and arrogance, the lawyers thought themselves irreplaceable at this historic moment in time. That as much as anything else galled Chavez and made him determined to prove otherwise.

The lawyers were not subtle. "Legal staff are organizing and pushing their feelings, e.g., waste of time to come to La Paz, Game isn't working, the real work of the union is 'out there,' La Paz staff are brown-nosing 'moonies,'" Hartmire reported to Chavez.

Their Games started shortly after *Time* picked up on recent stories about investigations into violence and child abuse at Synanon, which the magazine termed a "kooky cult"; in addition to mandatory vasectomies, Dederich had decided residents at Home Place should swap spouses. Dederich filed a $76 million libel suit against *Time*. Like Chavez, Dederich relished the idea of a good enemy: "The Holy War against Time unites people in Synanon as other battles did in the days that built Synanon," read an internal memo. Dederich announced a boycott against *Time* and asked Chavez for help. Chavez denounced the story as a vicious attack and asked the UFW board to offer Dederich full support, noting Synanon had supplied the union with $100,000 worth of cars and materials, plus, of course, the Game.

"How do we reconcile our belief in nonviolence with the fact that he has an armed camp now?" Cohen asked, referring to comments by Dederich about his specially trained weapons force. Hostility from neighbors and authorities had prompted Synanon to purchase $63,000 worth of guns and ammunition, including 235 pistols, rifles, and shotguns, Dederich said. Families told stories about children held in Synanon against their will and beaten up after escape attempts, and a Marin County grand jury was investigating allegations of child abuse.

Chavez said the *Time* magazine story represented an attack on religious freedom, and the UFW needed to help its friends. The board adopted the *Time* boycott. The next Saturday, the lawyers arrived at La Paz for their Game dressed in matching white shirts and black ties and marched in a serpentine line from the bus to the conference room carrying copies of *Time* and singing "Onward Christian Soldiers."

A few weeks later, Cohen approached Chavez with a request from several lawyers. Most earned $600 a month and depended on relatives or savings to get by. Forced to play the Game as they struggled to keep up with the mounting legal work, they had asked Cohen for an increase.

When he told Chavez, the union president saw an opportunity. Tell them to put it in writing, he said. Cohen did. He directed all the lawyers to submit requests and presented the letters to Chavez in one bundle. They asked for additional amounts that averaged just over $400 a month.

Doctors and lawyers had always been exempt from the $5-a-week system, a practical concession justified on the basis of their professional status. Plenty of other exceptions were made. When Chavez needed particular expertise—whether from a lawyer, a mechanic, or Fred Ross— he paid. But anytime a proposal to pay wages arose, he batted down the suggestion with vigor. As early as 1971 he had voiced concern that others would push to change the system. In 1973, he had warned that the volunteer policy would not outlast him. Since then, pressure had steadily increased. Longtime volunteers aged, had families, and outgrew the stage of life where they happily lived on food stamps and subsistence pay, dependent on La Paz for their children's shoes and clothing allowances.

The volunteer system had become central to Chavez's vision of community, as well as a test of his leadership. He had brought up the crucial question at each meeting since the first time he brought the board to Synanon. "I gather from all the discussion here, or do I, that we don't want to pay wages, we can't afford to pay wages, that it shouldn't be done now, maybe later?" he asked at one meeting. "I need to have a very clear-cut decision so that I know what to do." He had waited for an opportunity to force the issue, and the lawyers handed him that opening.

Chavez arrived at the June 16, 1978, executive board meeting fresh from a one-night stay in the Yuma County jail. Over Memorial Day weekend, Manuel Chavez had started a melon strike in Arizona. On June 7, a judge issued an injunction that barred all picketing, after hearing evidence that pickets threw rocks, blocked traffic, and threatened workers in the fields. Chavez was outraged by the no-picketing rule in his native county. He and Helen went to Yuma to disobey the injunction and face arrest. When they were released the next day and en route to a rally, Chavez had the driver detour and stop alongside a field in the North Gila Valley. For several minutes, he stared in silence across the field at the tree that marked the site of the old family homestead.

Two days later, Chavez opened the June board meeting with a poem by Mao Tse Tung. The tension showed in even minor discussions. A proposal to formalize a time-off policy degenerated into a debate about burned-out, frustrated staff. What was the point of giving people time off if they had no money to go anywhere on vacation? asked Gilbert Padilla. When

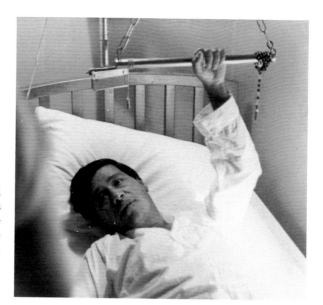

Chavez reaches for the bar installed above his bed in late 1968 when his back problems became so severe he could not sit up without assistance; he hung a rosary and a mezuzah on the metal bar. (Walter P. Reuther Library, Wayne State University)

Dr. Janet Travell examines Chavez in March 1969 in a Delano pool that was specially heated to ease his back pain; Marion Moses looks on. (Courtesy of Marion Moses)

Jane Fonda joins Chavez on a march through the Coachella Valley. (Walter P. Reuther Library, Wayne State University)

John Giumarra throws up his hands in mock surrender as he signs the historic grape contracts on July 29, 1970; his son, John Jr., looks on at far right. Celebrating victory, from left, are Jerry Cohen, Bishop Joseph Donnelly, and Monsignor George Higgins. (Cris Sanchez/Walter P. Reuther Library, Wayne State University)

Chavez in front of the Salinas jail, where he spent nineteen nights in December 1970 on a contempt charge for boycotting Bud Antle lettuce. (George Ballis/Walter P. Reuther Library, Wayne State University)

Salinas residents chant "Reds go home" as Ethel Kennedy walks with Dolores Huerta from an outdoor mass to the Monterey County jail to visit Chavez on December 6, 1970. (Gene Daniels/ Walter P. Reuther Library, Wayne State University)

Chavez waves an American flag as a lettuce worker addresses a Salinas rally of farmworkers eager to strike; Marshall Ganz looks on. (Courtesy of Bob Fitch photo archive © Stanford University Libraries)

Eliseo Medina, joined by Dolores Huerta, leads a march in Chicago to support the boycott. (Courtesy of Eliseo Medina)

Jessica Govea, smiling, at a rally in Delano on Mexican Independence Day, September 16, 1972; Virgina Jones on Govea's left. (Courtesy of Govea family)

Cesar looks on as Manuel Chavez shakes hands with William Kelly, a Coca-Cola executive, after signing a contract for orange workers in Florida in April 1972. (Hap Stewart/Walter P. Reuther Library, Wayne State University)

Chavez campaigns for the boycott on the Phil Donahue show in August 1972. (Walter P. Reuther Library, Wayne State University)

A farmworker reads *El Malcriado* in the waiting room of the UFW clinic in Calexico, under a larger-than-life poster of Chavez. (Glen Pearcy/Walter P. Reuther Library, Wayne State University)

Joan Baez and Taj Mahal sing at the funeral of Juan de La Cruz, a sixty-year-old farmworker shot on a picket line in August 1973. (Cris Sanchez/Walter P. Reuther Library, Wayne State University)

Chavez meets with striking Gallo workers. (Courtesy of Bob Fitch photo archive © Stanford University Libraries)

Juana Chavez joins her son on a march from San Francisco to Gallo headquarters in February 1975. (Courtesy of Bob Fitch photo archive © Stanford University Libraries)

Chavez was an amateur photography buff, a hobby he developed in the navy. (Walter P. Reuther Library, Wayne State University)

Richard Chavez, Cesar, and Fred Ross look grim as they contest the results of the Gallo election, which the UFW lost to the Teamsters. (© Rick Tejada-Flores)

Chavez walks at La Paz with California governor Jerry Brown, the only politician Chavez consistently praised, in February 1976, when the ALRB ran out of funds. (Cathy Murphy/Walter P. Reuther Library, Wayne State University)

Chavez jokes around with Chris Hartmire as they film a commercial for Proposition 14 in the fall of 1976. (Courtesy of Chris Hartmire)

Chavez with his mentor, Fred Ross, at the 1977 UFW convention. (© Cathy Murphy 1977)

Cesar and Richard Chavez on a ship during their October 1977 visit to the Philippines as guests of the Marcos government. (Walter P. Reuther Library, Wayne State University)

Chavez with his guard dogs, Boycott and Huelga, in the Tehachapi foothills above the La Paz compound where he often took morning walks. (Walter P. Reuther Library, Wayne State University)

Cesar and his son Paul consult on strategy on the handball court. (© Cathy Murphy 1976)

Chavez practicing yoga at La Paz. (© Cathy Murphy 1976)

Chavez poses with his son Fernando and parents in a picture that Cesar kept framed on his desk at La Paz. (Walter P. Reuther Library, Wayne State University)

Cesar and Helen at the wedding of one of their daughters at La Paz. (Walter P. Reuther Library, Wayne State University)

At the funeral of Rufino Contreras, a twenty-eight-year-old farmworker shot on February 10, 1979, during the lettuce strike; left to right, Governor Jerry Brown, Cesar, Helen, Richard Chavez, Dolores Huerta, Lupe Murguia, and Gilbert Padilla. (© Cathy Murphy 1979)

Chavez marches for the renewed grape boycott in 1987. (Walter P. Reuther Library, Wayne State University)

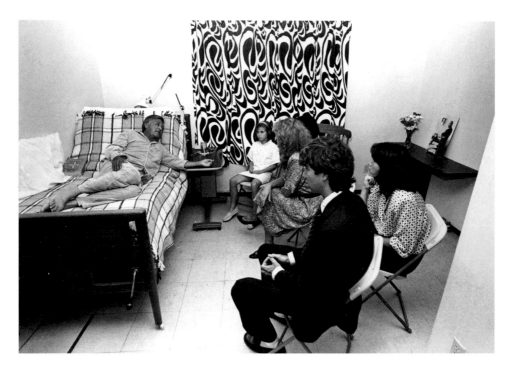

Three of Ethel and Robert Kennedy's children visit Chavez on August 4, 1988, during his last and longest fast. (Walter P. Reuther Library, Wayne State University)

Family and friends stand guard during the all-night vigil on April 28, 1993, as Cesar Chavez lay in a pine coffin built by his brother Richard. (© Cathy Murphy 1993)

the budget was presented for the next quarter, Chavez raised the requests by the lawyers for higher salaries.

"From where I stand, this represents to me two significant things. One is the money of course. But the other one is the philosophy." He equated philosophy with the commitment to subsistence wages and to a community like La Paz. "Is it really too late, or is it possible to try and get the legal department to live the kind of lifestyle that we do? And if we try to do that, what happens?"

Chavez insisted the question the board must decide was not how much to pay the lawyers but whether to pay staff at all. He spoke calmly, as he usually did once he had made a decision. "Every board meeting, it comes up. I think we should really make a decision."

For those who might not be swayed by philosophy, Chavez added a practical argument: if the lawyers received higher wages, other staff would renew requests for salaries. The union's perennially dire budget situation made that an impossibility, he said.

To leave no doubt, he coolly issued another ultimatum. "I also have my needs. Frankly, if we pay wages in this outfit, I'm leaving. I'm not going to be pissed off. But I don't want it. I have other things I want to do . . . I want to live in a community. I'll do anything to do that. Including leaving the union if I have to. I want to do that. It's not a good thing, because I'm probably overbearing on everybody else." Then he fell back on the pragmatic argument: "But really, you have no choice, moneywise, because it's there in black and white." Ganz laughed, recognizing the Hobson's choice.

"But if we had a choice," Chavez continued, "I can just see what the decision would be, philosophically, if we had a choice. If we had the money, this decision probably wouldn't stand too long . . . See, we really don't have a choice, right? We don't. And I don't know how long it will be before we have a choice."

Cohen gambled, in his cockiest style. He said most if not all the lawyers would leave rather than move to La Paz, especially the best ones. Knowing he could not win on philosophy, he appealed to the ever-pragmatic Chavez. You get what you pay for, Cohen said, and good lawyers won't work for free. "You may want to have some hired guns around," he said several times. He would help with a transition, but the pressures of his family, the need to pay college tuitions, and the desire to live in Monterey made a move to La Paz impossible. He would not raise his children like Dolores Huerta did, he said in a swipe at her notorious neglect.

Everyone in the room realized that Chavez could have easily and quietly reached an accommodation on the requests. His decision to frame the issue as a debate about philosophy signaled not only his willingness but his desire to sacrifice the legal department in the interest of establishing a principle.

"How do we resolve it?" Ganz asked, growing alarmed. "Because the price we pay then is losing a lot of immediate effectiveness, right?" If Cohen said he needed $20,000 a year, "are we really going to say, 'Well, that's too bad man'?" Ganz asked incredulously.

"I got an answer for you," Chavez responded. "If you don't resolve the philosophy, then I say, 'I want out.' I might just say that. Then you've got a real choice to make."

With clarity and prescience, he framed the decision as the watershed it would turn out to be: "When you make a philosophical decision, you either survive, or you fail . . . We're all somehow, maybe even subconsciously maybe, aware that it's one of those decisions that will make us or break us."

Padilla and Richard Chavez were ready to vote. Padilla defined the options as "pay or don't pay," and said the union could not afford to pay salaries. The younger board members pushed for a delay. We need time to think this through, Medina and Govea said. Cohen wanted to get the vote over with. He knew he had been outgambled. The board agreed to reconvene in a week and adjourned after midnight.

Chavez used the week to organize. Padilla read the lawyers' requests out loud at a community meeting and easily whipped up antagonism toward the greedy Anglo lawyers who demanded more money, made fun of La Paz, and thought they were better than everyone else. "The word that fits is 'blackmail,'" David Villarino wrote to his father-in-law. Chavez went to Salinas and met with the lawyers, an uncomfortable session that resolved nothing. They told him he should fire incompetent volunteers and pay people who could skillfully negotiate and administer contracts. He told them he wanted his lawyers at La Paz.

Chavez saw an opportunity to accomplish two goals: disband a legal department that had become at best out of step and at worst a threat, and reaffirm the principle of voluntary servitude.

When the executive board reconvened on June 25, Chavez again presented the question of whether or not to pay wages across the union. He dismissed pleas to consider only the lawyers' requests, a vote he might well have lost. He ruled out compromises, such as paying more money to fewer lawyers. They could defer paying wages until the union was on a sounder financial footing, but they had to make a philosophical decision. If they paid the attorneys, they would have to pay everyone, he repeated. "We have to really take a stand," he said. Huerta and Padilla agreed.

"I'm a leader," Chavez said. "I've been leading all of you guys all these years. And maybe you don't need me anymore. Really truly. And the way to put it is, my direction is just not satisfying you. Perfectly all right. I have another project I'd like to do."

"I think that's a big cop-out," Ganz replied. "I thought we were all committed to building a union. I thought that's why we were all here."

"And so far we've built a union largely based on my ideas, right?" Chavez said. "And we come now to a place where maybe my ideas maybe aren't working."

"Maybe other people have ideas . . . ways to make it better," Govea said.

Ganz faced the implications of all that Chavez had said in recent months, and the conflict with the reality in the fields. After almost a year of focusing on contract negotiations, the UFW still had scarcely more than a hundred contracts, representing a small fraction of the farmworkers in California. Now Chavez was about to jettison a legal department that was one of their key weapons. "We have always sort of prided ourselves on being different from the rest of the unions," Ganz said. "But there's one fact that keeps staring at me, which is that they are unions. And we're still not there. And I think that's where we want to get. And maybe the past experience of every other labor organization in the country just demonstrates that there comes a time when it has to happen. And I think we better face it, and I think we better deal with it."

The split had become public, and irreparable. They aired their different long-term visions. "Organize other poor people," Huerta said.

"That's your pot of gold," Ganz responded.

Huerta insisted she spoke for the members. "Organize the unorganized workers throughout the country. Maybe throughout the world. That was our goal. We all voted on that at the convention, and nobody opposed it. If that is really our goal, we can't talk about paying wages. It's just simple."

Medina looked at the same set of facts and reached the opposite conclusion. He, too, saw the question as one of philosophy. He was a farmworker, one of only two who had come out of the fields onto the board. He had worked toward building a union that would be run by farmworkers. There was no way talented farmworkers would come work for the union without pay. The students being trained in the Fred Ross school should be the best and the brightest from the ranch committees, he said—farmworkers, not the sons and daughters of union leaders. Look at the union staff in the field offices and La Paz, Medina said. "You think that's where the future of the union is? I disagree entirely. I think we need to realize that we're not going to be able to turn the union over to the workers on the same basis we started out. I think we should pay wages." The leaders in the fields were the ones with a personal stake in the union's success, he said. "We're kidding ourselves if we think that we're going to turn this union over to farmworkers on the basis of $10 a week and benefits."

Chavez had long played Medina and Ganz against each other, ensuring that his two strongest organizers never recognized their natural alliance. By the time they found themselves on the same side, Medina was on the verge of resigning. He had just finished managing a string of victories at eight citrus orchards that added more than twenty-four hundred new members and thousands of dollars in dues. He had figured out a way to forestall the lengthy delays growers often imposed: Medina kept workers on strike until the grower agreed to waive objections, certify the election, and bargain. Fresh from this success, he had presented Chavez with a modest budget to add a half dozen organizers to the staff. Chavez turned on Medina and denounced the proposal as ridiculous. Chavez attacked the young organizer in a manner he had often used on others, but never before on the respectful Medina.

Now, at what would be his final board meeting, Medina said he faulted himself. He had been derelict in his duties. Until now, he had gone along with whatever Chavez wanted, suppressing questions and doubts about the Game, the purges, mind control, community building. "Maybe, you know, we're all on different wavelengths," he said to Chavez. "Maybe part of it is that we don't understand where you're going. I sure as hell don't."

The vote split along generational lines. With some reluctance, Pete Velasco and Richard Chavez supported Cesar's proposal and voted to reaffirm the commitment to the volunteer system. Richard had been the strongest advocate of paying wages and becoming a business union, but in the end he could not vote against his brother.

Forcing a vote that amounted to a referendum on his leadership, Chavez had prevailed by the narrowest possible margin, a remarkably public schism. "Paying salaries, how stupid can they be," Chavez vented to Hartmire a few days later. "I am not going to risk my neck for that kind of organization . . . I can't keep risking my life when there is no idealism." He felt exactly the way he had felt in CSO, Chavez said. He was tired of forcing his will on everyone else and would step down as president in 1981. He added a major caveat: "Obviously if they all leave, then I will have to stay to develop the next group of leaders . . . Obviously I won't leave if there is a crisis or if I think the union can't survive. I don't want to give my life to a dead Dr. King movement."

Medina asked Chavez for a leave of absence a few days after the June board meeting, with the understanding he would not return. His departure removed the only credible alternative to Chavez, to the dismay of Ganz and Richard Chavez. They urged Cesar to reach out, but he made no effort to keep the young leader. Soon word emanated from La Paz: "Story already is that he [Medina] wasn't a good negotiator or organizer and all he wanted was money," Kirsten Zerger, one of the last lawyers left in Salinas, wrote in her diary. "How far from the truth. How sad we are at this state of revising history so soon."

Ganz and Govea went on loan to help Jerry Brown's reelection campaign, postponing a decision about their future with the union. Jim Drake had wrestled for more than a year before he could leave, feeling like he was resigning from his own family. In June, he finished negotiating a contract, walked into a meeting to announce the good news, received the traditional farmworker applause, walked out, and drove away. He went to work organizing woodcutters in Mississippi.

Even Hartmire thought about leaving, but he knew that his departure would send a terrible signal. "Somehow, the union has to make this transition from *la causa* to a bread and butter union and some old time people have to make it happen," he wrote his wife. "If it doesn't happen, there isn't going to be a farmworker union." Like many, he had worked himself to exhaustion. He ignored symptoms until he felt so ill he drove himself from La Paz to a Los Angeles hospital, where he collapsed with a bleeding ulcer.

By the time Hartmire had recovered, La Paz had stopped playing the Game, though there had been no formal announcement. Two high-profile tragedies contributed to the decision. In October, Paul Morantz, a Los Angeles lawyer who had successfully represented former Synanon residents seeking to recoup their life savings, was bitten by a rattlesnake that had been left in his mailbox. On November 18, 1978, Los Angeles police raided Synanon and seized incriminating evidence, including tape recordings of Dederich saying, "Don't mess with us. You can get killed dead, literally dead." The Old Man was found soon after in an alcoholic stupor in Arizona and arrested on charges of being an accessory to attempted murder; two of his followers were charged with placing the snake in Morantz's mailbox.

Four days after the police raid on Home Place, the charismatic cult leader Jim Jones coerced more than nine hundred of his followers to commit mass suicide by cyanide poisoning at the Peoples Temple in Guyana. The Peoples Temple had until recently been based in Northern California, where Jones was a well-known figure, active in Democratic politics and praised by prominent officials.

Both events had a sobering effect on La Paz. A Democratic assembly-man put out a press release comparing the cult of Chavez to Jonestown. Who wants to stay around only to find out in a year that there are five hundred suicides up at La Paz? Jerry Cohen said, half joking.

In Salinas, the legal department was phasing out. Cohen quietly resigned as general counsel and prepared to argue a case before the U.S. Supreme Court and help in contract negotiations. Half the lawyers left shortly after the vote by the executive board. The others stayed to wind up cases and hand off work to their successors. The transition to a volunteer legal depart-ment did not proceed as smoothly as Chavez had envisioned. He had difficulty recruiting talent. The new lawyers at La Paz were so inexperi-enced that the union paid more for outside counsel than they had paid the Salinas lawyers. The overwhelmed lawyers in La Paz pleaded for help.

Chavez went to visit Sandy Nathan, who had been Cohen's deputy overseeing all of the work before the ALRB. Nathan was packing up to leave. In a rare move, Chavez acknowledged he had erred. He had known the lawyers were good, he said, but he hadn't realized how good or how indispensable. He apologized for not having truly understood their work or its importance. The union needed help to rebuild, he said. He spoke in the persuasive, sincere manner that made people trust him and want to help. He asked Nathan to stay.

"He didn't need to come and lay himself open to me, and I wasn't going to extract anything from him," Nathan wrote that night. "I know it must have been hard for him, it must have been somewhat humiliating for him. I felt bad enough as it was. I felt this pervasive sense of sadness in there with him, that it was too late, where has he been, why didn't he come sooner . . . At one point I got this feeling of a person being offered something and you know you really can't accept it, you can't even talk about it in good faith anymore." He finished packing and headed east.

At La Paz, Chavez embraced the future that he had chosen. He orchestrated an elaborate graduation for the negotiators from the Fred Ross School—his son, son-in-law, Huerta's son, and eight other Mexican Americans, mostly children of movement volunteers. The ceremony began two hours late while seamstresses pressed into service only three days earlier finished sewing special shirts Chavez had requested. He wanted the graduates to wear matching manta shirts patterned after the one he had worn when he broke his Phoenix fast. He told them that manta, simple cotton, was the shirt of poor people.

In his homily, Chris Hartmire compared the graduates to the disciples of Jesus: "You are being sent out on this day by Fred, by Richard, by Cesar, by the board, by the whole union, that cares about what you do. At a deeper level, you're also being sent out by God, to serve the people and to announce the day of more justice."

Sensitivity about recent departures was near the surface. "When some of those of little faith and lots of mouth remark to you, 'Yeah, I guess the union is ok, but what about that second level of leadership?' I hope you just shove those words right down their mouth," Ross said in his remarks to the crowd. "Because that second level of leadership is sitting right in front of you right now."

In his commencement address, Chavez lauded the union's executive board for training a group that might challenge their leadership—secure in the knowledge that would never occur. "Very few unions would dare develop leadership without any restrictions," Chavez said. "We're not afraid of that . . . This decision was made by the leaders of the union knowing full well they were developing an awful lot of competition." More than a decade earlier, Chavez said, he had shared with Ross the dream of a school such as this one. "Some day, mark my words," he concluded, "we will see hundreds of farmworkers going through this school."

The eleven negotiators were the last class to graduate from the Fred W. Ross School.

PART V

November 1978–April 1993

CHAPTER 34

From Dream to Nightmare

I feel the way I never felt before. We have thirty years of struggle behind us, but I am spirited and encouraged. I feel I can fight for another hundred years.

Since his first forays into the Salinas Valley, Chavez had regarded the vegetable workers with a mixture of admiration and wariness. He respected their courage and willingness to engage in militant action. He boasted about "liberated ranches" where the *tortuga* forced recalcitrant supervisors to honor the contracts. He marveled at meetings where workers whipped copies of the UFW constitution out of their back pocket and quoted passages verbatim. But he also recognized that independence made the vegetable workers harder to control, and he understood the danger.

The lettuce workers, Chavez counseled the negotiation students at La Paz, were sharper and more likely than the grape workers to challenge authority. Most lechugueros were Mexican citizens with green cards. "Anybody with a green card—that's just an indication how on the ball they are. If you see a green card, rest assured they had to really hustle," Chavez advised. "Keep your eyes open, because they'll try to hustle you. If you don't know when to stand up, they'll get you. If you stand up too quickly, they'll get you."

In the fall of 1978, the UFW had thirty-one contracts covering roughly ten thousand vegetable workers. They were about one-third of the union's membership, and among the most highly paid. As the contracts neared expiration at the end of the year, the vegetable workers were not happy with their union.

The flash point for frustration was the UFW's Robert F. Kennedy health insurance plan, managed out of La Paz by volunteers with little training and minimal computer skills. They struggled to administer a complex medical plan for tens of thousands of workers. The union's eligibility lists were full of errors. Reimbursement checks arrived months late or never at all. Workers who took pride in managing their affairs found they had become credit risks. A report to Chavez by one of his chief negotiators in advance of contract talks called the RFK plan a "ticking time bomb."

Chavez dispatched Dolores Huerta and Richard Chavez to Salinas to scout out the situation in preparation for negotiations. They returned in alarm. Reimbursement checks for hundreds of dollars, issued more than a year earlier, gathered dust in an inch-thick pile of unopened envelopes. Two staff people struggled to service twenty contracts. Grievances piled up, unaddressed. The mood was ugly. "We are in serious trouble," Huerta reported. The only workers who showed up at union meetings were the most loyal Chavistas—and they came to yell at union leaders and plead for support. "We have very, very, big problems," Richard Chavez told his brother. At several ranches, they heard rumblings about moves to vote the union out.

Just as he had been impatient with grape workers' complaints about the hiring hall and back dues six years earlier, Chavez did not want to hear the vegetable workers' gripes. He first blamed the "assholes," left-wingers who he argued had infiltrated the union intent on sabotage. Even Huerta rejected that explanation. "You're very mistaken," Richard chimed in angrily. "We created the fucking problem. It's our problem . . . We had the same problem in Delano in '72. The same fucking problem." The militancy of the vegetable workers, Huerta added, made the situation in Salinas even worse.

Chavez tried to reassure them. The problem could never be as bad as in 1973, when the Teamsters took away all the UFW contracts. "If we lose contracts by decertification elections, that's going to be a bigger problem," Huerta responded. Under the ALRA, workers could decertify the union during the last year of a contract. Growers had already been capitalizing on the discontent by bringing unhappy workers from UFW companies to talk to workers during election campaigns. Of twenty-two elections held between June and September 1978, the UFW had lost two-thirds.

Chavez agreed to send a team to Salinas to iron out problems and soothe the ranch committees. What was the goal? asked Chavez. "The goal is to save those contracts," his brother answered. Cesar wanted to name the project. They decided on *"Plan de Flote."* The goal was to stay afloat.

With no negotiating team in place and the contracts expiring at year's end, Chavez stalled for time. Marshall Ganz had returned from the Brown campaign, and Chavez assigned Ganz to do an economic study of the vegetable industry. What he discovered gave Chavez hope and reignited his fighting spirit. During the double-digit inflation of the 1970s, profits for the growers had soared: Salinas lettuce growers cleared $71 million in 1978, a jump of 975 percent in eight years. During the same period, farmworkers' wages increased only 85 percent, to an average of $3.70 an hour. Farmworkers also lagged other employees of the lettuce companies, who had received much larger percentage increases.

Chavez seized on the statistics as a way to placate the angry vegetable workers. The numbers justified demands for major wage increases. He had long condemned the lechugueros for caring too much about money; now he hoped to turn that materialism to his advantage. He relished the impending showdown, a fight that would win back the workers' loyalty. In the past, Chavez had approached strikes with trepidation. Now he saw a strike as the only worthwhile gamble: "If they beat us, they beat us. We don't have a union. If we beat them, we have a union."

Board members cautioned that the medical plan caused the most complaints, not wages. Chavez insisted that large salary increases would solve all problems. A strike was the only route. "We're not going to get the money we need from those bastards unless we get into a big fight," he said. "I'm not going to settle for anything that's not going to give the workers some goddamn real money . . . Otherwise we're not going to have a union."

The UFW presented its economic demands on January 5, 1979, days after the contracts had expired. The opening package contained over-the-moon demands—an increase in the hourly wage to $5.25, higher salaries for specialty workers, overtime after eight hours, and dozens of other costly provisions. Chavez also insisted on full-time union representatives, paid by the company, a provision modeled on the UAW contracts.

Growers were taken aback. Their early meetings with Chavez had been amicable. Andrew Church, a Salinas attorney representing many of the more moderate growers, had assured Chavez the industry wanted a contract and would negotiate hard but in good faith. The vegetable growers split into factions, along geographic and philosophical lines. The moderate faction warned that the hardliners, who did not trust Chavez, would dominate the negotiations "if the Union comes in with a mau-mau" approach, reported Tom Dalzell, one of the last attorneys left in Salinas. In January, the union splashed its demands across the pages of a Mexicali newspaper. The hardliners crowed.

The industry countered with a proposal for a 7 percent raise, citing guidelines promulgated by President Jimmy Carter to stem the rampant inflation of the past decade. Union negotiators responded that Carter's guidelines did not apply to the lowest wage earners. On January 18, the two sides sat down for the first serious negotiation. The seventeen grower representatives arrived perplexed by the union's gambit but expecting to negotiate. As they watched Chavez talk past them, they realized he had other plans.

The strike began the next morning. The union called out one company each day—Cal Coastal, then Vessey, then Mario Saikhon, and then Sun Harvest, the giant company formerly known as Interharvest. Thousands of ripe heads of lettuce wilted in the fields. The price of lettuce soared. Growers brought in students, housewives, and even winos in a desperate attempt to salvage the crops. They deployed armed guards and dogs to protect the fields. Ganz estimated losses totaled $2 million during the first two weeks of the strike.

When Chavez visited the picket lines on February 1, 1979, about three thousand workers had shut down eight companies that normally supplied one-third of the nation's winter lettuce. He spoke to thousands of cheering workers and called the strike a "dream realized, a dream that at one time we thought impossible." The days "when people used to laugh at us" are over, he declared. The strike was the most organized he had ever seen. "I feel the way I never felt before. We have thirty years of struggle behind us, but I am spirited and encouraged. I feel I can fight for another hundred years."

Nine days later, Chavez sat down for the first one-on-one negotiations with Sun Harvest, with which the union held its largest and oldest vegetable contract. Talks had just begun in a Los Angeles church basement when word came that a farmworker had been fatally shot.

Strikers had rushed into the Mario Saikhon company fields, trespassing in an effort to drive out the scabs. The tactic was not officially sanctioned but widely used. A foreman and two other employees had opened fire. Rufino Contreras, twenty-eight, was struck in the head and collapsed facedown in the lettuce field. His father and brother watched him die.

Chavez prevailed upon angry workers to refrain from violence, just as he had after the deaths of Juan de la Cruz and Nagi Daifullah in 1973. Chavez eulogized Contreras that evening in front of more than a thousand workers. The next night, Chavez and Contreras's father led a silent three-mile candlelight procession. On Valentine's Day, more than seven thousand people walked for miles along rural roads in the funeral procession. Gov. Jerry Brown sat beside Chavez at the service. "Mi papi! Mi papi!" sobbed Contreras's five-year-old son.

The funeral was one of Chavez's last visits to the picket lines. His role, he told the strikers, was to raise money and outside support. "My job is in the cities," he said. "The large churches, labor unions and student groups in Los Angeles already are being contacted. We need to bring food and money in here, medical aid, all the things people need."

The union was spending between $300,000 and $400,000 a month on the strike. Two fund-raising appeals had generated minimal response. "Money's not coming in like it used to," Chavez told the board. He headed east on a fund-raising tour. He also began to lay the groundwork for a boycott of Chiquita bananas. Sun Harvest was owned by United Brands, which also owned Chiquita. Chavez was convinced a boycott would force Sun Harvest to settle.

At a fund-raiser at the New York apartment of Bob Denison, the investment banker who handled the union's funds, Chavez explained the difficulty of striking the most powerful industry in California. He sounded much as he had when people in the room first met him a decade earlier. "We've got to go out and use the boycott as a means of counteracting the pressure that comes because they have total control of the political life in the community," he said. "When you strike the growers, you strike the school board, you strike the water board, you strike the board of supervisors, the city police."

Denison acknowledged that generating interest in the farmworkers' cause had become difficult, even among New Yorkers who had supported the union for years. "Cesar Chavez and the grape strike and the farmworker union is a very old story," he told his guests. "And it's very difficult with a lot of people, unfortunately, to get them to feel as they did ten years ago, when people were more prone to become active. It's very difficult to stir people up now about anything."

Denison went further. He addressed the growing criticism that Chavez did not operate the union efficiently. Chavez rejected the life of a labor leader and the goals of the middle class, Denison said: "If the only way to be entirely efficient was to bring in a lot of outsiders who have a lot of special managerial skills and put them in charge of everything so the people involved in the union and the cause couldn't control their own destiny, that was too high a price to pay. So I'm not sympathetic to complaints." Then he handed Chavez a $1,000 check and told everyone else to donate before they walked out the door.

Back home, Chavez faced more problems. His dream strike had begun to disintegrate. Growers recruited scabs. Discipline on the picket lines broke down. Gambling and drinking increased. Ganz had started the strike with a structure that relied on captains at each company and a strike council that met twice a day to plan strategy. Chavez had replaced Ganz with a trusted friend from his teenage years in Delano, Frank Ortiz. Ortiz was close to Manuel Chavez. Ortiz refused to meet with the workers. His allegiance was to Manuel; the workers' allegiance was to Ganz. Friction between the factions deepened.

Manuel Chavez had been absent for several years from the union's official roster. In the fall of 1975, as election campaigns began, Manuel had disappeared, leaving behind large unpaid bills and a reported stolen car, with a loan cosigned by his cousin Cesar. "Dear Manuel," Cesar wrote in October 1975. "After some 20 telephone calls and various other ways of getting ahold of you, I finally decided to come and see you in Calexico. As expected I was not able to see you and I have given up hope of trying to reach you . . . For all intents and purposes, you have given up organizing for the Union, and God knows whatever it is you are doing. Therefore, I am replacing you of your duties with the Union." For years, Chavez would point to this as evidence that he was willing to fire anyone—even his own cousin.

By the time the 1979 strike began, Manuel had resurfaced in the Imperial Valley in an unofficial but significant role. "There are two cliques, two groups there," Chavez said. "They're there because we encourage them, because we allow them to happen." Chavez needed both. He relied on Manuel for intelligence, and he depended on Ganz for organizational assignments no one else could handle. To different degrees, Chavez had emotional bonds with both men, and he tolerated behavior from each that he would not have countenanced from others. But under the pressure of the strike, tension worsened. Jessica Govea was in charge of administering strike benefits; by March, two months into the strike, she and Ortiz were barely on speaking terms. Chavez called an emergency board meeting.

He did not address substantive problems with the strike. He had only one suggestion for brokering peace: "There's no way of cleaning ourselves up short of playing the Game . . . I've told you and I'll tell you again, without the Game, it's a problem."

The Game had not been played for months. Only Ortiz responded positively to Chavez's suggestion. Richard led the opposition. He did not need to yell and curse people out, he said; he relieved his frustrations by smacking golf balls. "Are we just concerned about you or are we concerned about the whole board?" Cesar asked.

"I don't know, they're free to go play golf, too, if they want," Richard said, eliciting laughter that broke the tension for a few seconds. Cesar was not amused. Only the Game would help, he insisted. "Some people are afraid of being told things that they're guilty of," he said. "Some are willing to take it for the goddamn cause and some are not.

"Fucking meeting of the executive board," Chavez concluded. "I'm going to bring the growers here and sell fucking tickets to raise money for the strike. Five dollars a ticket to every grower who comes and observes an executive board meeting."

Chavez had no coherent strike strategy. Disengaged from action on the ground, he made little effort to absorb important details, a skill at which he normally excelled. Ganz recited facts and figures about each company: number of machines and crews at work, boxes processed per hour, percentage loss in production. Chavez repeatedly asked which companies were on strike. He showed little concept of the relative size of companies or the degree of union support. When Chavez said the union had won elections at all but a handful of Salinas growers, board members immediately corrected him. The union had less than half under contract. "You're kidding!" Chavez said. "According to me, [speaking] on the East Coast, we have 90 percent."

Chavez saw no end game for the strike, which was draining the union's treasury. He pushed to shift resources to a boycott. "I want to go on the boycott!" Chavez told the board. "I love the boycott. Let me go on the boycott." Try it for three years, the others responded. The man who had built his union walking into barrios in the San Joaquin Valley and talking to workers one by one now felt more comfortable among the volunteers and boycott supporters.

Confident he would prevail, Chavez told his staff in La Paz to prepare for a boycott. "Funds are almost totally depleted," he said. "The strike has lost its punch. It's just not effective anymore." He said strikers were prepared to go out on the boycott, although vegetable workers had never endorsed that plan. "Everybody's unanimous that it has to be done," he said. "The question is when, how soon."

Chavez's decision met with anything but unanimous approval. First, the executive board balked. Ganz, in charge of the strike again once the harvest moved north into the Salinas Valley, argued they could win in the fields. Most board members agreed. They expressed doubts about boycotting lettuce, which had never been as successful as grapes. The heyday of the boycott had been before the passage of the ALRA. Since then, boycotts had helped pressure companies to negotiate, but they had supplemented, not substituted for, action on the ground.

Chavez had expected to face a more compliant board. He had replaced Eliseo Medina and Mack Lyons with two stalwart supporters—David Martinez, an intense young man who had dropped out of law school to join the boycott staff, and Ortiz, who had known Chavez for several decades. Neither man was likely to prove an independent thinker. "Lone rangers just aren't going to make it anymore," Chavez said, stressing the importance of unity. "Following the team concept is very critical in the union now."

When the board did not readily support his plan to phase out the strike in favor of a boycott, Chavez redirected his anger toward a favorite target—Dolores Huerta. They had been sparring partners since the earliest days of the union, but the fights had grown more personal and more intense. Like an old married couple, they knew each other's trigger points. Chavez could count on Huerta's loyalty; he was confident she would not leave, no matter how much abuse he heaped upon her. Her identity was completely tied to the union. Staff in La Paz became accustomed to late-night screaming matches in Chavez's office, which often spilled over into board meetings. There was little if any boundary between the private and professional, particularly since Huerta was Chavez's de facto sister-in-law. When he had pulled Huerta out of Sacramento as the union lobbyist in the midst of a key battle over the ALRA, she had angrily brought her case to the executive board and demanded a public explanation of why Chavez had taken unilateral action.

"You talk to Richard and find out why you were taken off," Chavez retorted. "Don't blame me. I had nothing to do with it."

"I am blaming you!" said Huerta, seven months pregnant with the couple's fourth child.

"Look, Richard wants you to stay home, you're going to have a baby, and goddamn it that's why I did it!" Cesar said, angry and patronizing at once. "I did it because he wanted me to do it. He was going out of his mind there in Delano."

When Chavez was under pressure, Huerta became what she called the "whipping girl," a role she leaned into just as Chavez leaned into the physical suffering of his fasts and marches. At the June 1979 board meeting, frustrated with the lack of progress in the Salinas strike and the board's reticence to shift resources to a boycott, Chavez exploded at Huerta for failing to turn in a few hundred dollars' worth of receipts, an omission she disputed.

"Don't you fucking lie! Why do you lie?" Chavez yelled at her. He questioned his brother about a missing receipt, and Richard joined the fray: "I'm fucking sick and tired of being harassed!"

"You're upset because she's screaming," Cesar taunted Richard, before turning back to Huerta: "You're the goddamn stupidest bitch I've seen in my whole life! . . . You're crazy. I can't deal with you on business . . . I don't want you on the board."

"You have my resignation," Huerta said as she walked out.

Board members sat in uncomfortable silence, waiting for the tirade to pass.

Chavez had demonstrated that one way or another, with time, he could get his way with the board even on the thorniest question. He proceeded with boycott plans.

In the Salinas fields, the talk was very different. Ganz had resumed daily meetings with the strike coordinators at each company. They pushed to expand the strike to all ranches with expired contracts, so that growers would have greater difficulty recruiting scabs. Aware that Chavez wanted to curtail the strike, Ganz improvised a "pre-strike" mode. Workers staged slowdowns and work stoppages. Rumors of an imminent full-scale strike brought growers back to the negotiating table.

On June 11, the eve of renewed negotiations, thousands of workers rushed the Salinas fields, wreaking havoc. More than seventy-five people were arrested and several workers hospitalized with stab wounds. Ganz and the strike leaders had instigated the violence in a preplanned, calculated attack, an effort to show strength.

Chavez chastised Ganz for rushing the fields without prior approval, in defiance of an agreement made after the death of Rufino Contreras. Chavez expressed particular annoyance about not having known about the action in advance, a function of his distance from the strike. "People get killed, Marshall, when you do that. You have to understand that. I don't want to be responsible for putting people in the field. Especially when I know nothing about it. It hit me like a ton of bricks . . . The risk to our people is very great . . . Especially if I don't know. I need to know. Don't you agree with that?"

After a long silence, Ganz agreed. "I think it was a mistake."

The effort to demonstrate the union's strength had backfired, Chavez said. The head of the vegetable growers association had turned to Chavez and said, "'Cesar, we just want you to know that terrorism and escalating terrorism are not going to work.'"

Growers were baffled by the union's mixed signals. Initially Chavez wanted to negotiate, then he triggered a strike with outrageous demands. Now he wanted to negotiate, and his chief lieutenant staged wildcat actions across the Salinas Valley. Growers speculated about power struggles. They thought Chavez wanted a perpetual strike to justify a boycott operation, which would turn into a presidential campaign for Edward Kennedy or Jerry Brown. The union's "outlandish demands" and erratic behavior were to blame for the growers' confusion, Ganz told Chavez: "I think a case can be made that they're as puzzled about what we want as maybe we are about what they want."

Richard Chavez agreed. The Salinas workers were clear: they wanted to use the strike to negotiate a contract, not launch a boycott. "It's our problem," Richard said. "Not the people's problem. Don't blame the people for this one . . . We made a mistake."

Cesar grew more adamant about ending the strike, taking control, and proving his course of action correct. "I think we should just stop screwing around and double guessing and we should go on the boycott," he said. "We're not going to beat them on the strike." He was convinced growers would not negotiate without a boycott. He pointed to his track record to bolster his case. "My gut feeling with me has been really good, most of the times in my life. My gut feeling is the employers don't want to negotiate a contract."

The union's semiannual convention approached. The board decided to hold a one-day meeting in Salinas on August 12 to show support for the strikers. Chavez proceeded as if the decision to boycott had been made. "On Aug. 13, 1979, hundreds of lettuce strikers will leave California and go to the cities of America to tell the story of their struggle and to seek support for the boycott of Chiquita bananas and non-union iceberg lettuce," he wrote, soliciting ads for the convention booklet.

The workers proceeded as if the convention would approve a resolution for a general strike against all the vegetable companies. Two marches began the week before the convention, heading toward Salinas from the north and south. They presaged the impending collision.

Chavez began a twelve-day march from San Francisco south through San Jose, hoping to draw the union's traditional supporters. On the sixth day, he began to fast. The walk only occasionally attracted more than a dozen marchers, including a handful of boycotters recruited for the exercise. At one point, on the outskirts of San Jose, they all suddenly fell down. A minor earthquake had rattled the ground. The others looked around in bewilderment; Chavez was already up and walking ahead, unfazed.

The marchers neared Decoto, the town where Ross had sent Chavez in 1953 on his first organizing assignment. Chavez turned to Scott Washburn and sent him ahead to drum up a crowd. Chavez did not want to return to the scene of his first solo triumph and walk through empty streets with a half dozen people. Washburn turned out a good crowd, and Chavez spoke from the roof of a car, reminiscing about his first house meeting campaign more than twenty-five years earlier.

The second march began in San Ardo, at the southern end of the Salinas Valley. Dozens, then hundreds of workers marched through the rich agricultural lands. As they passed fields, many workers walked out spontaneously and joined the march. "*Esta huelga está ganada*" (this strike is won), chanted Cleofas Guzman, a lechuguero from Sun Harvest who helped lead the march. The crowd swelled to thousands as they neared Salinas.

On August 11, the marchers joined forces, ten thousand strong, and rallied outside Sherwood Elementary School, next door to the UFW office. Chavez entered the rally with Gov. Jerry Brown, now a national celebrity whose recent African safari with girlfriend Linda Ronstadt had landed the couple on the cover of *Newsweek* and *People* magazines. Speeches by labor leaders and political supporters ran so long that the governor missed his flight. He stayed to cheer on the strikers: "Viva la raza. Viva Cesar Chavez. Go out and win. The victory is yours."

Hours later, Chavez briefed the executive board, in preparation for a meeting with leaders of the strike. He intended to explain to workers that the union had run out of money and must switch to a boycott. He would ask the strike leaders to recruit members to send on the boycott. Rarely had he so misjudged his audience.

In high spirits from the rally, the strike captains and members of the negotiating committee filed into the room and stood around the seated board members. Chavez updated them on negotiations with Meyer Tomatoes, which appeared close to agreement. His first surprise came when a worker asked who would sign off on the deal if members of the negotiating committee were all busy at the convention. Ganz explained the committee had agreed to review the first contracts, which would set precedents. Chavez made clear he felt the decision was his prerogative.

Warning that the discussion they were about to have should be kept confidential, Chavez launched into his pitch: "The union is broke," he told the two dozen workers. "We've spent $2.8 million. We've spent all our money on this strike. If we extend the strike and we don't win soon, then we have a big problem for the union. It's going to be hard. No, actually, it's impossible." They must go on the boycott, he said.

One by one, respectfully, workers disagreed. They told Chavez their colleagues expected a general strike. They repeated what Chavez had always said he wanted to hear: strikers were willing to sacrifice to win strong contracts for all workers, not just themselves, and they were committed to continue sacrificing for as long as it took. "We have to make a decision we will have to live with forever," said Chava Bustamante, who took the lead in the discussion.

"We've always gone to the boycott with the strikes we have lost," Chavez said. "It takes more time but it is easier to win . . . it is a sure win." The Gallo boycott had taken years, Bustamante pointed out. Boycotts cost money too, the workers said. They did not wish to give up jobs and travel across the country. With emotion, the strike leaders told Chavez that hundreds of workers were counting on them—and they believed the union could win.

"A general strike is for everyone, not just you," Chavez said. He could not in good conscience commit the resources of the union, he said. Then put the question to a vote at the convention, the workers urged.

Chavez fell back on delaying tactics. He was tired. The decision was too important to make in haste. At the convention the next day, he said, delegates would endorse a three-pronged strategy—strike, boycott, and legal action. They would resume the debate at some future date. When? workers asked. He declined to say. Chava Bustamante's older brother, Mario, a lechuguero who had been on the strike council since the start, had one parting comment: "If tomorrow there is a resolution from the Executive Board that there is going to be just a boycott, I'm going to oppose it," Bustamante warned. Chavez assured him that would not be the case.

The next morning, the Resolutions Committee took up Resolution 10, which proposed that the union commit its full resources to a boycott. Mario Bustamante was outraged. He rewrote the resolution to commit the union to expanding the strike. Hours later, Bustamante read the resolution on the convention floor, greeted by cheers. Chavez found himself chairing a runaway convention, unable to achieve the main goal he had come to Salinas to accomplish.

Then came a breakthrough that further undermined Chavez's strategy. The convention was winding down and delegates drifting out when Chavez took the microphone. "Fasten your seatbelts," he said. "There is an important announcement to come." Jerry Cohen and the negotiating committee from Meyer Tomatoes came conga-dancing down the middle aisle of the Hartnell College gym. They had reached agreement on a contract with a 43 percent raise over three years, increased medical and pension contributions, a cost-of-living increase, and a full-time union representative, paid by the company. "I think this is proof, proof of the kind of force we have when we use it," Cohen told the cheering workers.

Chavez never met again with the worker leadership. He called the executive board to a boycott-planning conference at La Paz. Ganz refused to leave Salinas. Workers at several companies that had been in "pre-huelga" mode staged wildcat walkouts. The weather cooperated: a heat wave caused ripe produce to rot in the fields. The Teamsters also helped, signing a contract at Bud Antle with starting wages of $5.00 an hour.

Two weeks after Chavez had told workers they could not win the strike, the UFW signed a contract with West Coast Farms, a major lettuce grower, with record wages and benefits. The nonunion lettuce growers immediately increased wages to keep the union out. That gave the UFW greater leverage, which Cohen used to finalize a deal with Sun Harvest on August 31, 1979. The front-page story in the Los Angeles Times noted the contract had been won through the strike, not the boycott. Strike leaders celebrated with drinks and then competed in sprints. Cohen pulled his Achilles tendon. He was so full of both alcohol and pain that he thought he had been shot.

After six days of work stoppages at the height of the season cost Mann Packing tens of thousands of dollars, Bill Ramsey and Don Nucci decided they could not afford any more losses. When the other vegetable growers walked out of a negotiating session, Nucci turned around and walked back in. The largest broccoli grower signed a contract on September 10, 1979. "There is no question, based on governmental guidelines, that this is an inflationary increase," Ramsey said. "We did the best we could."

Three days later, Cohen held court at the Towne House in Salinas, deliberately choosing the conference room where vegetable growers had cut deals with the Teamsters in 1970. "There was no negotiating," Cohen boasted as he recounted the contract-signing session to the executive board. "It was, 'There, this is what we want, and this is what we'll settle for.' And they settled . . . It was a run. They were lined up in the fucking parking lot like they were going to the dentist."

Cohen had urged Chavez to come to Salinas to sign the contracts. He sent his brother Richard instead. This was not Cesar Chavez's victory, and though no one would have pointed out that the union had won by defying his counsel, he had no wish to join the celebration.

Nor did he join another celebration two months later in the Imperial Valley, when the union took over El Hoyo (the Hole). Before the UFW contracts, El Hoyo was the Calexico parking lot along the border where workers waited in the early morning, hoping labor contractors would pick them for jobs. When Ganz had mentioned the possibility of renting the building in El Hoyo for the union office, Chavez had reacted with enthusiasm to the symbolic importance. That would signify the union had won, he said, directing Ganz to do whatever he could to procure the property. But when mariachis played and workers marched triumphantly to El Hoyo for the opening party in November 1979, Chavez stayed at La Paz.

At the executive board meeting a few weeks later, an atypical air of desperation permeated Chavez's reports. The union was broke from the strike. A number of significant vegetable growers still had not signed contracts. The computer system kept breaking down. His financial wizard was so frustrated by the lack of trained staff that she threatened to quit. A year after the negotiating class graduated, the union had only a handful of negotiators. After decades of denouncing scabs, Chavez argued against disciplining strikebreakers too harshly because the punishment might tarnish the union's image among outside financial supporters and trigger costly legal fights.

Badly in need of staff, he proposed recruiting alcoholics from cities and relocating them on farms, helping them dry out, and using them for the boycott. "I think that's the best, easiest and long-term way we should be moving," he told the board. "Who else is going to work for us? And stay, you know? These guys are forgotten. I really think we can get them. I really think we can build a strong base with them."

Only Ortiz and Martinez, the newest members, voiced support. Padilla, Ganz, Govea and Richard Chavez were incredulous. "We need to do a boycott. I don't know where we're going to get the people to do it," Chavez said irritably. "A shitload of people are alcoholics in this country. And nobody wants them." He rejected without explanation the suggestion they recruit help from the fields.

"Where we could pull people from is our membership, and the children," Govea said. "There's a tremendous amount of potential there."

The future leadership was not among the alcoholics, Richard scolded his brother: "I can tell you where the leadership is: The leadership is out there packing lettuce and carrots. We should invest some time and try to organize those people."

Discordant notes crept even into Chavez's sanctuary. Several dozen farmworkers finished a ten-week English class at La Paz. The advanced class prepared a slide show for the graduation ceremony. Their presentation concluded with a simple message: The union is not La Paz. The union is not Cesar Chavez. The union is the workers. The graduates gathered in the communal dining hall for a celebratory lunch with friends and family. Huerta rose and demanded to know who had put the workers up to that subversive message. Lunch went uneaten, and the crowd dispersed in confusion. Chavez fired two teachers. He sent a dual message that would grow more insistent in coming months: He did not believe farmworkers would articulate a challenge he viewed as treason; they must have been manipulated by someone else. And the union was Cesar Chavez.

CHAPTER 35

Una Sola Union

Our most serious and important internal struggle is over—at least for now . . .
It is a great relief to me.

Twenty-one farmworkers sat around a table listening intently as Cesar Chavez explained MBO, management by objective—in Spanish, *APO, administración por objetivos*. He told them about a soda-bottling plant that had hired management guru Peter Drucker, whose work Chavez greatly admired. Drucker asked the company to define its business. Bottling soda, the executives replied. He corrected them: You produce bottles. Your business is bottling. The company expanded, bottled various drinks, and made millions. We must decide what our business is, Chavez told the farmworkers.

The twenty men and one woman were ranch committee leaders from Salinas vegetable companies, elected to serve as union representatives under an innovative provision in the new contracts. Employers paid the farmworkers' salaries while they worked to resolve grievances and ensure smooth contract enforcement. Most of the newly elected representatives had been leaders in the strike. The paid reps, as they became known, were the first generation of farmworkers to earn full-time salaries to work on union business.

Chavez had lobbied for the new position, saying the union lacked sufficient staff to administer contracts without help among the crews. He brought the ranch leaders to La Paz for a five-day training session in May 1980. "Always ask questions, because this is how you learn; you learn more by participating," he told the paid reps. He tutored them on the history of the ALRA, the difficulties in administering the medical plan, and the importance of defining their mission. After a spirited give-and-take, Chavez guided them to the answer he sought: the union's mission was to give people quality.

When Chavez asked how they would explain to fellow workers the importance of delivering a quality product, the farmworkers turned to Cleofas Guzman. Guzman had emerged during the strike as a fearless, shrewd leader, with a keen mind and warm disposition. The lechuguero had easily won election as ranch committee president at Sun Harvest, the largest lettuce company, with 76 percent of the vote in a four-way race. If we pack the highest-quality vegetables, Guzman answered Chavez, "we'll have more work, a better future for our families, better benefits." The eagle, Guzman said, should symbolize the highest-quality produce. Everyone applauded.

On the surface, the scene resembled one of Chavez's long-held dreams: farmworker leaders, studying at La Paz, shaping the policies and future of their union. Their motivation, focus, and spirit invigorated Chavez—and stood in stark contrast to his own staff, increasingly tired, overworked, and directionless. "That week really charged me up," Chavez told the board members two weeks later. "I was on cloud nine because we were doing, I thought, some really effective work."

But these were the workers who had politely but firmly refused to give up their strike and go on the boycott. Now they had official titles, responsibilities, and power. Chavez's love-hate relationship with the vegetable workers shifted into a new phase.

The paid reps were a far cry from the sons and daughters of movement leaders whom Chavez had groomed at La Paz and tapped for training programs like the negotiations school. Mario Bustamante had worked odd jobs as a child in Mexico City to support his family, then crossed the border at fifteen to find his father, Salvador. Mario became a lechuguero like his father, who was buried in the UFW flag. Six feet tall, outspoken, and impetuous, Bustamante embraced the union first as a social club and then as a way to change his life. He was thirty-one when he became a paid rep. Sabino Lopez was the same age. He had come to Salinas as a sixteen-year-old with his father, an irrigator, and the teenager became an irrigator too, a steady job that suited his personality. For Lopez, the daily strike council meetings with Ganz became the classroom that Lopez had never attended. Both Bustamante and Lopez looked up to Guzman, a decade older. He lived across the border in Mexicali, like many of the vegetable workers. He was a champion runner, renowned for his speed as well as his strategic thinking. Guzman's clout was such that he could enforce discipline among workers without losing his popularity.

"Since this union was founded, it has been the dream of the leadership to build an organization led by farmworkers," Chavez had said at the 1977 UFW convention. Bustamante, Lopez, and Guzman took the union's founder at his word.

Ganz had become their mentor during the strike. At the beginning of 1980, he went on loan to Jerry Brown's short-lived presidential campaign. ("The governor wants Marshall Ganz more than Linda Ronstadt," Chavez told the board, relaying Brown's request for Ganz's help.) When he returned, Ganz considered leaving the union, baffled by his growing distance from Chavez. Ganz convinced himself that the chance to work with the paid reps and shape their new jobs was too important. They met each Saturday morning, along with Jose Renteria, a young farmworker who ran the Salinas field office. Ganz coached the paid reps on how to negotiate grievances, enforce discipline, promote quality, and iron out problems.

As Ganz built the paid reps into a force, his painful estrangement from Chavez widened. Ganz became more convinced the model he had developed in Salinas represented the only viable future for the union. He boasted to Chris Hartmire that if the minister wanted to see a *real* union, he should visit Salinas. Ganz also grew concerned the UFW needed to win more elections in the vegetable industry. The contracts put union companies at a financial disadvantage, which endangered the members' jobs. The paid reps could help organize the competition. Union growers would be helpful, too. Ganz wrote Chavez a memo urging an organizing campaign. He ended with a short reference to their increasingly tattered relationship: "The current situation is ridiculous and untenable. If you want my resignation—although I believe I can continue to make a valuable contribution to organize the UFW into a real national union and want to do so—just tell me."

Chavez never answered. In a final effort to convince Chavez to support an organizing effort in Salinas, Ganz expanded on his ideas in a twenty-one-page "Plan for the Vegetable Industry." Around La Paz, the document became known derisively as the "Marshall Plan." Chavez opposed the proposal as a recipe for decentralizing power. He marked up his copy and underlined objectionable sentences: "We must respect the membership's perception of its own interests and listen to this." *No*, Chavez wrote in red pen in the margin. He had long believed he knew the members' interests better than they did. Another no for Ganz's conclusion: "We should agree on the single goal of building a national farm workers union."

Chavez had made clear he found that goal too narrow. But he found himself again forced to protect the union's national turf. The claims he had staked a decade earlier had never materialized. In Texas and Arizona, former UFW officials had become impatient and split off new organizations. Both groups also had a philosophical difference with Chavez: they believed in organizing the undocumented and rejected Chavez's vision of the Mexican immigrants as a threat to local jobs. Chavez launched a counteroffensive against the splinter groups under a slogan he had once used against the Teamsters, "*Una sola union*"—"One union."

In Texas, Antonio Orendain, the original secretary-treasurer of the NFWA, had formed the Texas Farm Workers Union. "We decided the workers couldn't wait until Cesar Chavez was ready," Orendain said. "The workers don't even know who Cesar is." Chavez evicted Orendain from the building the Texas workers had constructed as the union office; Orendain refused to leave. Chavez condemned Orendain's union for violence; Orendain said he preferred to know about and control the violence rather than look the other way. When Orendain attempted to raise funds, Chavez branded the Texas organizers dangerous renegades and discouraged donations. Cesar and Manuel Chavez traveled to Texas and presided over an organizing convention that adopted the motto "Una sola union." But the UFW never followed up with the promised campaign, and Orendain continued to try to build an independent union.

In Arizona, Chavez faced a more significant threat. Gustavo Gutierrez, in whose Phoenix home Chavez had begun his 1972 fast, had left the UFW and helped form the Maricopa County Organizing Project (MCOP), a group that advocated for farmworkers' rights. Despite his reverence for Chavez, Gutierrez had always exercised a degree of independence. He felt Arizona farmworkers should have a say in their own future, rather than deferring all decisions to La Paz. Above all, MCOP was born out of frustration that the excitement generated by the 1972 fast had long dissipated—and the UFW showed no sign of moving into Arizona. Gutierrez and a few others thought they could lay the groundwork for what would eventually become a local of the UFW. Their organization focused initially on enforcing health and safety laws, calculating that enough agitation might persuade growers to sign contracts in exchange for labor peace.

At first, Gutierrez operated with the blessing of the UFW. But tension soon flared when a strike began among green onion workers. The UFW wanted to shut the strike down; Gutierrez insisted the workers had a right to decide. Manuel Chavez visited Gutierrez and told him to stop organizing. Gutierrez refused. His group developed innovative strategies, spending time in Mexico organizing workers and training leaders before they crossed into Arizona to work. MCOP made deals with law enforcement authorities to grant temporary work permits to undocumented workers in exchange for their testimony against smugglers who worked the border. MCOP focused on citrus workers, almost all of whom were undocumented. After a series of work stoppages, a large grower asked for a contract. Several more soon followed. The new union's success in winning strikes and contracts among an undocumented workforce drew national attention.

Chavez was nonplussed by the success, baffled that growers would sign contracts without the threat of the UFW coming in to organize. He set out to undercut the Arizona upstarts. UFW organizers threatened to have Arizona union members deported if they did not join the UFW. Gutierrez was accused of being a Communist. A clothing bank operated by his group was torched shortly after UFW officials charged the clothes were distributed only to illegal immigrants. UFW attorneys filed protests with state and federal authorities in an effort to nullify the Arizona farmworkers' contracts. The UFW intervened in an election and urged a "no union" vote. Chavez prevailed upon the Phoenix bishop to reverse a decision to award a $100,000 grant from the Catholic Campaign for Human Development to MCOP.

The loss of the grant was the last straw for Don Devereux, an investigative reporter who had been working with MCOP. Devereux called a colleague, Tom Barry, and asked him to investigate the UFW's actions. Barry knew nothing about the farm worker movement, but he was a skilled journalist with a social conscience. He hitchhiked the four hundred miles from his New Mexico home and listened to Gutierrez's tales about how the wet line had operated a few years earlier. Barry was outraged. He traveled with Gutierrez to border towns, where they heard story after story about immigrants terrorized during the wet line of 1974. Barry followed a trail of broken promises and unpaid debts left behind by Manuel Chavez.

Barry interviewed a woman who told him she took checks from Manuel and delivered bribes to the police chief and other officials in the

Mexican border town of San Luis. In a San Luis check-cashing shop, Alfonso Quintero showed Barry worthless checks for thousands of dollars cashed by Manuel. Quintero's attorney had repeatedly called La Paz, explained the problem, and asked to talk with Cesar Chavez. Cesar did not take the calls.

Chavez did not take Barry's calls, either. When Chavez went to a rally in Phoenix, Barry showed up. Manuel Chavez and a few others roughed up Barry and threw him out. He received threatening phone calls at home and moved out of his house for several months. He wrote a series of stories about Manuel and his business enterprises, the wet line, and the UFW's efforts to undermine farmworker groups outside California. None of the progressive magazines Barry approached accepted his stories. He handed his information over to a reporter for the *New York Times*.

In his letter "firing" Manuel Chavez after he disappeared in 1975, Cesar had added a postscript: "Rumors continue to persist that you have become a grower in Mexicali." Three and a half years later, Barry, and then the *New York Times*, confirmed the rumors. In the fall of 1975, Manuel Chavez, calling himself Manuel Camacho, had gone to a San Joaquin Valley grower named William Hamilton with a proposition. If Hamilton supplied the capital, Manuel would arrange to grow, harvest, and pack melons in Mexico and sell them to Hamilton to distribute. Not only were labor costs cheaper in Mexico, but the melon strikes that Manuel led in California and Arizona helped reduce competitors' supply. In effect, he started strikes that improved the market for his own produce. After a short time the deal fell apart, Hamilton recounted, when Manuel (who eventually revealed his true identity) delivered substandard melons and then sold them himself. In the end, the embarrassed grower lost $140,000.

The Arizona controversy caught the attention of muckraking journalist Jack Anderson, whose syndicated column appeared in dozens of papers. One of his researchers put together a column about complaints from the Arizona and Texas unions. "It saddens me to have to report that the United Farm Workers (UFW) union, which lifted so many stoop laborers out of peonage and degradation, has become a violence-prone, tyrannical empire under the iron-fisted rule of Cesar Chavez," Anderson's March 1980 column began.

Chavez called the column "a vicious attack on the United Farm Workers—perhaps the meanest and most deceitful barrage against the union that we have ever seen." The UFW threatened a libel suit. Chris Hartmire denounced Anderson as a "word merchant" who knew nothing about farmworkers. Hartmire compared Chavez to Jesus, St. Francis, and Gandhi, whose words mattered because of their actions: "Cesar Chavez does not write very often and he is not a particularly eloquent speaker, but his words have power and meaning because of the way he lives his life—simply and persistently on behalf of the poor."

Anderson recanted. "Flanked by three lawyers dressed in three-piece suits, a fuming Chavez sat in the hot California sun tearing clumps of grass from the ground as he spoke. He was angry. But he was also persuasive," the columnist wrote in a retraction.

Longtime UFW supporters dismissed Anderson's most inflammatory accusations, but many had reluctantly concluded the UFW stood little chance of expanding into a national union. Some, like the National Farm Worker Ministry, faced the question Chavez had worked hard to have them avoid: should they support other farmworker organizing? Local ministries had given up their independence on the assumption the UFW would become a national union. Hartmire's solution was to scale back the national ministry to conform with the UFW's reduced horizons. His close friend and a leader of the ministry, John Moyer, disagreed.

"The UFW does not have a monopoly on service and sacrifice," Moyer wrote to Hartmire. As long as Chavez was president, Moyer concluded, the UFW would never move beyond California. To expand would require that Chavez delegate power. A recent conversation with Chavez had confirmed Moyer's belief that the leader he so admired also had limitations: "I am the only one who is managing. Dolores comes over and helps me for ten days," Moyer quoted Chavez as saying. This, the minister said, was the problem. To organize other places required leaving someone else in charge of California. "Cesar knows this; he has said it; he has never been able to do it."

If anything, Chavez moved further away from delegating any power. His distrust of the vegetable workers and concern about a rival power base in Salinas deepened. Ganz's close relationship with Chavez in the past had generated jealousy. People were all too willing to feed rumors about insurrection back to La Paz. Ganz was plotting to start his own union, they told Chavez. A softball game and potluck dinner reunion of the old legal department was reported to Chavez as a "counter-organizing event" where allies of Cohen and Ganz planned strategy. Everyone in the union found themselves forced to choose sides.

Larry Tramutt was a true believer, a young Stanford-educated volunteer who had risen quickly on his intelligence and ability to deliver. He had taken over the boycott when Chavez purged Nick Jones, helped plan the Monday Night Massacre, and willingly played the Game. He did not shy away from the role of hatchet man and had little patience with inept or lazy volunteers. Tramutt liked living in La Paz because he found Chavez mesmerizing, even when he spoke of his "aura" or ability to cure illness by laying on hands. Chavez's eclectic interests and curiosity made him fun to be around. They made midnight trips to play handball in Bakersfield. Chavez fought for every point. On the handball court it was acceptable to challenge Chavez, and sometimes Tramutt won.

When wildcat strikes broke out in the summer of 1980 in the garlic fields of Gilroy, north of Salinas, Tramutt was sent to help. Growers raised their wages from $3.40 to $4.00 an hour and added an extra quarter per hamper. Workers saw the wage increase as proof of their power and pushed for elections. The paid reps came to help with the campaign. Tramutt had sat through the debates about whether to pay salaries and how to attract farmworkers to the UFW staff. He watched the paid reps work and grew excited. He thought the union had found the answer. The UFW petitioned for twenty-eight elections in the garlic fields and won all but two.

Tramutt was summoned to La Paz, and he looked forward to explaining to Chavez how the victories had been won with the help of the paid reps. When Tramutt saw the pursed lips, he knew. Only I call elections, Chavez said. He asked Tramutt if he were taking orders from Moscow. Tramutt resigned a few days later.

Jerry Cohen was next to go. Though he had resigned as general counsel in the transition that followed the dismantling of the Salinas legal department, Cohen had continued to negotiate contracts with vegetable growers. Several companies, particularly in the Imperial Valley, had held out long after the strike ended. Cohen became convinced Chavez thought additional contracts might strengthen Ganz's position. If they made concessions to get contracts, Cohen said, Chavez would say that Cohen and Ganz sold out the workers. Without concessions, he could not negotiate more pacts. "Cesar has them at checkmate," Kirsten Zerger, one of the ex-UFW lawyers, wrote in her diary after talking to Cohen. Cohen also expressed frustration that leaders such as Cleofas Guzman would not challenge Chavez or run for the executive board.

For his part, Chavez grew frustrated with the failure to sign contracts with Imperial Valley growers, a hard-line faction that was determined to hold out as long as possible. Chavez was particularly anxious to sign an agreement with the Bruce Church company, the largest grower in negotiations and most intransigent. "If we don't get Bruce Church, we might as well fold up," he said at a November 22, 1980, meeting, directing that the negotiating team be replaced. Two days later, Jerry Cohen resigned. He asked Chavez to meet. For more than three months, Chavez did not return Cohen's calls.

The vegetable workers had moved down to the Imperial Valley for the winter season. Chavez sent Oscar Mondragon to run the field office. Mondragon was a former farmworker who had risen in the union ranks. He was close to Manuel Chavez and had gone to jail for torching growers' buses during Manuel's 1974 strikes in the Imperial Valley. Mondragon made clear to the paid reps that he was in charge. He took away their keys to the office. The paid reps had little respect for Mondragon. Leaders such as Guzman and Bustamante did not shy away from fights. Bustamante confronted workers in the field office after hearing them conspire to make him look bad; they threw a chair and broke the lechuguero's nose. After hearing vague but worrisome threats, the paid reps decided to avoid the Mexican side of the border, where Manuel Chavez's connections were well known and vigilante justice was commonplace.

On January 23, 1981, Guzman was unexpectedly called to run a meeting in San Luis with Mondragon. Guzman never arrived. After searching every hospital and jail in Mexicali, where Guzman lived, his family found Guzman in the Mexicali general hospital. Police said Guzman had been heading east on the San Luis–Mexicali road when a cotton truck ran a stoplight as Guzman approached an intersection. His car hit the middle of the truck, sliding underneath. Guzman's head took the brunt of the collision.

Ganz and Govea were in a meeting at La Paz when Chavez took a phone call and came back looking shaken. He told them there had been an accident and sent them immediately to Mexicali. They drove all night, arrived at 5:30 A.M., and made arrangements for a neurosurgeon to examine Guzman. He was paralyzed and semicomatose.

Among what was known as Marshall's faction, no one believed the crash that had crippled the workers' most promising leader was an accident. The driver of the truck never surfaced. No one could explain the four-hour gap between when the collision occurred and when Guzman arrived at the hospital. No union official had looked for Guzman when he did not appear in San Luis.

Ganz and Govea had been planning to leave the union. They hastened their departure. As a farewell present, Chavez sent them to Israel for a month to research kibbutzim and collectives.

On February 10, 1981, two weeks after Guzman was crushed under the truck, Chavez went to the Imperial Valley for a memorial on the second anniversary of the shooting of Rufino Contreras. Ranch committee leaders demanded a meeting and peppered Chavez with questions: What was Manuel Chavez's role in the union? Why were the paid reps no longer allowed keys to the office? Why had Mondragon appointed Guzman's successor? Workers complained about a whispering campaign against Ganz and Govea, who were being blamed for the cost of the strike. Chavez told them all the politicking must stop. That included the gossip that Manuel had been involved in the car crash that crippled Guzman.

The vegetable workers returned to Salinas in the spring. Animosity increased. So did problems with the RFK health plan. Workers complained their credit was ruined because the plan paid claims so slowly. Every Saturday, the paid reps met to review cases and called La Paz with a list of complaints. Chavez was concerned and impatiently told his staff to fix the problems. He assigned people to clear up the backlog of claims. Delays and mix-ups persisted. Staff members blamed faulty computer programs.

Chavez called union staff to a meeting at La Paz on May 30, 1981. In a rambling speech, he warned of traitors and malignant forces. You are with us or against us, he told them. There was no middle ground. A faction was trying to overthrow the president and the board, Chavez warned. The plot was being masterminded by former union staff who were using the paid reps. Workers were tricked into selling out to the enemy, for money or for sex. Everyone must choose sides, he told them: stay and fight with, or get out. Renteria, the director of the Salinas field office, was forced to resign because he refused to help oust Bustamante and others identified as ringleaders.

The UFW's biennial convention was scheduled for September 1981, and three new board members would stand for election. Chavez had appointed three loyalists: his son-in-law, Arturo Rodriguez; Arturo Mendoza, an amiable organizer who had worked closely with the paid reps in Calexico; and Mondragon. There was no farmworker on the board. The paid reps decided to run their own slate. They chose Rosario Pelayo, who had worked in grapes and vegetables and been a strong UFW supporter for years, and Renteria, the ousted Salinas field office director.

Chavez had the votes, but the vegetable workers represented a sizable block of delegates. He could take no chances. He needed a crushing victory to discourage further challenges. Chavez dictated a new rule that would circumvent the delegates and effectively take away their votes. A petition signed by as few as 8 percent of the workers at a ranch could bind that ranch's convention delegates to vote for the Chavez slate.

Board members descended on Salinas with petitions: if you support Cesar, sign here. The paid reps were out to oust Chavez, Huerta and others told the workers. "How can they run the union?" an internal campaign memo asked, disparaging the paid reps as puppets of Ganz. Just as growers had once dismissed Chavez as a tool of Anglo outsiders, now he presumed farmworkers could not have initiated a significant challenge on their own.

Tensions were high as the delegates gathered in the Fresno convention center on September 5, 1981. The dissidents had been carefully seated in the back, as far as possible from any microphones. In his opening remarks, Chavez chronicled the history of the union's battles for survival against the growers and the Teamsters. Then he painted a dark picture of "malignant forces" out to destroy all that he had built:

"Now we come to this 1981 convention facing yet another assault on our beloved union. An assault even more menacing than the past conventions. More menacing because it is clandestinely organized by those forces whose every wish and desire is our destruction. Obstruction by those evil forces visible and invisible who work at every chance to destroy us—the growers, the teamsters, disaffected former staff, scoundrels, and God knows who, some unwittingly trying to reach the same goal—that is to bury our beloved union."

The rule to bind the delegates' votes had been adopted by the board as an emergency measure; the constitution required that the rule be ratified by the convention. Chavez called the resolution. Bustamante barreled up to the microphone. "To me, this resolution is unjust and undemocratic," he declared.

Chavez called a vote. "The matter looks very split," he said, looking at the show of hands. He postponed another vote until after lunch.

During the break, Chavez's team distributed leaflets accusing the dissidents of being tools of "the two Jews"—Ganz and Cohen. "Outside forces intend to force our President Cesar Chavez to resign." A memo in Spanish, handwritten in the distinctive lettering of one board member, laid out anti-Semitic arguments: The Jews want to take over the union. Ganz and Cohen, and the old legal department. The Jews

used our people—Jessica, Eliseo, Gilbert—to control the legal department and the negotiators. They think they are superior to Mexicans.

When Chavez called a second vote after lunch, the measure to bind the
delegates passed easily. The dissidents decided there was no point in staying. About fifty walked out. Someone shouted "Traitors," and a chant
began: "Down with the traitors." Bustamante broke the staff on his union
flag in two as he walked out with his brother Chava. "Death to the Busta-
mantes," Helen Chavez shouted from the auditorium balcony.

Chavez moved to finish off the paid reps. He sent Huerta, David
Martinez, and Arturo Rodriguez to Salinas. The board members visited
each vegetable company represented by the dissident paid reps and urged
them to oust the traitors who were out to destroy Chavez. When workers
stood by their elected leaders, Chavez fired the dissidents who served as
paid reps.

In Washington, D.C., Monsignor George Higgins grew alarmed. He
wrote Chavez on September 21, 1981, ticking off the recent departures and
allegations. "In my opinion, Cesar, even the slightest compromise on the
issue of anti-Semitism would seriously endanger the movement and
could conceivably destroy it . . . As I see it, the truth is that the UFW is in
serious trouble and that some of this trouble is strictly of its own making."

Chavez waited weeks to reply. Hartmire drafted a terse answer that
accused Higgins of jumping to conclusions without knowing the facts. By
October, the dissident leaders had all been fired, despite their protestations that they had been elected by their peers.

On October 24, 1981, Chavez addressed a group of leaders of the
United Church of Christ, reminiscing about how important they had
been in the early years of the struggle. He thanked John Moyer for being
a strong supporter ever since the minister came to Delano in 1965. Chavez
recalled the visit of the "Coachella 95" during the Teamster fight of 1973
as the "single most powerful example of the church's solidarity." Then he
addressed the present. He was relieved by recent changes, Chavez said,
though he did not mention the charges of anti-Semitism or the rebellion
by the paid reps. "Our most serious and important internal struggle is
over—at least for now," he said. At last, he said, he had an executive board
that shared his vision, after four difficult years and bitter fights. The union
had survived its early years "thanks to the sacrifices of the workers, and
the genius and courage of a group of heroic lone rangers," in which he
included Medina, Ganz, Drake, and Cohen. But the era of the lone ranger
was over, Chavez said. The executive board had adopted his new approach,

which he called TMT—top management team. "It is a great relief to me."

There was one more significant departure that tumultuous fall. Scott Washburn had been organizing farmworkers who lived in the canyons of northern San Diego, burrowed into the hillsides under tarps and in makeshift shacks. A few days before the Fresno convention, some of Washburn's organizers were called to a meeting with executive board member Frank Ortiz. Washburn went along. Ortiz was campaigning against the paid reps. He railed against Ganz and Cohen and said the Jews were out to take over the union.

Word got back to La Paz and Chavez asked for an explanation. Ortiz's clarification hardly helped: "I said, 'Too bad these two guys had to be two Jews because our best support all across the country comes from the Jewish people and organizations, also, that the Jewish people through all of history have been the most discriminated in the world and now we had Marshal[l] and Jerry working against us.'"

When Washburn saw the anti-Semitic flyers at the convention, he felt sick. He had watched his best friend, Joe Smith, be purged in 1976, had driven Jim Drake to the airport when he left the union, had listened in shock to Eliseo Medina announce his departure after a string of victories in the citrus orchards, and had seen Fred Ross grit his teeth as he tried to convince Gilbert Padilla not to resign. The anti-Semitic slurs were the last straw.

Chavez came to a meeting at the San Diego ALRB office in late October 1981. Washburn nervously pulled him into a conference room. He told Chavez that he, too, was leaving the union. Chavez did not mention all the other union leaders who had left in recent months. He just looked at Washburn and said, "They'll all be back."

CHAPTER 36

Playing Defense

We've been part of a very controversial organization since we started. We've been investigated up and down. I can truthfully say we've never been found lacking in any respect.

Outside the Salinas UFW office where they once worked, the farmworkers whom Chavez had fired from their leadership posts staged a fast in protest. "We're only doing what Cesar taught us," Mario Bustamante said during the eight-day fast. "To fight for justice."

The dissident farmworkers did not go quietly; unlike others who had been purged over the years, the workers had no incentive to keep silent and no place to go. Chavez had effectively blackballed them with both union and nonunion growers. The paid reps filed complaints with the Agricultural Labor Relations Board; state officials said the ALRB lacked jurisdiction. The workers filed internal charges against UFW board members; the executive board exonerated the leadership. The paid reps found an Oakland lawyer who specialized in union democracy and took their case pro bono. Nine farmworkers sued Cesar Chavez in federal court, claiming he had no right to fire them from positions to which they had been elected by their peers.

"The union has always been run according to the views of the President, Cesar Chavez. It became unable to deal with dissenting opinions," Bustamante said in his deposition. "There can be no doubt that the other plaintiffs and I were removed because Cesar perceived us to pose some kind of threat to his stronghold on the UFW, not because we failed to do our jobs."

The paid reps accused Chavez of using union funds to campaign for his slate on the executive board. He produced checks to show the union had been reimbursed for election-related expenses. The first check had been deposited after the paid reps had complained. They circulated a flyer claiming they had forced Chavez to repay the money. He sued for libel and slander, seeking $25 million in damages from nine farmworkers. In an unguarded moment with a reporter, Chavez acknowledged the suit was an effort to intimidate their lawyer.

The open dissension attracted the first prolonged spate of negative publicity for Chavez in two decades. Reporters from major news organizations asked about the paid reps, the departure of high-profile figures such as Marshall Ganz and Jerry Cohen, and the Synanon Game. Their inquiries were fielded by Chris Hartmire, who had resigned from the farmworker ministry to work full-time as Chavez's assistant. Hartmire's move to La Paz pleased Chavez, who was sensitive to the recent exodus. Hartmire had long been skilled in interpreting and justifying Chavez's actions. Now he used those talents in a more public forum. Unwittingly, some former staff might be "helping the enemy," Hartmire told the *Los Angeles Times*. He took notes on the messages he was to deliver: Jessica Govea sabotaged the medical plan. Marshall Ganz was trying to start his own union. Anti-Semitism was not tolerated in the union.

New York Times reporter Wayne King showed up at the La Paz gate and was turned away, but that did not deter him. Celebrity lawyer Melvin Belli threatened legal action on behalf of Chavez before the *Times* story appeared. King's front-page story focused on the "quashed rebellion" by the Salinas dissidents and allegations by former UFW officials that Chavez had become preoccupied with clandestine plots and traitors, at the expense of building the union.

When CBS television's *60 Minutes* expressed interest in profiling Chavez, aides coached him on how to counter charges of autocratic control. Chavez must take care not to appear hostile or aloof. He must rebut the idea that the union had not "lived up to the dreams and vision that people remember from the 1960s."

In a Salinas garage, *60 Minutes* correspondent Ed Bradley interviewed the paid reps who had sued their onetime leader. They, too, tried to be low-key, following their lawyer's advice. Finally, Bustamante could not help himself. Until 1979, he said, Cesar had been a good leader. "Now he is . . . *dictador!*"

Sitting outdoors at La Paz, the verdant hills as backdrop, Bradley asked Chavez how he felt being called a dictator. "Of course it bothers me,"

Chavez said, his expressive eyes looking pained. "But I think that our union is one of the most democratic unions in the country. They have a right to say whatever they want to say. That's the game. But I don't think too many people listen to them."

Of the top leaders who had left the union in recent months, only Gilbert Padilla talked to *60 Minutes* on camera. For more than two decades, Padilla had followed Chavez's lead. Padilla was on the first NFWA board. He and Chavez had shared rooms, cigarettes, and picket duty. In the last few years, Padilla had struggled to understand Chavez's behavior. Padilla had gone to all the other top leaders and said, Cesar's gone nuts. No one wanted to hear that. In October 1980, at a credit union board meeting, Huerta attacked Padilla and told him he should resign. He knew how Chavez operated. Padilla called Chavez and resigned the next day. Chavez had always been a dictator, Padilla told *60 Minutes*: "And we let him. Because we needed him."

Chavez shrugged off Padilla's criticism: "If he left without justifying, he'd be called a quitter."

Padilla and Govea were among several former union leaders who had found temporary work with California Rural Legal Assistance, the agency that Chavez had picketed in 1970 when he felt the group had become competition. After the 1981 convention, Cesar's son Paul led pickets at a CRLA office where Chava Bustamante worked. CRLA leaders were eager to stay on good terms with Chavez. Govea's and Padilla's contracts were not renewed.

In multiple arenas, Chavez found himself in the position he always tried to avoid: on the defensive. In the past, he had excelled at turning attacks to his advantage. When adversaries had lashed out at Chavez, their attacks boomeranged; the more vicious the attack, the more powerful Chavez appeared. When the Teamsters stole UFW contracts, the UFW became the sympathetic victim, standing up to bullies. When growers fired workers unjustly, farmworkers were heroes. When judges threw strikers in jail, the UFW's image soared. This time was different. Chavez found himself attacked for his own actions. With no external enemy to blame, he fingered the enemy within—traitors.

A story in *Reason*, a conservative magazine, charged the farm worker movement had improperly spent almost $1 million in federal funds. The story had a small audience, and the author had ties to the agricultural industry. But federal investigators and national reporters found that many of the magazine's conclusions checked out.

NBC correspondent Jack Perkins arrived at La Paz to interview Chavez and found an audience of fifty people. Perkins realized the WELCOME banners signaled anything but. Perkins could interview anyone he wanted, Chavez said—in front of the whole community. "We're not refusing an interview," Chavez repeated. The reporter explained he needed to speak with Chavez and other officials one-on-one. "Just do it in front of us," Chavez said. "What's wrong? What are you hiding? . . . You want an interview, I'll give you an interview. You're not going to tell me who's going to be around when the interview's done. They want to see, they have a right to see."

A flummoxed Perkins gave in. He would make clear that this was a stunt, he said. "You haven't met one like this, huh?" Chavez said with satisfaction as he got his way.

He gained little from the maneuver, however, since the facts were not on his side. Chavez feigned ignorance on details. He did not know whether the credit union had been computerized, how many health clinics existed, or locations of the union's service centers. The projects were all "coming along," he said. He casually informed Perkins at the conclusion of the interviews that the union might sue NBC for libel. "We've been part of a very controversial organization since we started," Chavez said. "We've been investigated up and down. I can truthfully say we've never been found lacking in any respect."

Chavez again unleashed a preemptive attack before the broadcast aired. He tried to deflect attention and discredit the report by attacking its sources and motivation. He alleged a grower conspiracy, threatened libel, and called for a White House investigation into improper ties between NBC and the Farm Bureau.

NBC did not mince words. Chavez's movement had been granted $796,000 to develop a microwave system to help the rural poor by connecting health clinics and service centers—but no health clinics existed and many service centers were shuttered. The credit union had been granted $349,115 to computerize and expand but had no computer or satellite offices.

Roger Mahony, now bishop of Stockton, watched the *Prime Time* report and recalled the early warnings from Jerry Cohen and AFL-CIO organizing director William Kircher about the need for professional staff. The controversy "will cause much misery and grief for the union that could have been avoided," Mahony wrote to Monsignor George Higgins.

Jimmy Carter, whose administration had been eager to fund Chavez's projects, had lost his reelection bid in 1980 to Chavez's old nemesis, Ronald Reagan. Reagan administration auditors concluded federal funds had been improperly used to support the UFW instead of nonprofit entities. A separate $347,529 grant from the U.S. Department of Labor for English classes was spent on students who did not qualify because they were not full-time farmworkers, earned too much money, or were undocumented. The government asked the union to return more than $255,000.

Chavez had brushed aside earlier warnings about sloppy bookkeeping and long operated as if rules did not apply. For years he had blurred the lines between the labor union and the nonprofit entities. When he needed money for the UFW, Chavez arranged transfers without regard to legal restrictions. One of the charities loaned the union $300,000 to buy computers, jeopardizing the charity's tax-exempt status. He had always bluffed his way past problems. Now the mistakes began to catch up with him. On top of the government's request that he return a significant portion of the grant, the IRS ruled that the union staff members were not legally volunteers. The UFW owed $390,000 in back social security and federal unemployment taxes.

Chavez also found himself on the defensive in the political arena at home. Here, too, the damage was self-inflicted. He had increasingly played the games he once abhorred. The union's fate was tied to the ALRA, and he needed political support to ward off attempts to water down the law. Huerta had returned to Sacramento as the UFW lobbyist. Instead of working on a shoestring, as she had decades earlier for the CSO, she had thousands of dollars in campaign funds. "Dolores should be able to hand the politicians the check, and then go see them in Sacramento for favors," Chavez said.

Assemblyman Howard Berman, a Los Angeles Democrat, had sponsored the ALRA. When Berman challenged Assembly Speaker Leo McCarthy for leadership of the house, Chavez relished an opportunity to pay back McCarthy for his role in defeating the UFW's Proposition 14. The UFW endorsed Berman's bid to oust McCarthy at the end of 1980. The union's political committee contributed thousands of dollars to Berman plus a $30,000 loan.

Neither McCarthy nor Berman prevailed. Instead, the fight marked the ascension of one of California's most powerful and colorful politicians, Willie Brown, who cobbled together a bipartisan coalition. Chavez's move had backfired: key Republicans threw their support to Brown because they feared that Berman would be beholden to Chavez. "I think it was an extremely dangerous threat to agriculture," said Assembly Republican leader Carol Hallet, explaining her support for Brown.

Chavez called Brown's pact with Republicans "an unholy alliance" and made veiled threats against two Chicano Democrats from Los Angeles, Assemblymen Art Torres and Richard Alatorre, who had supported Brown. An internal UFW memo was blunter: farmworkers had been betrayed by the two young legislators who supported "Farmer Brown." Torres had worked for the UFW and run for the Assembly with Chavez's support. Now the union leader vowed revenge. In the meantime, with Jerry Brown leaving the governor's office at the end of 1982, Chavez faced a bleak future in Sacramento.

Finally, Chavez found himself on the defensive in court. The Maggio company, a large vegetable grower, had sued the UFW for millions in damages from the 1979 strike, claiming the union had sanctioned reckless behavior that forced the grower to hire security guards and caused major losses. Maggio had substantial video and photographic evidence. Witnesses testified that strikers threw rocks, rushed the fields, and committed other violent acts. The UFW had rejected earlier overtures by Maggio to settle for $30,000. Several years into the case, the grower's attorneys again proposed a settlement. Chavez's counsel, Ellen Eggers, urged him to reconsider. Maggio offered to sign a contract on terms favorable to the union in exchange for a payment from the UFW of between $400,000 and $500,000, spread over five years. Eggers thought the amount could be bargained down and warned Chavez, "There is no question that so far they have the upper hand in this case." He declined to negotiate. In 1987, the UFW was found liable for $1.7 million in damages. Eventually the union exhausted its appeals and paid the court-ordered penalty. The UFW never signed a contract with Maggio.

Eggers faced another difficult defense of Chavez in the lawsuit filed by the paid reps. He seemed unconcerned about evidence that caused his legal team consternation. Chavez's defense was that the UFW constitution gave the president the right to fire staff, who served at his pleasure. But documents and witnesses supported the workers' contention that they had been elected, not appointed. Agendas for nominating meetings were entered into evidence along with memos from Ganz to Chavez announcing election results.

"I have never had any question whatsoever about whether the paid rep position is an appointed or elected position," Chavez said in a sworn deposition. "After the contracts were signed, I began appointing people to fill the positions pursuant to my authority." No paperwork existed to support his position. Shown a copy of a ballot, he said he had "no idea" how it had been prepared and only found out weeks later that there had been elections.

Chavez had grown accustomed to making statements that went unchallenged, whether the subject was how many schools he had attended, the number of health clinics, or whether vegetable workers were ready to go on the boycott. When confronted, he denounced doubters as tools of the growers. In the case of the paid reps, he confidently swore to facts unsupported by the record. In addition to his insistence that he had appointed the paid reps, he swore he had destroyed old tape recordings of executive board meetings.

On the central question of fact, U.S. District Court judge William Ingram unequivocally rejected Chavez's version of events. "I conclude they were elected," he wrote about the paid reps. "There is no evidence, contemporary with the events, that supports the contention that they were appointed." The judge noted in his November 16, 1982, ruling that Chavez was a busy man keeping track of many things, excusing him for testimony that could have constituted perjury. The paid reps, the judge wrote, had "every reason to believe that they are elective officials; they were led to believe that by their union leadership and by the duly published processes of election."

The second phase of the trial was to determine whether Chavez had a right to remove elected representatives. Chavez argued the workers were fired for "incompetence and insubordination." Again, Judge Ingram disagreed: "Although the court is hesitant to involve itself in intra-union disputes . . . the magnitude of the issues involved justifies such intervention . . . The court finds that defendant Chavez's interpretation was not reasonable. Summary removal of elected union officials is not warranted under any reading of the constitution."

The ruling proved a pyrrhic victory for the farmworkers. The union appealed, the case dragged on for years, and the workers ran out of time and money. After the initial burst of media attention, Chavez's skirmish with the rank-and-file leadership attracted little notice and did not tarnish his reputation outside the fields. In the cities, the baby boomers who had grown up boycotting grapes had moved into positions of leadership and power. They welcomed a chance to indulge in nostalgic support for *la causa* and their 1960s past. They gave money instead of walking picket lines.

Chavez, too, had aged, his thick hair showing touches of gray, his face considerably rounder. He found himself in demand to endorse baby boomers' other causes, such as the antinuclear movement. Jane Fonda and her husband, Tom Hayden, long-standing UFW supporters, formed the Campaign for Economic Democracy and asked Chavez to cochair their fund-raising dinner. In the summer of 1982, he was one of the few nonmusicians featured at Peace Sunday, a day-long event timed to coincide with the United Nations session on nuclear disarmament. More than eighty thousand people crowded into the Pasadena Rose Bowl and raised $250,000 for the antinuke movement at a concert full of 1960s legends— Crosby, Stills, and Nash, Jackson Browne, Stevie Wonder, Linda Ronstadt. Bob Dylan and Joan Baez harmonized on "Blowin' in the Wind." The crowd swayed to a rendition of "Give Peace a Chance" by John Lennon, who had been assassinated less than two years earlier.

For Chavez, 1982 marked a milestone: the twentieth anniversary of the union's first convention. One of Chavez's first secretaries, Susan Drake, organized a reunion in San Jose. Three hundred people crowded into a stiflingly hot church hall to relive the glory days, embrace old friends, shout "Viva," and sing along with Luis Valdez and the Teatro Campesino. "I've known Cesar for about 10 years," said singer-song writer Kris Kristofferson. "I think he's the only true hero we have walking on this Earth today."

In the souvenir program, Jacques Levy reminisced about flying home from Rome with Chavez, eight years earlier: "As a non-believer, I never thought I would reach this conclusion, but on the plane that day . . . I suddenly believed the impossible. Some day, long after both of us are dead, the Church might select the man sitting beside me for sainthood. And no matter what I read in the papers these days, I still believe so." Chavez autographed copies of Levy's book and posed for pictures with children on his lap.

"Together we joined to right a wrong," he told the crowd. "Together we brought the plight of the men, women and children who work in agriculture to the conscience of the country."

The twentieth-anniversary celebration at La Paz was timed for Founder's Day. Fred Ross and Chavez's siblings and children joined union staff members and close friends in a crowd of about 300 adults and 122 children. Chris Hartmire delivered the homily. He touched on the significance of the anniversary and past achievements and predicted a difficult future. "Some of the toughest times were the easiest for us," he said. "The dangers and the challenges were immediate and obvious. We were operating on all cylinders."

Now they sat behind desks and spent time at meetings rather than on picket lines. He compared Chavez to Paul in the Corinthians, when people began to challenge the apostle's teaching. Factions developed, and Paul was criticized for shortcomings. Those in the movement must hold on to each other and draw strength from Cesar's energy, Hartmire said. "I think there is something else that keeps us going, something we don't notice so much or talk about. It is both powerful and fragile. When it is gone, it is probably the beginning of our own leaving. One way of describing it is very simple: it's the feeling that what we are doing is right, that it is good, that for all the frustrations, it *matters*, it really matters, that it will make the world a little better for our children."

A few months later, Cesar Chavez buried his father. Librado Chavez died on October 12, 1982. The funeral was held in Our Lady of Guadalupe church in San Jose, around the corner from the family home on Scharff Street, where three decades earlier Cesar had first met Fred Ross. Fernando Chavez, a successful attorney, delivered the homily for his grandfather, who had never gone to school. Juana told her daughters not to wear black. All five children participated in the offertory. Vicky and Librado junior, the youngest, carried the bread and wine to the altar. Rita, the eldest, offered a watch, and Richard placed candles on the altar. Cesar offered a short-handled hoe, el cortito, the instrument that had tortured so many thousands of farmworkers. Because of the work of Librado's eldest son, el cortito had been banned from the fields of California, and the world was a little better for his children.

CHAPTER 37

Chicano Power

*I've traveled through every part of this nation. I have met and spoken with
thousands of Hispanics from every walk of life, from every social and
economic class. And one thing I hear most often from Hispanics, regardless of
age or position, and from many non-Hispanics as well, is that the farm
workers gave them the hope that they could succeed and the inspiration to
work for change.*

When Latinos in California were asked in 1983 to name the Latino they
most admired, the number one answer was Cesar Chavez. In a statewide
survey, Chavez scored twice as many votes as the runners-up, Dodgers
pitching sensation Fernando Valenzuela and actor Ricardo Montalban.

The poll itself reflected a coming of age for a once marginalized
community. The survey was commissioned by the *Los Angeles Times*,
which won a Pulitzer Prize for a series of stories that explored how the
fast-growing Latino population was shaping all facets of life in Southern
California. For six months, a team of reporters immersed itself in the
politics, culture, and lives of people who called themselves Latinos,
Hispanics, Chicanos, Mexicans, or Mexican Americans.

The rising generation of writers, actors, artists, and activists profiled in
the *Times* stories drew inspiration from Chavez's movement. Many traced
their success in the cities to his work in the fields. Luis Valdez, founder of
the Teatro Campesino, had become the first Chicano playwright on
Broadway with *Zoot Suit*, based on the story of a Mexican American gang
unfairly imprisoned for murder after a 1942 riot in Los Angeles. Edward
James Olmos had his breakthrough role as the narrator of the play. A few
years later, he was nominated for an Academy Award for his portrayal of
math teacher Jaime Escalante in the movie *Stand and Deliver*. Escalante
defied expectations and taught calculus to Mexican American students at
Garfield High, the East Los Angeles school whose graduates included

state legislator Richard Alatorre, boxer Oscar de la Hoya, and the founding members of the band Los Lobos.

Garfield High graduate Carlos Almaraz, whose paintings hung in major museums and galleries, credited his success directly to Chavez. Born in Mexico, raised in Chicago and Los Angeles, Charles Almaraz had thought of himself as a Mexican living in California until he met Luis Valdez in 1973. Almaraz changed his name to Carlos and headed to La Paz, following Valdez's advice to seek out the leader of the farm worker movement. Almaraz volunteered to paint the mural for the UFW's first convention, returned two years later with a team of artists to produce another mural, and worked intermittently for *El Malcriado*. When he found himself one semester short of his master's in fine arts, about to be kicked out of school for failure to pay tuition, Almaraz appealed to Chavez. He sent a $400 check. "Without you and the union this might not have been possible," Almaraz wrote Chavez upon graduating from Otis Art Institute. The artist painted a fifty-by-twenty-foot "Boycott Gallo" mural and wrote Chavez that his birthday present was waiting on a Los Angeles street corner.

Like Valdez and Almaraz, many Latino professionals were only a generation away from the fields. Since his early days of campaigning for Robert Kennedy, Chavez had been attuned to the affinity that Mexican Americans in the cities expressed for *la causa*. By the 1980s, Chicano Studies departments were common across California. MEChA (Movimiento Estudiantil Chicano de Aztlán) groups flourished on college campuses, where the number of Latino students inched up. Earlier Chicano movement leaders such as Reies Tijerina and Corky Gonzales, whom Chavez had denounced for their embrace of violence, had faded away. The migration of Latinos into the middle class, which Chavez had once deplored, now offered the UFW a wider base of support.

Though Latinos still registered to vote in disproportionately small numbers, their political impact had grown. By the early 1980s, four hundred Latinos held elected office in California, more than double the number ten years earlier. Chavez, who had begun his organizing career with the 1952 voter registration drive in Sal Si Puedes, grasped the implications. He moved to capitalize on the demographic shifts.

At the 1983 UFW convention, Chavez explained the movement's newest offspring, the Chicano Lobby. The nonprofit entity would advocate on issues of importance to Chicanos, a term Mexican American activists had adopted in the late 1960s. To help launch the Chicano Lobby,

San Antonio mayor Henry Cisneros addressed the convention, along with the recently elected president of the Mexican American Political Association, Fernando Chavez.

Fernando, the eldest of Cesar's children, had long been the most independent. His decision to refuse induction when he was denied conscientious objector status had landed him briefly in the spotlight when his case went to trial; he was acquitted after testifying he decided to become a pacifist after a talk with his father during the 1968 fast. Raised largely by his grandparents Juana and Librado, Fernando was the only one of Cesar's children to graduate from college. While most of his siblings worked in their father's movement, Fernando earned a master's degree in urban planning and then a law degree. He specialized in medical malpractice law. His San Jose office had no pictures of his father. He drove a Mercedes. "I'm a lot different from my father," he told an interviewer. "We have different sets of interests. I'm middle class. I *know* I'm middle class."

He had not been involved in public life, and his sudden elevation to president of the oldest Mexican American political group was seen as an attempt by the UFW to control the agenda. Fernando denied he was a stalking horse for the UFW. But his opponent, who lost by twenty-two votes, claimed the union paid dues for more than four hundred new members shortly before the MAPA election.

"I believe all political observers pretty much accept the theory that the Hispanic vote can be the pivotal vote in the 1984 presidential election," Fernando said when he took office. He promised a voter registration drive throughout the Southwest. That dovetailed with his father's agenda for the Chicano Lobby to generate money and support for the UFW.

Such support had become crucial to Chavez as he experimented with a new type of boycott. In the early years, he had counseled boycotters that success depended on one thing: dedicated people. "You start with people," he told a group of workers about to depart for boycott cities in 1969. "Whatever you do, you start with people." Now he had a different message: start with computers. He used one of his favorite words to describe the new boycott: scientific. For Chavez, science was yet another magic bullet; he had long believed that the right formula, carefully followed, would infallibly yield the correct answer.

He had been interested in computers before they became popular, and the union was buying its third system. Costs came down as manufacturers competed to produce more efficient mainframe computers. Desktop computers were being widely marketed for the first time. The personal computer had beat out human candidates to become *Time*'s "Machine of the Year," featured on the cover of the January 3, 1983, issue of the magazine. In politics, the new generation of computers enabled consultants to cross-reference voting patterns, household income, and census data to target direct mail. The religious right had been in the vanguard of using the emerging technology to proselytize. "Computers and sophisticated mail and TV messages have revolutionized business and politics," Chavez wrote in a May 1983 memo to executive board members. "Why should only the right-wingers benefit from the new ways?"

Sacramento consultant Richie Ross, a former boycotter turned political wizard, helped Chavez design a "high-tech boycott" to target consumers by direct mail rather than picket lines. "I told Cesar the old days of Xeroxed leaflets were over. The kids that used to march in parades against the Vietnam War are now driving BMW's and going out for Sunday brunch," Ross told a *New York Times* reporter. "You've got to do something different."

The union aimed the first high-tech boycott at Lucky, a California supermarket chain. UFW programmers mapped Lucky stores against census data, ranking each store according to the percentage of Latino residents nearby. They refined the list to target politically sympathetic neighborhoods by overlaying the map with election results on key measures, such as the UFW's Proposition 14 in 1976. Then they added data on household size, because large families could cost stores more business. Finally, volunteers visited stores with the highest ranking to verify that consumers were predominantly Latino and check whether alternative supermarkets were nearby. The UFW print shop prepared four glossy mailers explaining the union and the boycott, to be sent in succession to families who lived near the Lucky stores deemed most vulnerable.

The goal went beyond forcing Lucky to drop a specific product. Chavez's strategy was to gain long-term leverage with the threat that the UFW could damage the store's image among Hispanics. "This program is part of a campaign to mobilize the Hispanic community—and more specifically Hispanic consumers—in a way that has never been tried before," Chavez explained to the executive board in justifying a $1 million direct mail and television campaign. Marketing research showed that businesses of all kinds increasingly targeted Hispanics. The UFW had something unique to sell: its cachet. "Our own appeal strikes deep at the sense of cultural and ethnic identity felt by the overwhelming majority of

Hispanics in this state . . . No other organization (or product) can appeal to Hispanic consumers in this way."

Chavez's new enemy was California governor George Deukmejian, a Republican elected with support from the agricultural industry. When he took office in 1983, Deukmejian moved quickly to correct what he called an imbalance on the Agricultural Labor Relations Board and the ALRB. He restaffed the agency to favor the growers, cut the budget for investigations, and vetoed an appropriation to help clear a backlog of grievances. The political shift came as the union's power in the fields had eroded. The UFW had little ability to fight back by mobilizing workers who had once exerted pressure, even on friendly politicians such as Jerry Brown.

"If growers and their government close off the laws to us, let us take up arms again," Chavez said in his opening address to the 1983 UFW convention. He unveiled the high-tech boycott and asked consumers to boycott grapes and Red Coach lettuce, produced by the largest vegetable company that had refused to sign a contract, Bruce Church. The only contract that remained in table grapes was with Lionel Steinberg in Coachella, the first grower who had signed with the union in 1970.

"Today we are going back to where we left off in 1975," Chavez declared. "It's time for us to place our faith in the court of last resort once again." The union had given up hope of receiving a fair deal from the ALRB: "The governor can do whatever he likes to the ALRB, but he can't protect the growers from the boycott! . . . We built the union without the ALRB, and we can survive now without the ALRB."

In addition to targeting Hispanic consumers with a direct mail campaign, Chavez aimed the new boycott at the group he called the "Big Chill" generation, referring to the popular movie released in the fall of 1983 about a fifteen-year reunion of college friends. Chavez modulated his message to reflect the changing times and told the board the union must use different language. "Yesterday it was all right to talk about a union for farm workers and the right to organize," he said. "After all, with the war on poverty and the war in Vietnam, everyone was organizing. We could win the boycott by picketing stores because all our friends were in the streets anyway fighting the 'good fights.'" Now unions had fallen out of favor. President Reagan had broken the air traffic controllers union in 1981, a major blow to the labor movement. Chavez sought ways to cast the farmworkers' struggle in the rhetoric of the 1980s: Sexual harassment, a recent legal term that had become a focus of national attention and study, was rampant in the fields. Toxic chemicals, the new target of the environmental movement, poisoned farmworkers. The "gender gap," which had emerged for the first time in the 1980 presidential election when Democrat Jimmy Carter ran significantly better among women than men, offered "a sensational opportunity" for the UFW because women did most of the food shopping.

At La Paz, Chavez shuffled his staff yet again to accommodate the new priorities. Chris Hartmire became head of a new social marketing department, which included an expanded print shop with two high-speed presses, each able to print 80,000 four-color pieces per hour. The union began sending a small monthly magazine, *Food and Justice*, to financial supporters. Chavez also charged Hartmire with overseeing the design and purchase of a larger, sophisticated computer system for the union and its related entities.

Though he had announced the boycott months earlier, Chavez waited to get past the 1984 presidential election and the summer Olympics in Los Angeles before launching a full-scale campaign. By early 1985, the ribbon was cut on the new Sperry computer system and the print shop was complete. The UFW had filmed thirty-six different television spots, which consultant Ross grouped in three categories: "history," "didactic," and "emotional." The union bought $250,000 worth of time for 2,019 television commercials over fourteen weeks. The campaign commercials carried the tagline *"Como Siempre"* (as always)—a play for the sympathetic baby boomers of the early boycott years.

Chavez said the new boycott was aimed not at specific growers but at the ALRB. The commercials helped the union raise money. But Chavez never articulated a convincing connection between the boycott and forcing the state agency to act on farmworker concerns. In San Francisco, a bastion of support for the UFW, Mayor Dianne Feinstein vetoed a city council resolution in support of the boycott. She estimated the city had lost $17.5 million in convention business from the agricultural industry in the last five years because of support for the UFW. "If there is a problem with the ALRB, that is where the issue should be addressed," she wrote in a veto message, "not through a boycott which unwittingly hurts this city's number one industry [tourism] and largest employer."

The computer and printing presses also offered Chavez new options in the political arena. Politicians increasingly sought the endorsement of the preeminent Latino organization and the blessing of its founder. After his misstep in the Assembly speakership fight, Chavez had rebuilt the union's political clout, largely through substantial campaign contributions. In 1982, the UFW Political Action Committee handed out $780,000. The poorest workers in the state had become the second-largest political contributors, only a few hundred dollars behind the American Medical Association.

In the 1970s, the UFW had created a political fund by building into all contracts a holiday called Citizen Participation Day (CPD). Workers had the day off, usually a weekday in June, at the height of the season. But their salaries for that day went into a special union fund earmarked for political action. At first the donation was optional; at the 1977 convention the practice was made mandatory. "CPD is the farm workers' most powerful weapon at the present time," Chavez said at the time. "CPD stands as the only protection against these agribusiness interests determined to halt our progress and oppose justice."

After the record contracts signed with the vegetable workers at the end of the 1979 strike, the CPD funds soared. A worker earning $5 an hour would contribute approximately $40; under some of the 1981 contracts, the average payment per worker was more than $50. About thirty thousand workers under contract sent $1.2 million into the union's political campaign fund.

Chavez used the money to repair the breach with Willie Brown, whose support became crucial once Jerry Brown left the governor's office at the end of 1982. Without the backing of the Assembly Speaker, Chavez would be shut out. Over the course of two years, the UFW contributed $750,000 to Willie Brown's campaign committees. Brown protected the union's interests.

The extent of the union's donations to various candidates was hidden until long past the elections. For two years, the UFW filed sporadic and incomplete reports and ignored repeated warnings from the state agency that oversaw campaign disclosure. An early fine was waived based on an explanation from Dolores Huerta that the form had been sent by mistake to the Fair Employment and Housing office instead of the Fair Political Practices Commission because of "all the dumb clerical stuff we were doing wrong." Eventually the state commission concluded the union had "displayed a persistent unwillingness to comply with the laws" and had committed twenty-six violations.

"We are undeniably guilty of most, if not all, of the alleged violations," wrote UFW attorney Ellen Eggers. The fine was eventually reduced to $25,000, from a maximum of $52,000.

The violations involved more than sloppy paperwork. The union deliberately funneled money through intermediary committees to conceal the source of contributions. In three instances, the union secretly bankrolled the campaign of a candidate running against Assemblyman Art Torres, the Democrat who had provided a key vote for Willie Brown in the speakership contest. Despite Torres's long history as a UFW supporter and full-time staff member, Chavez attempted to extract vengeance for Torres's decision to switch support from Howard Berman. "We are very loyal to the people we support," Chavez said. "But also, when we get double-crossed, we can be pretty mean." Torres withstood the challenge, with the aid of Jessica Govea, who helped run his campaign, and the victory was widely reported as a blow to the UFW's prestige. Torres and Chavez never spoke again.

As the union lost more contracts and members, CPD contributions decreased. Richie Ross stepped in again to help. Ross had met his wife, a farmworker, in the Philadelphia boycott house during the first grape boycott. He had risen in Sacramento to become Willie Brown's top aide and had been dubbed Brown's "warlord" by a California magazine. Ross told Chavez that the UFW did not realize its own political strength. Rather than buying access with contributions, the union could trade on Chavez's prestige.

With its new $2 million print shop, the UFW could produce literature for candidates at half the commercial rate. The union should ask Democratic leaders for a list of priority campaigns and develop a "dirty dozen of supporters" who would be beholden to the union for its support, Ross advised. The UFW would gain a broader base of support, a bloc that could fend off harmful legislation. By printing campaign literature, the UFW would have candidates' mailing lists, Ross pointed out, "an implicit threat" that could be used to punish anyone who betrayed the cause.

Chavez implemented the Ross strategy. Instead of donating money, the UFW made money: the print shop produced campaign mailers, lawn signs, and posters. The UFW's political action committee (PAC) bought the material from the union and then reported the payment as an in-kind contribution for political candidates.

Politicians courting Latino voters came begging for the union's endorsement. Many were eager to purchase printing services from the union. As the UFW PAC ran low on funds because the deductions from union contracts evaporated, candidates paid the PAC for services. The PAC paid the union. The loss of contracts did not diminish Chavez's political clout.

In La Paz, a generational change began to take place. Paul Chavez, Cesar's middle son, became increasingly involved in the political operation. He worked during the early 1980s in Sacramento, and then took over running the print shop. His sisters Linda and Liz also worked at La Paz, as did their husbands. Richard Chavez's son Federico became a lawyer and worked for the union.

Richard Chavez resigned from the executive board at the end of his term in 1984. He had often talked of wanting to return to civilian life. When the time came, he found tears streaming down his face as soon as he drove through the gate at La Paz. He cried all the way to Mojave, he wrote to Huerta: "I guess when one puts 18 years of his life into something it does mean something."

On November 9, 1984, Chavez delivered a speech at the Commonwealth Club of California, the oldest public affairs forum in the country. He joined the ranks of presidents and foreign dignitaries who had addressed the political, social, and literary elite of San Francisco—"a different kind of audience than I am used to facing," he wrote Shirley Temple Black, the club president, in accepting the invitation. Chavez spoke of the miseries and exploitation of farmworkers, children working in the fields, and workers living in caves. Those injustices, he said, had driven him to his life's work.

Much of the address was upbeat. The number of workers under contract, the health of the UFW, even its very existence—those were not the most important issues, he said. The union by its presence forced growers to improve wages and conditions. The historic significance of the farm worker movement had been established. He took satisfaction in the changes spreading from California across the country. He delivered a prophetic vision of the future and an eloquent epitaph for the union he had created:

> I've traveled through every part of this nation. I have met and spoken with thousands of Hispanics from every walk of life, from every social and economic class. And one thing I hear most often from Hispanics, regardless of age or position, and from many non-Hispanics as well, is that the farm workers gave them the hope that they could succeed and the inspiration to work for change . . .
>
> Tens of thousands of children and grandchildren of farm workers and the children and grandchildren of poor Hispanics are

moving out of the fields and out of the barrios and into the professions and into business and into politics, and that movement cannot be reversed. Our union will forever exist as an empowering force among Chicanos in the Southwest. That means our power and our influence will grow and not diminish . . .

We have looked into the future and the future is ours. History and inevitability are on our side. The farm workers and their children and the Hispanics and their children are the future in California, and corporate growers are the past. Those politicians who ally themselves with the corporate growers and against farm workers and the Hispanics are in for a big surprise. They want to make their careers in politics; they want to hold power 20 and 30 years from now. But 20 and 30 years from now, in Modesto, in Salinas, in Fresno, in Bakersfield, in the Imperial Valley and in many of the great cities of California, those communities will be dominated by farm workers and not by growers, by the children and grandchildren of farm workers and not by the children and grandchildren of growers.

Regardless of what the future holds for the union, regardless of what the future holds for farm workers, our accomplishments cannot be undone. La causa, our cause, doesn't have to be experienced twice. The consciousness and pride that were raised by our union are alive and thriving inside millions of young Hispanics who will never work on a farm.

CHAPTER 38

Selling the Brand

A company can make a social contribution only if it is highly profitable.

At the end of the 1980s, Cesar Chavez asked a familiar question: what is our business? This time the query was largely rhetorical. There were no deep thinkers like Jim Drake around to draft passionate responses, and no soul-searching discussions about the merits of putting resources into organizing versus negotiating. Chavez answered himself with one word: "entrepreneurial."

"The purpose of a business: to create a customer," he wrote in longhand notes from a meeting to form yet another subsidiary, the Farm Workers Corporation. "A company can make a social contribution only if it is highly profitable."

Much of Chavez's attention was directed to raising money through commercial activities along with the union's more traditional routes. He explored radio and the increasingly popular market of cable television. He dabbled in real estate investments. He modeled experiments after his success in politics, pitching to the growing community of Latino professionals. The UFW sold its brand on T-shirts and mugs, at wine-and-cheese parties, and on scores of college campuses across the country. Cesar Chavez had become a marketable commodity.

His entrepreneurial ventures offered outlets for Chavez's curiosity. The projects also compensated for a precipitous decline in dues. From a high of $2.99 million in 1982, dues had fallen to $1 million just three years later. Contracts vanished, and those that remained covered fewer workers.

Companies went out of business, stalled on renegotiations, or found loopholes to move employees out of the bargaining unit. At some ranches, workers voted to decertify the UFW. Sun Harvest, the giant vegetable grower, had shut down at the end of the 1983 season; officials said the company never recovered from losses suffered during the 1979 strike.

Three years after Gov. George Deukmejian took office in January 1983, the number of jobs covered by UFW contracts had dropped from thirty thousand to fifteen thousand. Over the next six months, the union lost fifteen more contracts, leaving about seventy-five. Chavez railed against Deukmejian for destroying the ALRB and painted the union as a victim of an alliance between Republicans and growers. His former counsel, Jerry Cohen, saw things differently.

Cohen acknowledged that the Deukmejian administration had gutted the board that administered the best labor law in the country. But the attorney held Chavez responsible for his failure to continue organizing. The union achieved some of its greatest victories in the era of hostile politicians such as Nixon and Reagan, Cohen pointed out in an op-ed piece in the *Los Angeles Times*. "Junk mail doesn't organize people; people organize people," Cohen wrote. "Unions that do not organize, die."

Chavez tried to expand the membership outside the fields. The UFW created categories of associate membership in a project he dubbed "Crunch Bird." Anyone could join the "Community Union" for $5 a month and receive discounts at drugstores, travel deals, and real estate advice. The union targeted former farmworkers and consumers with the goal of signing up five thousand. A broader definition of membership, Chavez told farmworkers, would "open the doors of your union to everyone."

More members were badly needed to increase the pool of clients for struggling services, such as his beloved credit union. At the end of 1987, the credit union had only 1,063 members out of a potential of 3,500 (probably a more accurate figure of the UFW's membership than the higher numbers the union reported). Since the bank opened, it had handed out almost six thousand loans worth more than $7.7 million.

The print shop built on its political success by spinning off a commercial venture called El Taller Grafico Specialty Advertising Corporation (ETG), with Chavez as chair and Huerta as vice chair. ETG marketed UFW merchandise to the public and also sold T-shirts and specialty items for labor unions to distribute at conventions, a variation on Synanon's old distribution network. "When you order promotional items through us, it's a victory for all the unions," said a magazine ad for ETG

450 THE CRUSADES OF CESAR CHAVEZ

that featured an Olympic gold medal emblazoned with the UFW eagle. By 1988, sales topped half a million dollars. ETG added children's clothes, polo shirts, jewelry, buttons, and posters.

Chavez's most ambitious commercial venture took him far from the fields: he became a housing developer. The union's foray into housing grew out of a partnership with a Fresno businessman named Celestino Aguilar, who had approached Chavez in the early 1980s with a proposal. As a real estate appraiser, Aguilar heard about foreclosures in advance. If the union put up money to buy houses, Aguilar would oversee renovations and flip the house at substantial profit. He would take a commission, and he promised the union a return of 25 to 50 percent on its investment.

The partnership flourished. They moved from foreclosures to high-end custom-built homes and subsidized apartment complexes. Aguilar led the UFW executive board on tours of properties in Fresno. At the 1986 UFW convention, Chavez introduced the Fresno appraiser as a hero who had made a lot of money but never forgot his roots.

Homelessness had become a problem in the national spotlight, and the federal government allocated more funds for construction and rent subsidies for low-income housing. Aguilar and the UFW took advantage. Chavez shifted the focus of the National Farmworkers Service Center— his original entrepreneurial venture and "problem clinic"—to housing. In 1987, the real estate portfolio included 48 low-income apartments in Fresno and 81 apartments in Parlier, with 70 single-family homes and 226 apartments on the drawing board. Chavez and Aguilar formed American Liberty Investments, which helped shield the UFW from public exposure. To service the new apartments, Chavez and Aguilar formed Ideal Minimart Corporation, which built two strip malls and operated a check-cashing store. By 1987, Richard Chavez's company, Bonita Construction, had been hired for some of the work.

When the *Fresno Bee* reported that almost none of the UFW housing projects were built by union contractors, the revelation outraged the building trade unions. Construction unions had contributed thousands of dollars in the years when the UFW had survived on the generosity of organized labor. Dozens of union plumbers, bricklayers, and construction workers had volunteered time to help build projects like Forty Acres. Now the UFW, once the inspiration for a resurgent labor movement, built commercial housing with nonunion labor.

"The 6,800 members of the California State Conference of Bricklayers and Allied Craftsman have for years supported your union, as brothers should," the group's vice president wrote Chavez. "I am asking that you offer an explanation to my members. I believe they deserve one."

Chavez attacked growers for trying to discredit the UFW and the *Fresno Bee* for slanted coverage. He claimed the Service Center was "a completely separate and independent organization" from the UFW. The newspaper, he said, had written about the issue because the UFW supported the Newspaper Guild in a dispute.

Labor unions had long been wary of Chavez, and the UFW had earned a reputation for always having its hand out and doing little to help others. But outside the labor movement, the housing controversy did little to dull Chavez's luster. The union continued to market its most valuable asset—Cesar Chavez. He found particularly receptive audiences on college campuses across the country.

"As president of the United Farm Workers, Chavez has led a long struggle against injustice and unsafe food for over 30 years," read a "Dear Friend" letter from Arturo Rodriguez, sent to college students along with a "checklist for a successful UFW speaking event." Rodriguez had taken on more responsibilities since joining the executive board in 1981 and functioned increasingly as his father-in-law's chief aide. The letters ticked off some of Chavez's recent honors, including a National Hispanic Hero Award from the U.S. Hispanic Leadership Conference and a standing ovation from two thousand students at the University of Illinois at Urbana-Champaign. The union asked for a $5,000 honorarium for each appearance and offered suggestions on student and faculty sources to approach for contributions.

In 1990, Chavez spoke at sixty-four events, earning an average of $3,800 per appearance. He talked mainly to students, plus a mix of labor groups and special fund-raisers organized by longtime supporters. In Amherst, Massachusetts, Chavez presided over a chili cook-off festival coupled with a UFW fund-raiser. Closer to home, Chavez wrote a "wine and cheese marketing plan" that targeted VIPs from labor, religious groups, academia, and community organizations. He calculated the union could raise $480,000 in five months by holding 240 fund-raisers, though they never achieved close to that number.

In 1991, the union adopted a marketing plan to increase revenue as Chavez embarked on a "Public Action Speaking Tour." The plan calculated a "strategic marketing mix" and targeted the largest and most prestigious schools. The union appealed to the desire of colleges for diverse speakers and minorities. The goal was to raise $1.2 million, plus $60,000 by selling items produced by ETG.

Volunteers who hosted and facilitated Chavez's visits received detailed checklists with directions on how to set up the podium, how many cars to have available to shuttle Chavez between appearances, and what foods to have on hand for his macrobiotic diet: miso, tamari, tofu, garbanzo beans, adzuki beans, lentils, brown rice, buckwheat noodles, burdock, carrots, rutabaga, kale, collard greens, radishes, shallots, and parsnips. Two recipes for miso soup were also included in the packet, along with a reminder not to use salt in cooked food.

In his standard speech, Chavez talked about the problems of farm-workers, the dangers of pesticides, and the nefarious alliance between Republicans and the agriculture industry. He also spoke more broadly about social ills and his disillusionment with the political system. Government would never address problems of poverty, racism, or sexism, he said in an address at Harvard University. Even good candidates become corrupted by lobbyists. He had soured on the idea that voter registration was the key to power, because the votes of the poor did not count. "The more you own, the more your vote counts."

Only action like boycotts and marches would achieve social change, he told students. "If you take public action, you don't need 51 percent to win, and the polls never close, and you can vote more than once."

He was relaxed with student audiences, the master teacher in a new setting—mentoring in the halls of privilege rather than the fields of poverty. The nation's best and brightest called him a hero and role model, and Chavez graciously accepted their earnest accolades. He smiled and patiently answered questions. What would you do differently if you were starting out all over? "I'd use computers." How can we address the really big problems, like nuclear disarmament? "Stop paying taxes." Did he admire any politicians? "My friend Jerry Brown."

Students gave him standing ovations, spoke of their admiration for his dedication, and promised not to buy grapes. He said the question he was asked most often was how he stayed with the cause. "Very simple. Just stay with it. I have nothing else to do. Nothing else to do. I don't own a house, and I don't own a car. I don't have a bank account. I have nothing. But I have ideas, and I love to raise hell."

In 1988, the farm worker movement had grown to include eighteen nonprofit and commercial entities, in addition to the UFW. The entities grew more financially intertwined. The Service Center paid the

Education and Legal Defense Fund to provide social services at the field offices. The UFW paid La Union de Pueblo Entero to monitor grievance boards set up under contracts. The UFW, pension fund, and RFK plan paid rent to the Service Center. The other entities paid the union for computer services and printing. The Service Center bought $100,000 worth of stock in ETG, which paid 10.5 percent in royalties on sales to the UFW.

The older entities that still delivered services to farmworkers limped along. Health care and pension plans, ambitious and once-revolutionary ideas, suffered with few participants. By 1989, the RFK plan covered only between two thousand and four thousand workers per month, depending on the season. In 1983, Chavez had made a round of appearances to hand out the first pension checks. "At last, farm worker dignity is being recognized," he said in Oxnard. "No longer are they being put in the junk pile and forgotten." But with fewer contracts, the number of workers who could qualify dropped. The pension plan struggled to locate eligible beneficiaries, inching up from 690 retirees in 1989 to about 1,000 by 1992.

The fate of the Martin Luther King Jr. trust fund illustrated the trajectory of Chavez's movement over less than two decades. When he negotiated the first table grape contract with Lionel Steinberg in the spring of 1970, Chavez wanted to start an economic development fund. Steinberg's attorney suggested a trust fund jointly administered by appointees of the union and the growers. The trust fund, originally called the Farm Worker Fund, began with a 2¢-per-hour contribution for each worker at Steinberg's Coachella vineyard. In later contracts, the company contribution increased to 5¢ an hour.

In 1973, Chavez asked Coretta Scott King for permission to name the fund after her late husband. The nickel-an-hour MLK contribution became standard in UFW contracts. MLK would offer services for all farmworkers, but those under contract, who were sacrificing from their paychecks, would be the primary beneficiaries.

For the next decade, the MLK fund operated service centers, health clinics, and day care centers. Much of the money went unspent, accumulating interest. In the fall of 1983, Celestino Aguilar and Cesar Chavez spoke to the MLK board about the potential of investing in real estate. Soon the fund was investing millions of dollars in Aguilar's projects.

As the union lost contracts, MLK's income came primarily from interest on investments. By 1986, contributions from workers' salaries fell significantly below the one-third threshold required for the fund to quality as a public charity. On the advice of counsel, the MLK fund became a private foundation. The joint employer-union board was dissolved. Federal tax law required that the foundation spend its interest income each year.

By 1989, the Martin Luther King Jr. fund was a private foundation with $8 million in principal, effectively accountable to no one but Cesar Chavez. Each year, MLK doled out between $600,000 and $700,000 to other UFW-related enterprises. Money earned by a generation of farmworkers, who had been told their sacrifice would provide services for all farmworkers, had become a subsidy for a growing bureaucracy increasingly removed from the fields.

CHAPTER 39

The Last Fast

We built this union twice. We are now trying to build the union one more time.

As the union's twenty-fifth anniversary approached in 1987, Chavez obsessed over the smallest details of the celebration. Chris Hartmire was in charge of the festivities, and the minister grew annoyed at Chavez's intense interest and penchant to overrule decisions at the last minute. The celebration took on outsized importance for the movement's leader, who would turn sixty years old on Founder's Day. Hartmire found Chavez's focus disturbingly self-important.

"Come Join Us, Again, in Delano," began the invitation sent to 140,000 people, an appeal to history and nostalgia. Like all the union's fundraising letters, the mail was targeted. Attorneys received a letter that stressed how important lawyers had been to the UFW's success, while the appeal to politicians featured a support committee of elected officials. Religious leaders, environmentalists, Hollywood celebrities, and former volunteers each received a separate pitch. All were invited to join the "Eagle Club"—$5,000 bought Gold Eagle status and a full-page ad in the glossy seventy-six-page Commemorative Journal; smaller contributors were listed as Silver, Bronze, and Black Eagle sponsors.

On May 23, 1987, thousands paid the $25 admission fee to enter a large tent erected on the grounds of Forty Acres. Fred Ross chatted with Jacques Levy. Dozens of guests stopped by Juana Chavez's chair to pay respects to the family matriarch. Relatives of the five union martyrs planted trees in their honor as five bunches of red balloons were released into the sky. Luis Valdez and the Teatro Campesino drew cheers as they played familiar huelga songs. ETG sold anniversary shirts and hats, wine-glasses, and commemorative programs. Mariachis played all evening as the crowd ate barbecue and danced until midnight.

The cast of religious and labor luminaries was noticeably thinner than in earlier years. There was little in the UFW's recent past to celebrate. The union had won elections or fought off decertifications at thirty-two ranches in the past five years—and lost at thirty-nine. Chavez vowed to intensify the grape boycott and force growers back to the negotiating table. He summoned visions of the historic 1970 contract signing with John Giumarra that had taken place in the room where they partied: "We're predicting that growers will again come to this hall and sign sooner than they think."

Newspaper stories pegged to the anniversary painted a starkly differ-ent picture. "Twenty-five years after raising the plight of California's farmworkers to an international concern, Cesar Chavez has all but left the fields," began a story in the *San Diego Union-Tribune*. "Having fought so fervently to win collective-bargaining rights and the nation's first agri-cultural labor law, Chavez's United Farm Workers union now is nearly dormant, with past victories in wages and improvements in working conditions rapidly fading."

Reporters visited agricultural valleys around the state and found no sign of the UFW. Farmworkers had never seen union representatives. CRLA, Chavez's old adversary, held seminars to educate workers about minimum wage, overtime, and their rights to bathrooms and work breaks. Recent federal legislation had enabled undocumented immi-grants to legalize their status, and growers had set up a $1 million program to help their workers qualify. "If I were Cesar Chavez and I had a law like this, under the amnesty I would try to get all my people back," said Impe-rial Valley grower John Vessey. "And he's doing nothing. He's off on some tangent regarding pesticides and the grape boycott that is going to put his workers out of work."

Chavez's response defiantly acknowledged the decline in the union's membership: "We built this union twice. We are now trying to build the union one more time."

The last word in the *Union-Tribune* series went to Eliseo Medina, who was organizing immigrant janitors in San Diego for the Service Employ-ees International Union. "Organizing is always going to mean risks," Medina said. "The UFW was willing to take them in the early days. They need to go back to organizing. That's what they did best. There's a void, and if the UFW doesn't fill it, somebody else is going to step in."

Some months later, Chavez stopped by a fiftieth-birthday party in San Diego for the movement entities' longtime counsel, Frank Denison. Chavez stayed only a few minutes. Manuel Chavez told Denison that Cesar left when he saw Medina; he would not stay in the same room.

What Vesey called a "pesticide tangent" had become the center of the union's boycott, educational campaign, and fund-raising efforts. Decades before the organic food movement, Chavez argued that all pesticides were dangerous to farmworkers and consumers. He had expressed concern about pesticides in the earliest negotiations, and the 1970 UFW contracts banned the use of DDT—more than two years before the federal government outlawed the chemical. Pesticides had been a secondary issue for the union during the height of its organizing years. But in the mid-1980s, as he searched for a new villain, Chavez seized on pesticides as a way to again raise the national consciousness about farmworkers. Environmental disasters such as Love Canal, federal Superfund sites, and suspicions about ties between chemicals and disease had increased public awareness. Pesticides drifted from field to field, Chavez pointed out, and seeped into the ground, the water, the fruit, and the workers' clothes and skin. "We maintain that there are no safe pesticides," he said in a stump speech, "because the sole purpose of a pesticide is to kill living things."

Marion Moses, who had played an early and important role in Delano as Chavez's nurse and confidant, had graduated from medical school, specialized in occupational health, and returned to work for the UFW. Pesticides became her cause, and she helped Chavez identify five organophosphates to target in his campaign. Volunteers were given fund-raising scripts to use for phone-banking to solicit donations. The UFW raised more than $100,000 to build its own pesticide lab, and Moses obtained thousands of dollars of donated equipment. The facility never opened.

Back in the summer of 1983, parents in the small San Joaquin Valley city of McFarland had become alarmed about an unusual number of childhood cancers. They met with local and state officials and demanded an investigation. Cancer clusters had become an emotional debate around the United States, fueled by high-profile media stories. Experts differed widely on the dangers but agreed that proving a cause-and-effect correlation was difficult. In the fall of 1986, county officials announced McFarland was safe, a conclusion that pleased no one. Chavez saw an opportunity to humanize the pesticide issue and ratchet up the boycott.

Cancer was complicated, he said, but the suffering of small children was easy to understand. "These cancer clusters come because of the unregulated use of cancer-causing pesticides," Chavez said. The union prepared a seventeen-minute video called *The Wrath of Grapes*, narrated by actor Mike Farrell. The film featured some of the young victims, including five-year-old Felipe Franco, born without arms and legs. The pictures of Felipe were taken from a television broadcast and used without his parents' permission. Grape growers, outraged by Chavez's assertions and concerned about the economic impact, encouraged parents to protest the use of their children's images. Several parents sued the UFW and demanded the union stop showing the film. "Chavez has been exploiting our children to raise money for his troubled union," Connie Rosales, one of the mothers, wrote to universities where Chavez was scheduled to speak. "Although we respect the right of anyone to speculate, the UFW had crossed the line of speculation into exploitation."

Chavez asserted the union's First Amendment right to show the video and intensified his rhetoric. "The use of pesticides and the misuse of pesticides is the cause of all the problems in McFarland, and there is no other cause," Chavez said. Fred Ross conducted a house meeting campaign in McFarland, and Chavez addressed a community meeting. "The growers are using the pesticides to kill our people," he said. In nearby Earlimart, more cases of childhood cancer surfaced. At a press conference with several affected families, Chavez compared their plight to that of the canaries sent to die in the coal mines: "Farmworkers and their children are society's canaries."

Boycotting grapes to win contracts for farmworkers in the 1960s had been a clear and convincing message; the pesticide issue never resonated the same way. Chavez struggled to persuade consumers that if they stopped buying grapes, growers would stop using dangerous chemicals. He reassigned top staff to key cities. "I am sure that you agree with me that unless we assign everyone to the boycott and raise the money we could fail on the eve of some big successes," he wrote to the executive board members. Soon he called them back and announced the boycott would focus on specific supermarket chains. He asked shoppers to sign petitions calling on the stores not to carry grapes because of pesticides. He violated anti-picketing injunctions in Los Angeles to get arrested. He flew families of the cancer victims to New York to appear with him on television and radio programs.

"Our workers and their children are being poisoned in the killing fields of California's table grape industry," Chavez said at an Earth Day rally in New York City.

The lawsuit against *The Wrath of Grapes* was dismissed, but parents continued to allege that the union exploited grieving families for financial gain. When UFW members showed up with flags and joined the funeral procession for a fourteen-year-old cancer victim, her furious mother confronted Dolores Huerta and ordered them to leave. Parents, desperate for answers, argued that the UFW's focus on grapes took away attention from other potential carcinogens, such as pesticides in cotton fields or nitrates in the water.

Chavez dismissed the parents' criticism. "We know where it's coming from—from the growers," he told NPR reporter Scott Simon. Simon asked for proof. Furthermore, he pressed, why not take the children out of the film if their parents objected? Chavez bristled and refused to comment further. "I don't want you to do a job on me," he warned. Simon tried to ask questions about Chavez's leadership and inquired about Synanon and the Game. Chavez denied they had played the Game and denounced Simon as unprofessional. "I don't appreciate the interview at all. It's really, really disgusting to have you do that," Chavez said as he walked out and slammed the door. Simon and his crew were told to leave La Paz and informed that the union would sue if NPR aired a piece on Chavez. The threat did not stop the broadcast.

With the boycott failing to get traction, Chavez upped the ante. He resorted to his most dramatic move, a lengthy public fast. He chose a room at the Filipino retirement village on the grounds of Forty Acres and began his third major fast at midnight on July 16, 1988. He was sixty-one years old. The union had just thirty-one contracts.

"A powerful urge has been raging within me for several months," Chavez said in a statement on the third day of the fast. "I have been struggling against it. Toward the end of last week this urge became insistent. I resisted again but my efforts were in vain." He cited the panoply of issues affecting farmworkers that he had fought for decades, from the lack of fair elections to the dangers of pesticides. "This fast is first and foremost personal. It is something I feel compelled to do. It is directed at myself. It is a fast for the purification of my own body, mind and soul." He also criticized those he said had not done enough to help him, including farmworkers. "The fast is also an act of penance for those in positions of moral authority . . . who know that they could or should do more, who have become bystanders and thus collaborators with an industry that does not care about its workers."

He lay on a hospital bed, in white pajamas. He worked on a table across the bed until he became too weak and needed help to sit up. Throughout the fast, he allowed one of his staff members to film him. The physical pain became visible as the fast wore on. On the twelfth day, at the evening mass, a thirteen-year-old girl from McFarland who had benign thyroid tumors sang a song she had written for Chavez. On the nineteenth day, three children of Robert Kennedy arrived. Their presence generated the first major media attention.

Five days later, Chavez passed the record he had set during his 1972 Phoenix fast. Hartmire told the crowd gathered for nightly mass that Chavez had grown very weak. By the thirtieth day, he had lost thirty pounds, about 17 percent of his body weight. "We strongly urge Cesar to give serious consideration to discontinue his fast," Marion Moses said at a press conference. His nausea made it difficult for him to drink water. Chavez said he would break the fast in six days, the following Sunday.

The Rev. Jesse Jackson had visited some of the McFarland families. In his address to the Democratic National Convention, soon after Chavez began to fast, Jackson had spoken of farmworker children dying from pesticide exposure. He was invited to be the celebrity who helped Chavez break his fast.

On Sunday, August 21, gospel music played as Jackson made his entrance on the special stage erected at Forty Acres. Chavez was carried onto the stage by his sons Paul and Anthony, one arm draped around each, in a Christlike pose. The crowd of thousands stayed silent at his request. Major church leaders were notably absent, and the biggest names belonged to Hollywood stars. Ethel Kennedy gave him the host as he broke the thirty-six-day fast, with his mother, Juana, looking on. The ninety-six-year-old woman held up a small cross of twigs, made by one of Cesar's grandchildren. The cross would be passed on to others who pledged to continue the fast.

"The fast will go on in hundreds of distant places and it will multiply among thousands and then millions of caring people until every poisoned grape is off the supermarket shelves and the fast will endure until the fields are safe for farm workers, the environment is preserved for future generations, and our food is once again a source of nourishment and life," Fernando Chavez read in a statement from his father.

Hartmire had been present for all Chavez's major fasts, each different, but each beginning "inside Cesar's heart and soul," Hartmire said in his homily. "Many people cannot or will not understand his actions. But it should not be a surprise to anyone. He has always led us by his example. He has always led with his own body. Some people lead with their words or their promises or their threats. Cesar has always led us with his deeds, with his actions."

Hartmire's words masked some creeping doubts. Unlike the first two fasts, the drama of this longest, painful sacrifice had not produced significant movement. The growers ignored the fast. Hartmire, the true believer since 1962, began to wonder what Chavez could do next. Hartmire occasionally confided his doubts to his coworkers, including Paul Chavez. Yet when Dolores Huerta and Oscar Mondragon asked Hartmire to run for secretary-treasurer of the union at the convention a few weeks after the fast, he agreed.

In the wake of the fast and its lack of results came another round of purges at La Paz. The charges were familiar. Chavez accused staff members of sabotage and collaboration with growers. Some were accused of theft, charges that blocked them from collecting unemployment and saved the union money. In late 1988, Chavez called the FBI to investigate what he described as two threatening phone calls on his direct line that came from within La Paz. Chavez described one caller as "a white male about 30 years of age whom he envisioned as a college professor type because he was so articulate during his statements."

At the same time, through the circuitous route of a divorce case, the UFW was notified that a former accountant had embezzled hundreds of thousands of dollars. The money had been slated for the Fresno housing projects, and the fact that the theft had escaped notice for more than two years spoke to the movement's sloppy bookkeeping. Hartmire, now secretary-treasurer, had been in charge of financial management when the money disappeared. He tried to talk to Chavez as soon as the news broke, but the union president said they would discuss the theft at the upcoming board meeting.

Chavez sat in his special black rubberized rocking chair as he ran the January 1989 meeting of the UFW and its eighteen related entities. When the meeting turned to former accountant Bryce Basey and his embezzlement, Hartmire found himself the target of an orchestrated attack, almost like a Game: Hartmire had supervised Basey. Chavez had never trusted the accountant. How could he have pulled off the theft? Perhaps he had had help inside? One executive board member not in on the Game said no one could possibly think Chris Hartmire was involved. Silence.

Chavez appointed a committee to suggest how to proceed, and Hartmire left the meeting. It did not take him long to realize his life with the union was over. He called a family summit to explain. "I always figured that Hartmire and Chavez were for the ages, like Gilbert and Sullivan, bacon and eggs, gin and tonic," the Hartmires' eldest son, John, wrote to his father. "Perhaps Cesar has outgrown the struggle he gave life to. I think the growers sense that, which is probably why they have not made any move toward the bargaining table."

When Hartmire met with Chavez to formally resign, Huerta was there, too, to bear witness. They told Hartmire he had become disloyal—another Marshall Ganz. Helen Chavez cried as Chris and Pudge Hartmire packed up their trailer and left La Paz. Cesar had a worker follow their car.

The departure shocked even those who knew Chavez well. "It's difficult to believe that you of all people could ever have a taint on loyalty or trust," Marion Moses wrote Hartmire.

Richard Cook had succeeded Hartmire as head of the farmworker ministry and worked for the union for years. He grieved for his friend, and for the movement. "Cesar is just too complex. The little bastard is a genius but a destructive one," Cook wrote to Hartmire. "I expect he will eventually cut down everything and everyone until only he and Dolores are left. Right back where they began."

"In a way, I got what was coming to me," Hartmire wrote in his journal. "I went along with a lot of rotten stuff . . . I not only went along, I interpreted these events so that Cesar would be protected. I rationalized and excused many things he did for the sake of *la causa* and the NFWM. I ignored certain truths and told a lot of half-truths in order to show the UFW and Cesar in the best possible light."

Chavez turned on other longtime advisers, though none as publicly or viciously. At least one executive board member was sure his phone was tapped and that Chavez had people spy on board members. Chavez questioned the ethics of Frank Denison, who had done legal work for the corporations for many years. Chavez laid out a case against Denison on a series of three-by-five index cards, twisting the lawyer's counsel into conflict-of-interest charges. Denison had advised Chavez that the pension fund should not invest in housing, not reimburse the union for office space and other services, nor enroll the union's own staff in the pension plan—all sound recommendations, but not the advice Chavez wanted to hear.

Max Avalos had worked with Hartmire to raise millions of dollars in food contributions for strikers. At a meeting in 1981, he had pointed to a white wall and said that if Cesar said the wall was black, the wall was black. Eight years later, Chavez accused Avalos of Communist ties and severed all contact.

"Unity is our most valuable asset" was the slogan for the 1990 convention. Chavez warned that they must guard against a campaign to destroy the union through character assassination and infiltration. "That is why our unity is our most valuable asset. Viva la causa!" The unity slogan gave way to "The Indestructible Spirit," the theme of Founder's Day in 1991 and the 1992 convention. Chavez busied himself writing out instructions by hand on how the delegates should be selected. The convention began with an 8:00 A.M. mass and adjourned by 3:30 P.M.

The only deviation from routine resolutions came when Chavez announced that Huerta would take on a special title, vice president emeritus, and step away from her union job. On September 14, 1988, Huerta had been protesting outside a $1,000-a-person fund-raiser for President George Bush at the St. Francis Hotel in San Francisco. Bush opposed the grape boycott. Police told the crowd to move and when they did not disperse fast enough attacked several people with batons. Huerta, 110 pounds and just over five feet tall, suffered two broken ribs and a ruptured spleen. She sued and was awarded a record settlement of $825,000. Publicly, she explained her departure from the UFW as a time-out; others said she had rejected Chavez's insistence that the settlement money belonged to the union.

Gradually La Paz became a ghost town. Some, such as Father Ken Irrgang, who had lived at La Paz for many years, decided to leave. Others were thrown out. A mix-up about labels in the print shop one afternoon turned into an hour-and-a-half tirade from Chavez about the impropriety of a farewell lunch for his son Paul, who was moving to Fresno to oversee the housing projects. Some people quit before they could become targets, and others left under a cloud of suspicion.

"I keep hoping and praying CC will bounce back from whatever happened to him after the fast, but it sounds like he's worse if anything," Irrgang wrote to Hartmire. "I just can't shake my loyalty to the UFW cause, but CC's behavior is heartbreaking—especially how far he is in reality from the image so many good people have of him."

Chavez's image grew in strength with distance from the fields. He accumulated awards and honors at home and abroad. He was one of five celebrities honored with Univision's Premio Encuentro award, along with singer Celia Cruz and baseball star Fernando Valenzuela. The Mexican government bestowed on Chavez its highest prize, the Aguila Azteca. Most of his family and UFW board members accompanied Chavez to accept the award in November 1990. He had a private audience with Mexican president Carlos Salinas.

One of the most meaningful honors came in the Coachella Valley, where Filipino workers had gone on strike in 1965 for $1.40 an hour. For many years, Chavez's name had been anathema in the valley. Cities denied the UFW permits for rallies, judges enjoined Chavez from picketing, growers cursed him. On October 23, 1990, Coachella became the first district to name a school after Cesar Chavez.

"In this world it is possible to accumulate great wealth and to live in opulence, but a life built on those things alone leaves a shallow legacy," Chavez said at the dedication ceremony. Coachella school board president James Rice compared Chavez to Don Quixote, who dared to dream the impossible dream. Superintendent Al Mijares said Chavez touched the students' hearts.

He toured the school hand in hand with five-year-old Adam Rodriguez, posed with toddlers, signed autographs, shook hands, and answered questions. A fourth-grade class showed Chavez their pillow-lined bathtub, where students could relax with a book when they finished assignments. They asked him to jump in, and he smilingly obliged. He watched kids solve math problems and said math had been his favorite subject. He helped students plant a tree in his honor. "Mr. Chavez, you are an inspiration to all of us. We share your vision of a peaceful world, a world of understanding and hope," read ten-year-old Melanie Rodriguez.

"We want farmworkers' children to be just as proud of their parents' profession as other children are," Chavez said in his speech. He was introduced by nine-year-old Javier Reyes, who said: "He encourages me and so many people to do our best each day."

CHAPTER 40

Three Funerals

Death comes to all of us, and we do not get to choose the time or the circumstances of our dying. The hardest thing of all is to die rightly.

Cesar Chavez was at his mother's bedside on December 14, 1991, when Juana Estrada Chavez passed away. She was ninety-nine. She left behind five children, thirty-three grandchildren, eighty-three great-grandchildren, and two great-great-grandchildren.

The rosary was three days later at Our Lady of Guadalupe, the San Jose church around the corner from the Chavez home. The original church building, which Cesar had helped Father McDonnell put together, had become an auxiliary hall when a new church was completed in 1967. After an all-night vigil, Juana's funeral mass was held on the morning of December 18.

Mariachis played as one representative from each grandchild's family placed a long-stemmed red rose on the casket, where they were braided together to stay in place. Her grandchildren had compiled their recollections, delivered in a speech entitled "Remembering Nana" that recalled her love of mariachis, herbal remedies, and card games with Librado; her lectures about boys, her turkey stuffing, and her prayers for others; and above all her lessons about courage and respect and her refusal to allow her family to be victimized.

"She was a wise woman who fulfilled God's commandments by loving and serving her neighbors even to the point of sacrifice," Cesar said, delivering his eulogy first in English and then in Spanish, for the many farmworkers who crowded into the church. "We are here because her spirit of love and service touched and moved our lives. The force that is generated by that spirit of love is more powerful than any force on earth. It will never be stopped."

Cesar spoke of the richness of his mother's legacy, not in dollars but in inspiration. "She had the gift of faith, that gift of knowing what is truly important in this life." He looked up from the yellow-lined sheets of paper with his handwritten speech and added spontaneously, "And that's quite a gift." Then he resumed his stilted reading.

"Death comes to all of us, and we do not get to choose the time or the circumstances of our dying. The hardest thing of all is to die rightly. Juana Chavez died rightly. She served her God and her neighbor."

At the cemetery, Cesar lingered as he carefully spread his handful of dirt the entire length of his mother's casket. He stood alone for a long time, tan jacket over his white pinstriped shirt and black vest, watching as the long line of mourners passed, each throwing in dirt. His sister Rita, following her mother's wishes, wore a gray checked suit. Juana Chavez was buried alongside her husband under a headstone inscribed with an image of the Virgen de Guadalupe and a one-word epitaph: MOTHER.

By the following fall, another seminal figure in Chavez's life was near death. Fred Ross died on September 27, 1992, at the age of eighty-two. On Sunday, October 4, his family buried Ross's ashes under a tree on Mount Tamalpais near his home in Marin County, overlooking the Pacific Ocean. They reminisced and cried and sang some of his favorite songs, including "The Ballad of Joe Hill." Fred Ross Jr. told his nephew that the spirit of the boy's grandfather would never die, just like Joe Hill. The family sat down to plan a memorial service.

"Because you were so close to him and he so loved you, we would like you to honor him by giving the eulogy," Fred Ross Jr. wrote to Chavez. He enclosed the program they had planned, listing all the speakers.

Chavez might be forgiven his failure to respond promptly to the request. The list of names must have evoked complex feelings: Chris Hartmire, Jerry Cohen, Jessica Govea, Luis Valdez, Jim Drake, once so central to the movement in its moments of triumph. Chavez had sacrificed each of them in relentless pursuit of his vision. Now his top aides were largely relatives and hangers-on.

Chavez had no choice but to deliver the eulogy for his mentor. He wrote out seven pages of notes in pencil, tracing their friendship from the first encounter in San Jose. He wrote of his wonder when hundreds of people showed up at the first big CSO meeting. Cesar had gone home that night, he said, and told Helen, "What happened tonight is pure magic—and I'm going to learn it, come what may. I will not stop until I learn how to organize." To end the eulogy, he copied excerpts from letters that Ross had written in 1962 when Chavez began organizing in Delano, scared and alone.

The afternoon of the Ross memorial, guests milled about in the courtyard of the Delancey Street Foundation in San Francisco, many seeing one another for the first time in decades. There were hugs, tearful reunions, and some awkward greetings. Doug Adair, who once edited *El Malcriado* and now farmed dates in the Coachella Valley, shook hands with Paul Chavez, who had become one of his father's top aides. Liza Hirsch, thrown out of the union in 1978, arrived with Eliseo Medina, who was rising in the ranks of the Service Employees International Union. Larry Tramutt had changed his name to Tramutola and started a consulting business. Mario Bustamante came with his wife, Gretchen Laue, whom he met when she worked on the 1979 lettuce strike, and their three young children. Jerry Brown had just run for president a third time and came in cowboy boots, jeans, and a black jacket with his campaign's 800 number on the back. Marshall Ganz, who had graduated from Harvard after a twenty-eight-year leave of absence, talked with Tom Dalzell, who worked as an attorney for the electrical workers union. They shook their heads at the strangeness of the scene.

Jerry Cohen, master of ceremonies, opened with one of his favorite Fred Ross axioms: a good organizer is a social arsonist who goes around setting people on fire. Looking around the room, Cohen noted, "Even in death, Fred is a great organizer."

"We met in the trenches," Luis Valdez said, recalling the 1966 DiGiorgio campaign where Fred Ross became his teacher. Ross taught Valdez to bring people together, to be disciplined, and to follow through. Just months before Ross died, Valdez had approached him with the idea of making a movie about Chavez's early success organizing Oxnard farmworkers in the CSO. Ross had been enthusiastic, and the two men went to La Paz to talk with Chavez. He said he wanted the union to be remembered, not him, and vetoed the idea. He could not bring himself to cede control of his image.

At the Ross memorial, Valdez led the Teatro Campesino in songs from the DiGiorgio campaign. Everyone rose to their feet, locked arms, and swayed to "Solidaridad Pa' Siempre."

Speaker after speaker obliquely echoed Cohen's observation that Ross had brought them back together. Jim Drake, characteristically blunt, alluded most directly to the bitterness and anger of many who had been cast out of the union. Drake thanked Ross for reuniting them and paraphrased a line he attributed to the author Toni Morrison: we must lay down our sword and shield and come back to the family.

After a half dozen speeches, Cohen introduced the man who had torn the family apart. Chavez had a terrible cold, and his congestion made the speech more painful. He was so hoarse he could barely talk and punctuated the eulogy with coughs. His affection for Ross came through nonetheless. He ended with a typical Ross story about their last time together, true to the spirit of the visit if not the facts. Ross was as sharp as ever, Chavez said, and outwalked his visitors. "I shall miss him very much," Chavez concluded, and the audience rose to its feet in applause.

Chavez went to many funerals in the 1990s. He would call his brother Richard, who had built himself a house just a mile from La Paz, and drag him off to a rosary or vigil or mass. When Cesar was home, his days no longer filled up with meetings and calls. His office had no lines of people waiting for an audience. To Richard's surprise, Cesar took a week off and the two brothers went to Mexico. Cesar delighted in his grandchildren, many of whom lived at La Paz or nearby. He hiked the hills of La Paz with them, introduced them to jazz, and called the little ones his "skididobopi-deboppopbo." Some grandchildren spent more time with him than his own children had when they were young. Christmas and Easter were big family holidays at La Paz. On March 31, 1993, his sixty-sixth birthday, Chavez cooked an Indian feast for his extended family. Ten days later, he joined the children in the annual Easter egg hunt.

One particularly dark cloud hovered over La Paz: a trial that threatened to bankrupt the UFW. The Bruce Church company, one of the largest lettuce growers in California, had never signed a contract after the 1979 strike. The issue was not financial. Bruce Church offered to top wages in the UFW's other contracts. The primary disagreement centered on who could determine whether workers were in "good standing." The company insisted that paying dues should be the only criterion. The UFW wanted the right to discipline or fire workers who did not comply with other union requirements, such as attending meetings or protest rallies. The two sides had fought bitterly for more than a decade, before the ALRB, in the courts, and in the press.

Though the grape boycott had never gained traction in the 1980s, the UFW had more success targeting stores that sold Red Coach lettuce,

Bruce Church's top-of-the-line produce. When Chavez spent more than $1 million targeting Lucky stores with the high-tech boycott, the supermarket chain—which bought 10 percent of Bruce Church's lettuce—agreed to buy its produce elsewhere. Other stores followed.

Bruce Church sued, charging the UFW made libelous statements and illegally threatened supermarkets not to carry Red Coach lettuce. Bruce Church had substantial land in Arizona, which banned secondary boycotts, so the company filed suit in Yuma in 1984. Four years later, a jury returned a $5.4 million verdict against the UFW, concluding the union had used false and deceptive publicity to discourage consumers from buying Red Coach lettuce and had threatened stores that sold the lettuce. An appeals court found the underlying Arizona anti-boycott law was flawed and threw the verdict out. The case was remanded for a new trial on narrower grounds, and Chavez returned to court in 1993.

The union had assets of less than $2 million, and a loss could be crippling. Chavez had recruited Huerta to come back and help prepare the union's defense, tracking down witnesses who could bolster some of the union's claims, such as allegations that Bruce Church workers were sexually harassed. Chavez fasted for several days before he was due in court.

He was sworn in as a witness in the Yuma courtroom the afternoon of April 21 and grilled for several hours. He returned to court the next morning for a second day on the stand. James Clark, one of the Bruce Church attorneys, questioned Chavez from 9:30 A.M. to noon and again from 1:30 P.M. to 3:00 P.M. The testimony did not go well. Clark hammered home the points that had won the case for the company the first time: Had the union not threatened to ruin the reputation of stores if they carried Red Coach lettuce? How could the union accuse Bruce Church of condoning child labor, sexual harassment, and pesticide poisoning without offering examples? How could the union accuse supermarkets of supporting those abuses by buying Bruce Church produce?

Chavez was forced to acknowledge that the union had sent out mailings claiming Bruce Church had bargained in bad faith—even though that finding was overruled on appeal, and the union had actually been found guilty of the same charge.

Clark entered into evidence flyers with headlines such as "Alpha Beta Stores and Child Abuse," the UFW's effort to link supermarkets to unsubstantiated assertions about Bruce Church. Clark quizzed Chavez about his 1983 memo on the high-tech boycott, which had been strategically leaked to supermarket executives to warn them about the damage they faced if they did not stop buying Bruce Church lettuce.

Chavez tried to wriggle out of earlier assertions that the boycott had caused Lucky stores to remove Red Coach lettuce. He had claimed victory to motivate the troops, Chavez said, but he could not say for certain why Lucky had stopped buying Bruce Church lettuce.

Clark was incredulous. "Mr. Chavez, let me just ask you one more time, did you ever, before this date, testify that it was not your opinion and the opinion of the union that the cause of Lucky stopping to purchase lettuce from Bruce Church was your fault?"

"Yes, we said that," Chavez replied.

"This is the first time you ever took a position different from that?" Clark pressed.

"No, what I said was, Lucky said it wasn't because of us."

The Yuma courthouse where Chavez testified was about ten miles from the homestead where he had grown up in his grandfather's house along the Gila North Main canal. The crumbling ruins of the Chavez home and the fields his father once farmed were now owned by the Bruce Church company.

Chavez returned at the end of his second day in court to the small San Luis, Arizona, home of Doña Maria Hau, a former farmworker and long-time UFW supporter. She had given up her bedroom so that the UFW leader could be comfortable. He broke his fast with a light supper and retired to his room around 10:00 P.M.

Chavez was usually an early riser. When he did not appear by 9:00 A.M., UFW secretary-treasurer David Martinez entered the bedroom. Chavez was lying on his back in bed, fully clothed, union and court documents scattered about. Martinez tried to waken him, and realized Chavez was dead. When the paramedics arrived, a book on Native American art lay on his chest, upside down.

Cesar Chavez was sixty-six years old. Given his genes, he had often confidently predicted a long life. "If I don't get hit by a car or a bullet, I will live to be at least 100 and active through 95," he once said. "Death is nothing. I already took care of the fear. You cannot lead if you're afraid. And you cannot lead if you're not in front." In the end, he barely outlived his mother.

His body was flown in a chartered plane to Bakersfield, where Helen Chavez and her children waited on the tarmac. The news spread quickly. Marion Moses, working with a coffee cooperative in El Salvador, found an urgent message to call the Kern County coroner, who needed to speak with Chavez's personal physician. Luis Valdez, traveling in an entourage with the Mexican president, confirmed the news on a portable radio-telephone, and began to cry. He headed back to La Paz to help choreograph the funeral. At Helen's request, LeRoy Chatfield and Chris Hartmire returned to La Paz to help make arrangements.

Chavez's family commissioned an autopsy and said he died of natural causes. The evidence was inconclusive, but the circumstances of his death were consistent with an arrhythmia that could have been triggered by an electrolyte imbalance brought on by his fast.

Cesar had left two instructions about his funeral. He wanted the service at Forty Acres, and he wanted his brother Richard to build a simple pine coffin. Richard got specifications from the mortuary and went to work. The coffin took him thirty-eight hours to build.

Almost everyone came back to Delano. Chavez's body lay in state at Forty Acres, dressed in a white guayabera shirt, turquoise rosary beads in his hand. On the inside of the pine coffin lid was the red-white-and-black UFW flag. Tens of thousands of mourners streamed past from 10:30 A.M. on Wednesday, April 28, when the doors opened, through the all-night vigil.

They mourned a man who had changed their lives, treasuring private memories, often of moments more human than historic. Wendy Goepel would always remember the magic of taking Chavez to see Diego Rivera murals in Washington, D.C. Jerry Cohen went back to the room in the Stardust Motel where he and Chavez had met John Giumarra at two-thirty in the morning. Jim Rutkowski recalled waiting hours to brief Chavez before an important court appearance because he stopped en route to play handball with farmworkers; when he finally arrived, Chavez knowledgeably answered his lawyer's questions, standing on his head. Eliseo Medina remembered the leader who had slept on the floor of a Chicago apartment and kept boycotters awake with his snores.

As the three-mile funeral procession wound through the streets of Delano, Medina collected signatures on a UFW flag to save for his twelve-year-old daughter, Elena. One hundred twenty pallbearers took turns of three minutes carrying the heavy casket. Marchers were still lining up in Memorial Park when the procession reached Forty Acres, the banner of the Virgen de Guadalupe leading the way. Mourners carried ten thousand white gladiolas, Helen's favorite flower, an echo of the ten thousand roses distributed at Gandhi's funeral. In front of the large tent that covered much of the lawn at Forty Acres was a giant banner with a likeness of Chavez and the slogan VIVA CESAR CHAVEZ. Ten thousand rented chairs seated less than a quarter of the crowd, but many preferred the shade of the trees to the heat of the crowded tent. Cardinal Roger Mahony was the chief celebrant, joined by two dozen concelebrants. At the end of the stage, tall and gray, was Father Donald McDonnell.

The next day, Chavez was buried in a private ceremony at La Paz, next to the graves of his beloved dogs, Boycott and Huelga.

Epilogue

Forty years after she walked out of the fields on strike in September 1965, Consuelo Nuño picked grapes in a Delano vineyard. She worked for Hronis, a company owned by the family that *El Malcriado* had exposed in the early 1960s for cheating sugar beet workers.

Her arms ached after eight hours of harvesting grapes, but hot showers helped. She thought about retiring but enjoyed the camaraderie of the work. She had health insurance, though most of her coworkers did not. Like most growers, Hronis hired crews through labor contractors, the middlemen whom the UFW had once driven out of the fields.

Nuño lived just a few miles from Forty Acres. The old headquarters stood largely deserted in 2005, the front lawn overgrown. The UFW had no contracts in the Delano vineyards.

Chavez's legacy loomed large in Delano nonetheless. As he had foreseen, Mexican Americans once shut out of power had become the establishment—in city hall, on the school board, and in the courts, the venues that had once been bastions of Anglo power. Students attended Cesar Chavez High School, which had opened in 2003 on the east side of town. The school board chose the name although the decision cost $100,000; the grower who sold the land had specified he would collect damages if the school were named after a person he found objectionable.

"He's the most important citizen Delano has ever had," said grape grower Martin Zaninovich, who once led the fight against Chavez. "And we just have to acknowledge that." The UFW never won an election at Zaninovich's Jasmine Vineyards. His workers had an employee handbook and profit sharing, and many sent their children to college. In retrospect, Zaninovich said, Chavez had brought attention to some important issues, though he was never a labor leader.

In the Delano vineyards, younger workers knew little if anything about Cesar Chavez. Many were recent immigrants. They associated the name only with a famous Mexican boxer. But for older workers like Nuño, Chavez's lessons about dignity outlived his union. "They taught us how to defend ourselves," she said. She tried to pass that on to the next generation.

In the cities and on the college campuses where he so often spoke in later years, Chavez's face was painted on murals and etched in stone. His name was written on street signs, his words invoked to inspire young people, and his slogan "Si se puede" turned into a universal rallying cry.

Jared Rivera was fourteen years old when Chavez died. Jared's father had grown up in a migrant family; Jared attended the University of California at Berkeley, where the Cesar Chavez Student Center sits near the hall where Chavez asked the crowd to donate their lunch money in 1966 to bail his wife out of jail. Rivera joined MEChA, one of the few Chicano organizations that thrived into the twenty-first century. He studied Chicano history and decided to work as a community activist and labor organizer. Sixteen years after Chavez's death, Rivera pointed to a tattoo of the black eagle on his arm: "I'm an organizer because of him."

Around the country, thousands of people whose lives were shaped by Chavez worked to reconcile conflicting emotions. They had worshipped Chavez and become disillusioned, basked in his tutelage and endured his wrath, admired his courage and despaired his decisions. Each wrestled privately to come to terms with a personal sense of Chavez's legacy. For some, that struggle took many decades. For others, reconciliation came more easily.

Gustavo Gutierrez still lived in the Phoenix house where Cesar Chavez began his fast in May 1972. I interviewed him in his living room in the fall of 2011. His ample frame filled the chair, his large face encased in a bushy beard and white mane, a gray ponytail flowing down his back. Every so often he reached for a plastic water bottle, revealing the stumps on his hand where he lost fingers during an early accident in the fields. He lifted the water bottle over his enormous stomach and squirted a small dog he was training not to bark.

Gutierrez reminisced about the first time he met Chavez, in the spring of 1965. Chavez and Fred Ross conducted a training session at the Arizona migrant workers organization where Gutierrez worked. Ross came in with a scrapbook full of stories about the CSO. Chavez explained how to conduct house meetings. A year later, Gutierrez joined the last four days of the march to Sacramento, carrying a sign that said ARIZONA FARM-WORKERS SUPPORT CALIFORNIA FARMWORKERS. In 1970, he went to Delano to witness the grape growers sign the first contracts, and from there to Salinas to help with the lettuce strike.

The memories were still fresh, though Gutierrez was seventy-nine years old: The pride he felt marching in the *peregrinación*. The admiration when he watched Chavez plan strategy. The annoyance when Chavez challenged Gutierrez's car allowance. The disappointment when direct mail appeals began to carry Cesar Chavez's name as the return address, instead of the UFW's. The defiance when Manuel Chavez delivered the message that Gutierrez should shut down the Arizona farmworkers union. The anger when his efforts to help Arizona farmworkers were undermined.

Gutierrez smiled, at peace with his memories. He embraced Cesar Chavez in all his complexity. "Cesar was my mentor," Gutierrez said. Palms up, he held his right hand above his head and lowered his left near the floor. On balance, he said, the good outweighed the bad. It was not even close.

Acknowledgments

I am grateful to all the people who helped me over the last nine years to understand Cesar Chavez, who educated me not only about the farm worker movement but about agriculture, labor unions, organizing, social movements, California history, Catholicism, and Mexican culture. If I tried to thank everyone, I would surely leave some out. Many are cited in the list of interviewees; some whose contributions were immeasurable do not appear. My profound thanks for all the conversations and insights, the cups of tea and the glasses of wine.

I am indebted to those who made the history, and to those who preserved it. I am grateful that Cesar Chavez recognized the historic nature of his quest and that advisers such as LeRoy Chatfield and archivists such as Philip Mason helped preserve the documentation. Chatfield's work both in the early days of the movement and in more recent years has provided scholars with an invaluable resource. I owe special thanks to the staff at the Reuther Library at Wayne State, who have over the course of almost a decade of visits been unfailingly helpful and supportive, often under trying circumstances. My thanks to Elizabeth Myers, William LeFevre, and, especially, Mary J. Wallace, for her patience and unflagging help in untangling the audio archives that were so crucial to my research.

Jeffrey Burns at the archives of the Archdiocese of San Francisco guided me not only through relevant collections there but pointed me to others. Thanks also to Kevin Feeney, archivist at the Archdiocese of Los Angeles, and to Polly Armstrong and Ignacio Ornelas at the Green Library at Stanford. Several colleagues graciously shared observations and research. Thanks to Felipe Hinojosa, Gabriel Thompson, and Bruce Perry.

A fellowship from the National Endowment for the Humanities

enabled me to complete my research. A two-week stay at Mesa Refuge was a writer's dream.

For the photographic display, I'm indebted to Mary Wallace and to Wendy Vissar, whose creative counsel and technical expertise helped shape a compelling visual narrative.

Writing is a solitary pursuit, but I had a wonderful support team. My agent, Gloria Loomis, believed in the book from the beginning. At Bloomsbury, I'm indebted to Laura Phillips, Rob Galloway, and especially to Peter Ginna, whose thoughtful editing and guidance made this a far better book. John Hoeffel caught errors that no one else did. My three readers helped me think through both what I wanted to say and how to say it; many thanks to Sam Enriquez, Geoff Mohan, and above all to my husband, Michael Muskal, for his wise counsel and enduring faith and encouragement.

Thanks to everyone who understood the importance of this biography, and especially to those who trusted me to tell the story of someone who changed their lives.

Bibliography

This book is drawn chiefly from the extensive array of primary sources available in more than a dozen public archives. In addition to written documentation, the UFW archives at Wayne State University include hundreds of tape recordings of union board meetings, conferences, and conversations. In the course of my research, I listened to more than fifteen hundred hours of tapes, including recordings of thirty national executive board meetings between December 1973 and December 1980. Several dozen additional tapes of conferences, staff meetings, interviews, and public events between 1967 and 1981 also provided rich source material.

Audiotapes made between 1969 and 1975 by Jacques E. Levy, Chavez's official biographer, are also an invaluable resource, documenting many key junctures in the union's history. A third important source of tapes is available on the Farmworker Movement Documentation Project website; I relied in particular on a series of interviews conducted by Fred Ross, mainly in March 1969 (the Fred Ross Sr. Oral History Archive).

I was also privileged to have access to private collections of several key participants in the farm worker movement. In addition, Bruce Perry, who conducted research on Chavez for several years, generously shared with me written material and more than two hundred interviews recorded in the mid-1990s.

Over the last seven years, I have interviewed more than eighty individuals who knew Chavez in a wide range of capacities. Those conversations helped me craft the biographical narrative and provided essential background. They are cited where relevant and a full list of interviewees is included. All quotations in the book, however, are drawn from primary sources.

Abbreviations

Abbreviations for individual archives follow their identification below. The Walter P. Reuther Labor Library at Wayne State University in Detroit is the repository for archives of the UFW and more than a dozen related collections. I use the following abbreviations for collections cited:

ADMIN	UFW Administration
ADMIN3	UFW Administration Part III
CENT	UFW Central Administration
DH	Dolores Huerta Papers
GANZ	Marshall Ganz Papers
INFO	UFW Information and Research
NFWM	National Farm Worker Ministry
NFWA	National Farm Workers Association
OOP1	Office of the President, Part I
OOP2	Office of the President, Part II
OOP3	Office of the President, Part III
ROSS	Fred Ross Collection
TAY	Ronald Taylor Papers
UFWOC	United Farm Workers Organizing Committee
UFWA	United Farm Workers Audio archives

Other abbreviations in the notes and text:

NEB	National Executive Board of the United Farm Workers
ALRB	California Agricultural Labor Relations Board
ALRA	California Agricultural Labor Relations Act
NARA	National Archives and Research Administration

Archives

Jerry Cohen Papers, Amherst College Archives and Special Collections, Amherst College Library

El Teatro Campesino Papers, University of California at Santa Barbara (ETC)

Farm Labor Collection, Archives of the Archdiocese of Los Angeles, Los Angeles (AALA)

Field Foundation Papers, Briscoe Center for American History, University of Texas, Austin

Gerald Ford Presidential Library, Ann Arbor, Michigan

Herman Gallegos Papers, Special Collections, Cecil Green Library, Stanford University

Industrial Areas Foundation Records, University of Illinois, Chicago (IAF UIC)

Industrial Areas Foundation Records, Briscoe Center for American History, University of Texas, Austin (IAF Austin)

Jacques E. Levy Research Collection on Cesar Chavez, Yale Collection of Western Americana, Beinecke Rare Book and Manuscript Library (JEL)

Maricopa County Organizing Project Records, Arizona State University, Phoenix (MCOP)

Donald McDonnell/Spanish Mission Band papers, Archives of the Archdiocese of San Francisco, Menlo Park (AASF)

Ronald Reagan Presidential Library, Simi Valley, California

Fred Ross Papers, Special Collections, Cecil Green Library, Stanford University

San Joaquin Valley Farm Labor Collection, California State University, Fresno (SJVFLC)

Emil Schwarzhaupt Foundation Papers, University of Chicago, Chicago (ESF)

Synanon Foundation Archives, UCLA

United Packinghouse Workers of America Papers, Wisconsin Historical Society, Madison (UPWA)

United States Department of Labor, Record Group 174, Records Relating to the Mexican Labor ("Bracero") Program, National Archives and Research Administration, San Bruno

Private Collections

Cois Byrd papers

Tom Dalzell papers

Chris Hartmire papers

Eliseo Medina papers

Jessica Govea papers

Dissertations

Brown, Jerald. "The United Farm Workers Grape Strike and Boycott." Ph.D. diss., Cornell University, 1972.

Pitti, Gina. "To Hear About God in Spanish." Ph.D. diss., Stanford University, 2003.

Rose, Margaret. "Women in the United Farm Workers." Ph.D. diss., University of California, Los Angeles, 1988.

Thompson, Mark. "The Agricultural Workers Organizing Committee, 1959–1961." M.A. thesis, Cornell University, 1963.

Books

Bardacke, Frank. *Trampling out the Vintage.* New York: Verso, 2011.

Dunne, John Gregory. *Delano: The Story of the California Grape Strike.* New York: Farrar, Straus and Giroux, 1967.

Ganz, Marshall. *Why David Sometimes Wins.* New York: Oxford University Press, 2009.

Garcia, Matthew. *From the Jaws of Victory.* Berkeley: University of California Press, 2012.

Levy, Jacques. *Cesar Chavez: Autobiography of La Causa.* New York: W. W. Norton, 1975.

London, Joan, and Henry Anderson. *So Shall Ye Reap.* New York: Thomas Y. Crowell, 1970.

Matthiessen, Peter. *Sal Si Puedes (Escape if You Can): Cesar Chavez and the New American Revolution.* Berkeley: University of California Press, 1969.

Mitchell, Don. *They Saved the Crops.* Athens: University of Georgia Press, 2012.

Pawel, Miriam. *The Union of Their Dreams.* New York: Bloomsbury Press, 2009.

Ross, Fred. *Conquering Goliath: Cesar Chavez at the Beginning.* Keene, CA: El Taller Grafico Press, 1989.

Taylor, Ronald B. *Chavez and the Farm Workers.* Boston: Beacon Press, 1975.

Websites

Farmworker Documentation Project (FMDP), www.farmworkermovement.com

Fred Ross Sr. Oral History Archive (Ross Tapes), www.farmworkermovement
.com/media/oral_history

FBI files (only a fraction of the files are available online), http://foia.fbi.gov
/foiaindex/chavez.htm

California Agricultural Labor Relations Board, http://alrb.ca.gov

Interviews

Douglass Adair, August 15, 2010

Henry P. Anderson, March 31 and June 2, 2011

Tom Barry, January 20, 2012

Jim Braun, June 27, 2012

Kit Bricca, July 9, 2013

Wendy Goepel Brooks, August 19, 2011, and June 7, 2013

Mario Bustamante, May 13, 2005, June 22 and September 3, 2008

Chava Bustamante, June 17, 2008

Cois Byrd, February 19, 2008

Terence Cannon, June 14, 2012

Ron Caplan, November 28, 2011

William Carder, June 26, 2006, and June 18, 2008

LeRoy Chatfield, February 28, 2013

Anna Chavez, January 19, 2012

Librado Chavez Jr., March 7, 2012

Bob (Jasper) Coffman, December 17, 2011

Jerry Cohen, April 23 and June 5, 2008, June 5, 2009

Ida Cousino, September 17 and December 17, 2011

Jerry Cox, May 25, 2012

Tom Dalzell, June 26, 2006

Sue Carhart Darweesh, June 15, 2012

Mark Day, November 17, 2011

Alfredo DeAvila, February 2, 2012

Frank Denison, February 12, 2008

Don Devereux, August 31, 2011

Susan Drake, September 22, 2011

Peter Edelman, November 28, 2012

Ellen Eggers, May 7, June 28, and December 17, 2008

Bill (Rampujan) Esher, September 20, 2011

Bob Fitch, June 21, 2013

Ed Frankel, September 11, 2011

Herman Gallegos, March 31, 2011

Marshall Ganz, October 2, 2005

Margaret Govea, March 2, 2007, and June 9, 2008

Gustavo Gutierrez, November 1, 2011

Chris Hartmire, June 23, August 20, September 19, and October 31, 2006, and March 14, 2007

David Havens, September 26, 2012

Joe Herman, July 18, 2006

Ruben Hernandez, November 30, 2011

Fred Hirsch, September 22, 2011

Tom Hubbard, February 3, 2012

Donna Haber Kornberg, September 15, 2011

Henry Lacayo, November 21, 2011

Gretchen Laue, June 22 and September 3, 2008

Michael Lee, March 26, 2013

Sabino Lopez, August 5, 2005, and September 24, 2007

Howard Marguleas, February 2, 2006, and March 14, 2011

Philip Mason, October 20, 2008

Peter Mattheissen, July 15, 2013

Donald McDonnell, January 26 and November 11, 2011

Eliseo Medina, February 22, July 3, and December 29, 2008

Liza Hirsch Medina, May 8, 2006

Mike Miller, July 11, 2012

Crosby Milne, January 26, 2007

Marion Moses, June 20, 2006, January 27, 2011, and February 25, 2012

John Moyer, April 5, 2011

Kathy Murguia, November 25, 2011, and August 3, 2012

Tom Nassif, February 18, 2011

Sandy Nathan, May 17, 2007, February 25, 2008, and April 11 and June 18, 2008

Richard Ofshe, August 4, 2011

Antonio Orendain, December 11, 2011

Esther Padilla, May 21, 2008

Gilbert Padilla, June 20, 2007, May 21, 2008, and January 25, 2011

Rosario Pelayo, May 13, 2005

Jose Renteria, August 5, 2005

Cruz Reynoso, August 3, 2011

Virginia Rodriguez, March 30, 2011

Fred Ross Jr., February 24, 2005

Jim Rutkowski, September 12, 2011

Lloyd Saatjian, July 12, 2006

Joe Serda, July 11, 2006

Dave Smith, January 22, 2013

Bob Thompson, June 6, 2011

Art Torres, June 6, 2013

Larry Tramutola, January 26, 2011

Luis Valdez, August 14, 2011, and June 21, 2013

Don Villarejo, June 6, 2011

Scott Washburn, August 20, 2008, and November 1, 2011

Martin Zaninovich, October 2, 2006, and September 20, 2007

Notes

Prologue

1 **"mystical figure"** www.mindfully.org/Reform/Cesar-Chavez9nov84.htm

1 **argyle vest** Photo courtesy of Michael G. Lee

2 **pork tenderloin** menu from Commonwealth Club papers, Hoover Institution Library, Box 500, Folder 16

Chapter 1

Sources: Oral histories by Cesar, Rita, and Richard Chavez and other family members, the earliest and most complete conducted in the late 1960s by Jacques Levy. Primary interviews include: multiple interviews by Levy with Cesar Chavez; Chavez family interview by Levy, Jul. 1969; Rita Chavez interviewed by Levy, May 22, 1969; Bruce Perry, Aug. 7, 1995; Paradigm Productions, n.d.; Santa Clara County Oral History project, Aug. 22, 2011; National Park Service interview, Nov. 22, 2011; Richard Chavez interviewed by Levy, May 7, 1969, and Jun. 16, 1974; Ross, Mar. 1969; Cal State Northridge Oral History project, Mar. 14, 1997; Paradigm Productions, n.d.; Juana Chavez interviewed by Cesar, Sep. 5, 1984; author interviews with Hernandez, Mary Chavez, and Librado (Lenny) Chavez Jr.

7 **basic facts** 1930 Census

8 **crossed into Texas** In the 1930 census, Librado and Dorotea reported crossing the border in 1898. In later accounts, Librado offered slightly different dates, but 1898 appears most likely. Birthdates are similarly murky. Librado's obituary gave Aug. 17, 1881, as his birthday but in later records he gave his birth year as 1888, which would be more consistent with his accounts of crossing as a young child.

8 **thriving business** Tape of Juana Chavez interviewed by Cesar, Sep. 5, 1984, UFWA

8 **filed a claim** Deed, Yuma County Registrar-Recorder Office

8 **To the south** Map drawn by Richard Chavez, JEL, Box 20, Folder 430

9 **bought the cluster of buildings** Mortgages and deeds, Yuma County Recorder's office

10 **before she married** Details of Juana's life from Sep. 5, 1984, interview

13 **deeded the farm** Deed, Yuma County Recorder

13 **auctioned off** *Yuma Daily Sun*, legal announcements, Jul. 30, 1937; Oct. 29, 1937

13 **filed suit** *Yuma Daily Sun*, Dec. 7, 1937; Yuma County deeds

13 **sold the land** Yuma County deeds; *Yuma Daily Sun*, Jun. 9, 1939

Chapter 2

Sources: The account of the family's early years in California is drawn from multiple oral histories by Cesar, Rita, and Richard Chavez (see Chapter 1 notes); author interviews with Hernandez and Librado Chavez Jr.

15 **bestseller list** http://www.steinbeckinstitute.org/grapes_historical.html

17 **average student** Miguel Hidalgo Junior High school records, courtesy of Bruce Perry

18 **developed circuits** JEL, Box 5, Folder 181

19 **oversight in the grapes** JEL, Box 1, Folder 132

20 **dishonorably discharged** Manuel Chavez navy record, NARA

20 **one arrest** FBI files refer to a Jan. 24, 1944, arrest that was dismissed; no records from the case survive. Chavez never mentioned it other than noting on his navy application that he was arrested for "fighting." He often told a story about being arrested because he refused to sit on the Mexican side of the Delano movie theater, but I have found no documentation to support that incident.

20 **his application** Cesar Chavez Navy record, NARA

21 **honorably discharged** Ibid.

21 **Helen and Cesar** Helen Chavez interview, JEL, Folder 173; Rose, "Women in the United Farm Workers"

22 **they were married** Marriage certificate, Reno County Clerk

22 **$1.50 an hour** Hernandez interview

Chapter 3

Sources: Spanish Mission Band and McDonnell papers; Ross Papers; Pitti, Ph.D. thesis; *So Shall Ye Reap*; author interviews with McDonnell, Gallegos, Anderson, Librado Chavez Jr., and Cox.

25 147,000 Mexicans "Spanish Speaking Migrants in the Archdiocese of San Francisco," and "Report of the Missionary Apostolate, Pastoral Care of Spanish-Speaking People," AASF, Box A67

25 "Mitty saw the wisdom" Duggan autobiography, FMDP

25 to celebrate mass Leo Maher to McDonnell, Jan. 6, 1951, AASF, Box A67

26 unorthodox tactics Report of Spanish Mission Band, Sep. 7, 1950, AASF, Box A67

26 paid a call Ross diary, Ross Papers, Box 31, Folder 8

27 "Am I needed?" Ibid.

27 agreed to return Ibid. Whether Chavez ducked Ross that first night is unclear. In later years, he told an exaggerated version of the story. Richard and Helen Chavez both recounted that Cesar was skeptical of Ross initially, so it's possible Cesar's doubts as well as the late hour contributed to the cancellation of the first scheduled meeting. But the widely reported story about Cesar hiding for several nights from Ross is apocryphal.

27 dozen family members Richard Chavez, JEL, Box 5 Folder 176

28 "Chavez has real push" Ross diary, Jun. 9, 1958, Ross Papers, Box 31, Folder 8

28 two important qualities Ross, JEL, Box 6, Folder 196

29 Chavez later recalled Taylor, "Chavez and the Farm Workers," 81

30 "time for action" Address to the Catholic Council for the Spanish Speaking meeting in San Antonio, Texas, Apr. 1958, McDonnell archives, Box 10

Chapter 4

Sources: Chavez and Ross daily activity reports; Ross Papers; Ross interviews with Levy; author interviews with McDonnell and Gallegos.

32 Cesar dropped her off Ross, Apr. 4, 1969, JEL, Box 6, Folder 196

32 "question of power" Ibid.

33 "make up my mind" Chavez, JEL, Box 2, Folder 141

33 linoleum-floored front room Gallegos interview

34 "not good at speeches" "The Saga of Sal Si Puedes," 1953; Ross Papers, Box 22, Folder 15

35 four thousand new voters Ross to California Federation for Civic Unity, Nov. 17, 1952, CFCU Papers, Box 3, Folder 10, Bancroft Library

35 "most discouraging" "GOP Poll Check for Illiteracy Brings Protest," *San Jose Mercury News*, Nov. 5, 1952

35 "the potential leaders" Ross, n.d., IAF UIC, Box 12, Folder 189

36 "I share your feeling" Alinsky to Ross, Aug. 5, 1953, IAF UIC, Box 47, Folder 459

36 "nothing I'd like better" "Cesar Tries his Wings," Ross Papers, Box 20, Folder 17

37 Alinsky hired Chavez Ross to Chavez, Mar. 2, 1954, OOP1 Box 2, Folder 3

37 "one of the things he learned" Ross, May 28, 1969, JEL, Box 6, Folder 196

37 "man of sound principles" McDonnell, Jun. 21, 1954, OOP1 Box 2, Folder 4

38 made front-page news *Madera Tribune*, Jul. 14, 1954

38 "going from door-to-door" Ross to Chavez, Jul. 23, 1954, OOP1, Box 2, Folder 4

38 "interested in the Mexican vote" Chavez to Ross, Aug. 20, 1954, ROSS, Box 1, Folder 4

38 "tamales and buñuelos" Chavez to Ross, Dec. 21, 1954, ROSS, Box 1, Folder 7

38 Ross admonished Ross to Chavez, Apr. 6, 1955, OOP1 Box 2, Folder 6

38 demanded to know Chavez to Ross, May 15, 1955, ROSS Box 1, Folder 12

39 thought of Ross Linda Chavez, Paradigm Production transcript, FMDP

39 "were you on a diet" Alinsky to Chavez, Sep. 9, 1955, OOP1, Box 2, Folder 7

39 "feel like God" "Cesar Tries His Wings"

Chapter 5

Sources: Unless otherwise indicated, all details are from daily entries from Chavez journals/activity reports in 1956 in Ross collection, Wayne State, Box 1, Folders 18 thru 44, and Box 2, Folders 1 thru 6.

40 described a scenario Minutes of Jul. 1955 CSO convention, Ross Papers, Box 11, Folder 10

41 Alinsky observed Alinsky to Ross, Nov. 20, 1962, IAF Austin, Box 559, Ross folder

41 "It's a big problem" Chavez report, Mar. 26, 1956, ROSS, Box 1, Folder 26

42 sold nine thousand tickets Carl Tjerandsen notes, ESF, Box 33, Folder 4

43 "picked up ducks" Ross diary, Ross Papers, Box 30, Folder 2

44 "the Christmas tree sale" Chavez report, Dec.3–24, 1956, ROSS, Box 2, Folder 6

Chapter 6

Sources: Chavez and Ross activity reports; IAF archives in Chicago and Austin; Emil Schwarzhaupt Foundation archives; United Packinghouse Workers papers; author interviews with Gallegos, Margaret Govea, and Gilbert Padilla.

45 "people do it themselves" Chavez report, Jan. 29, 1957, ROSS, Box 2, Folder 9; Ross report, Feb. 26, 1957, ROSS, Box 2, Folder 13

46 "starting from the top" "Report of CSO Training," Bashford, Jan. 6–Feb. 14, 1958, ESF, Box 30, Folder 9

46 "plenty of time" Cassen, Jul. 6–Aug. 10, 1958, IAF UIC, Box 17, Folder 249

47 "No one was told" Lundgren, n.d., IAF UIC, Box 17, Folder 249

47 "I recall one night" Alberts, IAF UIC, Box 17, Folder 249

47 fifty-thousand-mile mark Chavez diary, OOP 1, Box 4, Folder 1

48 "People would come first" Chavez interview on FMDP at http://www.farmworkermovement.com/media/oral_history/swf/chavezintervieworgan.swf; for another version of the story, see Matthiessen, "Cesar Chavez," *New Yorker*, Jun. 21, 1968

49 "flat broke" Chavez report, Mar. 15, 1957, ROSS, Box 2, Folder 14

49 "this damn issue" Chavez report, Apr. 5, 1957, ROSS, Box 2, Folder 16

49 "mad at the world" Tape of Dec. 1971 conference at La Paz, UFWA

50 "for the privilege[d] few" Chavez report, Mar. 22–24, 1957, ROSS, Box 2, Folder 15

50 "adventurous thinking" IAF 1957–58 annual report, ESF, Box 30, Folder 3

50 "your salary increase" Alinsky to Chavez, Apr. 19, 1957, OOP 1, Box 2, Folder 10

51 lowered salaries Clive Knowles to Ralph Helstein, Jan. 30, 1959, UPWA, Office of the President, Box 143, Folder 15

51 had a deal Ross report, Aug. 17, 1958, ROSS, Box 2, Folder 41

51 "my big mouth" Ross to Tony Rios, Aug. 3, 1958, ROSS, Box 2, Folder 41

Chapter 7

Sources: Details from Chavez daily activity reports; Fred Ross Papers; UPWA Archives; ESF Archives; IAF Archives, Chicago; U.S. Department of Labor archives; *Oxnard Press-Courier*.

53 number of Mexicans employed "Foreign Labor Plan Abuse May Kill It, Farmers Told," *Oxnard Press-Courier*, Jan. 15, 1959

53 "whole day was spoiled" Chavez report, Oct. 17, 1958, ROSS, Box 2, Folder 45

53 "the most important thing" Chavez report, Sep. 29, 1958, ROSS, 2, Folder 43

54 bracero program The series of laws passed between 1942 and 1964 are collectively referred to as the bracero program. Many recent works have raised questions as to whether there was ever a labor shortage, even during the war. See, for example, Mitchell, *They Saved the Crops*.

55 should shun a program "The Braceros Must Go," *Monitor*, Jul. 29, 1960

55 "unspeakable cruelty" Reuther to Meany, Nov. 10, 1958, UPWA, Office of the President, Box 143, Folder 15

55 dramatic impact A.J. Norton to Glenn Brockway, Oct. 17, 1955, U.S. Dept. of Labor Archives, RG 174

56 alarming wage discrepancy Jan. 30, 1958, testimony, citing "Domestic and Imported Workers in Harvest Labor, Santa Clara County, California, 1954" by Varden Fuller, John W. Mamer, and George L. Viles, UPWA, Office of the President, Box 143, Folder 15

56 house meetings in 1957 Chavez report, Mar. 25, 1957, ROSS, Box 2, Folder 15

56 "looks almost impossible" Chavez report, Dec. 12, 1958, ROSS, Box 2, Folder 48

56 "Application For Work" Ross Papers, Box 10, Folder 4

57 Romulo Campos Chavez report, Dec. 29, 1958, ROSS, Box 2, Folder 49

57 "a dastardly thing!" *Oxnard Press-Courier*, Jan. 15, 1959

58 Zamora admitted George Duemler to Kenneth Robertson, May 28, 1959, Dept. of Labor Archives, RG 174

58 "come back tomorrow" Chavez report, Jan. 19, 1958, Ross papers, Box 11, Folder 5

58 a subsequent inquiry Kenneth Robertson to Albert Misler, Feb. 15, 1960, Dept. of Labor archives, RG 174

58 "I have no work" Ross papers, Box 11, Folder 5

58 two hundred farmworkers Ross diary, Feb. 26, 1959, Ross Papers, Box 5, Folder 18

59 "living as no American should" Mitchell address, Feb. 23, 1959, McDonnell papers

59 front-page reports "Abuse of Braceros Charged," *Oxnard Press-Courier*, Jan. 19, 1959

60 "Called Cesar" Ross Papers, Box 5, Folder 18

61 "six months of Headaches" Chavez to Ross, May 23, 1959, Ross Papers, Box 11, Folder 12

61 "I'll go at it alone" Chavez to Ross, May 7, 1959, ROSS, Box 3, Folder 3

62 "some of the small things" Chavez reports, Apr. 1–3, 1959, ROSS, Box 3, Folder 3

62 "life long desire" IAF annual report, 1959, ESF, Box 30, Folder 4

Chapter 8

Sources: Chavez-Ross correspondence; minutes of CSO meetings; McDonnell Papers; author interviews with Gallegos, Hartmire, Anderson, Carhart, and McDonnell.

63 close to arranging Alinsky to Helstein, Sep. 15 and Oct. 6, 1959, UPWA, Office of the President, Box 143, Folder 15

64 didn't bother making friends Fernando Chavez essay, http://www.voxxi .com/cesar-chavez-son-fernando-leader/

64 "scared stiff" Chavez to Gallegos, May 24, 1960, and Jun. 2, 1960, Gallegos papers

64 voter registration campaign Report on voter registration, ESF, Box 30, Folder 8

65 "a real fire-brand" Ross to Alinsky, Mar. 10, 1960, Ross Papers, Box 2, Folder 3

66 "never be used again" Transcript of Chavez talk, Oct. 4, 1971, La Paz, Hartmire papers

66 passed a resolution Minutes of CSO Executive board, Jul. 21–22, 1961, Gallegos papers

66 a workable deal Chavez to Ross, Jul. 18, 1961, ROSS, Box 3, Folder 4

66 "I personally can't see" Chavez to Louis Zarate, Aug. 3, 1961, ROSS, Box 3, Folder 4

67 commitments from 650 Minutes of Nov. 17–18, 1961, CSO Executive committee meeting, Gallegos Papers

67 **worth $3 billion** Thompson, "AWOC"

67 **by-laws spelled out** Copy of by-laws in possession of author

68 **"one remaining blot"** Jan. 8, 1959, meeting at AFL-CIO headquarters, UPWA, Office of the President, Box 143, Folder 15

69 **group was disbanded** McDonnell to San Diego Bishop Charles Buddy, Jun. 11, 1961, AASF, Box A67

69 **"who is going to help"** Chavez to Ross, Aug. 15, 1961, ROSS, Box 3, Folder 4

69 **"Oxnard is the place"** Chavez to Ross, Dec. 28, 1961, Ross Papers, Box 2, Folder 8

70 **"my latest dreams"** Chavez to Ross, Jan. 25, 1962, ROSS, Box 3, Folder 5

71 **Rios came charging** Gallegos interview

72 **"charity organization"** Minutes from CSO Executive Board, Jul. 21–22, 1962, Gallegos Papers

72 **he was resigning** Minutes from CSO board meeting, Mar. 16–18, 1962, Gallegos Papers

73 **"lost arms and feet"** Carhart to Hartmire, Mar. 19, 1962, NFWM, Box 45, Folder 15

Chapter 9

Sources: Ross-Chavez letters; Chavez-Huerta letters; Manuel Chavez interviewed by Levy and Ross; NFWA papers; author interviews with Anna Chavez, Hartmire, Orendain, and Padilla.

77 **took pictures** Photo archives, Reuther Library

77 **arrived on April 23** Chavez to Ross, Apr. 26, 1962, ROSS, Box 3, Folder 5

79 **"somebody had to do something"** Rose, "Women in the United Farm Workers"

80 **"one place not to start"** Chavez to Ross, Apr. 26, 1962

80 **"Cheque or no cheque"** Chavez to Ross, May 2, 1962, ROSS, Box 3, Folder 6

80 **"In your opinion"** NFWM, Box 45, Folder 15

81 **"take advantage of whatever publicity"** Chavez to Ross, May 2, 1962

81 **"wants very badly to find out"** Chavez to Ross, Jun. 13, 1962, ROSS, Box 3, Folder 7

81 **"the true workers"** Chavez to Ross, Aug. 7, 1962, ROSS, Box 3, Folder 9

82 **"again become slaves"** Chavez to Ross, Aug. 28, 1962, Ibid.

82 "this is a movement" Chavez to Ross, Aug. 7, 1962, Ibid.

83 offered financial support Chavez to Hartmire, Jul. 31, 1962, NFWM, Box 45, Folder 15

83 focus on the older children Rose, "Women in the United Farm Workers"

83 "his first big money" Chavez to Ross, Jul. 3, 1962, ROSS, Box 3, Folder 9

84 "if you did the begging" Chavez to Ross, May 16, 1962, ROSS, Box 3, Folder 6

84 outlined Chavez's plan Ross to Alinsky, Apr. 7, 1962, Ross Papers, Box 2, Folder 3

84 "Heard about your project" Abe Chavez to Cesar Chavez, May 20, 1962, NFWA, Box 7, Folder 19

84 "Talk about being hungry" Chavez to Ross, Jun. 19, 1962, ROSS, Box 3, Folder 7

85 "isolate the atom" Chavez to Ross, Jul. 11, 1962, ROSS, Box 3, Folder 8

85 "All is not well" Chavez to Ross, Jun. 19, 1962

86 blow-by-blow account Ross to Chavez, Jul. 9, 1962, NFWA, Box 12, Folder 13

86 "sacrifice the workers" Chavez to Ross, May 2, 1962, ROSS, Box 3, Folder 6

86 "conducting a little survey" Chavez to Ross, May 22, 1962, ROSS, Box 3, Folder 6

86 "Check the letterhead" Chavez to Ross, Sep. 18, 1962, ROSS, Box 3, Folder 10

87 working as a salesman Manuel Chavez in JEL, Box 5, Folder 173 and Ross Tapes, FMDP

87 "this sounds crazy" Chavez to Huerta, Sep. 17, 1962, JEL, Box 18, Folder 378

88 "*inspire* the workers" Chavez to Ross, Sep. 18, 1962

88 "10 fingers crossed" Ross to Chavez, Sep. 21, 1962, NFWA, Box 12, Folder 13

88 "striking gabachos" Ross to Chavez, Sep. 25, 1962, NFWA, Box 12, Folder 13

88 gathered at 10:00 A.M. on Sunday Agenda, minutes, NFWA, Box 3, Folder 8

89 idea of an eagle Chavez to Ross, Mar. 11, 1963, ROSS, Box 3, Folder 11

89 "fantastically wonderful job" Ross to Chavez, Oct. 3, 1962, NFWA, Box 12, Folder 13

89 "go down in California history" ROSS, Box 3, Folder 10

Chapter 10

Sources: Chavez-Ross letters; Chavez-Huerta letters; NFWA minutes and newsletters; Chavez interviews in Ross Tapes; author interviews with Esher, Goepel, Hartmire, Orendain, and Miller.

92 "nation of Mexicans" Huerta, Apr. 6, 1969, JEL, Box 5, Folder 183

92 started college TAY, Box 9, Folder 2; Huerta autobiography, DH, Box 1, Folder 5

92 "deserve the recriminations" Huerta to Chavez, Feb. 29, 1964, NFWA, Box 2, Folder 13

92 "quiet long suffering type" Huerta to Chavez, n.d., NFWA, Box 2, Folder 13

93 "Get out!" Chavez in Ross Tapes

93 "I am game" Huerta to Chavez, n.d., late 1964, NFWA, Box 2, Folder 13

93 second convention Minutes, Jan. 20, 1963, NFWA, Box 5, Folder 28

94 "Padilla was my discovery" Chavez in JEL, Box 1, Folder 133

94 "the same mistake twice" Chavez to Ross, Dec. 14, 1962, ROSS, Box 3, Folder 10

94 "the risky part" Chavez to Huerta, Jan. 24, 1963, JEL, Box 18, Folder 378

95 "Let's face it" Newsletter, Oct. 18, 1962, NFWA, Box 10, Folder 8

95 "gut tearing fear" Chavez to Huerta, Feb. 22, 1963, JEL, Box 18, Folder 378

95 signed an agreement Chavez to Huerta, Mar. 9, 1963, JEL, Box 18, Folder 378

96 Richard's house Richard Chavez interviews in JEL and Ross Tapes; mortgage records, Kern County Recorders Office, tape of Feb. 1976 NEB, UFWA

96 association's annual meeting newsletter, Feb. 4, 1964, NFWA, Box 10, Folder 8

97 "develop the newspaper" Chavez to David Burciaga, Jul. 26, 1963, Burciaga papers, Wayne State

97 "help with your newspaper" Esher to Chavez, Nov. 11, 1964, NFWA, Box 8, Folder 4

98 "The meaning is ill-bred" Chavez to Ross, Mar. 23, 1965, ROSS, Box 3, Folder 12

98 "I liked the general tone" Abe Chavez to Cesar Chavez, NFWA, Box 7, Folder 14

99 his first office News release, "Office Opens," NFWA, Box 10, Folder 8

100 "Manny the Mostest" Chavez to Ross, Oct. 18, 1962, ROSS, Box 3, Folder 10

100 Manuel bragged Manuel Chavez in JEL, Box 5, Folder 173

100 Manuel was arrested Manuel Chavez arrest record and probation report, in possession of author

101 doubled its income Jan. 3, 1966, Form 1024 Tax Exemption application, JEL Folder 410

101 "The most exciting thing" Chavez to Ross, Mar. 23, 1965, ROSS, Box 3, Folder 12

101 "the watch makers" Drake manuscript, in JEL, Folder 387

101 swear on a crucifix Chavez notes, minutes of meetings Apr. 11 and 20, 1963, NFWA, Box 11, Folder 13

101 declared *El Malcriado* *El Malcriado*, May 1965

102 "Urban support" Miller to Friends of SNCC, Aug. 18, 1965, NFWA, Box 13, Folder 22

102 "mass movement of farm workers" Leaflet in NFWA, Box 12, Folder 9

103 "a strike that had much success" *El Malcriado*, May 1965

103 "a pretty narrow squeak" Ross to Chavez, Aug. 17, 1965, NFWA, Box 12, Folder 13

103 "giving a lot of thought" Chavez to Ross, May 21, 1964, ROSS, Box 3, Folder 12

104 "too much democracy" Ross to Chavez, Aug. 17, 1965, NFWA Box 12, Folder 13

Chapter 11

Sources: NFWA Papers; Farm Labor Collection; Ross Tapes; Ganz, *Why David Sometimes Wins*; author interviews with Adair, Cannon, Esher, Goepel, Ganz, Havens, Medina, Murguia, and Valdez.

105 "All I could think" Dunne, *Delano*, 79

106 he addressed the workers Agenda for meeting, Sep. 16, 1965, and Chavez notes, NFWA, Box 13, Folder 20

106 said a Hail Mary Goepel interview

107 no ordinary strike "Guerilla Warfare in the Grapes," *Movement*, Oct. 1965

107 "We are stopping them" *El Malcriado*, no. 21

108 Hundreds rallied "Strike in the Grapes," *Movement*, Oct. 1965

108 "stay on the offensive" Tape of Jan. 27, 1969, meeting, UFWA

108 complaints were filed Kenny to FAA, Nov. 4, 1965, NFWA, Box 1, Folder 5

108 **"could well ruin farmers"** Willinger to Msgr. Cornelius Higgins, Diocese of Sacramento, Nov. 19, 1965, AALA, Folder 1965

109 **"troublesome days"** Bell to Willinger, n.d., AALA, Folder 1965

109 **"They have the money"** *El Malcriado*, no. 21

110 **"As a Mexican"** *El Excéntrico*, Feb. 5, 1964, ETC, Series 3, Box 1

111 **"unbourgeois theater"** "The Tale of La Raza," *Ramparts*, Jul. 1966

111 **"Here was Cesar"** Ibid.

112 **"civil rights forces"** Council of CA Growers newsletter, Nov. 1, 1965, SJVFLC

112 **158 job actions** Thompson, "Agricultural Workers Organizing Committee"

112 **"third force"** Council of CA Growers newsletter, Oct. 4, 1965, SJVFLC

112 **"A movement is underway"** Hartmire to action mailing list, Jan. 25, 1966, Hartmire papers

113 **arrested all forty-four** Arrest report, NFWA, Box 6, Folder 15

115 **"win this strike"** "Reuther Pledges Coast Strike Aid," *New York Times*, Dec. 17, 1965

115 **"We're poor"** Chavez, Ross Tapes.

115 **"felt like they were equal"** Ibid.

115 **"lost our independence"** Ganz, *Why David Sometimes Wins*, 144

115 **"in community organizing"** "Cesar Chavez Talks About Organizing," *Movement*, Dec. 1965

115 **"only way I know"** Ibid.

116 **"We're experimenting"** *Movement*, Oct. 1965

Chapter 12

Sources: *Movement*; author interviews with Cannon, Coffman, Cousino, Frankel, Goepel, Hartmire, Murguia, Valdez, and Zaninovich.

117 **"Without hesitation"** Goepel to Alinsky, mid-Nov. 1965, IAF Austin, Box 527

118 **"*Estimado amigo*"** Chavez, Oct. 6 1965, NFWA, Box 10, Folder 8

120 **"a real movement"** Chavez to Friends of SNCC, Oct. 5, 1965, Hartmire papers

121 **drew parallels** James Farmer to CORE chapters, Dec. 17, 1965, Mike Miller papers, FMDP

121 **"no relevant middle ground"** Hartmire, Jan. 1966, Hartmire papers

121 **used codes** Chavez notes, UFWOC, Box 2, Folder 2

122 **jumped a train** Coffman interview

123 **"here to help"** "Delano Farm Workers Get Kennedy Pledge of Help," *Fresno Bee*, Mar. 16, 1966

123 **"the simple truth"** Transcript of Mar. 16, 1966, hearing, NFWA, Box 6, Folder 15

123 **memorable exchange** Ibid.

125 **march became a pilgrimage** Chavez, in Ross Tapes; Ganz, 148

125 **"wanted us to arrest them"** Dunne, 132

125 **promised Cesar a crowd** Manuel Chavez, Ross Tapes

126 **"Walking along the freeway?"** *Huelga*, on FMDP

126 **"in the past"** Transcript in JEL Box 6, Folder 200

127 **"ours, all ours"** "Plan de Delano," in possession of author

127 **"more Mexican than Catholic"** "An Interview with Cesar Chavez," Jeff Dietrich, *Catholic Agitator*, May 1977

127 **"the penance part"** JEL, Box 6, Folder 200

127 **"every step"** Chavez in Ross Tapes

127 **Kircher put on old clothes** Kircher, Oct. 19, 1973, TAY, Box 9, Folder 16

128 **"more than 5,000"** Transcript of CA Grape and Tree Fruit League meeting, Mar. 24, 1966, SJVFLC

129 **"Labor history was written"** "Schenley to Bargain with Grape Union," *New York Times*, Apr. 7 1966

129 **sleeping arrangements** Logistics of march, notes, NFWA, Box 12, Folder 1

130 **"my wife, Helen"** Cassette tape, Apr. 10, 1966, UFWA

130 **"flames of class struggle"** *Delano Record*, Apr. 12, 1966

130 **"even the score"** Transcript of news conference, Oct. 23, 1966, Drake papers, Box 1, Wayne State

Chapter 13

Sources: Ross interviewed by Levy; NFWA papers; Ross Tapes; Dunne, *Delano*; Jon Lewis photographs on FMDP; author interviews with Chatfield, Cousino, Frankel, Ganz, Hartmire, Medina, Serda, and Valdez.

132 **The DiGiorgio empire** Robert DiGiorgio, Oral History, conducted 1983, Bancroft Library, UC Berkeley

132 **trying to convince** Ibid.

133 violent confrontation Ross, JEL, Box 6, Folder 196; "Grape Strike Brawl," *Los Angeles Times*, Apr. 22, 1966

133 "wants to be an organizer" Ross Papers, Box 24, Folder 2

134 "return the growers' violence" Quoted by John Moyer in *Journal of Current Social Issues*, Autumn 1972

134 "Ida had sat slumped" Ross Papers, Box 24, Folder 21

134 lock on the phone Minutes of meeting, Jul. 11, 1966, OOP1, Box 44, Folder 11

134 "It's tough enough" Dunne, *Delano*, 153

135 Serda decided to risk Serda interview

136 "strategic importance" Hartmire to Forrest Weir, Jul. 5, 1966, Hartmire papers

136 "a brilliant guy" Ross, Sep. 21, 1973, TAY, Box 9, Folder 17

136 "They're animals" Dunne, *Delano*, 140

137 "give up a lot" Ibid., 149

138 DiGiorgio handed out leaflets Ibid., 160

138 El Mosquito Zumbador NFWA, Box 12, Folder 1

139 $10,000-a-month subsidy Kircher to Meany, May 16, 1966, Meany Archives, AWOC: RG28-002

140 "servants of the union" Dunne, *Delano*, 156

140 going to get dirty Interviews with Frankel and Cousino

140 Jimmy the Greek Ganz, *Why David Sometimes Wins*, 197

140 "we will be victorious" Dunne, *Delano*, 163

142 "We didn't have the credibility" Chavez in JEL, Box 3, Folder 162

Chapter 14

Sources: Author interviews with Cousino, Esher, Goepel, Haber, Hartmire, Lynch, Orendain, Liza H. Medina, Moses, Murguia, and Valdez.

143 "has to work more" *Movement*, Dec. 1965

144 "the hardheaded guy" Tape of retreat, Jan. 27, 1969, UFWA

144 He divided people Ibid.

145 Richard Chavez recalled Richard Chavez, Ross Tapes

146 "only one name" Orendain Oral History, Jul. 20, 1971, University of Texas at Arlington

146 "never change our kids" JEL Box 1, Folder 134

146 **"tedious work"** JEL Box 1, Folder 138

146 **Day began his ministry** Delano Grapevine newsletter, Jan. 1968, in possession of author

146 **dozens of telegrams** AALA, Folder 1968

146 **"really like that a lot"** Mattheissen, *Sal Si Puedes*, 232

147 **"make the babies"** Several people quote Helen Chavez as saying this

148 **"this little hole"** Tape of Jan. 4, 1969, meeting, UFWA

148 **"never said no"** Ibid.

148 **"I may be wrong"** JEL Box 1, Folder 138

148 **on the payroll** List of salaries, UFWOC, Box 6, Folder 9

148 **"a paid staff"** *Movement*, Dec. 1965

148 **"a floor to sleep on"** Chavez letter, Oct. 6, 1965, NFWA, Box 10, Folder 8

149 **"pay is five dollars"** Diary of students, Apr. 12–19, 1966, NFWA, Box 10, Folder 8

149 **dues would total** 1967 UFWOC LM2 report, U.S. Department of Labor

151 **Kushner wrote** Kushner to Huerta, Jul. 27, 1967, OOP2, Box 46, Folder 10

151 **Chavez called Bill Esher** Account of board meetings from detailed minutes taken by Philip Vera Cruz, Vera Cruz papers, Wayne State, Box 2, Folder 7; Chavez index cards on meetings with those to be purged, Drake papers, Box 2, Folder 15; author interviews with Valdez, Goepel, Haber, and Esher

153 **"Cesar suspects"** Vera Cruz papers, Box 2, Folder 7

153 **Teatro traveled East** Newport Folk Festival program, news stories, ETC, Series 14, Box 1

154 **"best ones are still here"** Matthiessen, 173

154 **told she must choose** Vera Cruz minutes

154 **"farmworkers' cathedral"** Tape of Chavez and Chatfield, Nov. 19, 1968, UFWA

155 **"Very plain, but very beautiful"** Ibid.

156 **"the spiritual center"** Chavez interview, FMDP, http://www.farmworker movement.com/media/oral_history/swf/chavezinterviewA.swf

156 **"once seemed a dream"** Delano Grapevine newsletter, Jan. 1968

Chapter 15

Sources: Interviews on Ross Tapes with Cesar Chavez, Richard Chavez, Manuel Chavez, LeRoy Chatfield and Mark Day; Chavez interviews in JEL; Chatfield, Cohen, and Vera Cruz diaries; Kern County court records; author interviews with Chatfield, Cohen, Day, Drake, Edelman, Ganz, Hartmire, Hirsch, Moses, Murguia, and Orendain.

157 fine no-shows Minutes of Jan. 19, 1968, meeting, Drake papers, Box 2, Folder 37

157 "he made experiments" Chavez, May 6, 1969, JEL, Box 1, Folder 132

158 the "Research Committee" Interviews with Hirsch, Orendain; essays by Hirsch and Reyes on FMDP

158 "all the dirty work" Cassette tape, "Cesar—NY Boycott," UFWA

159 Giumarra charged Kern County Court records, *Giumarra vs. UFWOC*

159 Rumors circulated Tape of Ross, Day, and Chatfield, Mar. 1969, FWDP

159 "keep in mind" Ibid.

159 "fasting as a prayer" Moses letter, Marion Moses papers, Wayne State

161 "trying to play God" Huerta, May 7, 1969, JEL, Box 5, Folder 184

163 "playing for all the marbles" Cohen journal, Cohen papers, Box 2, Folder 8

163 "pray for me" Chavez to Manning, Feb. 20, 1968, AALA

163 "fast of Cesar Chavez" Cohen papers, Box 2, Folder 11

164 "expressed my amazement" Duggan autobiography, FMDP

164 Orendain refused Interview with Orendain

164 "Had Cesar the right" Vera Cruz journal, Vera Cruz papers, Box 3, Folder 8, Wayne State

164 "wholly irrational reversal" Hirsch, "Some personal notes on Delano," Jun. 2, 1968, Kircher papers, Box 13, Folder 2, Wayne State

164 "the redemption of Manuel" Cohen papers, Box 2, Folder 8

165 "gringo justice" Tape of meeting, Jan. 27, 1969, UFWA

166 "marred our image" Chatfield journal, Mar. 2, 1969, courtesy of Bruce Perry

166 "your ears pop" Chavez, Ross Tapes

166 "beautiful floating feeling" Ibid.

167 "Just pray to God" Richard Chavez, Ross Tapes

167 Kennedy expressed concern Peter Edelman Interview #1, Jul. 15, 1969, RFK Oral History Collection, JFK Presidential Library

168 **"on the way down"** Cohen journal, Box 2, Folder 11

168 **dodged a dozen questions** http://www.youtube.com/watch?v=XNJ_6KfnX8k

168 **What do you say** Chavez notes, OOP1, Box 5, Folder 7

168 **run for president** Edelman interview

168 **"I marched with Cesar"** Robert F. Kennedy Papers, Speeches, John F. Kennedy Presidential Library

169 **Juana Chavez sent** Bruce Perry taped interview with Helen Pedotti, n.d., courtesy of Perry

169 **Democratic registration** Office files of Marvin Watson, Box 2, LBJ Presidential Library

170 **Chavez blocked out May** Chavez 1968 datebook; Drake files, Box 2, Folder 34; Chavez, Ross Tapes

170 **"We were extremely popular"** Chavez, JEL, June 27–29, 1969, Box 1, Folder 134

170 **Sheridan watched Chavez** Walter Sheridan, Aug. 13, 1969, RFK Oral History collection, JFK Presidential Library

170 **On election eve** Ibid.

171 **"sooner or later"** Cohen to Roger, n.d., courtesy of Jerry Cohen

Chapter 16

Sources: JEL tapes; Farm Labor Files; Chatfield journal; author interviews with Chatfield, Hartmire, Mason, Matthiessen, and Moses.

172 **happy to help** Matthiessen interview

173 **"Indian's bow nose"** Matthiessen, *Sal Si Puedes*, 6

173 **"introduced as a saint"** Chavez, Dec. 8, 1969, JEL, Box 1, Folder 139

173 **confirmation name** Mark Hurley to Chavez, Mar. 27, 1970, ADMIN, Box 5, Folder 10

174 **called Bill Kircher** Kircher interview, Oct. 19, 1973, TAY, Box 9, Folder 16

174 **recite the Hail Mary** Chatfield journal, Sep. 12, 1968

174 **officer was stationed** Chatfield journal, Sep. 13, 1968

174 **Chatfield wrote twice** Chatfield to Manning, Jun. 14 and 21, 1968, AALA, Folder 1968

174 **"creating a crisis"** Chatfield journal, Sep. 15, 1968

174 **"sooner or later"** Huerta, Apr. 1969, JEL, Box 5, Folder 184

175 **"sounded like a messiah"** Ibid.

175 **"too saintly"** Drake interviewed by Pat Hoffman, on FMDP

175 **hung a photo** Matthiessen, 323

175 **read his draft** Matthiessen interview

175 **$900 check** Chatfield journal, Dec. 5, 1968

176 **"stab of genius"** Chatfield journal, Mar. 1, 1969

176 **"get everybody involved"** Chatfield and Chavez., tape, Nov. 19, 1968, UFWA

176 **"How in hell"** Itliong, Apr. 4, 1969, JEL, Box 5, Folder 185

176 **Meeting at his house** Tape of Jan. 14, 1969, meeting, UFWA

177 **"Cesar Chavez's union"** Ibid.

177 **"In a confrontation"** Ibid.

178 **raised his biggest threat** Chatfield journal; Kircher, Oct. 19, 1973, TAY Box 9, Folder 16

178 **"He sees himself"** Matthiessen, 284

178 **"pull a Joseph Stalin"** Jan. 14, 1969, tape

179 **"one man organization"** Itliong, JEL, Box 5, Folder 185

179 **"people of heart"** Jan. 14, 1969, tape

179 **"But he is a man"** Hirsch, "Some personal notes on Delano," Jun. 2, 1968, in Kircher papers, Box 13, Folder 2, Wayne State

180 **"some serious doubts"** Mason, Apr. 26, 1969, JEL Box 6, Folder 188

180 **"I'm single-minded"** Jan. 14, 1969, tape

181 **"As his leadership inevitably extends"** Matthiessen, 173

Chapter 17

Sources: Hartmire and Medina papers; author interviews with Cohen, Fitch, Ganz, Hartmire, Medina, and Serda.

183 **Giumarra owned** Brown, "The United Farm Workers Grape Strike"

183 **"their only weapon"** *UFWOC v. Superior Court of the State of California,* Aug. 28, 1967, court files

184 **they talked good-naturedly** Tape of boycotters meeting, Dec. 1967, FMDP, Ross Tapes

185 **"Cesar is the main reason"** *"Labor,"* 1969, Medina papers

187 **"They are immoral"** Notes from Jul. 5, 1968, cabinet meeting, Reagan Library, GO Box 24, Folder Jun. 1968

187 **"If the boycott spreads"** Notes from Jul. 16, 1968, cabinet meeting, Reagan Library, GO Box 25, Folder Jul. 1968

187 dipped precipitously Roger Mahony notes, Jan. 5, 1970, AALA, Folder 1970

187 "negotiating from power" Chavez, Jun. 26, 1969, JEL, Box 1, Folder 134

187 "created an image" Commonwealth Club of California minutes, Aug. 7, 1969, SJVFLC

188 ban grapes from dining halls "La Raza Comes to Campus," http://depts .washington.edu/civilr/la_raza2.htm

189 "do business with Hitler" *Food Merchants Advocate*, May 1969

189 "growers are bleeding" Chavez to Ganz, Mar. 9, 1969, ADMIN, Box 26, Folder 25

189 "left foot is considerably larger" Tape of Travell visit, Mar. 15, 1969, UFWA

191 "The Grapes of War" Defense Department fact sheet, Hartmire papers

192 conscientious objector Chavez, May 9, 1969, JEL, Box 1, Folder 132

192 "he is my son" Ibid.

193 "You do your trick" Chavez, JEL, Box 1, Folder 136

193 At a Chicago rally *Chicago Sun-Times*, Nov. 13, 1969

194 Chavez found time Chavez, JEL, Box 1, Folder 139

194 "Todos bien" Cesar to Richard, Helen Chavez, Dec. 15, 1969, INFO, Box 51, Folder 36

194 "I have grown" Govea, Montreal Boycott files, Box 3, Delano Correspondence folder

195 "bigger and better things" Chavez to Ganz, Feb. 4, 1970, OOP2, Box 19, Folder 3

196 "We go up and down" Chavez, Mar. 1970, JEL, Box 1, Folder 138

Chapter 18

Sources: Bishops' committee reports and Mahony notes; Levy notes on negotiations; Ross Tapes; Harvard Business School case studies; author interviews with Cohen, Marguleas, Moses, Reynoso, and Saatjian.

197 "going 80 miles" Chavez, Ross Tapes

198 price of Larson's grapes Harvard Business School case study 4-374-069, in author's possession

198 Saatjian's Methodist congregation Saatjian interview

198 Steinberg invited Chavez home Chavez, JEL, Folder 163

198 dropped from eighty-five "Grower Ranks Cut by Grape Boycott," *Los Angeles Times*, Mar. 24, 1970

199 "like a noose" Steinberg, Jun. 11, 1971, JEL, Box 6, Folder 198

199 "writing history" Lucey to Chavez, Aug. 13, 1968, AALA, Folder 1968

199 "no disposition" Mar. 3, 1970, Donnelly to bishops' committee, Report on Week of Mar. 2, 1970, AALA, Folder 1970

200 "As in the early days" Ibid.

200 "the word racism" "First Grapes With Union Label Shipped to Market," *New York Times*, May 31, 1970

200 bishops arranged separate meetings Account of negotiations from notes of Roger Mahony, AALA, Folder 1970, and Jacques Levy notes

201 "a lot like Vietnam" "Why They Signed with the Union," *Farm Quarterly*, Sep.–Oct. 1970

201 "learned to like Chavez" Ibid.

201 Giumarra Jr. was so angry Mahony to bishops' committee, Apr. 7, 1970, AALA, Folder 1970

201 "put the squeeze" Chavez to Mahony, May 13, 1970, AALA, Folder 1970

202 "Cesar couldn't bear" Matthiessen, 240

203 "wipe them out" May 11, 1970, memo, ADMIN3, Box 95, Folder 34

203 "power goes to the head" Chavez, JEL, Box 2, Folder 142

203 drew two ships Levy notes, JEL, Box 2, Folder 142

203 joined the betting "Date on which Giumarra calls Cesar," OOP1, Box 5, Folder 8

204 "a little push" Levy tape, n.d., circa Jun. 1970

204 "Some blue chips" Levy notes, Jul. 8, 1970, JEL, Box 2, Folder 145

204 "make a mint" Levy tape, n.d.

204 Feick agreed to ask Chronology from Mahony handwritten notes, in Folder 1970, and Mahony to Ad-hoc Committee on Farm Labor, Jul. 23, 1970, AALA; Levy notes, JEL Box 41, Folder 783

205 "this is like heaven" Jul. 16, 1970, JEL, Tape 57

206 "ever seen him as happy" Fred Ross Jr. to Chavez, Dec. 8, 1970, OOP2, Box 46, Folder 5

206 Tensions at the school Mark Day, *Forty Acres* (Praeger, 1971), 80; *El Malcriado*, Apr. 1, 1969, and Jul. 1, 1970

207 "over-played and over-bluffed" Mahony to bishops' committee, Jul. 23, 1970

208 Chavez became angry Levy notes on negotiations, JEL, Box 41, Folder 783

208 "You are a new union" Transcript of contract signing and press conference, JEL, Box 2, Folder 149

Chapter 19

Sources: Court records and transcripts, Superior Court of Monterey County; records of the bishops' committee and Mahony notes; Levy notes, tapes, and interviews; Cohen journals; author interviews with Carder, Cohen, Ganz, Hartmire, Lopez, Medina, and Valdez.

214 "feel out the Teamsters" Cal Watkins declaration, Aug. 31, 1970, in *Mann Packing v. Cesar Chavez*, Superior Court of Monterey County files

215 "Above all, the workers want" *El Malcriado*, Aug. 1, 1970

215 "Two Anglos got together" Levy tape, Jul. 28, 1970, JEL, Box 2, Folder 148

215 Levy noted Levy notes, Jul. 29, 1970, JEL, Box 2, Folder 148

216 "time has passed" *El Malcriado*, Aug. 1, 1970

216 "we all signed cards" Declaration of Mann Packing workers, n.d., in Mann Packing v. Cesar Chavez, Superior Court of Monterey County files

216 enough money for six weeks Levy notes, Aug. 2, 1970, JEL, Box 2, Folder 149

217 wedding reception Chavez, JEL, Box 4, Folder 165

217 called Monsignor Roger Mahony Mahony to Ad-hoc Committee on Farm Labor, National Conference of Catholic Bishops, Aug. 26, 1970, AALA, Folder 1970

217 Higgins's discretion Higgins press conference, Aug. 12, 1970, and Levy notes, JEL, Box 2 Folder 149

218 never announced the vote Higgins, Apr. 11, 1994, JEL, Box 37, Folder 743

218 "not like a spiritual fast" Chavez, JEL, Box 4, Folder 165

218 "a totally new ball game" Driscoll, Sep. 10, 1970, JEL, Box 3, Folder 153

219 "a monastery in Tibet" "Judge Calls Chavez 'Star of Radio, TV,'" *Los Angeles Herald Examiner*, Sep. 11, 1970

219 "call a boycott" Levy tape, Sep. 15, 1970, JEL, Box 3, Folder 153

219 "They were unafraid" Govea journal, in possession of author

220 "there will be retaliation" Cohen diary, Sep. 24, 1970, Cohen papers, Box 1, Folder 5

220 "Dolores has mismanaged" Higgins to Mahony, Sep. 24, 1970, AALA, Folder 1970

221 "A confession?" Cohen diary, Sep. 28, 1970, Cohen papers, Box 1, Folder 5

221 roughed-up Dolores Bruce Perry interviews with Cynthia Bell, Aug. 22, 1993, and Daneen Montoya

221 fighting Chavez in court *Bud Antle vs. UFWOC*, Complaint for Injunction and Damages, Aug. 24, 1970, Superior Court of Monterey County files

222 "we are being persecuted" Chavez deposition, Nov. 23, 1970, ADMIN3, Box 70, Folder 3

222 "essence of Christ's teaching" "Chavez asks lettuce boycott support," *New York Times*, Nov. 30, 1970

222 Inside Judge Campbell's chambers Transcript of court proceeding, Dec. 4, 1970, ADMIN3, Box 69

223 booked him Monterey County Sheriff booking sheet, OOP1, Box 5, Folder 1

224 "Jail is a small price" Levy tape, Dec. 5, 1970, JEL, Box 7, Folder 256

224 "brown and black workers" Levy tape, Dec. 1, 1970, JEL, Box 86, Tape 2

224 Ethel Kennedy marched Levy tape, Dec. 6, 1970, JEL, Box 86, Tape 4

226 "with you till the end" Petition, Calexico, Dec. 8, 1970, OOP1, Box 5, Folder 1

226 Letters to Chavez Ibid.

226 "hearing aid battery" George Nelson to Chavez, Dec. 8, 1970, courtesy of Bill Carder

226 "my husband had great admiration" Levy tape, Dec. 19, 1970, JEL, Box 86, Tape 5

226 Helen wrote Cesar Letters in UFW archives, Wayne State, accessed at http://chavez.cde.ca.gov/researchcenter

227 "My spirit was never in jail" "State Court Lets Chavez Out of Jail," *Salinas Californian*, Dec. 24, 1970

Chapter 20

Sources: Hartmire papers; Levy tapes; author interviews with Cohen, Hartmire, Murguia, and Smith.

229 averaged seventy visits Tape of conference NYC, Nov. 19, 1971, UFWA

229 he questioned Lewis Lewis interview, http://www.jayvigon.com/portfolio/DesignStudio-Videos-Chavez-LaPaz.html

229 bought the parcel Deed, Kern County Recorder's Office

230 named the complex with care Chavez, JEL, Box 2, Folder 141

230 lists of items Minutes of NFWM meeting, May 2–4, 1971, Hartmire papers

230 Chavez had big plans Hartmire notes, Hartmire papers

231 "we call that education" Tape of Chavez with students at La Paz, Jan. 1973, UFWA

231 "If the workers are not liberated" Tape of conference, La Paz, Dec. 2, 1971, UFWA

231 **"the important qualities"** Tape with students, Jan. 1973

232 **"national union of the poor"** Transcript of meeting, Jun. 5, 1970, Hartmire papers

232 **"When people sacrifice"** Chavez remarks, "On Money and Organizing," Oct. 4, 1971, Hartmire papers

232 **"very difficult question"** Ibid.

233 **"The moment we stop sacrificing"** Ibid.

233 **"at heart an experimenter"** Tape of Chavez with students, n.d., UFWA

233 **"Power also comes out of credit"** Chavez, Jun. 24, 1970, JEL, Box 2, Folder 143

233 **restart** *El Malcriado* Levy tape of meeting Sep. 17, 1971, La Paz, JEL, Tape 10

234 **"The whole game"** Tape of Dec. 73 NEB meeting, UFWA

234 **$90,000 loan** Tape of conference, Dec. 2, 1971

234 **"it may seem artificial"** Dunbar to Chavez, Aug. 6, 1969, Field Foundation, Box 2T143

234 **Chavez assured Dunbar** Chavez to Dunbar, Aug. 28, 1969, Field Foundation, Box 2T143

235 **"a lot of problems"** Tape of Chavez with students, Feb. 10, 1978, UFWA

235 **"a mystic bit"** Kircher interview, Oct. 19, 1973, TAY, Box 9, Folder 16

235 **"slight bit of trauma"** Moyer to Drake, Mar. 22, 1971, OOP1, Box 47, Folder 25

236 **an assassination plot** Account drawn from extensive files on the Shears case in UFW archives, including Cohen memos, copies of affidavits by ATF officials in ADMIN3, Box 32, Folder 5; Levy notes, JEL Tape 119; and FBI files

237 **"Cesar objected to paying"** Cohen to file, Feb. 3, 1972, ADMIN3, Box 32, Folder 5

237 **patrolled the perimeter** Interview with Dave Smith

237 **"On her birthday"** Chavez to Anna Puharich, Jan. 29, 1971, OOP2, Box 48

237 **"eat honey"** Jan. 13, 1974, TAY, Box 9, Folder 1

237 **"built sort of a community"** Tape with students, La Paz, Jan. 1973, UFWA

Chapter 21

Sources: Levy daily journals of negotiations; Mahony reports to bishops' committee; author interviews with Chatfield, Cohen, Eggers, Gutierrez, Hartmire, Moses, Rutkowski, and Washburn.

240 no evidence Interview with Gutierrez

240 "show our love" Tape of rally, May 12, 1972, UFWA

240 "pretty stubborn guy" Associated Press story, May 28, 1972

241 Chavez told Hartmire Hartmire notes, Hartmire papers

241 "they have caught the fire" Hartmire to boycotters, May 19, 1972, Hartmire papers

241 "brings tears to my eyes" Levy tape, Jun. 4, 1972, JEL, Box 86, Tape 14

241 "He went to Delano" Ibid.

242 prevailed on a 14-5 vote Minutes of NFWM meeting, May 2–4, 1971, Hartmire papers

243 "a miserable performance" Higgins to John Cosgrove, Jan. 15, 1971, in AALA, Folder 1971

243 "The myth is shattered" Taylor interview, Apr. 3, 1971, TAY, Box 8, Folder 13

243 "it's been my life" Transcript of Chavez talk, Jan. 3, 1970, UFW Archives, accessed at http://chavez.cde.ca.gov/researchcenter

243 Thirteen labor bills Mahony to bishops' committee, Jun. 4 and Jul. 20, 1972, AALA Folder 1972

244 "There's no limit" Tape of conference, La Paz, Dec. 2, 1971, UFWA

244 "pretty realistic view" Cohen, Nov. 1971, JEL, Box 4, Folder 165

244 "at a crossroads" Cohen journal, Cohen papers, Box 1, Folder 5

244 Cohen looked for plaintiffs Levy notes, Jun. 11, 1971, JEL, Box 3, Folder 160

244 the bulletin board clause Tape of conference, Dec. 2, 1971

245 "guy named Nixon" Ibid.

245 "we're in trouble" Transcript of conference, Aug. 5–6, 1972, CENT, Box 4, Folder 51

245 "you know he's special" "The Anglo Army Behind Cesar Chavez," *Los Angeles Times*, Apr. 6, 1972

246 "Cesar spoke very softly" Chatfield, *Cesar 1968*, courtesy of Bruce Perry

247 "a guy who starts juggling" Tape of conference, NYC, Nov. 19, 1971, UFWA

Chapter 22

Sources: Levy files and tapes; Mahony files in Farm Labor Collection; Cohen papers; author interviews with Bricca, Cohen, Medina, and Marguleas.

248 **"the most terrible two weeks"** Quotes and description of Richard Chavez's experience come from Jun. 14, 1974, interview by Levy, JEL, Box 4, Folder 173 unless otherwise indicated

250 **"a gentle intimidator"** Cohen diary, Sep. 10, 1970, Cohen papers, Box 1, Folder 5

250 **"we were in a bind"** Tape of conference, La Paz, Dec. 2, 1971, UFWA

250 **"a step above"** Ibid.

251 **"We never educated them"** Tape of conference, NYC, Nov. 19, 1971, UFWA

251 **"we must not be afraid"** Minutes of Sep. 19, 1970, meeting, INFO, Box 51, Folder 59

252 **"they react against the union"** Tape of conference, Dec. 2, 1971

252 **"the vegetable people began to make us understand"** Ibid.

253 **"increasing animosity towards the UFWOC"** Mahony to Chavez, Nov. 15, 1971, AALA, Folder 1971

253 **"I have your letter"** Chavez to Mahony, Nov. 27, 1971, OOP1, Box 47, Folder 9

254 **long lists of complaints** Mahony to Ad-Hoc Farm Labor Committee, Jun. 4, 1972, AALA, Folder 1972

254 **Chavez responded** Chavez to Mahony, Jun. 14, 1972, AALA, Folder 1972

254 **"Something has to be done"** Mahony to Kircher, Jul. 3, 1972, AALA, Folder 1972,

254 **"Why is there such hostility"** D'Arrigo to Richard Chavez, Jun. 14, 1972, AALA, Folder 1972

255 **"unreasonable, capricious, and hostile"** Larson to Chavez, Apr. 24, 1972, AALA, Folder 1972

255 **"destroying all the good work"** Steinberg to Chavez, Mahony, May 16, 1972, AALA, Folder 1972

255 **"never been so disgusted"** Marguleas, Jun. 7, 1972, JEL, Box 42, Folder 811

255 **he had no crews** Roberts, Marguleas telegrams to Mahony, Oct. 3, 1972, AALA, Folder 1972

256 **"According to the report"** Tape of conference, Dec. 2, 1971

257 **"let me know if you're quitting"** Chavez to Huerta, Dec. 15, 1972, ADMIN, Box 11, Folder 5

258 **"the decision had been made"** Mahony to bishops' committee, Feb. 5, 1973, report, AALA, Folder 1973

258 **"it's going to be a great miracle"** Chavez with students, Jan. 1973, La Paz, UFWA

258 "we'll come beat their brains out" Chavez memos, ADMIN, Box 11, Folder 18

258 they met on April 5 Transcript of meeting, ADMIN3, Box 28, Folder 56

259 only passages that Cesar censored Tape of Dec. 16–23, 1974, NEB, UFWA

Chapter 23

Sources: Documents and audiotapes, UFW archives; *Fighting for Our Lives*; Levy daily journal and tapes; Farm Labor Collection; FBI Files; Byrd papers; author interviews with Byrd, Carder, Cohen, Dalzell, Hartmire, Moyer, and Nathan.

260 "we have the villain" Chavez, Mar. 17, 1974, JEL, Box 4, Folder 169

260 "justice for farmworkers" *Fighting for Our Lives*

261 bulges under their jackets Lt. Yoksimer to Deputy Sheriff Cois Byrd, Apr. 12, 1973, Byrd papers

261 overtime bill Records of Riverside sheriff department, Byrd papers

261 "You rotten bum!" *Fighting for Our Lives*

262 "We've got this great villain" Chavez, Mar. 17, 1974, JEL, Box 4, Folder 169

262 "They had to pick on something" Chavez, JEL, Box 4, Folder 168

262 "a non-white union" Interview with Gerard Sherry, NC News Service, Jun. 1973, AALA, Folder 1973

263 "Things have really escalated" Tapes of Jun. 25, 1973, in UFWA and JEL Tape 84

263 "Organizing is a gamble" "Interview with Cesar Chavez," by John Moyer, *Impact*, Aug. 1971

264 "Must gamble daily" Cohen diary, Box 1, Folder 5 Vol. 2, Cohen papers

265 "The crippling injunction is dissolved" Cassette tape, n.d., UFWA

265 increased pay to $90 Tape of Jun. 13–18, 1975, NEB meeting, UFWA

266 "This is our entire life" "Chavez Vows to Continue Fight," *Los Angeles Times*, Jul. 22, 1973

266 olive-green jailhouse dress Gerard Sherry, "Dorothy Day Speaks from Jail," Aug. 10, 1973, Catholic News Service

267 Chavez was suddenly optimistic Levy diary, Jul. 20–30, 1970, JEL Tape 120

267 "learned more about concern and solidarity" Tape of Cleveland rally, Jun. 29, 1973, UFWA

267 "it's our strike too" Tape of Chavez speech, Jun. 25, 1973, UFWA

267 **"It's not that serious"** Interview with Sherry, Jun. 1973

268 **"whores in the camps"** Levy notes and diary of negotiations, JEL Tape 120

269 **"make them feel small"** Quigley, Dec. 9, 1973, TAY, Box 9, Folder 10

269 **"arming of the strikebreakers"** *Fighting for Our Lives*

269 **"series of beatings"** Ibid.

270 **died at 1:00 A.M.** FBI report, in Stanley Pottinger papers, Folder 126b, Ford Library

270 **Daifullah wrote home** Daifullah letters, Hartmire papers

271 **"We are going to win"** De la Cruz eulogy, Hartmire papers

271 **Chavez was out of money** Pottinger papers, Ford Library

271 **"the cops were behind it"** Tape of Chavez interviewed by Winthrop Griffith, n.d., UFWA

271 **"how can I be discouraged?"** Jan. 13, 1974, TAY, Box 9, Folder 1

272 **spent more than $5 million** UFW LM2 report to U.S. Department of Labor, 1973

272 **"This is our work"** Tape of press conference in Salinas, 1973, UFWA

Chapter 24

Sources: Transcript and tapes of 1973 founding convention; UFW Constitution; tapes of NEB meetings, Dec.17–23, 1973, Mar. 27–Apr. 1, Oct. 12–15, and Dec. 16–23, 1974, and Mar. 25–28, 1975; Levy tapes and notes; Taylor files; author interviews with Dalzell, Ganz, Medina, Orendain, and Padilla.

273 **sown the seeds** Levy notes, Sep. 23, 1973, JEL, Box 6, Folder 205

274 **16-by-24-foot mural** Almaraz explanation of mural, on FMDP website

274 **"win or lose"** Sep. 21, 1973, JEL Tape 17b

275 **"they believed that power corrupts"** Tape of Chavez with students, Feb. 10, 1978, UFWA

275 **crafted the brief preamble** Ibid.

276 **"Some of the best people"** Levy tape, Sep. 23, 1973, JEL, Tape 18A

277 **"All colors, all shapes, all sizes"** Transcript of convention proceeding, in possession of author

278 **more than eighty budgets** Quigley interview, Dec. 9, 1973, TAY, Box 9, Folder 10

278 **"you deal with the problem"** Chavez, May 15, 1969, JEL, Box 1, Folder 133

278 **"he must get control"** Levy notes, Nov. 13, 1973, JEL, Box 4, Folder 164

279 Quigley made decisions Quigley interview, Dec. 9, 1973

279 "whole idea of administration" Chavez with boycotters, Mar. 16, 1974, JEL, Box 4, Folder 168

280 "they knew all these things" Tape of Mar. 25–28, 1974, NEB, UFWA

280 "biggest problem is car and telephone" Tape of Dec. 1973 staff meeting, UFWA

280 "making you guys responsible" Tape of Dec. 17–23, 1973, NEB, UFWA

281 "This week is my week" Ibid.

281 "We'll know what to do" Tape of Dec. 16–23, 1974, NEB, UFWA

281 "give me some time to be in La Paz" Ibid.

282 Ross chastised Chavez Tape of Oct. 12–15, 1974, NEB, UFWA

283 "nobody is going to work against you" Richard Chavez to Levy, Jun. 1974, JEL, Box 4, Folder 173

284 "unity is more important" Tape of Mar. 25–28, 1975, NEB, UFWA

Chapter 25

Sources: Maricopa County Organizing Project archives; Yuma *Daily Sun*; Levy tapes of European tour; tapes of NEB meetings, Mar. 27–Apr. 1, Jun. 11–14, Oct. 12–15, and Dec. 16–23, 1974; author interviews with Barry, Devereux, Gutierrez, Liza Hirsch Medina, and Padilla.

285 the headline Winthrop Griffith, "Is Chavez Beaten?" *New York Times*, Sep. 15, 1974

286 "that didn't indicate much support" *Sacramento Bee*, Feb. 23, 1974

286 "We bought a goddamn strike" Tape of Mar.27–Apr. 1, 1974, NEB, UFWA

286 "I don't ever get tired" Chuck Powers, "Chavez and the State of his Union," *Los Angeles Times*, Jun. 23, 1974

286 "I kidded myself" Levy tape, Oct. 9, 1974, JEL Tape 112

286 In a dozen speeches Levy tapes, Sep. 16–24, 1974, JEL Tapes 108–9

287 "there stood Monsignor Higgins" Chavez report to NEB, Dec. 1974, Hartmire papers

288 "We were overjoyed" Levy tape, Sep. 27, 1974, JEL Tape 110

288 "It was recognition for us" Levy tape, Oct. 9 1974, JEL Tape 113

288 spent $80,000 a week Details of wet line from tapes of Oct. and Dec. 1974 NEB, UFWA

289 denounced the wet line "UFW Expects to Hear," *Yuma Daily Sun*, Nov. 18, 1974

289 "They bought off the police" Stories by Tom Barry, MCOP, Accession 1994-1302, Box 4

289 the simple mechanism Riverside Sheriff department reports, Byrd papers

290 Manuel provided entertaining accounts Tape of Dec. 16–23, 1974, NEB, UFWA

290 "activity has got to stop" "3 Convicted UFW Members," *Yuma Daily Sun*, Jan. 14, 1975

290 Manuel and Cesar tacitly acknowledged Tape of Dec. 16–23, 1974, NEB

291 held him in jail Ibid.

291 "he started buying everybody off" Barry stories, MCOP papers

291 "some mind-boggling stuff" Hartmire to Chavez, Dec. 24, 1974, OOP2, Box 44, Folder 10

292 "It's like playing poker" Tape of Dec.16–23, 1974, NEB

292 "all sorts of grief" Ibid.

292 "Cesar forgives Manuel" Matthiessen, 332

292 "don't make people any better" *American Labor Magazine*, Feb. 1971

293 He dismissed questions "Chavez Offers Olive Branch," *Yuma Daily Sun*, Oct. 17, 1974

293 the "Illegals Campaign" Tape of Jun.11–14, 1974, NEB, UFWA

294 "get the illegals out of California" Chavez memo to all entities, May 24, 1974, in possession of author

294 directed Jerry Cohen to retaliate Tape of Oct. 12–15, 1974, NEB, UFWA

294 "let's go after them" Tape of Jun. 11–14, 1974, NEB

294 "come here to become rich" Chavez, Mar. 17, 1974, JEL, Box 4, Folder 171

294 one of his companions disappeared "UFW Brings Picketing Back," *Yuma Daily Sun*, Jan. 6, 1975

295 dismissed questions about violence "Chavez Accepts $5,000 Check," *Yuma Daily Sun*, Jan. 10, 1975

295 Cesar appeared with Manuel "Police Brutality is Chavez's Complaint," *Yuma Daily Sun*, Jan. 31, 1975

295 vegetarian diet Taylor interview, Oct. 14, 1973, TAY, Box 8, Folder 18

296 the royal "we" President's Oct. 1974 report to NEB, in possession of author

296 Paul Hall lectured Chavez Levy notes, Sep. 26, 1973, JEL Tape 123

296 "trying to build a union" Richard Chavez to Levy, Jun. 1974, JEL, Box 4, Folder 173

297 "Poor Peoples Union" Tape of Dec. 16–23, 1974, NEB

297 meeting with Fred Ross Notes on Jan. 29, 1975, meeting, Ross Papers, Box 12, Folder 3

298 "life can have meaning" Hartmire, "The United Farm Workers Are Alive and Well," Oct. 1974, Hartmire papers

298 "he's an idealist" Meany interview, Aug. 29, 1974, AALA, Folder 1974

298 told Sally Quinn "Indefatigable Cesar Chavez," *Washington Post*, May, 4, 1975

298 "God and his wife, Helen" *La Voz de Pueblo*, Nov/Dec. 1972

298 "just the same old guy" Jan. 13, 1974, TAY, Box 9, Folder 1

Chapter 26

Sources: Levy interviews with Cohen and Nathan; Tapes of NEB meetings, Dec. 17–23, 1973, Jun. 11–14, Oct. 12–15, Dec. 16–23, 1974, and Mar. 25–28, 1975; author interviews with Cohen, Dalzell, and Nathan.

299 sick to his stomach Cohen interview and tape of Jun. 30–Jul. 2, 1977, NEB, UFWA

300 "run out of time" Tape of Dec. 17–23, 1973, NEB, UFWA

300 hold firm Tape of Jun.11–14, 1974, NEB, UFWA

301 "get those bastards out" Tape of Dec. 16–23, 1974, NEB, UFWA

301 "We have to introduce legislation" Tape of Oct. 12–15, 1974, NEB, UFWA

302 inaugural address http://governors.library.ca.gov/addresses/34-Jbrown01 .html

302 "problem is going to be our friends" Tape of Dec. 16–23, 1974, NEB

303 "go after Gallo" Tape of Oct.12–15, 1974, NEB

303 "self-confident picture" Mahony report to Ad-Hoc Farm Labor Committee, Jan. 27, 1975, AALA, Folder 1975

304 invited Zaninovich Mahony to Zaninovich, Mar. 8, 1975, AALA, Folder 1975

304 Gallo also told Mahony Mahony notes, Jan. 7, 1975, AALA, Folder 1975

304 marchers reached Modesto Tape of rally in Modesto, Mar. 1, 1975, UFWA

305 phones began to ring Dalzell to Chavez, Mar. 7, 1975, Dalzell papers

305 Chavez told the board Tape of Mar. 25–28, 1975, NEB, UFWA

305 "farmworkers are not the status quo" Brown, Paradigm Productions, 1995, FMDP

305 "we made some deals" Tape of Mar. 25–28, 1975, NEB

306 Brown asked Chavez Details of negotiation from Levy interview with

Chavez, Aug. 1, 1975, JEL, Box 29, Folder 572; Brown interview, Paradigm; and Mar. 1975 NEB

306 Chavez sent back word Dalzell to Chavez, Apr. 11, 1975, Dalzell papers

307 "That is part of their plan" Mahony to Manning, Apr. 27, 1975, AALA, Folder 1975

307 argument he had used with growers Brown interview, Paradigm Productions

308 "The whole fight's going to change" Chavez, May 17, 1975, JEL, Box 29, Folder 575

Chapter 27

Sources: Transcript of UFW 1975 convention; transcripts of ALRB hearings and election records of the ALRB; Govea papers; tapes of NEB meetings, Jun. 13–18, Sep. 22, and Oct. 10, 1975; author interviews with Cohen, Ganz, Medina, Nathan, and Washburn.

311 "I said, 'March!'" Chavez, Aug. 1, 1975, JEL, Box 29, Folder 572

311 "like a common language" Ibid.

312 "incredibly chaotic" Tape of NEB, Jun. 13–18, 1975, UFWA

315 "The sacrifice, they understand" JEL interview, Aug. 1, 1975

315 assigned Medina to handle Jun. 13–18, 1975, NEB

316 Cathy Murphy's first impression http://infocus.gettyimages.com/post /cathy-murphy-how-photographing-cesar-chavez-changed-my-life

316 "the dignity of the worker" Press conference, Sep. 14, 1975, JEL, ALRA Tape 11

316 "our time has come" Transcript of 1975 UFW Convention, WORK, Box 7, Folder 7

318 "This one breaks my heart" Tape of Oct. 10, 1975, NEB, UFWA

318 "a reign of terror" Chavez press conference, Sep. 10, 1975, JEL, ALRA Tape 11

318 "most frustrating in the history" Tape of Sep. 22, 1975, NEB, UFWA

319 "just get the Chicano community" Oct. 10, 1975, NEB

320 conducted 329 elections Records of the ALRB

320 "you win them, or you lose" Tape of Feb. 15–21, 1976, NEB, UFWA

320 "It changed everything" Chavez interview in *Sojourners*, Oct. 1977

321 "People will sacrifice" Tape of Jul. 23–24, 1976, NEB, UFWA

321 "What kind of time schedule" Sep. 22, 1975, NEB

321 "a Christmas present" Gardner to Ross, Dec. 20, 1975, Ross Papers, Box 2, Folder 4

322 "what made the movement" Tape of Jun. 13–18, 1975, NEB

322 192 victories First Annual Report of the ALRB, ALRB

Chapter 28

Sources: Tapes of NEB meetings, Feb. 16–21, Jun. 13–15, Jul. 24, Sep. 14–15, 1976, and Mar. 14–16, 21, 1977; Medina papers; author interviews with Cohen, Ganz, Hartmire, Medina, and Milne.

323 "We're people people" Tape of Feb. 16–21, 1976, NEB, UFWA

324 Milne was sold Milne interview

324 Chavez told the board Feb. 16–21, 1976, NEB

326 "We must be missionary" Transcript, Jul. 6–8, 1976, ADMIN, Box 29, Folder 21

326 only fifteen contracts Feb. 16–21, 1976, NEB

326 "string around your neck" Tape of Mar. 14–16, 1977, NEB, UFWA

327 "delegate more" Tape of Chavez and staff, n.d., 1976, UFWA

327 West Foods Medina notes, Medina papers

328 "no surprises" Chavez to Medina, Jul. 21, 1976, Medina papers

328 he recalled happily Tape of Sep. 14, 1976, NEB, UFWA

328 "The first contract" Ibid.

328 Harris poll *Long Beach Telegram*, Oct. 20, 1975

328 "one remarkable leader" Jack Newfield, *Village Voice*, May 10, 1976

329 "We're here to stay" "After Push, After Shove," *Chicago Tribune*, May 9, 1976

329 he wanted to proceed Medina notes, Medina papers

329 "all of us grabbed hoses" Minutes of May 3–4, 1976, debriefing, UFW 1986 Accession Box 55 [Note: The 1986 Accession has been recently combined with the UFW Administration Records; I use the box numbers where I originally found the documents.]

330 the arguments against Tape of Jun. 13, 1976, NEB, UFWA

330 Democratic National Convention Tape of Jul. 24, 1976, NEB, UFWA

331 Can we win? Ibid.

332 "a real problem" Transcript, Jul. 27, 1976, UFW 1986 Accession, Box 54

332 "We're getting burned" Tape of Sep. 15, 1976, NEB, UFWA

333 spearheaded the opposition Advertisement from NFWM newsletter, Fall 1976, Hartmire papers; Kubo interview, courtesy of Bruce Perry

333 "don't be bitter" "Farmworkers Cheer Chavez," *Los Angeles Times*, Nov. 4, 1976

334 Chavez had been fasting Maddock interview, Paradigm Productions, FMDP

Chapter 29

Sources: Tapes of NEB meetings, Jun. 13–15, Jul. 24, Sep. 14–15, Nov. 18, 24, and Dec. 15–16, 1976, and Mar. 14–16, 21, 1977, and Apr. 4, 1977, community meeting; Hartmire papers; author interviews with Ganz, Hartmire, Jones, Liza Hirsch Medina, Moyer, Gilbert Padilla, and Rodriguez

336 "live and die in the movement" Tape of Jones interviewed by Walter Taylor, Jul. 24, 1976, UFWA

336 Ross observed Ross discussing the fast, Ross Tapes, FMDP

337 she ran into Joe Smith Chronology based on correspondence between Smith, McCarthy, and Hartmire and notes of Hartmire's interviews about the Smith/Jones purges, Hartmire papers, and tape of Jun. 30–Jul. 2, 1977, NEB, UFWA

337 "a fantastic idea" Tape of Feb. 16–21, 1976, NEB, UFWA

337 "Cesar understands" Tape of Smith interviewing job candidates, Jul. 1976, UFWA

337 "a beautiful paper" Tape of Sep. 14, 1976, NEB, UFWA

338 "It's a fucking game" Tape of Sep. 15, 1976, NEB, UFWA

338 "shattering phone conversation" Jones to Hartmire, Oct. 7, 1976, Hartmire papers

339 "We are deeply concerned" Joneses to executive board, Nov. 14, 1976, Hartmire papers

339 "right to fire me" Smith to Padilla, Nov. 17, 1976, Hartmire papers

340 "I've been fired" Tape of Nov. 18, 1976, NEB, UFWA

341 "I work every day" Tape of conference, La Paz, Dec. 2, 1971, UFWA

341 "reminiscent of McCarthyism" Tape of Dec. 1976 NEB, UFWA

341 "Somebody fingered Nick" Hartmire to Chavez, Dec. 1, 1976

341 Chavez offered explanations Hartmire notes on conversations with Chavez, Hartmire papers

342 Moyer focused on Chavez Moyer to Hartmire, Nov. 23, 1976, Hartmire papers

342 "Following orders is a gift" Tape of Mar. 14–16, 21, 1977, NEB, UFWA

342 his brother returned the memo Richard to Cesar Chavez, Mar. 17, 1977, INFO, Box 5, Folder 36

343 "we bullshit about democracy" Tape of Mar. 1977 NEB meeting

343 the Monday Night Massacre Tape of Apr. 4, 1977, community meeting, UFWA

345 "such a fearful night" Godfrey to NEB members, Apr. 18, 1977, Hartmire papers

346 "a mini-cultural revolution" Hartmire to NFWM staff, May 31, 1977, Hartmire papers

346 "the heart and soul" Tape of Nov. 18, 1976, NEB

346 Medina had been right Tape of Jun. 30–Jul. 2, 1977, NEB, UFWA. In fact, many tapes of Milne's sessions are at Wayne State.

347 "a certain degree of paranoia" Moyer to Hartmire, Nov. 23, 1976, Hartmire papers

Chapter 30

Sources: Tapes of NEB meetings, Feb. 25–27, Mar. 14–16, 21, and Jun. 30–Jul. 2, 1977; tapes of the Game played at La Paz, May and Jul. 1977; Ofshe articles; Synanon Foundation archives; author interviews with Cohen, Ganz, Hartmire, Medina, and Ofshe.

348 without phones or distractions Tape of Chavez and staff, Feb. 3, 1977, UFWA

348 Synanon had grown Background on Synanon from Richard Ofshe, "The Social Development of the Synanon Cult," *Sociological Analysis*, 1980; Ofshe and David and Cathy Mitchell, *The Light on Synanon* (Wideview Books, 1982)

349 "when I sit down" "Charles Dederich, 83, Synanon Founder," *New York Times*, Mar. 4, 1997

350 radically reshaped the organization Ofshe, "Social Development"

351 the board assembled at Home Place Tape of NEB, Feb. 25–27, 1977, UFWA

354 "the game will help" Chavez to Dederich, Mar. 14, 1977, Synanon archives, Box 105

354 donating excess goods Ofshe, "Social Development," and Stephen Trott, assistant attorney general, to William Webster, FBI director, Mar. 16, 1984, FBI files on Synanon

354 "orange crate mentality" Jady Dederich interview, Sep. 18, 1996, courtesy of Bruce Perry

355 proposed a joint venture Board of Directors meeting, Apr. 25, 1977, Synanon archives, Box 255

355 Dederich made the offer Ibid.

355 "He is a genius" Tape of Mar. 14–16, 21, 1977, NEB, UFWA

356 "They expect a return" Hartmire to Chavez, Jun. 2, 1977, Hartmire papers

356 "a revolutionary concept" Chavez to staff, Sep. 1977, Hartmire papers

356 "trained seals" Ofshe, "Social Development"

356 hoped to groom Mar. 14–16, 21, 1977, NEB

356 "broke down and cried" Tape of Jun. 30–Jul. 2, 1977, NEB, UFWA

356 Matt Rand cited Matt Rand to Chavez, May 6, 1977, Hartmire papers

357 a waiting list Presidents report, Jun. 1977, in possession of author

357 Helen watched a Game Tape of Jun. 30–Jul. 2, 1977 NEB

357 "had a good cry" Ibid.

357 described an incident Ibid.

358 "unthinkable to me" Ibid.

358 "it would be chaotic" Transcript of Organizing Department Conference, Jul. 6–8, 1976, ADMIN, Box 29, Folder 21

358 "the vanguard of this movement" Chavez report to UFW convention, Aug. 26, 1977, in possession of author

359 "You're the sparks" Tape of Jun. 30–Jul. 2, 1977, NEB

Chapter 31

Sources: President's newsletters; tapes of NEB meetings, Mar. 14–16, 21, Jun. 30–Jul. 2, Oct. 23, 1977, and Mar. 23–25, Apr. 3–5, Jun. 15–16, 1978; Hartmire papers; author interviews with Cohen, Ganz, Hartmire, Moyer, and Padilla.

360 the March 31, 1977, celebration President's newsletter, Mar. 11 and Apr. 15, 1977, in possession of author

360 "It is, in fact, the day" Chavez memo to staff, n.d., Hartmire papers

361 "building communal living" Jeff Dietrich, "An interview with Cesar Chavez," *Catholic Agitator*, May 1977

361 "to have a mecca" Tape of Mar. 14–16, 21, 1977, NEB, UFWA

361 Los Menos Notes from Hartmire, Chavez conversations Jun. 25–Jul. 23, 1976, Hartmire papers

362 "we can live a little better" Tape of Mar. 14–16, 21, 1977, NEB

362 he and Chavez discussed Hartmire notes from conversations, Hartmire papers

363 "This is a people's movement!" Tape of UFW 1977 convention debrief, n.d., UFWA

363 "force yourself to be with the people" Tape of Jul. 24, 1976, NEB, UFWA

363 "just plain folk" Tape of Oct. 23, 1977, NEB, UFWA

363 "life of the union" Tape of Jun. 15–16, 1978, NEB, UFWA

364 "don't take one plugged nickel" Tape of speech, Sep. 28, 1972, JEL Tape 107

364 "things have changed" Tape of Mar. 23–25, 1978, NEB, UFWA

364 "thirteen-year-old cause" Tape of Jun. 30–Jul.2, 1977, NEB

364 phase out its subsidy Woodcock to Chavez, Feb. 14, 1976, OOP2, Box 26, Folder 4

364 60 percent of the union's income UFW 1977 LM2 report, U.S. Department of Labor

364 "we don't have a movement" Tape of Mar. 14–16, 21, 1977, NEB

365 "It is not helping people" Hartmire notes, Hartmire papers

365 "We're all afraid" Tape of Mar. 14–16, 21, 1977, NEB

366 "disaster area" Leo and Mary Jane Nieto to Hartmire, May 24, 1977, Hartmire papers

366 "a real struggle" Moyer to Hartmire, Jul. 11, 1978, Hartmire papers

367 "don't think much of the idea" Richard Chavez to Cesar, Apr. 1, 1977, INFO, Box 5, Folder 36

367 a royal greeting Detailed itinerary of trip, OOP2, Box 36, Folder 8; DH, Box 19, Folder 21

367 "a hell of a lot better" Bernard Wideman, "Cesar Chavez Hails Philipine's Rule," *Washington Post*, Jul. 29, 1977

368 "clear the record" Higgins to Chavez, Jul. 29, 1977, AALA, Folder 1977

368 "Ninety percent support" Tape of Chavez talking to NY boycotters, n.d., UFWA

368 "Mistakes were made" Moyer to Hartmire, Sep. 19, 1977, Hartmire papers

368 "I did not praise martial law" Gerard Sherry, *Monitor*, Oct. 27, 1977

368 "don't own your own soul" Higgins, JEL, Box 37, Folder 743

369 "We're experimenting" Tape of Jun. 30–Jul. 2, 1977, NEB

369 "everyone's in the garden" Tape of Mar. 14–16, 21, 1977, NEB

370 "our dream is a Poor Peoples Union" Transcript of Ross speech, May 1977, Ross papers, Box 1, Folder 8

Chapter 32

Sources: Tapes of NEB meetings, Mar. 14–16, 21, Jun. 30–Jul. 2, 1977; Drake oral histories on FMDP; Ganz, "Plan for the Vegetable Industry"; author interviews with Cohen, Ganz, Hartmire, Medina, and Esther and Gilbert Padilla.

371 "come to the crossroads" Tape of Mar. 14–16, 21, 1977, NEB, UFWA

372 "incapable of moving" Ibid.

373 "I give an order" Ibid.

373 "What is our union business?" Chavez to staff, Jul. 13, 1977, OOP2, Box 18, Folder 44

373 "I'm rotting away" Drake to Chavez, Jul. 1977, OOP2, Box 18, Folder 44

374 "being absolutely incredulous" Tape of Jun. 30–Jul. 2, 1977, NEB, UFWA

374 "part of history" Tape of Mar. 14–16, 21, 1977, NEB

374 "shadow of the law" Ibid.

375 He opened the meeting Tape of Jun. 30–Jul. 2, 1977, NEB

376 "I used to do that" Ibid.

380 one-sentence oath Copy of oath, UFW 1986 Accession, Box 54

380 signed the oath Tape of Jun. 30–Jul. 2, 1977, NEB

380 a love letter Tape of Jun. 30–Jul.2, 1977, NEB, and interviews with Esther Padilla, Gilbert Padilla, and Hartmire

381 Chavez's infidelities Based on interviews with more than a dozen key union staff members who lived in Delano and La Paz between 1964 and 1988.

381 "a natural attraction" Tape of organizing conference, 1967, Yinger archive, on FMDP

381 "My marriage is on the rocks" Tape of Jun. 30–Jul.2, 1977, NEB

382 Cesar prepared notes "My Marriage Meeting," Jul. 4, 1977, UFW 1986 Accession, Box 54

382 "she is just so damn real" Tape of Helen's birthday, Jan. 1978, La Paz, UFWA

383 "most productive in the movement's history" President's Newsletter, Jul. 22, 1977, in possession of author

Chapter 33

Sources: Tapes of NEB meetings, Mar. 23–25, Apr. 3–5, Jun. 15–16, 25, 1978; Govea and Hartmire papers; Kirsten Zerger journals; author interviews with Cohen, Dalzell, Ganz, Hartmire, Medina, Nathan, Rutkowski, and Tramutola.

384 told Jacques Levy Levy notes Sep. 23, 1973, JEL, Box 6, Folder 205

385 Ganz responded Ganz to Chavez, Feb. 27, 1978, Govea papers

386 "He's not your father" Tape of Mar. 23–25, 1978, NEB, UFWA

386 "Let me run union" Chavez notes, OOP 2, Box 18, Folder 16

386 "Let's go play" Tape of Apr. 3–5, 1978, NEB, UFWA

388 "prune them ruthlessly" Chavez report to convention, Aug. 26, 1977, OOP2, Box 38, Folder 19

388 "It's a mistake" Tape of Jun. 15–16, 1978, NEB, UFWA

388 "guys that have words" Tape of Jun. 30–Jul. 2, 1977, NEB, UFWA

389 "brown-nosing 'moonies'" Hartmire to Esther Winterrowd, May 8, 1978, Hartmire papers

389 "The Holy War" Mitchell, "The Light on Synanon," 264

389 "an armed camp" Tape of Apr. 4, 1978, NEB, UFWA

389 $63,000 worth of guns "What's Happening Inside Synanon?" *Los Angeles Times*, Jan. 31, 1978

390 "we don't want to pay wages" Tape of Mar. 14–16, 21, 1977, NEB, UFWA

390 stared in silence Interview with Rutkowski, who was in the car

390 opened the June board meeting Tape of Jun. 15–16, 1978, NEB

392 "'blackmail'" Villarino to Chavez, Jun. 23, 1978, OOP2, Box 36, Folder 26

393 "I'm a leader" Tape of Jun. 25, 1978, NEB, UFWA

394 "Paying salaries, how stupid" Hartmire notes from conversations with Chavez, Jul. 8 and 12, 1978, Hartmire papers

395 "revising history so soon" Zerger diary, Sep. 6, 1978, courtesy of Zerger

395 "union has to make this transition" Chris to Pudge Hartmire, Feb. 1, 1978, Hartmire papers

396 five hundred suicides Zerger diary, Nov. 22, 1978

396 "He didn't need to come" Nathan memo, Jun. 4, 1979, courtesy of Nathan

397 an elaborate graduation Tape of negotiators' graduation, Nov. 11, 1978, UFWA

Chapter 34

Sources: Tapes of NEB meetings, Sep. 15–18 and Dec. 1978, Mar. 11, Apr. 22, Jun., and Aug. 11, 1979; tape of Aug. 11, 1979, meeting with workers; transcript of 1979 UFW convention; Govea and Hartmire papers; author interviews with Chava Bustamante, Mario Bustamante, Cohen, Ganz, Hubbard, Laue, Lopez, Nassif, Gilbert Padilla, and Washburn.

401 quoted passages verbatim Tape of Jun. 13–15, 1975, NEB, UFWA

401 "they'll try to hustle you" Tape of Chavez and students, May 15, 1978, UFWA

402 "ticking time bomb" Ann Smith to Chavez, Jul. 1978, report on negotiations, in possession of author

402 "serious trouble" Tape of Sep. 10, 1978, meeting, UFWA

402 had lost two-thirds Tape of Sep. 15–18, 1978 NEB, UFWA

403 "save those contracts" Tape of Sep. 10, 1978, meeting

403 "If they beat us" Tape of Dec. 1978 NEB, UFWA

404 The moderate faction Dalzell to Cohen, Oct. 26, 1978, Dalzell papers

404 losses totaled $2 million "Chavez Taunts Growers," *Los Angeles Times*, Feb. 2, 1979. In fact, UC Berkeley economists later concluded Imperial Valley growers had record profits. The price of lettuce increased nearly 400 percent. Growers—with the exception of Sun Harvest—had formed a strike insurance cooperative though a Bermuda firm, which protected the struck growers against losses.

404 "a dream realized" *Los Angeles Times*, Feb. 2, 1979

405 "Mi papi! Mi papi!" "7,000 Attend Funeral Mass," *Los Angeles Times*, Feb. 15, 1979

405 "My job is in the cities" *Los Angeles Times*, Feb. 2, 1979

405 "Money's not coming in" Tape of Jun. 1979 NEB, UFWA

406 Denison said Tape of fund-raiser in NYC, Apr. 1979, UFWA

406 unpaid bills and a reported stolen car UFW Work Department Papers, Box 2, Folder 22; OOP2, Box 44, Manuel Chavez folder

406 "Dear Manuel" Cesar to Manuel Chavez, Oct. 10, 1975, UFW 1986 Accession, Box 15

406 "two cliques" Tape of Mar. 11, 1979, NEB, UFWA

407 "You're kidding!" Tape of Apr. 22, 1979, NEB, UFWA

407 "I love the boycott" Ibid.

408 "strike has lost its punch" Tape of Chavez and staff, Jun. 1979, UFWA

408 "Lone rangers" Tape of Dec. 1978 NEB, UFWA

408 "talk to Richard" Tape of Feb. 16, 1976, NEB, UFWA

409 "whipping girl" Huerta to Levy, JEL Box 5, Folder 184

409 "Why do you lie?" Tape of Jun. 1979 NEB

409 wreaking havoc "UFW Clash in Salinas," *Fresno Bee*, Jun. 12, 1979

410 "a mistake" Tape of Jun. 1979 NEB

410 **"My gut feeling"** Ibid.

410 **"boycott of Chiquita bananas"** Chavez to supporters, Jul. 27, 1979, OOP3, Box 32, Folder 29

411 **The marchers** Accounts of the march in the *Fresno Bee* and *Salinas Californian*, Aug. 7–11, 1979

412 **"The union is broke"** Tape of Aug. 11, 1979, NEB, followed by meeting with workers, UFWA

413 **"Fasten your seatbelts"** Transcript of UFW 1979 Convention, Aug. 12, 1979, in possession of author

414 **"inflationary increase"** "Broccoli Grower, UFW OK Pact," *Los Angeles Times*, Sep. 11, 1979

414 **"going to the dentist"** Tape of Dec. 1979 NEB, UFWA

414 **reacted with enthusiasm** Tape of Feb. 16–21, 1976, NEB

414 **air of desperation** Tape of Dec. 1979 NEB

415 **"These guys are forgotten"** Ibid.

Chapter 35

Sources: Transcript of 1981 UFW convention; tapes of NEB meetings, Dec. 1979, Jun. 1980; tape of May 1980 conference; Hartmire papers; MCOP Archives; author interviews with Adair, Barry, Bustamante, Cohen, Devereux, Ganz, Gutierrez, Hartmire, Lopez, Pelayo, Renteria, Tramutola, and Washburn.

416 **"Always ask questions"** Tape of conference, May 19–23, 1980, UFWA

417 **76 percent of the vote** Tape of Dec. 1979 NEB, UFWA

417 **"on cloud nine"** Tape of Jun. 1980 NEB, UFWA

418 **"organization led by farmworkers"** Chavez report to convention, Aug. 26, 1977, OOP2, Box 38, Folder 19

418 **"more than Linda Ronstadt"** Tape of Dec. 1979 NEB

418 **"ridiculous and untenable"** Ganz to Chavez, Sep. 26, 1980, GANZ, Box 1, Folder 7

418 **marked up his copy** "Plan for the Vegetable Industry," Oct. 7, 1980, UFW 1986 Accession, Box 17

419 **"the workers couldn't wait"** Orendain, in Jack Anderson column, Mar. 1980

420 **undercut the Arizona upstarts** *UFW v. AERB*, Mar. 1980, MCOP, Box 28, Acc 1990-402; Campaign for Human Development Grant, MCOP, Accession 1990-402, Box 58

420 Barry followed a trail Interviews and drafts of Barry stories in MCOP, Accession 1994-1302, Box 4

421 "Rumors continue to persist" Cesar to Manuel Chavez, Oct. 10, 1975, UFW 1986 Accession, Box 15

421 confirmed the rumors "Criticism of Chavez takes root in farm labor struggle," *New York Times*, Feb. 7, 1979; Barry stories, MCOP Accession 1994-1302, Box 4

421 "a vicious attack" Chavez, Mar. 19, 1980, OOP Box 27, Folder 8

422 "his words have power" Hartmire response to Anderson, Mar. 1980, Hartmire papers

422 a retraction Jack Anderson column, *Washington Post*, Jun. 7, 1980

422 "a monopoly on service" Moyer to Hartmire, Dec. 9, 1980, Hartmire papers

422 "counter-organizing event" Memo to Chavez, May 24, 1981, UFW 1986 Accession, Box 54

423 He asked Tramutt Tramutola interview

423 "at checkmate" Zerger diary, Oct. 6, 1980, courtesy of Zerger

424 "If we don't get Bruce Church" Tape of Nov. 22, 1980, NEB, UFWA

424 did not return Cohen's calls Cohen to Chavez, Mar. 4, 1981, courtesy of Cohen

424 Guzman never arrived Govea and Ganz to Chavez, Jan. 31, 1981, Govea papers

425 politicking must stop Chavez meeting notes, Feb. 10, 1981, UFW 1986 Accession, Box 54

425 Everyone must choose Agenda for May 30, 1981, meeting, JEL, Box 33, Folder 694

426 dictated a new rule Chavez memo, Sep. 1, 1981, UFW 1986 Accession, Box 54

426 puppets of Ganz David Martinez memos, Aug. 24, 1981, JEL, Box 33, Folder 694

426 "to bury our beloved union" Transcript of UFW convention, Sep. 5–6, 1981, in possession of author

426 anti-Semitic arguments Campaign flyer, UFW 1986 Accession, Box 54

427 Higgins grew alarmed Higgins to Chavez, Sep. 21, 1981, Hartmire papers

428 "a great relief" Transcript of Oct. 24, 1981, speech, Hartmire papers

428 Ortiz's clarification Ortiz to Chavez, Sep. 11, 1981, UFW 1986 Accession, Box 54

428 "They'll all be back" Washburn interview

Chapter 36

Sources: U.S. District Court files; Hartmire papers; author interviews with Bustamante, Eggers, Hartmire, Laue, Lopez, Padilla, and Torres.

429 "what Cesar taught us" *Salinas Californian*, Dec. 10, 1982

429 "some kind of threat" Bustamante declaration, May 18, 1982, in *Hermilio Mojica et al v. United Farm Workers* C82-0512 (hereafter, "court files")

430 sued for libel *United Farm Workers v. Mojica et al.*, C82-644

430 effort to intimidate Jeff Coplon affidavit, in court files

430 He took notes Hartmire notes, Hartmire papers

430 turned away Ibid.

430 front-page story "Chavez Faces External and Internal Struggles," *New York Times*, Dec. 6, 1981

430 "lived up to the dreams" Marc Grossman to Chavez, Aug. 5, 1983, on http://chavez.cde.ca.gov/researchcenter

430 Bradley asked Chavez CBS, *60 Minutes*, broadcast Dec. 25, 1983

432 Perkins arrived at La Paz Tape of Perkins filming interviews, UFWA

432 preemptive attack Chavez response, Jan. 27, 1980, OOP3, Box 32, Folder 44

432 NBC did not mince words *Prime Time* segment aired at various times during early Jan. 1980; "U.S. Confirms Inquiry into UFW's Handling of Funds," *Los Angeles Times*, Jan. 26, 1980

432 "misery and grief" Mahony to Higgins, Jan. 27, 1980, AALA, Folder 1980

433 improperly used Barbara Macri to 1988 convention, OOP3, Box 21, Folder 16

433 Chavez arranged transfers Loan to buy computers, Hartmire papers

433 owed $390,000 "IRS Says Chavez's Union Owes $400,000," *Los Angeles Times*, Jul. 19, 1980

433 "hand the politicians the check" Tape of Apr. 5, 1978, NEB, UFWA

433 a $30,000 loan Loan agreement, Sep. 12, 1980, DH, Box 22, Folder 19

434 "Farmer Brown" Memo, n.d., DH, Box 2

434 rejected earlier overtures Eggers, Jun. 2, 1994, JEL, Box 33, Folder 696

434 Maggio offered to sign Eggers to NEB, Jun. 6, 1985, DH, Box 32, Folder 7

434 "never had any question" Chavez deposition, May 1, 1982, court files

435 "they were elected" Judge William A. Ingram, Nov. 16, 1982, court files

435 "incompetence and insubordination" *Fresno Bee*, Nov. 20, 1982

435 **Judge Ingram disagreed** Ingram order, Nov. 30, 1984, court files

436 **found himself in demand** Hayden invitation, DH papers, Box 26, Folder 18; Peace Sunday, *Pacifica Radio* report, Jun. 6, 1982

436 **"the only true hero"** Account of reunion from souvenir program, in possession of author; UPI May 29, 1982; *San Jose Mercury News*, May 23, 1982; KQED California public radio report, FMDP

436 **celebration at La Paz** Hartmire notes, homily, Apr. 3, 1982, Hartmire papers

437 **Chavez buried his father** Notes and program for Librado Chavez funeral, Hartmire papers

Chapter 37

Sources: State campaign finance reports; Hartmire papers; author interviews with Hartmire and Torres.

438 **The poll** "Latino Heroes: Few and Far Between," *Los Angeles Times*, Aug. 5, 1983

439 **Almaraz changed his name** Almaraz oral history, Feb. 6, 1987, Archives of American Art

439 **"Without you"** Almaraz to Chavez, Apr. 16 and Nov. 19, 1974, OOP2, Box 43, Folder 9

439 **Chicano Lobby** Chavez often used the terms Chicano, Hispanic, Latino, and Mexican American interchangeably, sometimes referring to the same group by different terms in one speech.

440 **"different from my father"** "He Is His Own Man," *Los Angeles Times*, Jul. 27, 1983

440 **the union paid dues** "Chavez and Farm Workers Adapt Tactics to the Times," *New York Times*, Jul. 31, 1983

440 **"the pivotal vote"** "New President of MAPA Seeks to Boost Political Clout," Associated Press, Dec. 4, 1983

440 **"start with people"** Tape of Chavez with boycotters, Jan. 27, 1969, UFWA

441 **"revolutionized business"** Chavez to NEB, May 27, 1983, DH, Box 30, Folder 18

441 **"do something different"** "Chavez and Farm Workers Adapt Tactics to the Times," *New York Times*, Jul. 31, 1983

441 **"mobilize the Hispanic community"** Chavez to NEB, May 27, 1983

442 **"take up arms again"** Chavez report to 1983 UFW convention, Hartmire papers

442 "back to where we left off" Chavez statement, Jul. 11, 1984, in possession of author

442 "Yesterday it was all right" Chavez to NEB, Feb. 3, 1984, DH, Box 30, Folder 18

443 different television spots Ross to Chavez, Mar. 22, 1985, OOP3, Box 5, Folder 7

443 veto message Feinstein press release, Jul. 18, 1985, in possession of author

444 second-largest political contributors Campaign finance records, California Department of State records, State Archives

444 "most powerful weapon" President's newsletter, Aug. 7, 1978, in possession of author

444 more than $50 Emilio Huerta to Barbara Macri, Aug. 1972, DH, Box 22, Folder 44

444 contributed $750,000 UFW PAC filings, California State Archives, Sacramento

444 state commission concluded FPPC report, DH papers, Box 22, Folder 39

444 "undeniably guilty" Eggers to NEB, Jun. 9, 1983, UFW 1986 Accession, Box 26

445 "when we get double-crossed" "Chavez Puts Prestige on Line to Aid Garcia," *Los Angeles Times*, May 30, 1982

445 never spoke again Torres interview

445 beholden to the union Ross to Chavez, Nov. 7, 1983, OOP3, Box 8, Folder 54

446 cried all the way Richard Chavez to Huerta, n.d., DH, Box 21, Folder 64

446 "different kind of audience" Chavez to Temple Black, Oct. 24, 1984, Commonwealth Club papers, Hoover Institution Library, Box 500, Folder 16

446 eloquent epitaph Nov. 9, 1984, Commonwealth Club address, Commonwealth Club papers

Chapter 38

448 longhand notes Chavez notes on first meeting of Farm Worker Corp., Mar. 25, 1989, OOP3, Box 8, Folder 1

448 dues had fallen UFW LM2 reports, U.S. Department of Labor

449 jobs covered by UFW contracts Chavez to 1986 convention, OOP3, Box 10, Folder 14

449 lost fifteen more contracts Jan. 26, 1987, report, DH, Box 18, Folder 34

449 op-ed piece "UFW Must Get Back to Organizing," *Los Angeles Times*, Jan. 15, 1986

449 expand the membership Convention call for Sep. 4, 1988, OOP3, Box 7, Folder 7; Community union memo, OOP3, Box 8, Folder 1

449 only 1,063 members Credit Union minutes, Mar. 20, 1988, OOP3, Box 19, Folder 31

450 sales topped half a million Nov. 29, 1989, minutes of ETG, OOP3, Box 12, Folder 50

450 a return of 25 to 50 percent Minutes of MLK Trustees, Oct. 17, 1983, OOP3, Box 9, Folder MLK

450 introduced the Fresno appraiser Transcript of 1986 convention, OOP3, Box 11, Folder 1

450 shifted the focus Memos, OOP3, Box 32, Folder 18

450 real estate portfolio Detailed in DH, Box 18, Folder 28

450 Bonita Construction Payment to Bonita Construction, OOP3, Box 12, Folder 38

450 "explanation to my members" Bill Armstrong to Chavez, Mar. 15, 1988, OOP3, Box 8, Folder 9

451 Chavez attacked growers Chavez to Stan Smith, Building Trades Council, Mar. 28, 1988, Ibid.

451 "Dear Friend" letter OOP3, Box 4, Folder 21

451 spoke at sixty-four events OOP3, Box 4, Folders 10, 13, 47

451 marketing plan OOP3, Box 5, Folder 4

452 detailed checklists OOP3, Box 4, Folder 21

452 "the more you own" Chavez speech at Harvard Kennedy School, Feb. 27, 1990, http://forum.iop.harvard.edu/content/it-us-policy-v-public-solution-pesticide-poisoning

452 "the polls never close" Chavez speech at Harvard Kennedy School, Apr. 6, 1992, http://forum.iop.harvard.edu/content/reflections-social-justice

452 "I have nothing else to do" Ibid.

452 eighteen nonprofit and commercial entities Documents for Jan. 1989 NEB, Hartmire papers

453 first pension checks Chavez notes, Jun. 28, 1983, UFW 1986 Accession, Box 2

454 private foundation with $8 million Details of MLK fund in Chavez to NEB, Oct. 20, 1992, OOP3, Box 42, Folder 10; NEB memos, OOP3, Box 9, MLK folder; DH, Box 32, Folder 9

Chapter 39

Sources: Hartmire papers; ALRB records; Court files; *The Wrath of Grapes*; www.cesarslastfast.com; author interviews with Hartmire and Moses.

455 "Join Us, Again, in Delano" Invitation, OOP3, Box 21, Folder 5

455 five union martyrs In addition to De la Cruz and Daifullah in 1973 and Contreras in 1979, Nan Freeman, 18, was hit by a truck on a Florida picket line in 1972 and Rene Lopez, 21, was shot on a picket line outside a Fresno dairy in 1983.

456 "We're predicting" Description of event from Hartmire notes; *Food and Justice*, June 1987; Commemorative Journal, in possession of author; quote from *San Diego Union-Tribune*, May 24, 1987

456 "We built this union twice" *San Diego Union-Tribune*, May 24, 1987

457 "go back to organizing" *San Diego Union-Tribune*, May 25, 1987

457 Chavez told Denison Denison interview

457 "no safe pesticides" Chavez speech at Harvard Kennedy School, Feb. 27, 1990,http://forum.iop.harvard.edu/content/it-us-policy-v-public-solution-pesticide-poisoning

457 fund-raising scripts OOP3, Box 12, Folder 36

457 more than $100,000 Ibid.

458 "These cancer clusters" Chavez at Harvard, Feb. 27, 1990

458 "exploiting our children" Rosales to college administrators, Apr. 30, 1991, OOP3, Box 5, Folder 36

458 "no other cause" Chavez, Jun. 4, 1988, Hartmire papers

458 "assign everyone to the boycott" Chavez to NEB, Sep. 4, 1988, Hartmire papers

459 "the killing fields" Scott Simon report, *NPR*, Jun. 2, 1990

459 confronted Dolores Huerta Richard Steven Street in *California Farmer*, Jul. 16, 1988

459 "I don't appreciate the interview" Scott Simon, *NPR*, Jun. 2, 1990

459 thirty-one contracts UC Davis study cited in "Fast by Chavez Passes 29th Day," *New York Times*, Aug. 16, 1988

459 "something I feel compelled to do" Chavez statement, in possession of author

461 "always led us by his example" Account of fast from newspaper stories, Hartmire notes, detailed chronology by Pat Hoffman for NFWM, Hartmire papers

461 called the FBI FBI report, Dec. 1988, SC-9A-1191

461 former accountant had embezzled *U.S. v. Bryce Basey*, court records, U.S. District Court, Fresno

462 "Hartmire and Chavez" Account of meeting from Hartmire notes and interview; John Hartmire to Chris Hartmire, Jan. 26, 1989, Hartmire papers

462 "difficult to believe" Moses to Hartmire, n.d., Hartmire papers

462 "Cesar is just too complex" Cook to Hartmire, Feb. 20, 1989, Hartmire papers

462 "got what was coming to me" Hartmire journal, Hartmire papers

462 case against Denison Index cards, OOP3, Box 32, Folder 13

463 "Indestructible Spirit" "Indestructible Spirit," OOP3, Box 43, Folder 39; 1992 convention program, OOP Box 43, Folder 40

463 vice president emeritus 1990 convention proceedings, OOP3, Box 21, Folder 18

463 "hoping and praying" Irrgang to Hartmire, May 12, 1990, Hartmire papers

464 Aguila Azteca Memos on Aguila Azteca and trip, OOP3, Box 41, Folder 25

464 "He encourages me" *Coachella Valley Sun*, Oct. 24, 1990

Chapter 40

Sources: Video of Juana Chavez rosary, funeral mass and burial, Wayne State; video of Fred Ross memorial, on FMDP; author interviews with Chatfield, Hartmire, Moses, and Valdez.

465 "Remembering Nana" Details of rosary and mass from video, UFWA

465 "a wise woman" Chavez handwritten eulogy, OOP3, Box 7, Folder 45

466 buried Ross's ashes Fred Ross Jr. to Chavez, Oct. 9, 1992, OOP3, Box 32, Folder 20

466 seven pages of notes OOP3, Box 32, Folder 20

467 the Ross memorial Quotes and details from video

468 went to many funerals Chavez family interview, JEL, Box 31, Folder 672

468 delighted in his grandchildren Eric Chavez, on http://chavez.cde.ca.gov /researchcenter

468 cooked an Indian feast Richard Chavez, Paradigm Productions interview, FMDP

469 sworn in as a witness Court transcript of Apr. 21 and 22, 1993, in possession of author

470 David Martinez entered the bedroom *Los Angeles Times*, Apr. 24, 1993

470 upside down Bruce Perry interview with paramedics, courtesy of Perry

470 "Death is nothing" "Cesar Chavez's Causa," *Washington Post*, Apr. 22, 1979

471 took thirty-eight hours to build Richard Chavez, Paradigm Productions interview FMDP

471 funeral procession Funeral description from interviews, newspaper accounts, and Hartmire planning notes, Hartmire papers

Epilogue

473 chose the name "School Named After Cesar Chavez," *Los Angeles Times*, Jul. 12, 2002

473 "most important citizen" Interview with Zaninovich

474 "They taught us" Author interview with Nuño, Aug. 2005

474 "I'm an organizer" Author interview with Rivera, May 8, 2010

Index

A NOTE ON THE AUTHOR

Miriam Pawel is the author of *The Union of Their Dreams*, widely acclaimed as the most nuanced history of Cesar Chavez's movement. She is a Pulitzer Prize–winning editor who spent twenty-five years working for *Newsday* and the *Los Angeles Times*. In 2013, she was awarded a National Endowment for the Humanities fellowship. She lives in Southern California.